COLLECTED ESSAYS

VOLUME I

THE LITTMAN LIBRARY OF JEWISH CIVILIZATION

Dedicated to the memory of
LOUIS THOMAS SIDNEY LITTMAN
who founded the Littman Library for the love of God
and as an act of charity in memory of his father
JOSEPH AARON LITTMAN
and to the memory of
ROBERT JOSEPH LITTMAN
who continued what his father Louis had begun
יהא זכרם ברוך

'Get wisdom, get understanding:
Forsake her not and she shall preserve thee'
PROV. 4:5

The Littman Library of Jewish Civilization is a registered UK charity
Registered charity no. 1000784

COLLECTED ESSAYS

VOLUME I

HAYM SOLOVEITCHIK

London
The Littman Library of Jewish Civilization
in association with Liverpool University Press

The Littman Library of Jewish Civilization
Registered office: 4th floor, 7–10 Chandos Street, London W1G 9DQ

in association with Liverpool University Press
4 Cambridge Street, Liverpool L69 7ZU, UK
www.liverpooluniversitypress.co.uk/littman

Managing Editor: Connie Webber

Distributed in North America by
Oxford University Press Inc., 198 Madison Avenue
New York, NY 10016, USA

First published in hardback 2013
Hardback reprinted 2015
First published in paperback 2019

Catalogue records for this book are available from the British Library and the Library of Congress

ISBN 978–1–786941–65–7

Publishing co-ordinator: Janet Moth
Copy-editing: Agnes Erdos
Proof-reading: Philippa Claiden
Indexes: Itamar Rosenzweig and Agnes Erdos
Designed and typeset by Pete Russell, Faringdon, Oxon.

Printed and bound by CPI Group (UK) Ltd, Croydon, CR0 4YY

TO

JOSEPH AND ESTHER

Preface

GATHERING TOGETHER ESSAYS written over many years always leads the author to ponder whether these varied studies have an inner coherence. Do they reflect a preoccupation (conscious or not) with some underlying set of problems that found expression in what were seemingly unrelated research projects? I always knew that my attention as a historian was not held by pure studies in intellectual history, such as would be had, for example, by studying the gradual unfolding of many aspects of the Sabbath or Passover. Most of these observances were under no particular pressure, and their regulations grew and developed as legal ideas naturally do over the course of time. Not that I neglected studying these areas, but when I researched them, my purpose was more to see how the halakhah evolved in neutral, laboratory-like conditions as it were, so as to better recognize elsewhere when there was a deviation from its normal course—some uncharacteristic swerve in the unfolding of halakhic ideas and rulings that pointed to an undetected force at work there. I later termed this swerve 'measurable deflection' and discuss it in some of the essays that follow.

I equally had no interest in topics where social or economic pressures were so great that halakhah, in effect, abdicated its regulatory role. This took place in Poland, for example, towards the close of the sixteenth century, when the *heter 'iska* was introduced. The ban on intra-Jewish usury was effectively eliminated, and the various strategies that were proffered and those that were chosen to better effect this circumvention had no purchase on my interest. I was attracted to issues of resistance and accommodation, to cases where strong forces impinged upon halakhic observance, and both the scholarly elite and the community as a whole had to grapple with upholding observance while maneuvering to adapt to the new set of adverse circumstances. The line between adaptation and deviance is a fine one, and where a society draws that line is revelatory of both its values and its self-perception. Was there a sense of loss, of religious erosion, in these adjustments, or did the performance of those on the periphery reasonably conform to the expectations of those at the center?

It was no surprise, then, that I took *yein nesekh* (Gentile wine or wine touched by Gentiles) as the subject of my MA thesis, and the topic of *ribbit* (usury) for my doctoral thesis. Lurking inevitably on the borders of both topics were the questions: how widespread was the nonconformism, how was it viewed, and how great a need did the Ashkenazic elite feel to police group boundaries and behavioral codes? I had, however, no notion at the time that the subjects of Gentile wine and Jewish usury may have been causally related; that the Jewish involvement in moneylending may have been linked to Jews' long-standing engagement in viticulture—a Jewish profession some half a millennium old that had hitherto gone undetected. This occurred to me only decades later. The examination of this connection makes for a better-integrated volume of essays, but was, from the point of view of authorial intent, wholly unpremeditated.

The opening section of the volume is a survey, a brief description and characterization, of the dramatis personae of these essays: Rashi and the Tosafists. The first two essays complement one another; the third draws attention to a singular facet of the halakhic culture of the Tosafists, one to which I will return in the next volume of this series. The second and third sections primarily contain two in-depth thematic studies, one in the field of usury (*ribbit*), the other in that of *yein nesekh*. Though I have placed the usury essays first for organizational reasons, the one on *yein nesekh* is a step-by-step interrogation of every Ashkenazic halakhic source on the topic and best illustrates my approach to the history of halakhah. The method employed is implicit in everything else that I have written, but is set forth most clearly there. The reader interested in methodology would do well to begin with this essay and then turn to the studies of *ribbit*. The book concludes with four studies of the communal self-image of Ashkenaz and its attitude to normative nonconformance. Appended to these studies is a review essay that addresses such problematic Ashkenazic customs as the ban on eating legumes (*kitniyot*) on Passover and the practice of eating in the *sukkah* on Shemini Atseret.

Other than the essay on pawnbroking, which has been much expanded and rewritten, none of the previously printed essays have been altered. Any additions or changes in opinion are noted either in an Afterword or enclosed in { } in the footnotes. The additions to the footnotes are generally ones of fact; those in the Afterwords are mostly my current reflections on the subject, responses to criticism, or reactions to other scholars' treatment of the material. All bibliographical additions have also been placed in { } with one exception. The last thirty years have seen a flood of scholarly editions of medieval halakhic works; I have updated these references without marking them. For example, a citation of the *Ḥiddushei ha-Ramban* has automatically been updated from the Meltzer edition of 1928 to the relevant volume in the series of the *Shas ha-Yisra'eli ha-Shalem*.

The last two studies, on deviance, in the volume are new, and the one preceding them is a free translation of a chapter in my *Ha-Yayin bi-Yemei ha-Beinayim: Yein Nesekh—Perek be-Toledot ha-Halakhah be-Ashkenaz bi-Yemei ha-Beinayim* (Jerusalem, 2008). As closely as the previously published studies hew to the original formulations, I did not perceive them as masoretic texts, demanding absolute fidelity of transmission. If I or the editors at Littman found a phrase infelicitous, we edited it out; if a clause seemed overcomplicated, we simplified it. I did alter two overstatements. In one, I changed 'never' to 'rarely' ; in the other, I changed '[wine was] the most important article of trade' to 'one of the most important articles of trade'. (I tell my students to avoid, as much as possible, the use of 'ever', 'never', and the superlative form of comparison, but in preparing this volume I discovered that occasionally I had failed to practice what I preached.) The page numbers of the original essays have been supplied in the text thus |75| to enable readers to swiftly find references to passages in these articles registered in the scholarly literature of the past.

Written, as these essays were, at different times and for different audiences—some for scholars of rabbinic literature, some for laymen or for scholars not necessarily Jewish who were interested, for example, in the medieval Jewish attitude to usury—there are occasionally explanatory asides which may appear to the better-informed reader to be superfluous; I have left them untouched. Several of the essays began as lectures. In these oral presentations, I sometimes borrowed an apt phrase or sentence or two from a previous article and subsequently published the presentation. When several of these lectures are placed side by side, the occasional repetition can be jarring. In one instance, I have altered the formulation (and so noted in a footnote); in the two or three other instances, I have let them stand, and appeal simply to the reader's forbearance.

Acknowledgments

ANY ACKNOWLEDGMENT in a series of collected essays whose publication stretches back some forty-five years should begin with the 'creditors' who can never be repaid, not simply because they are no longer with us, but because their perspectives and ways of thinking are embedded in everything that one has written. First and foremost is my father, who bestowed upon me no less than decade and a half of talmudic instruction—and much more; then Jacob Katz, from whom I learnt historical method. I am also under obligation to Hayyim Hillel Ben-Sasson and Joshua Prawer, under whom I studied at the Hebrew University in Jerusalem. Not all learning takes place in the classroom, and I would be sorely remiss if I did not record my obligations to Michael Bernstein, Eliezer Shimshon Rosenthal, Shraga Abramson, and Saul Lieberman. For reasons best known to them (certainly not because of any merit of mine), they privileged me with hundreds of hours of conversation. What those sessions imparted to me, both in knowledge and method, has nourished every aspect of my scholarly life.

The idea of collecting my essays of some forty years, scattered in books and journals both known and unknown (some in works possibly deserving oblivion), was first suggested to me by my cousin, Morry Gerber. When I broached the idea to Connie Webber, the managing editor of Littman, she received it enthusiastically; without her involvement, the project would not have come to fruition. I had heard from colleagues about the superb editing at Littman; what I received exceeded all expectations. I had not one, but two editors. Agi Erdos did painstaking and meticulous work, and Janet Moth then provided me with the finest English editing that I have ever received. Philippa Claiden's patient checking of the Hebrew and correcting the proofs was likewise much appreciated; Pete Russell's design has improved the readability of the text, for which I am grateful; while Ludo Craddock's handling of the bureaucratic technicalities has made them less bureaucratic and technical.

I hired Hanna Caine-Braunschvig of Jerusalem, an experienced Hebrew editor, to check all the titles, places of publication, and pages of the articles and books cited, and to keep a watchful eye on some of the other paraphernalia of scholarship. However, the intelligence of her comments on the articles and our conversations about the manner of their improvement has turned our relationship from that of author/assistant to one of collegiality. Ezra Merkin, Jerry Balsam, and Sheon Karol read and commented perceptively on every essay in the collection. I am indebted to all of them. (Jerry's eye for errant commas proved a further blessing.) Elisabeth Hollender graciously checked my German references (especially their case endings).

Without the assistance of the staffs of the Gottesman and Pollack libraries of Yeshiva University, little of my research would have been possible. I would like to single out Zvi Ehrenyi, John Moryl, and Mary Ann Linahan for special thanks. The Institute of Advanced Studies (IAS) at the Hebrew University has been my home away from home for the past twenty-five years, and much of the writing in these volumes took place within the four walls of that institution. I owe a special debt to Penina Feldman, the past associate director of the IAS, who unfortunately did not live to see the present volume.

Given the state of the currently printed medieval rabbinic texts, no serious research is possible without sustained recourse to manuscripts. Everything that I have written over the past forty-five years is based, without exception, on the treasures of the Institute of Microfilmed Hebrew Manuscripts at the National Library of Israel in Jerusalem. Their holdings and their catalogue provide countless scholars with undreamt-of riches. The helpfulness of their staff, especially their cataloguers, is fabled. I am obliged to each and every one of them; however, I would like to note my special indebtedness to Binyamin Richler and Ezra Chwat.

I wish to thank Itamar Rosenzweig and Agi Erdos for their fine work in preparing the indexes. Most of the sources referred to in the lengthy essay on pawnbroking are available in PDF form online at <haymsoloveitchik.org>. I would like to acknowledge the assistance of both Menachem Butler and Frank Guelpa in preparing the PDF.

Other than the obligation that I owe to my teachers, my greatest debt is to the president of Yeshiva University, Richard Joel, and its provost, Mort Lowengrub. The new president of Yeshiva University, Rabbi Dr. Ari Berman, and his provost, Dr. Selma Botman, have continued their policy of allowing me to devote myself full-time to study and writing. Tim Stevens, Special Assistant to the Provost, has eased for me for the technicalities of the administrative transition. Without their gift of time and resources, this entire project —a multi-volume series of my collected essays—would simply have been inconceivable.

Contents

Note on Transliteration and Conventions Used in the Text xv

PART I

OVERVIEW OF THE TOSAFIST MOVEMENT

1. The Printed Page of the Talmud: The Commentaries and their Authors 3

2. Catastrophe and Halakhic Creativity: Ashkenaz—1096, 1242, 1306, and 1298 11

3. The Halakhic Isolation of the Ashkenazic Community 31

PART II

USURY AND MONEYLENDING

4. Usury, Jewish Law 41

5. The Jewish Attitude to Usury in the High and Late Middle Ages (1000–1500) 44

6. Pawnbroking: A Study in *Ribbit* and of the Halakhah in Exile 57

PART III

THE BAN ON GENTILE WINE AND ITS LINK TO MONEYLENDING

7. Can Halakhic Texts Talk History? 169

8. Halakhah, Taboo, and the Origin of Jewish Moneylending in Germany 224

PART IV

SOME GENERAL CONCLUSIONS

9. Religious Law and Change: The Medieval Ashkenazic Example 239

10. 'Religious Law and Change' Revisited 258

11. A Note on Deviance in Eleventh-Century Ashkenaz 278

12. On Deviance: A Reply to David Malkiel 283

REVIEW ESSAY

Yishaq (Eric) Zimmer, *'Olam ke-Minhago Noheg* 294

Bibliography of Manuscripts 309

Source Acknowledgments 316

Index of Names 317

Index of Places 324

Index of Subjects 327

Note on Transliteration and Conventions Used in the Text

THE transliteration of Hebrew in this book reflects consideration of the type of book it is, in terms of its content, purpose, and readership. The system adopted therefore reflects an academic approach to transcription, such as that of the *Encyclopaedia Judaica* or other systems developed for text-based or linguistic studies. The aim has partly been to reflect the pronunciation prescribed for modern Hebrew, as well as the spelling or Hebrew word structure, and to do so using conventions that are generally familiar to the English-speaking reader.

In accordance with this approach, no attempt is made to indicate the distinctions between *tet* and *taf*, *kaf* and *kuf*, *sin* and *samekh*, since these are not relevant to pronunciation. The *dagesh* is indicated by double consonants, except when the doubling would result a string of consonants unacceptable to the English reader's eye, as in *kitstsur*. Following the principle of using conventions familiar to the majority of readers, however, transcriptions that are well established have been retained even when they are not fully consistent with the transliteration system adopted. On similar grounds, the *tsadi* is rendered by 'tz' in such familiar words as barmitzvah. Likewise, the distinction between *ḥet* and *khaf* has been retained, using *ḥ* for the former and *kh* for the latter; the associated forms are generally familiar to readers, even if the distinction is not actually borne out in pronunciation, and for the same reason the final *heh* is indicated too. Although in Hebrew no capital letters are used, the transcription of titles and names in lower case may be strange to the English-speaking reader's eye and in this volume we therefore adopt the English system of capitalization (for example, *Shulḥan 'Arukh*).

No distinction is made between *'alef* and *'ayin* in the intervocalic position: both are represented by an apostrophe; *'ayin* is also marked at the beginnings and ends of words.

The *sheva na'* is indicated by an *e*—*perikat 'ol*, *reshut*—except, again, when established convention dictates otherwise.

The *yod* is represented by *i* when it occurs as a vowel (*bereshit*), by *y* when it occurs as a consonant (*yesodot*), and by *yi* when it occurs as both (*yisra'el*).

The definite article and those conjunctives and prepositions that in

Hebrew are attached to the word have been separated by a hyphen in our transcription to help distinguish the individual elements.

Medieval Hebrew names follow the above system, whereas contemporary names are transcribed as they appear in Western literature.

The names of scholars who have published in European languages are given in Latinized form, even when referring to Hebrew articles of theirs. Thus Yaakov Katz is uniformly referred to as 'Jacob Katz' and registered in bibliographical entries as 'J. Katz'. Similarly, Yoel Miller is registered as 'J. Müller'.

YIDDISH

The transcription of Yiddish in this volume follows the conventions of the YIVO Institute.

PART I

OVERVIEW OF THE TOSAFIST MOVEMENT

CHAPTER ONE

The Printed Page of the Talmud

The Commentaries and their Authors

THIS ESSAY was written for a volume accompanying an exhibition of the printed Talmud at the Yeshiva University Museum. Brevity was then the order of the day, and this study should be complemented by the next essay, 'Catastrophe and Creativity', which, its title notwithstanding, contains a detailed survey of the Tosafists.

OPEN ANY COPY OF THE TALMUD printed within the past half-millennium and you will find on the inner side of the page the commentary of Rashi (1040–1105), and on the outer side of the page *Tosafot*, the glosses of the French Talmudists of the twelfth and thirteenth centuries. Why did Rashi and *Tosafot* become so central to talmudic study and why is their study the core of the traditional Jewish canon?

If one reads an accurate translation of the Talmud, such as the translation published by the Soncino Press, one will understand all the words of the text and the general line of argument, but the individual steps lack clarity and the argument as a whole hangs loosely together. The reason is that the Talmud is, as it were, a 'telegrammatic' text: the main points are stated, but the flow, the linkage of the various points, is left up to the reader to reconstruct. It is this flow and linkage that Rashi supplies, and with remarkably few words. Rashi was gifted with an inordinate ability to detect both minor gaps in a presentation and the slightest ambiguity of language, and to correct them succinctly. Realizing the cumulative effect of trivial errors, he deftly guides the student through the text with a mere word or two, preventing a host of possible misunderstandings. So definitively did Rashi solve these problems that no one ever attempted again to write a similar commentary on the Talmud, and all dissimilar ones—regardless how prestigious—were swiftly consigned to oblivion. Provence discarded its classic commentary, that of R. Avraham ben David of Posquières (d. 1198), and even Yemenite Jewry, which revered Maimonides (1135–1204) as few other Jewish cultures have venerated a scholar, allowed Maimonides' commentary on the Talmud to disappear.

Rashi's commentary did not arise out of nowhere. Genius alone could never discern the meaning of the innumerable Persian, Greek, and Latin words that abound in the Talmud. Behind Rashi stood the traditions of talmudic interpretation of the academies of the Rhineland, the famed yeshivot of Mainz and Worms that Rashi attended as a youth. Those traditions are now known as the *Commentaries of Rabbenu Gershom Me'or ha-Golah* (Light of the Exile). Like the ban on polygamy that is attributed to Rabbenu Gershom but is actually a longstanding communal ban, the *Commentaries* are not his but rather the collective work of the academy of Mainz in the eleventh century.[1] The commentary on several tractates has been preserved, and a comparison with that of Rashi is illuminating. Most of the exegetical material by Rashi is already found there, but the commentary lacks those crucial words and comments that give bite and tightness to the talmudic arguments. Much as a great lawyer takes the brief of a colleague and, with the insertion of a phrase or two, transforms a reasonable argument into a convincing one, so Rashi transformed his heritage. The bricks and mortar of his oeuvre are to be found in the works of his predecessors. What those commentaries lack is the magic touch of Rashi's masonry.|37|

The commentaries of Rashi democratized talmudic scholarship. Prior to his work, the only way to master a tractate was to travel to a talmudic academy and study at the feet of a master. No written work could systematically convey with any degree of sustained accuracy the precise line of a talmudic argument. That could be conveyed only by oral instruction, by the vibrant voice of gifted teachers. With the appearance of Rashi's work, anyone, regardless of means, could by dint of talent and effort master any talmudic topic, and could do so with far greater precision than had previously been possible. This was true for the beginner and equally so for the accomplished scholar, who could for the first time enlarge the scope of his knowledge beyond what he had acquired in his student days. The lifelong study of Talmud, the constant conquest of new tractates, and the unlimited personal acquisition of knowledge were in many ways the consequence of Rashi's inimitable work of exposition.

That is not to say that Rashi's explanations were definitive. Far from it.

[1] A. Epstein, 'Der Gerschom Meor ha-Golah zugeschriebene Talmud-Commentar', *Festschrift zum achtzigsten Geburtstage Moritz Steinschneiders* (Leipzig, 1896), 115–43. Translated into Hebrew in *Netu'im*, 6 (2000), 107–33.

For some 300 years scholars scrutinized his commentary, criticized innumerable passages, and demanded their reinterpretation. Yet all realized that the problem that had confronted scholars for close to half a millennium—how to turn the abrupt and sometimes gnomic formulations of the Talmud into a coherent and smoothly flowing text—had been solved definitively by Rashi. The subsequent task of scholars, therefore, was to emend and add to his interpretations. Thus came into existence the subsequent genre of talmudic commentary, the *Tosafot*, or 'additions' to Rashi that are printed alongside his commentary.

What are the *Tosafot*? They are the glosses (additions written in the margin) of scholastic dialectics, the product of collation, contradiction, and distinction. The Talmud is a vast, loosely organized corpus with many overlapping discussions. The Tosafists undertook, on each and every topic, to collate all the discussions of a given issue in the entire Talmud, note any contradictions between the different passages, and resolve them by distinguishing between the cases under discussion. Not that the Tosafists were the first to note contradictions in the Talmud. Contradictions have been noted from the moment that the Talmud became normative. The approach that had previously prevailed was to follow, in cases of contradiction, the *sugya de-shema'tta* (dominant discussion). There is generally one major treatment of an issue in the Talmud, though that issue may reappear in the course of many other discussions. When confronted with a contradiction, one should follow the conclusions of the dominant discussion, even if other talmudic discussions of the problem would seem to imply a different outcome. The premise of dialectic is, however, that there are no 'major' and 'minor' passages in the corpus. All passages are equally valid. The Talmud in its totality is a harmonious whole. Talmudic discussions are indeed 'telegrammatic', and thus, though certain conditions of the case at bar are not always expressly spelled out, they are inferable from the discussion. The task of the scholar is to ferret out the distinctiveness of each of the seemingly similar cases under discussion and, thereby, restore harmony to an apparently dissonant corpus. Not that the Tosafists were the first people to distinguish between seemingly similar cases. Just as contradictions were noted from the very outset of talmudic study, so too were distinctions made and contradictions resolved from the beginning. Maimonides often quietly resolved contradictions with an added word or two, and few scholars quietly anticipated and resolved more questions that way than did Rashi. Anyone familiar with the super-commentarial works on Rashi knows how frequently the authors note, 'and Rashi forfended |38| the problem by . . .'. What was new in the dialectical approach of the Tosafists is the *systematic* quest for, and resolution of, contradictions. It demanded a new mode of study; in a sense, even a new curriculum. The Talmud could no longer be studied vertically, or consecutively, line after line, page after page, as had been done previously. It demanded 'horizontal' study, where each line of the Talmud was systematically collated with all parallel passages found in the vast talmudic corpus, and contradictions were uncovered and resolved. The fruit of their labor of some two centuries was *Tosafot*, the glosses printed alongside Rashi in all editions of the Talmud since the 1520s.

Anonymity reigns in the *Tosafot*. Only too often questions are raised without the name of the interlocutor. We find simply, *ve-teimah* (objection) or *im tomar* (should you say, i.e. object). Nevertheless, the acronyms of two speakers do stand out: ר"ת and ר"י. The former designates Rabbenu Tam, the universally accepted moniker for R. Ya'akov ben Me'ir of Ramerupt (1100–1171); the latter indicates his nephew, R. Yitsḥak of Dampierre (d. 1189).[2] Most of the famed thought of the Tosafists is actually the product of these two men. Who were they, and why their prominence?

The dialectical method, omnipresent in the Talmud, was revived by Rabbenu Tam. Dialectic was the dominant mode of scholastic thinking in the Middle Ages—it obtained in Roman and canon law and in theology. Was Rabbenu Tam influenced by developments in his surroundings? The revival of Roman law had not come to Champagne by the second or third decade of the twelfth century when Rabbenu Tam began his revolution, and the dialectics of canon law did not appear until later. In theology, dialectics was indeed emerging in northern France at this time, but its concepts and vocabulary were so technical, alien, and, in one sense, repugnant to Jews, that, even if we overlook the fact that these discussions were conducted in Latin, 'the language of the priests' as Jews called it, it seems rash to attribute influence to them without concrete evidence. One can, of course, invoke the zeitgeist (spirit of the age), but that is simply another way of saying that we know of parallel developments without having any evidence of contact.

In one sense the question is bootless. The greatness of Rabbenu Tam did not lie in his discovery of dialectic—that is systematically employed in most discussions of the Talmud—but rather in the scope and depth of his use of it. Rabbenu Tam's influence extended over the entire talmudic corpus; he scarcely treated a topic that he did not revolutionize by dialectic. He was able to offer many hundreds, probably thousands, of legal distinctions that subsequent thinkers found, and to this day still find, essential for any understanding of talmudic law. So fecund were his ideas and so productive was his mode of

2 On Rabbenu Tam, see E. E. Urbach, *Ba'alei ha-Tosafot*, revised edn. (Jerusalem, 1980), 60–113.

thinking that this type of analysis has continued to the present day. In brief, Rabbenu Tam rewrote halakhic thought by his revival and use of dialectic and made this method an indispensable tool of talmudic study.

Though extraordinarily creative, Rabbenu Tam wrote very little. The one small work he authored himself, *Sefer ha-Yashar*, was first printed in 1811 and remains unused to this day.[3] Words came easily enough to Rabbenu Tam when engaged in polemic or in the niceties of polite correspondence, but when called upon to express ideas, the sentences swiftly break down. The flow of words is unable to keep pace with the speed of his thought and with the leaps of his creative association. It is |39| ironic that the one significant Tosafist who wielded the metrics of Spanish poetry with any degree of skill was unable to pen a clear sentence, even by the abrupt and inelegant standards of dialectical writing.

Rabbenu Tam's thoughts have come down to us via the agency of his nephew, R. Yitsḥak of Dampierre (Ri). Indeed, were it not for Ri, not only Rabbenu Tam's work, but the very dialectical revolution itself might well have had no lasting impact. The nephew was the equal of the uncle in genius, but wholly opposite in character. Not for him the communal involvements, the sound and fury of scholarly controversies, the threats of excommunication that characterized the career of his stormy and imperious uncle. Quiet and unassuming, and without any desire to bend others to his will, Ri passed his entire life teaching and writing in a two- or three-street hamlet in Champagne.[4] We know little more of his self-effacing life other than that he studied with his uncle, Rabbenu Tam, and lived in Dampierre. This meek exterior, however, hid an iron will and a relentless dedication to his craft that few have equaled in Jewish history. Just as his great-grandfather, Rashi, humbly but steadfastly sought to explicate the entire Talmud, Ri undertook the protean task of elucidating the entire Talmud in light of dialectic and equally succeeded in his goal. In his school and under his tutelage every line of the Talmud was subjected to the probing light of the newly revived method. The slightest whisper of contradiction was noted and solutions were proffered; solutions and distinctions that have proven so suggestive and fruitful that their study is the staple of the talmudic curriculum to this day. Rightly, Naḥmanides entitled Ri Ba'al ha-Tosafot, the author of the *Tosafot*.

[3] *Sefer ha-Yashar* (Vienna, 1811). The work is divided into *ḥiddushim* (novellae) and *teshuvot* (responsa). Each was subsequently edited: *Sefer ha-Yashar: Teshuvot*, ed. S. F. Rosenthal (Berlin, 1898); *Sefer ha-Yashar: Ḥelek ha-Ḥiddushim*, ed. S. S. Schlesinger (Jerusalem, 1959). On the work, see Urbach (above, n. 2), 93–106; A. Reiner, 'Rabbenu Tam u-Venei Doro: Kesharim, Hashpa'ot ve-Darkhei Limmudo ba-Talmud' (Ph.D. diss., Hebrew University, 2002), 23–68.

[4] See Urbach (above, n. 2), 226–60.

Though an easy writer, Ri himself wrote little. He adopted the widely used method of composition, the *reportatio*.[5] The *magister* (master) would select a student to prepare a report of his teaching that he then would correct and certify, or the master would dictate the text himself. While Latin circles attributed these reports to the teacher, the Tosafists credited them to the pupil. Nevertheless, all recognized that the work was an accurate report of the master's teachings.

Over the course of his life, Ri used four students to write *reportatio*s. The first, his son, R. Elḥanan, was in the midst of composing a commentary on the tractate *'Avodah Zarah* when he was murdered in a pogrom in 1184. That truncated work is the only one of his many *Tosafot* that has come down to us.[6] R. Shimshon of Sens picked up where his fallen colleague had left off and wrote *Tosafot* on much of the Talmud. Only seven of his original *Tosafot* have survived, those on *Pesaḥim*, *Rosh ha-Shanah*, *Megillah*, *Ketubbot*, *Menaḥot*, *Bekhorot*, and parts of *'Avodah Zarah*.[7] R. Yehudah of Paris penned a third set of *reportatio*s, and those on *Berakhot*, *Megillah*, and *'Avodah Zarah* have come down to us.[8] One student, R. Barukh, who penned our printed *Tosafot* on *Zevaḥim*, also felt the need to bring the new discussions and conclusions of the dialectic to a wider audience and to draw practical conclusions from them, that is to say, translate the new ideas of Dampierre into religious practice. He chose a number of select topics, such as the laws of the Sabbath and *kashrut*, and

[5] B. Smalley, *The Study of the Bible in the Middle Ages*, 2nd edn. (repr. Notre Dame, 1964), 200 ff. {P. Glorieux, 'L'Enseignement au Moyen Âge: Techniques et méthodes en usage à la Faculté de Paris au XIIIe siècle', *Archives d'histoire doctrinale et littéraire du Moyen Âge*, 43 (1968), 175–7, 185–6.}

[6] *Tosfot R. Elḥanan 'al 'Avodah Zarah* (Husiatyn, 1901). {It has recently been reissued on the basis of a more accurate transcription of MS Montefiore 67 from which it was originally published—together with notes by A. Y. Kreuzer (Benei Berak, 2003).}

[7] *Tosfot Rashba 'al Massekhet Pesaḥim*, ed. E. D. Rabinovitz-Te'omim (Jerusalem, 1956); *Tosfot Rashba mi-Shants 'al Massekhet Ketubbot*, ed. A. Liss (Jerusalem, 1973); *Tosfot R. Shimshon ben Avraham mi-Shants 'al Massekhet 'Avodah Zarah*, in *Shitat Kadmonim 'al Massekhet 'Avodah Zarah*, ed. M. Y. H. Blau, i (New York, 1969). {The standard *Tosafot* on *Rosh ha-Shanah*, *Menaḥot*, and *Bekhorot* are also those of R. Shimshon, as are considerable sections of the *Tosafot* on *Shabbat* and *Bava Batra*. See Urbach (above, n. 2), 600–75. The original text registered only those *Tosafot* of Ri's pupils—mentioned here and in the next two notes—that were published separately. Dr. S. Pick drew my attention to the misimpression created by such a restricted listing. For a full listing of all the *Tosfot Shants* including published fragments, see now Y. Kohen, 'Keta'im mi-Tosfot Shants le-Massekhet Kiddushin', *Yerushatenu*, 6 (2012), 15–18.}

[8] First published as *Tosfot R. Yehudah Ḥasid* in *Berakhah Meshuleshet* (Warsaw, 1860), subsequently from a fuller manuscript in the Bodleian Library, Oxford, as *Tosfot R. Yehudah Sir Leon 'al Massekhet Berakhot*, ed. N. Sachs, 2 vols. (Jerusalem, 1969, 1972); *Tosfot R. Yehudah Sir Leon 'al Massekhet 'Avodah Zarah*, in *Shitat Kadmonim 'al Massekhet 'Avodah Zarah* (above, n. 7). {The standard *Tosafot* on *Megillah* were penned by R. Yehudah; see Urbach (above, n. 2), 617–18.}

composed, under Ri's direction or at |40| least inspiration, a *reportatio* elucidating Ri's teachings regarding these matters. Entitled *Sefer ha-Terumah*, the work is in every sense a *Tosafot* from the school of Ri.[9]

Two areas of Jewish law are not found in either Rashi or *Tosafot*: agricultural law and the laws of purity. The former, discussed in *Zera'im*, primarily obtain in the Land of Israel, while the latter, addressed in *Toharot*, are operative only when the Temple in Jerusalem is standing. These tractates consist only of *mishnayot*. Both Rashi and the Tosafists restricted their work to talmudic tractates and therefore left these areas untreated. Ri's pupil, the aforementioned R. Shimshon of Sens, penned a vast commentary on these *mishnayot*, a work that has not been superseded to this day.[10] His departure for Israel in 1211 effectively ended the creative period of tosafist thought.

Most intellectual revolutions take a century or so to be absorbed, not only by the public but also by the discipline itself. Such was the case with the joint labors of Rabbenu Tam and Ri. Put differently, intellectual revolutions are by definition large-scale and their implications far-reaching; they achieve their full impact only when these new insights and their consequences are split up into smaller, more manageable units, retailed, as it were, to the larger community. The thirteenth century witnessed the division, repackaging, and delivery of the thoughts of the great men of the twelfth century. This took two forms: the writing of codes and the editing of the *Tosafot* that had issued forth from Ri's academy in Dampierre.

The first task, foreseen by R. Barukh, was undertaken on a grand scale by R. Mosheh of Coucy, Tosafist, preacher, and disputant at the trial of the Talmud in Paris in 1240. Organizing his work according to Maimonides' count of the biblical commandments, he reproduced under the rubric of each commandment the extensive discussions of the *Tosafot* of his teacher, R. Yehudah of Paris. The end product was a massive two-volume work entitled *Sefer Mitsvot Gadol*, which was accessible only to scholars.[11] The need for a briefer, practical guide to the tosafist teachings was immediately felt and swiftly met. R. Yitsḥak of Corbeil penned a much shorter work called *Sefer Mitsvot Katan*, which was widely diffused and very influential.[12]

9 There is no critical edition of *Sefer ha-Terumah*, which was first published in Venice in 1523. The 1897 Warsaw edition has appeared frequently as a photo offset. {For the standard *Tosafot* on *Zevaḥim*, see Urbach (above, n. 2), 661–2.}

10 On R. Shimshon of Sens, see Urbach (above, n. 2), 261–313.

11 The most recent complete edition is that of E. Schlesinger, 3 vols. (Jerusalem, 1995–9).

12 Though it is officially called *'Amudei ha-Golah*, I have never seen it referred to by anything other than *Sefer Mitsvot Katan*, or by its acronym, *Semak*. There is no critical edition of this much-used work, which was first published in Constantinople in 1509. The 1820 Kapost and 1935 Satmar editions have been frequently photo-offset.

The editing and abridging of the Dampierre *Tosafot* occupied such mid- and late-thirteenth-century Talmudists as R. Perets and R. Eli'ezer of Touques. Their works are known, not surprisingly, as *Tosfot R. Perets* and *Tosfot Touques*. Oddly enough, these thirteenth-century abridgments became the basis for our printed *Tosafot*, not the original *Tosafot* that issued forth from Ri's academy in Dampierre. In Italy in the late fifteenth century, the *Tosafot* of R. Shimshon of Sens were generally available, but by a strange twist of fate this classic set of *Tosafot* did not make it into the canon. Gershom Soncino, the printer of the first published Talmud, had somehow heard that the *Tosafot* of Touques and other late *Tosafot* were the most reliable. So he disregarded the *Tosafot* of R. Shimshon that lay readily to hand and, at personal risk, traveled to France to find those reputedly superior *Tosafot*. As he wrote thirty years later in a somewhat garbled note:

> יגעתי ומצאתי ספרים [ש]היו סתומים וחתומים (ו)מאז, והוצאתים לעין השמש הזאת [ש]יזהירו כזוהר הרקיע כמו התוספות מטוך של הר"י ורבינו תם. הלכתי עד צרפת וקמברי וזיניברה אל חדרי הורתם למען זכות בהם את הרבים, כי בספרד ובאיטליא ובכל הארצות לא שמענו אלא משאנץ של רבי פרץ ורבי שמשון וחבריהם.

I toiled and found books that were previously closed and sealed, and brought them forth to the light of the sun, to shine in the firmament, as the *Tosafot* from Touques of R. Yitsḥak and Rabbenu Tam [?!]. I traveled to France, Chambéry, and Geneva, the places where [the books] were conceived, so that the public might benefit from them, for in Spain, Italy, |**41**| and all the lands, we have only heard of the [*Tosafot*] of Sens, of R. Perets, and R. Shimshon and their colleagues.[13]

What he brought back from his foray to France was an assorted mixture of *Tosafot* from a variety of schools,[14] and this late medley of *Tosafot*, wholly derivative of those of Dampierre, is what he (and subsequently all other printers of the Talmud) published. It is these that have become the canonical *Tosafot* of the printed page. The caliber of Rabbenu Tam and Ri was such, however, that their thinking, even in a somewhat abrupt and abbreviated form, was powerful enough to shape the course of talmudic thought for close to a millennium. |**42**|

[13] See M. J. Heller, *Printing of the Talmud: A History of the Earliest Printed Editions of the Talmud* (New York, 1992), 102–3.

[14] See Urbach (above, n. 2), 600–75.

CHAPTER TWO

Catastrophe and Halakhic Creativity

Ashkenaz—1096, 1242, 1306, and 1298

THE TITLE of this essay is, in a sense, a misnomer; most of it is a survey of the Franco-German Tosafists and complements the preceding essay, 'The Printed Page of the Talmud'. The study assumed the form that it did as I sought to rectify a growing misconception that the massacres of the First Crusade precipitated an intellectual crisis. Traumatic the events of 1096 certainly were; psychological shock, however, is not the same as intellectual decline or stagnation. I found the notion of either of these consequences without foundation, indeed, contrary to everything that we know about the tosafist movement of the twelfth and thirteenth centuries and its immortal achievements. So I decided to preface the argument with a brief survey of that famous movement. (To some of the readers, this preface may be the essay's real *raison d'être.*) To broaden somewhat the scope of the study, I addressed four crises of the Ashkenazic community in the high Middle Ages and their significance in its intellectual history.

THE TITLE 'Catastrophe and Halakhic Creativity' is a misnomer—the dead don't think. The actual question being posed is: is the loss of creativity occasioned by death significant? This, in turn, hinges on where the field stood when catastrophe struck. For example, had a plague hit London in the year 1600, its effect on English literature would have been devastating, whereas had this happened in 1630, the impact would have been minimal. So the question we have to address is: where did halakhic creativity stand, in

An earlier version of this essay was presented at 'Crusades and Crusaders': An International Conference, Ben-Gurion University of the Negev, Beersheba, 17–19 June 1996, and again at the Twelfth International Congress of the World Union of Jewish Studies, Jerusalem, 25 July–3 August 1997. Sections were also presented at the Conference in Honor of the 850th Birthday of Rashi, held in Paris in late November 1990. My thanks are extended to Professors Gerard Nahon and Daniel Lasker, who graciously hosted the respective conferences in Paris and Beersheba. {An expanded version of this essay is found in my *Ha-Yayin bi-Yemei ha-Beinayim: Yein Nesekh—Perek be-Toledot ha-Halakhah be-Ashkenaz* (Jerusalem, 2008), 115–32.}

France and Germany, when catastrophe struck: in 1096—the Crusade massacres of German Jewry; in 1242—the burning of the Talmud; in 1306—the expulsion from France; and, finally, the corresponding destruction of the German cultural community in the closing decades of the thirteenth century and the early years of the fourteenth—by the imprisonment of R. Me'ir of Rothenburg in 1286, soon followed by his death in 1293, by the martyrdom of R. Mordekhai in the Rintfleisch pogroms in 1298, and, some six years later, in 1304, by the flight to Spain of R. Asher and his son, the future author of the Tur?

To answer these questions, I need to present, in encapsulated form, my perceptions of the Ashkenazic (Franco-German) culture of the high Middle Ages. Such a presentation entails an attempt, perhaps hubristic, to find some patterns in the amorphous, winding, glossatorial literature of the period, and to offer, at the same time, some preliminary characterization of some of the seemingly faceless figures and anonymous voices that confront us whenever we open a printed page of the Talmud.

I shall begin with the twelfth and thirteenth centuries—the age of the Tosafists—and conclude with my understanding of the eleventh century and the cultural impact of the massacres of 1096. |71|

When we speak of the Tosafists, we refer to the great school of talmudic glossators who flourished in the twelfth and thirteenth centuries, first in Champagne (Troyes, Ramerupt, and Dampierre), then in Île-de-France and Normandy. Great, in that their glosses shaped halakhic thought in the Middle Ages, have been published alongside the Talmud ever since the 1530s,[1] and are indissolubly associated with every attempt to understand that corpus to this very day. Indeed, if, as Whitehead once aphoristically said, all philosophy is a series of footnotes to Plato, we can say, with far less exaggeration, that all subsequent halakhic thought has been a series of footnotes to the Tosafists.

Origins tend to be obscure, and the origins of the tosafist method are no

[1] True, the Soncino printings had, from the outset (1484), always contained *Tosafot*, as did, of course, the benchmark printings of Daniel Bomberg. However, the pre-Expulsion printings in Spain and Portugal and that of Fez in the 1520s had the text of the Talmud with Rashi's commentary alone. Still, no text of the Talmud has been published in the past 475 years without the glosses of the Tosafists. See R. N. N. Rabbinovicz, *Ma'amar 'al Hadpasat ha-Talmud: Toledot Hadpasat ha-Talmud*, ed. A. M. Habermann (Jerusalem, 1965); and the introduction of H. Z. Dimitrovsky to *Seridei Bavli* (New York, 1979), 1–48. Even the Iberian printings say less than they appear to do. This format was probably determined by the students of R. Yitsḥak Campanton, the dominant halakhic figure in 15th-century Spain. In his academy, the Talmud was studied with Rashi's commentary and the novellae of Naḥmanides, rather than with the *Tosafot*. However, as Naḥmanides' *Ḥiddushim* are based on the *Tosafot*—indeed, are an extrapolation of tosafist thought—the Talmud was being studied, in Iberia no less than in France, through the writings of the Tosafists and through the lens of their thought.

different. Suffice it to say that, in the course of the first half of the twelfth century, halakhah undergoes, as does Christian theology, canon law—and Roman law, somewhat earlier—the transition from exegesis to dialectics.

If the origins of the dialectical movement are obscure, the person in whom it is first fully embodied, indeed, who placed dialectic decisively on the intellectual map, is anything but obscure. That role is occupied by the imperious figure of R. Ya'akov of Ramerupt (d. 1171), more commonly known as Rabbenu Tam—Rashi's grandson and the only Tosafist whose remarkable force of character was capable of piercing the thick veil of impersonality that envelops the glossators of the Middle Ages.[2]

Rabbenu Tam wrought a revolution and was well aware of the fact: through him flowed the imperious sense of bringing a newly wrested vision of truth to the world. His contemporaries, even his critics, sensed this, and their relationship to him was not simply one of respect or reverence, but of awe—awe before the unforeseeable and the unique. Fear of his intellectual thunderbolts and the force of his leonine personality often made timid men of those who had dealings with him.[3] Yet, despite his seminal labors, next to nothing of his writing

[2] This determination is independent of the question where talmudic dialectic first emerged—in France or in Germany. Let us even grant that the origins of dialectic are to be found in late 11th-century German thought—and I believe this not to be the case—nevertheless, its historical impact is via the work of Rabbenu Tam and Ri. It is their glosses that came to dominate all other halakhic cultures of Europe, that of Provence, Christian Spain, and even that of Germany (see H. Soloveitchik, 'Three Themes in *Sefer Ḥasidim*', *AJS Review*, 1 [1975], 349; id., 'Can Halakhic Texts Talk History?', *AJS Review*, 3 [1978], 148–9; repr. Chapter 7 below). And it is French *Tosafot* that have been published alongside the Talmud for close to half a millennium. In addition, there is no evidence that Rabbenu Tam or Ri drew their inspiration for dialectic from the writings of the first German Tosafist, R. Yitsḥak ben Asher (Riva), not to speak of any of his predecessors. Indeed, Rabbenu Tam had almost no knowledge of the writings of Riva, and Ri's acquaintance with them, though wider, was still patchy. Indeed, from the point of view of historical impact, the significance of German dialectics was minimal. The writings of the German Tosafists, Riva, Rivam, Ravyah, and R. Yitsḥak Or Zarua', scarcely ever crossed the cultural borders of the German Empire and swiftly fell into disuse even within the Empire, for the reasons spelled out below. Through florilegia as the *Mordekhai* and *Haggahot Maimuniyot*, many doctrinal *positions* of German thought did influence eastern Europe, but the German works themselves were unknown there. Both the dialectical method and the dialectical texts adopted in the study of the Talmud were, in eastern Europe as the world over, those of the French Tosafists (see below). {For a discussion of Riva's role in the rise of dialectic, see the Afterword to this essay. I have set forth my reasons for discounting the alleged 11th-century German origin of dialectics in 'Berurim ba-Halakhah shel Ashkenaz ha-Kedumah 2: Di'alektikah, Sekholastikah ve-Reshitan shel "ha-Tosafot"', *Sidra*, 24–5 (2009–10): *Zvi Steinfeld Festschrift*, ed. D. Henschke (Ramat Gan, 2011), 267–71. A translation of the article will appear in the second volume of this series. That essay also addresses the alleged influence of scholasticism, exemplified by Anselm, on the new dialectic of the Tosafists.}

[3] Here and in the next paragraph I have borrowed several formulations from my essay 'Can Halakhic Texts Talk History?' (above, n. 2).

has come down to us. A single elliptical and enigmatic work, first published only in 1811, entitled the *Sefer ha-Yashar*, constitutes his literary remains, and it would seem that this is not simply what survived but almost all that he wrote. That work is divided into two parts: responsa and novellae. The responsa are clear on the whole, the novellae often anything but. This is not due to scribal error, for when we have testimonial evidence, as from the *Sefer Ravyah* or the *Yiḥusei Tanna'im ve-Amora'im*, the text cited differs little from ours.[4] Some of the difficulty is clearly attributable to the fact that certain sections are the garbled writings of pupils. Other problems stem from the *Sefer ha-Yashar*'s additional role as Rabbenu Tam's notebook: it contains personal jottings that take on meaning only when placed in a wider context.[5]

However, the major source of obscurity lies in the simple fact that Rabbenu Tam was a great thinker but a poor |72| writer—at least of reasoned argument. Words came readily enough to Rabbenu Tam in the social aspects of correspondence, complimentary or derogatory, or when expressing himself briefly and succinctly to a knowledgeable inquirer. But when confronted with the task of full-scale exposition of text and ideas, the sentences seem to break down under the speed and weight of tumbling thought, and their texture is made yet rougher by an abruptness bred of impatience and imperiousness. It is ironic that the only Tosafist of stature who could wield with any degree of skill the metrics of Spanish verse[6] was rarely capable of writing a clear expository sentence, even by glossatorial standards.

The combination of restless creativity with difficulties in writing, especially of sustained composition, often leads to a dangerous disproportion between personal accomplishment and literary legacy, an imbalance that is strikingly noticeable in the works of Rabbenu Tam's great contemporary, Rabad of Posquières, whom he resembled in so many ways. Anyone who has

[4] Both works occasionally cite passages not found in our edition, hardly a surprising fact in view of the unedited and agglomerated state of the *Sefer ha-Yashar*. However, the new passages cited by them are no more felicitous in expression than are the old.

[5] e.g. *Sefer ha-Yashar: Ḥelek ha-Ḥiddushim*, ed. S. S. Schlesinger (Jerusalem, 1959), #344. The entry contains notes explaining how various talmudic passages are to be understood in light of Rabbenu Tam's doctrine of *belilato rakah*; however, the doctrine itself is not set forth there. If we did not know it from the writings of the Dampierre school (e.g. *Tosafot*, *Pesaḥim* 37b, s.v. *de-khulei*), the passage in the *Sefer ha-Yashar* would be nigh incomprehensible.

[6] R. Efrayim of Bonn (fl. mid-12th century) did indeed wield Spanish metrics more gracefully than did Rabbenu Tam; however, he was not in Rabbenu Tam's league as a Tosafist. That in itself may yet say little, for few people in the past millennium were in that league. More to the point, R. Efrayim of Bonn, as dialectician, did not have the stature of his contemporaries, R. Efrayim of Regensburg or R. Yo'el ha-Levi, not to speak of that of the latter's son, Ravyah (R. Eli'ezer ben Yo'el ha-Levi, died *c.*1225).

repeatedly experienced the voltage of Rabad of Posquières' brief notes and then surveys his literary legacy will feel that the creativity of the man was far greater than his actual oeuvre. Unlike Rashi or Maimonides, Rabad never found an appropriate format in which to systematically cast his life's work. Like Rabad, Rabbenu Tam's genius was of the type that needs a better receptacle for his insights than he was able to provide. And one wonders what the final image and impact of Rabbenu Tam would have been had he not been followed by the more orderly genius of Dampierre.

But followed he was by his nephew, R. Yitsḥak of Dampierre (Ri) (d. 1189). And the happy conjunction of uncle and nephew, so different in temperament, but equal in genius—even more significantly, equal in their mutually complementary geniuses—propelled halakhah to an unparalleled half-century of development, possibly the greatest half-century since Abbaye and Rava transformed their tannaitic heritage in the fourth century. By the year 1184 at the latest, the tosafist dialectic was, as we shall see, fully developed. What was left, at most, was its systematic application to the entire talmudic corpus, and this R. Yitsḥak of Dampierre accomplished with an awesome relentlessness that wholly belied his mild manner and soft-spoken deportment. His systematic labors and his unending attention to detail stood in sharp contrast to the free-wheeling thunderbolts of his uncle Rabbenu Tam, though, in his own quiet way, R. Yitsḥak of Dampierre brought about no less a number of *bouleversements.*

Though apparently an easy writer, Ri nevertheless wrote little, or perhaps his works have simply not survived. He certainly adopted the widespread method of *reportatio*.[7] The teacher or master would either dictate his teachings to a select student or a select student would write up the master's teachings; the master |73| would then check, if necessary emend, and then approve the text. The subsequent work went, in Latin sources, generally under the name of the master; in Jewish sources it would be called **תוספות או פירוש ר' פלוני שנכתב לפני ר' אלמוני**—the *Tosafot* or commentary of 'X' (the name of the student) written before (i.e. at the feet of) 'Y' (the name of the teacher). The hallmark of a *reportatio* was the two-letter abbreviation at the end: **מ"ר**, i.e. **מפי רבי** (from the mouth of the master).

Ri's teachings have come down to us through four primary channels, via the writings of four pupils: the *Tosafot* of his son, Rabbi Elḥanan, those of the

[7] On *reportatio*, see B. Smalley, *The Study of the Bible in the Middle Ages*, 2nd edn. (repr. Notre Dame, 1964), 200 ff. {P. Glorieux, 'L'Enseignement au Moyen Âge: Techniques et méthodes en usage à la Faculté de Paris au XIIIe siècle', *Archives d'histoire doctrinale et littéraire du Moyen Âge*, 43 (1968), 175–7, 185–6.}

great Rabbi Shimshon of Sens (d. 1214) and Rabbi Yehudah of Paris (d. 1224), and, finally, the code of his pupil, Rabbi Barukh[8] of Worms (d. 1211), the author of the *Sefer ha-Terumah*, who, though of German origin, is a French Tosafist to his fingertips.

The earliest *reportatio* was apparently that of his son, Elḥanan, who was killed in a pogrom in the year 1184, while in the midst, it would seem, of glossing the tractate *'Avodah Zarah*.[9]

These glosses have survived, and they manifest an already fully developed dialectic,[10] thus providing us with a *terminus ad quem* for the fruition of tosafist dialectic. Rabbi Shimshon of Sens picked up the pen of the fallen colleague R. Elḥanan, and proceeded under Ri's direction to compose glosses on much of the Talmud. And these glosses served as the basis of much of the *Tosafot* as we know them today, and as they have been known for close to half a millennium. Ri's German pupil, R. Barukh of Worms, sensed the need to translate current theory into practice, to align current practice with the new thought of the Tosafists, and composed the *Sefer ha-Terumah*. The work is not a code in the standard sense of the word, but rather a discursive analysis of the most significant issues in a number of important, select areas of Jewish law, such as the Sabbath, *kashrut*, *tefillin*, divorce, and, interestingly enough, the contem-

[8] The dates of death of the three figures in this paragraph are taken from the short chronicle published by I. M. Ta-Shma, 'Kheronikah Ḥadashah li-Tekufat Ba'alei ha-Tosafot mi-Ḥugo shel ha-Ri', *Shalem*, 3 (1981), 319–24. {Emanu'el has demonstrated that the German origins of R. Barukh are illusory. It is never mentioned in any medieval chronicle and first appears in the *Sefer Yuḥasin* of R. Avraham Zakut (Constantinople, 1576). My remarks here and in the next paragraph ('Ri's German pupil') thus need correction. See S. Emanuel, '"Ve-'ish 'al Mekomo Mevu'ar Shemo": le-Toledotav shel R. Barukh b. Yitsḥak', *Tarbiz*, 69 (2000), 423–40. One should note that the correction is genealogical only. That R. Barukh was a pupil of Ri and a French Tosafist to his fingertips has always commanded universal assent.}

[9] E. E. Urbach, *Ba'alei ha-Tosafot*, revised edn., i (Jerusalem, 1980), 254. That he was killed while composing the *Tosafot 'al 'Avodah Zarah* seems to emerge from the following: in 1182, two years before his death, he was writing on that tractate, as is evident from his remarks in his *Tosafot* at 9b, s.v. *hay*. Our text of this work stops abruptly, in mid-tractate, at fo. 35a. R. Asher ben Yeḥi'el (Rosh), who had the full literature of the French Tosafists at his disposal and selected the best of the *Tosafot* to edit, would seem to have no more than we do of R. Elḥanan's work on that tractate. In the *Tosfot ha-Rosh 'al 'Avodah Zarah*, R. Elḥanan's work is continually drawn upon until fo. 35a and then the citations abruptly disappear. Apparently R. Elḥanan's tragic death prevented the completion of this work. The *Tosfot ha-Rosh* on the first and second chapters of the tractate *'Avodah Zarah* have been erroneously published as the *Ḥiddushei ha-Rashba 'al 'Avodah Zarah* (Jerusalem, 1966); see the review of this work by A. Rosenthal in *Kiryat Sefer*, 42 (1967), 137–9.

[10] *Tosfot R. Elḥanan 'al 'Avodah Zarah*, ed. D. Fränkel (Husiatyn, 1901). {Urbach has already drawn attention to defects in Fränkel's transcription (*Ba'alei ha-Tosafot*, see above, n. 9). A superior edition based on MS Montefiore 65, which Fränkel had also used, was published by A. Y. Keuzer (Benei Berak, 2003).}

porary status of the sanctity of the Land of Israel, a topic possibly connected with his and some of his colleagues' intended emigration to the Holy Land. Limited as these issues are, R. Barukh of Worms's treatment of them faithfully reflects the teachings of Ri. *Sefer ha-Terumah* is, for all intents and purposes, another version of the *Tosafot* of R. Yitsḥak of Dampierre.

Rabbi Shimshon of Sens continued the commentarial enterprise of Rashi when he fused the exegetical base of Rabbi Yitsḥak of Simponte with his own insights and the full range of tosafist dialectic and produced a work on the two orders of the Talmud left uncommented by Rashi—*Zer'aim* and *Toharot*—a commentary that remains unrivaled to this day. His labors completed, he left Sens to settle in the Land of Israel, and with his departure in the year 1211 one may say that the *creative* period of the Tosafists came to an end. The thirteenth century simply arranged and packaged the intellectual revolution of the twelfth. |74|

An intellectual revolution often takes a century or so to be digested. So it was with the Newtonian revolution and, similarly, with that of Rabbenu Tam and Ri. Little new was accomplished in France in the thirteenth century, as any comparison of twelfth- and thirteenth-century *Tosafot* will indicate. Our printed *Tosafot* or those of R. Perets of Corbeil (both works of the late thirteenth century) add little or nothing to what we find in the *Tosafot* of the Dampierre school, such as the *Tosfot Sens* or *Tosfot Ri Sir Leon*, written a century earlier. Similarly, there is little in the *Sefer Mitsvot Gadol* of R. Mosheh of Coucy, written in the mid-thirteenth century, not found already in the Dampierre *Tosafot*. R. Mosheh's originality lies not in his creative dialectics but in the use that he made of Maimonides and in his fusion of the latter's work with that of the Tosafists.[11] The efforts of the thirteenth century were devoted to editing, abridging, and codifying the intellectual accomplishments of the twelfth. The burning of the Talmud in 1242 precipitated *no* intellectual crisis, opinion to the contrary notwithstanding, only an institutional one. Paris ceased to be what it had been for two generations, the major talmudic center in France. The schools moved out to the periphery, primarily and surprisingly to Normandy, Evreux, Touques, and Falaise, escaping somehow the ever-watchful eye of the much-feared *bailli*, Juan de Peronne, and, for equally incomprehensible reasons, to the southern outskirts of Paris, in Corbeil, eluding

[11] The controlled and careful use of the *Mishneh Torah* by R. Mosheh of Coucy is now clearly discernible in A. Merzbach and I. Peles's recent edition of the *Sefer Mitsvot Gadol* (Jerusalem, 1993). As only one volume of that edition has appeared, E. Schlesinger's *Penei Mosheh: Leshonot ha-Rambam ba-Semag* (Jerusalem, 1996) is also useful. {A second volume appeared in 2003. However, as the two volumes only go as far as Injunction #127, Schlesinger's work retains its utility.}

in some mysterious way the scrutiny of both the clergy and the inquestors of the king.

The code of Ri's pupil, *Sefer ha-Terumah*, had covered only select topics. The need for a comprehensive code translating the new Talmud of the Tosafists into halakhic practices became progressively more insistent. This task was undertaken by Rabbi Mosheh of Coucy, a participant in the Paris disputation of 1240. A scholar and an itinerant preacher, he was the one Tosafist who had ventured out of his homeland down to Spain, and in the year 1236 had there preached to the wayward. He says in his preface that he was prompted to record practical halakhah by the requests of his auditors, who had asked for some written halakhic guide to which they could refer.[12] Whether the ensuing work of R. Mosheh would have been comprehensible to those auditors I very much doubt. It rapidly proved too detailed and discursive for most—even in the author's native France. This should serve as a warning of the dangers in taking prefaces seriously. Authors are often the last people to be aware of the true nature of their work.

Almost immediately upon its appearance, abridgments were made: some proved ephemeral, such as that of R. Avraham ben Efrayim;[13] one, that of Rabbi Yitsḥak of Corbeil (*c.*1280), was an instant classic. Dividing the commandments into seven units and eliminating all dialectic and any Maimonidean traces, Rabbi Yitsḥak penned the definitive handbook of French halakhic practice. It rightly earned its |75| wide dissemination and influence. Indeed, no other tosafist work has survived in so many manuscripts. The *Semak*, as it was called,[14] was completed by the closing decades of the thirteenth century, as were the labors of the Tosafists in Normandy who edited and compressed the twelfth-century *Tosafot* of Dampierre into the format that was destined to be printed, centuries later, in the Talmud. With the completion of the *Semak* and the editorial work of Normandy in the third quarter of the thirteenth century, the French tosafist movement may be said to have come to its close. The expulsion of 1306 had no impact upon Jewish intellectual life; it simply sealed what the inner dynamic of Jewish life had already

[12] *Sefer Mitsvot Gadol* (*Lo Ta'aseh*), introduction (Venice, 1547), fo. 3a; ed. A. Merzbach and I. Peles, *Sefer Mitsvot Gadol* (Jerusalem, 1993), p. 13; ed. E. Schlesinger (Jerusalem, 1989), p. 5.

[13] The work is still in manuscript, though sundry passages have been published, e.g. A. Y. Ḥavatselet's edition of the first twelve sections published in the *Sefer ha-Zikaron la-Rav Yedidyah Frankel* (Jerusalem, 1992), 281–304. On the two differing versions of this work, see E. Kupfer, 'Me-raḥok u-mi-Karov', *Sefer ha-Yovel li-Khevod N. M. Gelber* (Tel Aviv, 1963), 217–19. {The work has since been printed: *Kitsur Sefer Mitsvot Gadol*, ed. Y. Horowitz (Jerusalem, 2004–5)}.

[14] An acronym for *Sefer Mitsvot Katan*. Interestingly, the author entitled his work *Sefer 'Amudei ha-Golah*; however, the name never caught on. Indeed, I know of no medieval author ever referring to it by this name.

tentatively closed. At most, it guaranteed, as did the terms of the subsequent readmission, that there would be no French Renaissance in Jewish history.

Germany, no less than France, experienced in the twelfth century the shift from exegesis to dialectic. The developments east of the Rhine were less concentrated and dramatic, but no less far-reaching. Beginning in the first decades of the twelfth century, not surprisingly in Speyer, the only major Jewish settlement that was spared the massacres of the First Crusade, dialectic spread in the next generation to Mainz and Regensburg, and then on to Bonn and Cologne. Creativity may have peaked in France at the turn of the thirteenth century, but in Germany it continued unabated throughout that century, though it assumed different forms and expressions. It is this, generally unnoted, dissimilarity that now merits our attention.[15]

The German and French dialectic, while identical in method, differed in their focus and ultimate impact. France, in the eleventh century, had no indigenous tradition. Intellectually, it was a backwater. The Torah centers from time immemorial were two cities in Lotharingia, Worms and Mainz, and in its revered academies Rashi himself had received his education. The French tradition, on the other hand, was the creation of Rashi and his family, Rabbenu Tam and Ri, and its intellectual ambiance was determined by the interests of those three central figures. Rashi focused on exegeting the text of the Talmud; Rabbenu Tam and Ri then focused on collating all discordant passages of the Talmud and resolving these contradictions. The labors of Rashi, Rabbenu Tam, and Ri became paradigmatic for the entire culture. French thought is focused on *explication de texte*. The text of the Talmud and it alone occupied French halakhic thought—to the point of exclusion of all other intellectual endeavors. No doubt they knew, as did their German and Provençal contemporaries, many responsa of the Ge'onim, not to speak of those of the leading scholars of Early Ashkenaz, yet one will search the tosafist literature in vain for any substantive references to them. Indeed, their preoccupation with the brave new world of dialectic contributed to their not attaching importance even to their *own* responsa. It is an obvious, but scarcely noted, fact that with the exception of |76| Rabbenu Tam, who was unique in more than one way, not a single collection of responsa of any French Tosafist has survived. A solitary attempt *was* made to preserve the responsa of the great R. Shimshon of Sens, but, significantly, no one considered such a

15 The only person to remark on some of these differences has been Y. Sussman in his 'Efrayim Elimelekh Urbach: Bio-Bibliografyah Meḥkarit', *Musaf Mada'ei ha-Yahadut: Bamat ha-Iggud ha-'Olami le-Mada'ei ha-Yahadut*, 1 (1993), 48–53, esp. nn. 63, 82, 83. I am gratified that, working independently, we arrived at similar conclusions.

collection important enough to be preserved.[16] Even Rashi's responsa were not preserved in France, indeed, were scarcely known by the French Tosafists, many of whom were his own descendants. Over the course of centuries, innumerable questions were naturally asked, and innumerable answers written, but these replies were viewed as *livres de circonstance*. Unlike commentary, responsa were simply not viewed as being a genre of literary expression.

Preoccupation with dialectic and text-fixation rendered the French oeuvre monochromatic. It was, however, what ensured its immortality. The Talmud was relentlessly scrutinized, interrogated, and collated, and the resultant product was an exhaustive, line-by-line analysis with which no student could dream of dispensing. Thus, the French glosses became *the* indispensable accompaniment to the talmudic text from the thirteenth century to our own day. The German glosses, as we shall see, with their heterogeneous nature and topical arrangement, never constituted a running commentary. They were a rich lode to be mined, indeed, to be exploited. And that is precisely what transpired. The German works were swiftly epitomized, and from florilegia, notably the *Mordekhai*, *Haggahot Maimuniyot*, and the *Haggahot Asheri*, their ideas entered the halakhic mainstream, but the massive tomes themselves lay generally unused and uncopied. Indeed, many were first printed only in the twentieth century.

To return to Germany chronologically. Heir to a long and variegated tradition, Germany never became halakhically single-minded. First, the Talmud was not the sole object of the German commentaries. Commentaries on the *midreshei halakhah*—*Sifrei*, *Sifra*, and *Mekhilta*—were written, as well as on tractate *Shekalim* of the Yerushalmi.[17] Liturgical texts, long objects of detailed study in Ashkenaz, continued to attract the attention of the German Tosafists:

[16] The responsa of R. Shimshon of Sens were gathered by R. Ya'akov of Courçon. There are one or two references to it in the tosafist literature and then it is heard of no more. Apparently no one saw fit to preserve it. See Urbach, *Ba'alei ha-Tosafot* (above, n. 9), 316–17.

[17] On *Sifra*: those of R. Simḥah of Speyer and R. Shemu'el he-Ḥasid and the pupil of R. David ben Kalonymus (published as the *Perush ha-Rash 'al Torat Kohanim*, Warsaw, 1866); on *Sifrei*: R. Me'ir ben Kalonymus; on *Mekhilta*, that of R. Shemu'el he-Ḥasid and, possibly, R. Me'ir ben Kalonymus (Urbach, *Ba'alei ha-Tosafot* [above, n. 9], 194–5, 312–18, 364–5, 418–19). On Yerushalmi *Shekalim*, that of R. Mosheh Tachau (Urbach, *Ba'alei ha-Tosafot* [above, n. 9], 422) and the two commentaries published by A. Sofer in *Massekhet Shekalim 'im Shenei Perushim le-Rabbotenu mi-Kadmonei ha-Rishonim* (Jerusalem, 1954). The German provenance of both commentaries was established by E. E. Urbach in his review of Sofer's work in *Kiryat Sefer*, 31 (1955–6), 326–8; and see Urbach, *Ba'alei ha-Tosafot*, 432. As Urbach notes (ibid. 422, 432) both R. Mosheh and R. Meshullam may have also written on other tractates of the Yerushalmi. {Urbach notes this possibilty only with regard to R. Meshullam. He states specifically in his introductory volume, *'Arugat ha-Bosem*, iv (Jerusalem, 1963), 157, that there is no evidence of commentaries by R. Mosheh Tachau on other tractates of the Yerushalmi.}

the twelfth century witnessed the composition of R. Eli'ezer of Mainz's (Ravan's) commentary on prayers, and the thirteenth the even greater work of R. 'Azri'el of Bohemia, the *'Arugat ha-Bosem*.[18] Halakhic biography in the guise of the *Yiḥusei Tanna'im ve-Amora'im*, even a dictionary of talmudic realia, were composed in this period in Germany.[19] And when they addressed the Talmud, as often they did, it was not in the spirit of relentless *explication de texte* as in France. To be sure, Ravyah (d. *c.*1225) and R. Yitsḥak Or Zarua' (d. *c.*1250) often explicated talmudic passages and brilliantly so, but, as often as not, they used the text simply as a point of departure and moved into associated topics. And responsa, |77| while never fully achieving the status of a genre of literature as in Spain, nevertheless had a respectable place in the German canon. The writings of the French Tosafists on the Talmud represent the sum total of explications of a specific talmudic *sugya* (passage); the cumulative works of the German Tosafists (such as the *Sefer Ravyah* and *Or Zarua'*) represent the sum total of known *discussions* on the specific *topic*, part of which is under discussion in a talmudic passage.

The mid-thirteenth century witnessed a shift in the direction of the creative energies of Germany, and much of this new orientation was accomplished by—or took place in the school of—R. Me'ir of Rothenburg (d. 1293). Responsa-writing, which had always had a respectable place in the German canon, achieved full stature and recognition in that figure's works, and in him Germany found her greatest respondent, the only one who bears comparison with the great respondents of Spain. A major attempt was made by a pupil of his, R. Me'ir ha-Kohen, to effect some sort of *reception* of the Maimonidean Code, a work that had hitherto gone almost unnoticed and certainly had been without influence in Germany.[20] And a massive florilegium of French and

[18] See E. E. Urbach's discussion, ibid. 3–127. The liturgical commentary of R. Eli'ezer of Mainz (Ravan) has been erroneously published by Mosheh Hershler as *Siddur R. Shelomoh mi-Germaiza* (Jerusalem, 1972). Rashi, raised in the traditions of the Rhineland and trained in its academies, actively engaged in liturgical commentary, as did members of his circle, as A. Grossman has detailed in his *Ḥakhmei Tsarfat ha-Rishonim: Koroteihem, Darkam be-Hanhagat ha-Tsibbur, Yetsiratam ha-Ruḥanit* (Jerusalem, 1995). However, once the dialectic revolution took hold, halakhists in France lost interest in such exegesis.

[19] R. Yehudah ben Kalonymus, *Yiḥusei Tanna'im ve-Amora'im*. The edition of Y. L. Maimon (Jerusalem, 1963) contains the entries for the letters *bet* to *tet*. The entries of letter *yod* have been published in two volumes by M. Y. H. Blau under a different title, *'Erkei Tanna'im ve-'Amora'im* (New York, 1994). On talmudic realia, see Urbach, *Ba'alei ha-Tosafot* (above, n. 9), 378.

[20] In the *Or Zarua'*, vols. i–ii (Zhitomir, 1862) and iii–iv (Jerusalem, 1887), the Maimonidean citations are peripheral at best. The author of the *'Arugat ha-Bosem* (ed. E. E. Urbach, vols. i–iii [Jerusalem, 1938–63]), R. 'Azri'el ben Avraham of Bohemia (fl. late 12th and early decades of the 13th century) is clearly intrigued by Maimonides' philosophical remarks in *Sefer Mada'*, but Maimonides'

German traditions was attempted by yet another pupil, R. Mordekhai ben Hillel. But outside events—the rapid decline in Jewish status in the closing decades of the thirteenth century, the successive, widespread massacres of the Good Werner (1287) and the Rintfleisch (1298)—put an end to this new flowering. R. Me'ir was incarcerated in 1286 and languished in prison till his death in 1293, his pupil, R. Mordekhai, was massacred in 1298, and in 1304 his other pupil, R. Asher (Rosh), fled with his son, the future author of the *Tur*, to Spain. With that flight, Germany lost two of the greatest halakhic jurists and codifiers of the Middle Ages. Few cultures could sustain four such losses over little more than a decade. Whatever chances there might have been for a rebirth were ended by the wholesale massacres of the Armleder and those during the Black Death. Germany lapsed into a decline that lasted for several centuries. Catastrophe, which struck the French community only after its intellectual work had been done, struck down German culture in its prime.

And what of the earlier catastrophe—that of 1096? From all the above, it is clear that Germany did not sink into any Dark Age in the years following 1096. Far from it: the centuries of lasting halakhic creativity were the twelfth and thirteenth, not the eleventh. It is the works of Ravan and Ravyah, R. Me'ir of Rothenburg and R. Asher, that are the staples of talmudic study to this day, not the *Sefer ha-Pardes* and the *Sefer ha-Oreh*, or the other anonymous florilegia of the eleventh century. That the First Crusade was traumatic is unquestioned. It was wholly unexpected, and unprecedented in its frightening scope. That it subsequently became emblematic in popular memory of the striking decline in Jewish status that followed in the twelfth century is |78| equally understandable, as the mind naturally runs along the line of *post hoc ergo propter hoc*.[21] The question, however, is not what it came to represent, but what it really was, what influence it actually had on the course of halakhic thought. From all that we know of the twelfth and thirteenth centuries, the answer is—clearly—little to none. Yet that clear answer raises an equally clear question: How could that be? How could the sudden, swift destruction of the central seats of learning of Ashkenaz be without impact? Why *did* no decline set in

halakhic positions do not bulk seriously in his work. {On the reasons for the failure of R. Me'ir's attempt to 'Ashkenize', as it were, *Mishneh Torah* and absorb it into the new, halakhic culture of the Tosafists, see my suggestion in '*Mishneh Torah*: Polemic and Art', in J. M. Harris, ed., *Maimonides 800 Years After: Essays on Maimonides and his Influence* (Cambridge, Mass., 2007), 339–55, to be reprinted in the second volume of the present series.

[21] On aspects of its image in Ashkenazic memory, see the Master's thesis of D. Wachtel (written under the direction of Yosef Hayyim Yerushalmi), 'The Ritual and Liturgical Commemoration of Two Medieval Persecutions' (Columbia University, 1995).

after the wholesale massacres of the intellectual centers of German Jewry in the early summer of 1096?[22] The answer, I believe, is simple.

In the eleventh century, Jews everywhere were engaged in explicating that massive, baffling work, the Talmud. The Mainz traditions took literary form in this century in what—much later—came to be known as the *Commentary of Rabbenu Gershom*, but more accurately should be called the *Anonymous Commentaries of Mainz*. The commentarial work of this school was superseded by the luminous commentary of Rashi as he summed up, transmuted, and transformed the commentarial traditions of Ashkenaz. With his work, exegesis came to an end, and the ground was prepared for the next stage of halakhic development, that of dialectic, which began some quarter of a century after his death. Had the devastating massacres occurred some forty years earlier, in 1056, it would have spelled disaster for the intellectual history of Ashkenaz. Rashi would have had no place to learn the exegetical traditions of the Rhineland, and the centers themselves would have been destroyed, their commentarial traditions lost forever. The bloodbath occurred, however, in 1096—at the end of a cultural era, in an intermission between two stages of halakhic development. By the final decade of the eleventh century, as Rashi (d. 1105) was nearing completion of his oeuvre, the age of talmudic exegesis was drawing to a close, and the importance of Germany to the commentarial enterprise had already ceased. A new age was dawning—that of dialectic—and its impetus and determining force came from France, in the Promethean figure of Rabbenu Tam and his unassuming, but no less intellectually formidable nephew, R. Yitsḥak of Dampierre, or R. Yitsḥak Ba'al ha-Tosafot—'R. Yitsḥak, the author of the *Tosafot*', as Naḥmanides aptly entitles him.

[22] The issue of the general significance of the First Crusade has been much discussed in recent years. Robert Chazan and Simon Schwarzfuchs have contended that 1096 had little long-term effect upon German Jewry. Avraham Grossman has argued that it had a major impact upon intellectual developments. Both Chazan and Schwarzfuchs have pointed to the tosafist movement as evidence of the continued intellectual vitality of Germany after the First Crusade. Needless to say, I share their views, and seek in these concluding paragraphs to address both the consequent question of why there was no decline and the new arguments that have been advanced for the pivotal role of 1096 in halakhic history. Cf. R. Chazan, *European Jewry and the First Crusade* (Los Angeles and London, 1987), 197–216; S. Schwarzfuchs, 'Mekomam shel Masa'ei ha-Tselav be-Divrei Yemei Yisra'el', in R. Bonfil et al., eds., *Tarbut ve-Ḥevrah be-Toledot Yisra'el bi-Yemei ha-Beinayim: Sefer Zikaron le-Ḥayyim Hillel Ben-Sasson* (Jerusalem, 1989), 251–68; Grossman, *Ḥakhmei Ashkenaz ha-Rishonim: Koroteihem, Darkam be-Hanhagat ha-Tsibbur, Yetsiratam ha-Ruḥanit mi-Reshit Yishuvam ve-'ad li-Gezerot Tatnu (1096)*, 3rd edn. (Jerusalem, 2001), 435–40, and more extensively in id., 'Shorashav shel Kiddush ha-Shem be-Ashkenaz ha-Kedumah', in Y. Gafni and A. Ravitzky, eds., *Kedushat ha-Ḥayyim ve-Ḥeruf ha-Nefesh: Kovets Ma'amarim le-Zikhro shel 'Amir Yekuti'el* (Jerusalem, 1993), 99–130, esp. pp. 101–5.

Two arguments have been advanced for the intellectual significance of 1096: first, Rashi's dramatic emergence as *the* commentator par excellence of the Talmud and the consequent shift of learning from Germany to France came in part as a result of the First Crusade. Second, the rapid emergence of dialectic and its swift monopoly on halakhic thinking was possible only because the old traditions and the venerable seats of learning of Worms and Mainz were obliterated by the events of 1096. |79|

Rashi emerged as the commentator par excellence, not because he stood on any mound of corpses, or because his platform was the ruins of Mainz and Worms, but simply because he was immediately *recognized* as being—and remains to this very day—the commentator par excellence. Rashi's work consigned the commentarial labors of R. Yehudah of Barcelona and of Rabad of Posquières, and even the talmudic commentaries of Maimonides, to the dustbin of history, and in an astonishingly brief period of time. To give two simple examples: R. Yehonatan of Lunel was a pupil of Rabad, a man viewed as the greatest of Provençal commentators (*gedol ha-mefarshim*, as Me'iri called him); yet Rabad's interpretations are absent from R. Yehonatan's commentaries. He follows Rashi entirely, one might say even slavishly, for he reproduces Rashi's remarks even in places where the version of the text upon which he is commenting differs from that of Rashi![23] Nor was the powerful presence of Maimonides a bar to Rashi's commentarial conquests, even in Maimonides' inner circle. R. Ḥanan'el ben Shemu'el was both Maimonides' in-law, his daughter being married to Maimonides' son, and a member of Maimonides' court (*bet din*). Yet in his published commentary on *'Eruvin*, he transcribes Rashi's remarks systematically; indeed, Rashi's words form the very basis of R. Ḥanan'el's work.[24] True, in the next generation, R. Peraḥyah restored Maimonides' commentaries to pride of place;[25] however, the restoration was fleeting. Maimonides' work swiftly fell into desuetude. So salient was Rashi's commentarial superiority that even the Yemenite community, which revered

[23] *Perush R. Yehonatan mi-Lunel 'al Bava Kamma*, ed. S. Friedman (Jerusalem, 1969), introduction, 8–13. (See I. M. Ta-Shma's interesting suggestion for this strange conduct in his *Rabbenu Zeraḥyah ha-Levi—Ba'al ha-Ma'or u-Venei Ḥugo* [Jerusalem, 1992] 156 ff.)

[24] *Perush R. Ḥanan'el ben Shemu'el 'al Massekhet 'Eruvin*, ed. A. Shoshanah (Jerusalem and Cleveland, 1996). The same holds true for his commentary on *Kiddushin*, published by Y. Suna in 1975—not surprisingly, as this commentary is, apparently, later than that on *Shabbat*. (See Suna's introduction to *R. Ḥanan'el ben Shemu'el—Perush 'al ha-Rif: Massekhet Kiddushin* [Jerusalem, 1975], 13.) In these commentaries, Maimonides' exegesis is salient, Rashi's pervasive.

[25] *Perush R. Peraḥyah ben Nissim 'al Massekhet Shabbat*, ed. A. Shoshanah (Jerusalem and Cleveland, 1988). Even this restoration is not all that it seems, for R. Peraḥyah regularly uses the commentary of R. Yehonatan of Lunel, who, as I noted in the text, faithfully reproduces the words of Rashi.

Maimonides as did no other and treasured every word that he wrote, allowed Maimonides' talmudic commentaries to totally disappear.[26] Rashi, as I have said, consigned competing commentaries to oblivion. It is difficult to imagine that someone who easily disposed of the commentaries of Rambam and Rabad 'needed' pogroms to overcome the *Anonymous Commentaries of Mainz*. Indeed, these commentaries disappeared with equal speed even within Germany, whose scholars had every reason to treasure them. Had these commentaries been composed in Regensburg, whose community, however unwillingly, had ended up at the baptismal font during the events of 1096, these works might have been ipso facto compromised. The vast majority of Mainz's Jews, however, had memorably given the ultimate measure of devotion, and by means of chronicle and liturgy the martyrs were swiftly enshrined in German Jewish memory as *the* exemplars of sacrificial fidelity. If anything, the First Crusade should have enhanced the aura of that city and of all that emanated from it, and in all probability it did. Commentaries, however, survive not because of their aura, but because of their utility; and the far greater utility of Rashi's work was apparent to all, even in Germany—German literature of the twelfth and thirteenth centuries yields few, if any, citations of the old Rhineland commentaries. Germany in the twelfth century, like |**80**| Provence, Spain, Italy, and even Egypt, in the thirteenth century, employed Rashi to the practical exclusion of all others, for one and the same reason: he was far and away the best.

As for 1096 clearing the ground for the rapid emergence and conquests of dialectic, it emerged most swiftly and dramatically in France—in the giant figures of Rabbi Ya'akov Tam and R. Yitsḥak of Dampierre. The center of talmudics shifted to France because of the astonishing succession of three figures of genius—Rashi, Rabbenu Tam, and Ri—whose thought swiftly dominated every subsequent halakhic culture of Europe—Germany, Provence, and Spain —whose writings have been printed alongside all editions of the Talmud since the 1530s,[27] and whose works dominate the halakhic scene to this very day.[28]

[26] Ta-Shma has suggested that Maimonides' commentary on the Talmud was an unfinished work that never circulated and was kept entirely within his family. I. M. Ta-Shma, 'Perush ha-Rambam la-Talmud—Ḥidah u-Fitronah', *Shenaton ha-Mishpat ha-'Ivri*, 14–15 (1988–9), 299–305 {reprinted in id., *Kenesset Meḥkarim: Iyyunim ba-Sifrut ha-Rabbanit bi-Yemei ha-Beinayim*, ii (Jerusalem, 2004), 309–16}. It's an interesting idea, and, if correct, would account, independently of the spread of Rashi's work, for the absence of any extant copies, even in the Yemenite community. It would not, however, explain the near-instantaneous disappearance of Maimonides' commentary from the writings of his inner circle to which I have drawn attention. At any rate, it remains, as Ta-Shma himself notes, an idea, and only time will tell if it is ultimately validated.

[27] See above, n. 1.

[28] See above, n. 2.

I opened by saying that if all philosophy is a series of footnotes to Plato, halakhic thought has certainly been a series of footnotes to the French Tosafists. I would close by simply adding: 'And 1096 had nothing to do with it.'

AFTERWORD

1. In a recently published essay in *Sidra*, I questioned the view that dialectic arose in the Worms school in the last third of the eleventh century, specifically in the academy (*bet midrash*) of R. Shelomoh b. Shimshon (Rabbenu Sasson).[29] A translation of that article will appear in the second volume of this series, as one of eight studies re-evaluating eleventh-century Ashkenaz. I would like to address here the notion that has gained traction these past two decades that the tosafist dialectic originated a generation before Rabbenu Tam (d. 1171) in Speyer, in the academy of R. Yitsḥak b. Asher, Riva, who died before 1133. This is factually true, yet historically problematic.

It is true in the sense that we know of *Tosafot* emanating from his academy (*Tosfot Rivam she-nikhtav lifnei Riva*, or *Tosfot Riva*), and these reasonably antedate any writings of Rabbenu Tam. It becomes problematic once we ask what it means to have 'originated' the dialectical method of the *Tosafot*. The method itself is found on every page of the Talmud, as *amora'im* scoured the tannaitic literature for even the slightest contradiction and resolved those they found by distinctions (*ukimtot*). The dialectical method was not new; it had lain dormant and was revived by the Tosafists. In saying this, I am distinguishing between a 'dialectical resolution' and dialectic as a method of study, a sustained mode of interrogating and understanding a corpus. People have resolved contradictions found in the Talmud from the moment of its 'publication'. This is hardly surprising, as the Talmud is rife with them. We find such resolutions in the Ge'onim, in R. Yosef Ibn Megas, in Maimonides, and frequently if unobtrusively in Rashi, as his super-commentators have long noted.[30] However, as I have already noted in the essay 'The Printed Page of the Talmud', these men did not study the Talmud comparatively, horizontally, as it were; they did not set out to *systematically* collate parallel passages of the

29 Above, n. 2—see the end of the essay.

30 See my *Yeinam: Saḥar be-Yeinam shel Goyim—'al Gilgulah shel Halakhah be-'Olam ha-Ma'aseh* (Tel Aviv, 2003), 20–2.

Talmud and resolve the contradictions they found. They studied the Talmud sequentially, vertically, as it were, one *sugya* after the other in the order in which they appear in the Talmud. Resolving contradictions that one has noted in the course of study of the Talmud is one thing; systematically scouring the Talmud *for* contradictions is another. Only those who practiced the latter are dialecticians. Only when the very study of Talmud means the systematic quest for contradictions and their resolution can one speak of a 'dialectical movement'.

It is difficult to place Riva with certainty on either side of the dividing line, as we have yet to find any manuscript containing his *Tosafot* on so much as one chapter of the Talmud, let alone on an entire tractate. There are citations of Riva in the tosafist literature and many of them contain proffered resolutions of contradictions; however, this, after all, is what the Tosafists, dialecticians all, *would* cite of his work. How representative of his corpus were these questions? How large a role did dialectics play in Riva's thought? We simply don't know.

Let us even assume, and I believe the assumption to be reasonable, that Riva did indeed occupy himself with the classic triad—collation, contradiction, and distinction—which would make him the first dialectician in Ashkenaz. We are still left, however, with the question of caliber. It is not difficult to make a distinction between two ostensibly similar cases. (Lawyers do this daily in the briefs that they submit to any court.) It is difficult, however, to endow a suggested distinction with significant judicial meaning. It is immensely difficult to endow hundreds upon hundreds, indeed thousands, of distinctions with significant judicial meanings. Only figures of towering genius could do so; Rabbenu Tam and Ri had that necessary stature. The questions that they asked and the innumerable distinctions that they made have been scrutinized by subsequent halakhic thinkers for close to a millennium and have proven to be endlessly rich in meaning. Indeed, acquiring knowledge of these distinctions came to be viewed as the first step towards any understanding of halakhah.

One may reasonably question whether the *Tosafot* of Riva were of similar stature. This is not to denigrate Riva; few if any in the past millennium *could* compete with the joint efforts of Ri and Rabbenu Tam. First, let us note how little of the *Tosfot Riva* has survived: nothing in manuscript and relatively little in citation. The *Tosafot* emanating from Dampierre (either in their original or edited form) have come down to us, indeed, in many different forms—the standard, printed *Tosafot*, *Tosfot Shants*, *Tosfot R. Yehudah mi-Paris*, *Tosfot R. Perets*, and the like. Further, there are probably thousands of quotations and citations of their positions in the Franco-German literature of the Middle

Ages. No *Tosafot* of Riva whatsoever have survived—not even in fragmentary form, and the citations of them in medieval rabbinic writings are very few and quite far between.[31] That French scholars do not refer to the *Tosfot Riva* is understandable, but why do the German Tosafists refrain from citing him? Even Ravyah, who does quote Riva far more frequently than most, cites many more of his specific interpretations of talmudic passages and individual rulings (*pesakim*) than his dialectical resolutions of contradictory discussions in the Talmud.[32] This tells us something of the *relative* worth of Riva's dialectic. Apparently few of his distinctions were worth repeating, once (and I emphasize *once*) one was acquainted with those of Rabbenu Tam and Ri.

Indeed, from the *Tosfot ha-Rav* cited in our printed *Tosafot* on *Mo'ed Katan*, which J. N. Epstein has shown to be that of the Riva,[33] one can get a sense of the caliber of that scholar's *Tosafot*. I doubt whether anyone using those citations will improve his grasp of the tractate. Admittedly, there is little dialectic in *Mo'ed Katan*; this, however, should not mislead us. Significance is a function of intellect, and intellect will out, will manifest itself in exegesis, dialectics, judicial rulings, or whatever. There are jurisprudential problems in *Mo'ed Katan*, as in any other tractate, and these are simply not addressed by Riva, at least not in what has come down to us. Compare the insights into the issues of mourning (*avelut*) of the *Tosfot ha-Rav* with those of Rabad, for example, found in the numerous citations of his lost commentary in the *Hilkhot Semaḥot* of R. Me'ir of Rothenburg and in the *Shitah* that emanated from the academy of Rabbenu Yeḥi'el of Paris.[34] The intellectual power of Rabad's insights is manifest. Does anyone doubt that, had Rabad written *Tosafot* on a tractate, *his* distinctions would have been jurisprudentially significant? Caliber is caliber, and what we have of Riva in *Mo'ed Katan* is deficient in this regard. We also know that Rabbenu Tam twice found Riva's resolutions incomprehensible and told his students:

> **ומה שתירץ הרב ר' יב"א---הוא לא תירץ והוא לא עשה אותם התוספות המעתיקים קראום על שמו. ולא תסמכו עליהם כי רובם (שגיגות) [שגויות].**

[31] It won't do to attribute this loss to the effects of the First Crusade, as that occurred in 1096 and Riva died a generation later, sometime prior to 1133. Cf. I. M. Ta-Shma, 'Review of Ḥ. Soloveitchik's *Yeinam: Saḥar be-Yeinam shel Goyim*', *Zion*, 69 (2004), 507–8.

[32] See V. Aptowitzer, *Mavo le-Sefer Ravyah* (Jerusalem, 1938), 239, 287, 296.

[33] J. N. Epstein, *Meḥkarim be-Sifrut ha-Talmud u-ve-Safot Shemiyot*, ii: 2 (Jerusalem, 1988), 942–4.

[34] R. Me'ir mi-Rotenburg, *Teshuvot, Pesakim u-Minhagim*, iii: *Hilkhot Semaḥot*, ed. Y. Z. Cahana (Jerusalem, 1963); *Otsar Rishonim 'al Mo'ed Katan: Shitah le-Talmido shel R. Yeḥi'el mi-Paris* (Jerusalem, 1937).

The resolution of Riva is not his resolution [i.e. he never said it] and he never wrote those *Tosafot*. It was the copyists who attributed them to him and do not rely on them for most of them are shot through with errors.[35]

No one could appreciate better than Rabbenu Tam Riva's pioneering attempt at dialectic, but no one knew better than he just how far it fell from the mark. He took care to cast no aspersions on his predecessor, and his formulation was notably polite for that sharp-tongued genius; its import, however, seems clear.

If one measures innovation by the simple criterion of who tried it first, Riva probably was the first dialectician; though seeing that dialectic is found on every page of the Talmud and noting how rife that corpus is with contradictions, one may well assume that many people attempted dialectic before him. Here and there, Riva, together with these anonymous Talmudists, may have made some important distinctions; however, they were incapable of doing so systematically. Rabbenu Tam and Ri succeeded in reviving dialectic and making it the basic tool of talmudic analysis to this day because they demonstrated on every page of the Talmud just how productive, indeed indispensable, the approach was. No Jewish scholar in the Middle Ages discovered dialectic; two scholars revived it and proved its indispensability; neither of them was Riva.[36]

2. Joseph Dan, in his recently published *Toledot Torat ha-Sod ha-'Ivrit bi-Yemei ha-Beinayim* (Jerusalem, 2011), 12, n. 2, has demurred from my assessment of the consequences of 1096 on Jewish intellectual history. While admitting that the twelfth and thirteenth centuries were ones of outstanding creativity, he argues that any statement that the First Crusade had little effect is 'what-if history'. Who is to say that the German late eleventh and twelfth centuries might not have been the equal of the French ones had Mainz and

35 I take *sheguyot* as being a stronger term than *ta'uyot* or *mut'ot*. If the reader feels differently, he may strike the words 'shot though' from the above sentence. *Sefer ha-Yashar, Ḥelek ha-Ḥiddushim*, #315. See also *Or Zarua'*, iv (Jerusalem, 1887), *'Avodah Zarah*, #284 about the report of another ruling of Riva

וגם כשנאמרו דברים לפני ר"ת היה תמה והיה אומ[ר]: פה קדוש יאמר דבר זה!? הלכך אין לסמוך על המכתב.

When these words were reported to Rabbenu Tam, he said, 'Such a holy mouth [i.e. wise person] should say such things?!' Therefore, do not rely upon the letter.

36 Perhaps there is some rush to judgment in my remarks. After all, there are not that many citations of the *Tosfot ha-Rav* in *Mo'ed Katan*. The new set of *Tosafot* on *Shabbat* being published by A. Shoshanah (*Tosfot Ri ha-Zaken ve-Talmido*, i [Jerusalem, 2007], ii [Jerusalem 2010]) will provide us with a far larger number of such reports. After an in-depth study of that work, I may have to revise my judgment; until then, I stand by this assessment. For a differing view of Riva, see Y. Sussman, 'Efrayim Elimelekh Urbach' (above, n. 15), 47–8, n. 78.

Worms not been destroyed? It is a possibility, to be sure; but, to my mind, it is an implausible one. Allow me to make an analogy. In one (admittedly limited) sense, Mozart emerged from the Mannheim school. Suppose Mannheim had later been destroyed, and someone had commented that this was of little matter to music, for Mozart had already transformed and transfigured the Mannheim legacy and, soon after that, Beethoven proceeded to revolutionize music entirely. To this contention the following objection was raised: who can say that Mannheim would not have produced a second Mozart and Beethoven of its own? The chances of a second Mozart and a second Beethoven appearing alongside the first Mozart and the first Beethoven are as great as that of Germany producing another Rashi, Rabbenu Tam, and Ri alongside the original ones. This triad will figure in any count of the half-dozen greatest Talmudists of the past millennium. Titans aren't born twinned.

CHAPTER THREE

The Halakhic Isolation of the Ashkenazic Community

THIS ESSAY was written for a conference on why science made so few inroads into medieval Ashkenazic culture. The scientific corpus was readily available in the Middle Ages, and some of it seems to have circulated in Ashkenaz, yet it remained without cultural resonance. I was surprised to be invited to this conference since, as I told its organizers, I knew nothing about science in Ashkenaz. However, I added that the phenomenon of cultural isolation held true for Ashkenaz even in halakhah, and they asked me whether I would give a presentation on that. The following paper was the result. As noted below, I drew freely here on previous studies, and whatever merit the essay has lies in the recasting of old material (together with some new data) to portray to what degree Ashkenaz chose to be indifferent to the accomplishments of other halakhic cultures.

I HAVE NO GOOD TIDINGS |41| to bring to the conference. Indeed, I have, perhaps, no tidings at all. I know nothing about science in Ashkenaz, nor in any other Jewish culture for that matter. I can speak only of matters halakhic, and can only point out the isolation of Ashkenaz in that area, too.

Let me begin at the end. The lights were going out for the Jews in Ashkenaz in the closing years of the thirteenth century. They were expelled from England in 1290, and from the royal kingdom of France in 1306. In Germany, the collapse of the strong imperial government exposed the Jews to two

I have in this essay drawn freely, both in substance and in formulation, upon two previous studies of mine, 'Catastrophe and Creativity: 1096, 1240, 1306', *Jewish History*, 12 (1998), 71–85 (Chapter 2 above), and '*Mishneh Torah*: Polemic and Art', in J. M. Harris, ed., *Maimonides 800 Years After: Essays on Maimonides and his Influence* (Cambridge, Mass., 2007), 339–55. (The essay will appear in the second volume of this series. Given the nature of the audience here addressed, I saw little reason to burden my essay with numerous halakhic citations. The reader who seeks such documentation will find it in the above-mentioned studies.)

murderous waves of pogroms, that of the Good Werner in 1287 and the Rintfleisch in 1298, which devastated some 140 Jewish communities. R. Me'ir of Rothenburg was imprisoned in 1286 and lingered in confinement for a decade until his death in 1293. His pupil, R. Mordekhai, fell victim to the Rintfleisch massacres, and his other famed pupil, R. Asher, fled south with his young son, the future author of the *Arba'ah Turim*, and in 1306 he became the rabbi of the Jewish community of Toledo in Spain.

In Toledo, Rabbenu Asher penned his famous *Sefer Pesakim*. A generation later, his son, R. Ya'akov, authored the classic *Arba'ah Turim* (more commonly called simply *Tur*) which formed the basis of the famous sixteenth-century code, the *Shulḥan 'Arukh*. R. Asher arrived at a time when the Catalonian school of Naḥmanides was flourishing, and his works were widespread in Spain. R. Asher's colleague and political patron was the great R. Shelomoh Ibn Aderet of Barcelona, Rashba, whose novellae are to this day staples of talmudic studies. And the contemporary of the author of the *Tur* was no less a figure than R. Yom Tov Al-Sevilli, more commonly known as Ritva, whose works are on the desk of all students of the Talmud.

|42| The *Sefer Pesakim* of Rabbenu Asher (Rosh) swiftly made its way back to Germany, as did subsequently the *Arba'ah Turim*. The first was accorded great weight in subsequent Ashkenazic thought, the second work somewhat less. Its easy accessibility, its readability even for a layman, made it somewhat suspect in some elite rabbinic circles,[1] but its readership was widespread indeed. Yet the great novellae of the Catalonian school, the *ḥiddushim* of Ramban, Rashba, Rah, and Ritva, remained completely unknown in Ashkenaz. Not that their way of thinking was new or alien to Ashkenaz, quite the contrary. Naḥmanides' school was the natural offshoot—indeed, the second stage—of the tosafist movement. The true intellectual successors of Rabbenu Tam and Ri of Dampierre were not R. Yehudah or R. Yeḥi'el of Paris, or R. Perets of Corbeil, but the great halakhists of Catalonia whose works I have just enumerated. Indeed, in Ritva's writings, the Franco-German dialectic received its most literate and sophisticated expression. Yet Ashkenaz ignored them totally. Not for lack of availability. The same travelers who brought back to German Jewry the writings of their exiled intellectual leaders, Rabbenu Asher and R. Ya'akov Ba'al ha-Turim, could equally well have provided them with the Catalonian writings, which constituted the culmination of Ashkenaz's intellectual aspirations. But this culmination was foreign, and was totally ignored for centuries.

[1] See the appendix to my essay, '*Mishneh Torah*: Polemic and Art', cited above in the unnumbered note (p. 31).

Is this because we are dealing with little men? The scholars of fourteenth- and fifteenth-century Germany were indeed small in comparison with the titans of the twelfth and thirteenth. Is it because we are dealing with men too fearful of any change to their cultural heritage, even if, in retrospect, we can see that it would not have been a change but rather the apogee of their traditions of thought? Possibly; let us, however, step back two centuries, to a time when giants still walked the lands of Ashkenaz, and see if the situation was any different. The first decade of the thirteenth century saw the appearance of the *Mishneh Torah* in northern Europe. One of the very first scholars to receive a copy of that work, or at least parts of it, was R. Shimshon of Sens, the third figure in the triumvirate of genius that, to all intents and purposes, created the tosafist corpus: Rabbenu Tam (R. Ya'akov of Ramerupt, d. 1171), Ri (R. Yitsḥak of Dampierre, d. 1189) and Rash mi-Shants (as R. Shimshon of Sens is called in Hebrew sources, d. *c.*1220). We know that he received the first book of Maimonides' opus and was aware of the work's scope. Had he wished, he could easily have received its seventh and ninth books, those codifying and explicating the talmudic orders of *Zera'im* and *Toharot*. Perhaps he actually did, but we shall never know, for he made not the slightest use of them. His interpretations |43| of those two orders of the Talmud of fabled difficulty would be the product of *his* skills, the dialectic of his masters, Rabbenu Tam and Ri, and the Italian traditions from Simponte to which Ashkenaz was heir. The writings of some Spanish or Egyptian scholar were of no interest to him, regardless of how great the latter's command of the Talmud may have been. Was this perhaps an idiosyncrasy of R. Shimshon? Some artists find stimulation in the works of contemporaries, as did Mozart for example; others, such as Beethoven, feel that the compositions of others cramp their own creativity. Beethoven listened to, or rather read the scores of, Handel, but of almost no one else. Was R. Shimshon a kindred soul of Beethoven? Let us look at his successors. In the course of the entire thirteenth century, Maimonides' *Mishneh Torah* had almost no impact on French thought. There is scarcely a single reference to *Mishneh Torah* in the standard *Tosafot* on the Talmud, which fill some twenty-two volumes. To be sure, one Tosafist, R. Mosheh of Coucy, who had preached in Spain in the 1230s, had to acquaint himself with *Mishneh Torah* in view of Maimonides' influence in that country. From his readings, he realized two things: first, that Maimonides' extraordinary organization of large and complicated topics in halakhah, as *Hilkhot Shabbat*, for example, should be utilized; second, that Maimonides had formulated in crystalline Hebrew prose many obscure Aramaic dicta, and even gnomic Hebrew ones found in the Talmud, and that these well merited reproduction.

He proceeded to do so in his massive, two-volume *Sefer Mitsvot Gadol*, better known by its acronym, *Semag*. However, his approach to Maimonides' work is essentially that of scissors and paste: occasionally he borrows the structure; very frequently he lifts sections, sentences, or even apt phrases from Maimonides' work and uses them for his own purposes. Does he ever come to grips with Maimonides' *own* thought, with the innumerable distinctive views that he introduced into halakhah, not to speak of the conundrums that Maimonides created with some of those views—with which scholars have wrestled for centuries? Almost never.

Even this limited infusion of non-Ashkenazic material was short-lived. No sooner was R. Mosheh of Coucy's detailed, two-volume work 'published' in the mid-thirteenth century than abridgments were made, such as the widely disseminated *Sefer Mitsvot Katan*, more commonly called (by its acronym) *Semak*, or the less known abridgment of R. Avraham ben Efrayim. The first thing that the condensers did was to throw out the Maimonidean formulations—lock, stock, and barrel. And they weren't missed. No work was more copied and none more glossed and annotated than the famed abridged code, *Semak*. Scribe after scribe, owner after owner added to and emended its formulations; but rare is the gloss |**44**| in any manuscript of that work that restores a Maimonidean formulation. French halakhic culture had no use for Maimonidean thought, and could do quite well, indeed, without so much as a line of Maimonides' famed prose.

In Germany the situation was not essentially different. The author of the *'Arugat ha-Bosem*, R. 'Azri'el of Bohemia, a man of extraordinarily wide knowledge, was acquainted with the *Mishneh Torah*, and cites passages from the first three books of that work, but other than some passages in the *Sefer Mada'* that treated topics that he had not heard of before, the citations are inert references, not components of R. 'Azri'el's dynamic thought. The same holds true for R. Yitsḥak Or Zarua' of Vienna (d. *c.*1250), the great encyclopedist of the Ashkenazic world. He cites many more Maimonidean rulings than do his *confrères*, but again they are technical citations of agreement and disagreement; there is rarely any *engagement* with Maimonides' talmudic views, with the singular positions that he occasionally adopted that have fascinated Talmudists for close to a millennium.

Germany's unconcern with—indeed, immunity to—Maimonidean influence is more telling than is the same indifference in France, for French halakhic culture was monochromatic and even, if you wish, provincial. A few words about the difference between these two halakhic cultures are now in order.

The German and French dialectic, while identical in method, were different in focus and ultimate impact. France, in the eleventh century, had no indigenous tradition. Intellectually, it was a backwater. The Torah centers from time immemorial had been the two revered academies in Worms and Mainz, where Rashi himself had received his education. The French tradition, on the other hand, was the creation of Rashi (d. 1105) and his descendants—his grandson, Rabbenu Tam, and great-grandson, Ri—and its intellectual ambiance was determined by the interests of those three central figures. Rashi focused on exegeting the text of the Talmud; Rabbenu Tam and Ri then focused on collating all discordant passages of the Talmud and resolving these contradictions. Put differently, Rabbenu Tam and Ri concentrated on the dialectical exegesis of the Talmud. The labors of Rashi, Rabbenu Tam, and Ri became paradigmatic for the entire culture. French thought is focused on *explication de texte*. The text of the Talmud and it alone occupied French halakhic thought—to the extent of excluding almost all other interests. Codes were written, such as the *Sefer ha-Terumah* and the *Sefer Mitsvot Gadol*, but these focused far more on dialectic than on codification. Indeed, one has to wait until the close of the thirteenth century, with the appearance of the *Sefer Mitsvot Katan*, for anything that resembled what we would call a 'code', namely, a straightforward series of 'dos' and 'don'ts', without elaborate discussions of their talmudic origins and alternative views.

No doubt, the Tosafists knew, as did their German and Provençal contemporaries, |45| many responsa of the Ge'onim, not to speak of those of the greats of Early Ashkenaz, yet one will search in vain the tosafist literature for any substantive references to them. Indeed, their preoccupation with the 'brave new world' of dialectic contributed to their not attaching any importance even to their *own* responsa. Even Rashi's responsa were not preserved in France, indeed, were scarcely known by the French Tosafists, many of whom were his own descendants. Over the course of centuries, innumerable questions were naturally asked and innumerable answers written, but these replies were viewed as *livres de circonstance*, to be discarded and forgotten after they had served their purpose. Unlike commentary, responsa were simply not viewed as being a genre of halakhic creativity and expression.

Preoccupation with dialectic and text-fixation rendered the French oeuvre uniform and single-minded. This, however, ensured its immortality. The Talmud was relentlessly scrutinized, interrogated, and collated, and the resultant product was an exhaustive, line-by-line analysis with which no student could dream of dispensing. The French glosses thus became *the* indispensable accompaniment to the talmudic text from the thirteenth century to our own day. French thought was indeed inward-turning and totally self-preoccupied, exclusivist to the point of hubris; however, its genius was such that it turned the city of Troyes and the tiny hamlet of Dampierre into the capitals of the halakhic world for close to a millennium.

So exclusivist were the French Tosafists that they remained indifferent even to the great dialectical works of their German brethren. German students flocked to French academies in the thirteenth century, bringing with them the works of their teachers. Yet the French scholars ignored them almost entirely. Given such a complete absorption with the new world of talmudic thought, which they believed that they and they alone had uncovered, it is not at all surprising that the French were not interested in the works of other cultures. The German cultural exclusivity is, however, puzzling.

Heirs to a long and variegated tradition, German scholars never became halakhically single-minded. First, the Talmud was not the sole object of their commentaries. Commentaries on the *midreshei halakhah—Sifra*, *Sifrei*, and *Mekhilta*—were written, as well as on tractate *Shekalim* of the Yerushalmi. Liturgical texts, long the object of detailed study in Ashkenaz, continued to attract the attention of the German Tosafists: the twelfth century witnessed the composition of a commentary on prayer by R. Eli'ezer of Mainz (Ravan), and the thirteenth an even greater commentary by R. 'Azri'el of Bohemia, the *'Arugat ha-Bosem*. Halakhic biography in the guise of the *Yiḥusei Tanna'im ve-Amora'im*, even a dictionary of talmudic realia, were composed in this period in Germany. Moreover, when German Tosafists addressed the Talmud, as they often did, it was not in the spirit of relentless *explication de texte* as in France. To be sure, Ravyah (d. *c.*1225) |46| and R. Yitsḥak Or Zarua' (d. *c.*1250) often explicated talmudic passages, and brilliantly so, but as often as not they used the text simply as a point of departure and moved into associated topics. Finally, responsa, while never fully achieving in Germany the same proud status of a halakhic genre as they did in Spain, nevertheless occupied a respectable place in the German canon. The German library is a vast one, rich in midrashim and geonic works many of which are lost to us, and its range of interests was truly encyclopedic; but German thinkers were interested in every aspect of their *own* multifaceted literature and traditions; they were uninterested in the literature and thought of Provence and Spain.

Let us remember that the twelfth century witnessed the spread of Rashi's commentaries and those of his grandson, Rashbam (d. *c.*1140), to Provence and beyond. During this same period, R. Zeraḥyah ha-Levi of Lunel, *Ba'al ha-Ma'or*, spread the teaching of Rabbenu Tam far and wide, and by the thirteenth century the literature of both Provence and Catalonia was saturated by the writings of Rashi and the French Tosafists. Far more than simply numerous citations, these writings form the warp and woof of the halakhic literature of those cultures. The movement of ideas, however, was always from north to south, never the reverse. Little to nothing of the writings of Rabad of Posquières or R. Zeraḥyah ha-Levi of Lunel ever traveled up the Rhone–Saône valley, and despite the growing emigration of Ashkenazic Jews to the more hospitable lands of southern Europe, nothing of the writings of Naḥmanides and his school ever moved north. Provence and Catalonia drank avidly at the wells of Ashkenaz. Ashkenaz remained ignorant of, and willfully indifferent to, the great creative achievements of Provence and Catalonia throughout the entire Middle Ages.

Only one figure in the history of Ashkenaz was free of this cultural chauvinism (and chauvinism it was): R. Me'ir of Rothenburg. Unique in many ways, he also recognized greatness when he saw it and availed himself of it from whatever source he could. The tractate *Mo'ed Katan* had, for whatever reason, never received proper commentary and exposition from the Tosafists, and R. Me'ir used, extensively and unhesitatingly, the commentary on that tractate of the great Provençal scholar, Rabad of Posquières. In the same ecumenical spirit, he instructed or inspired his student R. Me'ir ha-Kohen to write a massive Ashkenazic gloss to the *Mishneh Torah*, known as the *Haggahot Maimuniyot*. R. Me'ir of Rothenburg realized that Maimonides' work was not to be scissored and pasted, nor even to be excerpted or epitomized, but in view of the grandeur of its scope it deserved, indeed demanded, to be taken in its entirety—in all its massive, fourteen-volume entirety. It only required updating—that is to say, it needed to be annotated and emended with tosafist notes—and then incorporation into the Ashkenazic canon. In other words, he was to gloss and 'Ashkenize' it, in much the same fashion as R. Mosheh |47|
Isserles of Cracow was to do in the latter half of the sixteenth century with the next great Sefardic code, the *Shulḥan 'Arukh*. In fact, his emendations had served to canonize the *Shulḥan 'Arukh* in eastern Europe.

At the time, and even in retrospect, there was every reason to believe that the cultural barriers would at last come down, at least in part: that the effect of the *Haggahot Maimuniyot* on *Yad ha-Ḥazakah* would be the same as that of Isserles' *Mappah* on the *Shulḥan 'Arukh*—reception through emendation and update. Behind the *Haggahot Maimuniyot* stood the authority of R. Me'ir of Rothenburg, the last of the German Tosafists, the greatest decisor (*posek*) of Ashkenaz, and one whose personal conduct and rulings were scrupulously reported and generally viewed as normative. Yet this attempt to breach the walls of cultural isolation, this valiant effort to incorporate the greatest work of

Andalusian halakhah into the Ashkenazic canon, was a failure. Never—to the slightest extent—did the *Yad ha-Ḥazakah* (or its relevant sections) become the basis of an Ashkenazic code. The *Haggahot Maimuniyot* did not become the *Mappah* to the *Mishneh Torah*. It soon served simply as a source of information for Franco-Germanic works that were either lost—as were the *Or Zarua'* and *Sefer Ravyah*—or hard to come by, as was the *Semag*. In other words, the *Haggahot Maimuniyot* served only to teach Ashkenaz more about itself, about some of its past thoughts that it had been in danger of forgetting. R. Me'ir of Rothenburg's revolutionary vision went unrealized. Ashkenaz, to its own detriment, remained as indifferent to Maimonides in the sixteenth century as it had been in the thirteenth.

By way of conclusion, and in fairness, I should add: the failure of the *Haggahot Maimuniyot* was not entirely the fault of Ashkenaz, indeed, it was not entirely the result of any *fault* whatsoever. The reason why R. Me'ir's dreams were for naught had as much to do with the unique nature of *Mishneh Torah* as it did with the lamentable cultural insularity of his countrymen. This, however, is a different story, and one that I have recently told elsewhere.[2]

[2] See '*Mishneh Torah*: Polemic and Art' (above, p. 32 n.).

PART II

USURY AND MONEYLENDING

CHAPTER FOUR

Usury, Jewish Law

USURY is defined in talmudic law as 'wages for waiting', that is, money paid for deferred repayment of a loan. Usury is viewed as a violation of the pentateuchal injunction (Exod. 22: 24; Lev. 25: 37). Rabbinic law extended the range of this injunction to include forms of commodity loans and mortgages. The line distinguishing the pentateuchal from the rabbinic injunction is not always clear, though the difference is far-reaching. While the courts will not enforce collection of interest on a loan that contravenes either a pentateuchal or rabbinic injunction, restitution is enforced only if a pentateuchal law has been breached.

The usury injunction covers five major areas: (1) money repaid at a later date, (2) commodities lent and repaid with increment at a later date, (3) deferred payments of purchase, if the price paid at the later date is higher than the one that obtained at the time of sale, (4) possessory mortgages, or antichresis, that is, the creditor takes possession of a house or field of the debtor for the period of the loan and resides there or utilizes his crop, without deducting the rent or produce from the principal, and (5) *commenda*, a silent partnership in which one person provides the capital, the other the initiative and labor.

Such restrictions posed serious obstacles to most forms of business enterprise or merchant and agricultural credit. Certain allowances are already to be found in the Talmud, and numerous (though not all) medieval commentators and jurists raised these allowances to normative status. Purchasing on credit was allowed with a price higher at the time of repayment than the one at the time of sale, on condition that no explicit statement was made at the time of sale that were it to be paid then the price would be lower—even though this was clearly understood. Some authorities ruled that symbolic deduction of rent or produce from the capital sufficed to allow possessory mortgages. *Commendas* were allowed if the active partner received symbolic wages.

The pentateuchal injunction forbade interest between Jews but allowed the taking or paying off to a foreigner (*nokhri*). Both Christians and Muslims were viewed as foreigners. Rabbinic law forbade such interest but made exceptions if no other means of subsistence was available. The frequent summary taxation and impositions coupled with the progressive exclusion of Jews from trade and commerce led R. Ya'akov ben Me'ir (Rabbenu Tam) to write: 'We may allow taking interest from non-Jews because there is no end to the yoke and the burden king and nobles impose upon us. Everything we take is thus needed for subsistence. Moreover, we are condemned to live in the midst of other nations and cannot earn our living in any other manner [except by moneylending].'

As Jews in medieval Europe were engaged in moneylending, liquidity was essential, and replenishment of assets through direct borrowing was a major problem. The most important means of circumvention, developed by Rashi and simplified by Rabbenu Tam, was the use of a Gentile straw man. A Jew would ask a Gentile to serve as his intermediary in requesting a loan from another Jew. Legally two loans had taken place: the first from Jew to Gentile, the second from Gentile to Jew.

In Muslim countries Jews were not restricted to moneylending, and what lending took place elicited little comment. In Europe, however, Jewish moneylending was a frequent object of attack by Christian writers from the latter half of the twelfth century on. In modern times, some historians have averred that Jews entered this field not simply because of the pressure of circumstances, but also against the wishes of leading rabbinical authorities. There is no evidence for this claim. In Jewish law no special stigma attaches itself to the injunction against usury, just as none exists in Babylonian, Roman, Byzantine, or Muslim law. Indeed, there was none in western Europe until the latter half of the twelfth century. The intensely negative connotations that still attend the term 'usury' are a unique creation of the high Middle Ages and the period of the Reformation.

BIBLIOGRAPHY

Bernfeld, I., *Das Zinsverbot bei den Juden nach talmudisch-rabbinischem Recht* (1924).

Cohen, B., *Jewish and Roman Law*, ii (1966), 433–56.

Cohen, H. H., 'Usury', *Encyclopaedia Judaica*, xvi (1972).

Hoffmann, M., *Der Geldhandel der deutschen Juden während des Mittelalters bis zum Jahre 1350* (1910).

Langmuir, G., 'The Jews and the Archives of Angevin England: Reflections on Medieval Anti-Semitism', *Traditio*, 19 (1963), 183–244.

Marcuse, J., *Das biblisch-talmudische Zinsenrecht* (1895).

Rabinowitz, J. J., 'Some Remarks on the Evasion of Usury Laws in the Middle Ages', *Harvard Theological Review*, 37 (1944), 49–59.

Soloveitchik, H., 'Pawnbroking: A Study in *Ribbit* and of the Halakhah in Exile', *Proceedings of the American Academy for Jewish Research*, 38–9 (1972), 203–68.

Stein, S., 'The Development of the Jewish Law of Interest from the Biblical Period to the Expulsion from England', *Historia Judaica*, 18 (1955), 3–40.

—— 'Interest Taken by Jews from Gentiles', *Journal of Semitic Studies*, 1 (1956), 141–64.

Udovitch, A. L., 'At the Origins of the Western *Commenda*: Islam, Israel, Byzantium?', *Speculum*, 37 (1962), 198–207.

CHAPTER FIVE

The Jewish Attitude to Usury in the High and Late Middle Ages (1000–1500)

THE ISSUE of Jewish usury has provoked more heat than light, the object of both prejudice and apologetics. The issue does not depend on an imagined essence of Judaism, whose discovery was the figment of some scholar's imagination,[1] but on reasoned inference from the available evidence.

If we be guided by this evidence, a discussion of the Jewish attitude towards usury in the high and late Middle Ages must treat four kinds of data: legal sources (halakhic sources), ethical and philosophical writings, biblical commentaries, and the literature of polemics.[2] Let us take each in turn. |115|

[1] I refer, naturally, to W. Sombart, *Die Juden und das Wirtschaftsleben* (Leipzig, 1911), a work that received far more scholarly attention than it ever merited. Sombart's thesis has generated a large literature; I will draw attention only to a few works. P. R. Mendes-Flohr, 'Werner Sombart's *The Jew and Modern Capitalism*: An Analysis of its Ideological Premises', *Leo Baeck Yearbook*, 21 (1976), 87–107; D. S. Landes, 'The Jewish Merchant, Typology and Stereotypology in Germany', *Leo Baeck Yearbook*, 19 (1974), 22–3; F. Raphael, *Judaïsme et capitalisme: Essai sur la controverse entre Max Weber et Werner Sombart* (Paris, 1982).

[2] This essay introduces no new material, though it does offer a number of different readings of the sources. These sources have been gathered and analyzed by a number of fine scholars, most notably J. Rosenthal in his extensive study, 'Ribbit min ha-Nokhri', first published in *Talpiot: Rive'on le-'Inyanei Halakhah, Aggadah u-Musar*, 5 (1952), 472–92; 6 (1953), 130–52, subsequently reprinted in an expanded form in his *Meḥkarim u-Mekorot*, i (Jerusalem, 1966), 253–323. Some new material and differing emphases are also found in S. Stein's two essays written contemporaneously with those of Rosenthal, 'The Development of the Jewish Law of Interest from the Biblical Period to the Expulsion of the Jews from England', *Historia Judaica*, 17 (1955), 3–40; 'Interest Taken by Jews from Gentiles: An Evaluation of Source Material (Fourteenth to Seventeenth Centuries)', *Journal of Semitic Studies*, 1 (1956), 141–64. Important, too, is D. B. Ruderman's discussion in his *The World of a Renaissance Jew: The Life and Thought of Abraham ben Mordecai Farissol* (Cincinnati, 1981), 85–97. Though the 17th century is beyond the time frame of my essay, reference should be made to B. Ravid's fine, well-annotated essay, 'Moneylending in Seventeenth Century Jewish Vernacular Apologetica', in I. Twersky and B. Septimus, eds., *Jewish Thought in the Seventeenth Century* (Cambridge, Mass., 1987), 257–83.

Jewish law divides all religious imperatives into two major classes: pentateuchal and rabbinic. Pentateuchal injunctions are those found in the Bible—as understood by the Oral Law—and are viewed as of Divine origin. Rabbinic imperatives are those instituted by talmudic sages. Their transgression is no minor matter, to put it mildly; nevertheless, they remain but man-made laws. The Bible states (Deut. 23: 20–1): 'You should not lend at interest to your brother . . . To the foreigner you may lend at interest.' As the word *nokhri* (which the King James Version (vv. 19–20) translates as 'stranger') was taken by the Oral Law throughout the Bible (not just in the matter of usury) as meaning 'non-Jew', interest from a Christian, or Muslim, or heathen for that matter, was viewed by the halakhah as being allowed by the Bible.

The Talmud reports one view that there is a rabbinic injunction against lending to Gentiles at interest, unless such a transaction is necessary for simple subsistence (*kedei ḥayyav*). Another opinion denies the existence of such an injunction and holds that usury to a 'foreigner'/'stranger' is allowed without qualification.[3]

In the great talmudic glosses of the twelfth and thirteenth centuries, the *Tosafot*, written in northern France and of incalculable influence in the Middle Ages, one does find the widespread practice of lending to Gentiles put to legal question. The text reads (and this text is cited endlessly throughout the Middle Ages):

או[מר] ר"ת . . . וקי[ימא] ל[ן] כאידך לישנא . . . לא אסרו מעולם . . . רבית דנכרי. ואפי[לו] ללישנא קמא יש להתיר לפי שיש עלינו מס המלך ושרים והכל הוי כדי חיינו. ועוד שאנו שרויין בין האומות ואי אפשר לנו להשתכר בשום דבר אם לא נישא וניתן עמהם, הלכך אין לאסור רבית שמא ילמד ממעשיו יותר משאר משא ומתן.

Rabbenu Tam says [Rabbenu Tam being the sobriquet given to the towering figure R. Ya'akov of Ramerupt, the creator of the dialectical movement in northern France; d. 1171] that we now allow taking interest from Gentiles because we rule like the other view in the Talmud that interest-taking from Gentiles is permitted . . . However, interest-taking is now permissible even according to the view that holds that it was forbidden by rabbinic injunction, for we have exactions of the king and lords [to pay] and all the money we have is deemed 'necessary for simple subsistence' [*kedei ḥayyav*]. Another reason [for allowance]: [The Talmud says that the reason that usury from Gentiles was forbidden was 'lest he have too much to do with Gentiles and learn their [wicked] ways', which made sense in talmudic times when Jews were all living together so they could support themselves by trading with one another.] We [however] live amidst the Gentiles, and we cannot earn a living other than by business

[3] *Bava Metsi'a* 71b–72a.

dealings with Gentiles; there is therefore no reason to forbid usury any more than trading [with Gentiles. Hence the law is today inapplicable.][4] |116|

It has been claimed—more understandably by the scholars living in the antisemitic atmosphere of Wilhelminian Germany,[5] less so by those in Anglo-Saxon countries—that Jews lent to Gentiles at interest only as a result of *force majeure*, for lack of any alternative. However, if one studies the responsa literature, one discovers quickly enough that Jews lent to Gentiles at interest from the very outset of their documented existence in Europe, long before their economic marginalization and restriction to moneylending. The earliest responsa that have come down to us—whether from Lucca or Mainz at the end of the tenth century,[6] or from northern France from the latter half of the eleventh,[7] or from Provence in the early twelfth[8]—all indicate that no one ever imagined that usury from Gentiles was forbidden by Jewish law. It is assumed by all to be permissible. Indeed, the entire strategy of both businessman and Talmudist in the Middle Ages to alleviate or obviate the ban on intra-Jewish credit was by involving the Gentile as fictitious intermediary in the arrangement.[9] |117|

[4] *Tosafot*, *Bava Metsi'a* 70b, s.v. *tashikh*. In reality, only the first explanation is that of Rabbenu Tam. The latter explanations (that of simple sustenance and that usury ought not to be different from other business dealings) are those of Rabbenu Tam's great pupil, R. Yitsḥak of Dampierre (d. 1189). However, this became clear only at the end of the 19th century with the publication of the third volume of the huge medieval compendium, *Or Zarua'* (at *Bava Metsi'a*, #208). During the entire period discussed in my essay (and many centuries after), the doctrine went under Rabbenu Tam's name, and I have so cited it. On the differing approaches of Rabbenu Tam and of R. Yitsḥak of Dampierre, see S. Albeck, 'Yaḥaso shel Rabbenu Tam li-Ve'ayot Zemano', *Zion*, 19 (1955), 106–8.

[5] e.g. M. Brann, 'Geschichte der Juden in Schlesien', in *Beilage zum Jahresbericht des jüdisch-theologischen Seminars* (1901), 82; A. Kober, 'Die rechtliche Lage der Juden im Rheinland während des 14. Jahrhunderts im Hinblick auf das kirchliche Zinsverbot', *Westdeutsche Zeitschrift für Geschichte und Kunst*, 28 (1909), 245.

[6] See the responsum of R. Meshullam ben Kalonymus in *Teshuvot Ge'onim Kadmonim*, ed. D. Cassel (Berlin, 1846), #141. The text should be emended according to J. N. Epstein, 'Die Rechtsgutachten der Geonim, ed. Cassel nach Cod. Berlin und MS Michael', *Jahrbuch der jüdisch-literarischen Gesellschaft*, 9 (1911), 299 (translated into Hebrew and reprinted in id., *Meḥkarim be-Sifrut ha-Talmud u-vi-Leshonot Shemiyot*, i [Jerusalem, 1984], 215) and L. Ginzberg, ed., *Ginzei Schechter*, ii (New York, 1929), 209. (A translation of this responsum is found in I. A. Agus, *Urban Civilization in Pre-Crusade Europe*, i [New York, 1965], 318–19. The translations, while often loose, are on the whole accurate; the analyses have been well assessed by R. Lopez in his review in *Speculum*, 42 [1967], 342–3. Questions have been raised whether this and other responsa of R. Meshullam are from his Lucca period or that of Mainz, hence the formulation in the text; see the entry *Meshulam* [*sic*] *ben Kalonymos* in *Encyclopaedia Judaica*, xi [Jerusalem, 1971], col. 1401–2.)

[7] *Teshuvot Rashi*, ed. I. S. Elfenbein (New York, 1943), ##49, 229 correct the garbled text according to *Sefer ha-Terumot* (Venice, 1622), 46: 4: 10; (Jerusalem, 1988), 933. {The fully corrected text together with a translation is found in Ch. 6, below, pp. 77–8.}

[8] *Sifran shel Rishonim*, ed. S. Assaf (Jerusalem, 1935), #36.

[9] See Ch. 6 below.

The remarks of the glossators are very much after the fact. They simply reflect a well-documented phenomenon: the systematic attempts of the northern French glossators to justify, if at all possible, the long-established conduct of their communities.[10]

Not only was usury to Gentiles viewed as fully permissible legally, there was also no perception whatsoever that there was any moral taint to such an activity or that Jews lent to Gentiles only because there was no other way for them to earn a living, as Abelard—a brilliant debater—would have us believe.[11] Admittedly, when Jews were banned from trade, agriculture, and the crafts, they concentrated on lending for lack of any alternative; however, there is no indication in Jewish sources that they saw any moral taint to this enforced activity.

The remarks of Rabbi Yosef Bonfils (Tov 'Elem) of early to mid-eleventh-century Anjou are often cited as evidence of the opposition of rabbinic authorities to the growing Jewish involvement in usury.[12] However, his oft-cited remark: 'Those who eat [the fruit of] usury [do blaspheme and] make Moses into a fool and his Torah [teachings] nonsense, saying had Moses known how easy it was, he would never have forbidden it', is simply a quotation of a talmudic remark.[13] Nor does his citing this biting statement evince a negative attitude towards usury. The question at bar in the responsum of Rabbi Yosef Bonfils is whether the community can tax land held for agricultural purposes at the same rate that it taxes capital that is lent out at interest. Rabbi Yosef replies in the negative. He feels that it is unfair to tax land used for agriculture,

[10] J. Katz, 'Ma'ariv bi-Zemano ve-Shelo bi-Zemano: Dugma le-Zikah bein Minhag, Halakhah ve-Ḥevrah', *Zion*, 35 (1971), 35–60; reprinted in id., *Halakhah ve-Kabbalah: Meḥkarim be-Toledot Dat Yisra'el 'al Medoreiha ve-Zikatah ha-Ḥevratit* (Jerusalem, 1984), 175–200; English translation in J. Katz, *Divine Law in Human Hands: Case Studies in Halakhic Flexibility* (Jerusalem, 1998), 88–110; H. Soloveitchik, 'Religious Law and Change: The Medieval Ashkenazic Example' (Chapter 9 below); {'"Religious Law and Change" Revisited' (Chapter 10 below)}.

[11] Petrus Abaelardus, *Dialogus inter Philosophum, Judeum et Christianum*, ed. R. Thomas (Stuttgart and Bad Cannstatt, 1970), 51; see Peter Abelard, *Collationes*, ed. J. Marenbon and G. Orlandi (Oxford, 2001), 20–1 and notes ad loc. There is no contemporary record of, or subsequent reference to, any of these restraints on landholding mentioned by Abelard. The evidence in France, though not in Germany, does point to Jewish concentration in moneylending at this time, but not for the reasons advanced by the Jewish disputant in Abelard's work. Cf. R. Chazan, *Medieval Jewry in Northern France: A Political and Social History* (Baltimore and London, 1973), 33–4; K. Stow, *Alienated Minority: The Jews of Medieval Latin Europe* (Cambridge, Mass., 1992), 216. I incline to their dating, though the eminent Salo Baron in his *Social and Religious History of the Jews*, iv (Philadelphia, 1957), 206, dates this concentration to the closing years of the 12th century. Needless to say, this would preclude any merit to Abelard's claim.

[12] Agus, *Urban Civilization* (above, n. 6), ii. 445. I too had previously misconstrued his remarks: see 'Pawnbroking' (above, n. 7), n. 104.

[13] *Bava Metsi'a* 75b.

which entails |118| great effort, expense, and risk, at the same rate as capital lent out at interest, which, while entailing some risk, does not involve any similar exertion or demand further expense. To prove his point, he cites long lists of talmudic passages which speak of the backbreaking exertions needed to make land yield its produce, and then proceeds to quote the above-cited passage to show that moneylending is an easy profession. The purpose of the passage is to demonstrate the effortless nature of moneylending rather than its immorality—an issue that is never at bar in the responsum.[14]

There is equally no ground for claiming that the German Pietists opposed usury.[15] In a large, multifaceted, and formless work such as the *Sefer Ḥasidim* (Book of the Pious) one can find any and every idea. The controlling question is what degree of importance this idea has in the movement's ideology, and if it is not important, whether it at least has a distinct, clear place in their thought. *Sefer Ḥasidim* is, furthermore, amorphous and associative: central assertions and parenthetic asides are found alongside one another and their disentanglement poses major methodological problems. For our present discussion, three criteria may serve to winnow the trivial from the essential: intent, repetition, and intensity. That is to say: What is the purpose of the passage? Does the idea expressed there recur with any degree of frequency in the literature of the movement? Finally, does one sense in its formulations an emotional involvement, whether of identification or disgust?

In light of these considerations let us investigate the remarks of *Sefer Ḥasidim* cited as proof of the Pietists' opposition to usury. They are found in the section entitled 'On Torah Study':[16]

> **'מרבה הונו בנשך ובתרבית לחונן דלים יקבצנו, מסיר אזנו משמוע תורה גם תפילתו תועבה' (משלי כח, ח–ט) סמכם להודיע שלא יאמר אדם 'אני לוקח ריבית וחפץ אני לתת הריבית לגבאי צדקה למי שיחונן דל', מוטב שלא יקח ריבית. לפי שכתוב (ויקרא כה, לז) 'ובמרבית לא תתן אכלך', וכתיב 'תרבית' (הרי כתיב) לגבי ריבית לכך בתחיית המתים יהיה מת 'ולא יחיה' שכתוב ביחזקאל (יח, יג) ובנשך נתן ותרבית לקח וחי לא**

[14] *Teshuvot R. Me'ir mi-Rotenburg* (Prague and Budapest, 1895), #941; translation in Agus, *Urban Civilization* (above, n. 6), ii. 438–41. For an extended analysis of this responsum, see H. Soloveitchik, *Shut ke-Makor Histori* (Jerusalem, 1990), 54–65. {On the nature of the Prague–Budapest edition, see Ch. 6, below, n. 38(*b*).}

[15] Cf. Y. Baer, 'The Socioreligious Orientation of *Sefer Hasidim*', *Binah*, 2 (1989), 79 (This is a slightly modified translation, without footnotes, of Baer's influential Hebrew article, 'Ha-Megamah ha-Datit-Ḥevratit shel Sefer Ḥasidim', published in *Zion* in 1938. Our passage is found in the Hebrew version at p. 30).

[16] *Sefer Ḥasidim*, ed. Y. Wistinetzki, 2nd edn. (Frankfurt am Main, 1924), #808. The redundant phrase **הרי כתיב**, placed in parentheses, is found in MS Parma, de Rossi 1133, from which Wistinetzki published.

יחיה את כל התועבות האלה עשה מות ימות דמיו בו. לכך 'מרבית' 'תרבית' ראשי תיבות מת. ואל יאמר אקח ריבית ואתן ללומדי תורה. 'ובתרבית' ב' יתר: שני ריביות--מישראל ואף מגוי, מי שיכול להתפרנס משדותיו. ועוד ב' ריבי[ו]ת--מוקדמת ומאוחרת.

'He that augmenteth his substance by interest and increase, gathereth it for him that is gracious to the poor. He that turneth away his ear from hearing the law, even his prayer is an abomination' (Proverbs 28: 8–9). The two verses were joined together so that one should not say, 'I want to give money earned in usury to charity'.

'You should not lend thy food at interest [*marbit*]' (Leviticus 25: 37); and elsewhere (Leviticus 25: 36) usury is called not *marbit* but *tarbit*, the first letters of the two words spell 'MeT' |**119**| ['dead' in Hebrew]—to teach you that the usurer will not be resurrected as is clear from Ezekiel (18: 13): 'He [that] hath given at interest and hath taken interest, shall he live? He shall not live!' That is why the beginning letters of the two words '*m*arbit' and '*t*arbit' spell *met* (dead). One should never say, 'I will take interest and give it all to charity'. And in that verse it further says *u-ve-tarbit*; the *bet* in that word is superfluous. *Bet* numerologically is 2; this is a numerological reference to a twofold ban: on usury from a Jew and that from a Gentile for one who can support himself from his fields [i.e. has no need to take Gentile usury for his sustenance]. It also refers to the twofold ban on both 'advance' and 'delayed' usury.

Having previously emphasized in #807 the importance of supporting scholars, he hastens to add in #808 that this support should not come from usury.[17] Then he proceeds to decode, in good hasidic, numerological fashion, the various hints and references embedded in this verse. One is the non-resurrection of those guilty of the sin of usury, the second is the ban on both Jewish and Gentile usury, and, in addition, the ban both on 'early usury', i.e. interest paid prior to the repayment of the capital, and on 'late usury', i.e. interest paid well after the repayment of the capital. The purpose of the passage is not to condemn Gentile usury; this injunction is mentioned in passing as one of several numerological hints found in the biblical verses about usury. There is nothing unique in this use of the numerological reference of *ke-neged*: it was a favorite hermeneutical device of the Pietists. Literally hundreds of similar numerological allusions are expounded in the pages of *Sefer Ḥasidim*. Nor is there any further criticism of usury from a Gentile in the vast literature of that movement. Quite the contrary: in the only other place where usury is mentioned, in #1958, it is described as a 'fence' (*seyag*) against charging interest to another Jew. In other words, usury from a Gentile was forbidden by rabbinic

[17] For the tendency of some Jews and Christians to give money earned by usury to charity, see S. Baron, *Social and Religious History of the Jews*, xii (Philadelphia, 1967), 330, n. 53, and the remarks of the *Nizzahon Vetus* in D. Berger, *The Jewish–Christian Debate in the High Middle Ages: A Critical Edition of the Nizzahon Vetus* (Philadelphia, 1979), 134, 292.

law not because it was intrinsically wrong, but for fear that the Jew would get accustomed to practicing usury and would eventually, from habit, charge Jews too.

The polemical literature is equally unenlightening. An attorney for the defense answers accusations; one can never know what he personally thinks of the case at bar. True, R. Mosheh of Paris debated with Christians in the thirteenth century whether Jews and Christians were still brothers, as the verses from Obadiah (1: 10, 12) would seem to indicate, and hence the Jews were constrained from lending to Christians at interest, for it is written, 'but to your brother you |**120**| should not lend at interest' (Deut. 22: 20).[18] It is no less true that the geographer R. Avraham Farissol (*c.*1450–*c.*1525) discussed at length whether contemporary Christians were or were not the actual 'sons of Edom', whom the Bible had termed 'brethren' of the Jews (Deut. 23: 8).[19] However, no Jew in the long Middle Ages doubted for a moment that the Christian was not his brother. An anonymous polemicist expressed well, I think, the general feeling, writing: 'You yourselves call us "dogs" and not "brothers" [why are you suddenly insisting in moneylending that we are brothers?].'[20]

Substantive conclusions can be drawn only from the 'internal literature': from the works that Jews wrote for their own consumption and not to answer Christian attacks. In that literature we find no substantive discussion of Gentile usury—neither by halakhists nor by kabbalists, and not even by ethicists, philosophers,[21] or exegetes. They simply saw no problem in usury. Kimḥi and Naḥmanides expressed the dominant perception when they commented on the passage in Deuteronomy (23: 21) that not charging interest on a loan is an

[18] Cited by Yosef Ofitsial in his *Sefer Yosef ha-Mekkane*, ed. J. Rosenthal (Jerusalem, 1970), 61–2.

[19] S. D. Loewinger, 'Likkutim mi-Sefer Magen Avraham shel Avraham Farissol', *Ha-Tsofeh le-Ḥokhmat Yisra'el*, 12 (1928), 294 ff. On Farissol's discussion, see Ruderman, *The World of a Renaissance Jew* (above, n. 2), 87 ff. On the identity of Edom and Christianity, see the classic essay of G. D. Cohen, 'Esau as Symbol in Early Medieval Thought', in A. Altman, ed., *Jewish Medieval and Renaissance Essays* (Cambridge, Mass., 1967), 19–48, reprinted in the author's *Studies in the Variety of Rabbinic Cultures* (Philadelphia, 1991), 243–70.

[20] Rome, Vittorio Emanuele, MS 53, fo. 25a, ed. Y. Rosenthal, in 'Vikuaḥ Dati bein Ḥakham be-Shem Menaḥem u-vein ha-Mumar ve-ha-Nazir ha-Dominikani Pablo Kheristiani (ha-Maḥatsit ha-Sheniyah shel ha-Me'ah ha-Yod-Gimel)', in M. Zohori, A. Tartakover, and H. Ormian, eds., *Hagut 'Ivrit be-Amerikah* (Tel Aviv, 1974), 72. I was referred to this source by Berger, *The Jewish–Christian Debate* (above, n. 17), 291. {As to the ascription to 'Menaḥem', see Berger's remarks, p. 36, n. 104. On Jews as dogs, see K. Stow, *Jewish Dogs: An Image and its Interpreters: Continuity in the Catholic–Jewish Encounter* (Stanford, 2006).}

[21] Barring, of course, those few passages in philosophical works which have a clear polemical intent. These passages have been identified and discussed by Berger, *The Jewish–Christian Debate* (above, n. 17), and by Stein, 'The Development of the Jewish Law' (above, n. 2), and 'Interest Taken by Jews' (above, n. 2).

act of charity, and one is obligated to act charitably only towards one's brother (co-religionist) but not towards a stranger (*nokhri*).[22]

The Pentateuch strictly forbids usury between one Jew and another, and medieval scholars took this injunction very seriously indeed. However, they perceived it not as a social |121| moralism (*mishpat*) but a Divine fiat (*ḥok*), similar to the laws forbidding non-kosher food, for example, which is a Divine decree that must be obeyed because of the divinity of the legislator, not because it possesses any intrinsic moral force.[23] Put differently, the usury injunction was never perceived, as was the Seventh Commandment, as a Divine commandment confirming what natural law had already long legislated.[24] As charging interest was never perceived as an injustice, the freedom to charge interest to Gentiles aroused neither questions nor uneasiness—except in a polemical setting.

The Talmud had already adopted this neutral stance towards usury in commercial transactions between Jews, for example in mortgage and installment payments.[25] In straightforward loans between Jews, this came to be the view of halakhists from the twelfth century on. However, even for those scholars of the preceding century who viewed the injunction against intra-Jewish usury as

22 Ramban (Naḥmanides), *Commentary on the Torah, Deuteronomy*, translated and annotated by C. B. Chavel (New York, 1972), 23: 20. Naḥmanides' remarks are taken from Kimḥi's commentary on Psalms, *Ha-Perush ha-Shalem le-Sefer Tehillim*, ed. D. Darom (Jerusalem, 1972), 15: 5. Kimḥi's remarks have a clear polemical intent, not surprisingly as the verse in Psalms, rather than the verses in Exodus, Leviticus, or Deuteronomy, is the *locus classicus* of the Christian discussion of usury. {See also Yitsḥak ben Yeda'yah's remarks cited by M. Saperstein in *Decoding the Rabbis: A Thirteenth-Century Commentary on the Aggadah* (Cambridge, Mass., 1980), 134–5. (The passage is cited in translation. I would like to thank Dr. Saperstein for providing me with a transcription of the original Hebrew text still in manuscript.)}

23 H. H. Ben-Sasson, *The Middle Ages*, in id., ed., *A History of the Jewish People* (Cambridge, Mass., 1976), 391–2.

24 The much-discussed problem in Jewish legal literature whether pentateuchal usury constitutes theft is beside the point. The question arises in Jewish law only as a result of the biblical ban. At bar is the issue: though interest is paid willingly, it is nevertheless forbidden by the Bible. Does this ban simply forbid its receipt, with the money willingly given to the lender remaining the property of the lender? Or does this injunction cancel out the transference of ownership by the borrower and its retention by the lender then constitute theft? Theft may be a *consequence* of the biblical ban; it is not anterior to it as would be any injunction arising from natural law. Were this to be an issue of natural law, usury from Gentiles would equally be forbidden, when in fact the entire discussion is only about intra-Jewish credit forbidden by the Bible. See e.g. *Shitah Mekubbetset* (Jerusalem, 1961), *Bava Metsi'a* 61b, s.v. *sheken*; *Mishneh le-Melekh*, 'Hilkhot Malveh ve-Loveh', 4: 3.

25 This was first pointed out by Jacob Katz in a lecture at the Third World Congress for Jewish Studies held in Jerusalem in 1961. He stated it in print only some thirty-five years later in 'Hirhurim 'al ha-Yaḥas bein Dat ve-Khalkalah', in M. Ben-Sasson, ed., *Dat ve-Khalkalah: Yaḥasei Gomlin* (Jerusalem, 1995), 37.

an expression of an economic moralism, their aversion never equaled nor even remotely resembled the revulsion elicited by *usura* or *foenus* in the Christian world. Consequently, this transformation, when it did occur—in the late eleventh and early twelfth centuries—was seen as a minor one, occurring often imperceptibly, without the awareness of most halakhists. If discerned at all, it was perceived as a loss of distaste for—indeed, an acceptance of—relationships that were substantively (though not formally) usurious, and there was a corresponding shift in evaluating usury by a purely legal yardstick rather than by an economic one as had previously been the case. It was not a major transformation of values as it was |122| in the Christian world.[26] And this radical difference in the perception of usury between the two religions should give us pause.

In one sense, the source of the difference is obvious. One will look in vain in Jewish literature for any of the reasons found in canon law or in Christian theological writings for the ban on usury. For example, that the seller in effect sells time which is not his but God's, or that money is barren, or that since the borrower acquires the money lent, one is asking him to pay double: once for the acquisition of the loan, namely the repayment of the principal, and then again for the use of what is now his own, namely the principal, for the interest charged is for the use of the principal that he already acquired when he received the loan. Arguments such as these sound quite simple: they make a black and white case against usury, and can be used by handbooks and preachers to present usury as theft pure and simple, and, in the ubiquitous compounding of interest, a theft that grows greater daily and increases inexorably against the now helpless borrower.[27] Arguments of this type—that present usury as an injustice and as a breach of natural law—are entirely missing from Jewish literature. If one turns to chapter 'Eizeh hu Neshekh' in *Bava Metsi'a* to study the talmudic laws of usury, one immediately encounters a ruling that defines the illicit interest that would arise in certain speculative maneuvers in the Roman commodity market. It reads:

> לקח הימנו חטין בדינר זהב הכור, וכן השער. עמדו חטין בל' דינרין, אמר לו תן לי חטיי, שאני רוצה למוכרן וליקח בהן יין. אמר לו הרי חטיך עשוייות עלי בשלשים והרי לך אצלי בהן יין, ויין אין לו.

[26] See my essay 'Pawnbroking: A Study in *Ribbit* and of the Halakhah in Exile', *Proceedings of the American Academy of Jewish Research*, 38–9 (1972), 224–42. {Indeed, in the revised version of the essay (Chapter 6 below, pp. 121–2), I reject the very term 'economic moralism' in favor of 'legal formalism'.}

[27] J. T. Noonan, *The Scholastic Analysis of Usury* (Cambridge, Mass., 1957), 11–38; T. P. McLaughlin, 'The Teachings of the Canonists on Usury (XII, XIII and XIV Centuries)', *Mediaeval Studies*, 1 (1939), 98–125; O. I. Langholm, *Economics in the Medieval Schools: Wealth, Exchange, Value, Money and*

If a man bought wheat at a golden *denar* (= 25 silver *denars*) the *kor* when such was the market price, and the wheat rose to thirty [silver] *denars*, and he said 'Deliver me my wheat since I would sell it to buy wine with the price', and the other said 'Let your wheat be reckoned to me at thirty *denars*, and thus you have a claim on me for wine!'—although he has no wine.[28]

The case is as complicated (and obscure) in the original Hebrew as it is in the English translation. As one progresses in 'Eizeh hu Neshekh', the degree of complexity (and obscurity) thankfully diminishes, but the nature of the treatment of usury remains unchanged. It is uniformly technical—one formal definition after another. There isn't a line that speaks of usury as intrinsically immoral, as depriving another of what is rightfully his. Not a line that subsequent preachers could seize upon and elaborate movingly to illustrate its inherent criminal nature.

However, if truth be told, it is not the Jewish attitude to usury that needs explaining but rather that of Latin Christendom since the middle of the twelfth century. The Jewish position on usury is simply one variation of the common stances towards usury since |123| ancient times. Namely: lending at interest is both an economic and a social necessity, yet at the same time potentially dangerous. Some societies forbid it outright and then turn a blind eye to its more commonly practiced forms. Others forbid it and then employ legal fictions to allow those instances viewed as practically necessary. Yet others permit it, but limit the rate of interest that may be charged, as did Hammurabi and the Romans, as does the Greek Orthodox Church to this day.

Until the twelfth century the Catholic Church was generally indifferent to usury.[29] If she addressed it at all, it was in reference to the clergy. Admittedly, in Carolingian times, for a number of reasons, the Church, even Charlemagne himself, did indeed legislate against usury. This, however, was but a passing phase, and the eleventh century and the early twelfth saw the monasteries in parts of northern France function as major lenders at interest and even openly sign documents *ad usuram*.[30] In southern France, in Toulouse for example, so

Usury according to the Paris Theological Tradition 1200–1350, Studien und Texte zur Geistesgeschichte des Mittelalters 29, ed. A. Zimmermann (Leiden, New York, and Cologne, 1992), 48–52, 56–9.

28 *The Mishnah*, trans. H. Danby (repr. Oxford, 1932), *Bava Metsi'a* 5: 1, p. 355; *Bava Metsi'a* 60b.

29 The basic works on the subject remain M. Neumann, *Geschichte des Wuchers in Deutschland bis zur Begründung der heutigen Zinsengesetze (1654)* (Halle, 1865); F. Schaub, *Der Kampf gegen den Zinswucher, ungerechten Preis und unlautern Handel im Mittelalter. Von Karl dem Grossen bis Papst Alexander III. Eine moralhistorische Untersuchung* (Freiburg im Breisgau, 1905); E. Leiber, *Das kanonische Zinsverbot in deutschen Städten des Mittelalters* (Ph.D. diss., Freiburg, Ueberlingen, 1926); G. Le Bras, 'Usure', *Dictionnaire de théologie catholique*, xv (Paris, 1950), cols. 2336–72.

30 R. Genestal, *Le Rôle des monastères comme établissements de crédit étudié en Normandie du XIe à la*

widespread was usury until its conquest by the Capetians in the 1220s that one historian has labeled the period 'the Golden Age of usurers'.[31] Jews entered moneylending in the early twelfth century, as Gavin Langmuir pointed out long ago, for the simple reason that there was little stigma attached to this profession.[32] Nor had canonists or theologians given it much thought. Let us recall that in Gratian the discussion is brief, indeed skeletal—all sources cited are 500 to 600 years old, and the definition given to usury is rudimentary. The first general council to treat usury was in 1139: it was equally the first council that applied the injunction not only to the clergy but also to laymen.

In the second half of the twelfth century there was a dramatic |124| change. The group that gathered around Peter Chanter (d. 1197) was the moving force in this development. These men saw usury not as a venal sin, a trivial lapse, but as a major evil and its eradication as a social and religious imperative.[33] In the thirteenth century, usury became a central topic of European discourse.[34] This process continued—with ups and downs—for several centuries until the sixteenth century, by which time usury had assumed almost demonic proportions—the scourge of society and the major social dissolvent—as is evidenced by the pamphlet literature in Germany at the time of the Reformation and in Italy by the preaching, for example, of Bernard de Feltre. The question naturally presents itself: Why did an injunction which for a millennium was far more honored in the breach than the observance suddenly become a cardinal sin and acquire a moral repugnance, some of which has lasted to this very day? The real riddle is not the Jewish position on usury but what came to be the Christian one, the why and the how of this major transformation in the *mentalité* of western Europe.

At the same time, one must emphasize that one cannot find the slightest evidence in medieval Jewish writings of the Middle Ages of any capitalist or even pre-capitalist outlook.[35] Admittedly, a capitalist outlook will see nothing

fin du XIIIe siècle (Paris, 1901); H. van Werveke, 'Le Mortgage et son rôle économique en Flandre et Lotharingie', *Revue belge de philologie et d'histoire*, 8 (1929), 53–91.

[31] M. Castaing, 'Le Prêt à interêt à Toulouse aux XIIe et XIIIe siècles', *Bulletin philologique et historique* (1953–4), 273–8.

[32] G. Langmuir, 'The Jews and the Archives of Angevin England: Reflections on Medieval Anti-Semitism', *Traditio*, 19 (1963), 213.

[33] J. W. Baldwin, *Masters, Princes and Merchants: The Social Views of Peter Chanter and his Circle* (Princeton, 1970), i. 296–311; ii. 204–11.

[34] J. Le Goff, *Your Money or Your Life: Economy and Religion in the Middle Ages* (New York, 1990), 10.

[35] Cf. Stein, 'Interest Taken by Jews' (above, n. 2), 153; id., *Jewish–Christian Disputations in Thirteenth-Century Narbonne: Inaugural Lecture* (London, 1969), 15–16.

wrong with usury; however, seeing nothing wrong with usury does not in itself constitute a capitalist outlook.

The argument for a capitalist viewpoint is based on citations drawn from the same dubious source—the polemical literature. Yet even in this literature there is no support for such an argument. R. Me'ir ben Shim'on of Narbonne argued against the anti-usury ordinances of St. Louis that society cannot exist without credit and that credit has its price.[36] However, he was only echoing what Louis's own counselors had contended.[37] His contemporary, R. Ya'akov |125| ben Elyah, in replying to the convert Pablo Christiani, observed that without credit, palaces could not be built nor monasteries erected, and that royal palaces could never be maintained.[38] However, he was only stating what every intelligent person knew. Don Yitsḥak Abravanel (1437–1508) defended Jewish usury against Christian attacks by insisting, among other things, that 'usury was not an unfit [i.e. an immoral] thing'.[39] Let us grant for the sake of argument that he was sincere about this, though his other three arguments are patently apologetic and in the first and uncensored edition of his work he openly stated so.[40] Nevertheless, it is difficult to see what this statement has to do with the *Weltanschauung* that sees in man's unbridled economic activity a good in itself, or with one that advocates that the purpose of profit is not its consumption, but rather its constant reinvestment so as to widen evermore the scope of man's economic activity. Finally, not a line is to be found in Jewish

[36] S. Stein, 'A Disputation on Moneylending between Jews and Gentiles in Me'ir ben Simeon's *Milhemeth Miswah* (Narbonne, 13th Century)', *Journal of Jewish Studies*, 10 (1959), 45–61, esp. pp. 52–3.

[37] R. Chazan, 'Anti-Usury Efforts in Thirteenth-Century Narbonne and the Jewish Response', *Proceedings of the American Academy of Jewish Research*, 41–2 (1973–4), 61–2.

[38] *Iggeret (Vikuaḥ) R. Ya'akov mi-Venetsyah*, in J. Kobak, *Ginse Nistaroth: Handschriftliche Editionen aus der jüdischen Literatur*, 1–2 (Bamberg, 1868), 16.

[39] *Mirkevet ha-Mishnah* (Sabbioneta, 1551), 23: 16. {This was the title given to Abravanel's *Commentary on Deuteronomy* in the *editio princeps*. The passage is found in the widely photocopied 1962 Jerusalem edition, *Perush Abravanel 'al ha-Torah: Devarim*, at p. 216a.} This passage was not added when the author arrived in Italy after the exile from Spain in 1492, as some have conjectured, for the argument is equally found in the recently published first draft of Abravanel's commentary. See S. Regev, 'Nusaḥ Rishon shel Perush Abravanel le-Sefer Devarim', *Kovets 'al Yad*, NS 15 (2001), 358–9.

[40] Already noted by Stein, 'Interest Taken by Jews' (above, n. 2), 151. The concluding remarks in subsequent editions of the Commentary read: 'From these four answers it has been shown that Moses our Teacher justly enjoined [what he enjoined] and that all his utterances are just and without warp or crookedness (Deut. 32: 5). However, the truth is that we should believe in this matter according to the traditions of our Sages.' The contrast introduced by 'however' is incomprehensible. In the *editio princeps* there is a middle sentence that reads (fo. 76c–d): 'Behold, I gave these answers to Christian sages for the sake of peace and to mollify the rulers.' The next sentence introduced by 'however' then follows naturally. On the differences between the several editions of Abravanel, see S. Z. Leiman, 'Abarbanel and the Censor', *Journal of Jewish Studies*, 19 (1968), 49–61.

writings that so much as hints that worldly activity, let alone worldly success, is an indication of an individual's elected or redeemed state.[41] Indeed, these very categories do not exist in Judaism.

Moneylending was seen neither as disreputable nor as some pre-capitalist activity. It was simply a way of earning a living. This profession had both its drawbacks—it contributed to the ever-growing |126| antisemitism[42]—and its advantages—it allowed much free time for Torah study.[43] But still, it was simply a livelihood and nothing more.

[41] This was already noted by J. Katz in *Tradition and Crisis: Jewish Society at the End of the Middle Ages* (New York, 1993), 52–61. Katz's work first appeared in Hebrew in 1958. It was translated into English, poorly and without footnotes, in 1961. In the 1990s it was translated again, this time superbly, with all of its footnotes and with a fine afterword by B. Cooperman in which he surveyed the extent to which the numerous theses advanced by Katz in 1958 had held up in the ensuing thirty-five years. It is to this translation that I refer.

[42] The most recent study is that of C. Cluse, 'Zum Zusammenhang von Wuchervorwurf und Judenvertreibung im 13. Jahrhundert', in F. Burgard, A. Haverkamp, and G. Mentgen, eds., *Judenvertreibungen in Mittelalter und früher Neuzeit* (Hanover, 1999), 135–63.

[43] Yosef ben Mosheh in 15th-century Germany in his *Leket Yosher*, i (Berlin, 1903) 118–19, in the name of R. Shalom ben Yitsḥak Zekel; Yitsḥak ben Yeda'yah in 13th-century Provence in Saperstein, *Decoding the Rabbis* (above, n. 22), 135, and note ad loc. Needless to say, free time could be used for good or ill, and we need not be surprised if we encounter a writer or two decrying its frivolous misuse.

CHAPTER SIX

Pawnbroking

A Study in Ribbit *and of the Halakhah in Exile*

BARRING a brief study of some fine point in the esoteric lore of German Pietism, this was my first article in Jewish studies, and in many ways it remains the densest and most multi-layered. This is a result of both the nature of the topic and its target audience. An analysis of pawnbroking requires parsing simultaneously three areas of Jewish law: debt, pawns, and usury, none of which are simple. Any analysis must also incorporate the practices of moneylending in medieval France and Germany and equally the laws governing pawnbroking in these countries.

Every essay is written for an imagined audience, and mine was intended for the eyes of Jacob Katz, Saul Lieberman, and my father. Knowing that all three appreciated brevity, I tried to say as much as possible in as few words as possible. I may have succeeded, but short writing makes for long reading, and I have long since regretted the terseness of the formulations. When I submitted the Hebrew version for publication some five years later (it took another six years for it to appear[1]), I expanded the presentation somewhat and incorporated numerous points that had been clarified in my seminars. While not pursuing any further research on the topic, I have, over the years, chanced upon various materials and registered them on the margins of my Hebrew copy. The study thus reflects systematic research up to the mid-1970s. Upon republishing my essays, it seemed foolish to reproduce the original English version when an expanded one existed in Hebrew. So I have freely translated many passages of the Hebrew text, incorporated my notes and jottings, and tried to further loosen

All manuscripts except those of Cambridge University, Hechal Shelomoh, Jerusalem, and the Jewish Theological Seminary of America were viewed at the Institute of Microfilmed Hebrew Manuscripts of the Jewish National and University Library in Jerusalem.

As readers will notice, some of the quoted material in the notes below is in Hebrew only. I have only provided English translations for those citations which would be of interest to the general reader. The rest are technical proofs of halakhic arguments. Anyone who cannot follow the Hebrew will not be able to follow the legal argument.

[1] H. Soloveitchik, *Halakhah, Kalkalah ve-Dimuy 'Atsmi: ha-Mashkona'ut bi-Yemei ha-Beinayim* (Jerusalem, 1985).

the tautness of the original presentation. Barring two points, that of 'economic moralism' and the length of German resistance to certain French allowances, most of the changes are expositional or they elaborate and nuance points in the original essay, so the reader is receiving, in a more accessible form I hope, the substance and the argument of that essay. Indeed, many pages hew closely to the original. To better orient the reader, I have prefaced the essay with some brief general remarks about pawnbroking, drawn from the Hebrew. (As to the significance of recent research in Germanic law, see the Appendix.)

The first thing the reader will notice is that the analysis of eleventh-century developments takes up some 60 percent of the essay. The same ratio applies to the other in-depth analysis in this volume, 'Can Halakhic Texts Talk History?', for eleventh-century Ashkenazic texts are the most difficult in the halakhic literature. People tend to think that the complicated text is the difficult one. This is rarely the case. The most complicated analysis by the Maharam Schiff, a seventeenth-century super-commentator of the *Tosafot*, for example, is often far easier than a seven-line passage in the *Ma'ase ha-Ge'onim*. The thought of the Maharam Schiff may be complicated, even convoluted, to our way of thinking; but we know his frame of reference and the precise meaning of each and every term that he uses. All that is necessary is to familiarize ourselves with his mode of reasoning, *derekh ha-pilpul*, and that is something that one can set about learning. The difficult text is the one that appears from nowhere, the first utterance of its kind in a culture. One has no background against which to set those words and no assurance of their precise meaning. This is one source of the difficulties in reading *Sefer Ḥasidim*, and it is doubly true of halakhic works that antedate Rashi. What precisely did a halakhic term invoked by R. Yitsḥak ha-Levi of Worms mean to him? How exactly did R. David ha-Levi of Mainz understand the talmudic passage that he cited? How does one go about answering either of those questions? Probing the pre-Crusade literature, one discovers that the meanings of its words have nebulous borders and its technical terms are often labile. One phrase can be used for several different notions, and, conversely, one and the same notion can have different appellations. (Indeed, one of Rashi's major and unappreciated accomplishments was giving point and clarity to legal terms and fixing their denotation for posterity.[2]) Finally, the literature of the eleventh century expresses itself, it does not explain itself. It takes its frame of reference for granted and is unaware of alternatives. Deceptively simple, eleventh-century German texts are treacherous; one has to tread there very carefully.

One has to be equally sure that one is treading in the eleventh century, analyzing a text of that period, and not some edited later version thereof. Other than the early volumes of *Ravyah*,[3] no Ashkenazic work of the high Middle Ages (*c*.1000–1300) has

[2] I have elaborated on this point in *Yeinam: Saḥar be-Yeinam shel Goyyim—'al Gilgulah shel Halakhah be-'Olam ha-Ma'aseh* (Tel Aviv, 2003), 62–3. For an example in our topic, pawnbroking, see below, p. 121.

[3] *Sefer Ravyah*, ed. V. Aptowitzer, 4 vols. (Berlin and Jerusalem, 1912–36).

received a truly critical edition; there is no escape, then, from textual reconstruction in any study of medieval Ashkenazic thought. Few texts, however, are in a worse state than those of the eleventh century, writings that have been neglected for close to a millennium. Rashi rendered much of their thought obsolete and the tosafist revolution relegated it to total irrelevance. Most were not published until the late nineteenth and early twentieth centuries; hence the detailed attention to textual issues in the footnotes.

The halakhic culture of Early Ashkenaz leaves something to be desired in terms of articulation and precision, but not in its adaptive handling of contemporary problems as it grappled with a commercial landscape radically different from the Bavli's agricultural milieu. In dealing with the shift from the Babylonian economy, where the large Jewish population interacted mostly with its co-religionists, to that of the medieval world, where Jews were a minute percentage of the population and trade was between Jew and Gentile, that is to say, between an individual within the halakhic system and one outside it, the scholars of Early Ashkenaz have the confident steps of the practiced and the surefooted. The seasoned hand is equally displayed in their loosening of the severe restrictions that classical halakhah had placed on the mobility of credit. Their talmudic exegesis was to be improved upon and some of their judicial analogies would be challenged, but apart from one tractate (which I discuss in a subsequent essay[4]), they moved with confidence and ranged with ease over the entire Talmud, and their intuitions were flawless. Indeed, there is little in creative, judicial elasticity that later Talmudists could teach the scholars of Early Ashkenaz. The bold, new form of credit transfer that they intuited was later shown by Spanish Talmudists to be implicit in the Talmud. The notion of 'halakhic federalism' which will emerge from our analysis of the decisions of Ravyah and Ri[5] is already reflected in the rulings of R. Yehudah Ba'al Sefer ha-Dinim in the second quarter of the eleventh century. When the curtain rises on Ashkenaz in the last quarter of the tenth century, its halakhists are engaged, in the so-called *Perush Rabbenu Gershom*, in exegeting the entire Talmud including its most esoteric tractates—those of *Seder Kodashim* (the Order of Temple Service)—and its decisors (*poskim*) are moving over the new European terrain not with the hesitant steps of the beginner but with the assured stride of the experienced. This is all the more remarkable as only a generation earlier Ashkenazic halakhic thought had been non-existent.

The essay also highlights, as does 'Can Halakhic Texts Talk History?' below, the revolutionary role of Rashi in both halakhic theory and practice. His mildness and reticence are deceptive. He was as innovative as he was *un*obtrusive; his grandson, Rabbenu Tam, was as innovative as he was obtrusive. The two dominate the landscape of pawnbroking and usury, as they do that of *yein nesekh* (Gentile wine), the subject of the next essay in this volume.

[4] Below, pp. 177–8. [5] Below, pp. 147–50.

In this essay, as in the study of *yein nesekh*, Rashi is in constant dialogue with his predecessors and contemporaries. Indeed, it is impossible to get a view of Rashi's doctrines in their fullness, not to speak of their startling consequences when he first articulated them, without reconstructing the halakhic world in which he was raised and situating his views as richly and as deeply as possible in the traditions of Early Ashkenaz.

It is sometimes said that Rashi was influenced by Andalusian sources. This may be true in biblical exegesis, but it is hardly so in halakhic matters. I am not stating that instances of such influence do not exist, only that I have never chanced upon them. I do not know of a single case where knowledge of the positions of Alfasi, Maimonides, or R. Yosef Ibn Megas sheds light on Rashi's doctrines. If we seek new insight into Rashi's words, we will find it only after those words are placed in their proper framework: the teachings of the institutions in which Rashi had studied, the famed academies of Worms and Mainz, the fountainheads of Ashkenazic culture.

Finally, two remarks on method.

Alongside uncovering latent economic outlooks, I have also sought to detect personal posture, the hesitations and ambivalences of such Talmudists as Rashi and Rabbenu Tam. To this end, I have employed the method that I have described, in 'Can Halakhic Texts Talk History?', as the 'measurable deflection'.[6] There I speak about detecting social or economic influences upon halakhic thought; the same criterion holds true for evidence of individual ambiguity. To avoid a simplistic sociology of law, anyone claiming that a jurist's thought has been influenced by outside forces or inner ambiguities must be able to point to some obvious flaw in the thinker's argument, a measurable deflection from the expected line of reasoning that indicates that something impinged upon the mind of the jurist and diverted his thought from its normal course. Much, of course, hinges on knowing what the 'obvious', the 'expected', or the 'the normal' course of thinking of a specific jurist is. Only too often it is a difficult, if not impossible, task. Not so with Rashi and the Tosafists. We have been reared from childhood on their words and views, printed alongside the text of the Talmud since the 1520s, and we 'naturally' read the Talmud through this lens. So thoroughly have we internalized their mode of reasoning that the major methodological problem for the historian of the halakhah is to free himself from their tacit assumptions and way of thinking.

Eleventh-century literature speaks but does not explain, and thus requires interrogation if its underlying assumptions are to be elicited. One must guard, however, against anachronisms, finding for an eleventh-century position a rationale that is seemingly plausible to our way of thinking, or even to that of the Tosafists, and retrojecting it upon their predecessors. As most legal rulings can be justified by a number of different arguments, the only valid approach is to analyze all proposed solutions—to examine each step of the several arguments, testing its consonance with the litera-

[6] Below, p. 198.

ture of pre-Crusade Ashkenaz and equally with *its* mode of reasoning. In the body of the essay I have presented what I believe are the underlying rationales of early Ashkenazic thought. I have probed alternative explanations in the footnotes. This resulted in some notes of noticeable corpulence. I trimmed down those that I found of indecent girth by assigning parts of them to an appendix, as supplements to specific notes. Some of these supplements contain, as usual, additional information; others (such as the supplements to notes 80, 81, 117, and 181) contain discussion that is essential to my argument. Without them, the essay would lack analytical rigor.

THE BUSINESS OF PAWNBROKING A BRIEF INTRODUCTION

A STUDY OF JEWISH PAWNBROKING in the high Middle Ages yields much insight into the workings of Jewish law, but uncovers little new about Jewish economic history. Such famous moneylenders as Aaron of Lincoln,[7] Creslin of Provence,[8] Vivelin of Strassburg,[9] and the Cavalleria and Alconstantini families of Spain,[10] who played so significant a role in the economies of their respective countries, make no appearance in the halakhic sources; just as few, if any, traces are to be found in the rabbinic literature of early modern Poland of the transactions of the great international lumber merchants who operated out of Danzig in the late sixteenth and early seventeenth centuries. These palpable absences are due partly to the operation of these powerful figures outside the control of the Jewish community, but equally to the fact that these potentates preferred to settle their problems among themselves. They sought to function far from the communal limelight so as not to awaken envy which might lead to someone informing on them (*mesirah*) to the Gentile authorities, and strove, above all, to shelter the scope of their activities from the public eye lest discovery lead to further taxation. When rabbinical adjudication proved unavoidable, care was taken not to leave a paper trail. The questions posed were oral and the disposition summary.

7 C. Roth, *A History of the Jews in England*, 3rd edn. (Oxford, 1964), 15–16, and literature there cited; H. G. Richardson, *English Jewry under the Angevin Kings* (London, 1960), *passim*.

8 R. Chazan, *Medieval Jewry in Northern France: A Political and Social History* (Baltimore, 1973), 77, 95.

9 S. W. Baron, *A Social and Religious History of the Jews*, xii (New York and London, 1967), 135 and notes ad loc.

10 Y. Baer, *A History of the Jews in Christian Spain*, ii (Philadeplia, 1966), index, s.v. Alconstantini, Cavalleria.

Thus, the highest economic echelons of Jewish society are rarely reflected in the responsa literature.

As the responsa literature primarily treats problematic situations, the middle echelon of creditors, those who lent, not fortunes but sums still large enough to make it worth their while to pay a notary or to draw up a promissory note, equally do not appear on the halakhic register. (These mid-level creditors included such figures as Vitalis Salamon Mayr of Perpignan, more commonly known as R. Menaḥem ha-Me'iri, or Morel de Falaise, also known as R. Shemu'el of Falaise—editor of the standard *Tosafot* on *'Avodah Zarah*.[11]) Since Jews were forbidden to lend at interest to their co-religionists, one who did could scarcely turn to halakhists to right any wrong he believed he had suffered. Jews were permitted to lend to Gentiles, but any problems that arose would be settled by the Gentile authorities. Only if a Jew transferred the promissory note of a Gentile to another Jew could the case reach a Jewish court. However, Germanic law, which in the high Middle Ages obtained through much of western Europe and certainly throughout what Jews called Ashkenaz—England, northern France, and the German Empire north of the Alps—did not recognize such transfers, certainly not without the debtor's consent, and the Gentile debtor would refuse to pay the new creditor.[12] In some places, for example in England where there was a vibrant traffic in promissory notes,[13] no problems of usury could emerge as Jews viewed such sales as

[11] R. W. Emery, *The Jews of Perpignan in the Thirteenth Century: An Economic Study Based on Notarial Records* (New York, 1959), 28; E. E. Urbach, *Ba'alei ha-Tosafot*, revised edn. (Jerusalem, 1980), 461–2, and the literature there cited.

[12] R. Huebner, *A History of Germanic Private Law* (Boston, 1918), 553 ff.; G. Kisch, *The Jews in Medieval Germany* (Chicago, 1949), 228. On the overwhelming dominance of Germanic law until the latter half of the 12th century in the Midi (what Jews called 'Provence', the ancient 'Provincia Romana', i.e. Rousillon, Languedoc, Comtat Venaissin, and, strictly speaking, Provence), see e.g. M. L. Carlin, *La Pénétration du droit romain dans les actes de la pratique provençale* (Paris, 1967), 2–7, and bibliography there cited. Carlin's book and the works she cites chart the initial penetration of Roman law; it should be emphasized, however, that even after such ingress, local, customary law often predominated. See e.g. J. Rogozinski, *Power, Caste and Law: Social Conflict in Fourteenth-Century Montpellier* (Cambridge, Mass., 1982), 107–13. In matters of pawnbroking, to judge by rabbinic sources, Germanic law prevailed well into the 13th century, if not up to the expulsion of 1306; see Carlin, p. 170. (For the scope of the term 'Provence' in medieval Hebrew sources, see H. Gross, *Gallia Judaica: Dictionnaire géographique de la France* [Paris, 1897]; with supplement by S. Schwarzfuchs [Amsterdam, 1969], 489–91, 632–3. Y. Assis, 'Les Juifs de Montpellier sous la domination aragonaise', *Revue des études juives*, 148 [1989], 5, n. 1, includes Cerdagne within that appellation. I am not familiar with such a use.)

[13] On England, see Richardson, *English Jewry* (above, n. 7), 71–6; V. D. Lipman, *Jews of Medieval Norwich* (London, 1967), 81 ff. and the sources there cited. (For a study of the history and significance of these assignments from the point of view of development of English law see S. J. Bailey, 'Assign-

halakhically valid. The purchaser was now the direct creditor of the Gentile and the charging of interest was permitted. Needless to say, if the initial note contained a clause saying 'pay the bearer',[14] the Gentile debtor stood in direct relationship to whoever had legal possession of the note and the ban on usury once again did not apply.

Pawnbroking, however, did generate problems. An item might be pawned by a prince, an abbot, a wealthy burgher, a peasant, or even a passing stranger, for people of every rank are occasionally confronted with an urgent need for cash. However, one should emphasize that making loans that are secured by a pawned item and pawnbroking are two different businesses. When a bank, for example, lends money, it generally expects to be repaid; it takes collateral in the event that the debtor fails to meet his obligation. Such institutions or individuals tend to lend sizeable sums, to creditworthy people, and the loans are relatively long-term. A pawnbroker, on the other hand, frequently gives cash to people with poor or no credit history and whose entire bearing suggests little prospect of repayment. He knows in advance that his reimbursement will often come from the sale of the pawned item. Such loans tend to be short-term (for several weeks or months) and of small, indeed often tiny, sums of money on pawns of trivial value.[15] One who lends money on collateral will

ment of Debts in England from the Twelfth to the Twentieth Century', *Law Quarterly Review*, 47 [1931], 516–35; *Law Quarterly Review*, 48 [1932], 248–71.) How frequently Jews in Germany used promissory notes in their loans to Gentiles is a subject of controversy. See G. Caro, *Sozial- und Wirtschaftsgeschichte der Juden im Mittelalter und der Neuzeit*, i (Leipzig, 1908), 437 ff.; see, however, Kisch, *The Jews in Medieval Germany* (above, n. 12), 225 ff. The impression given by rabbinic sources corroborates Caro's view. It's difficult to speak with any certainty about the situation in France, as few if any Jewish loan documents have come down to us; see Chazan, *Medieval Jewry* (above, n. 8), 105, 109, 138. The only discussion of a sale of a Jewish–Christian promissory note is by R. Yitsḥak of Corbeil in the late 13th century—see my *Halakhah, Kalkalah* (above, n. 1), 95, n. 49. His stringent demand for renunciation (*silluk*; for the meaning of the term, see below, pp. 133–5) stemmed, perhaps, from the fact that by his time such documents had no validity, and certainly were not transferable.

14 e.g. A. Gulak, *Otsar ha-Shetarot* (Jerusalem, 1926), 206–7; Rabad on 'Hilkhot Mekhirah', 6: 12; Kisch, *Jews in Medieval Germany* (above, n. 12), 228–9; Emery, *Jews of Perpignan* (above, n. 11), 38, n. 2; I. Baer, *Die Juden im christlichen Spanien*, i (Berlin, 1929), *passim*, esp. p. 1057 ff.

15 R. de Roover, *Money, Banking and Credit in Medieval Bruges: Italian Merchant Bankers, Lombards and Money-Changers* (Cambridge, Mass., 1948), 99–167, esp. p. 124; R. W. Patterson, 'Pawnbroking in Europe and the United States', *Bulletin of Department of Labor*, 21 (1889), 179, 189, 204, 227; Emery, *Jews of Perpignan* (above, n. 11), 31–3; A. Holtmann, *Juden in der Grafschaft Burgund im Mittelalter*, Forschungen zur Geschichte der Juden 12 (Hanover, 2003), 234–8, 241. For the nature of the pawned objects, see e.g. de Roover, 120–4; J. Quesnel, *Le Gage mobilier dans l'ancienne Bourgogne*. Collections d'études sur l'histoire du droit et des institutions de la Bourgogne 20 (Dijon, 1910), 54–76; M. Hoffmann, *Der Geldhandel der deutschen Juden während des Mittelalters bis zum Jahre 1350* (Leipzig, 1910), 74, 98; G. Nahon, 'Le Crédit et les juifs dans la France du XIIIe siècle', *Annales ESC*, 24 (1969),

occasionally even waive the collateral and settle for an ironclad promissory note. He is a 'banker', that is to say, an extender of credit, who seeks only to ensure repayment of his loan. The pawnbroker, in contrast, relies primarily on the item that has been pawned, for its sale is the sole sure source of his reimbursement. He deals in objects as much as in credit. It was not by accident that trade in used goods—the inevitable corollary of pawnbroking—became a traditional Jewish occupation.

This distinction, like all others, should not be pressed too far. There were many people who engaged in what we would call banking and who still kept a hand in pawnbroking; conversely, there were many pawnbrokers who were only too happy to lend sizeable sums to creditworthy individuals. However, if one attends closely to the words of the speakers in the responsa literature of medieval Ashkenaz, one generally feels that they are parties to pawnbroking and not to bankers' loans. The impression arises from the mention of '2*d.*' or '4*d.*', which means '[at a weekly rate of interest of] 2 *denarii* or 4 *denarii* [per pound, which had 240 *denarii*]. (The old English system of coinage, which was discarded there only in the late 1960s, was introduced in continental Europe by Charlemagne and obtained throughout much of western Europe during the Middle Ages.) It is further indicated by such phrases as 'and I lent him for a week' or 'and I deposited the pawn for a month'; from the objects pawned, such as clothes, household items, and agricultural tools; from the occasional feeling that the creditor doesn't want the debt to be paid and, at times, that he even seeks to prevent repayment—for a pawned object was invariably worth more than the debt, often twice as much. The atmosphere of most of the responsa fits the world of pawnbrokers portrayed by de Roover far more than that of the great bankers of England and tax farmers of Spain, or of the middle-echelon creditors that appear in the registers of Perpignan and are described so well by Emery.[16]

1132; R. Kohn, *Les Juifs de la France du Nord dans la seconde moitié du XIVe siècle*. Collection de la Revue des Études Juives 5 (Louvain and Paris, 1988), 137–42; A. Holtmann, *Juden in der Grafschaft Burgund*, 233–6.

[16] Emery subsequently synthesized his work and that of others undertaken in the wake of his study (above, n. 11) in 'Le Prêt d'argent juif en Languedoc et Roussillon', in *Juifs et judaïsme de Languedoc*, Cahiers de Fanjeaux 12 (Toulouse, 1977), 85–96. A more recent study of Jewish moneylending activity in Catalonia as reflected in notarial records is Y. Assis, *The Jews of Santa Coloma de Queralt*, Hispania Judaica 6 (Jerusalem, 1988). Assis's portrait has much in common with that of Emery, though caution should be exercised as to his conclusions about the importance of Jewish moneylending activity in the overall economy of Santa Coloma de Queralt. See M. B. Milton, 'Christian and Jewish Lenders: Religious Identity and the Extension of Credit', *Viator*, 37 (2006), 301–18.

Accordingly, the halakhic literature deals with a profession that left few documentary traces.[17] Why spend money on a notary to record the loan of a pittance? If one held a pawned object, moreover, what could a notarized piece of paper, as a rule, add to the assurance of repayment? That pawnbroking was significant is unquestionable; but how widespread was it? What percentage of the Jewish community was engaged in it? What percentage of the lenders were Jews? The historian has no clear answer to these questions.

Unfortunately, the responsa literature is of little help here. One thing, however, is clear. A peripheral occupation could scarcely give birth to an entire literature, and would not generate several hundred pages of legal discussions, certainly not in the medieval period when halakhic writings inclined strongly to brevity.[18] If the very first German Tosafist, R. Yitsḥak b. Asher (d. before 1133), wrote a brief handbook on the laws of pawnbroking,[19] if one of the very first works that have come down to us from Provence is a work on pawnbroking by R. Meshullam of Lunel (d. 1160s),[20] these are sure signs that pawnbroking was a significant enterprise in those areas. If Naḥmanides (d. 1270) broke once, and only once, the literary structure of his novellae to insert a very lengthy discussion of pawnbroking which has little to do with the talmudic discussion at hand, and if his disciples, and their disciples in turn, followed in his footsteps and did the same in their novellae,[21] it is clear evidence that in

[17] See e.g. Richardson, *English Jewry* (above, n. 7), 76, Emery, *Jews of Perpignan* (above, n. 11), 76, and F. Irsigler, 'Juden und Lombarden am Niederrhein im 14. Jahrhundert', in A. Haverkamp, ed., *Zur Geschichte der Juden im Deutschland des späten Mittelalters und der frühen Neuzeit*, Monographien zur Geschichte des Mittelalters 24 (Stuttgart, 1981), 131. The *reconnaissances*, i.e. pawn tickets, mentioned by de Roover (above, n. 15) are what the German Pietist (MS Oxford, Bodley, 1566, fo. 178a) had in mind when he taught his daughters how to write *ketavim le-mashkonot* rather than pawn contracts, so one cannot infer from his remarks that pawn contracts were frequently used. (An almost identical passage was cited from a different manuscript by M. Güdemann in his *Geschichte des Erziehungswesens und der Cultur der Abendländischen Juden*, i [Vienna, 1880], 230, n. 5. Our passage is from a pietistic work entitled *Sefer ha-Ne'elam*, his from a work entitled *Ḥiddushim be-Otiyot Ḥaserot*.)

[18] The medieval source reader that I compiled in the early 1970s for my seminar on the halakhic analysis of pawnbroking, *Halakhah ve-Khalkalah bi-Yemei ha-Beinayim*, had some 220 pages, and it made no claim to completeness.

[19] See below, p. 118.

[20] This work has been preserved in two sources: the 13th-century Provençal work printed as the *Ḥiddushei ha-Ritva 'al 'Avodah Zarah* (Amsterdam, 1729), fo. 40c–d, see below, n. 98(*d*), and in the Catalonian *Sefer ha-Terumot* (Saloniki, 1596), fo. 81a–d; edn. *Giddulei Terumah* (Venice, 1643), 46: 4: 10, fos. 235d–236c; ed. A. Goldschmidt (Jerusalem, 1988), vol. ii, 986–9.

[21] *Ḥiddushei Ramban 'al Bava Metsi'a*, ed. I. Z. Meltzer (repr. Jerusalem, 1972), 71b, s.v. *u-var*; ed. E. R. Hishrik (Jerusalem, 2002), 454–61; *Ḥiddushei ha-Rashba 'al Bava Metsi'a*, ed. E. Lichtenstein (Jerusalem, 2006), 71b, cols. 588–91; *Ḥiddushei ha-Ran 'al Bava Metsi'a*, 71b, s.v. *ve-katav*; ed. Y. G. Grossberg (Jerusalem, 1994), 247–50; *Perush ha-Ran 'al ha-Rif, Bava Metsi'a* 71b (Vilna edn., fo. 42a–b).

Aragon, or in Catalonia and Roussillon at the very least, Jewish involvement in pawnbroking was considerable. However, what percentage of the Jewish population engaged in this profession? What percentage of Jewish capital was invested in this enterprise? Our sources afford no answer. The rabbinic literature attests to the significance of pawnbroking, not to its relative weight in the economic activity of the Jews.

I noted above that there is a marked similarity between the picture that emerges from the Ashkenazic sources of the eleventh and twelfth centuries and the portrait that de Roover has drawn of pawnbroking in Bruges in the fourteenth and fifteenth centuries. Indeed, the medieval picture in its broad outlines is reproduced in the studies of pawnbroking in both Europe and America in the late nineteenth and early twentieth centuries.[22] Pawnbroking is based on the occasional need of the rich and powerful to meet some sudden, urgent demand for liquidity, and the far more frequent need of people of limited means to cover a chronic shortfall, to make ends meet until the next paycheck—*prêt à la petite semaine*, as the French say, or *ligmor et ha-ḥodesh* (to finish the month), as the Israeli expression goes. The closer one gets to the subsistence line, the smaller the difference between one age and another and between one culture and the next.[23]

I have mentioned '2*d.* or 4*d.* [per £] a week'. These terms yield an annual interest rate of 43 or 86 percent (e.g. 52 × 2 = 104; 240*d.* = £1; 104 ÷ 240 = 43%). These sums are often quoted as the going rate of interest in medieval times. This is correct, yet misleading. Pawnbroking usually involves short-term loans, measured in weeks or months, rarely in years. The modern credit card is probably the best analogy; indeed, it now often serves as a substitute for pawn-

[22] See the studies listed in the bibliography of de Roover, *Money, Banking and Credit* (above, n. 15): L. N. Robinson and R. Nugent, *Regulation of Small Business Loans* (New York, 1935); R. C. Raby, *The Regulation of Pawnbroking* (New York, 1924); D. G. Orchard and G. May, *Moneylending in Great Britain* (New York, 1933). A fine summary of the studies of pawnbroking in France, Germany, Belgium, and the United States in the 1880s and 1890s may be found in R. W. Patterson, 'Pawnbroking in Europe' (above, n. 15). The noticeable differences between the rates of interest in the 19th century reported by Patterson and those of the Middle Ages (and concomitantly the differing rates of redemption of pawns) are primarily because the institutions surveyed by Patterson were governmental, i.e. subsidized, which was scarcely the case for the medieval pawnbrokers discussed in this essay. Note that in the United States, where the institutions studied were in private hands (pp. 257–8), the interest rates are similar to those of the Middle Ages, both as to the percentage charged and to the sharp differences of rates between the various locales.

[23] For an excellent description of pawnbroking and its impact on daily life—its weekly rhythm, its role in the household budget, its emotional and economic costs—both from the points of view of the continually hard-pressed clients and that of the lenders, see M. Tebbutt, *Making Ends Meet: Pawnbroking and Working-Class Credit* (Leicester, 1983).

ing. If the credit card is used to tide over a temporary, recurrent gap in the monthly cashflow, it is a useful means of getting by, of somehow matching income to expenditure. However, if the debt is allowed to accumulate, the rates are destructive. At this moment (July 2009), I hold in my hand a bill from a well-known department store for $209. There are two pages of text. Towards the end of the first page, the note informs me (in small print) that if the stipulated minimum payment is not made for a year, the accumulated interest and penalties will amount to 123 percent of the original debt. True, this is on the harsh side, but even without monthly penalties, sums that in their original dimensions seem manageable and reasonable, if left unpaid, compound and grow like a virulent cancer.

During the early decades of the twentieth century the Russell Sage Foundation initiated studies in Britain and the United States to determine the minimum interest rate necessary for a pawnbroking operation simply to turn a profit. The conclusion was between 30 and 36 percent.[24] Besides covering the fixed costs of plant maintenance and fees that the government may have imposed, the income must also pay the salaries of the workers. If the business is family-owned and -run—working behind the counter, doing the bookkeeping, taking care of the storeroom, wrapping and tagging the pledges—the income from the loans has to match the salaries that these people would have earned working elsewhere. The income must equally compensate for what the moneys lent out could otherwise have earned in investments, in addition to the income lost by the moneys 'lying around', lying idle in the coffers of the pawnbroker waiting to be lent out. To all this should be added the considerable expense of safely storing the pawned goods (some of which are of significant worth).[25] Studies made of the European *monts-de-piété* (small loan institutions, generally church- or government-run) yielded roughly the same figure.[26] This is minimal profit; if one seeks, understandably, to do somewhat better, the interest rate must necessarily rise. In 1916 some honest and responsible lenders from the American Association of Small Loan Brokers, together with the Russell Sage Foundation, sought to limit predatory lending to small businessmen and needy individuals and drew up a series of equitable regulations for loans under $300. They further succeeded, by 1930, in having no fewer than twenty-five states adopt their proposal, which became known as the Uniform Small Loan Law and regulated some 3,000 agencies. These included personal finance companies that made loans on household goods, the

24 de Roover, *Money, Banking and Credit* (above, n. 15), 131, and the literature cited above, n. 22.

25 See de Roover's discussion, ibid. 127–31.

26 See Patterson, 'Pawnbroking in Europe' (above, n. 15).

hallmark of consumer pawnbroking. One such company had 263 subsidiaries in 228 cities, and in 1930 extended credit totaling $56 million. (Remember the buying power of a dollar in the Great Depression.) The rate of interest allowed by the Small Loan Law was 3.5 percent a month, which comes to 42 percent a year (without compounding). A recent study by the Russell Sage Foundation yielded the following maximum annual interest rates permissible by law, as of the end of 1991: New York 36 percent, Pennsylvania 36 percent, Indiana 69 percent, California 82 percent, Oregon 91 percent, Illinois 167 percent, Texas, Wyoming, and Oklahoma 240 percent, North Carolina 264 percent, and Georgia 340 percent.[27] If one adds to the underlying minimum of some 40 percent the uncertainties of life, property, and government enforcement in the Middle Ages generally, and for Jews in particular, 43 percent seems reasonable, to put it mildly. In situations of poor security, even ones fraught with danger for the Jews—frequent forced exactions and confiscations by rulers, punctuated by pogroms by the populace—the rate charged could readily double itself, and did.

Our study is of pawnbroking, but the reader should be aware that not every instance of pawn-taking that we will encounter in our sources is evidence of such an occupation. Indeed, some such cases do not even document an instance of moneylending. In the Middle Ages, to extend credit without receiving some security in return was viewed as folly. The security could be either a guarantor or a pawn. As a dearth of currency was common enough in the Middle Ages, and income was often received in the form of produce (what is called payment in kind) rather than in coin, purchases frequently could not readily be paid for by cash; rather, the commodity was sold on credit until the necessary quantity of coin was obtained. In such cases a pawn was given to guarantee the payment. One of the earliest instances of pawning in the Midi, dating from 962, was to insure payment in a horse sale.[28] In fact, the most common form of credit in English villages in the Middle Ages was credit extended in the context of a sale.[29] The giving and taking of pawns is evidence of the extension of credit, not necessarily of moneylending.

Conversely, lending money is not always evidence of professional moneylending. In the earliest stage of commercial development in the overwhelm-

[27] S. Tenenbaum, *A Credit to their Community: Jewish Loan Societies, 1885–1945* (Detroit, 1993), 44–6; John P. Casey, *Fringe Banking: Check-Cashing Outlets, Pawnshops and the Poor* (New York, 1994), 40–1.

[28] M. Castaing-Sicard, *Les Contrats dans le très ancien droit toulousain: Xᵉ–XIIᵉ siècles* (Toulouse, 1959), 102.

[29] C. Briggs, *Credit and Village Society in Fourteenth-Century England* (Oxford, 2009), 63, 97.

ingly agricultural economy of the eleventh century, the knight and noble received their payment in kind, while the peasant retained some of the produce for his own use. The merchant was thus the only person who had silver coins, ready cash, and one naturally turned to him for loans. In this phase of economic development, one cannot easily separate the merchant from the moneylender, the trader from the money changer.[30] It will be wise to remember these cautionary remarks when we come to analyze Jewish economic activity in Champagne in Rashi's day.

PAWNBROKING IN ASHKENAZIC HALAKHIC THOUGHT

Background

The Economic Context

In Babylonia the Jews were overwhelmingly an agricultural class;[31] when the Ashkenazic community first comes into view, around the turn of the first millennium, the Jews are predominantly involved in commerce.[32] Commercial enterprise requires initial financing, and business demands ongoing credit. One's own money rarely suffices; other people's money must be used, and one pays for this use. Such payments are called in English interest or usury; in Hebrew the term is *ribbit. Ribbit* from a Gentile was viewed as permissible. Admittedly, there is a view in the Talmud that there is a rabbinic injunction against such loans, but all the evidence indicates that this view never obtained any purchase on the European Jewish community. In the earliest documents that we possess from Christian Europe, beginning with the closing decades of the tenth century, the permissibility of lending at interest between Jews and Gentiles is taken as a given.[33]

30 J. Kulischer, 'Warenhändler und Geldausleiher im Mittelalter', *Zeitschrift für Volkswirschaft, Sozialpolitik und Verwaltung*, 17 (1908), 29–71, 201–54.

31 Y. Gafni, *Yehudei Bavel bi-Tekufat ha-Talmud: Ḥayyei Ḥevrah ve-Ruaḥ* (Jerusalem, 1991), 130–1.

32 See, most recently, M. Toch, 'The Jews in Europe, 500–1050', in P. Fouracre, ed., *The New Cambridge Medieval History, ca. 500–700* (Cambridge, 2005), 558–61; for some of the older studies see below, n. 37.

33 (A) On the rabbinical injunction against lending to a Gentile at interest, see J. Rosenthal, 'Ribbit min ha-Nokhri', *Talpiot: Rive'on le-'Inyanei Halakhah, Aggadah u-Musar*, 5 (1952), 475 ff.; 6 (1953), 130 ff. (reprinted in an expanded form in J. Rosenthal, *Meḥkarim u-Mekorot*, i [Jerusalem, 1966], 253–323); S. Albeck, 'Yaḥaso shel Rabbenu Tam li-Ve'ayot Zemano', *Zion*, 19 (1954), 106–8; S. Stein, 'The Development of the Jewish Law of Interest from the Biblical Period to the Expulsion from England', *Historia Judaica*, 17 (1955), 3–40. (B) On the presumption of the permissibility of taking interest from

The ample resources of monasteries, possibly the major source of credit in the eleventh century, were thus available to Jewish businessmen, and they could equally supply credit to Gentiles in all walks of life. Liquidity is always a problem in business, and doubly so in a society such as that of eleventh-century north-western Europe, which did not have sufficient silver (let alone gold) to provide the currency it needed. Europe awakened to the biblical ban on usury only in the latter half of the twelfth century.[34] In the eleventh and early twelfth centuries, monasteries lent openly *ad usuram*; indeed in Normandy they were the major moneylenders in the economy.[35] Gentiles thus had access to both Jewish resources and those of their co-religionists; Jews did not. The Jewish businessman had to be placed on an equal footing with his Gentile competitor, otherwise he would not survive. He too needed access to the capital of other Jews. How was the ban on Jewish usury to be sidestepped?

Not only was intra-Jewish credit essential, it also had to be made mobile. Credit is almost universal: neighborhood groceries, for example, regularly sell on credit. They do not, however, employ the housewives' debts as the basis of obtaining new funding. In business, debts are also assets. To be sure, they exist to be collected; however, they equally exist to be sold, to be transferred to other parties in return for new money, new goods, or new credit. Money expended in loans must be susceptible of replenishment by sale of the debt, by transfer of the collateral provided by the original debtor. Without such continuous recouping of capital, there can be no commercial life. Yet classical halakhah is notoriously restrictive of debt transfer. Debts either cannot be transferred or can be transferred only in the most cumbersome fashion.[36] The mobility of credit was the second problem that confronted the sages of Early Ashkenaz.

Supply of capital, furthermore, had to be better linked to demand, and often only Jewish middlemen could accomplish this task. In eleventh-century Ashkenaz, Jews still handled the business dealings of some nobles and monasteries, serving as their factotums and exclusive agents. From this perch they provided Jewish businessmen with precious access to Gentile capital, but could their functioning be made consonant with Jewish law? Could the Jewish factotum, the *ma'arufya*, as the Jews somewhat mysteriously called these middlemen,[37] lend at interest to his co-religionists and receive from their

Gentiles current in the European Jewish community from its earliest days, see my essay, 'The Jewish Attitude to Usury', Chapter 5 above, and n. 6 ad loc.

34 See the references ibid. 52–4, and the literature cited in nn. 29–34.

35 R. Genestal, *Le Rôle des monastères comme établissements du crédit étudié en Normandie du XIe à la fin du XIIIe siècle* (Paris, 1901).

36 See below, pp. 88–9.

37 M. Hoffmann, *Der Geldhandel* (above, n. 15), 94–7; B. Blumenkranz, *Juifs et chrétiens dans le monde occidental, 430–1096*, Études juives 2 (Paris, 1960), 18 ff.; I. A. Agus, *Urban Civilization in Pre-*

hands payments of *ribbit*? Finally, the halakhists of Early Ashkenaz had to confront the problems of debt repayment in a society that suffered from a chronic lack of currency: remuneration frequently took the form of paying off one debt with the money obtained by incurring another. Could Jews participate in this debt cycle, in this widespread arrangement called *Schadennehmen*?[38]

The Halakhic Context

Controlling Rulings

As two laws figure prominently in all discussions of pawnbroking, it will be best to explain them and provide a diagram at the outset, rather than break the flow of analysis with their explication.

It is an accepted principle in Jewish law that a Jew cannot serve as an agent (*shaliaḥ*) for a Gentile, nor can a Gentile serve as an agent for a Jew.[39] Any

Crusade Europe, i (New York, 1965), 187–255; S. Eidelberg 'Maarufia in Rabbenu Gershom's Responsa', *Historia Judaica*, 15 (1953), 59–67, reprinted in id., *Medieval Ashkenazic History: Studies on German Jewry in the Middle Ages* (New York, 1999), 11–20. On the term *ma'arufya* see A. Grossman, *Ḥakhmei Tsarfat ha-Rishonim: Koroteihem, Darkam be-Hanhagat ha-Tsibbur, Yetsiratam ha-Ruḥanit mi-Reshit Yishuvam ve-'ad li-Gezerot Tatnu*, 2nd edn. (Jerusalem, 2001), 556, n. 61 and R. Steiner, 'Ikvot Leshoniyim shel Soḥarim Yehudim me-'Artsot ha-Islam be-Mamlakhah ha-Frankit', *Leshonenu*, 73 (2011), 352–7.

[38] (A) On *Schadennehmen* or *Schadenklausel* see M. Neumann, *Geschichte des Wuchers in Deutschland bis zur Begründung der heutigen Zinsengesetze* (Halle, 1865), 159 ff., 393 ff. A full bibliography is to be found in G. Kisch, *Jews in Medieval Germany* (above, n. 12), 486, n. 115; see esp. O. Stobbe, *Die Juden in Deutschland während des Mittelalters in politischer, socialer und rechtlicher Beziehung* (Braunschweig, 1866), 114–15. See also J. J. Rabinowitz, 'Some Remarks on the Evasion of the Usury Law in the Middle Ages', *Harvard Theological Review*, 38 (1944), 49 ff. For 11th-century Germany see *Teshuvot Rabbi Me'ir mi-Rotenburg* (Prague and Budapest), #893. For the subsequent period, see M. Hoffmann, *Der Geldhandel* (above, n.15), 98, to which add *Mordekhai, Bava Batra*, #554; *Teshuvot Rabbi Me'ir mi-Rotenburg* (Prague and Budapest), ##748, 817 (see editor's note); *Sefer 'Ets Ḥayyim* in *Ḥamishah Kuntresin*, ed. N. N. Coronel (Vienna, 1864), fo. 102b. (B) Bibliographical information: (1) Zunz already identified ##873–914 in *Teshuvot R. Me'ir mi-Rotenburg* (Prague and Budapest) as being responsa from the 11th-century *Sefer ha-Dinim* of R. Yehudah ha-Kohen of Mainz in his *Literaturgeschichte der synagogalen Poesie* (Berlin, 1865), 611. See in detail A. Grossman, *Ḥakhmei Ashkenaz ha-Rishonim: Koroteihem, Darkam be-Hanhagat ha-Tsibbur, Yetsiratam ha-Ruḥanit mi-Reshit Yishuvam ve-'ad li-Gezerot Tatnu (1096)* (3rd edn., Jerusalem, 2001), 196–201. (2) The various collections of responsa attributed both in print and in manuscript to R. Me'ir of Rothenburg are in reality responsa of Ashkenazic scholars, 1000–1350. The reader should not be surprised if on numerous occasions a responsum of Rashi or of Rabbenu Tam or Ravyah is sourced in some compilation entitled 'Teshuvot R. Me'ir mi-Rotenburg'. The single largest collection is the *Teshuvot R. Me'ir mi-Rotenburg* (Prague, 1607). The text is poor, the citations are unsourced, and the print abominable. M. A. Bloch published a far superior edition in Budapest in 1895. All citations were checked in the first edition; throughout the essay, however, reference is made to that of Bloch, and I have registered its place of publication as 'Prague and Budapest'.

[39] *Bava Metsi'a* 71b.

action performed by such 'agents' is viewed as being performed on their own initiative, i.e. they, the agents, are viewed as the principals. This would open the gate for the simplest ploy in allowing intra-Jewish usury. A Jew could appoint a Gentile as his agent to get a loan at interest from another Jew. Though the Gentile is an agent in every real sense of the word, he would legally be viewed as a principal. Thus the loan would not be from Jew to Jew via a Gentile, but two separate loans would legally have taken place: the Gentile (on his own initiative, as it were) took a loan from the second Jew and then turned around (again, on his own initiative) and lent that money to the first Jew.

The Talmud foresaw and forbade such an arrangement.[40] The rather strange term used (which we will explain later) for this injunctive ruling is לחומרא (*le-ḥumra*, i.e. stringency), and the ban of *le-ḥumra* looms as a 'brooding omnipresence' over all the halakhic discussions of intra-Jewish credit and its necessary mobility.

The second ruling is that of Rava. אמר רבא שרי ליה לאיניש למימר ליה לחבריה הילך ד' זוזי ואוזפיה לפלניא זוזי, לא אסרה תורה אלא רבית הבאה מלוה למלוה.[41] ('Rava said: One may say to his neighbor, "take these four *zuz* and lend money to so-and-so", [for] the Torah forbade only usury which comes from the borrower to the lender.') This dictum states that usury is a bilateral affair: the debtor and

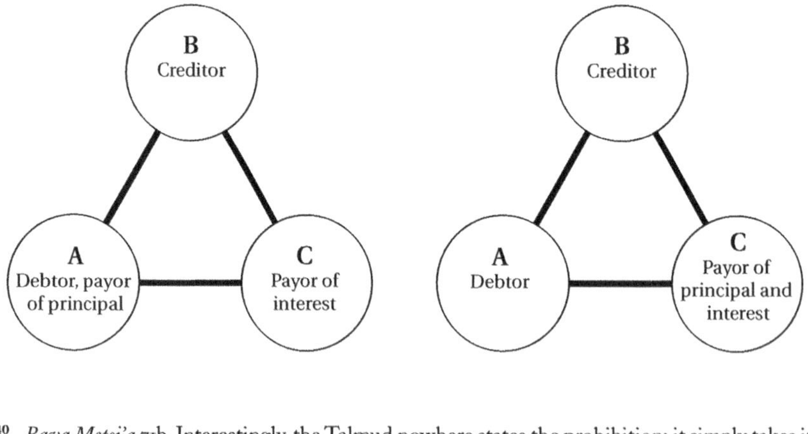

[40] *Bava Metsi'a* 71b. Interestingly, the Talmud nowhere states the prohibition; it simply takes it as a given in its discussion of a Tosefta in the cited passage: *bi-shelama sefa* [*shel ha-Tosefta*] *le-ḥumra*. See below, p. 106. On the Tosefta itself (ed. M. S. Zuckermandel, repr. Jerusalem, 1963, 5: 17), see S. Lieberman, *Tosefta ki-Feshutah, Nezikin: Bava Metsi'a* (Jerusalem, 1988), 221–3 and see below, n. 179(*f*).

[41] *Bava Metsi'a* 69b. (The reading of MS Munich 95, *Dikdukei Soferim*, ed. R. N. N. Rabbinowicz, Munich 1882, ad loc. is an instance of *homoioteleuton*.)

payor of interest must be one and the same person. If, however, the arrangement is 'triangular', that is to say, A takes a loan at interest from B and repays only the principal while C independently (i.e. not per instruction of A) pays the interest, the injunction against *ribbit* has not been breached. Neither has it been breached if A takes a loan at interest from B, and C independently repays the principal together with the interest. This principle will be continually invoked in Ashkenaz. Indeed, the strategy of allowance of the next two centuries is to create such triangular situations by legally sundering the payor from the borrower, and the claim that an interest payment is not 'from borrower to lender' (*ribbit mi-loveh le-malveh*) will be encountered with regularity.

Frequently Repeated Cases

As *Schadennehmen* and the most common form of credit mobility, the 'pawned pawn' (*pignus pignoris*), will figure prominently in all discussions, it may prove best to describe and even illustrate them at the outset. These illustrations may seem to reveal a lack of high-minded seriousness. However, the serious reader who does the heavy lifting in the footnotes and appendix—with their alternative interpretations and variant readings—may come to appreciate that he obtained a clear picture of the cases at bar with childish ease.

Let us begin with the 'pawned pawn':

> On January 1, a Jew (Jew 1) lends £100 for two months to a Gentile at, shall we say, 4 percent a month. On February 1, he finds himself in need of capital, goes to another Jew (Jew 2), and says, 'Lend me £100. As collateral I give you the Gentile's pawn and we will split the interest that I will receive from him next month. In other words, when the Gentile redeems the pawn on March 1, he will give me £108 (i.e. the principal of £100, plus two months' interest). I will give you £104 of that sum (i.e. the principal of the loan between us [Jew 1 and Jew 2], and the £4 interest for the month of February).' At face value, this arrangement should be forbidden. The first loan (on January 1) between the Jew and the Gentile is, of course, permissible; however, the second loan (on February 1) between Jew 1 and Jew 2 is usurious. True, Jew 1 pays (on March 1) with money that he has just received from the Gentile. However, he legitimately acquired that money from the Gentile, as it was paid willingly, per contract. Thus, when Jew 1 uses this money to pay his co-religionist, he is paying both the principal of *his own* loan and its interest with *his own* money. The ubiquitous pawned pawn, the major instrument of credit mobility, is, at first blush, usury pure and simple.

The Pawned Pawn

January 1

February 1

March 1

Schadennehmen

January 1

A note about the illustrations: Jews in the German Empire commonly wore a distinctive hat (*Judenhut* or *pilleus cornutus*) and grew a beard. The hat was viewed as part of the national dress and had initially no negative connotations. Lay Gentiles in western Europe were usually clean-shaven, at least from the latter half of the eleventh century. On the hat and beard as national dress, see G. Kisch, *The Jews in Medieval Germany* (Chicago, 1949), 292–6, 341; on the Jewish hat, see R. Straus, The "Jewish Hat" as an Aspect of Social History', *Jewish Social Studies*, 4 (1942), 59–72; on Gentile beards and absence of beards, see G. Constable, 'Introduction on Beards in the Middle Ages', in R. B. C. Huygens, ed., *Apologiae Duae*, Corpus Christianorum. Continuatio Medievalis 62 (Turnhout, 1985), 94–102. See also p. 54, n. 25 for further literature on Jewish beards, and see E. Horowitz ''Al Mashma'uyot ha-Zakan bi-Kehilot Yisra'el', *Pe'amim*, 59 (1994), 124–48.

February 1

March 1

Let us now turn to *Schadennehmen*:

> A Jew borrowed money from a Gentile; when the bill became due, he was not liquid and was unable to meet the payment. Instead, he gave his Gentile creditor an object of value and told him to pawn it with another Jew at interest and to keep the money for himself, saying 'I will worry about redeeming my pawn.' In other words, 'I accept, agree to the loss of money that I will suffer at the time of redemption in paying the interest that has accrued.' Whence, the term *Schadennehmen*—'acceptance of loss [resulting from the accrued interest]'.

Is the Gentile creditor seeking to act as an agent of the Jewish debtor in obtaining a loan from the second Jew? Or is he more accurately seen as borrowing the Jewish debtor's pawn and with it obtaining on his own a new loan, leaving the Jewish debtor (upon the latter's own suggestion) with the problem of getting his property out of hock? The legitimacy of this institution will hinge on these different constructions, and each construction has further implications.

Ideally, we should begin with the earliest halakhic documents that have come down to us from Ashkenaz: the writings of Rabbenu Meshullam and Rabbenu Gershom and those of their pupils. However, it seems best to begin with the French sources of the eleventh century, as the presentation of the issues there is fuller, and then to proceed and integrate the scattered and occasionally fragmentary reports of Early Ashkenaz into our analysis.

As this essay is an attempt to discern unarticulated assumptions and implicit doctrines and, at the same time, to detect the personal posture of famed halakhists, it entails a sustained engagement with the primary sources. Most of them, both those in print and those still in manuscript, have been scanned and brought together in a file entitled *Pawnbroking and Ribbit—A Source Book* (it can be downloaded from my website, <www.haymsoloveitchik.org>). Armed with this compilation, the critical reader can evaluate my readings of the occasionally gnomic sources, test my inferences, and stalk my errors with minimum physical effort. (The original pagination of the essay is marked thus |**100**|. As the study has been considerably expanded—over and above the added fifteen-page introduction—any exact correlation with the original is impossible. The page markings simply provide the parameters within which a cited passage can be found. One passage—treating Rashbam—has been transposed; the original page numbers of that discussion therefore appear below out of sequence.)

The Eleventh Century

Eleventh-Century French Thought—Rashi

The |205| earliest discussion in France that we possess about these matters is from Rashi (d. 1105), that is to say, almost as far back as we possess written records of Jewish thought north of the Loire. The responsum is one written by Rashi fairly early in his career. Though sure enough of his own opinions when confiding them to his inner circle, he did not yet have the authority or inner confidence to bruit them about when they ran counter to prevailing opinion. The letter is somewhat brief, but with a little effort the line of reasoning may be reconstructed.

**וששאלתם: אם ישראל נותן משכונות לגוי ב[על] ח[ובו] למשכנן לישראל אחר תחת יד גוי, אם מותר לאותו ישראל אחר לגבות הרבית מן הגוי כיון שיוצא מכיסו של ישראל או לא. תשובה: זה ששאלת[ם] הוי יודע שמות[ר], והמונע הרי זה חסיד שוט[ה]. ובלבד שלא יתכוין מתחיל[ה] על כך, אבל הכיר במשכונו של ישראל בתחילה קנסינן ליה.
ומה ששאלת[ם]: אם ישראל נותן משכון שיש לו מגוי ואמר לישראל: 'הלוה לי מה שיש על המשכון ואקבל ממנו הרבית שעלה עליו עד אותו היום, ומכאן ואילך תעלה לך רבית', ששאלתם: אם מותר לישראל זה לקבל הרבית מיד הגוי ולתנו לחברו? הוי יודע שמות[ר], של[א] אסר[ה] תור[ה] אלא ריבית הבאה מלוה למלוה.
ושתי תשובות הללו אני יודע התירן, ומונע אני להורות מפני לעגי שפ[ה] עד שמצאתי סייג לדברי ממורי ר' דוד הלוי שהורה לי הלכה למעש[ה].**[42]

[42] *Sefer ha-Terumot* (Saloniki, 1596), 46, fo. 80b end; edn. *Giddulei Terumah* (Venice, 1643), 46: 4: 10; ed. A. Goldschmidt (Jerusalem 1988), p. 933, with three emendations from *Issur ve-Heter*, ed. Y. Freimann, 52–3; *Sefer ha-Oreh, Ḥelek Sheni*, ed. S. Buber (Lemberg, 1905), 217–18. Parallel passages are cited by I. S. Elfenbein in *Teshuvot Rashi* (New York, 1943), ##49, 229, to which should be added MSS Cambridge Add. 667, fo. 71b; Cambridge Add. 2580, fo. 108a (gloss); Oxford, Bodley 566 fos. 11b–12a.

Text: No version is free from errors. Corrections: (1) *taḥat yad* in the *Sefer ha-Terumot* makes no sense; (2) **שלא יתכוין מתחילה קנסינן ליה** (thus in the Saloniki edition) of the *Sefer ha-Terumot* is a *homoioteleuton* of the fuller passage in the *Sifrut de-Vei Rashi* as the poor syntax indicates. The printers of the 1605 Prague edition sensed the difficulty, as did a generation later R. Azaryah Figo. Lacking the *Issur ve-Heter* and *Sefer ha-Oreh*, the former could only emend the text to *de-'az kansinan leih*, the latter to *de-kansinan leih*. (3) *ve-akabbel* as found in the *Sifrut de-Vei Rashi*, rather than the meaningless *u-mekabbel*. (4) The *Sefer ha-Terumot* reads *she-moreh halakhah le-ma'aseh* while the *Sifrut de-Vei Rashi* has *she-horah lo halakhah le-ma'aseh*. The text of the *Sefer ha-Terumot* at any rate needs correction (*she-moreh ken halakhah le-ma'aseh*) and, since we know (see below) that Rashi did correspond with R. David on matters of usury, I saw no reason, while emending, not to accept the reading of the *Issur ve-Heter* and *Sefer ha-Oreh*. If one wishes to insist that Rashi at the time of this responsum knew of R. David and only later received an actual reply from him, I have no objection. (5) From the *Kitsur Sefer Mitsvot Gadol* of R. Avraham ben Efrayim (Jerusalem, 2005), 217–18, Injunction #99; *Mordekhai, Bava Metsi'a*, #338 (Vilna edn.), 156b, ll. 19–22, it would appear that R. Tuvyah ben Eliyahu of Vienne did not have the words *ba'al ḥovo* in the first line of our responsum. Rashi would then not be dealing with *Schadennehmen*, but with the Gentile straw man (see below, p. 103). It is difficult to accept this version contrary to the consensus of all other sources.

For bibliographical information, see the Appendix, note 42.

|206| *Query*: If a Jew gives pledges to his Gentile creditor to pawn them to another Jew as the Gentile's property [i.e. under the pretense of it being the property of the Gentile],[43] is it permissible for the other Jew [the creditor] to collect the interest from the Gentile inasmuch as it comes out of a Jew's pocket, or is it not permissible?

Reply: Be assured that the above case is permissible; and he who refrains practices a foolish piety; provided that he [the creditor] did not initially so intend [i.e. to take interest from the Jew]. If, however, he recognized at the outset that the pledge was a Jew's, we penalize him.

[*Reply to a*] *further query*: If a Jew gave a Gentile pawn in his possession and said to another Jew: 'Lend me what I have on this pledge [i.e. the sum of the debt], and I shall receive from him the interest that has accrued until today, but from now on the interest will accrue to you', and your question is: is it permissible for this Jew to receive the interest from the hands of the Gentile and to hand it over to the other Jew? Be assured that it is permissible for the Torah forbade only interest from debtor to creditor [*ribbit mi-loveh le-malveh*].

I know the permissibility of both these responses [i.e. cases] but have refrained from so ruling because of a strong negative reaction [*la'agei safah*] until I found support[44] for my opinion in my teacher, |207| R. David, who instructed me to decide thus in practice.[45]

The two questions posed to Rashi concern, not surprisingly, the permissibility of those two essential credit operations—*Schadennehmen* and the 'pawned pawn'. While Rashi firmly believed that both cases are permissible, he was far more emphatic about the first, *Schadennehmen*, than the second. Indeed, so self-evident did the matter of *Schadennehmen* appear to him that he

43 תחת יד גוי = *sub christiano*. For the use of *sub* in connection with fronting (*sub judaeis ponere*), albeit from a later period, see the documents published by P. Lefèvre in 'A propos du trafic de l'argent exercé par les juifs de Bruxelles au XIVe siècle', *Revue belge de philologie et d'histoire*, 9 (1930), 911.

44 For *seyag* as *ḥizzuk* ('support'), see *Teshuvot Rashi*, introduction, p. 40; *Ḥullin* 46b, s.v. *heinu* end. The use is predominantly pre-tosafist, though one occasionally finds it as late as the early 15th century (MS Montefiore 108, fo. 75b). Its origin apparently lies in equating the two talmudic expressions: חכמים עשו חזוק לדבריהם and חכמים עשו סייג לדבריהם. S. Lieberman drew my attention to Rashi, *Niddah* 3b, s.v. *seyag*. Similarly, see the so-called Rashi commentary to *Avot* 3: 13 and in *Ḥukkei Torah* in: S. Assaf, *Mekorot le-Toledot ha-Ḥinnukh be-Yisra'el*, revised edn., ed. S. Glick, i (Jerusalem, 2002), 205. As the use of *seyag* in the sense of support became more rare, copyists began to emend texts that had employed the term in this sense. For example in *Orḥot Ḥayyim*, *Ḥelek Sheni*, ed. M. Schlesinger (Berlin, 1902), 464, our *seyag* was changed to *siyyu'a*, as was *seyag* in a pre-Crusade responsum found in *Teshuvot R. Ḥayyim Or Zarua'* (Jerusalem, 2002), #176 (corroborated by *Sefer Asufot*, MS London, Montefiore 134, fo. 126d), emended in the *Pardes* (Constantinople, 1802, fo. 16a; Warsaw, 1870, #259) to *semekh*. (The above passage in the manuscript of *Sefer Asufot* is reproduced in my *Ha-Yayin bi-Yemei ha-Beinayim—Yein Nesekh: Perek be-Toledot ha-Halakhah be-Ashkenaz* [Jerusalem, 2008], plate 21.)

45 Possibly: 'who decided an actual case of mine thus'.

neglected to inform us of the rationale for his decision. Fortunately, Rashi felt the second case, the 'pawned pawn', to be somewhat less obvious, and he cited book and verse. The passage invoked by Rashi is Rava's ruling, cited above, that payment of interest to the creditor is not forbidden *per se* but only if performed by the debtor.[46] A bilateral relationship ('interest from debtor to creditor') is necessary for the injunction of *ribbit* to be breached, and the pawned pawn fails to meet this requirement.

It is clear, then, that in the pawned pawn, Rashi did not envisage the payor as being legally the debtor. The party paying the debt physically (on March 1 in our illustrated example) is clearly the Jew (Jew 1 of the illustration), and as the talmudic principle that a Jew cannot serve as the agent of a Gentile (*ein sheliḥut le-goy*) is, as I have stated, unquestioned in this period, this Jew remains, perforce, the legal payor, despite the fact that he may have been acting on Gentile instructions. If so, Rashi could not view the Jew (Jew 1) as the legal debtor, despite his having asked (on February 1) for money, given collateral, and received a sum of money in return. That left only one person in the arrangement who could be the debtor, namely, the Gentile (the debtor to Jew 1), who now found himself in terms of Jewish law (though he probably never knew it) in a direct debtor relationship to the current pledge-holder (Jew 2). In other words, Rashi assumes that Jew 1 (on February 1) did not take a loan on a |**208**| pawn, but rather sold the debt owed to him to Jew 2 for a sum of money. The money given to him by the second Jew was not a loan, as we might understandably have thought, but rather a payment for the debt that he had just acquired by the acquisition of the pawn. If this be so, the case conforms paradigmatically to the talmudic one that Rashi referred to: a debtor relationship exists between A (the Gentile debtor) and C (the second Jewish creditor), but payment of the interest takes place only between B (the first Jewish debtor) and C (the second Jewish creditor). In other words, B pays off A's debt to C, and thus no usury injunction has been transgressed (see illustration on p. 80).[47]

The leap from a loan with a second pledging to the sale of a debt is a large one, to put it mildly, yet Rashi has no doubts about its having transpired, and his certainty (*ani yodea' heteran*) finds its echo in a contemporary responsum. Rashi informs us that R. David ha-Levi of Mainz arrived at the same conclusion, and it would seem that we are fortunate enough to have a copy of his

46 Above, pp. 72–3.

47 Seeing that the Gentile is now viewed as the debtor, the question naturally arises why Rashi and, as we shall immediately see, R. David of Mainz both chose to invoke the triangular principle (*ribbit mi-loveh le-malveh*) rather than the equally applicable one that Jewish–Gentile usury was permissable. It seemed best, however, to address it at a somewhat further stage of the analysis: see the Appendix, note 66.

ruling. He had received a query about a pawned pawn identical with the one that Rashi had addressed and replied thus:

חזרתי על כל צידי ריבית ואין איסור כיון דמשך שמעון המשכון דלא אסרה תורה אלא ריבית הבאה מלוה למלוה

I have considered [the arrangement] from every [possible] angle of *ribbit* and [find that] it is perfectly permissible, seeing that Shim'on has dragged the pawn [*de-mashakh ha-mashkon*] [and acquired it], for the Torah only forbade usury from the lender to the borrower [*ribbit mi-loveh le-malveh*].[48]

[48] (A) Text and attribution: MS *Haggahot Mordekhai*, Jewish Theological Seminary, Rabbinica 673, fo. 280c (= MS Oxford, Bodley 678, fo. 281c), printed by I. A. Agus, *Teshuvot Ba'alei ha-Tosafot* (New York, 1954), 49. *U-de-lo asrah* in the printed text is an error; the editor inadvertently added a superfluous *vav*; the manuscript, however, reads simply and correctly *de-lo asrah*. The editor attributes all three pieces that appear in the manuscript under the rubric הגה to Rabbi Ya'akov

The writer is dealing with no fewer than six pentateuchal injunctions forbidding usury and permits them all by invoking the principle of *ribbit mi-loveh le-malveh*. How the case of a pawned pawn yields the triangular relationship described by Rava is explained by two words, *de-mashakh ha-mashkon*, which, strictly speaking, is meaningless. First, it is a halakhic commonplace that a Jew cannot acquire any property rights in a pawn belonging to a Gentile (see below). Second, even granting the acquisition of such property rights, how does this alter who the parties to the debt are? Yet not only does the respondent permit all these pentateuchal injunctions, but he also announces that by no stretch of the imagination could the pawned pawn be forbidden.[49] Charted on purely halakhic co-ordinates the responsum is incomprehensible. Clearly, the respondent has in mind some obvious facts of life to which reference is made by the phrase *meshikhat ha-mashkon* and from which the conclusion of *eino ribbit mi-loveh le-malveh* is self-understood.

Fortunately, two words provide us with an indication of how this transference of debt is effectuated, something noticeably missing from Rashi's responsum. R. David speaks of *meshikhat ha-mashkon*, pulling or dragging the pawn—*meshikhah* being one of the formal acts by means of which one acquires mobilia. The same doctrine of permissibility by means of the sale of the pawns appears explicitly in the responsum of R. Meshullam b. Kalonymus in the late tenth century, who speaks of the permissibility of the pawned pawn seeing

b. Yitsḥak ha-Levi on the basis of the signature at the end of the note. This manner of attribution is perhaps not without some danger in a work as eclectic as the *Haggahot Mordekhai*, though the middle piece is in fact attributed to R. Ya'akov in the *Teshuvot ha-Rashba*, vii (Warsaw, 1868; new edn. Jerusalem, 2001), #505; MS Cambridge, Add. 498, fo. 10b; MS Montefiore 131 of the *Orḥot Ḥayyim, Ḥelek Sheni*. See the addenda to this work, p. 632 (s.v. addendum to p. 469). It is perhaps safer to judge each piece on its own merits, and, since respondents, like other entities, should not be multiplied beyond necessity, I have attributed the missive to R. David, who we do know wrote on this topic and so ruled. If one insists on claiming R. Ya'akov as the author, I have no quarrel, for that would mean yet a fourth party to this doctrine. (MS Oxford, Bodley 678 and MS New York, Jewish Theological Seminary, Rabbinica 673 are identical, line for line, and were copied by the same scribe.) (**B**) On R. David of Mainz, see A. Grossman, *Ḥakhmei Ashkenaz ha-Rishonim* (above, n. 38(*b*), 258–64. (**C**) As to Rashi's remarks in *Kiddushin* 8b s.v. *be-mashkon*, see the Appendix, note 81, item 2. (**D**) On the composite nature of what is commonly called 'volume 7 of the *Teshuvot ha-Rashba*', see the editor's introduction to the Jerusalem edition, p. 9, and S. Z. Havlin's introduction to the reproduction of the *Teshuvot u-She'elot le-Rashba, Rome c.1490*, published by the National Library of Israel (then the Jewish National and University Library), (Jerusalem, 1977), p. 25.

49 For a similar 11th-century use of *ḥazarti 'al kol tsidei ribbit ve-ein issur* to express a halakhic truism, *sheluḥo shel adam ke-moto*, see *Teshuvot Ḥakhmei Tsarfat ve-Lotir*, ed. J. Müller (Vienna, 1881), #98. Its author is most probably R. Gershom Me'or ha-Golah. The phrase *ḥazarti 'al kol tsidei . . . ve-lo matsati* is taken from *Shabbat* 139a.

that the creditor sold the pawn to the other party.[50] With R. David proclaiming this as self-evident in the early days of the German Ashkenazic community, with Rashi assuming as much[51] at the dawn of the French one, and R. Meshullam speaking of it in the primeval tenth century, one may |209| say without exaggeration that the doctrine was co-extensive with Jewish legal thought in Europe. Clearly all three halakhists were referring to some self-understood reality which explains this 'obvious' allowance. What, however, was it?

Acquisition of Pawns

In a world governed by halakhah, the chances for the transformation of a transferred pawn into the sale of a debt were slight. First it should be noted that the pawn was taken from a Gentile. This, if anything, should have diminished the chances of sale, for sale presupposes ownership, and, while it is correct that Jewish law confers limited ownership to the pledge-holder, this is true only for pledges taken from Jews. Ownership of pawns taken from Gentiles is a subject of controversy in the Talmud. The majority opinion is that, while the creditor takes legitimate possession of such pawns, he acquires no rights of property in them.[52] This doctrine held undisputed sway in France and Germany from the earliest reports in the eleventh century till the close of

[50] (A) Text: *Teshuvot Ge'onim Kadmonim*, ed. D. Cassel (Berlin, 1848), #141, correct according to J. N. Epstein, 'Die Rechtsgutachten der Geonim, ed. Cassel nach Cod. Berlin und MS Michael', *Jahrbuch der Jüdisch-Literarischen Gesellschaft*, 9 (1911), 299 (translated into Hebrew and reprinted in id., *Meḥkarim be-Sifrut ha-Talmud u-vi-Leshonot Shemiyot*, i [Jerusalem, 1984], 215), and L. Ginzberg, ed., *Ginzei Schechter*, ii (New York, 1929), 209. The text reads *makhar lo shelish ha-mashkon*. It would be implausible to emend *makhar* to *masar* for reasons spelled out in the Appendix, note 80, item 4. (B) Context: The question is obscure because it seems to be a stenographic report of the words of the different parties and has the loose, ungrammatical pattern of oral speech. The parties, furthermore, spoke in the vernacular and the scribe translated their words into Hebrew as literally as he could. Legally, the question at bar was whether an intra-Jewish loan had taken place and interest was thus forbidden, or whether the original loan was between a Jew and a Gentile (and usury was permitted) and the second Jew had served simply as an intermediary. For a detailed reconstruction, see my *Shut ke-Makor Histori* (Jerusalem, 1990), 41–5. (C) On R. Meshullam, see Grossman, *Ḥakhmei Ashkenaz ha-Rishonim* (above, n. 38(*b*)), 48–78.

[51] We are analyzing here the common assumptions of the 11th century. For presentational purposes I have grouped Rashi with R. David and R. Meshullam and, possibly, R. Ya'akov b. Yitsḥak ha-Levi. Actually, Rashi based his rulings on the upshot of these common assumptions and thought them plausible enough. Ever the intellectual and terminological purist, Rashi took care not to articulate these assumptions and never spoke of *mekhirat ha-mashkon* as did R. Meshullam b. Kalonymus, or of *meshikhat ha-mashkon* as did R. David of Mainz. See below, n. 93. On the terminological purism of Rashi, see my *Yeinam* (above, n. 2), 61–2.

[52] *Pesaḥim* 31b, and parallel passages.

our period at the dawn of the fourteenth.[53] Even if we were to admit the existence of a subterranean school to which our respondents adhered that equated Gentile pledges with Jewish, all property rights in pledges existed only in pledges taken in distraint (*shelo bi-she'at halva'ah*), not those given as accessorial security at the time of the loan (*bi-she'at halva'ah*). On this point all agreed, and we possess a responsum of Rashi himself ruling out any ownership in the pledges taken at loan time.[54] |210|

As the debtor in this case was a Gentile, and the pledge his, any litigation

[53] R. Yehudah Ba'al Sefer ha-Dinim, in *Teshuvot R. Me'ir mi-Rotenburg* (Prague and Budapest), #875; for authorship, see above, n. 38(*b*); *Ravan*, i, ed. S. Albeck (Warsaw, 1905), #112 (= *Teshuvot R. Me'ir mi-Rotenburg* [Prague and Budapest], #409); *Ravan*, ii, ed. S. Z. Ehrenreich (Simleu Silvaniei, 1926), *Shevu'ot* 43a, fo. 234d; R. Yo'el ha-Levi, MS Paris, Bibliothèque Nationale 1408, fo. 154b; R. Eli'ezer b. Yo'el, ibid.; *Ravyah*, ii, ed. V. Aptowitzer (repr. New York, 1983), *Pesaḥim*, #465. (The decisions of R. Yo'el and Ravyah in the aforementioned manuscript are immediately followed by the ruling cited below, n. 214. It is not clear whether this holding was authored by either of these two scholars. If it is indeed anonymous, the ruling is evidence of yet another voice against property rights in Gentile pawns.) *Teshuvot R. Me'ir mi-Rotenburg*, ed. R. N. N. Rabbinowicz (Lemberg, 1860), #86 (= *Mordekhai, Bava Batra*, #611); *Mordekhai, Kiddushin*, #486; ed. Y. Roth (New York, 1990), 110–11; E. Kupfer, ed., *Teshuvot u-Fesakim me'et Ḥakhmei Tsarfat ve-Ashkenaz* (Jerusalem, 1973), #139 (authored possibly by R. Simḥah of Speyer); *Or Zarua'*, iii (Jerusalem, 1887), *Bava Metsi'a*, #215; *Teshuvot Maharaḥ Or Zarua'*, ed. M. Avitan (Jerusalem, 2002), #203; Rosh, *Pesaḥim*, 2: 10 (see also *Bet Shemu'el, Even ha-'Ezer*, #28: 33). The one exception is R. Shelomoh of Château-Landon, below, p. 148. (I was referred to the Bibliothèque Nationale manuscript by an article of C. Sirat, 'Le Manuscrit Hébreu 1408 de la B. N.', *Revue des études juives*, 123 (1964), 356. Binyamin Richler of the Manuscript Microfilm Division of the National Library of Israel was kind enough to transcribe for me immediately the relevant lines and subsequently sent me a photostat.) Bibliographical information: I have used the 1887 Jerusalem edition of the *Or Zarua'* on *Nezikin* throughout. The recent three-volume edition of Machon Yerushalayim (Jerusalem, 2009) claims to have based *Seder Nezikin* on (unspecified) manuscripts. However, it has used them negligibly, if at all, and has little scholarly merit.

[54] See previous note, to which add *Ravan*, i, #111 (see *Shakh*, 'Ḥoshen Mishpat' 72: 9). (**A**) The responsum of Rashi may be found with his full signature **ושלום שלמה בר' יצחק** (lest someone suspect a natural enough interchange of **'רש** and **רש"י**) in *Teshuvot Maimuniyot, Mishpatim*, #2; MS Oxford, Bodley 641 fo. 231a, #251; *Mordekhai, Shevu'ot*, #775 (the last has the acronym only). (This responsum was not reproduced by Elfenbein in his edition of *Teshuvot Rashi*.) *Teshuvot Rashi*, #240 proves nothing. At bar there is the non-acquisition of Jewish gages by Gentiles, a matter agreed upon by all—see *Pesaḥim* 31b. (**B**) Only in the third quarter of the 12th century, on the basis of multi-textual dialectics, did some faint property rights begin to be attributed to loan-pledges (*Tosfot Shants, Pesaḥim* [Jerusalem, 1956], 31b, s.v. *minayin*, see below, n. 208), and then only in France. See the remarks of the Ravan and Ravyah in the sources cited in the previous note. (**C**) The doctrine of the *Halakhot Gedolot* cited in *Or Zarua'*, #276 and *Teshuvot R. Me'ir mi-Rotenburg* (Prague and Budapest), #288 (taken from the little-known late 13th-century work, *Nimukei R. Kovil*; see S. Emanuel, 'Teshuvot Maharam mi-Rotenburg she-Einan shel ha-Maharam', *Shenaton ha-Mishpat ha-'Ivri*, 21 [1998–2000], 177–9), was academic and struck no roots. Be that as it may, there is no *shetar* in the cases under discussion, nor were *shetarot* issued when pawns were given; see de Roover, *Money, Banking and Credit* (above, n. 15), 143 ff.

would be decided by Gentile courts and according to Gentile law, unless the Jewish community had obtained a *privilegia* which stated otherwise.[55] If recourse to courts was rare in this period, we may say, at the least, that unless the debtor otherwise stipulated, he would act according to his Gentile conceptions, and that the forms of coercion which could be brought to bear upon him, being predominantly Gentile, would be in accordance with Gentile usage.

Until well into the thirteenth century, Germanic law (that is to say, the law of the Germanic tribes that conquered the Roman Empire and which obtained throughout north-west Europe in the Middle Ages) in the matter of pledges differed radically from its Jewish counterpart. To the halakhah, pawns are accessorial; that is to say, a personal obligation exists upon the debtor to pay, in default of which the creditor acts upon and acquires the pledge. In Germanic law, a pledge is pure *Sachhaftung* without any personal liability. The debtor is under no obligation whatsoever to make any payment.[56] 'By being

[55] Kisch, *Jews in Medieval Germany* (above, n. 12), 87 ff., 209, 217–23; A. Hilgard, ed., *Urkunden zur Geschichte der Stadt Speyer* (Strasbourg, 1885), 11–12, #11.

[56] (A) Since the publication of K. von Amira, *Nordgermanisches Obligationenrecht* (Leipzig, 1882–5), and A. Heusler, *Institutionen des deutschen Privatrechts* (Leipzig, 1885–6), this point has won universal assent. A vigorous statement of the matter is to be found in J. H. Wigmore's article 'The Pledge-Idea: A Study in Comparative Legal Ideas', *Harvard Law Review*, 10 (1897), 321 (esp. pp. 326–33). For later discussion and bibliography, see O. von Gierke, *Deutsches Privatrecht*, ii (Leipzig, 1895–1917), 809 ff., 955 ff.; R. Huebner, *A History of Germanic Private Law* (above, n. 12), 374–7, 440–5, 463–76; R. Schröder and E. Frhr. von Künßberg, *Lehrbuch der deutschen Rechtsgeschichte*, 7th edn. (Berlin and Leipzig, 1932), 300 ff., 780 ff., 1038, 1068. The subtleties of conditional forfeit or provisional payment which gave rise to disputes amongst German historians need not concern us here. The medieval Jew made no systematic survey of Germanic law, not to speak of the Scandinavian (north German) one, which has yielded up to modern scholars so many secrets of the past. He knew the law from everyday encounter. It is the salient features of this law and its simplest translation into halakhic terms that I am concerned with. And these facts (if not their exact significance) are agreed upon by all hands. For recent developments in the field of Germanic law, see the Appendix, note 56. (B) The absence of any outstanding debt in the instance of a pledge is wholly independent of the issue of one's general acceptance of *Schuld* and *Haftung* as the basis of the Germanic law of obligations. Even those who deny its centrality admit that a loan on collateral was a *transaction au comptant* (e.g. J. Yver, *Les Contrats dans le très ancien droit normand* [Caen, 1926], 4–9, 145 nn. 7, 25–6). (C) The claim of Re'uven in *Teshuvot Ge'onei Mizraḥ u-Ma'arav*, ed. J. Müller (Berlin, 1888), #152 *may* equally reflect *Sachhaftung*. The query is clearly from 11th-century France. It is drawn from MS Montefiore 98, from which *Teshuvot Ḥakhmei Tsarfat ve-Lotir* was printed. Indeed, it is found in that manuscript at fo. 95a, immediately following the cluster of responsa (##47–56) that appears in the latter collection. Why the editor excluded it from that collection, I don't know. See below, n. 120(*a*). (D) *Sefer ha-Yashar, Ḥelek ha-Ḥiddushim* (ed. K. Schlesinger [Jerusalem, 1959], #603) אע"ג דבדיניהן אין בעל חוב קונה משכון means, as in *Bekhorot* 13a: מאי 'בדיניהן'? שפסקה להם תורה, i.e. according to the rules that bind them in Jewish law, in the case at hand, the ruling is that Gentiles do not acquire Jewish pawns. See above, n. 53. If he refers to the law of the Gentiles of his time, his words go against everything that we know about the Germanic law of gages in the Middle Ages, both from Gentile and Jewish sources.

given |211| the pledge the creditor received absolute satisfaction; thenceforth there was nothing more for him to claim from the debtor.'[57]

For the Jews this was not theory but cold fact of everyday business. If they were to rule in their civil courts on cases involving Christian–Jewish loans, as rule they must, they would have to translate, if only rudimentarily, the contemporary pledge into halakhic terms. The conclusions were ineluctable. For Jewish law, at least in its final unfolding, is incurably obligational. That money should be transferred from one hand to another with no obligation of repayment imposed was inconceivable, unless, of course, something had been acquired, and that something could only be the pledge.

If some thinking scholar had demurred that the reason the creditor cannot bring an action for payment is not because there is no debt outstanding, but simply because he has in his hand the means of satisfaction and should look to that for payment, two other salient features, perhaps the most significant ones in the pawn business, would allay any of his doubts as to the nature of the pledge. If the pledge is less, or has become less in value at the time of the maturity, than the original claim, the creditor has no way of recovering the deficit.[58] Conversely, if the pledge be worth more than the debt, |212| the

[57] J. Brissaud, *A History of French Private Law* (Boston, 1912), 584.

[58] Sources cited in Wigmore, 'The Pledge-Idea' (above, n. 56), 330; see subsequent literature in the sources, cited ibid. As to *Lex Visigothorum* 5: 6: 3, see V. von Meibom, *Das deutsche Pfandrecht* (Marburg, 1867), 257 ff. The Hebrew sources, too, speak of the inability to recover the difference should the pawn of the Gentile have been worth less than the debt. See the famous proclamation of Rabbenu Tam (below, pp. 133–6) cited in the *Or Zarua'*, *Bava Metsi'a*, #202, *Teshuvot R. Me'ir mi-Rotenburg* (Prague and Budapest), #796, where he speaks of a creditor who took a pawn worth only half the debt. The correct text reads thus:

שהלוה על משכונות שוים י' ליטרא (ק) [ת] דינרים [= כ' ליטרא] ואבד המשכונות וצעק [המלוה] ע"י גוי ולא נענה, כי (י)אמר [הלוה] מן הגוים לקחתם.

He lent 400 *dinarim* [= 20 *litra*] [to another Jew via a Gentile intermediary] on pawns worth [only] 10 *litra* [= 200 *dinarim*]. The pawns were lost and the creditor—via the Gentile [intermediary]—insisted vociferously [on repayment of the balance of the debt] and received no satisfaction, for the [debtor] said, 'you took them [the pawns] from Gentiles' [so there is no balance owed, for the pawns are quit-payment].

As already noted (above, p. 64), the monetary system that obtained in England until the end of the 1960s was that instituted by Charlemagne at the close of the eighth century. 1 *libra* (*litra* in medieval Hebrew or pound (£) in modern English) equaled 20 *solidi* (*dinarim* in medieval Hebrew or shillings in modern English). 1 *solidus* equaled 12 *denarii* (*perutot* in medieval Hebrew or pence in modern English). 1 *libra* equaled 240 *denarii*. (One has to remember at all times that *denarius* in Latin was the term for penny—whence the '1*d*.' to signify one penny in the old English currency—and *dinar* in Hebrew was the term for *solidus*/shilling. Jews used *dinar* thus because in the monetary system employed by the Mishnah the *dinar* was worth more than the *perutah*.) (A) The natural confusion between **ת** and **ק** in the printed text was further facilitated by common practice. A pledge as a rule

surplus value is his.[59] If this does not imply ownership, then nothing else can.[60] True, the debtor has the right of repurchase, |213| but the arrangement of acquisition with the residual right of seller repurchase is a known halakhic

was worth twice the debt, and a pawn valued at 10 *libra*/*litra* (= 200 *solidi*/*dinarim*) would ordinarily fetch a loan of 100 *solidi*/*dinarim* (see Hermannus Quondam Judaeus, *Opusculum de Conversione Sua*, ed. G. Niemeyer [Weimar, 1963], 73). And so ק (= 100) seemed to the scribe the natural reading of the ambiguous letter. (B) Despite the fact that *ve-tsa'ak ha-loveh* is found in the fine text of the *Or Zarua'*, the *malveh* is clearly intended, and so reads the text in *Teshuvot R. Me'ir mi-Rotenburg* (Prague and Budapest), #796. A similar slip occurs in the same section of the *Or Zarua'* some thirteen lines prior, as the editor has already noted. (C) On the general confusion of *loveh* and *malveh* in Ashkenazic texts, see the Appendix, note 58.

59 Sources are found in Wigmore, 'The Pledge-Idea' (above, n. 56), 331, and in the subsequent literature cited in that note.

60 (A) The fact that the creditor was held responsible in Germanic law for the pledge (in the event that the debtor sought to redeem it), even for loss resulting from *force majeure* (sources in Wigmore, 'The Pledge-Idea' [above, n. 56], 329, and in F. Pollock and F. W. Maitland, *History of English Law*, ii [Cambridge, 1898], 170–5), again indicates ownership; see Rashi, *Bava Metsi'a* 82a, *Pesaḥim* 31b, s.v. *koneh* and *Shakh*, 'Ḥoshen Mishpat' 72: 9, and below, n. 207. See, though, R. Avigdor's remarks cited in *Teshuvot ha-Rosh* (Jerusalem, 1994), #35: 1, p. 154b, s.v. *ve-im*. (B) Whether the doctrine of *force majeure* in and of itself indicates on Rashi's part a pawn theory similar to the Germanic one of the time seems to me rather dubious. One might note, if only to illustrate the recurrent patterns of legal thought, that it has been so construed by a 20th-century *rosh yeshivah*, who was above any suspicion, God forbid, of historical leanings. See Y. M. Shurkin, *Shi'urei Rabbi Ya'akov Mosheh Shurkin*, i (Lakewood, 2002), *Kiddushin* 8b, s.v. *ve'al pi*:

> [והנה] דתוס' ס"ל דהמלוה חייב בגניבה ואבידה של המשכון ורש"י ס"ל דחייב אפילו באונסין, ובמה פליגי? . . . וי"ל דרש"י ס"ל דמשכון שלא בשעת הלואה הוי פרעון על החוב אלא יש זכות ללוה דיכול לפדות המשכון עם המעות. וכיון דהוי פרעון על החוב הוי המשכון ממון המלוה ואם היה אונס על המשכון הוי אונס על ממון המלוה. אבל מתוס' משמע . . . דאינו פרעון אלא שיש למלוה שעבוד בהמשכון אבל בעצם הוא ממון הלוה, ולפיכך פטור מאונסין.

(C) Again (see above, n. 58), the Hebrew sources reflect the nigh-total ownership of Gentile pawns. It comes to the fore unintentionally in a remark of R. Yitsḥak of Dampierre, the great Ri, about the firstborn's double portion of inheritance (MSS Oxford, Bodley 683, fo. 62b; Cambridge, Oo 6.70.1, fo. 104c). The double portion applies only to *muḥzak* of the deceased, not to *ra'uy*. (The two terms can be roughly translated as 'chose in possession' and 'chose in action', see below, n. 79.) Rashbam (*Bava Batra* 125b, s.v. *ve-ein*) was of the opinion that a pawn is a 'chose in possession' and thus subject to double inheritance; Ri believed it to be a 'chose in action', and his position is reported in these words (the reporter may be R. Ḥezkiyah of Magdeburg): אין בכור נוטל פי שנים במשכון ואפי' דגוי ואפילו משכנו שלא בשעת הלואתו, כן פי' ר"י. ('The firstborn does not take a double portion of a pawn, even one of a Gentile or even a distraint pawn.') Why Ri said 'even a distraint pawn' is understandable, for halakhah vests the creditor with certain property rights in the distraint pledge (above, n. 54). Why, however, 'even one of a Gentile'? Quite the contrary; halakhically there is not a scintilla of ownership in a Gentile pawn (above, n. 53). Ri is here thinking in contemporary terms, and there were far greater rights of ownership in the pawn of a contemporary Gentile than there ever were in the distraint pawn of a Jew, contemporary or otherwise. (As to the question in and of itself of a firstborn's rights to double portion in a Gentile pawn, see the literature cited in *She'elot u-Teshuvot Maharam Mints*, ed. Y. S. Domb [Jerusalem, 1991], #66: 4, p. 278, n. 87 and in S. Emanuel, *Teshuvot Maharam u-Venei Doro* [Jerusalem, 2012], ii, #382, pp. 749, 751–2.)

phenomenon (certain forms of *hekdesh* or *battei 'arei ḥomah*, for example), and does not necessarily impugn the fullness of ownership.[61] Defects to title in the contemporary pawn there were,[62] but far less than in the Jewish counterpart. The Germanic |214| contract pledge, which theoretically should have been doubly disqualified from ownership, both because it came from a Gentile and by virtue of the time of its deposit, and hence should have been beyond the power of the creditor to transfer, was, in fact, more fully the lender's property than the Jewish distraint pledge, to which adhered unquestioned property rights with the concomitant susceptibility to sale.

This is the first fact of life being referred to by R. David of Mainz and Rabbenu Meshullam b. Kalonymus when they wrote of acquisition of the Gentile pawn (*meshikhat ha-mashkon*) and sale of the Gentile pawn (*mekhirat ha-mashkon*).[63] Pledges were re-pledged, given as gifts, and provisionally sold in the normal course of business,[64] and the rabbis of the tenth |215| and eleventh centuries could not restructure European business practices to align them with the halakhah. If they were to rule that the transference of pledges was not valid, then Jews would simply cease to have their cases adjudged by Jewish law, and the end of Jewish autonomy in the Middle Ages would soon be in sight. The ubiquitous pledge had to be given recognition. As its actual contours more than corresponded halakhically to the effectively acquired Jewish distraint pledge, this structural similarity, hand in hand with habit, assured it a smooth assimilation.

Incorporating this double transformation into halakhic decision-making contained a dual admission. The breakdown of the distinction between Jewish and Gentile pledges was simply recognition of the fact that Jewish commerce was no longer endogamous as it had been in talmudic times, and that

61 See also *'Arakhin* 31a, *Megillah* 27b. One should not be misled by the injunction of *ribbit*. The point is that *ribbit* defines its own categories of loan and sale, but what may be regarded as loan *sub specie usurae* may often be a full-fledged sale in terms of civil law. See *Milḥamot*, *Bava Metsi'a* 67a; *Tosafot*, *Megillah* 26b, s.v. *ogorah*. One should not go so far as to view the terminology that evolved with regard to pawns, though similar to *hekdesh* and *battei 'arei ḥomah*, as having been consciously patterned upon them. The term *pidyon* comes most probably from the Latin *redemptio* and its reverse *ḥalut* (e.g. *Teshuvot Ḥakhmei Tsarfat ve-Lotir*, #98, *Teshuvot Rashi*, ##178, 240), as S. Lieberman pointed out to me, from *shetarei ḥiltata* (*Bava Metsi'a* 16b). Whatever the origins be, the constant use of such terms would only reinforce the analogy to *hekdesh*.

62 Strictly speaking, full title was acquired only after the formal ceremony of *Auflassung*. This requirement, however, seems to have been more honored in the breach than the observance, and often the borrower waived the requirement of *Auflassung*. For details, see the Appendix, note 62.

63 Above, pp. 81–2.

64 Responsum of Rashi in *Teshuvot Maimuniyot*, *Mishpatim*, #2; MS Oxford, Bodley 641 fo. 231a, *#251*; *Mordekhai*, *Shevu'ot*, #775; responsum of R. Yehudah, Ba'al Sefer ha-Dinim, in *Teshuvot R. Me'ir mi-Rotenburg* (Prague and Budapest), #880; for authorship, see above n. 38(*b*).

commercial relationships between Jew and Gentile would have to be pragmatically treated by rabbinical authorities in ways that differed little from those between Jew and Jew. The equation of deposit pledges with those of distraint—as in Germanic law—was but the admission that Jews were no longer a host nation whose law bound strangers who wandered into its midst. It was the Jews who now lived on sufferance, and it was they who would have to adapt their categories to the prevailing ones. But if the rabbis could not alter reality, neither would they yield to it in principle. The recognition they extended to Exile was *de facto*, not *de jure*. Sale of pledges was admitted as a fact, but its premise, ownership—so contrary to talmudic dictum—was never enunciated as a doctrine, nor was it extended beyond necessity. The very same men who spoke in money matters about pledge-sales, when asked to rule on affairs removed only slightly from commerce, as for example inheritance of Christian pledges, would speak of the complete absence of any property rights in such pawns and the consequent illegality of their transfer as self-evident principles of halakhah.[65] On this I shall have more to say later.

Assignment of Debt |216|

The sale of the pledge in the case under discussion was, it will be remembered, but a means to an end, and that end was the assignment of the debt. The second Jew acquired the debt from the first one and thus became the direct creditor of the Gentile, and the Jew destined to pay off the debt (the original creditor) now became a third party. Debtor and payor of the interest were thus separate and distinct parties, and the interest given could not be considered as a payment of *ribbit* by debtor to creditor (*ribbit mi-loveh le-malveh*).[66]

Talmudic law recognizes only two forms of assignment of debt: either a formal assertion of assignment in the joint presence of all three parties, i.e. debtor, creditor, and creditor-to-be (*ma'amad sheloshtan*, 'triple presence'),[67] or transfer of the note of indebtedness by the creditor (*mesirah*) with or without an accompanying note affirming the assignment of the debt (*ketivah*).[68]

[65] Rabbi Yehudah, Ba'al Sefer ha-Dinim in *Teshuvot R. Me'ir mi-Rotenburg* (Prague and Budapest), #875; for authorship, see above, n. 38(*b*). See also item 3 in the Afterword to 'Halakhah, Taboo, and the Origin of Jewish Moneylending' (below, p. 235).

[66] Above, p. 79. My remarks henceforth refer to R. David and Rashi. One cannot reconstruct R. Meshullam's argument as a line is missing in our text as a result of a *homoioteleuton*. Compare *Teshuvot Ge'onim Kadmonim*, #141 with the genizah fragment published by Ginzburg in *Ginzei Schechter* (above, n. 50), ii. 209, ll. 32–3. See the Appendix, note 66 for why Rashi and R. David of Mainz invoked the principle of *ribbit mi-loveh le-malveh* rather than the allowance of Gentile usury.

[67] *Gittin* 13b–14a.

[68] *Bava Batra* 76a–77a and commentaries ad loc. *Agav* is of course more than questionable; see also below, n. 73(*b*).

That assignment of debt could be effected equally by sale of the pledge is nowhere to be found in the Talmud.

This new form of debt sale appears in the eleventh century, not only with respect to Gentile pledges, but also with respect to Jewish ones, in wholly intra-Jewish transactions. Thus little can be attributed to Germanic pledge-law. Indeed, the latter's famous |217| ruling, *Hand muß Hand wahren*, namely, that the original owner of the pawn has no means of recovery from a third party,[69] the very person whom we wish to place in a direct creditor relationship to him, would have militated strongly against the emergence of any such doctrine. Its origins lie elsewhere.

The traditional forms of debt assignment were ill suited to the needs of pre-Crusade Jewry. Trade and loan were conducted primarily by word of mouth, and the absence of written instruments is one of the most striking features of the period.[70] Transfer via the note of indebtedness was, accordingly, of limited application. 'Triple presence' worked well enough in a sedentary society where all the parties were at the call of one another, and where a fairly infrequent sale of debts was presupposed.[71] But eleventh-century Jewry was commercial and constantly on the move.[72] |218| Even if loans were made to borrowers residing in one place, in an economy of rapid credit turnover, a debtor could hardly be expected to run around to sessions of 'triple presence' every time his debt changed hands. Credit had to be made more mobile.

[69] See below, n. 206, and the literature cited there.

[70] This has already been noted by R. S. Lopez in his review of Agus's book *Urban Civilization* (above, n. 37) in *Speculum*, 42 (1967), 342.

[71] Significantly, when Shemu'el ruled (*Bava Metsi'a* 20a) **המוכר שטר חוב לחבירו וחזר ומחלו מחול**, he did not append to it any suggested remedies as, for example, clauses to order or to bearer, as did Rabad in his gloss to Maimonides' Code ('Hilkhot Mekhirah', 6: 12): **לפיכך אם כתב לו בשטר חובו הריני משועבד לך ולכל הבאים מכחך אינו יכול למחול כשמכר שטר חובו**, and as is found in both Jewish and Christian European formularies (Gulak, *Otsar ha-Shetarot* [above, n. 14], 206–7; Brissaud, *French Private Law* [above, n. 57], 536–7). Apparently the ruling did not appear to him to be particularly disruptive. Three generations later, Rabbah b. Rav Huna advised (*Ketubbot* 86a) **אי פקח הוא מקרקש ליה בזוזי**, but this is a suggestion for novation (to another specific party naturally) and not for the creation of a negotiable instrument.

[72] **כשרציתי להחזיק בדרך כשאר בני אדם**, as a plaintiff put it in a responsum of R. Yehudah, Ba'al Sefer ha-Dinim, in *Teshuvot R. Me'ir mi-Rotenburg* (Prague and Budapest), #880; for authorship see above, n. 38(*b*). See Caro, *Sozial- und Wirtschaftgeschichte der Juden* (above, n. 13), i. 191–7; Hoffmann, *Der Geldhandel* (above, n. 15), 7–15; Blumenkranz, *Juifs et chrétiens* (above, n. 37), 13–21; Agus, *Urban Civilization* (above, n. 37), i. 53–309; M. Toch, 'Pe'ilutam ha-Kalkalit shel Yehudei Germanyah', in Y. T. Assis et al., eds., *Yehudim mul ha-Tselav: Gezerot Tatnu ba-Historiyah u-va-Historiografyah* (Jerusalem, 2000), 32–54; id., 'The Jews in Europe 500–1050' (above, n. 32), 557–62. I am not concerned here with the significance of Jewish trade in general economic life—on this opinions differ widely—but rather with the significance of trade in Jewish economic life, which by all accounts was sizable.

People had begun on their own to assign debts by cash sale[73] and equally by pawn transfer.[74] Credit was regularly replenished by transfer of the pawn which accompanied every debt at the time, and with the transferred pawn went the debt. This was the second fact of life taken for granted in the responsa of Rashi and R. David, and it alone makes sense of both the brevity of their response and their confidence in its self-evidence. To give a modern analogy: it may well be that the *ketivah u-mesirah* demanded for the transfer of notes of indebtedness (*otiyot*)[75] does not require a separate bill of transfer, and endorsing the original note (as we do today) suffices halakhically. Suppose a leading talmudic authority of our day received an inquiry about payment of *ribbit* involving a Gentile check which had been endorsed by the Jewish debtor, Shim'on, to the Jewish lender, and that scholar replied, much as R. David of Mainz did:[76] 'I have considered [the arrangement] from every [possible] angle of *ribbit* and [find that] it is perfectly permissible seeing that Shim'on endorsed it [*ḥatam me-aḥorav*], for the Torah only forbade usury from the lender to the borrower [*ribbit mi-loveh le-malveh*].' Nine hundred years from now, when personal checks have ceased even to be a memory and are known only as a legal concept of *ḥayyav ani lekha maneh bi-shetar*, this responsum is discovered and read. It would equally seem nonsense. (If one attempted to analyze the response in classical halakhic terms, one would do so in terms of the talmudic categories of *katav bi-khetav yado*, *get pashut*, and *ḥayyav ani lekha maneh bi-shetar*, and the more comprehensive the analysis, the less comprehensible the ruling would be.) The decision is self-evident, however, in a world where endorsed checks are the standard form of credit transfer.

73 (A) R. Yehudah, Ba'al Sefer ha-Dinim, in *Teshuvot R. Me'ir mi-Rotenburg* (Prague and Budapest), #880; for authorship, see above, n. 38(*b*). Note R. Yehudah's silence on the non-halakhic mode of debt transfer. He adjudicates the issue at bar but says not a word about the non-halakhic manner of the debt transfer. This phenomenon repeats itself in the responsa literature. I will discuss it below, pp. 146–9. (B) One may feel confident that *agav* was equally employed, though I have not as yet discovered any overt reference to it in 11th-century sources (see *Ravan*, i, #48). (*Teshuvot Rashi*, #255 should be used very carefully for practical inference, and if there be any inference, it may very well refer exclusively to *harsha'ah*.)

74 See Rashi's responsum cited above, n. 64. To my mind, the responsum of R. Yehudah Ba'al Sefer ha-Dinim in *Teshuvot R. Me'ir mi-Rotenburg* (Prague and Budapest), #893—for authorship, see n. 38(*b*)—is also an instance of sale of debt via transfer of pawn. Note Levi's language: *be-ḥovi she-hayita ḥayyav li mi-kodem*. The phrase in Levi's initial conversation with Re'uven, *she-atah ḥayyav le-Shim'on*, simply identifies the pawn and the debt; it does not connote that at this stage, the debt is still owed to Shim'on. However, opinions could differ on the matter.

75 *Bava Batra* 76b–77a.

76 Above, p. 80. Strictly speaking, a check is, as Izhak Englard pointed out to me, not a note of indebtedness, but a written order drawn on banks. Though not exact, the example is, I believe, still apropos.

To return to the eleventh century. Transfer of debts by transfer of pawn was not only an unalterable fact of medieval life, it also had an inner suasion to it; indeed, it lent itself, after a fashion, to halakhic validation. |219|

Two things had contributed above all to the profound reluctance on the part of talmudic law to allow debt transfer. First, a debt was conceived as some personal obligation between creditor and debtor. The debtor had yielded a personal lien to a particular creditor alone, and it was felt that it should not and could not be transferred to another. Second, a debt is a lien, an obligation, something incorporeal, and talmudic law is extremely severe on transactions involving 'thingless' things.[77] |220|

[77] (A) Rashi, *Ketubbot* 85b, s.v. *maḥul*; *Mahadurah Kamma shel Rashi*, *Shitah Mekubbetset*, *Ketubbot* (Amsterdam, 1721), ad loc. (= *Perush Rivan* in J. N. Epstein, *Meḥkarim be-Sifrut ha-Talmud u-vi-Leshonot Shemiyot*, iii [Jerusalem, 1991], 170). See Rabbenu Gershom, *Bava Batra* (Romm), 175b top, s.v. *shi'abuda*; ed. T. Y. Leitner, 2 vols. in 1 (Jerusalem, 1999), ii. 217 (reference to *Sanhedrin* 31b), phrased more pungently by Rabbenu Tam (*Tosfot ha-Rosh*, *Ketubbot* [Jerusalem, 1999], 85b, s.v. *ha-mokher*; *Piskei ha-Rosh*, *Ketubbot*, 9: 10) and by Rabad ('Hilkhot Mekhirah', 6: 12). This is not to say that Rashi's doctrine is identical with those of Rabad and Rabbenu Tam—perish the thought—or even that the last two are, necessarily, identical with one another, but they share the same basic aperçu of the private nature of the obligation, be it contract or lien. Admittedly, *lav ba'al devarim didi at* may be invoked in matters of sale, where no obligation whatsoever exists (e.g. *Bava Metsi'a* 14a), which proves that it is a wider principle of 'lack of standing'. The issue here is not whether Rashi has adequately explained Shemu'el's strange ruling, but whether he is attempting to do so by introducing this principle. *Lav ba'al devarim didi at* is clearly not the claim of the former debtor after the waiver; his claim is simply 'I owe you nothing'. It is introduced by Rashi to express the personal element of debt that underlies Shemu'el's dictum. That *lav ba'al devarim didi at* may also be invoked in matters of land sales demonstrates that it is too broad a principle to fully explain Shemu'el's enigmatic ruling. This led Rabbenu Tam to create the terminology of *shi'abud ha-guf* and *shi'abud nekhasim*. However, unless one creates a new set of categories, as did Rabbenu Tam, the principle of *lav ba'al devarim didi at* is the principle that comes closest to expressing the ineradicable personal element that exists in indebtedness. (B) Rashbam on *Bava Batra* 148a, s.v. *be-ma'amad*, s.v. *halva'ati*; Rabbenu Gershom, *Bava Batra* (Romm), 147b, s.v. *ve-ha-amar*; ed. Leitner, vol. ii. 145 ad loc. Other theories have been advanced, but we are here concerned with the reasons why Ashkenaz viewed assignment as impossible, and the above sources are the earliest we possess in France and in Germany. (*Ravan*, i, ##47–8, is his own rationale, and not a tradition.) Interestingly their reasoning coincides with that of several historians of law as to the origin of similar rulings in other systems. See W. W. Buckland, *Main Institutes of Roman Private Law* (Cambridge, 1931), 238, 298–9; Pollock and Maitland, *History of English Law* (above, n. 60(*a*)), ii. 226, and references there cited. (For the restrictions on and ineffectiveness of debt transfer in Germanic law see Huebner, *History of Germanic Private Law* [above, n. 12], 553 ff.; Kisch, *Jews in Medieval Germany* [above, n. 12], 228.) (C) Menahem Elon pointed out to me that the term *shi'abud ha-guf* is not wholly an invention of Rabbenu Tam. It appears in approximately this form in a responsum by Alfasi in *Teshuvot R. Me'ir mi-Rotenburg* (Cremona, 1557), #146: *ha-loveh meshu'abad la-malveh, mamono ve-gufo*. To my thinking, viewing these two concepts as Rabbenu Tam's creation is still justified. Two different terms may or may not mean two different legal categories; the test of the matter is divisibility. When one says that the debtor is obliged *mamono ve-gufo* to pay his creditor, this may simply be an emphatic way of stating the weighty obligation of payment on the part of the

Both these problems were sharply diminished, if not eliminated, by the pledge. First, with the pledge the sense of personal indebtedness was absent. The creditor might never see the debtor again and couldn't care less whether he did. He held in his hands the wherewithal of collection and it was to this that he looked for satisfaction.[78] Second, with the lien focused in the pledge, the sense of intangibility was dulled, for only a thin line divides inherence from incorporation. A lien concentrated can only too easily become a lien concretized. How long, to invoke the language of common law, can one hold a 'chose in action' in one's possession and not think of it as a 'chose in possession'?[79] There may be little legal difference between the lien created |221| by a banker's loan and that of a pawnbroker, but it is a fact that a banker thinks in terms of debts, and a pawnbroker in terms of objects.

The sensed corporeality of the lien and the absence of the personal nature of indebtedness, coupled with the need for more mobile credit, yielded the doctrine of assignment via pledge.[80] Nor was their legal vision false. Some century and a half later in Spain this form of credit sale was detected as having actually been presumed in a talmudic discussion,[81] an insight given to the

debtor. If, however, one maintains that A retains the *shi'abud ha-guf* (and therefore may waive the debt) while B has acquired the *shi'abud nekhasim* (and therefore may collect the debt if no waiver takes place), we are then dealing with separate and distinct categories. To the best of my knowledge, Rabbenu Tam is the first to invest each of these two terms with differing legal quiddity.

[78] I assume that Rabbenu Kalonymus's remarks—preserved in *Or Zarua', Bava Metsi'a*, #89; *Mordekhai, Bava Metsi'a*, #401; *Teshuvot R. Me'ir mi-Rotenburg* (Prague and Budapest), #700; MS Oxford, Bodley 678, fo. 370c–d—refer, despite his phrasing, to a distraint pledge. If it does refer to a contract pledge then a severe restriction, in practice, though not in theory, has been introduced in personal obligation. See *Ravan*, i, #111; *Temim De'im* (in *Tummat Yesharim* [Venice, 1622]; as a separate work, Warsaw, 1897), #50. For a similar perception in a different context, see *Teshuvot, Pesakim u-Minhagim shel R. Me'ir mi-Rotenburg*, ed. Y. Z. Cahana, ii (Jerusalem, 1960), *Teshuvot*, #75.

[79] (A) Chose in action (a thing in action): a personal right not reduced into possession, but recoverable by a suit at law; a right of proceeding in a court of law to procure payment of a sum of money. Opposite—chose in possession: a personal thing of which one has possession (excerpted from *Black's Law Dictionary*, abridged 5th edn. [St Paul, 1983], 124). (B) The doctrine of concretized lien also explains why no objection was raised in the post-Rabbenu Tam period as to the non-transferability of intangible Gentile debts, analogous to 'triple presence' (*ma'amad sheloshtan*). (C) As to the apparent dissent registered in *Mordekhai, Bava Batra*, #614, see the Appendix, note 79.

[80] Before commiting ourselves to this interpretation, it is essential, if our argument is to have methodological rigor, to consider other possibilities of validating the transfer of debt and see whether any of them offers a more plausible alternative to my proffered reconstruction of the path taken by 11th-century Ashkenazic Talmudists. See the Appendix, note 80 for alternative explanations such as *dina de-malkhuta dina*, *situmta*, and *otiyot niknot bi-mesirah*.

[81] *Kiddushin* 8a–b. **איתביה רבא לרב נחמן: 'קדשה במשכון מקודשת', התם במשכון דאחרים וכדרב יצחק, דאמר רבי יצחק מנין לבעל חוב שקונה משכון וכו'**. For a discussion of the significance of these two lines for the business of pawnbroking and, far more significantly, from the perspective of analyti-

halakhists only because of centuries of common practice, but a perfectly valid one nevertheless.[82] It passed all halakhic muster and went on into |222| the code of Jewish civil and criminal law, the 'Ḥoshen Mishpat', where it remains unchallenged to this day.[83]

cal rigor, my reasons for believing that one of these inferences—though intuited—was not drawn by the scholars of Early Ashkenaz, see the Appendix, note 81, items 1 and 2.

[82] The mode of inference from *Kiddushin* by R. Shemu'el ha-Sardi, author of the *Sefer ha-Terumot*, 51: 4: 7 (ed. Goldschmidt, p. 1199), is a consequence of his intuitive agreement with the universal practice of his time of transfering debts by transfer of the pawn. This can be seen by analyzing its unarticulated premises. Underlying the conclusion drawn by the author of *Sefer ha-Terumot* from the passage in *Kiddushin* (see the Appendix, note 81, item 1) is the assumption that the property rights that a creditor has in a pawn exist only for the creditor *qua* creditor. These rights do not have an independent existence, as do, for example, the property rights of a craftsman in the artifact that he created from the raw materials of others (*uman koneh be-shevaḥ keli*). These rights arise from his having mixed his labor with the object. A creditor has mixed no labor with the pawn he received. His rights stem from the debt owed to him. Put differently, the rights of a craftsman arise from a creative act; those of a creditor from a legal status. He who lacks the status lacks the rights that accompany it. For another person to acquire those rights, he must acquire that debt. From this it follows that transfer of the pawn must, of necessity, entail transfer of the underlying debt.

Yet even this plausible legal assumption does not lead ineluctably to a conclusion that the transfer of the debt comes automatically with the transfer of the pawn. Had R. Shemu'el ha-Sardi intuitively felt that debts could not be assigned via pledge transfer, he could simply have said that the issue at bar in the talmudic discussion in the passage in *Kiddushin* is the validity of *mashkon* as *kesef kinyan*. If its validity presumes a prior transfer of debt, then such a transfer, by *ma'amad sheloshtan* for example, is presumed to have taken place. The necessary attendant circumstances are no more spelled out in the discussion of *mashkon* in this *sugya* than is the necessary statement by the man (and *not* the woman) of *harei at mekuddeshet* in the previous *sugyot* of *'arev* or *'eved kena'ani* (*Kiddushin* 7a). See Rashi, s.v. *ve-akadesh, heilakh*; other talmudic commentators ad loc. and Rambam ('Ishut', 5: 21). All this does not detract, however, from the doctrine's validity. The assumption of automatic debt transfer allows the passage in *Kiddushin* to be read in the simplest fashion.

To what extent inference is a function of habit is well illustrated by this case. The author of the *Sefer ha-Terumot* found debt transfer the natural implication of the *sugya* in *Kiddushin*, and a century later R. Ya'akov Ba'al ha-Turim concurred. In 1961 in America, where pawnbroking had ceased to be even a memory, one of the most famous talmudic scholars of the previous generation understood Rashi in that very *sugya* (s.v. *be-mashkon*) to be saying the same thing (see previous note) and was at a loss as to its basis. This was his reaction (I cite verbatim lecture notes shown to me by his pupils): **ואף במשכון דאחרים דפירש"י שקדשה בחוב דאחרים אלא שע"י משיכת המשכון קונה את החוב,ואף זי[?] מחודש[!] דלא מצינו הקנאת חוב בש"ס אלא ע"י מעמד שלשתן או כתיבה ומסירה . . . אבל לא מצינו שע"י משיכת המשכון יקנה כל החוב.**

[83] 'Ḥoshen Mishpat' 66: 8. I have been asked both by Jay Rosen and Berachyahu Lifshitz: if, as I claimed, Early Ashkenaz, in dealing with Gentile pawns, silently incorporated the status of such pawns in Germanic law: seeing that in that legal system a pawn was a quit-payment and the debt extinguished, how could that pawn be used for the transference of a debt? The answer appears, to me at least, quite simple. In order to regulate the monetary affairs of their community, Talmudists had to silently incorporate only as much as was necessary for the halakhah to function realistically. Nor would they in any way wish to incorporate more of the contemporary Gentile reality than

However, all this was in the future. In Rashi's time no such proof was known, and we well understand now the vigorous resistance to Rashi's ruling on the *pignus pignoris*, the pawned pawn. The decision to forgo both the non-acquisition of Gentile pledges and the traditional modes of debt transfer of classical halakhah is precisely the type of ruling that will not be accepted coming from a young man and must come from a well-known and venerated decisor (*zeken hora'ah*). One can hear the opposition contending against Rashi:

Who are you, young man, to ignore *yisra'el mi-goy lo kani mashkon*, *ma'amad sheloshtan*, and *ketivah u-mesirah*, and speak of pawn acquisition and new forms of debt sale? If a well-known decisor from the great talmudic centers of Mainz or Worms says so, we might well listen to him, for such a ruling would fall under the rubric of *horah zaken*.[84] However, we won't risk violating no fewer than six pentateuchal injunctions on the basis of the intuition of a tyro.

To this objection Rashi had no answer for he realized just how many halakhic rules would be violated by this decision. Rashi gives no reasons in his responsum for he has none, other than the conviction that one cannot act daily on the

was absolutely necessary. Every silent incorporation was an infusion of an alien element into the halakhah, and the fewer of these the better. In the case of the pawned pawn, they had only to extend to Gentile pawns the same rights that a creditor had in a Jewish distraint pawn (*shelo bi-she'at halva'ah*). Thus, after pawning, the Gentile remained the debtor of the first Jew and subsequently of the second one. Concomitantly, upon payment of the debt, he could have demanded from the second Jew the return of his pawn. The Gentile may have been unaware of this fact, and as pawns were usually worth far more than the debt, it was not in the interests of the Jew to inform him of this right. That right existed nevertheless.

I should add that Rabbenu Tam's doctrine of *silluk* eliminated that right. It turned the pawned pawn into the *de facto* property of the creditor. Note, however, that he did not allow the status of the pawn in Gentile law—a fact of life—to translate itself automatically into Jewish law. That would have meant surrender to Exile, to permit the surrounding society to impose its legal categories on the halakhah. He insisted that Jewish law create or, more accurately, ratify the actual situation by *silluk*. Without such ratification, the halakhah would not recognize the *de facto* ownership of the pawn. See below, pp. 148–50.

84 Indeed, Rashi was powerless until he was able to invoke the authority of Rabbi David of Mainz, and note should be taken of a similar appeal to R. David by Rashi on the matter of *basar be-ḥalav be-shishim*, when the latter was again battling the regnant halakhic view at the time: *Teshuvot Rashi*, ##46, 81, 382. One of Rashi's pupils records that Rashi addressed three queries to R. David, ibid. #46 and MS Cambridge, Add. 667.1, fo. 69b. From MS Oxford, Bodley 566, fos. 11b–12a, we know that the author had in mind *basar be-ḥalav be-shishim* and and the double query about *Schadennehmen* and the pawned pawn. In fact, Rashi further corresponded with R. David on the no less important and sensitive subject of whether the Jewish factotum (*ma'arufya*) of a wealthy Gentile was permitted to lend the Gentile's money to a fellow-Jew at interest (see below, p. 107). However, the pupil who made the count was unaware of it.

basis of one reality and proceed to rule on the basis of another. Halakhah must base itself upon 'the plain, plump facts' and incorporate them willy-nilly into its decision-making process. Rashi's conduct here is part of the same phenomenon that I will draw attention to in my discussion of Ri[85] and which is operative to this day among halakhic decisors. Suppose a Jewish court was called upon to rule upon the inheritance of a Rothschild. Would it dream of saying that there was no wealth to distribute seeing that most of Rothschild's wealth was in stocks and bonds, intangibles (*davar she-ein bo mamash*) which cannot be sold or acquired? There is no difference between the necessity for contemporary halakhists to take legal cognizance of the stock market and the need of *rishonim* to factor into their rulings the realities of the medieval pawn market—the market that underlay most extension of credit in north-west Europe at the time.[86]

What transpired in eleventh-century Ashkenaz may have been simply a replay of what had occurred in the classical period of halakhah, the period of the Sages (*tekufat ḥazal*), for the non-transferability of debts had long hung around the neck of Jewish merchants like an albatross. According to many views, the very assignment of debts is of rabbinic origin. By pentateuchal law (*mi-de-oraita*) debts cannot be sold or transferred.[87] The Sages had realized that business demanded assignment, and they instituted it by means of transfer of the bill of indebtedness with or without an accompanying note (*mesirah* or *ketivah u-mesirah*).[88] As Ashkenazic scholars noted, this rapidly proved too cumbersome,[89] and so the Sages then instituted transfer by triple presence, which they admitted had no legal foundation, but which the Tosafists noted had a very practical purpose.[90] Rashi's grandson, Rashbam, added that the Sages had chosen the form of triple presence because this was the custom of merchants at the time,[91] what in his time was called *jus mercatorum*. The

85 Below, pp. 145–7.

86 See my remarks in 'A Response to Rabbi Ephraim Buckwold's Critique of "Rabad of Posquières: A Programmatic Essay", Part I', *Torah U-Mada Journal*, 14 (2006–7), 194–6. (The essay will appear in the third volume of this series.)

87 e.g. Alfasi on *Ketubbot* 85b (Vilna edn., fo. 44b); Maimonides, 'Hilkhot Mekhirah' 6: 12, 'Zekhiyah u-Matanah' 10: 2; Ri, *Tosafot*, *Ketubbot* 85b, s.v. *ha-mokher*; Rabbenu Tam (initially) ibid.; *Tosfot Shants*, *Ketubbot*, ed. A. Liss (Jerusalem, 1973), 85b, s.v. *ha-mokher*; Rashba, *Ḥiddushim*, *Bava Batra* (Jerusalem, 1960), 147b, s.v. *ve-nir'eh li*.

88 *Bava Batra* 75b–76a.

89 Rashbam, *Bava Batra* 144a, s.v. *kanah*: **כך תקנו חכמים לפי שהדבר תדיר הוא בין הבריות לא הזקיקו חכמים להקנות בקנין ובעדים**. The context there strictly speaking is bailments, but the formula applies both to bailments and debts.

90 *Tosafot*, *Gittin* 14a, s.v. *ke-hilkhata*: **כהלכתא בלא טעם, פ' מה שמועיל לקנות, אבל טעם יש למה תקנו חכמים מעמד שלשתן, תקנו שלא יצטרך לטרוח ולעשות קנינים**.

91 *Bava Batra* 148a, s.v. *be-ma'amad*: **ולפי שהדבר נהוג בין סוחרים והחנונים תקנו את הדבר**.

problems confronted by eleventh-century scholars were identical with those confronted repeatedly by the Sages of talmudic times; the technique, if Rashbam is historically correct, was equally the same—incorporation of dominant practices. What had changed was the status of this incorporation. *Ḥazal* had extended *de jure* cognizance to the new procedures. Men of the Middle Ages did not see themselves as empowered to institute (*le-taken*) a new and binding form of debt assignment; they could extend to the new only recognition *de facto*. That they did; indeed, they turned that restriction into a statement about themselves and the Exile—about which I shall have more to say later.[92]

Attitude towards Usury

An Unarticulated Premise. Besides the premises of pledge-ownership and debt assignment, there remains a third assumption in the responsa of R. David and Rashi[93] and with it we come to the |223| posture of these scholars towards

[92] Below, pp. 147–50.

[93] (A) In Rashi's case there are only two assumptions in his responsum. It will be noticed that while R. Meshullam spoke of *mekhirah* and R. David of Mainz of *meshikhah*, Rashi keeps absolutely silent and speaks only of the upshot, the assignment of the debt. Nor is his reticence coincidental. Rashi realized that the transfer of debt, which he did not for a moment doubt, could not be rooted in acquisition of the pawn, for no such rights were attained by Jewish creditors (see *Mordekhai*, *Shevu'ot*, #775), and so talk of *meshikah* and *mekhirah* was out of place. (B) If acquisition of the pawn was precluded, what was the basis of the assignment? One might contend on the basis of the ruling of *otiyot niknot bi-mesirah* and argue that Rivan's and Rashbam's concurrence (see the Appendix, note 80, item 3) reflects Rashi's attitude. I think, however, that this is not the case. First, a doctrine of *mesirah* might well require a direct transfer from hand to hand (see *Tosafot*, *Bava Batra* 76a, s.v. *iy*; *Kiddushin* 25b, s.v. *behemah*), something about which we haven't a whisper in the sources, not even a *ve-hamaḥmir* or *tov ha-davar*. Moreover, it assumes that *otiyot niknot bi-mesirah* does not entail acquisition of the document. See, however, Rashi on *Ketubbot* 86a, s.v. *magbei* (second occurrence) and *Mahadurah Kamma* or *Perush Rivan* (above, n. 77(*a*), ad loc., and see Rashba's remarks in the *Shitah Mekubbetset* ad loc.), and one would have to say that Amemar's ruling was only in the instance of *ketivah u-mesirah*, where he wrote *keni lakh ihu ve-khol shi'abudeih* (see Rashbam, *Bava Batra* 76a, s.v. *katav*, *otiyot*, *u-vi-shetar*), but not according to the ruling of *otiyot niknot bi-mesirah*—all of which is highly implausible. While the precise rights of the creditor in the paper of the note of indebtedness became subsequently a much-disputed and obscure issue (see *Shitah Mekubbetset* ad loc., 'Ḥoshen Mishpat' 66: 23, and commentaries ad loc., esp. the *Shakh* and the *Ketsot ha-Ḥoshen*; see also *Tosafot*, *Bava Batra* 76a, s.v. *iy*, and *Ḥiddushei Ramban* ad loc. in conjunction with *Teshuvot Maharaḥ Or Zarua'*, #211), I am reluctant to read any of this into Rashi. The same holds true for distinctions between possession and ownership, with only the former being necessary for the assignment of debts. The tenor of the *sugya* in *Bava Batra* is of ownership, as are the words of Rashbam, and also those of Rashi in *Ketubbot*, and historically, I would leave it at that. Rashi's silence is best understood as a simple, perspicacious realization that transfer of debts by pledges had to be assumed for such was the reality at the time, and halakhah must respond on the basis of the cold facts of life. It was best, however, not to spell out the premises that such a debt assignment entailed, for it would expose the non-talmudic nature of this unavoidable ruling. See below, pp. 147–50.

usury. Despite the fact that the original creditor asked his friend for a loan (*halveh li*)[94] and made no mention of a sale, a sale none the less was said to have taken place. Strictly speaking this is not an assumption, but rather a construction, the interpretation which the courts choose to give to this type of transaction, and, like all constructions, it reflects as much the predisposition of the judges as the nature of the matter at hand. Had the first Jew said, 'Give me [*ten li*] $100 [for] this pawn', the judicial construction of a sale would have been within the parameters of the ordinary. Construing 'Lend me $100 [on] this pawn' as a sale rather than a loan falls well beyond these parameters. Since this radical reinterpretation of the transaction permitted the taking of interest, clearly Rashi and his older mentor were strongly, indeed boldly, inclined to allowance. However, we must be careful not to attribute to this ruling more leniency than it possessed. Their ruling expressed an awareness of the cardinal fact of the case, namely, that in reality the interest was coming out of the Gentile's pocket and not the Jew's, and no intra-Jewish interest had been given. It was because of the halakhic formality of Gentile non-agency (i.e. that the Jewish agent of a Gentile is viewed as the principal to the transaction) that *ribbit* had reared its ugly head. Usury was present procedurally, but not substantively. And if *ribbit* be transgressed only formally, the courts should make every effort to construe the relationship so that the underlying economic reality re-emerges—which is precisely what they did. |224|

Had we nothing else from the pens of R. David and Rashi, one might take this to be the whole of their position on usury. It is congruous, as we shall see, with much of the attitude of their predecessors, among whom numbered no less a figure than Rabbenu Gershom Me'or ha-Golah (d. 1028). However, R. David of Mainz and, above all, Rashi wrote on more than one problem, and if we turn to these decisions we will discover that their posture with respect to *ribbit* was more complex, and, in the final analysis, considerably different.

***Schadennehmen* and its Implications.** In the first half of his responsum, Rashi discussed the frequent *Schadennehmen*, as did R. David.[95] A debt falls due, and the Jewish debtor is unable to meet payment (as mentioned above, there was a chronic dearth of currency at the time). He gives some valuable object to his creditor and authorizes him to pawn it at interest for the sum of the debt. The Gentile having received satisfaction has no interest in redeeming it, but, as pledges are invariably worth more than the debt (often twice the amount),[96]

94 See text above, p. 77.

95 Above, p. 85, n. 58(*a*).

96 Hermannus Quondam Judaeus, *Opusculum de Conversione Sua* (above, n. 58(*a*)), 73; F. Schaub, *Der Kampf gegen den Zinswucher, ungerechten Preis und unlautern Handel im Mittelalter: von Karl dem Großen bis Papst Alexander III* (Freiburg, 1905), 47; *Teshuvot Rashi*, #241; *Ravan*, ii, *Bava Metsi'a* 35a

the Jew will seek to get back his pawn, paying principal and interest. Two paths were open to him. If he wished, he could go to the creditor directly, but if he sought to get it out of hock before much interest had accumulated, the creditor would be loath to surrender the pawn, which was worth much more, and could plead *Hand muß Hand wahren*, namely, he had received the pledge from a Gentile, and, by Gentile law, only the bailor (*ha-mafkid*) had remedy from the bailee (*ha-nifkad*). A third party, even the original owner himself, had no claim against him: neither the right of redemption nor even the claim of unlawful detention.[97] True, R. Gershom (d. 1028) had declared that such a ruling was contrary to Jewish law, |225| and that if the original owner was a Jew and the present bailee a Jew, the object would have to be surrendered to its lawful owner. But people don't yield business advantages that easily. Rashi had to make the same point in two separate responsa and his younger contemporary, Riva, R. Yitsḥak of Speyer (d. before 1133), felt the need to reiterate Rabbenu Gershom's ruling. A hundred and fifty years later the great R. Me'ir of Rothenburg (d. 1293) was still arguing against this misconception, and a generation or two after his death we find R. Elḥanan, the teacher of the editor of a collection of R. Me'ir's responsa, informing defendants that *Hand muß Hand wahren* had no standing in halakhah.[98] Moreover, the bailee could simply

(= *Teshuvot R. Me'ir mi-Rotenburg* [Prague and Budapest], #774); Hoffmann, *Der Geldhandel* (above, n. 15), 68–9; *Teshuvot R. Me'ir mi-Rotenburg* (Prague and Budapest), #963; de Roover, *Money, Banking and Credit* (above, n. 15), 133; R. B. Pugh, 'Some Medieval Moneylenders', *Speculum*, 43 (1968), 278; G. Nahon, 'Le Crédit et les juifs' (above, n. 15), 1133; P.-C. Timbal, *Les Obligations contractuelles dans le droit français des XIIIe et XIVe siècles d'après la jurisprudence du Parlement*, ii (Paris, 1977), 435, 437; see above, n. 58. (*Or Zarua'*, #202 should be seen as an intra-Jewish loan, though there too the pawn was usually worth more than the debt, e.g. *Teshuvot R. Me'ir mi-Rotenburg* [Prague and Budapest], #209, authored by R. Ḥayyim Ḥefets Zahav; see Emanuel, 'Teshuvot Maharam mi-Rotenburg' [above, n. 54(*c*)], 188, n. 169.)

97 See below, n. 206, for bibliography.

98 (A) *Shibbolei ha-Leket II*, ed. M. Z. Ḥasida, p. 80, ll. 18–22; new edn., p. 170, ll. 15–18; *Temim De'im*, #158, the so-called *Ḥiddushei ha-Ritva, Bava Metsi'a* (Amsterdam, 1729), 71b, s.v. *kuti*; see below, n. 140(*a*). Rashi argued against the notion of *Hand muß Hand wahren*, with its implicit denial of ownership as against possession in mobilia (see below, pp. 145–6), in his responsum in *Teshuvot Maimuniyot, Mishpatim*, #2 (see above, n. 64, for parallel passages), and again at length in *Teshuvot Rashi*, #241 (p. 276): **שכל מקום שהגזילה שם ברשות בעלים עומדת ואין כח ללוקח לעכבה על מעותיו דאיתמר המוכר שדה לחבירו. . .ונמצאת שאינה שלו. . .ואם תאמר אין דין זה נוהג במטלטלין, הרי שנינו אמר לו מכור לי בני מעיה . . . ועוד שנינו המכיר כליו וכו'**. Why would anyone imagine that halakhically there could not be ownership of mobilia without possession? Rashi sought here to forestall such an assumption in Jewish law only because such was the nature of ownership of mobilia in the surrounding society. (His phrase *ein din zeh noheg be-mittaltelin* corresponds to the later formulation of *Hand muß Hand wahren—mobilia non habent sequelam*; Brissaud, above, n. 57, p. 288.) *Teshuvot R. Me'ir mi-Rotenburg* (Prague and Budapest), #728; MS Oxford, Bodley 641, fo. 174a. This point was made again by R. Yitsḥak of Oppenheim in MS Hamburg, Staats- und Universitätsbibliothek 45,

challenge the claimant's ownership, forcing the owner to produce proof thereof—not always a simple matter in mobilia. The simplest course, if possible, was to request the Gentile to redeem it for him, and to this case Rashi addressed himself and stridently insisted upon its permissibility.

Rashi's certainty stemmed from the fact that here one need invoke neither triple-decked premises nor judicial constructions, but simply |226| the famous talmudic ruling of the incapacity of Gentiles to function as agents for Jewish principals. Any action performed by them is regarded as independently initiated, with the Gentile the principal and not the agent. Since, in the case under consideration, the Gentile received the money and returned it, the entire transaction was a Jewish–Gentile one and free from the ban of usury, even though interest, in the words of Rashi's interlocutor, would be 'coming out of a Jewish pocket'. Note however, that *Schadennehmen* entailed an economically usurious relationship between two Jews; nevertheless, since legally the Gentile and not the second Jew was the debtor, Rashi was of the opinion that the injunction against usury did not apply.

Rashi's Interpretation of the Gnomic Ruling of *le-ḥumra*. Rashi, however, appended an important qualification to his ruling on *Schadennehmen*, namely, that the creditor should not be aware at the time of the loan that the pawn is a Jew's, i.e. that the interest will inevitably be paid by a Jew. If he was so aware,

fo. 177d, #198: **וישראל שמוסר משכונו ללות מישראל נרא' לי שצריך ליתן לו לפדותו, מידי דהוי אמכיר כליו וספריו ביד אחר שצריך להחזיר לו** and in MS Cambridge, Oo.6.70, 1, fo.105a (gloss). R. Elḥanan's remarks are found in MS Parma, de Rossi 86, fo. 2: **ואין יכול לומר לו לאו בעל דברים דידי את ... ולא גרע מגזלו גוי דצריך להניח לו לפדות ולהחזיר לו במעות שקנה**. These texts have been recently published in Emanuel, *Teshuvot Maharam u-Venei Doro*, i, #205; ii, 403: 4. On R. Yitsḥak of Oppenheim and R. Elḥanan, see ibid. i. 108–9, 120–2. (B) Whether, despite all strictures, *Hand muß Hand wahren* left its mark on daily rulings is problematic and I tend to be dubious. Rabbenu Tam was unquestionably aware that the ordinary debtor would have two titles to redemption of a pawn: that of depositor and that of owner, and most probably intended the renunciation (*silluk*; see *Or Zarua'*, #215; below, n. 195) to surrender both these rights. I doubt very much, though, that most people were aware of the necessary dual renunciation when they performed *silluk*. As to the case of the Paris courts in the 13th century, see the Appendix, note 189. (C) On the two editions of *Shibbolei ha-Leket II* which I cite throughout the essay, the first by M. Z. Ḥasida, the second by Y. Ḥasida—to which I refer as 'new edn.'—see the Appendix, note 98. (D) My reference to the *Ḥiddushei ha-Ritva 'al Bava Metsi'a* does not refer to the authentic work of the *Ḥiddushei ha-Ritva 'al Bava Metsi'a* edited by S. Rafael (Jerusalem, 1992), but to the book published under that name in Amsterdam in 1729. This work was not authored by Ritva and is clearly of medieval Provençal origin. Nevertheless, it continued to be reprinted under the name of Ritva and was included in the *Kur le-Zahav* edition of Ritva's works (Warsaw, 1879–83), which for close to a century was the most widely used text. For the Provençal origin of the so-called *Ḥiddushei ha-Ritva 'al Bava Metsi'a*, see *Ḥiddushei ha-Ritva ha-Ḥadashim* ed. A. Halperin (London, 1962), introduction, 8–11; *Me'iri 'al Bava Metsi'a*, ed. K. Schlesinger (Jerusalem, 1969), introduction, 9.

the loan was then forbidden as usury, for the Talmud had ruled in its doctrine of *le-ḥumra* that the principle of Gentile non-agency could be suspended if its application resulted in interest being paid by one Jew to another.[99] Significantly, however, Rashi did not |227| view this ruling as a general hedge (*gezerah*) against actual usury, and hence operable under all circumstances and

[99] (A) See above, p. 72. I have taken Rashi's *kansinan leih* as a reference to this talmudic ban on Gentile intermediaries for the following reasons: first, Rashi's certainty in *Schadennehmen* stems from several considerations. It is quite possible that the Gentile is to be viewed as acting on his own initiative altogether and not as anyone's agent. Even if he be seen as acting upon Jewish initiative (it's at least an open question), nevertheless, there is no agency for Gentiles and he is, perforce, the principal. If this is so, the objection of *le-ḥumra* immediately raises its head. One can hardly give a blanket allowance of *Schadennehmen*, much less berate the opposition, without disposing of the obvious argument of *le-ḥumra*. The responsum *must* contain a reference to it. Secondly, if this be not a reference to *le-ḥumra*, what is this penalty (*kenas*), of which Rashi speaks with such simplicity and certainty? It is clearly not the common ruling in Champagne, for that forbade all forms of *Schadennehmen* on the strict grounds of full-fledged usury (*me-'ikra de-dina*). It must, then, be Rashi's own private penalty. On what basis does the young, hesitant Rashi impose penalties upon people for practicing what he vigorously insists is permissible? This immediate translation of private opposition into absolute, unquestioned legal penalty would not be surprising in so imperial a temperament as that of Rabbenu Tam; I find it totally out of character with Rashi, not to speak of its taking place at so early a stage in his career. Finally, viewing *le-ḥumra* in this light provides us with a key to Rashi's subsequent far-reaching ruling on the Gentile straw man. See text below. (See *Or Zarua'*, #212, below, n. 190, for a similar interpretation of *le-ḥumra* by Ri.) (B) In his commentary on *le-ḥumra* in *Bava Metsi'a* 71b, Rashi wrote (and the manuscripts of the commentary accord fully with the printed text), **דמשמע שנכרי זה חשוב שלוחו של ישראל לחומרא**, i.e. the doctrine of *le-ḥumra* reinstituted agency, and this interpretation dominates halakhic thought to this day. Rashi makes no reference to agency in his earlier responsum, and I suggest that at the time he had not yet evolved this doctrine of agency, but viewed it simply as an ad hoc penalty (see below). I would add that J. Fraenkel, in his *Darko shel Rashi be-Ferusho la-Talmud ha-Bavli* (Jerusalem, 1975), has argued on wholly different grounds that the commentary to *Bava Metsi'a* does not belong to Rashi's early period. See his summary on p. 284. {I assumed here that Rashi's remarks in his commentary signaled a shift away from the doctrine of *le-ḥumra* as a penalty (*kenas*). This implies a major change in his perspective on *ribbit*. I am now inclined to view it less as a change in Rashi's thinking than as a reflection of his hermeneutical fastidiousness and his aversion to incorporating personal views into his commentary. Rashi continued to hold, as before, that the goal of *le-ḥumra* was to penalize circumventions; however, that was a personal opinion not implicit in the text and should not, therefore, appear in his explication.} (C) For those who find it difficult to separate *le-ḥumra* from agency—for the identity of the two has become a halakhic truism—I would point out that the notion of agency is missing in R. Ḥanan'el, though in the course of time some halakhists in Ashkenaz in the 12th and 13th centuries unwittingly attributed this notion to him. Compare the actual language of R. Ḥanan'el as cited in *Or Zarua'* (#210 end) with the reports of his doctrine in the *Yere'im ha-Shalem*, i (Vilna, 1892), fo. 45, and the *Semag*, ed. E. Schlesinger (Jerusalem, 1989), 341, Injunction #191. Agency is equally and conspicuously missing in the *ribbit* handbook of Rashi's younger German contemporary, Riva (see below, p. 118), found in the *Shibbolei ha-Leket II* (above, n. 98(*a*)), 79, ll. 11–14; new edn., p. 168, ll. 1–6; the so-called *Ḥiddushei ha-Ritva* (above, n. 98(*d*)), fo. 40c, ll. 12–13; and *Temim De'im* (above, n. 78), fo. 30b, ll. 45–6 (missing in *Shibbolei ha-Leket II*, p. 80, ll. 17–18; new edn. p. 170, l. 15, as its author, R. Tsidkiyahu ha-Rofe, abridged slightly

intents (even when the loan had been given to the Gentile in good faith and only later was its ultimate destination discovered). He saw it rather as a penalty (*kenas*), and hence only applicable in cases of complicity. The purpose of the rabbinic ordinance of *le-ḥumra* was not to guard against the formation of real usurious relations, in which case the intent of the parties would be irrelevant, but to preclude attempts by one of the parties to circumvent the injunction. To Rashi's mind, there was clearly less to be said against usury than against the attempts to set it at naught. Practicing usury is not as serious as thwarting the law against it.

Put differently: usury is forbidden, severely forbidden, by the Torah; however, it is not inequitable, not inherently wrong, and so there is no need to 'erect any fences' (*seyyagim*) to insure against its breach. The goal of the rabbinic hedge of *le-ḥumra* was not to secure an economic moralism—for there is none—but to preserve the integrity of halakhic observance. To Rashi's thinking, the injunction against *ribbit* is a *ḥok* (a dictate of the law of Revelation, as is the ban on consumption of non-kosher foods), not a *mishpat* (a dictate of the law of reason against breaches of the social order such as theft).[100]

Let us be clear as to what is being said here. Whether usury is theft became subsequently a disputed issue in Jewish law.[101] This famous discussion, however, is entirely after the fact, after Revelation. Once the Torah has banned usury, does practicing usury, taking another person's money to which one is not entitled, constitute theft or not? (One argument against theft is that the lender has willingly paid the interest. How can one commit theft by taking something that has been given voluntarily?) The issue at bar is whether the Divine law against usury created a new category of theft. The question of *ḥok* or *mishpat*, on the other hand, is pre-Revelation, as it were, and addresses the inherent nature of usury. Had the Torah not legislated against usury, would it have been banned, as would theft and rapine, because it was intrinsically unjust? Rashi here answers in the negative.

That this conception of *ribbit* differed notably from the prevailing one is obvious from the sharp opposition that Rashi's views encountered in his home town of Troyes—recall his phrase 'and I refrain from so ruling because of a strong negative reaction' (*mi-shum la'agei safah*); indeed, this is the only time

the original text; see below, nn. 140, 144, 146). Finally, see *Teshuvot, Pesakim u-Minhagim shel R. Me'ir mi-Rotenburg*, ii, *Teshuvot*, #75, and note that neither R. Me'ir's report of Riva nor his own interpretation of the Tosefta invokes agency.

100 *Yoma* 67b; *Sifra*, ed. I. H. Weiss (Vienna, 1862), 'Aḥarei Mot', 86a: *she-ilu lo nikhtavu, be-din hayah le-khotvan, kegon ha-gezelot*.

101 e.g. *Shitah Mekubbetset 'al Bava Metsi'a*, 61b, s.v. *she-ken*; *Mishneh le-Melekh*, 'Hilkhot Malveh ve-Loveh', 4: 13.

that I know of that he makes such a remark—and explains why he was powerless at the early stage of his career to have his way until supported by R. David ha-Levi of Mainz.[102] The extent of Rashi's break with tradition will become clear only after we analyze the dominant view of usury at that time in Germany, in the ancient seats of learning of Worms and Mainz where he himself had studied. However, let us continue with our analysis of Rashi, for that gentle revolutionary had not yet finished his work.

The Economic Significance of Rashi's Rulings and their Practical Limitations. Before moving on to Rashi's final position on matters of usury, let us shift our attention from the legal (and, if you wish, philosophical or moral) implications of the above responsum of Rashi to its commercial ones. What did Rashi's dual allowances mean in monetary terms? The unqualified allowance of lending to Gentiles at interest was, in reality, a mixed blessing. While it provided an important outlet for Jewish capital, at the same time it placed Jews seeking credit in an intolerable position. Who would lend to his co-religionist at no interest when he could loan the same sum profitably to a Gentile? How did Rashi's (and R. David's) rulings ameliorate this problem? The allowance of *Schadennehmen* meant that the financial resources of the Jewish community could be freely drawn upon—with payments of competitive interest—to liquidate debts owed to Gentiles; while that of the pawned pawn meant that credit extended to Gentiles at interest could be replenished at prevailing interest rates from Jewish |228| sources. Economically, a tight money situation had been eased as both Gentile assets (money owed by Jews to Gentiles) and Gentile debts (money owed by Gentiles to Jews) could now serve amongst Jews as the basis for loans at interest. The ban on intra-Jewish usury had been lifted to the extent of the sum total of the current Jewish–Gentile money traffic.

Yet even this partial alleviation went against the grain in Troyes. Rashi dared not proclaim his allowance until he had the authority of R. David behind him. We know from the Rhineland in this period that when moneylending was rife, leniency in popular practice appears to have been a step ahead of formal halakhic argument.[103] We may have here an indication that though Jews in Champagne were engaged in moneylending in the first quarter of the eleventh century, their involvement in this field a half-century later was not yet significant.[104]

The partial alleviation provided by R. David of Mainz and Rashi proved progressively insufficient. It was of use to a businessman seeking to get out of a

[102] Above, p. 77.

[103] See below, p. 110.

[104] For the involvement in moneylending, see the responsum to Troyes of R. Yosef Tov 'Elem in *Teshuvot R. Me'ir mi-Rotenburg* (Prague and Budapest), #941; the parallel text in *Mordekhai, Bava*

pressing debt or a moneylender needing capital quickly; but what of initial business financing, the lifeblood of commerce? Were Jews, moreover, to be disadvantaged in the availability of this credit *vis-à-vis* their Gentile competitors? Halakhah here was caught in a bind. The wider the allowance of taking usury from Gentiles, the greater the economic pressure on the Jewish businessman. His Gentile competitors in the eleventh century could obtain credit from both Jewish and Gentile sources, while the Jew was denied the opportunity to draw upon the financial resources of his co-religionists. The ban on *ribbit* was an ever-increasing hindrance to Jewish commercial enterprise. Jewish–Gentile competition doomed the usury injunction amongst Jews well before the devolution of Jewish status in the twelfth century. This is a point which cannot be overemphasized. As the Gentile mercantile classes gathered strength in the decades preceding the Crusades, so did the pressures upon the halakhists to equalize the terms of Jewish and Gentile financing, to level the playing field, and to provide Jews with access to capital comparable to that available to their Gentile competitors.

The Gentile Straw Man. It was Rashi who, in his later years, created (or validated) the central fiction of Jewish credit operations in the Middle Ages, the use of a Gentile straw man. A Jew was permitted to obtain a loan at interest from another Jew by the simple expedient of having a Gentile serve as intermediary. |229| A Jew could request a Gentile employee of his to go and request money at interest from another Jew, obtain it, and return with the money. [105]

What Rashi now allowed with this so-called intermediary was a far cry from what he had permitted in his youth. Then, in the instance of *Schaden-*

Batra, #481 informs us that the city in question was Troyes. As to the dates of R. Yosef Tov 'Elem, see F. G. Hirschmann, *Stadtplanung, Bauprojekte und Großbaustellen im 10. und 11. Jahrhundert: vergleichende Studien zu den Kathedralstädten westlich des Rheins*, Monographien zur Geschichte des Mittelalters 43 (Stuttgart, 1998), 178–9, 412, n. 2970 (*sic*). I should here correct what I wrote in the original article (p. 228): 'though Jews in France had begun, much to the uneasiness of R. Yosef Tov 'Elem, to turn to moneylending'. I was here following, albeit in somewhat more temperate language, I. A. Agus, *Urban Civilzation* (above, n. 37), i. 445, and indirectly S. Baron, *A Social and Religious History of the Jews*, iv (New York, 1957), 157. In fact, R. Yosef Tov 'Elem was neither denigrating moneylending nor praising and encouraging agriculture. See my remarks in Chapter 5 above, 'The Jewish Attitude to Usury' (pp. 47–8).

105 *Teshuvot Rashi*, #175. (A) I assume that this responsum was written much later in Rashi's life than the one that I have just analyzed. In the latter responsum Rashi was unable to announce the narrow allowances of *Schadennehmen* and of the pawned pawn until he had the backing of R. David ha-Levi of Mainz. In the responsum I am about to discuss, Rashi proclaims without the slightest hesitancy the sweeping, central fiction of Jewish moneylending of the Middle Ages. This was written at a stage of his career when he clearly had nothing to fear from opposition, had no need for outside

nehmen, it had been a case where the Jew had entered a genuine debt relationship with a Gentile and, at a later date, when unable to meet payment, gave him a pawn and told him to take his payment from a loan that would be given to him on the basis of the pledge. In such a case, it was an open question of judicial construction whether the giving of the pawn was a creation of agency, an authorization to take a loan for the debtor and from that loan to take his payment, or whether it was a loan (*hash'alah*) of a pawn to an independent party to take a loan on his own and to let the original debtor worry about getting his pawn back.[106] Personally I suspect that part of Rashi's certainty in *Schadennehmen* stemmed from his conviction that the latter interpretation was equally a plausible construction of the transaction.[107] Be that as it may, the role

support, and didn't feel under any pressure to hold back in order to avoid 'strong, negative reaction' (*la'agei safah*). (B) I open the possibility of Rashi's responsum being a validation of an extant practice only because in the Rhineland, as we shall see (below, p. 110), a radical allowance of Rabbenu Gershom and his successors seems not to be an innovation of their own, but rather validation of a contemporary business practice. However, we have no data about any such business practice in Champagne in Rashi's time. (C) The original text of the responsum is that of the *Sefer ha-Terumot*, 46: 1: 5, ed. Goldschmidt, p. 847, is confirmed by the *Sifrut de-Vei Rashi* and MSS Oxford, Bodley 566, fo. 59b; Parma, de Rossi 86, fos. 6b–7a, #10. The text of our responsum, found in several collections of responsa attributed to R. Me'ir of Rothenburg (*Teshuvot R. Me'ir mi-Rotenburg* [Prague and Budapest], #799; MSS Parma, de Rossi 1033, fo. 17d–e; Oxford, Bodley 692, fo. 229a, #209; Oxford, Bodley 884, fo. 164c–d, from *ve-im ba be-mirmah*), would seem to be a later expansion. It accurately reports, however, that Rashi's allowance was made in cases where the creditor was unaware that the pawn belonged to a Jew. The absence of this qualification in the original responsum is indeed surprising. We must, however, remember that all that we possess is a brief reply which plunges *in medias res* and that we lack the initial query which probably outlined the circumstances of the creditor's ignorance. Unless one is willing to assume that Rashi rejected *le-ḥumra* as later his revolutionary grandson, Rabbenu Tam, did—and no one to the best of my knowledge has dreamt of such a thing—we must assume such unawareness on the part of the creditor. (D) I am aware that as a result of the researches of A. Sofer (*Teshuvot Ḥakhmei Provintsiyah* [Jerusalem, 1967], introduction, p. 7) the reliability of the *Sefer ha-Terumot* for direct quotation has been somewhat lessened. However, when it is confirmed by passages from works issuing from Rashi's own school, I feel that full credence should be given to his citations. (E) One should caution that the Rothenburg expansion is not uniformly reliable. Though correct in perceiving that the responsum dealt with a creditor caught unawares, it misunderstood Rashi's ruling as being addressed to the problem which plagued German business in later times—that of false fronting. See below, nn. 145, 168.

[106] See the remarks of Riva, *Shibbolei ha-Leket II*, p. 80, ll. 4–17; new edn., p. 170, ll. 1–15. For parallel passages, see below, n. 140.

[107] (A) The objection that if the construction be of loan (*hash'alah*) then the qualification of *le-ḥumra*, namely creditor's ignorance, has no place is correct, if one assumes that Rashi is operating with a principle of reinstated agency; see above, n. 99(*b*). If, however, Rashi views this simply as a penalty imposed upon the creditor for seeking to benefit from usury (ibid.), then the construction given to the debtor's actions may well be irrelevant. See text below. (B) If the loan aspect played a decisive role in Rashi's allowance of *Schadennehmen*, I would then have to retract my analysis of Rashi's ruling as

of the |230| Gentile was sufficiently natural and his conduct sufficiently appropriate that such a construction could at least have been entertained. No such thing existed in his new allowance of *ribbit* by the simple means of a Gentile intermediary. This newly inserted Gentile is a 'straw man'; he never had, nor has he now, an independent role in the transaction. In his request for and receipt of money, he is, in every sense, acting as agent between two Jewish principals. To interpose this errand-boy between the two and then proclaim him a principal is legal fiction, pure and simple.

Put differently, the intermediary is in fact an agent; and as for pleading the rule of 'no Gentile agency' (*ein sheliḥut le-goy*), this was precisely what the law of *le-ḥumra* had been intended to prevent. One could not use a Gentile go-between (and invoke the absence of Gentile agency) to evade the usury injunction.[108]

Yet Rashi obviously saw his ruling as being fully consonant with the dictates of the Talmud. On closer inspection, Rashi's new and radical allowance seems not only not to have been in contradiction with *le-ḥumra*, but, indeed, the logical outcome of his old understanding of that ruling! Though, one should add, time had to elapse before he realized its full implications. Or, perhaps, time had to elapse before he himself was willing to accept its full implications.

I have already mentioned that, as a consequence of his economic outlook, he had seen *le-ḥumra* not as a hedge (*gezerah*) against the formation of economically usurious relations but as a penalty (*kenas*) for attempting to circumvent the usury ban. *Kenas* in Jewish law is generally restricted to monetary (or material) penalties. If so, it can here be applied to the creditor only, who will lose his interest as a consequence, for the halakhah, while strictly forbidding the debtor to pay any *ribbit*, never imposes upon him financial penalties, even if he transgresses the injunction in its most severe pentateuchal form. As he is beyond the pale of any *kenas*, his actions and intentions should be irrelevant to the application of the *kenas*. Only the intent of the creditor, the sole subject of the penalty, should be reckoned with. Thus the debtor should be able to initiate any step he wishes to circumvent the injunction. Personal outlook yielded

reflecting a rejection of *ribbit* as an economic moralism. This would not affect my final analysis of Rashi or of his break with the Rhineland tradition, for in the responsum under discussion, Rashi certainly has abandoned any such notion of substantive usury and is advocating legal fiction pure and simple in an economically usurious relationship. At bar here is not Rashi's final and most influential position, which is crystal clear, but whether or not Rashi began moving towards that position early in his career.

108 Above, p. 72.

Rashi the interpretation that the rabbinic ban of *le-ḥumra* was a penalty for circumvention, circumstances abetted good logic in transforming it into profitable circumvention, and the gate of legal fiction opened wide to all borrowers.

I have said that 'personal outlook yielded the interpretation', for the talmudic ruling of *le-ḥumra* is an empty box which the interpreter can fill only with his own viewpoint. It is not, indeed cannot here be, text-driven. The Talmud cites a tannaitic source (*beraita*) that gives two arrangements which are forbidden because of usury, the second of which is the instance of a loan between two Jews with a Gentile go-between. The Talmud then questions the reason for the injunctions and says, we well understand the second case as the ban is well known (*bi-shelama sefa le-ḥumra*), and then goes on to analyze the first case.[109] It never returns to the second arrangement, nor is there any other place in the Talmud where such an arrangement is discussed. Most commentators have noted that the Talmud does not speak of an outright injunction (i.e. doesn't say *bi-shelama sefa asur*), and from this inferred that the injunction here is not pentateuchal but only rabbinic.[110] The Sages forbade the subterfuge of a Gentile middleman in a loan between two Jews, but the three words—*bi-shelama sefa le-ḥumra*—provide no hint as to the reason. Whether they forbade it so as to prevent the formation of an economically usurious relationship between two Jews or to punish attempted circumvention of the law will depend entirely on the commentator's outlook, what he believes to be the soundest reason for such a ban.

Towards the end of this revolutionary decision, Rashi appended the following proviso:

אם ישראל עצמו . . . בא לפדות משכונו אל יזכור לו שום ריבית אלא יאמר לו קנהו בדמים מידי בכך וכך.

If the Jew himself [i.e. the debtor] . . . should come to redeem his pledge, let him not mention any usury, but he [the Jewish creditor] should say, 'Buy it from me for such and such a sum'. |**231**|

This appendage is very difficult to sustain logically. How can any deed done at the time of redemption, let alone any words then uttered, affect the existence of usury? If the creditor's ignorance, at the time of the loan, of the fact that the Gentile is acting on Jewish behalf annuls the ban of *le-ḥumra*, and the principle of Gentile non-agency retains its pristine strength, the subsequent direct

[109] *Bava Metsi'a* 71b.

[110] The exception to this viewpoint being Maimonides, who sees the situation as involving a pentateuchal injunction and attaches no importance to the strange wording of *le-ḥumra*. See 'Hilkhot Malveh ve-Loveh' 5: 3.

payment by the Jew should in no way impair the allowance. The debtor was the Gentile straw man and the Jew legally a third party. One does not need, for the purpose of allowance, Gentile interposition both in loan and repayment; one side will suffice, and the case under consideration possesses that by all accounts. Was Rashi in doubt whether the creditor's ignorance sufficed to maintain Gentile non-agency, since a usury situation was in fact being created? If so, why then did he have no qualms if the payment, too, was made by the Gentile straw man? If his legal interposition is in doubt, and we fear that he is not a principal but an agent, it is in doubt whether he acts once or twice. Furthermore, how does mentioning the word *ribbit* affect anything? If the relation is usurious, circumlocutions don't help; if it's not usurious, one can call it whatever one wishes.

Clearly, this was an emotional qualification to a legal fiction which rested uneasily on Rashi's mind. So long as Rashi treated real situations and *bona fide* parties, though the relationships were economically usurious, he was confident and unqualified in his rulings. But when his principles led him ineluctably to legal fiction, a crucial one which would lift the ban of usury and place Jewish and Gentile financing on an equal footing, legalist and realist that he was, he openly allowed it, yet recoiled from the scene of one Jew handing over interest to another and openly calling it usury. The injunction against *ribbit* was dying, but the simple mention of its name still evoked abhorrence. Half a century or so later, when the next major legal fiction (*torat ha-silluk*) was introduced by Rabbenu Tam, the boldest halakhist of the Middle Ages, he too shied away from explicit reference to the real party to the debt even in a side document to the transaction.[111] Another hundred years had to elapse before this verbal reticence was discarded, and people in the mid- to late thirteenth century could call a licit payment of interest by its real name.[112]

Ma'arufya. The doctrine of legal formalism in matters of usury and |232| the principle of Gentile non-agency were, however, a double-edged sword, and Rashi realized it early in his career. Gentile non-agency meant not only that a Gentile could not serve as an agent to a Jew, but also that he could not appoint a Jew as his agent.[113] This meant that under Jewish law, Jewish administrators of Gentile estates were to be viewed as principals to any transaction, and any

[111] *Or Zarua'*, #202 end, cited below. p. 136.

[112] *She'elot u-Teshuvot Or Zarua' u-Maharam b. Barukh*, #478, recently reprinted in Emanuel, *Teshuvot Maharam u-Venei Doro*, i, #92: וכן ישראל ששלח בידי גוי משכונו או בגדיו או בגדי אשתו לישראל חבירו יכול ליקח הריבית דמצי א"ל ישראל לאו בעל דברים דידי [את] ואין לי עסק [עמך] אע"פ שידע שהיה של ישראל דאי[ן] חילוק בזה... אע"פ שבא ישראל לפדו' ואומ' שיש לו ליתן הריבית, מותר.

[113] *Bava Metsi'a* 71b.

money they lent to other Jews was an intra-Jewish loan and so fell within the ban on usury. Admittedly, no usury was coming 'out of the Jewish administrator's pocket', but formally it was he who was the borrower or the lender and, as such, fell afoul of the usury injunction. Knowledge of trade and finance was relatively rare in feudal and certain ecclesiastical circles at that time, and Jewish expertise had long found there an outlet. The *ma'arufya*, the Jewish factotum or exclusive agent of wealthy Gentiles, played a large role in Jewish economic life in this period,[114] and many a Jewish merchant and tradesman—and pawnbroker, too—received his financing from the good offices of these intermediaries. The ruling of Gentile non-agency would cut the sources of available credit in half, and halve the potential market of these agents and estate managers.

This Rashi perceived early in his career and, perplexed at universal practice[115] yet fearing to disallow something so entrenched and widespread, he dispatched a second inquiry to R. David of Mainz. That authority replied again with an allowance, on the basis of the law that only interest that was paid directly from debtor to creditor (*ribbit mi-loveh le-malveh*) had been forbidden. Rashi could not comprehend this reasoning, for the interest in this case was direct. Since the Jewish manager was viewed as the principal, the money he lent out was his loan and the money he received was a direct payment to the creditor. Yet, deferential, as always, to authority, and not wishing to criticize established forms of activity if they had only some sanction, Rashi ruled likewise. He ruled in this manner in his youth and continued to do so later when he had become famous, though to his inner circle he confided his misgivings.[116] |233|

Summary. The picture which emerges of Rashi's attitude towards usury is of one who sees in the injunction a religious proscription rather than an economic moralism, with a corresponding de-emphasis in his treatment of the real in favor of the formal. If good law was on the side of the genuinely usurious *Schadennehmen*, he championed it vigorously, even characterizing those who forbade it as practitioners of a 'foolish piety'. If but a poor case could be made for the economically innocuous *ma'arufya*, he was then basically opposed. He was unquestionably of a bold bias in favor of allowances to ease

[114] See above, n. 37.

[115] *Teshuvot Ḥakhmei Tsarfat ve-Lotir*, #56; see below, p. 111.

[116] **(A)**

פסק ריב"ן: והשתא אסקינן מילתא [דאין] שליחות לגוי לא אנן לדידהו ולא אינהו לדידן ולית ליה נמי זכייה, הלכך אסור לישראל לקבל מעות מן הגוי ולתנם לחבירו בריבית אפילו העמיד את חבירו אצל הגוי דהאא לית ליה זכייה. ודבר זה שאל ר' את ר' דוד הלוי והתיר לו אפי' לא העמיד חבירו אצל הגוי, ולא אמר טעם אלא משום דלא אסרה תורה אלא ריבית הבאה מיד לוה למלוה, (ור"י) [ור'] נוהג בו היתר על פיו ולבו מגמגם ונוקף.

Jewish credit, if only it was feasible within the accepted canons of halakhic thought. Pledge-sale, *Schadennehmen*, and even the radical straw man all were; *ma'arufya* was not. But his allowances were new, and possessing a temperament devoid of extremism, he confined his judicial constructions to *bona fide* relationships and shied away from the realization of his own legal fiction in its most explicit form.[117] |234|

Eleventh-Century German Thought (*c.*980–1090)

Early on in his career, it will be recalled, Rashi refrained from making allowances out of fear of 'a strong negative reaction [*la'agei safah*]' until he obtained the support of R. David of ha-Levi of Mainz. In the matter of the pawned pawn, extending legal cognizance to property rights in Gentile pawns and admitting a new mode of transfer of debts by transfer of pawns were just the sort of steps that could be taken by a recognized and widely respected jurist, but not by a neophyte, as promising as he may have been. Rashi also encountered opposition when he allowed *Schadennehmen*. As northern France (*Tsarfat*) had few, if any, indigenous traditions, if we seek the source of this opposition we must turn to the Rhineland, the cradle of Ashkenazic culture, in whose famous academies (*yeshivot*) Rashi himself had studied, and which had long provided religious guidance to the Ashkenazic community. |235|

At the dawn of Ashkenazic legal thought, Rabbenu Gershom Me'or ha-Golah (d. 1028) had wrestled with the problem of loans made to Gentiles via Jewish middlemen. Only too often a non-Jew would turn to a Jewish friend or his *ma'arufya* and ask him to obtain a loan at interest from another Jew. Since *ein sheliḥut le-goy* (a Gentile can neither serve as the agent of a Jew, nor commission a Jew to be his agent), Jews could not legally be Gentile agents.

Semak Zurich, ed. Y. Y. Har-Shoshanim (Jerusalem, 1988), iii. 201–2. The text appears anonymously in MS Jewish Theological Seminary, Rabbinica 673, fo. 280 a–b, the latter half of which was published by I. S. Elfenbein, astonishingly enough, as a parallel reading to *Teshuvot Rashi*, #49. See above, n. 42. (B) The concluding phrase would seem to mean לבו מגמגם להלכה ונוקפו למעשה. *Lev* as the seat of the intellect is standard in talmudic literature (W. Hirsch, *Rabbinic Psychology* [London, 1947], 150) and Rashi employs it regularly in his personal remarks. See Y. Avineri, *Heikhal Rashi* (Tel Aviv, 1940–60), i. 269; iv. 125. *Gimgum* means cognitive doubt and disagreement and is frequently joined by Rashi with *lev* (ibid., and vol. i, p. 95). In its second occurrence (with *nokfo*), *lev* is used descriptively. This term, *libo nokfo*, denotes in classical usage a fear of committing a dangerous or forbidden act, though Rashi does employ it as synonymous with *gimgum* in *Rosh ha-Shanah* 25a, s.v. *'edei*. It would be best translated there as 'I fear it be an error'. If it is here being used in its traditional sense, as I believe the case to be, there *may* then be a hint that Rashi personally refrained from benefiting from any *ma'arufya* arrangement; see *Niddah* 3b, 12a, 65b: *libo nokfo u-foresh*.

[117] I have not addressed *Teshuvot Rashi*, #177, as I do not believe it to be authentic for the reasons set forth in the Appendix, note 117.

The Jewish intermediary was perforce a principal, and the loan thus took place in two stages: first, from Jew to Jew, then, from Jew to Gentile. The loan, however, was one at interest, and the first phase was thus forbidden.

Rabbenu Gershom re-established the desired agency by a simple, ingenious construction.[118] True, when the Gentile asked the Jew to |236| obtain a loan, no agency (of acceptance, *sheliḥut le-kabbalah*) was created, for *ein sheliḥut le-goy*. However, Rabbenu Gershom asked, when the Jewish creditor gave the money to the Jewish go-between to give to the Gentile, why should it not be viewed as a commission of agency (of delivery of an object, *sheliḥut le-holakhah*)? The Jewish intermediary was the agent of the Jew to lend his money to a Gentile. In Rabbenu Gershom's construction there was no agency in the request for money, but there was in the giving of the money. The Jewish go-between should be seen not as the agent of the Gentile debtor (as was in fact the case), but of the Jewish creditor. Jurists as a rule do not switch principals in cases of agency for no good reason, do not get up and turn an agent of one party doing one thing (*kabbalah*) into the agent of the opposite party doing another (*holakhah*), unless there are good and pressing considerations. Ashkenazic scholars two generations later inform us that borrowing from and lending to Gentiles via Jewish intermediaries was an accepted and widespread practice.[119] I am inclined to think that this was equally the case some fifty years before, and that Rabbenu Gershom's judicial construction of reverse agency was more the ratification of a widespread contemporary practice than a spontaneous, theoretical allowance which generated a new one.

Rabbenu Gershom's construction won wide acceptance in Germany, but

118 (A) *Shibbolei ha-Leket II*, p. 79, ll. 21–5; new edn. (see Appendix, note 98), p. 169, ll. 1–5; see nn. 140, 141 for references and discussion of the text of Riva's work and its transmission. (*Ve-halveh* is a typographical error for *ve-tilveh*—thus in MS Oxford, Bodley 658, fo. 38a, from which M. Z. Ḥasida published—cf. line 19. The parallel passages in the sources cited below, n. 140, read *u-leveh*.) (B) I have construed the phrase וכן מצא רבי בפסקיו של רבינו הגדול רבינו גרשון (*Shibbolei ha-Leket II*, p. 80, l. 22; new edn., p. 170, l. 19) as referring only to the case of *Hand muß Hand wahren*, ll. 18–21; new edn., ll. 15–18, see Appendix, note 98. From the words that follow *me-hatam nami mashm'a*, it is clear that Rabbenu Gershom also ruled on the case of poor judgment on the part of the agent, discussed by Riva on p. 79, l. 40–p. 80, l. 3; new edn., p. 179, ll. 16–29 (see below, n. 147). One could contend, I suppose, that the intervening discussion of *Schadennehmen* (p. 80, ll. 4–17; new edn., p. 170, ll. 1–15) was also part of Rabbenu Gershom's discussion and to it does the writer refer in the phrase *ve-khen matsa rabbi*. I have declined to do so on principle, though I will be the first to admit that Rabbenu Gershom would have forbidden *Schadennehmen*; see below, n. 138. Attributions should be read strictly and, whenever possible, not expanded beyond the bounds of certainty. (C) I have not employed the text of the responsum found in *Teshuvot Rabbenu Gershom Me'or ha-Golah*, ed. S. Eidelberg (New York, 1956), #25, for the reasons enumerated in the Appendix, note 118.

119 *Teshuvot Ḥakhmei Tsarfat ve-Lotir*, #56.

there were dissenting voices.[120] In Worms some two generations later we hear R. Shelomoh b. Shimshon (Rabbenu Sasson), and most probably R. Yitsḥak ha-Levi, asserting that any such tacit inversion of agency was incorrect. If |237| any such agency was desired then the creditor had to specifically appoint the go-between as his agent. They admitted, however, that people were lending to Gentiles at interest and borrowing from them at interest via Jewish intermediaries without a thought of such appointments. Despite their objections and misgivings, they would not order disgorgement of the interest, even if halakhically it was in order,[121] since in the final analysis, the interest passed from Gentile to Jew and not from Jew to Jew. |238| The halakhic categories of agency, they asserted, did not reflect the economic reality of the case at hand, and enforcement, in practice (if not in theory), should be confined to instances that were genuinely usurious. Interestingly, they called this doctrine of economic realism *ribbit mi-loveh le-malveh* (interest passes directly from debtor to

120 Ibid. (A) The editor, J. Müller, in his introduction (p. 30) correctly attributed the responsum to the above respondents as one of a group of ten replies written to a R. Yitsḥak b. Yitsḥak, as a glance at the manuscript (Jews' College 98, fos. 90b–95a) will indicate. In his notes, especially to section 52, he lapsed into a possible attribution to Rashi, on which basis Elfenbein incorporated it as responsum #79 of his edition of *Teshuvot Rashi*. I make reference to the manuscript because no argument from contiguity can be made on the basis of the printed text, as Müller did not publish the manuscript in its entirety—at times, not even consecutively; see Grossman, *Ḥakhmei Ashkenaz ha-Rishonim*, above, n. 38(*b*), 24. (B) On its authorship, see ibid. 341–2. I have stated that most probably R. Yitsḥak ha-Levi was also a respondent, seeing that we know that R. Sasson consulted with him on a responsum or two in this cluster, and that R. Yitsḥak's son, R. Ya'akov, upheld this position a generation later (see below, n. 123). (C) The anonymous responsum found in *Teshuvot R. Me'ir mi-Rotenburg* (Lemberg), #177, reflects a similar view, denying reverse agency in repayment. The responsum, both in style and in content, appears to be of the 11th century, but I have been unable to ascertain its authorship. Simcha Emanuel of the Hebrew University, the leading authority on the responsa collections of R. Mei'r of Rothenburg, informs me that he has no information as to its source. (The signature at the end, *mi-ketivat yado shel R. Ḥayyim Palti'el*, is actually the heading of the next responsum, as is common in manuscripts and early printings. To give an example from the narrow compass of my study: *Teshuvot R. Me'ir mi-Rotenburg* [Prague and Budapest], #794 is a responsum of Rabbenu Gershom Me'or ha-Golah—see below, n. 129. At the end appears the signature *teshuvat Rabbenu Yitsḥak b. Shemu'el*. This is the heading of the next responsum—see below, n. 197. In situations where an attribution may refer either to a preceding or a subsequent responsum, provenance can be determined only by content. Cf. S. Emanuel, 'Kovtsei Teshuvot Maharam mi-Rotenburg' [MA thesis, Hebrew University, 1988], 78, n. 13.)

121 (A) I have construed the unusual phrase **אבל אין כדי להפקיע הרבית** to mean that the courts should not order restitution of the interest, which is usually called *le-hotsi be-dayyanim*. See a similar use of the phrase, albeit much later, in *Teshuvot ha-Rosh* 108: 26: 2 in the Venice 1607 and all subsequent editions (the responsum is missing from earlier ones). On the loose terminology employed occasionally by pre-Crusade Askenazic Talmudists, see *Yeinam* (above, n. 2), 62–3 and below, p. 121. (B) Line 9 of our responsum should read: **(וגוי) [וישראל] אינו סומך על ישראל [אלא] מה שיתן לו הגוי מרבית יקבל הימנו**, i.e. the Jewish creditor does not rely upon the Jewish intermediary [for payment,

creditor), only in their hands it meant not the legal debtor and creditor, as it did in the hands of Rashi and Rabbenu David, but the actual, fiscal ones, the individuals from out of whose pocket the money comes and into whose pocket the money goes. This is a point to which I will return.

According to the construction of Rabbenu Gershom, the conduct of the Ashkenazic community was wholly in accord with the halakhah, while according to the Worms scholars it left something to be desired. The Ashkenazic community had from the very outset a self-image of religious scrupulousness—though one should not exaggerate this, as some, such as myself, have done[122]—small wonder that Rabbenu Gershom's view carried the day, and other than one brief responsum of R. Yitsḥak's son reflecting his father's views,[123] the Worms doctrine disappeared from the halakhic horizon.|239|

R. Shelomoh b. Shimshon's contemporary, R. David of Mainz, was among those who accepted R. Gershom's ruling, but remained perplexed by the universal practice of invoking it even when a Gentile gave a Jew a loan via a Jewish intermediary. Rabbenu Gershom's construction, he realized, was valid only if a Gentile requested the loan. Then the giving of the money by the Jew could be constructed as a creation of agency. If, however, the Gentile gave *his* money to his *ma'arufya* to lend to another Jew, the latter's acceptance could hardly be construed as agency. A can authorize B to give A's money to C; he cannot authorize B to give C's money to him.[124] Such distinctions, needless to

but knows that] what the Gentile debtor will give of the interest to him [the intermediary], he [the creditor] will receive from him [the intermediary].

122 See my discussion and qualifications in *Ha-Yayin bi-Yemei ha-Beinayim* (above, n. 44), 358–69 and in '"Religious Law and Change" Revisited' (Chapter 10 below).

123 *Teshuvot Ba'alei ha-Tosafot*, #7, and MS Cambridge, Add. 498, fo. 10b. (In the printed text an ellipsis is found in the next to last line, as if to indicate some lacuna. There is no such gap in the MS Jewish Theological Seminary, Rabbinica 673, from which the responsum was taken. The dots there are simply a scribal flourish of the type found in the hundreds in that manuscript.) The query is abbreviated in the above texts. The full transcription is found in MS London, Montefiore 131 of the *Orḥot Ḥayyim, Ḥelek Sheni*. See the addenda of this work, p. 631 (s.v. addendum to p. 465). It is clear from the fuller version that the case under discussion is not an instance of a pawned pawn but the one discussed by Ravan (vol. i, #103), where he allowed receiving interest. He argued that although the payment was from Jew to Jew, the initial debt had been between Jew and Gentile as a consequence of Rabbenu Gershom's doctrine of reverse agency. R. Ya'akov b. Yitsḥak ha-Levi's decision makes sense only if he assumed that the loan legally was from Jew to Jew, i.e. he denied Rabbenu Gershom's construction, as did his father. (Ravan did not mention Rabbenu Gershom as the author of the doctrine of reverse agency for after Riva's discovery and interpretation of the Tosefta, this doctrine became a truism in Germany. See below, pp. 123–4.)

124 To be sure, one could contend that the debtor-to-be commissioned the *ma'arufya* to obtain a loan for him from the Gentile. (Riva in *Shibbolei ha-Leket II*, p. 79, ll. 26–30; new edn., p. 169, ll. 5–10, clearly saw it that way.) Let us, however, remember that in most cases the *ma'arufya* already had the

say, were beyond the people and their needs, and no heed was paid to them. R. David, no less than Rabbenu Gershom, shared the Ashkenazic communal self-image, and his solution was to combine R. Gershom's judicial construction with the talmudic ruling that only interest passing directly from debtor to creditor (*ribbit mi-loveh le-malveh*) was forbidden. True, he reasoned, the recipient of the loan was totally passive and could initiate nothing, and the loan was thus from Jew to Jew. Note, however, the mechanics of the payment: here the Jewish debtor was the initiating party; he gave the money to the Jewish *ma'arufya* and hence could commission agency. And if the debtor could, then he did, by virtue of Rabbenu Gershom's construction. When the Jew returned the money via the Jewish middleman, he did not intend the payment for the middleman—as he never considered him his creditor—but for the Gentile. So in no sense would it be a forced construction to see his giving the money to the intermediary as a creation of agency to pay off the Gentile. Legally, R. David reasoned, money had been lent from Jew to Jew; but repayment had been made, not to the legal creditor, but to a third party (the Gentile). The parties of payment were not those of the loan; interest had thus never passed from debtor to creditor, and the universal practice stayed comfortably within the confines of the permissible.[125]

Rashi, we know, found R. David's ingenious allowance of *ma'arufya* unconvincing. Was this because Rabbenu Gershom's construction of inverted agency was unknown in Champagne country (Rabbenu Gershom's influence in the eleventh century was far less than has been generally supposed[126]) or, as

Gentile's money in his possession. It is stretching judicial construction to its limits to view him now as suddenly obtaining (so as to loan to a would-be debtor) money long in his possession.

125 R. David's invocation of *ribbit mi-loveh le-malveh* cannot be construed as economic usury similar to that of R. Sasson (above, p. 111), seeing that R. David dissented from that definition in his allowance of *Schadennehmen*.

126 Stripped of their polemical exaggerations, Agus's remarks on the restricted influence of Rabbenu Gershom (Agus, *Urban Civilization* [above, n. 37], i. 38–41) are on target, as any unprejudiced reading of the sources will verify. France in the 12th century was still unaware of Rabbenu Gershom's doctrine of reverse agency. See Rabbenu Tam's remarks in *Sefer ha-Yashar*, *Teshuvot*, ed. S. Rosenthal (Berlin, 1898), #76: 7; *Temim De'im*, #157; *Kovets 'al Yad*, 7 (17) (1968), 99, #16 (*ve-tihyeh sheluḥi le-hava'ah/le-havi* in all three texts); *Sefer Yere'im ha-Shalem*, ii, fo. 45, where R. Eli'ezer raises the same question as Riva, namely that the Tosefta contradicted the Bavli's ruling of *le-ḥumra* and, unaware of Rabbenu Gershom's doctrine, he could only emend the text from *mutar* to *asur*. R. Mosheh of Coucy in the mid-13th century (*Semag*, 341, Injunction #199) rejected R. Eli'ezer's emendation and offered an alternative explanation, without any mention of reverse agency. Indeed, to the best of my knowledge, reverse agency never makes an appearance in the French tosafist literature.

For further remarks on the reputation of Rabbenu Gershom in eleventh-century Germany, see the Appendix, note 126.

intimations in the writings of Rashi's pupils may hint,[127] because Rashi had detected some basic flaw[128] as to its |240| application to the case at hand? His diffident decision not to bruit his objections abroad makes it impossible for us to speak with certainty.

Rabbenu Gershom's doctrine of inverted agency formed the basis of R. David's allowance of the *ma'arufya*; another ruling of Rabbenu Gershom will round out our picture of his posture towards usury and, at the same time, throw light on the opposition that Rashi encountered in Troyes in his ruling on *Schadennehmen*.

Rabbenu Gershom was asked to rule on the instance where a Jew had guaranteed to another Jew the loan of a nobleman. The Gentile debtor died prior to repayment and the creditor exacted full payment and interest from the guarantor. He ruled:

> **ושמעון [המלוה] עבר על מה שכתוב לא תקח מאתו נשך ו[תרבית] ובדין הוא שיחזיר שמעון כל הריבית . . . לפי שעכשיו שמת השר ולא פרעו נעשה שמעון מלוה וראובן לוה משום דהוי ערב והוי ליה רבית מלוה למלוה הואיל ולא יצא מכיסו של גוי אסור לשמעון לקבלו וחייב להחזירו דהו[י] ל[יה] רבית קצוצה . . . ואתם אנשי קדש עשו גדר ביניכם שלא יבא הדבר לידי קלקול שלא ילוה אחד ברבית ע[ל] י[די] ערב.**[129]

Shim'on [the creditor] transgressed the pentateuchal injunction (Lev. 25: 36), 'take no usury from him or increase', and Shim'on is duty-bound to return the entire interest . . . For seeing that the nobleman died without paying, Shim'on has become the credi-

[127] Rivan writes (above, n. 116), **אסקינ[ן] מילת[א] דאין שליחות לגוי . . . ולית ליה נמי זכייה, הלכך אסור לישראל לקבל מעות מן הגוי וליתנם לחברו בריבית**. Had there only been a principle of Gentile non-agency, but acquisition (*zekhiyah*) on their behalf were valid, then the *ma'arufya* would be permissible, for the parties to the loan would be Jew and Jew but those of payment Jew and Gentile. Hence Rashi adds that there is no acquisition on their behalf and the payment legally is from Jew to Jew. Rashi thus seems to be aware of the possibility of winning the allowance by focusing on the return path of the money.

[128] That flaw being simply that to pay off another man's debts is to pay him (see *Tosafot*, *Bava Metsi'a* 71b, s.v. *metsa'o*). If the principle of non-agency is admitted on the loan side, then there are two stages—(1) loan from Gentile to Jew and (2) loan from Jew to Jew—and thus Jew 1 is legally in debt to the Gentile. When Jew 2 (the actual debtor) repays the money directly to the Gentile, he pays off the debt of Jew 1, and that is the same as paying him. From *Ravan*, ii, *Bava Metsi'a* 71b, fo. 204b, s.v. *ve-asur* end: *ve-im shagag*, we can see that this aperçu still eluded German scholars a century later. Or it may be that Rashi sensed the textual difficulties that the presumption of inverted agency would create in the talmudic passage in *Bava Metsi'a* 71b, if one assumed, in the case there under discussion, that the repayment followed its natural course (see *Ravan*, i, #103). See the observation of R. Yitsḥak Or Zarua' about Rivan's interpretation of the *beraita*, *yisra'el she-lavah ma'ot min ha-goy*, *Or Zarua'*, #210. Caution must be used since we have not been provided with a verbatim citation.

[129] *Teshuvot R. Me'ir mi-Rotenburg* (Prague and Budapest), #794; MS Bodley 641, fol. 186a, #142; authorship of Rabbenu Gershom in MSS Cambridge, Oo.6.70,1, fo. 105b (gloss); Oxford, Bodley 683, fo. 64b.

tor and Re'uven the debtor, and it [the payment] is usury between lender and creditor [*ribbit mi-loveh le-malveh*] since it does not come out of the Gentile's pocket. It is forbidden to Shim'on to accept it and he must return it, as it is pentateuchally forbidden usury [*ribbit ketsutsah*].

And you, men of holiness, make a fence among yourselves that it lead not to a breach, that one would lend at interest by means of a surety.

Rabbenu Gershom is of the view that with the death of the debtor the surety becomes (retroactively) the debtor, and thus any payment between him and the creditor would be *ribbit mi-loveh le-malveh*.[130] Since the interest 'is not coming out of the Gentile's pocket', the creditor is forbidden to accept it. However, if the debtor does not die but is simply unable to pay, the surety remains but a surety and, strictly speaking, is permitted to pay the debt of a third party, i.e. that of the borrower.[131] Unless preventive action was taken and a fence (*gader*) was erected around what was legally permitted, *ribbit* would be openly practiced by the simple expedient of having a Jew serve as the surety for a penniless Gentile debtor.[132] It was against this eventuality that Rabbenu Gershom warned his interlocutors.

Note Rabbenu Gershom's remark about whose pocket had been emptied by the interest payment. Interest is here strictly enjoined since it 'came out of the Jew's pocket'. Were the payment, in the final analysis, to come from that of the Gentile, Rabbenu Gershom implies that some allowance could be found. This is the same outlook that underlay his bold construction allowing the credit activities of the Jewish *ma'arufya*.[133]

The controlling consideration in Rabbenu Gershom's outlook is whether an economically usurious relationship between two Jews has been created. If no such relationship has sprung into existence, the courts should make every effort to allow the arrangement and construe the formal relations between the parties to reflect the innocuous reality. If, however, *de facto* usury did emerge

130 Rabbenu Gershom's overall position on surety in matters of usury is anything but clear. See my article ''Arev be-Ribbit', *Zion*, 36 (1972), 1–21, esp. pp. 1–6, 20–1. (I have suggested that the new role of 'lender' is retroactive so as to facilitate the holding of *ribbit ketsutsah*.)

131 *Bava Metsi'a* 71a–b: *aval 'atah na'aseh lo 'arev*.

132 Indeed, just such a fiction or its legal equivalent came into use in 13th-century Germany, not for personal profit, but as an aid to the communities in paying the mounting taxes and imposts of their rulers. See *Teshuvot Maharaḥ Or Zarua'*, #168, echoed by R. Ḥizkiyah of Magdeburg in MSS Cambridge, Oo.6.70.1, fo. 103b (gloss); Oxford, Bodley 683, fo. 61b: **על מה שהקהל כשצריך להן מעו[ת], לוים מישר' בריבית ונותן לו גוי ערב ומתירין לו ליקח הרבית. נר' שהורגלו בו מכיו[ן] דדיני דגוי בתר ערב אזיל (ב"מ עב ע"ב) ואם מת הגוי, אין לתבוע מהישר[אל] כלום. ואע"ג שהלוה לו מיד ליד, מ"מ על גוי סמך, ומסתמא לה[י]תר נתכוין**. See below, n. 192.

133 He probably would have invoked the same judicial construction of viewing the Jewish intermediary not as a guarantor but as an agent of the Jewish lender.

between two Jews (what I will call henceforth 'economic usury', as opposed to the formal definition of usury proposed by Rashi), not only was it strictly forbidden, but communal steps should further be taken to forbid arrangements where the formal halakhic categories of 'debtor' and 'creditor' might obscure the unacceptable fiscal realities.

Rabbenu Gershom called economically usurious relations those in which 'moneys come out of the Jew's pocket', which, if we will recall, is exactly the term used by Rashi's interlocutor in describing *Schadennehmen*.[134] When Rashi ruled that *Schadennehmen* was permitted, even though 'it [the money] came out of the Jew's pocket', he was dissenting pointedly from the dominant view of the Rhineland, from the view of Rabbenu Gershom, Rabbenu Sasson, and R. Yitsḥak ha-Levi, all of whom had emphasized the determinative role of the fiscal over the formal. It would scarcely be surprising, then, if a similar conception obtained in Troyes in Rashi's early years, and generated the 'strong negative reaction' (*la'agei safah*) to his allowance, a reaction so strong that Rashi was powerless to overcome it until he found the support of R. David ha-Levi of Mainz, the one Rhineland figure who had broken ranks with the general consensus. Whether R. David's breach was a harbinger or an anomaly, we shall see as we turn to the developments in the Rhineland in the next century. Before doing so, however, we may cast one final glance at Rashi.

Rashi characterized the position adopted by the Troyes opposition as that of a 'pious fool' (*ḥasid shoteh*),[135] a term that conveys a high-minded but irritating obtuseness. The argument of the opposition has not been preserved, and any suggestion as to its nature remains conjectural. However, had it contended, as Rabbenu Gershom had done implicitly—and as his younger contemporary, R. Yitsḥak ben Asher (Riva) of Speyer, was to do explicitly—that the rabbinical ban of *le-ḥumra* was not a penalty (*kenas*) but a fence (*gader*) against *de facto* usury, one might well think the view mistaken, but scarcely obtuse, and certainly not irritating. Though Troyes was far from being a city of scholars,[136] its fund of religious idioms, its stock of halakhic phrases, were one and the same as those of the wider Ashkenazic culture. We have already noted that one of the terms current for economic usury was *ribbit mi-loveh le-malveh*.[137] If Rashi's opponents kept insisting that *Schadennehmen* was

[134] Above, pp. 77–8. [135] Ibid.

[136] The rustic image of Troyes a generation before Rashi emerges from the responsum of R. Yehudah Ba'al Sefer ha-Dinim and of R. Eli'ezer ha-Gadol in the *Kol Bo* (Naples, 1490), #142. (On the date of the responsum, see *Shut ke-Makor Histori* [above, n. 50(*b*)], 99–102.)

[137] It was thus used by R. Sasson and possibly R. Yitsḥak ha-Levi; see above, p. 113. One could argue that Rabbenu Gershom used the phrase similarly in the responsum that we have just discussed

forbidden because it was *ribbit mi-loveh le-malveh*, when to Rashi's mind that norm—when properly understood—was the basis of the allowance, his exasperation is understandable. The battle cry of the disallowers was in fact the very rationale of the practice's permissibility. No amount of argument could suffice to persuade the nay-sayers that *loveh* did not mean a pocketbook or purse, but a legal party. At his wits' end, Rashi did the rarest of all things for him—he uttered a sharp, derogatory epithet. A conjecture on my part, to be sure, but one which allows us to round out our picture of France and Germany in the eleventh century and to turn to their attitude towards usury in the next century, in the age of the Tosafists.

The Tosafist Period

Germany *c.*1090–1225 |243|

A stubborn and unyielding resistance to ever-growing economic pressures is the tale told by halakhic developments in Germany during the next century. This is all the more surprising as this recalcitrant posture was not in the least the consequence of any immanent halakhic development. To the contrary. Rabbenu Gershom had opened halakhic discourse in Ashkenaz with a bold construction to allow genuinely non-usurious transactions. Actual usury between Jew and Jew he would not brook, and he advised communal leaders to repress any subterfuge that might result in one Jew paying interest to another. The Worms court disagreed with his judicial construction but agreed that the courts did not need to force restitution of interest that had ultimately come out of a Gentile's pocket. R. David carried Rabbenu Gershom a step further and allowed *Schadennehmen*—a genuinely usurious transaction—but only within the context of non-fictitious business relationships between Jew and

in the text. The key sentence is concatenated and reads: לפי שעכשיו שמת השר ולא פרעו נעשה שמעון מלוה וראובן לוה משום דהוי ערב והוי ליה רבית מלוה למלוה הואיל ולא יצא מכיסו של גוי אסור לשמעון. By standards of modern Hebrew a *vav* is missing, and one doesn't quite know how to interpret the lengthy, rolling sentence. Does הואיל ולא יצא מכיסו של גוי refer back to the preceding clause or forward to the subsequent one? If to the preceding clause, then 'not coming out of the Gentile's pocket' defines *ribbit mi-loveh le-malveh* (and the next clause should begin [*ve*]-*asur le-Shim'on* etc.) and the phrase *ribbit mi-loveh le-malveh* means economic usury. However, it is equally possible, and I incline to this interpretation, that 'not coming out of the Gentile's pocket' should be joined to the next clause (and the opening word should read [*ve-*]*ho'il*), as it opens a new line of thought, namely, had there not been a usurious relationship, a judicial construction would be in place for its allowance. If so, *ribbit mi-loveh le-malveh* would not be synonymous with de facto usury. The obscurity cannot be clarified by parallel sources, as I have found none in print or manuscript. The summary of Rabbenu Gershom's ruling found in two manuscripts (above, n. 129) is too brief to allow any inference.

Gentile.[138] R. David's |244| position was, in effect, Rashi's point of departure: from there he moved on in time to legal fiction and created the crucial Gentile straw man, hedged at first with emotional qualifications, but very much there all the same. The thrust of eleventh-century thought is from realism to formalism. It moved from viewing usury as an economic moralism—which, to be properly upheld, demanded that the distortions of law should not be allowed to obstruct the flow of legitimate credit, nor illicit credit to be sanctioned by legal ingenuity—to seeing the ban on usury as a purely religious injunction which could be transgressed or annulled by a technicality. I would have expected that beginning, as did Rashi, with R. David's, or even possibly Rabbenu Gershom's, position, German thought would have moved in the same direction. Certainly the economic forces at work for allowance in Germany in the twelfth and early thirteenth centuries were as powerful as those in the eleventh. At the very least, stabilization at the level of permissibility achieved in R. David's time could be anticipated, but hardly a regression.

Riva's Handbook: The Ban on the Straw Man and a Redefinition of the German Posture towards Usury

The work which dominated Ashkenazic thought on these matters for well over a century is a little handbook of Rabbi Yitsḥak ben Asher (Riva) of Speyer (d. before 1133) which, like many other influential works in the Middle Ages, barely escaped with its life.[139] Ravan (R. Eli'ezer b. Natan of Mainz, *c.*1090–1160) based his discussions upon it, and his grandson, the great Ravyah (R. Eli'ezer b. Yo'el, *c.*1140–1225) made an annotated summary of it which achieved wide circulation.[140] So popular did the abridgment become |245| that

[138] I would hesitate to attribute Riva's position on *Schadennehmen* to Rabbenu Gershom. True, in light of Rabbenu Gershom's opposition to any arrangement that entailed interest payment from one Jew to another, a disallowance of *Schadennehmen* on his part would only be natural. However, had there been such an explicit ban by him, I do not think that R. David could have allowed that arrangement with the simplicity that he did. R. David did move away from Rabbenu Gershom's position. However, there is all the difference in the world between overruling a precedent, and a slow, often unconscious, shift in attitude over the course of a generation, which finds expression in ruling on a new case that has just come before the courts. The latter I feel reflects more the atmosphere of the correspondence. If someone feels that I am being over-cautious and wishes to include an injunction against *Schadennehmen* amongst Rabbenu Gershom's decisions, he is quite welcome to do so. See above, n. 118(*b*).

[139] I. Twersky, *Rabad of Posquières* (Cambridge, Mass., 1962), 94–5.

[140] (A) Riva may have written the opening paragraph himself (see below, n. 155(*b*)), but the rest of his thoughts, as is common with the Tosafists, were put in writing under his direction by a pupil. The text has been preserved in *Shibbolei ha-Leket II*, pp. 79–80; new edn., pp. 167–72 (see Appendix, note 98), and in two Provençal collections: the so-called *Ḥiddushei ha-Ritva 'al Bava Metsi'a* (above, n.

by the end of the thirteenth century the original work was forgotten, and was unknown even to such a figure as R. Me'ir of Rothenburg. Fortunately, an Italian with good German contacts picked up a copy in the mid-thirteenth century before it went out of circulation, while another, somewhat fuller, version made its way to southern France, gained a measure of currency, and entered some Provençal collections which have come down to us.

Riva's handbook is a quiet polemic against the new allowances of Rashi and R. David, and at the same time a guide to problems of agency and usury in the pawnbroking business. Besides citing the basic texts (one of them, the Tosefta, newly discovered and now introduced for the first time in halakhic thought[141]) and enunciating the fundamental principles, it discussed the Gentile straw man,[142] the Jewish middleman,[143] *Schadennehmen*,[144] and the problem which was to plague Jewish business and perplex Jewish courts: that of misrepresentation and false fronting.[145] Riva stated and then reiterated his opposition to the allowance of *Schadennehmen* and to the use of a Gentile straw man.[146]

98(*d*)), fo. 40b, and *Temim De'im*, #158. (As copies of the work were circulating in Provence, Me'iri obtained one and, as was his wont, summarized its contents in *Bet ha-Beḥirah 'al Bava Metsi'a*, ed. K. Schlesinger [Jerusalem, 1963], 271–3.) The text of the *Shibbolei ha-Leket* is slightly abridged; see below, nn. 144, 146–7. In addition, it suffers in one place from a *homoioteleuton* (below, n. 162 end). Nevertheless, whenever possible I have referred to it, since the lines in that edition are numbered and the passage more easily found. The attribution found in the *Haggahot ha-Rosh* 5: 54 assigning the entire work of Riva to Rabbenu Gershom should, of course, be discounted. (**B**) Ravyah's summary (with parenthetic notes of his own) is found in *Teshuvot R. Me'ir mi-Rotenburg* (Lemberg), #445–8; *Or Zarua'*, ##212–15; *Mordekhai*, #337 end. Sections of it are also cited in 'Piskei Rabbenu Yosef', in M. Y. H. Blau, ed., *Shitat Kadmonim* (New York, 1992), #306, pp. 384–5. (M. Z. Ḥasida, the editor of the *Shibbolei ha-Leket*, says the original is located in *Ravyah* 1072. I was unable to find anything there or in its environs.) From *Teshuvot, Pesakim u-Minhagim shel R. Me'ir mi-Rotenburg*, ii, *Teshuvot*, #75, it is clear that R. Me'ir knows not of the original text of the Riva, but only of that of the Ravyah.

141 *Shibbolei ha-Leket II*, p. 79, ll. 13, 26; new edn., p. 168, l. 6, p. 169, ll. 6–7. From the context and subsequent discussion it seems clear that Rabbenu Gershom did not cite this Tosefta, but rather it was Riva's discovery. Moreover, had the Tosefta served as the basis of Rabbenu Gershom's ruling, it is difficult to imagine that Rabbenu Sasson of Worms (and possibly Rabbi Yitsḥak ha-Levi) could have dissented without accounting for the Tosefta (see above, p. 111).

142 *Shibbolei ha-Leket II*, p. 79, ll. 8–19; new edn., p. 168, ll. 1–12.

143 Ibid. 79, ll. 21–43; new edn., p. 169, ll. 1–24.

144 Ibid. 80, ll. 3–17; new edn., p. 170, ll. 1–15; continuation: *Temim De'im*, #158, and so-called *Ḥiddushei ha-Ritva*, fo. 40b. See below, nn. 146, 161.

145 *Shibbolei ha-Leket II*, p. 80, ll. 29–49; new edn., p. 171, l. 3–p. 172, l. 2.

146 אבל כשישראל נתחייב מעות לע"א ונתן לו עליהם משכון, התם **ודאי** הע"א מתחילה לצורך ישראל לוה, ואע"ג דאין שליחות לע"א, אפילו הכי כיון שמיד ישראל באו ליד ע"א ולצורך ישראל, **ודאי נראה לר[בי] דאסור** [emphasis added]. In *Temim De'im*, #158 and with minor variations *Ḥiddushei ha-Ritva*, fo. 40b. This reiteration was omitted by the author of the *Shibbolei ha-Leket* at p. 80, l. 17; new edn., p. 170, l. 15 (see above, n. 144; below, n. 161). Note the repetition of the ruling, the repetition of the emphatic

Moving on to a practical plane, he struck out from the strict path of usury to deal with some of the recurrent problems of agency and pawn-lending, such as the measure of good judgment and discretion on the part of the |**246**| agent[147] and the efforts by the creditor to resist redemption of the valuable pledge by pleas of *Hand muß Hand wahren*.[148]

The Gentile straw man, the major fiction for freeing Jewish credit, was disallowed, and the doctrine of a ban on real usurious relations asserted. I would give much to know whether Riva was here opposing established practice, or, as I suspect, the straw man was only a recent innovation, a French one perhaps, which had not yet penetrated too deeply into Rhenish business habits. At any rate a firm 'no' was laid down, and it was certainly maintained as long as Germany preserved her halakhic distinctness and traditions, that is, until the second quarter of the thirteenth century and, most probably, for seventy-five to a hundred years after that.[149] It is noteworthy that Riva does not call usuri-

vaday, and the use of the same emphasis in the first discussion of *Schadennehmen* (l. 11; new edn., l. 8). Riva is clearly polemicizing against an opposite view, i.e. that of Rashi and R. David.

147 *Shibbolei ha-Leket II*, p. 79, l. 40–p. 80, l. 3; new edn., p. 169, ll. 21–9. The Provençal texts, *Temim De'im* and the so-called *Ḥiddushei ha-Ritva* (above, n. 98(*d*)), which are fuller than the abbreviated text of the *Shibbolei ha-Leket* (see preceding note), conclude: *aval mi-shelo asur likaḥ me-'olam*, implying that a matter of usury is at hand. This, however, is difficult to maintain since the initial loan was from Jew to Gentile, so any repayment by the middleman would be payment by a third party and permissible. (See Riva's remarks in the parallel Provençal texts coming after *likaḥeno* at p. 80, 1. 28, or after *litlo* in new edn., p. 172, l. 2, cited by both editors, M. Z. Ḥasida in his notes on p. 81 and S. Ḥasida in his notes ad loc.) It may be that we have the same psychological phenomenon occurring with Riva as was detected in Rashi (above, pp. 106–7). The radical allowance of split interest (see below, p. 124) rests uneasy on his shoulders, and so begin emotional qualifications. This, however, would restrict Riva's remarks on non-payment to matters of split interest and the text does not warrant it. I believe that on this occasion the text in the *Shibbolei ha-Leket* is not an abridgment but is the original one. The point at issue is not the permissibility of payment in view of *ribbit*, but the obligation of repayment on the part of the agent because of poor judgment in the execution of his responsibilities. At least this is how Riva was subsequently understood. Ravan (ii, *Bava Metsi'a* 71b), writing with Riva's handbook before his eyes and paraphrasing it into his work (see below, n. 162), wrote: **וכיון דשליחו של מלוה הוא אם הגוי אנס הוא דלא יהיב רבית אין ישראל השליח חייב ליתן למלוה כלום דהא שלוחו הוא**, and his grandson Ravyah registered his disagreement with the ruling of Riva in this language: **ואפי' אם הגוי אלם ולא יפרע לראובן, יטול שמעון הריבית. אבל אם הזכיר לו שם הגוי האלם הרי ידע שאין דרכו לתת רבית כולי האי, לא יתן ראובן משלו דידע ומחל** (*Teshuvot R. Me'ir mi-Rotenburg* [Berlin, 1891], #56 [p. 20]; *Or Zarua'*, #211; *Mordekhai*, #337; *Teshuvot ha-Rosh* 108: 5).

148 *Shibbolei ha-Leket II*, p. 80, ll. 18–21; new edn., p. 170, ll. 15–18; on *Hand muß Hand wahren*, see above, p. 98. Seeing that the usury paid in the instance of a pawned pawn came out of the Gentile's pocket, Riva naturally allowed the arrangement (p. 80, l. 29 ff.; new edn., p. 171, l. 3 ff.).

149 In the *Or Zarua'* (##202, 209–11) the French and German schools are given an equal hearing. If anything, the emphatic language of Rabbenu Tam (*Or Zarua'*, #202) would carry the day. On the fall of Germanic traditions before the French wave, see my essays 'Can Halakhic Texts Talk History?'

ous relations *ribbit mi-loveh le-malveh* as did his predecessors in the eleventh century. Indeed, while the doctrine of economic usury continued for another century, no one ever again called it by that name. Though failing in his youth to persuade the good burghers of Troyes, Rashi did succeed in persuading posterity that *ribbit mi-loveh le-malveh* was not a principle of bookkeeping but of law, and demanded juridic definition. This is another example of one of Rashi's major contributions to halakhah which we, as the unwitting beneficiaries, take for granted, namely, the establishment of precise terminology for halakhic discourse.[150] Anyone who studies closely the texts of the eleventh century (most of which have only been published within the last century), with their fluid and often opaque terminology, and compares them with the precise language of the post-Rashi literature, will see the difference immediately.

To return to usury. Riva disagreed strongly with Rashi's allowances, yet his language is restrained, to say the least. To be sure, Rashi was an older and much-revered figure, and Riva took care to criticize the position, not the person. His tone, however, is one of intellectual and not of moral disagreement. At stake is the proper understanding of the nature of the passage of *le-ḥumra* in light of the Tosefta (see below), not the allowance of an ethical outrage. One has no sense when reading Riva's dissenting remarks of any clash of basic values. I have used the term 'economic moralism' to describe the position of the Rhineland, but is this an accurate term or is it one mistakenly borrowed from descriptions of the Christian literature against usury? In Latin Europe, at least after the twelfth century, usury took on the visage of legalized theft, pure and simple, and a sin against natural law, an outrage to man's inborn, divinely instilled sense of right and wrong.[151] This generated a passion and intensity

(Chapter 7 below, pp. 221–2) and 'Three Themes in *Sefer Hasidim*', *AJS Review*, 1 (1976), 347–52 (to be published in the third volume of this series). An exception would seem to be R. Barukh of Mainz in his *Sefer ha-Ḥokhmah*, a section of which has been preserved in the *Haggahot Mordekhai*, #439. However, despite the fact that the printed text is corroborated by MS Vienna 72, a *homoioteleuton* has certainly occurred between the word *le-haḥmir* and the words *ve-khen piresh*. All medieval scholars report that R. Ḥanan'el ruled in favor of *le-ḥumra*, and R. Yitsḥak Or Zarua' (#210, end) has been kind enough to reproduce his remarks. After citing Rabbenu Tam's opinion, R. Barukh told of those who disagreed and ruled, ע"כ יש להחמיר, and added, וכן פירש ר' חננאל. The scribe jumped a line from *le-haḥmir* to *le-haḥmir*, with the resultant confusion. For the continuance of the ban of the 'French' straw man into the 14th century, see text below, p. 128.

150 See my remarks in *Yeinam* (above, n. 2), pp. 62–3.

151 See T. P. McLaughlin, 'The Teachings of the Canonists on Usury (XII, XIII, XIV Centuries)', *Medieval Studies*, 1 (1939), 98–125; J. T. Noonan, *The Scholastic Analysis of Usury* (Cambridge, Mass., 1957), 11–38; O. I. Langholm, *Economics in the Medieval Schools: Wealth, Exchange, Money, and Usury according to the Paris Theological Tradition, 1200–1350*, Studien und Texte zur Geistesgeschichte des Mittelalters 29, ed. A. Zimmermann (Leiden, New York, and Cologne, 1992), 48–52, 56–9.

in the preaching on and discussion of the issue that have no parallel in any Jewish source. Even when a doctrine of economic usury is being criticized, as it is here in Riva's handbook, the arguments advanced are so low-key—they do not rise above a reiterated *vaday*—that if the reader is not properly cued to the innovatory rulings of Rashi, he would not notice the critique at all. For over a century, Germany and France disagreed whether to define usury legally or economically, yet at no time do we find in Germany the slightest expression of moral rectitude or hear of any outrage at the iniquitous French allowances. Not encountering any sign whatsoever of two differing moral perspectives, not finding a hint of discordant views on commercial activity, investment, or on the barrenness or productivity of money, we must conclude that usury was not viewed by either culture as a sin against nature, but only as a sin against God's will. Indeed, there is nothing in the talmudic treatment of *ribbit* which would indicate that the taking of interest was inherently unjust. The heavy Jewish involvement in trade and commerce in the high Middle Ages would certainly not have generated any change in this perspective. It is not that Germany held *ribbit* to be a *mishpat* and France took it to be a *ḥok*; in both cultures *ribbit* was but a *ḥok*. The issue that divided them was how to define that which God forbade: by legal or by fiscal categories? Germany's doctrine may be called economic realism; it should not be described, as I have done up to now, as upholding an economic moralism.[152]

Riva's Handbook—Content and Influence, Theory and Practice

The bans on *Schadennehmen* and the Gentile straw man reimposed by Riva were very serious restrictions; at the same time, however, |247| Rabbenu Gershom's construction of inverted agency, which had allowed the uninhibited functioning of the non-usurious Jewish middleman or *ma'arufya*, was reinforced by Riva and raised to the level of a halakhic truism.[153] These two

[152] The central passage reflecting the talmudic attitude towards usury is *Bava Metsi'a* 61a. See the commentators ad loc., esp. *Ḥiddushei Ramban*, ed. I. Z. Meltser (repr. Jerusalem, 1972), s.v. *mikhlal*; ed. E. R. Hishrik (Jerusalem, 2002), 366–8 (note also Ramban's ending); *Ḥiddushei ha-Ritva*, ed. S. Rafael (Jerusalem, 1992), s.v. *mah le-hanakh*. See A. Kirschenbaum, 'Jewish and Christian Theories of Usury in the Middle Ages', *Jewish Quarterly Review*, 75 (1985), 276–89, and my discussion in 'The Jewish Attitude to Usury in the High and Late Middle Ages' (Chapter 5 above).

[153] To be sure, the Tosefta (ed. Zuckermandel, 5: 18, p. 382; ed. Lieberman, 5: 18, p. 91) rejected the practice on the basis of *mar'it 'ayin*, as noted by Riva (p. 79, ll. 30–4; new edn., p. 169, ll. 10–14), who was slightly perplexed by the common allowance. But clearly it did not bother him deeply for his pupil writes: **וגם הוא בעצמו נהוג לעשות כן להלוות לגוי ע"י ישראל**. Anyone possessing any familiarity with history and halakhah knows that few people went to the poorhouse because of the ban of *mar'it 'ayin*.

developments were occasioned by the introduction of the Tosefta into discussion hitherto dominated by the Babylonian Talmud.

The Tosefta had ruled: 'If a Jew said to a Gentile, "Go and lend my money at interest to a Jew", it is forbidden. If a Gentile said to a Jew, "Go and lend my money at interest to a Jew", it is permitted.'[154] It was not in the nature of the Tosafists, nor of any good jurist for that matter, to create controversy where none had existed before or to place the Babylonian Talmud in a position of disagreement with the Tosefta. The alignment of the first half of the Tosefta with the Talmud was not difficult, for it expressed only what the Talmud had said in *le-ḥumra*. However, Riva noted that in the language of the Tosefta there was no mention of stringency (*le-ḥumra*) or of penalty, all of which had provided the opening wedge for Rashi's allowances. The Tosefta spoke the language of a flat, comprehensive injunction which to Riva meant that that, too, was the intent of the Talmud. If so, it meant that the object of the talmudic ban was not complicity, but rather any real usurious relationship between |**248**| Jew and Jew.[155] Seeing that the term *le-ḥumra* had invited Rashi's interpretation of penalty, Riva omitted all mention of the *sugya* in *Bava Metsi'a* and cited the Tosefta and the Tosefta alone. However, how could the second half of the Tosefta be made compatible with the well-known talmudic ruling that Gentiles could not create agency? Only by Rabbenu Gershom's inverse construction! The Tosefta could easily be interpreted very differently and, in other places, it was.[156] But a mind habituated to the doctrine of reverse agency could

[154] *Shibbolei ha-Leket II*, p. 79, ll. 13–14, 26–7; new edn., p. 168, l. 6, p. 169, ll. 6–7. Source: Tosefta 5: 18 (ed. Zuckermandel, p. 382; ed. Lieberman, *Nezikin*, pp. 90–1).

[155] (A) From Riva's language it is clear that he conceived of it as a ban on real usurious relations. The pupil to whom he dictated it realized that all cases in the Talmud and Tosefta contained at least an element of complicity on the part of the debtor. He asked, then, what the case would be if no authorization for a loan from a Jew had been given, i.e. if a usurious situation had been created without the principals being aware of it. To this an anonymous annotator of the *Mordekhai* replied permissively. What Riva's apt pupil had detected was that logically his rulings perhaps contained an element of penalty, but clearly Riva did not view it that way and intended to forbid Jews to pay interest to their co-religionists. (B) In the *Temim De'im*, #158, after *lil'vot* in line 19 of the *Shibbolei ha-Leket II*, p. 79 (new edn., p. 168, l. 12), the signature מר' יצחק is found; the subsequent *mesapka li* is that of the pupil. The continuation in the *Mordekhai*, #337, *ve-li nir'eh de-shari*, is neither a part of Riva's handbook, nor a note of Ravyah (cf. *Teshuvot R. Me'ir mi-Rotenburg* [Lemberg], #445). Indeed, it is not even a remark of R. Mordekhai but of a glossator to the *Mordekhai* as MS Jewish Theological Seminary, Rabbinica 673 fo. 280c indicates: מספקא לן[!]. הג"ה ונ"ל דשרי. Thus the text of the work of Riva found in the *Mordekhai* is a glossed 14th-century copy of a 13th-century abridgment of a work written in the late 11th or early 12th century. The text of Riva's handbook that Me'iri possessed (above, n. 140(*a*)) had Riva's student's question, but not, understandably enough, the anonymous, 14th-century, German response to it.

[156] See the interpretation given by the various authors cited in S. Lieberman, *Tosefet Rishonim*, ii (Jerusalem, 1939), 117; id., *Tosefta ki-Feshutah, Bava Metsi'a*, pp. 223–4 (ad ll. 44–6).

see in the Tosefta's words only validation of the accepted theory and practice and confirmation of the intuition of its forefathers.

With the doctrine of inverted agency now on firm, indeed incontestable, grounds,[157] Riva felt secure enough to expand its allowance to the outermost limits of plausibility. Very frequently a Jewish middleman would receive money from a Jewish creditor at a lower rate of interest than he proceeded to charge the Gentile. Making a profit from services supplied is natural enough, but the different rates of interest made it difficult to view this as anything other than two separate loans, the first of which, being from Jew to Jew, was usurious. Nevertheless Riva permitted it, insisting upon the existence of only a single loan between creditor and Gentile and on the role of the middleman as agent. The interest differential was |249| to be viewed simply as payment for services rendered.[158] But note that it was the Gentile who made the payment. Despite the fact that the Gentile debtor was now paying the middleman that he himself had commissioned, that middleman, Riva now claimed, was still to be viewed as the agent of the Jewish creditor.[159] So long as no usurious situation existed fiscally, Riva was willing to push judicial construction to its outer limits, and, possibly, even a touch beyond.

Turning to the popular and usurious *Schadennehmen*, Riva denied any judicial constructions in favor of its permissibility and thus struck down the previous allowances of Rashi and R. David. If a Jew specifically loaned an object to his Christian creditor to take a loan at interest on his own account from another Jew, then, of course, it was permissible. But if no such explicit loan took place, and the Jew simply gave the pawn to his Gentile creditor to obtain with it a loan from another Jew, then the transaction was to be viewed as agency and was forbidden out of hand.[160] Riva then proceeded to reiterate his doctrine against *Schadennehmen* and the Gentile straw man, and his proscription of economically usurious relations.[161]

Riva had banned the straw man and imposed stringent restrictions on *Schadennehmen* but had, at least, expanded the allowance of Jewish middlemen to cases of varying interest rates. Ravan, the leading spokesman of the next generation, accepted his predecessors' restrictions in full,[162] but added his own

[157] See n. 153.

[158] For the middleman's commissions in percentages, albeit from the creditor, see *Teshuvot Rashi*, #80.

[159] *Shibbolei ha-Leket II*, p. 79, ll. 34–40; new edn., p. 169, ll. 15–21.

[160] Ibid., p. 80, ll. 4–18; new edn., p. 170, ll. 1–15.

[161] *Temim De'im*, #158, so-called *Ḥiddushei ha-Ritva* (above, n. 98(*d*)), ad loc., after what is in the *Shibbolei ha-Leket II*, p. 80, l. 18; new edn., p. 170, l. 15. See above, nn. 144, 146.

[162] *Ravan*, ii, *Bava Metsi'a* 71b. Ravan's writings in *Bava Metsi'a* are a summary of Riva's handbook and his own prior responsa (see *Ravan*, i, #103). Ravan in *Bava Metsi'a* 82a (ed. Ehrenreich, fo.

restriction on transactions with differing rates of interest on the basis of another newly discovered Tosefta. Ravan's grandson, R. Eli'ezer b. Yo'el, the last great representative of the German school, made, as I have already remarked, the popular abridgment of Riva's handbook and would appear to |250| have concurred, generally, with the rulings it contained.[163] We know at least from his other writings that he fully endorsed the ban on the Gentile straw man in the face of attempts by the great Rabbenu Tam to allow it.[164]

The twelfth century witnessed an ever-growing dependence of the Jew upon moneylending; yet the course of German thought was, in general, in the direction of stringency. One old allowance (*Schadennehmen*) was struck down, as was a new one (the Gentile straw man); another (reverse agency) was validated, expanded, retracted, and, finally, perhaps expanded again; but new and necessary allowances were consistently denied. The posture of the German Tosafists towards usury, towards reality itself, while perhaps not as quixotic as that of Rashbam—who, as we shall see, forbade all the above and the *ma'arufya* too—was, nevertheless, still measured and stubborn, and governed more by text and logic than by experience.

205b–c) seems no more ready than Riva to draw new conclusions from the Tosefta (above, n. 154, at ll. 24–5) as to the controlling role of *aḥarayut* in determing the identities of debtor and creditor in a loan, as does later, for example, R. Yitsḥak of Corbeil in his *'Amudei ha-Golah*, more commonly known as *Semak* (Constantinople, 1509), #259; (Satmar, 1935), #260. (The numerous editions of *Semak* show a fluctuation of three or four in the section numbering, e.g. #259 in one edition may be anywhere from 258 to 263 in another.) Riva's analysis of a loaned pawn was continued, apparently, by the anonymous respondent in *She'elot u-Teshuvot Or Zarua' u-Maharam b. Barukh*, #479, recently reprinted in Emanuel, *Teshuvot Maharam u-Venei Doro*, i, #93. Note, however, his restrictive proviso towards the end, **עד כדי דמיו של חפץ**, which may or may not be a consequence of Riva's remark in the *Temim De'im* and *Ḥiddushei ha-Ritva*: **והרי הוא עכשיו כמו שמוכרו לישראל בקרן ובריבית**, a conclusion that Riva himself never drew. (The passage in the two Provençal texts is found after the penultimate word in l. 18 of p. 80 in the *Shibbolei ha-Leket II*. Its absence from the latter work is simply the result of a *homoioteleuton* of *u-ve-ribbit*.)

[163] Ravyah's abridgment (as distinct from his own writings) is found in *Mordekhai*, ##337–8 (Vilna edn., p. 156a–b); *Teshuvot R. Me'ir mi-Rotenburg* (Lemberg), ##445–8; *Or Zarua'*, ##211–15. At the end of the abridgment he appended the following note (*Mordekhai*, #338, Vilna edn., p. 156b, l. 1): **ע"כ שורש דבריו והוא האריך ואני קצרתי ובמקצת הפסקים האלו לבי מהסס ויש להשיב והמשכיל יבין**. We know from his other writings (cited above, n. 147 end) that he differed in the assessment of the responsibility of the agent for poor judgment and, more significantly, in the thorny problem of false fronting. I assume that it is to these rulings that he referred. If he had other reservations they were not very strong ones, as he never bothered to enunciate them. His two pupils, the one who transcribed his rulings that appear in *Teshuvot R. Me'ir mi-Rotenburg* (Lemberg) and the great R. Yitsḥak Or Zarua', felt justly free to omit his qualifying note altogether.

[164] *Or Zarua'*, #210; *Teshuvot R. Me'ir mi-Rotenburg*, ed. M. A. Bloch (Berlin), #56, (p. 20). Note his language: **מיהו נראה דאזלי' לחומרא, גם (בפרקי) [בפסקי] זקיני פסק כדברי**. He does not concur with past decisions; he feels rather that they coincide with his.

So much for German thought, but what of practice? Did the German community uphold the restrictive doctrines of its tradition and deny itself the unfettered access to Jewish capital that the Gentile straw man provided? Our evidence is entirely indirect, and it seems to point, surprisingly enough, to overall compliance throughout the tosafist period, that is, through the first decade of the fourteenth century.

The descriptions of moneylending in the writings of Ḥasidei Ashkenaz speak of intra-Jewish loans only by means of the cumbersome, *commenda*-like arrangement, *maḥatsit sekhar, maḥatsit hefsed.*[165] There is never a mention of any Gentile straw man. Indeed, from the tale told in #1423 of the subterfuges of the cunning Jew who seeks to lend his surplus cash to other Jews and must deceive them as to its origins, it is clear that the writer is not even aware of the stratagem of the straw man. Otherwise, a simple and legitimate avenue would have presented itself to the would-be lender at interest. In the writings of the German Pietists, usury does not figure as one of the serious breaches in religious observance or ethical conduct. To be sure, there are references to such violations, but they are few in number and without any intensity or resonance.[166] Unlike dishonest business practices or sexual relations with Christian women, against which the Pietists railed constantly, violation of the *ribbit* injunction does not loom in their writings as one of the widespread sins of the time.[167]

One might yet write this off as a quirk of the Pietists (which I scarcely think it is); however, the absence of the Gentile straw man in twelfth-century Germany would explain the strange pattern of discussion of 'misrepresentation'. From the days of Riva on, the German authorities wrestled with the problem of borrowing under false pretenses. A Jew would approach his co-religionist and present himself as an agent for a Gentile needing a loan and offer the Gentile's pawn as security. When the bill became due, he would announce that there was no Gentile: the pawn was his, and payment of interest

[165] (A) Roughly put: *maḥatsit sekhar maḥatsit hefsed* is a silent partnership where one partner invests funds and the other manages them. The manager receives a percentage of the profits and is responsible for some of the loss. The percentage for which he is responsible in case of loss is, in effect, a loan. The manager's service to the investor, if performed gratis, would be *ribbit*. The manager, therefore, must be paid for his service. This may be done outright by his receiving a salary or by giving him a greater percentage of the profit than that of his silent partner (two-thirds to one-third, for example), while the percentage of the losses is split equally between the two. See also Finkelstein's note cited below, n. 171. (B) *Sefer Ḥasidim*, ed. Y. Wistinetzki, 2nd edn. (Frankfurt am Main, 1924), ##864, 889, 774, 1205, 1209, 1233, 1678, 1682. Note the wide spread of the texts. They are not taken from one or two scrolls (*megillot*) of *Sefer Ḥasidim*.

[166] Ibid. ##111, 1232, 1295, 1422; see below, n. 193.

[167] As to the alleged opposition of the German Pietists to any form of interest taking, see 'The Jewish Attitude to Usury' (Chapter 5 above).

was therefore out of the question as it would constitute usury. No one wanted him to get away with his ruse, yet, on the other hand, how could the courts enforce payment of interest if the claimant could demonstrate, as he usually could, that he was now telling the truth? Things got so bad that there was even a communal ordinance dealing with the problem. In France, on the other hand, with two peripheral exceptions, there is no mention of the problem[168]—certainly no mainstream discussion of it, which is very puzzling. In the course of several centuries, cases of misrepresentation did crop up in France, but they were not endemic to business enterprise. It was not a recurrent problem that one had to expect and address beforehand, as in Germany.

[168] Misrepresentation: *Riva in Shibbolei ha-Leket II*, p. 80, ll. 29–49; new edn., p. 171, l. 3–p. 172, l. 2; *Teshuvot R. Me'ir mi-Rotenburg* (Prague and Budapest), #737, taken from the *Sefer ha-Ḥokhmah* of R. Barukh of Mainz (Emanuel, 'Teshuvot R. Me'ir mi-Rotenburg' [above, n. 54], p. 159, n. 46); MS Jewish Theological Seminary, Rabbinica 673, fo. 280d (it is clear from that passage that R. Eli'ezer of Metz never discussed misrepresentation; rather, the aforementioned R. Barukh inferred his position from his remarks in *Bava Metsi'a*); MS Hamburg, Staats- und Universitätsbibliothek 45, fo. 155; *Teshuvot, Pesakim u-Minhagim shel R. Me'ir mi-Rotenburg*, ii, *Teshuvot*, #79 (and see ##76–8, 80–1); Emanuel, *Teshuvot Maharam u-Venei Doro*, i, #363; *Teshuvot ha-Rosh*, 108: 1, 3, 11, 12, 31. Communal ordinance: *Mordekhai*, #338 end (Vilna edn., p. 156b near bottom). France: MS Hamburg, Staats- und Universitätsbibliothek 45, fo. 183c–d, recently published in Emanuel, *Teshuvot Maharam u-Venei Doro*, ii, #411; MS London, Montefiore 108, fo. 102b; R. Menaḥem Vardimas cited in *Teshuvot Maharaḥ Or Zarua'*, #180. (Norman Golb's claims for the importance of this scholar in his *Jews of Medieval Normandy: A Social and Intellectual History* [Cambridge, 1998], 387–97 and *passim*, should be taken with a grain of salt. Suffice it to say that this Talmudist's name is never mentioned in either Urbach's *Ba'alei ha-Tosafot* [above, n. 11], or in S. Emanuel's *Shivrei Luḥot: Sefarim Avudim shel Ba'alei ha-Tosafot* [Jerusalem, 2007]). *Piskei Rabbenu Ri mi-Corbeil*, in *Sefer Ner li-Shema'ayah: Sefer ha-Zikaron le-Zikhro shel ha-Rav Shema'ayah Sha'anan* (Benei Berak, 1988), 14, #18. (The variant *ha-ribbit ve-ha-shevaḥ 'al ha-mashkon*, cited in n. 34 from MS Paris, Bibliothèque Nationale 380, is the consequence of a gloss creeping into the text. The text originally has just *shevaḥ*, which is a translation of *lucrum*, i.e. usury, a term used frequently in the *shetarot* of English Jews. See M. D. Davis, *Hebrew Deeds of English Jews* [London, 1888], 29, 31, 54, 64, and *passim*. A scribe glossed *shevaḥ* as *ribbit* and the gloss subsequently entered the text.) On the various editions of the *Piskei Ri mi-Corbeil*, see S. Emanuel, *Shivrei Luḥot*, 201–7. The passage here under discussion is reproduced by Emanuel at p. 203. (I have difficulty identifying R. Yitsḥak of Corbeil's teacher, R. David, with R. David of Metz as Urbach contends in *Ba'alei ha-Tosafot* [above, n. 11], 571. The time frames do not match.) Despite the language of R. Me'ir of Rothenburg in *Teshuvot, Pesakim u-Minhagim shel R. Me'ir mi-Rotenburg*, ii: *Teshuvot*, #78, a close examination of the writings of the French school shows that Rabbenu Tam never ruled on misrepresentation. R. Me'ir inferred his position on misrepresentation from Rabbenu Tam's remarks about *prozbol hayah li ve-ne'evad* (*Gittin* 37a). Seeing that a distinctive German halakhic culture ceased to exist by the second quarter of the 13th century (above, n. 149), one might ask why misrepresentation is still found in the responsa of R. Me'ir of Rothenburg some forty to fifty years later. The answer is that the history of misrepresentation stretched back for 100 to 150 years in Germany, and entrenched practices don't die quickly. Moreover, it is far from clear that the German resistance to the Gentile straw man crumbled in the second quarter of the thirteenth century. See text below, p. 128.

The difference is easily explained, however, if Germany actually refrained from using the Gentile straw man while France employed it, for the social and commercial penalties for misrepresentation would be radically different in the two countries. If one could readily obtain credit at interest from another Jew, the attempt to acquire the money without interest was outright fraud. Few businessmen thought that money thus obtained was worth their reputation. If, on the other hand, no Gentile straw man was available, there was no simple and direct way of getting credit from other Jews. As the payment of interest is precluded in these circumstances, and as no one lends money for nothing, misrepresentation took on a wholly different visage. The ruse, one could claim, was employed not because its practitioner wished to deprive another of his just profit, for he would gladly have rendered his due—had it only been permissible. The lender was a victim of circumstances. He needed money badly and, regrettably, no other way to obtain it was available other than by misrepresentation.[169] One could be believed or not, but that was a risk that some were willing to take. Thus, the question of misrepresentation arose in Germany and not in France.

In the second quarter of the thirteenth century French influence rose appreciably, and Germany as a distinct halakhic culture began to disappear.[170] People began employing the Gentile straw man, and against this new and growing practice was directed, around the year 1220, one of the decrees of the famous Rhineland communities, Speyer, Worms, and Mainz, known as the *Takkanot Shum*: 'One should lend to his fellow Jew [at interest] only by means of *mahatsit sekhar, mahatsit hefsed*.' How effective the ordinance was we do not know; what we do know is that Rabbenu Asher (Rosh), writing in Spain in the first quarter of the fourteenth century, speaks of the Gentile straw man as a misguided practice of the French Jews. It may well be that the German community held fast to the old injunctive outlook of its founders throughout the era of the Tosafists. Despite a very heavy dependence by the mid-thirteenth century on moneylending for their economic survival, many, perhaps even most, German Jews declined to avail themselves of the major allowance of intra-Jewish credit throughout that century and into the next.[171]

[169] Note the language in *Teshuvot R. Me'ir mi-Rotenburg* (Prague and Budapest), #737: **והטעיתיך מפני אונסי**, and that of Riva (*Shibbolei ha-Leket II*, p. 80, ll. 30–1; new edn. p. 170, ll. 3–4): **ישראל שנצרך למעות ולא היה יכול ללוות על ערבונו מישראל בלא ריבית.**

[170] See above, n. 149.

[171] (A) L. Finkelstein, *Jewish Self-Government in the Middle Ages* (repr. New York, 1964), 225. For the meaning of the Hebrew term, see above, n. 165(*a*), and Finkelstein's remarks at p. 234, n. 1. The ordinance against allowing Gentiles to tread the grapes used in the making of Jewish wine, p. 225, was equally directed against the growing French influence; see my essay 'Can Halakhic Texts Talk

Twelfth-Century French Thought: Rashbam, Rabbenu Tam, and Ri |251|

Rashbam's Reversion

In France things fell out quite differently. There was a momentary, sharp reversion to the old injunctive view of the Rhineland which was followed by a sustained, open, and avowed quest for allowance, almost to the point of halakhic abdication. The change in direction of French thought was, in all probability, due to the towering figure of Rabbenu Tam, who, with his intense awareness of people's needs and his unparalleled boldness in acting out his convictions,[172] determined in *ribbit*, as in so many other areas of halakhah, both the general attitude of the Tosafists and the main direction of their thought |241|.[173]

Rashi had rendered tacit deference to entrenched business practice and also to the traditions of the Rhineland academies in which he had studied by not challenging the commercial dealings of the ubiquitous Jewish manager or *ma'arufya*. His grandson, pupil, and amanuensis, Rashbam (*c.*1080–1140), neither had Rashi's awareness of the need for occasional forbearance nor felt that he owed the academies of Mainz and Worms any compliance. Seeing no justification for the *ma'arufya*, he forbade this lending out of hand. That not being enough, he broke away from Rashi's interpretation of *le-ḥumra* as a penalty imposed upon the creditor, and saw it as a general fence against any real usurious relations between Jew and Jew. Thus he struck down the central legal fiction of the Gentile straw man, hobbled Jewish managership, tied up Jewish credit, and obstructed any possible fronting with Gentile money,[174] all this in a period when moneylending was fast becoming the staff of Jewish

History?' (Chapter 7 below, pp. 214–15). (B) See *Teshuvot ha-Rosh*, 108: 11: *ve-da' ki ha-tsarfatim be-artsenu nohagim kula be-ribbit, u-ve-maklo yaggid lo* (Hosea 4: 12), *ki amru Rabbenu Tam amar . . .*

172 (A) S. Albeck, 'Yaḥaso shel Rabbenu Tam li-Ve'ayot Zemano' (above, n. 33(*a*)), 104–41; Urbach, *Ba'alei ha-Tosafot* (above, n. 11), 60–113. One need not agree fully with their respective portraits to admit the truth of Rabbenu Tam's social awareness and boldness of thought and deed. On Urbach's portrait of Rabbenu Tam, see H. H. Ben-Sasson, 'Hanhagatah shel Torah', *Beḥinot*, 9 (1956), 46–9. (B) One could, of course, attribute it in part to Rashi's spirit (see above, pp. 108–9); personally, I doubt it.

173 At this point I have slightly restructured the essay and moved some material here from earlier pages. This explains the disruption in the original page numbering.

174 Jewish fronting at this early date was probably not so significant an enterprise in France as it became in the latter half of the century, when influential religious figures began a vigorous campaign against any Christian lending at interest. See Schaub, *Der Kampf gegen den Zinswucher* (above, n. 96), 143–51; J. W. Baldwin, *Masters, Princes, and Merchants: The Social Views of Peter the Chanter and his Circle*, i (Princeton, 1970), 296–343, and my essay, 'The Jewish Attitude to Usury' (Chapter 5 above), nn. 29–34.

life.[175] The rulings of Rashbam should put us on our guard against any facile equation of halakhic developments and economic realities. There are times and temperaments when halakhists will insist upon legal purity in the face of all the facts. Yet when they do attempt to |242| turn back the tide, they should not be surprised if their words, like those of Rashbam, become engulfed and their wreckage first surfaces some two hundred years later.[176]

Rabbenu Tam and Le-ḥumra |251|

Rashbam had forbidden the use of the Gentile straw man, and if many did not change their ways as a consequence of his ruling, there were those who did, and not without hardship. Others felt uneasy at the use of a legal fiction and resorted to it only reluctantly.[177] Moreover, even Rashi's allowance was prov-

[175] I incline to the view of Chazan and Stow that the major involvement of French Jews in moneylending had occurred by the 1140s. See R. Chazan, *Medieval Jewry in Northern France: A Political and Social History* (Baltimore and London, 1973), 33–4; K. Stow, *Alienated Minority: The Jews of Medieval Latin Europe* (Cambridge, Mass., 1992), 216. Salo Baron delays their deep involvement in this field until after the Third Crusade; see his *Social and Religious History of the Jews* (above, n. 104), iv. 206.

[176] (A) A headless fragment of Rashbam's work is found in *Teshuvot R. Me'ir mi-Rotenburg* (Lemberg), #444 (corroborated by MS Parma, de Rossi 651, fo. 151b–d, #495). The anonymous torso may be identified by comparing it with Rivan's remarks cited above, n. 116. Rashbam here, as on other occasions, took his uncle's commentaries as the basis for his work, correlated them with remarks of R. Ḥanan'el, struck out *ve-rabbi noheg bo heter*, and wrote in its place *ve-ḥas ve-shalom ein linhog heter ba-davar*. The fact that Rashbam refers to Rashi as *rabbi zekeni* and not *rabbi*, as in his commentary on *'Avodah Zarah*, corroborates my impression that this piece was not written under Rashi's tutelage. (See e.g. the language of Rashbam cited by the so-called *Tosfot Shants 'al Makkot* [Benei Berak, 1973], 20a, s.v. *ve-'al*.) Indeed, the citations of R. Ḥanan'el would indicate that it was composed after Rashi's death. On Rashbam's use of Rivan's work, see Chapter 7, 'Can Halakhic Texts Talk History?', below, n. 31.

Emanuel has conjectured (*Shivrei Luḥot* [above, n. 168], 97, n. 202) that #444 in *Teshuvot R. Me'ir mi-Rotenburg* (Lemberg) was originally found in Ravyah's *Sefer Avi'asaf*, seeing that the next three sections in the Lemberg collection are taken from that work; see above, n. 140(*b*). If this conjecture be proven correct, my formulation will have to change from 'their wreckage first surfaces' to 'make a solitary appearance in a lost work of Ravyah'. (B) Needless to say, one cannot assume that since the concluding section of Rashbam's remarks was taken from Rivan, the same holds true for the preceding ones—the doctrine of *le-ḥumra* and the disallowance of a straw man all militate against such an arbitrary assumption. See also *Or Zarua'*, #210, for Rivan's interpretation of the *beraita*, which Rashbam does not reproduce. (As to the latent problem of the undisclosed principal, see *Bava Kamma* 102b, *Teshuvot R. Me'ir mi-Rotenburg* [Prague and Budapest], #285. *She'elot u-Teshuvot Or Zarua' u-Maharam b. Barukh*, #481, recently reprinted in Emanuel, *Teshuvot Maharam u-Venei Doro*, i, #94, is unique and clearly tendentious.)

I do not believe that Rashbam's position is related to Christian–Jewish polemic, nor do I think that the re-emergence of Rashbam's position in the 13th century is related to the decline of the *ma'arufya*. I have set forth my reasons for these views in the Appendix, note 176.

[177] *Or Zarua'*, #202; *Teshuvot R. Me'ir mi-Rotenburg* (Prague and Budapest), #796; MSS Cambridge, OR 786, fo. 183c–d; Oxford, Bodley 641, fo. 187a, #144; *Mordekhai*, #338: **הרי לך שאין המלוה על הלוה כלום ואין כאן הערמה . . . למען דעת כל אדם שהוא היתר גמור**. See below, p. 133.

ing inadequate in many cases. Rashi had demanded that the creditor should remain in ignorance as to the agency of the Gentile and genuinely believe that the latter was acting on his own initiative. But in the tiny Jewish communities pawned items could often be identified, as could the Gentile helper who was frequently sent to pick up the loan. When a Jew needed credit to take advantage of a business opportunity, he would have to wait around until he could find a Gentile willing to serve as his intermediary. He could not call immediately upon his household staff.[178] Such delays were intolerable and often fatal.

Witnessing the growing dependence of his people on moneylending, Rabbenu Tam (d. 1171), |252| with characteristic boldness, sought to wipe *le-ḥumra* off the books, asserting that it had only been a temporary supposition by the Talmud rather than a final conclusion.[179] This was one of Rabbenu Tam's most tendentious doctrines. The ruling of *le-ḥumra* had won universal assent among talmudic commentators for it had been framed as a *bi-shelama* (roughly translated: 'we well understand that . . .'). When posing a question, the Talmud often says—indeed, the Bar Ilan Responsa Project gives no fewer than 1,265 instances of it in the Bavli—'we well understand A, but B is problematic'. The matter well understood, the subject of a *bi-shelama* is invariably something agreed upon by all. Rabbenu Tam demonstrated that there is an instance in tractate *Yevamot* where the subject of a *bi-shelama* proves to be

178 *Teshuvot R. Me'ir mi-Rotenburg* (Lemberg), #444: **אסור לישראל לומר לעבדו עכו"ם קח משכון ולוה עליו מעות בריבית מישראל**. *Or Zarua'*, #202: **שיתן הלוה המשכונות ליד גוי ואפי' עבדו ושפחתו**.

179 (A) *Bava Metsi'a* 71b; see above, p. 72, and n. 40 ad loc. (B) *Sefer ha-Yashar*, ed. S. F. Rosenthal (Berlin, 1898), #76: 7; *Temim De'im*, #157; *Sefer Yere'im ha-Shalem*, i, 88–9; *Semag*, 341, Injunction #191; *Tosafot*, *Bava Metsi'a* 71b, s.v. *ke-gon*; *Tosfot ha-Rosh 'al Bava Metsi'a*, ed. M. Hershler and Y. D. Grodzinski (Jerusalem, 1959), 71b, s.v. *ke-gon*; *Tosfot R. Perets 'al Bava Metsi'a*, ed. H. B. Hershler (Jerusalem, 1970), 71b, s.v. *shenatan*; *Or Zarua'*, #210; *Rosh* 5: 54; *Teshuvot ha-Rosh* 108: 4, 11; *Haggahot Mordekhai*, ##438, 456; *Haggahot Maimuniyot*, 'Hilkhot Malveh ve-Loveh', 5: 4, n. 6. (C) R. Me'ir of Rothenburg's position in *Teshuvot, Pesakim u-Minhagim shel R. Me'ir mi-Rotenburg*, ii, #75, cannot be adduced as supporting Rabbenu Tam. R. Me'ir's inclination to allowance at the end of his responsa is based upon the new, 13th-century awareness of the determinative role of parties to the collection (*geviyah*) in determining the parties to the debt. See my *Halakhah, Kalkalah* (above, n. 1), 82–97. I do not understand the remarks of R. Me'ir of Rothenburg in his *Ḥiddushim* cited by the *Haggahot Maimuniyot*, ibid. (D) The problematic text of the *Haggahot Mordekhai*, #456, in which R. Eli'ezer of Metz supports the position of Rabbenu Tam, though corroborated by MS Jewish Theological Seminary, Rabbinica 674, fo. 42a, is most probably, as R. Eliyahu of Vilna suggested, the product of an elision. See *Haggahot ha-Gra* on 'Hilkhot Malveh ve-Loveh', 5: 4, n. 6, in *Yad ha-Ḥazakah, Mishpatim*, ed. S. Frankel (Jerusalem, 1989). (E) One should add that there is no indication whatsoever that Rabbenu Tam based his doctrine on the Yerushalmi; see *Ḥiddushei Ramban 'al Bava Metsi'a*, ed. E. R. Tselniker et al. (Jerusalem, 2002), 71b, s.v. *ela*. (F) The doctrine formulated by the anonymous respondent in *Teshuvot u-Fesakin me'et Ḥakhmei Tsarfat ve-Ashkenaz*, #124, is highly original; it is not based, however, on Rabbenu Tam's position. (See Lieberman's interpretation of the Tosefta in light of the Yerushalmi; above, n. 40.)

incorrect. Let us grant Rabbenu Tam his point;[180] all it proves is that there is a very distant *possibility* that here *le-ḥumra* is only a talmudic hypothesis. How does Rabbenu Tam know that this is in fact the case? The odds are over a thousand to one that it is not. There is no difficulty whatsoever in the *sugya* which would lead us to conclude or even make us suspect that the *bi-shelama* of *le-ḥumra* is rejected. Not surprisingly, subsequent opinion in France tended to reject Rabbenu Tam's radical position.[181]

However, the doctrine did answer people's needs, and it found a wide following. In England, where dependence among the Jewish community on moneylending was almost universal, the unqualified use of the straw man seems to have become, by the mid-thirteenth century, the standard form of intra-Jewish credit.[182] As the community in England was but an offshoot of the French one, it is not surprising to discover that its practices only reflected those of the homeland.[183]

[180] Even that was questioned; see *Teshuvot ha-Rosh*, 108: 11.

[181] Despite R. Yitsḥak Or Zarua's remarks (#214) I believe that R. Shimshon of Sens simply endorsed Rabbenu Tam's views on *le-ḥumra*. Text in *Or Zarua'*, #214; *Teshuvot R. Me'ir mi-Rotenburg* (Prague and Budapest), #797; MS Cambridge, Or. 786, fo. 183b; MS Oxford, Bodley 641, fo. 187b; Oxford, Bodley 692, fo. 229b, #208; *Mordekhai*, #338; *Shibbolei ha-Leket II*, p. 82; new edn., p. 174; *Teshuvot Maharam*, MS Parma, de Rossi 86, fo. 6b, #8; *Teshuvot Rashi*, #367. Little significance need be attached to Recanati's report of R. Shimshon of Sens (*Piskei Halakhot* [Bologna, 1538], #339). The author was far removed in time from the period under discussion and cannot always be relied upon. See e.g. his immediately following remark about R. Me'ir of Rothenburg and R. Me'ir's own writings in *Teshuvot, Pesakim u-Minhagim shel R. Me'ir mi-Rotenburg*, ii, *Teshuvot*, #75; though see R. Me'ir's problematic remarks in his *Ḥiddushim*, cited in the *Haggahot Maimuniyot*, 'Hilkhot Malveh ve-Loveh', 5: 6 (see n. 179(*d*)). Other than R. Shimshon of Sens's approval, the doctrine is generally rejected in the sources cited in n. 177. To the large group of rejectionists, one should add the anonymous ר' (most probably R. Yeḥi'el of Paris) in MS Hamburg, Staats- und Universitätsbibliothek 45, fo. 183c; recently published in Emanuel, *Teshuvot Maharam u-Venei Doro*, ii, #411 (see below, Appendix, note 189).

[182] (A) Davis, *Hebrew Deeds of English Jews* (above, n. 168), 70–4; J. M. Riggs, *Select Pleas, Starrs and Other Records from the Rolls of the Exchequer of the Jews, A.D. 1220–1284*, Publications of Selden Society, 14 (London, 1902), 65; Rabinowitz, 'Some Remarks' (above, n. 38), 49–59; Stein, 'The Development of the Jewish Law of Interest' (above, n. 33), 35–7. (B) I have not addressed R. Ya'akov of Orleans's allowance remedy found in the *Haggahot Mordekhai*, #455, as it seems to have been without any influence; see the Appendix, note 182.

[183] (A) *Tosfot R. Perets 'al Bava Metsi'a* 69b, s.v. *lo: nahagu le-halvot be-ribbit le-yisra'el 'al yedei goy*; *Teshuvot, Pesakim u-Minhagim shel R. Me'ir mi-Rotenburg*, ii, *Teshuvot*, #75: *u-ve-khol Tsarfat nahagu le-hatir ke-divrei ha-Tosafot*; and the disapproving remarks of Rabbenu Asher, writing in Spain (*Teshuvot ha-Rosh* 108: 11): *ve-da' ki ha-tsarfatim be-artsenu nohagim kula be-ribbit, u-ve-maklo yaggid lo* (Hosea 4: 12), *ki amru Rabbenu Tam amar*. (B) See A. M. Fuss, 'Inter-Jewish Loans in Pre-Expulsion England', *Jewish Quarterly Review*, 65 (1975), 229–35. A simpler reading of the English documents would construe it as a prior, anticipatory authorization of *Schadennehmen*, in which all three parties will be Jews; whence the need for a Gentile straw man in accordance with the doctrine of Rabbenu Tam.

Rabbenu Tam and the Proclamation of Silluk *(Renunciation, i.e. Non-Relationship between the Parties)*

We come now to a second step taken by Rabbenu Tam, the *silluk* doctrine. Let us first address its target audience. The doctrine was announced in a proclamation whose candor has no parallel in the medieval talmudic literature. He began by openly avowing that he was instituting a radical judicial construction in order to provide much-needed economic relief for the Jewish community: **נראה בעיני היתר גמור ומצוה מן המובחר לתת מחייה לבני ברית** ('I deem it perfectly permissible, indeed a Divine mandate, so as to provide sustenance for my co-religionists'). He then outlined the construction at length (at great length, in fact, for that brief and abrupt writer), described in detail how he himself had employed it in a case involving a member of his family, emphasized **שהריוח שנותן הלוה למלוה בהיתר גמור הוא** ('that profit which the debtor pays the creditor is perfectly permissible'), and concluded: **ולמען דעת כל אדם שהוא היתר גמור הארכתי בדבר** ('I have dwelt on this arrangement at length so that everyone should know that it is perfectly permissible'). Note the word 'everyone' (*kol adam*) and the reiterated 'perfectly permissible' (*heter gamur*). People seeking an allowance need not be assured repeatedly that something is perfectly permissible; the word 'permissible' from no less a figure than Rabbenu Tam would have more than sufficed.

Rabbenu Tam is seeking here to persuade people who hesitate to use devices about which there is even a shadow of doubt, to reach those who do not wish to live by the standard of the common herd with its run-of-the-mill religiosity. Rabbenu Tam knows that an allowance that is not good enough for himself, which he himself would not rely on, will not be good enough for them. For that reason he emphasizes that he and his court have so ruled in a case involving his own son-in-law. His words are addressed to his compatriots who have declined to take advantage of Rashi's fiction of the Gentile straw man, not to speak of his own radical annulment of *le-ḥumra,* which most of his colleagues and pupils rejected. He is reaching out to the conservative and deeply religious (call them, if you wish, hyper-scrupulous) who still abide by the restrictions of the Rhineland, and possibly even by the disallowances of Rashbam, and seek to eke out their living in a time when moneylending is becoming, or has already become, the primary source of Jewish sustenance.[184]

Rabbenu Tam's radical doctrine canceling *le-ḥumra*, unlocking Jewish capital, and abolishing the usury restrictions on intra-Jewish credit was addressed to the needs of the entire community. His second step, the doctrine of *silluk* (which I am about to discuss in detail), with its striking proclamation, was

[184] See above, p. 130, and n. 175.

directed towards segments in the community that saw fictions and radical interpretations as little better than a whitewash and willingly paid the price for their belief. It was their refusal to take advantage of existing allowances, their sorry self-chosen lot, that elicited his *cri de coeur* and led him to see the alleviation of their plight as a Divine mandate. This reaction repeats itself over the centuries, albeit in less explicit and dramatic form. The less the aspiration to allowance, the greater the level of observance and inclination to stringency, the swifter and more flexible the response of the halakhists. I have discussed this at length elsewhere;[185] here I simply make note of it.

Let us now turn to the substance of the proclamation of *silluk*—non-relationship between the parties. |253| Seeking to give sustenance to these self-denying, devout souls, these *âmes d'élite*, Rabbenu Tam decided to bring the straw man to life.[186] If he could not destroy Gentile agency by textual interpretation, he would do it by court rulings.

[185] See 'Religious Law and Change' (Chapter 9 below), and my qualification in *Ha-Yayin bi-Yemei ha-Beinayim* (above, n. 44), 362–71, and in '"Religious Law and Change" Revisited' (Chapter 10 below).

[186] *Or Zarua'*, #202; *Teshuvot R. Me'ir mi-Rotenburg* (Prague and Budapest), #796; MSS Cambridge, Or. 786, fo. 183c–d; Oxford, Bodley 641, fo. 187b, #145; London, Montefiore 108, fos. 101b–102a; *Mordekhai*, #338; 'Piskei Rabbenu Yosef', #304, pp. 383–4. (A) Text: Both cases given in the proclamation are difficult. The problems of the second case arise from textual corruption (see my emendations above, n. 58). The first case, involving the pawning of the *Sefer he-'Arukh*, appears enigmatic due to the oral nature of the report. Rabbenu Tam seems to have dictated the proclamation, and it includes his side-remarks, which are easily recognizable as such in speech by a change in tone and inflexion. The written word cannot reproduce these vocal markers, and the asides appear to be part of the narrative with the resulting confusion.

The facts of the pawned *'Arukh* were the following: The brother-in-law of R. David of Brienne took a loan from R. Shemu'el of Joinville and also entered into a *commenda* arrangement with him, that is to say an *'iska*, in which half the sum is a loan and half an investment. (The loan portion must be repaid under all circumstances; the investment portion is the stake of the investor in the venture, and placed at the investor's own risk.) R. David graciously consented to deposit his *'Arukh* in the hands of R. Shemu'el as security for his brother-in-law's loan. R. Shemu'el had no use for the *'Arukh* and, not wishing to be held responsible as bailee (*shomer*) for the costly book, 'returned' it to R. David as bailment. He, R. Shemu'el, was legally the bailor (*mafkid*) and R. David was the *shomer*. R. David's brother-in-law lost everything and could repay neither the loan nor the loan portion of the *'iska*. When R. Shemu'el heard of the loss, he turned to R. David and asked for the *'Arukh* to be returned to him. Upon receiving it, he declared that he would not return the book unless the brother-in-law repaid both the loan and the entire sum that he, R. Shemu'el, had put into the *'iska*, that is to say both the loan portion to which he had a right of reimbursement and the investment portion to which he had no right at all. The court of Rabbenu Tam ruled that, unjust as R. Shemu'el's demand might, he nevertheless was entitled to keep the *'Arukh* seeing that he had received it from a Gentile intermediary who is considered the sole bailor, and R. David had no claim to the pawned book. In the middle of the narrative Rabbenu Tam remarked, '[Indeed], the *'Arukh* is still in his hands . . . [In fact], I don't know whether he has returned it [to the heirs of R. David,] when he [i.e. R. David] recently passed away.]', and then returned to his description of the case.

The principle of *le-ḥumra*, of Gentile agency in usurious relations, had consequences not only within the injunctive realm of *ribbit* but also in the general aspects of law of the case at hand. Since agency existed, the two Jewish principals could take action against one another directly. The creditor could bring suit against the debtor according to Jewish law, while the latter could insist upon all the rights of pawn redemption given to him by the halakhah. The Gentile as agent had neither rights nor obligations.

Rabbenu Tam instructed the courts to rule henceforth in matters of debt collection and pawn redemption as if the Gentile were the principal, and to allow no suit between the Jewish parties to be admitted regardless of the loss suffered by either side. If the courts would not recognize agency generally, it could scarcely exist with respect to usury. One could hardly deny to the two Jewish parties any redress at law from one another and yet claim that their relationship was one of privity of contract and hence within the proscription of *ribbit*. The Gentile was in fact now the principal and the loan genuinely two-staged, Jew to Gentile and then Gentile to Jew, and thus permissible. Rabbenu Tam was ordering the courts to undo the commission of agency that had actually taken place and the talmudic consequence of such a commission. But this gave his bold soul no pause and he went on to claim that not only was the transaction allowable, but it was even without the stigma of legal fiction (*ve-ein kan ha'aramah*), for it was truly on the Gentile's shoulders that the rights and duties[187] of principalship lay.

The words *ve-eini yodea'* should be added to Rabbenu Tam's remarks in l. 32 of the *Or Zarua'* on the basis of the reading in the *Teshuvot R. Me'ir mi-Rotenburg*. The phrase appears in brackets in Bloch's edition, as if it were entirely an editorial invention, which it is not. It is rather a minor emendation. As there is no extant manuscript, Bloch worked from the first edition of this massive compilation, that of Prague, 1608. It read here *eino yodea'*—which makes no sense—and he correctly emended it to *ve-eini yodea'*. (B) The entire tenor of Rabbenu Tam's lengthy proclamation, with the details and emphases that I have outlined above, implies to my mind that Rabbenu Tam is not simply publicizing his old doctrine that denied *le-ḥumra*, but is here taking a bold new step—instructing the courts to implement *silluk* at all costs, to disallow any and all suits between the would-be Jewish principals. This interpretation links the proclamation with its constant refrain of *silluk* with Rabbenu Tam's famous transaction with Ri with a similar demand for *silluk* (below, p. 140; I characterize it as famous because of its widespread dissemination documented in n. 195). However, I should note that R. Mosheh Isserles, possessing only the abbreviated report of the *Haggahot Asheri*, 5: 46 and the even briefer one in *Tosafot* 71b, s.v. *kegon*, took Rabbenu Tam's words as little more than restating his disallowance of *le-ḥumra* ('Yoreh De'ah', 169: 9).

187 'Duties' is perhaps an inaccurate word, for Rabbenu Tam studiously emphasizes the non-role of the two Jews rather than the intervening role of the Gentile, though the latter is logically entailed. He does this for two reasons. First, to have spoken of duties would have pointed out the fictitious nature of the arrangement, for the Gentile never assumed any such debt and would justly refuse to repay. Second, payment of debt was generally less discussed in medieval France than we might imag-

In reality, however, the arrangement was more of a sham than before. The full and absolute right to redeem the gage was now given to the Gentile, and to him exclusively. Given this situation, there was every reason to fear that he would seek to exercise it for his own profit. A Jew seeking credit would now never entrust a pawn to a Gentile over whom he did not have full control. Rabbenu Tam's ruling guaranteed that only Gentiles who were wholly dependent on Jews would ever be employed as middlemen. Legally, by turning the intermediary into the one and only party to the loan Rabbenu Tam may have eliminated fiction; practically, he only increased it. You can't have it both ways: the more you copperplate a fiction, the more fictitious it becomes.

Nor was Rabbenu Tam entirely unaware of this fact, at least unconsciously. Towards the end of the proclamation, he admonished against stating that pawned items were received 'from a Jewish debtor' in a subsequent bill of bailment—a document wholly extraneous to the lending:

The bailor should write . . . 'I received the aforesaid pawns on behalf of X son of Y' . . . He should not write, 'I received the aforesaid pawns on behalf of X son of Y, the Jew'. He should rather leave out the term 'Jew' or write 'from X the Gentile', but he should not label the pawns as coming from the [Jewish] debtor.

This is a startling requirement. Spelling out the ownership of the pawns in the loan contract itself would not create usury if none existed. Such labeling is all the more irrelevant in a subsidiary document. This concluding proviso belies the confident, assertive tone of the rest of the declaration. It indicates, as did Rashi's similar ban on mentioning the word *ribbit*, that for all Rabbenu Tam's repeated pronouncements of *heter gamur* (perfect permissibility), the boldest iconoclast of the Middle Ages was as uneasy with his new-begotten fiction of *silluk* as his soft-spoken grandfather had been with his newly found Gentile straw man.[188]

Ri and the Presumption of Legality (le-hetera ka-mikhaven)|254|

Whether the courts in France followed Rabbenu Tam's guidelines we do not know,[189] but that titan succeeded in imparting his authority to common prac-

ine. The creditor possessed the pledge, worth considerably more than the debt, and was not too concerned with repayment. For this reason, a debt is usually measured and discussed in terms of right of redemption. This is how Rabbenu Tam expressed it here, and Ri elsewhere (below, n. 202).

[188] **יכתוב הנאמן . . . קבלתי משכונות (ב)כך וכך לצורך פלוני בן פלוני . . . ואל יכתוב קבלתי משכונות כך וכך מפלוני בר׳ פלוני ישר[אל] אלא או יכתוב סתם כאשר כתבתי או יכתוב מפלוני גוי, אך שם הלוה לא יזכיר על המשכונות**. For Rashi, see above, pp. 106–7.

[189] For a discussion of the passages which might indicate such compliance, see the Appendix, note 189.

tice and his spirit to his pupils. His nephew, Ri (R. Yitsḥak of Dampierre, d. 1189), unable to assent to |255| Rabbenu Tam's bold dismissal of Gentile agency, took up his own cudgels against *le-ḥumra*. He advanced a doctrine, identical with that of Rashi, that conspiracy was necessary for *le-ḥumra*'s invocation.[190] He then advanced the doctrine of 'presumption of legality' to find allowance for cases of the creditor's complicity. Rather than disregard the initial intent as Rabbenu Tam had urged, he advised the courts to interpret it. Any two contracting parties naturally wish their transaction to be legal. Any construction necessary to bestow legality upon it should therefore be made.[191] The best way to sever the injunctive link between lender and borrower, in Ri's opinion, was to transfer the ownership of the pawn to the agent. The Gentile agent would then be (much to his surprise, had he known of it) the principal to the loan in every sense of the word. If such a transfer was necessary, we may assume that it took place. Since every lender wants to act within the dictates of the halakhah, we may presume that he intended to transfer the pawn, even though he never so stated and, perhaps, never even knew of such a requirement. The same presumption of like-minded intent would hold true for any new legal demand. A self-canceling clause had in effect been appended to halakhic requirements. And, indeed, no fewer than three new exactions were imposed on pawnbroking in this period: the need for conveyance of the pawn by Ri, the need for renunciation (*silluk*) in pawn transfers by Rabbenu Tam, which I will discuss shortly, and a renewed demand, a century later, by the author of the *Semak* for conveyance of the pawn (on the basis of the Tosefta). Each and every one of these |256| was swiftly and effectively neutralized by Ri's construction.

Nor did it stop there. It was further invoked for the very surety subterfuge that Rabbenu Gershom had attempted to forfend.[192]Admittedly, this fiction was employed in Ashkenaz not for private benefit but for the public good, as a way of meeting the ever-growing demands of taxes and imposts. Still, a fiction

[190] *Or Zarua'*, ##212–14; *Teshuvot Maharaḥ Or Zarua'*, #211; *Mordekhai*, ##338, 438 (read Yitsḥak, not Yonah); MS London, Montefiore 108, fo. 102a–b; R. Ḥayyim b. Shemu'el b. David of Tudela, *Tseror ha-Kesef*, ed. M. Y. H. Blau (New York, 1984), 382–3; *Tosfot ha-Rosh Bava Metsi'a* 71b, p. 194; *Rosh* 5: 55; *Teshuvot ha-Rosh*, 108: 11, 18; *Sefer ha-Terumot* 46: 4: 10; ed. Goldschmidt, p. 935; *Ḥiddushei Ramban, Rashba, Ran, Nimukei Yosef*, ad loc.; *Perush R. Avraham ben Yom Tov mi-Tudelah*, MS Oxford, Bodley 446, fo. 155a–b; *Teshuvot ha-Rashba*, vii, ##320, 503. (Ri was unaware of Rashi's responsum. For this general ignorance on the part of the Tosafists, Rashi's own grandchildren, of the *Sifrut de-Vei Rashi*, see *Ha-Yayin bi-Yemei ha-Beinayim* [above, n. 44], 348–9.)

[191] The word 'necessary' should, nevertheless, be emphasized. There are limits to judicial construction.

[192] Ri neutralized his own requirement of *hakna'ah* (transfer of pawn). A half a century or so later, R. Yitsḥak Or Zarua' neutralized Rabbenu Tam's requirement of *silluk*; see *Or Zarua'*, #215 end, #216;

that had been decried by Rabbenu Gershom was communally legitimated, as most anything could be, by this presumption of legality.

Ri did far more than foster an automatic nullifier of halakhic demands. The full ingenuity of the scholarly community was placed by his ruling at the automatic disposal of the businessman, and, with this, the role of halakhah shifted from adjudication to advocacy. A judge weighs one's actions; a lawyer finds, if he possibly can, the means of attaining one's ends within the letter of the law. It was just this latter function—furnishing the technique of allowance—that R. Yitsḥak of Dampierre had now assigned to the halakhists. In the realm of *ribbit*, halakhic thought was to be the automatic barrister of the businessman in the courts of man and God.

Not that Ri's assumption was without basis. The Ashkenazic community was generally God-fearing, far more so than most,[193] and who would not wish

Mordekhai, #338; *She'elot u-Teshuvot Or Zarua' u-Maharam b. Barukh*, #447. In the following generation, R. Perets neutralized R. Yitsḥak of Corbeil's renewed demand for *hakna'ah* in *Semak* (Constantinople, 1509), #259 (Satmar edn., #260) with his gloss ad loc. These glosses were penned soon after the book's appearance and became inseparable from it. For Rabbenu Gershom's warning against employing a Gentile straw man as surety for usurious loans, see above, pp. 114–15. For the use of just such a straw man by Jewish communities when the ever-increasing taxation demands of the authorities compelled them to draw upon short-term, intra-Jewish loans to meet these exactions, see the ruling of R. Ḥezkiyah of Magdeburg in MSS Cambridge, Oo.6.70.1, fo. 103b (gloss); Oxford, Bodley 683, fo. 61b: **על מה שהקהל כשצריך להן מעו[ת], לוים מישר' בריבית ונותן לו גוי ערב ומתירין לו ליקח הרבית. נר' שהורגלו בו מכיו[ן] דדיני דגוי בתר ערב אזיל (ב"מ עב ע"ב) ואם מת הגוי, אין לתבוע מהישר[אל] כלום. ואע"ג שהלוה לו מיד ליד, מ"מ על גוי סמך, ומסתמא לה[י]תר נתכוין**. R. Ḥezkiyah was drawing upon the remarks of R. Ḥayyim Or Zarua' in his responsum, *Teshuvot Maharaḥ Or Zarua'*, #168, but with none of the hesitations of the latter.

[193] As I noted above (p. 112), the degree of this religiosity should not be exaggerated; see my remarks in *Ha-Yayin bi-Yemei ha-Beinayim* (above, n. 44), 362–71, and in my essay '"Religious Law and Change" Revisited' (Chapter 10 below), though in matters of usury the level of observance seems to have been reasonably high. The case under discussion here is a good example of this. See the remarks of the inquirer in Spain in *Teshuvot ha-Rosh*, 108: 11: **אבל קשה לי לסמוך על היתר זה (ד"א להיתרא קמיכוין) במקום שאינם בני תורה, ואין חוששין בדבר עד ששולחין ע[ל] י[די] סרסורים יהודים ואינן חוששין**. A reasonable presumption in France was an improbable one in Spain. It is possible, of course, that the inquirer was romanticizing the French experience. I don't believe this to be so, as I have not come across any mention in medieval Ashkenazic sources, in print or manuscript, of breaches in the maintenance of the *ribbit* injunction, not even in the writings of the censorious German Pietists, who castigated their contemporaries relentlessly for their religious infractions (see above, p. 126). Undoubtedly, there were such breaches, perhaps even quite a few in the aggregate, and *Sefer Ḥasidim* records some of them (see above, n. 166), as does *Sefer ha-Tashbets ha-Katan: Nusaḥ Maharam Mints u-Veit Yosef*, ed. S. M. M. Schne'orson (Jerusalem, 2005), #509. (The printed editions lack this passage, but the text published by the editor, from MS London, Montefiore 130, is corroborated by MS Oxford, Bodley 800, fo. 48a, #507.) However, to all appearances they were either not numerous enough, or not sufficiently concentrated in a specific period or locale, to be perceived as an erosion or to present themselves to contemporary observers as a social or religious problem. The one

to turn a profit and abide by the law at the same time? But to assume a measure of religious aspiration on the part of the ordinary merchant is one thing; to treat it as an absolute and unvarying premise is another. To reckon with this presumption of observance as one factor amongst many is one thing; to seize upon it as a mechanism of automatic sanction is wholly another. With this ruling, Ri, in effect, had halakhah |257| relinquish its regulative role. It was no longer to sit in stern or benign judgment on the affairs of men, but was to serve, rather, as their handmaiden!

In conclusion, one should add that there are few better ways to illustrate the different yardsticks of significance employed by law and history than to contrast Ri's construction of intention of legality with Rabbenu Gershom's construction of 'reverse agency'. Legally the latter is far more radical; the reverse is true historically. That a *shaliaḥ le-kabbalah* is actually a *shaliaḥ le-holakhah*, as Rabbenu Gershom claimed, is startling, to say the least. That religious people prefer to act within the dictates of the law is quite plausible. Historically, the situation is reversed. The scope of Rabbenu Gershom's construction was local and simply represented a concession in an enterprise that was still closely regulated by halakhah; R. Yitsḥak's construction, however, being catholic, constituted an abdication of the controlling role of halakhah in the business of pawnbroking.

Rabbenu Tam and the Pawned Pawn and Ma'arufya

The second area of moneylending that Rabbenu Tam turned to was the widespread practice of pledge transfers. That transaction, it will be remembered, had been viewed by Rashi and R. David not as a new loan, but as an assignment of debt and, hence, beyond the pale of usury. Most people knew of the allowance but not of the construction and proceeded in their business dealings to act as if a loan had taken place rather than a debt sold.[194] This expressed

instance of reproof for such a breach that I have found is from the close of the Middle Ages, a letter of the famed Rabbi Ya'akov Weil (d. mid-15th century) exhorting a colleague to desist from borrowing at interest (MS Oxford, Bodley 1606, fo. 158b):

> והי' שלו' בחיליך אהו' הר"ר שמואל שיחי'. בנך הגיד לי איך שמנשה הלוה לך מידו לידך על משכונו' ואת' נותן לו ריבי'. תמהיני עליך הלא שנית ושלשת בשלהי פ' איזהו נשך (ע"ה ע"ב) מלוה עובר בכולן, לוה עובר משו' לא תשיך ולפני עור. ואמור רבנ' ריבי' קצוצ' יוצ' בדייני' (ס"א ע"ב). חזור בך ואם לא, צריכי' אנו לחשוב מחשבו' שלא יעש' תור' פלסתר (ע"ה ע"ב) וצדיק באמו[נ]תו יחיה. נאו' הקט' יעקב ווילא. העתקתי מן העתקה אשר נעתק (נעתק) מכתיבת ידו של (מהרי"ל) מהר"י ווילא.

194 See above, p. 97. My words may contain a simplification. It may also be that they were generally aware that a sale took place, but, as habits die slowly, they assumed that this was a sale with the right of redemption, which pretty much was the case in Gentile gage-law. As far as usury goes this makes no

itself primarily in the continued right of Jew 1 (in the illustration above, p. 74) to redeem his pawn from Jew 2, a right which the initial creditor, Jew 1, clung to tenaciously, since the pledge was worth far more than the loan and a tidy profit could be had from its recapture. But redemption implied loan and loan meant usury, and so Rabbenu Tam insisted that any transfer of a pawn must explicitly deny the right of redemption, deny the existence of any debt, indeed, deny any continuing relation between the two parties.[195] This doctrine of renunciation, of non-relation between the parties (*silluk*), became the dominant doctrine in Ashkenaz wherever word of Rabbenu Tam's decision reached. It achieved this dominance partly because of its intrinsic persuasiveness, partly because of its author's authority, |258| and partly because Ri reported that Rabbenu Tam had conducted a pledge transfer to him on these conditions. This report of an actual transaction between the great is almost a *unicum* in medieval halakhic literature, and it would have been a bold man indeed who challenged the legality of a transaction between the giant of Ramerupt and the no lesser one of Dampierre.

It may be that Rabbenu Tam also addressed the problem of *ma'arufya* and Jewish fronting.[196] So, at least, the *Sefer ha-Terumot* reports.[197] Seeing that for every other ruling in moneylending that the great Rabbenu Tam handed

difference, for sale with resale (*Kauf auf Wiederkauf*) is viewed as a loan and is subject to usury. Hence, regardless of what was commonly assumed to be the nature of the transaction, Rabbenu Tam had to object.

[195] (A) *Or Zarua'*, #215; *Mordekhai*, #338; *Shibbolei ha-Leket II*, p. 81; new edn., p. 173; *Teshuvot R. Me'ir mi-Rotenburg* (Prague and Budapest), ##795, 360; *Temim De'im*, #156; *Sefer ha-Terumot*, 46: 4: 10; ed. Goldschmidt, p. 934; *Teshuvot Maimuniyot, Mishpatim*, #30; *Teshuvot u-Fesakim le-Ri ha-Zaken*, in *Shitat ha-Kadmonim 'al 'Avodah Zarah*, ed. M. Y. H. Blau (New York, 1991), iii. 241, #132; MSS Oxford, Bodley 641, fo. 186b, #143; Oxford, Bodley 692, fo. 225b, #197; Oxford, Bodley 1408, fo. 38a, #137; London, Montefiore 108, fo. 102a. (B) I have been unable to determine whether or not the proclamation of Rabbenu Tam preceded the transaction between him and Ri. *Silluk* in the case of Rabbenu Tam and Ri was renunciation by the parties themselves of any further relationship. *Silluk* of the proclamation was an instruction to the courts to treat the two parties to any repawning as having no further relationship. An express, voluntary renunciation was clearly preferable to a court-proclaimed and court-enforced one, and this famous transaction may have taken place after Rabbenu Tam's proclamation. It is equally possible that the notion of *silluk* began as an express statement, as in his transaction with Ri, and in the course of time, Rabbenu Tam decided that this arrangement should become public (i.e. court) policy. (C) For the authorship of *Teshuvot u-Fesakim le-Ri ha-Zaken*, see S. Emanuel, 'Teshuvot Maharam mi-Rotenburg she-Einan shel ha-Maharam' (above, n. 54(*c*)), 160–4. (D) The printed *Or Zarua'* has mispunctuated and left unamended a central passage in Ri's report. The correct reading is **ולא תענה לי עוד ממנו אם אינך רוצה, [ו]אני פוטרך שלא וכו'**. **תענה ממנו** = respondere de = respondeo de (see R. E. Latham, ed., *Revised Medieval Latin Word List* [London, 1965], 405) = to be answerable for. (The emendation is based on the parallel sources cited above.)

[196] See above, n. 37.

[197] 46: 7: 3; ed. Goldschmidt, p. 1049.

down we have at least three or four French and German sources, it is astonishing that for this major decision we have none. While it is true that on occasion we find in Provençal sources responsa and rulings of French and German scholars that are not found in Ashkenazic sources, such an absence in matters of usury is notable. Without questioning the overall accuracy of R. Shemu'el ha-Sardi, I am somewhat hesitant to base any analysis of the cardinal scholar of northern France on a lone Catalonian source, especially as I do not understand the line of reasoning found in the report. The reported decision, however, is wholly in character with Rabbenu Tam's attitude to *ribbit*. He permits *ma'arufya* and fronting, even when the Jew takes a percentage of the loan as commission. For those not as overly cautious as myself and willing to give full credence to the report, what emerges is simply a fuller picture of Rabbenu Tam's activity. We see him addressing himself to all four major problems of moneylending and usury—intra-Jewish credit (the Gentile straw man), intra-Jewish collateral (the pawned pawn), Jewish managerial activity, and finally fronting—and finding allowances for them all. The absence of any ruling by Rabbenu Tam, according to my reading, on the last two problems is not so surprising. In the mid-twelfth century Jewish activity in these areas was in transit. *Ma'arufya* in France was not a shadow of what it had once been and fronting was not yet what it was to become.[198]

Ri, the Challenge to Credit Replenishment, and the Halakhah in Exile

But the underlying assumption of pledge transfer (see illustrations above, p. 74), perhaps the most basic premise of pawnbroking, the assignment of debts via this transfer, was one which could not escape scrutiny for long. Ri soon received a letter challenging this universal practice,[199] and it is one to which all who are interested in the history of halakhah would do well to pay heed. Not that either the plaintiff or the defendant had the slightest interest in the finer points of Jewish law. They probed the law only out of self-interest. A lawsuit had arisen between a creditor who sought to retain a pawn worth far more than the initial loan[200] and a debtor who sought to redeem it without paying the interest that had been agreed upon at the time of the second pawning. To this end the debtor argued that since Jews do not acquire property rights in Gentile gages, they cannot sell them, and without |259| assignment of the gage there was no assignment of debt.[201] This being the case, the giving

[198] See above, n. 174, and the Appendix, note 176, item 2.

[199] *Or Zarua'*, #215; *Mordekhai*, #338; *Teshuvot R. Me'ir mi-Rotenburg* (Prague and Budapest), #795; MS Oxford, Bodley 641, fo. 186a–b, #143.

[200] See above, nn. 58, 96.

[201] Since the assumptions that underlay debt transfer were never spelled out, the author of the query may have envisaged another rationale for assignment and it was against this that he addressed

of the pledge by the creditor to a third party must be an act of re-pledging, and the money received in exchange a loan, and one at interest between Jew and Jew—which naturally he could not pay. The upshot was that the pawned pawn, the basic instrument of credit mobility, the major means of credit replenishment, was illegal.

It is in the nature of religious law (and halakhah, in both its civil and its ritual spheres, is religious law) that an assumption that simply incorporates reality can be silently assimilated into the decision-making process, but can never be articulated. For, once it has been formulated, it would stand against dicta of immutable authority and imply a challenge to the timelessness of the law's mandate. Such assumptions, once challenged, were assumptions discarded, and so Ri, in his search to justify universal practice, fell back upon Rabbenu Tam's doctrine of renunciation (*silluk*). He suggested that when the first Jew (Jew 1 in the illustration above, p. 74) receives money from the second Jew (Jew 2 in the illustration) and gives him the pledge in return, the first Jew should renounce any right of redeeming the pledge and the second Jew any right to demand the repayment of the sum given.[202] Since the first Jew owed nothing |260| to the second one and could not, upon presentation of the sum, recover the pledge, no loan had been made and no usury existed, regardless of the first Jew's non-ownership of the pledge. For immediately upon the reciprocal exchange of money and gage, the two stood in no legal relationship whatsoever.

But the application of Rabbenu Tam's ruling was more than problematic. Rabbenu Tam had assumed a sale and spoken of it outright (*ve'anani* [i.e. Rabbenu Tam to Ri]: *ani mokher lekha kol ha-mashkon*—and he [Rabbenu Tam] said to me [Ri] 'I sell you the entire pawn').[203] Indeed, all his directives

his objections. He, or whoever argued his case, may have reasoned, as did later the author of the *Sefer ha-Terumot* (above, n. 82), that as the creditor has undeniable property rights in the pawn, he can unquestionably alienate the gage (*Kiddushin* 8a–b). But those rights premise a continued lien and can exist only for he who possesses that lien, i.e. the creditor, for they are distinctly creditor's rights. Hence the validity of a property sale necessitates the assignment of debt. If one infers the necessity of assignment from the transfer of property, once the sale is denied, so too is the assignment.

202 Strictly speaking, Ri does not mention renunciation of debt, but his authority and precedent is Rabbenu Tam, and he demanded it explicitly as Ri immediately proceeds to relate. Ri omits mentioning debt, for people did not think in terms of lien, but of redemption (see above, n. 187). He was asked about redemption of the pawn and it was to this query that he replied.

203 (A) *Or Zarua'*, #215 (and all parallel texts cited above, n. 195). (B) Once the question of Gentile non-acquisition had been raised, subsequent reports of Rabbenu Tam's ruling, as opposed to verbatim transcriptions of Ri's letter, might naturally contain some modification of his original sweeping remark, especially as this would in no way affect the practical demand of *silluk*. One can see this process already at work in *Teshuvot u-Fesakim le-Ri ha-Zaken* (above, n. 195), 232, #132, if one contrasts

were for the purpose of ensuring that a sale actually took place and that the buyer received an absolute title. But Ri had just admitted to his inquirer the impossibility of a sale (for Jews could have no property rights in Gentile pawns), and if that was so, the whole transaction was pointless, and the suggested renunciation was in fact criminal. For what had taken place when the second Jew gave the first one money and received an object in return? Not a sale, for Jew 1 had no property rights in the object. A loan—God forbid!—had not taken place either. What had the second Jew received for his money? Not ownership, for it was beyond the first Jew's power to bestow it. A lien in the object? Again no, |**261**| for no loan had taken place.[204] True, the first Jew cannot

the 'as-if' heading of the section written by a pupil of R. Yitsḥak, ***ke-mokher lo et ha-mashkon***, with the words of Ri that follow: *ani mokher lekha kol ha-mashkon*. In this manner arose the various formulations that one finds, towards the close of our period, in the works of the school of R. Me'ir of Rothenburg. See *Rosh* 5: 55; *Teshuvot ha-Rosh* 108: 5 (*hareini mokher lekha kol zekhut ve-shi'abud she-yesh li 'al ha-mashkon*); *Sefer Tashbets* (Warsaw, 1876), #485, end; ed. S. M. M. Schne'orson, #102; ed. S. Angel (Jerusalem, 2011), #487; *Teshuvot, Pesakim u-Minhagim shel R. Me'ir mi-Rotenburg*, ii, *Pesakim*, #141 and sources there cited, to which add *Semak Zurich*, iii. 200. In MS London, British Library 532 of the *Tashbets*, fo. 132a, #75, the offending phrase ***ve-domeh ke-ilu*** *mekharo lo* is missing altogether, and equally so from MS Cambridge Or. 791, fo. 37c, though the latter is probably a *homoioteleuton* of *maskon*/*mashkon*, as the redundant *kelal* would indicate (*mistalek le-gamrei me-ha-mashkon kelal, az yesh lo*). The version of the printed text, however, cannot be discounted, as it is corroborated by all the above-cited printed sources and numerous other manuscripts of the *Tashbets* (e.g. Oxford, Bodley 800, fo. 25b, #102; London, Montefiore 130, fo. 78b, #51; Hamburg, Staats- und Universitätsbibliothek 152, fo. 263f, #68; Paris, Alliance Israélite 482, fo. 477a, #261). French and German thought tended throughout to focus on the parties to the *ribbit* transaction. It was only by accident that their attention was drawn to the ownership of the pledges employed. The Provençal school, for reasons which lie beyond the scope of this essay, concentrated upon the pawns from the outset. Their earliest discussions of pawnbroking assume non-acquisition of Gentile gages (and Gentile non-acquisition of Jewish gages) as a matter of course. (See *'Ittur*, ed. Me'ir Yonah [repr. New York, 1955], *Hilkhot Bi'ur Ḥamets*, fo. 126a; R. Meshullam b. Asher in the so-called *Ḥiddushei ha-Ritva* [above, n. 98(*d*)], fo. 40c; *Sefer ha-Terumot* 46: 4: 10; ed. Goldschmidt, pp. 936–9; Rabad in *Temim De'im*, #43. A possible exception is the anonymous author of the query found in the responsa of R. Avraham, *av-bet-din* of Narbonne, in *Sifran shel Rishonim*, ed. S. Assaf [Jerusalem, 1935], #1.) When reports of Rabbenu Tam's doctrine of *silluk* penetrated Provence—and we can catch echoes of it in R. Avraham's reply ibid.—Rabbenu Tam's original remarks began to be similarly modified in Provence. See the edited transcription of R. Yitsḥak's note in *Temim De'im*, #156: *ani mokher lekha kol ha-mashkon ve-khol mah sheyesh li 'alav*. (c) On the Provençal treatment of the halakhic status of the Gentile pawn, see my *Halakhah, Kalkalah* (above, n. 1), 102–12 and Appendix, note 215, item 3.

[204] The right of possession suggests itself immediately. For a pledgee has three titles to a pledge: ownership (in certain cases), lien, and the right of possession. The third is indeed the essence of a pledge. However, it is not at all clear that these three titles are independent. Can one transfer to another the right of possession while retaining the lien for oneself? The right to possess flows from its status as pledge. One retains it *qua* lien. Without the lien, there should be no retention. Arguments can be made for a different view, and a number have (see *Netivot ha-Mishpat*, #66: 12; *Ḥiddushei ha-Rim*, *Hilkhot Kiddushin* 28: 26), but the fact that Ri did not make short shrift of his questioner by

reclaim the object, as he has renounced this right, but with a title as obscure as that of the second Jew, just what is to prevent a third party from appropriating it from him? Not perplexity but improbity envelops the renunciation. The first Jew as bailee (*shomer*) was duty-bound to return the gage to the Gentile (upon payment). He deposited it with the second Jew and then renounced his rights of recovery, and thus renounced the means of executing his obligation, of ful-

replying: נהי דגופו של משכון לא מצי למכור, תפיסת המשכון מיהו מכר ליה, shows clearly where he stood on this matter.

Shifting the sale to titles other than that of ownership is the thrust of *Teshuvot u-Fesakim le-Ri ha-Zaken*, *Tashbets*, R. Asher, and R. Avraham, *av-bet-din* of Narbonne, cited in the previous note. Their reformulation, however, is not without problems. What does the phrase *ke-mokher lekha et ha-mashkon* in the *Teshuvot u-Fesakim* mean, and just how does one go about transacting a *ke-mekhirah*? How is the sale of the lien, in Rosh's formulation, effectuated if the pawn remains unsold? Just what *zekhut* is being referred to in his formula—*hareni mokher lekha kol zekhut ve-shi'abud she-yesh li 'al ha-mashkon*—and what is the mechanism of its sale? (If it is synonymous with *shi'abud*, its addition has solved nothing.) What both writers are seeking to avoid is perfectly clear; what they are proffering in its place is anything but that.

Jay Rosen has questioned the cogency of the questions that I posed regarding Ri's application of Rabbenu Tam's doctrine of *silluk*. While it is true that a bailee cannot alienate the property entrusted by him, bailees do have the right to stipulate their conditions of bailment, as stated in the Mishnah in *Bava Metsi'a* (94a). Seeing that bailments could be alienated in Germanic law, why should the bailment by a Gentile of a pawn not be considered an implicit consent to the right of alienation? To the bailor's thinking, you could alienate the pawn, so why isn't his acceptance of the right of alienation the equivalent of stipulation?

The instances of stipulation given in the Mishnah in *Bava Metsi'a* are those affecting the degree of liability. A bailee who serves *gratis* (*shomer ḥinnam*) is generally responsible only in cases of negligence. A hired bailee (*shomer sakhar*) is generally responsible for theft; a borrower (*sho'el*) is liable even in case of *force majeure*, and so on. There is nothing intrinsic to bailment that dictates any specific level of liability; there is no inherent reason why a *gratis* bailee should be precluded from accepting liability for theft or why a hired bailee should insist that he will accept the post only if his liability is restricted to instances of negligence. Such stipulations run counter to nothing affecting the essence of the transaction. However, the very definition of bailment in Jewish law means that the bailee cannot appropriate the bailment for himself, but must either return it or give it to some designated third party. Bailment requires accountability. Indeed, the right to demand such an account defines the 'bailor': whomever the bailee is accountable to, whether the person who entrusted it to him or the party to whom he must deliver it, is legally the bailor (*Bava Kamma* 93a). If the bailee is accountable to no one, as under Germanic law, he is no bailee under Jewish law. As a creditor who receives a pawn as security is deemed *ipso facto* a bailee (*shomer sakhar*), the right of conversion (*sheliḥut yad*), not to speak of alienation, is by definition precluded.

(This is entirely independent of the issue of the *sheliḥut yad* in bailment of bills [*shetarot*] and real estate [*karka'ot*]; see *Ḥiddushei ha-Rashba 'al Shevu'ot*, ed. Y. D. Ilan [Jerusalem, 1995], 42b, s.v. *mat-nitin*, and editor's notes ad loc. There may be limited or quasi-bailment in matters of [*shetarot*] and *karka'ot*, a question that has occupied halakhists since Maimonides' controversial ruling on liability for negligence in real estate ['Hilkhot Sekhirut', 2: 3]; right of alienation, however, precludes any possibility of bailment.)

filling his duty of return. Ri quite accurately says that after renunciation 'it is as if he had sold it', but seeing that the first Jew is a bailee, this is outright theft.[205] To avoid usury Ri had pointedly cut the first Jew out of the picture, but by doing so he had deprived the Gentile of his pledge and had denied to the second Jew, despite the good money he had spent, any title to it.

What underlay Ri's ruling were the realities of the twelfth century. Surprising as it may be to the modern mind and inconceivable as it is to one raised upon halakhic thinking, where the |262| distinction between loan (*halva'ah*) and bailment (*pikkadon*) (the former consisting of a transfer of ownership to the borrower, while the latter is a transfer of possession only, thus the ownership always remains with the bailor [*mafkid*]) is as clear as day and night, Germanic law imposed no obligation upon the bailee (*shomer*) to return the object deposited with him. He could, if he wished, return its equivalent.[206]

[205] Conversion (*shelihut yad*; see *Tosafot, Bava Metsi'a* 41a, s.v. *she-netalah*) does not apply to Gentile bailments (Maimonides, 'Hilkhot Sekhirut', 2: 1; see *Minhat Hinnukh*, #57).

[206] (A) Pollock and Maitland, *History of English Law* (above, n. 60(*a*)), ii. 149–83, see esp. pp. 153, 155–6, 178–9, 182. See Heusler, *Institutionen* (above, n. 56(*a*)), 205; Brissaud, *French Private Law* (above, n. 57), 288 ff.; Huebner, *Germanic Private Law* (above, n. 12), 407 ff. This is the logical consequence of *Hand muß Hand wahren*, the literature of which is enormous. See ibid.; Gierke, *Deutsches Privatrecht* (above, n. 56), ii. 552, 558 ff.; Schröder and von Künßberg, *Lehrbuch* (above, n. 56), 777 ff., 1068 ff. for references. (The vigorous objections of P. Van Bemmelen, *Le Système de la propriété mobilière, droit antérieur système du code civil, droit futur* [Leiden, 1887], and E. Champeaux, *Essai sur la vestitura ou saisine et l'introduction des actions possessoires dans l'ancien droit français* [Paris, 1899], have received a cold reception from historians.) The Hebrew sources equally explain themselves best in light of the doctrine of *Hand muß Hand wahren*; see above, n. 98(*a*). (B) Before one starts in astonishment at this ruling, it would be wise to recall that the principle of conversion had not penetrated popular consciousness in talmudic times. See *Bava Metsi'a* 5b **התם נמי מורה [היתירא] ואמר דמי קא יהיבנא ליה**. Nor had this mentality disappeared in the Middle Ages. R. Yitshak Or Zarua' (*Bava Kamma*, #413), discussing some matter in litigation in Prague, overruled R. Yitshak ben Mordekhai, quite possibly his own teacher, on the basis that the agent (bailee of principal's funds) had intended to repay **ולא תגזול לאינשי על מנת שלא לפרוע משמע להו בהדיא בפ"ק דמציעא... אלמא היכא דיהיב דמי משמע להו לאינשי דלא עברי אלא תגזול**. True, he had talmudic precedent, but unless it reflected contemporary mentality he was under no pressure to invoke this psychological rule of thumb, let alone to overturn a previous decision on this basis. (See Urbach, *Ba'alei ha-Tosafot* [above, n. 11], 437, n. 9.) (C) Once again, the Hebrew sources of the 12th and 13th centuries reflect their medieval surroundings and the notion that bailment means loss of ownership. Ravan, when discussing a Jewish gage in Gentile hands (and note that the pledgee is not a gangster, *goy anas*, as e.g. in his discussion above, n. 147), wrote (vol. i, #112): **אפילו אם תמצא לומר דכיון שנתן המשכון ביד גוי הפקירו, אתה למד מכאן שלא הפקירו אלא אדעתיה דגוי** (And if you will contend that since he entrusted the pawn to a Gentile, he abandoned it, know that he abandoned to the Gentile only.) Who would ever suggest, in a world regulated by Jewish or Roman law, that someone who gives a pledge to an honest pledgee abandons it? The same question presents itself when reading the words of the respondent in *She'elot u-Teshuvot Or Zarua' u-Maharam*, #479; recently reprinted in Emanuel, *Teshuvot Maharam u-Venei Doro*, 1, #93:

This may indicate that there was no ownership of mobilia in Germanic law. There was only possession, and 'he who of his own free will parts with the possession of his chattel, parts with the chattel itself. In exchange he takes a mere right *in personam*, a mere "contractual right", a promise that after a certain lapse of time the chattel, or its equivalent, shall be returned to him'. Or it may be, as Maitland contends, not that Germanic law rejected ownership in favor of possession but rather that it contained no clear idea of either; 'owe' and 'own' were fused somehow in its thinking. There is little doubt that to Ri's mind, as to any halakhic one, the possibility of sale and transfer implied |263| ownership on the part of the bailee. At any rate the fact remained that the bailee could alienate what had been entrusted to his care[207] and that the third party entered into full possession of the bailment as a consequence. It was this course of action that Ri had counseled.

What had transpired was that the objection of the inquirer had stripped property rights from Gentile gages and had reduced them to pure bailments, but bailments by law could be sold, and so no one was any the worse for the change. Since one foreign assumption had been discovered and had to be discarded, Ri simply substituted another one in its place. The difference was only that while the old assumption of ownership of pledge corresponded so closely to halakhic principles that it could be incorporated with ease into decisions and the resultant product formed a natural whole, the alienability of bailments was a halakhic outrage, and could not even be hinted at indirectly. Yet it was a fact of life that neither Ri nor the best-intentioned pawnbroker could alter. To reply on the basis of any other assumption would have been to retreat to a fool's paradise and to forswear halakhic governance of the world of affairs

וששאלתם על ראובן שהשאיל חפץ לגוי . . . כך נ[ראה] ל[י] . . . וראובן שמסר החפץ לגוי הפקי[ר] ממונו

And you inquired about Re'uven who loaned an object to a Gentile . . . [Reply:] Thus it [the matter] appears to me: . . . and Re'uven, who handed over the object to the Gentile, abandoned his property.

Note again, there is not the slightest indication in the text that the Gentile is in any way disreputable.

[207] Alienation would be breach of contract, no more. See Pollock and Maitland, *History of English Law* (above, n. 60(*a*); the quotations in the text are taken from pp. 155–6, 178); Heusler, *Institutionen* (above, n. 56(*a*)), 407 ff.; Brissaud, *French Private Law* (above, n. 57), 289, n. 2. This gave Jewish creditors little pause, as it was the common practice among lenders. Anyway, it was better than violating the *ribbit* injunctions. If they attempted to translate this into their own terms, it would have appeared to them as something analogous to the law of *ein ha-sokher rasha'y le-haskir*. See *Terumat ha-Deshen*, ed. S. Avitan (Jerusalem, 1991), i, #210: **אע"ג דאמרינן בגיטין אין השואל רשאי להשאיל ואין השוכר רשאי להשכיר, היינו לכתחילה אבל אם עשה [כן] לא מיקרי גזלן בהכי**.

altogether. And so Ri wrote of the pledge with no reference to whence it came and no word as to its fate. In a world in which civil society was ordered along the lines of halakhah, the responsum was truncated nonsense; but in a world where halakhah was being superimposed |264| upon a reality bound by other rules it was very much to the point, and it was not by accident that his words received widespread dissemination and became in many places the dominant form of pawn transfer.

Ri's conduct highlights one of the major problems that confronted the keepers of the law in the Middle Ages: how to bring an alien reality to norm and reason without compromising the law's purity. By silent assumption, by judicial construction, without any overt reference, and in a circuitous fashion, a mute but far-reaching cognizance was extended to the intractable world around them. But deeply as medieval realities penetrated the very fiber of rabbinic adjudication, the theoretical foundations of halakhah were maintained by these men almost untouched. In an age when pledges were being bought and sold like peaches, the status of these pawns was being determined in the very same academies of Dampierre and Sens by the scholarly collation of all relevant talmudic texts and the sustained effort at their harmonization. The baffling slips of ownership that were attached to the contract pledge (*bi-she'at halva'ah*) were a consequence of textual analysis and dialectic and bore no relation, to put it mildly, to any actual need,[208] while the developments in the distraint pledge (*shelo bi-she'at halva'ah*) ran counter to all reality. Ri denied to this gage one of the basic traits of property and, as his words won acceptance, further losses in its sensed ownership soon made themselves felt in tosafist thought.[209]

208 *Tosfot Shants*, *Pesaḥim* (Jerusalem, 1956), 31b, s.v. *minayin*; *Tosafot*, *Gittin* 37a, s.v. *sha'ani*; *Tosfot ha-Rosh 'al Gittin*, ed. H. B. Ravits (Jerusalem, 2004), 37a, s.v. *ela me-'atah*; *Tosafot*, *Kiddushin* 8b, s.v. *mashkon*; *Tosfot ha-Rosh 'al Kiddushin*, ed. D. Metsger (Jerusalem, 2006), 8b, s.v. *ḥatam*. The difficulties in the argument advanced by *Tosafot* (*migo dekani*) were pointed out sharply by Ramban, *Milḥamot*, *Pesaḥim* 31b (Vilna edn., fo. 9b), **אומר הכותב אלו דברי הבאי, וכי בשביל שהוא קונה במקום א', יקנה כאן שלא כדין**, and have not been satisfactorily explained to this day. Jews did not need property rights in such pawns for the purpose of wedding rings, Passover observance, and sabbatical years, and rights in these areas did the Tosafists give to them. These are ad hoc rights created to resolve textual difficulties and neither flow from any central conception nor reflect any need.

209 One of the basic characteristics of ownership is that of *force majeure* (*onsin*). The owner suffers the loss in the event that his object is destroyed. If someone else takes the loss (in our case the debtor, pledgor) then apparently the object was his. Ri's restriction of responsibility of the creditor (pledgee) to cases of *gezelah ve-avedah*, and his transfer of the responsibility in case of *force majeure* to the debtor (*Tosfot Shants* in *Shitah Mekubbetset* [Amsterdam, 1721], *Bava Metsi'a* 81b, s.v. *divrei*; *Tosafot* 82b, s.v. *aimur* and parallel passages), seem to have been a break with French tradition (see above, n. 60(*a*)) and a clear attenuation of the old simple sense of pledge ownership. (Ramban's significant correlation

Despite, again, the universal traffic in |265| non-Jewish pledges, and the convolutions that were required to explain it, no one in France and Germany suggested that perhaps the decision lay with that opinion in the Talmud which had claimed property rights in Gentile pawns.[210] Only the little-known R. Shelomoh of Château-Landon, as obscure then as now, thought it proper to infer the law from day-to-day conduct.[211] Ashkenazic Jewry lived in |266| two worlds, in their countries of exile and in the land of the Talmud. As adverse circumstance only deepened their allegiance to their 'portable homeland', concession and stubbornness paradoxically increased conjointly. Allowances were made and sanctioned, but alterations of principles were not forthcoming. The recognition which they extended to their environment, to Exile itself, was never *de jure* and so their concessions were always local and of an ad hoc character. Once outside the area of ineluctable pressure, the received

with *uman koneh bi-shevaḥ keli* in *Milḥamot, Shevu'ot* 44a [Vilna edn., fo. 25a], which forms the basis of any construction of *jus in re aliena* as regards pawns—see *Ketsot ha-Ḥoshen*, #306: 4—was unknown to the Tosafists.) The effects were not long in becoming apparent. First, passages in the Talmud that spoke of lien with respect to pledges, which previous generations (Rabbenu Tam in *Teshuvot R. Me'ir mi-Rotenburg* [Cremona, #75]; *Ravan*, i, #112) had taken as a matter of course as referring to contract pledges, were now applied to those of distraint. See *Tosafot, Bava Kamma* 49b, s.v. *mashkono*, and *Tosafot R. Perets, Bava Kamma*, ed. B. Z. H. Pereg (Jerusalem, 1984), ad loc. Note also that the Tosafists did not explain, as did R. Aharon ha-Levi of Barcelona (*Shitah Mekubbetset, Bava Kamma* [Venice, 1762], ad loc.), that there is a tug of war between unequal rights of property, but simply dissolved the ownership into lien. True, the Talmud mentions lien, but that hardly prevented R. Aharon ha-Levi, who had a lively sense of the property rights in gages, from interpreting the passage in his terms, and, this certainly wouldn't have stopped the Tosafists had they felt the same way. Second, the new predominance of lien over ownership manifests itself in the ruling of R. Me'ir of Rothenburg (*Mordekhai, Sanhedrin*, #681) that renunciation (*meḥilah*) is effective without *kinyan* even in debts involving distraint pledges. Contrast this with R. Aharon ha-Levi (above) and note that both scholars argued from the identical passage of *'eved 'ivri gufo kanuy*, only that R. Aharon ha-Levi saw ownership as predominating in gages and hence saw the analogy to *'eved 'ivri* as valid, while R. Me'ir saw gages as primarily lien, and hence no different, with respect to renunciation, to any other form of debt. See Heusler, *Institutionen* (above, n. 56(*a*)), 203–4. (The formulations—similar to those in the printed *Tosafot*—found in *Tosfot Talmid Rabbenu Tam ve-Rabbenu Eli'ezer* in *Shitat ha-Kadmonim 'al Bava Kamma*, ed. M. Y. H. Blau [New York, 1976], 49b, s.v. *mashkono*, do not conflict with my analysis. The work was not penned by a pupil of Rabbenu Tam. It is a late mélange of tosafist material unrelated to Ri's great predecessor; see Urbach, *Ba'alei ha-Tosafot* [above, n. 11], 643–5.)

210 All the more remarkable since no reinterpretation of any talmudic passage would have been required, simply a ruling in favor of a minority view in the Talmud, examples of which we have in the hundreds.

211 M. Y. L. Zachs, 'Piskei ha-Rash mi-London', *Sinai*, 13 (1944), 233, #26. MS National Library of Israel, 8vo 90, fos. 57a–59b, from which the text with its oddities was published, is corroborated in our passage by MS Oxford, Bodley 781, fo. 68a (MS London, British Library Or. 1073, fo. 2b is a 19th-century copy of a manuscript written in Avignon in 1391). On R. Shelomoh of Château-Landon, see Urbach, *Ba'alei ha-Tosafot* (above, n. 11), 456, n. 33.

heritage, the immutable truths reasserted themselves. The very same men in pre-Crusade Jewry, it will be recalled, who when treating moneylending spoke freely of sales of Gentile gages, were guided in cases of inheritance by the law of non-acquisition of these pledges.[212] Ri, reporting his arrangement with Rabbenu Tam, speaks freely of the sale of Gentile pawns, yet equally denies any ownership of such pawns in matters of inheritance of the firstborn.[213] Ravyah, in the same spirit, would, when speaking of *ribbit*, compare the sale of non-Jewish pawns with that of cows, yet in other areas would deny any claim to a title of property in these very same pawns.[214]

Yet when all is said and done, a large number of prestigious responsa in the areas under pressure were written and piously preserved; responsa with assumptions and judicial constructions so radical that as time passed and the conditions which brought them forth receded from memory, their cumulative impact upon the expanding corpus of halakhah should have been great. Yet it is a remarkable fact that when these rulings were read by men of later generations and of different milieus, men with no knowledge of history, with a deep reverence for the words of their predecessors and with a profound drive towards legal harmonization, they never incorporated these dicta, whose peculiar origin in Germanic law they did not dream of, into their vast synthesis of halakhah. In the understandable efflorescence of pledge-law which took place in the long Jewish Middle Ages, and which finds expression in the great section 72 of the 'Ḥoshen Mishpat', drawn up in the late sixteenth century, one will search in vain for any influence of the numerous rulings of R. David, Rashi, Riva, Rabbenu Tam, and Ri, which figure so prominently in the laws of usury. In reply to the problem of accommodation and purity, the halakhists

212 See above, pp. 82–3.

213 See above, n. 60(*c*) and similarly my observations about Rabbenu Tam in n. 83.

214 Cow (*maknei kefeila*): *Or Zarua'*, #211; *Mordekhai*, #337; *Teshuvot R. Me'ir mi-Rotenburg* (Berlin), #56 (pp. 20–1); *Teshuvot ha-Rosh* 108: 5 (slightly abbreviated). Other matters: *Ravyah*, ii, *Pesaḥim*, #465; MS Paris, Bibliothèque Nationale 1408, fo. 154b; *Teshuvot R. Me'ir mi-Rotenburg* (Lemberg, 1860), #86; *Mordekhai*, *Bava Batra*, #611; *Mordekhai*, *Kiddushin*, #486; ed. Y. Roth (New York, 1990), pp. 110–11. In the above-mentioned manuscript of the Bibliothèque Nationale, the following ruling appears immediately after the holding of Ravyah against acquisition of Gentile pawns:

> פסק דישראל אינו קונה במשכון דגוי כלל . . . ופסק ראה שהעולם רגילים לתת משכונות זה לזה כשמשדכין ביניהם כדי שלא [יחזרו] בהן. ואם הקנה זה לזה משכונות של גוי וחזרו בשידוכין אינו קנין כדפרשית לעיל, אבל אם לא אמ[ר] בשעת קנין שהוא היה משכון של גוי וחזר בו בשידוכין, קנה זה שכנגדו המשכונות, ואין זה נאמן אפילו בשבוע' [לומר] שהמשכונות של גוים היו כדי שלא יקנה זה שכנגדו המשכונות, דלא מצינו נשבע ונוטל כי האי גוונא.

It is not clear from the context whether or not this passage was equally authored by Ravyah (see above, n. 53). See *Ravan*, i, #112, and my remarks in the Appendix, note 80, item 5.

evolved alongside their very conscious synthesis an intuitive system of legal federalism, allowing each area a measure of autonomy to achieve its own equilibrium, to evolve its own principles, and to make its own ad hoc rulings, fully prescriptive within their own sphere, but which, if they could not be squared with the classic texts, could never acquire general binding force.[215] Of all the positions adopted |267| by the men of this period about pawnbroking and usury that I have chronicled at such length, only one, the transfer of debts via pawns, was later discovered to be implicit in talmudic discussions, and this alone ascended to the status of a general and controlling principle of halakhah.[216]

[215] See above, pp. 82–3, 87–8. (A) One might object that the ruling in 'Ḥoshen Mishpat' 66: 8 was expanded beyond its classic source, for no mention is made of any restriction as to Gentile pledges (see *Urim ve-Tumim* ad loc.). I have my doubts as to the validity of this inference even legally; historically, I would very much hesitate to see the different formulations in 'Ḥoshen Mishpat' and 'Even ha-'Ezer' as originating from anything other than mechanical copying. The *Tur* is clearly copying from *Sefer ha-Terumot* (51: 4: 7; ed. Goldschmidt, p. 1199), who in turn argues from *Kiddushin* 8b, which automatically restricts him to Jewish pledges. The matter at issue was the validity of debt transfer and not whose pawns were being used, so R. Shemu'el ha-Sardi didn't qualify his statement, and unqualified it entered the *Tur*. This automatic incorporation might very well have been facilitated by the fact that in practice Jews transferred Gentile debts in an identical fashion as they did Jewish ones, but I do not believe that R. Ya'akov ever intended in his work to extend formal recognition to assignment of non-Jewish debts by means of pawns. (B) On the recurring pattern of 'halakhic federalism' and other uses of this term, together with a brief note on the sharply contrasting path in matters of pawnbroking taken by Provençal halakhah, see the Appendix, note 215, items 2 and 3.

[216] See above, pp. 92–3.

APPENDIX

SUPPLEMENTARY NOTES TO CHAPTER SIX

NOTE 6

Adiel Schremer in 'Shikkul Da'at Hilkhati: "Pelugat ha-Re'ah" u-Meḥkar ha-Halakhah ha-Bikorti', *Diné Israel: Studies in Halacha and Jewish Law*, 28 (2011), 100, n. 6, claims that my demand for 'measurable deflection' reflects my philosophy of legal formalism to which Y. Lorberbaum and H. Shapira drew attention in 'Maimonides' *Epistle on Martyrdom* in the Light of Legal Philosophy' in a previous essay in the same journal, 25 (2008), 123–69. Whether or not I actually hold the legal philosophy attributed to me by my two colleagues has been addressed in my reply 'A Response to Lorberbaum and Shapira, "Maimonides' *Epistle on Martyrdom* in the Light of Legal Philosophy"', *Diné Israel*, 28 (2011), 123–62. (This essay will appear in the second volume of this series.) Be my legal philosophy as it may, my remarks about 'measurable deflection' reflected my views on how history should be written and not how law is actually made. The issue is one of evidence not of jurisprudence. The question is not how a judge consciously or unconsciously arrives at a verdict, but on what basis a historian may legitimately make a claim as to how a specific judge arrived at a specific ruling. Even a judicial realist has to prove his case. In the absence of external sources such as letters and diaries, the only internal evidence that comes to mind is that of 'measurable deflection', especially when dealing with 99 percent of medieval halakhists about whose personal life and outlook we know nothing and of whose writings we have little but the impersonal, near-formulaic reports characteristic of medieval sources.

NOTE 42 **Bibliographical Information**

1. The first edition of the *Sefer ha-Terumot* (Saloniki, 1596) has been used throughout in preparation of this study. Since, however, copies of this are hard to come by and the print is very poor, where no significant variants have been found I have cited the Venice edition, which has been photo-offset. Goldschmidt's edition, while useful, has its occasional problems. For example, the editor confronted here with a responsum of Rashi did not check *Teshuvot Rashi*, let alone utilize the *Sifrut de-Vei Rashi* for superior readings of that responsum. The one extant manuscript of the *Sefer ha-Terumot*, MS Cambridge, Add. 489, stops at Gate 45 and is, thus, of no use for our study, as the laws of *ribbit* begin in Gate 46.

2. In the 1930s J. Freimann began to publish the *Issur ve-Heter* of the Rashi school from copies of the MS Frankfurt am Main, Stadts- und Universitätsbibliothek 8vo 69. He saw about fifty pages through galleys before the printing was interrupted. The galleys, bound in book form and classified as Rara, were available in the Jewish National and University Library in Jerusalem. They were photostatted and disseminated in 1973 and have recently been reprinted as part of a five-volume set entitled *Sifrei Rashi* (Benei Berak, 1999), in the volume entitled *Sefer ha-Sedarim*. It is also available online at the Digitalized Book Repository of the National Library of Israel.

3. The *Sefer ha-Oreh*, as published by Buber, has two parts, each containing a separate work. The second section, termed *Ḥelek Sheni*, is nothing but the *Issur ve-Heter* of the Rashi school in a different sequence, as was noted by S. Albeck in his introduction to *Sefer ha-Eshkol* (Jerusalem, 1935), 37. Not surprisingly, a text parallel to our passage is found in the *Issur ve-Heter* published by J. Freimann.

4. Y. Kleinman, the editor of the *Mordekhai ha-Shalem 'al Betsah*, published a version of

Mordekhai: Eizehu Neshekh in *Netser Matt'ai 'al Massekhet Bava Metsi'a: Sefer Zikaron le-Natan Tsevi Rakov* (Jerusalem, 1991), 87–124. In his rush to meet the publication date of the memorial volume, he omitted any apparatus and failed in his brief introduction to clarify his editorial policy in the single text that he chose to print. As it stands, it is not an edition of the *Mordekhai*, and I have not cited it.

NOTE 56 Recent Developments in the Study of Germanic Law of the Middle Ages

To someone reared in the Lithuanian tradition of talmudics, reading Heusler, Gierke, and Huebner is a joy, as is the vigorous restatement of their positions by Wigmore. The categories are sharply defined, the distinctions clearly articulated, and their analyses and presentations have a strong inner consistency. Admittedly, at times they may seem to go a bit overboard and assert that everything in law is determined by the immanent logic of the system, even linguistic developments that seem clearly a result of lexical ambiguity. For example, in the appendix to note 58 below I discuss how the terms debtor, debitor, *deteur*, and *ba'al ḥov*, because of their inherent ambiguity, could denote both the borrower (he owes a debt) and the creditor (he owns the debt, has the payment of the debt coming to him) in Hebrew, koine Greek, Latin, and medieval French and German. The German school will have none of this. The common terminology denotes a shared, reciprocal obligation. Just as the debtor is duty bound to pay the debt, so the creditor is obliged to accept the payment. In Huebner's words (*A History of Germanic Private Law* [footnote 12], 466–7):

> The legal duty of the obligee (Gläubigerschuld). Just as the word *Schuld* raises in our minds, in the first place, the conception of the obligor's legal duty, so in the original meaning of the word, as a matter of usage, a *Schuld* was first conceived as a duty to perform. But modern Germanistic legal theory has established the important and pregnant fact that in both law and speech of the primitive Germans, and even of the later Germans, the obligee (*Gläubiger*) was also thought of as a *Schuldner*, and was so designated. This was possible because the conception of *Schuld* was based upon the wholly general idea of a duty legally prescribed. Even in our sense of the word there is a duty, legally determined, on the part of the creditor: equally, as respects him there results from the obligational relationship a legal command, namely, to accept the performance to which the other party is obligated. He too 'shall' do something; it is his duty to receive what is owed to him. To the obligation of the obligor, namely a legal duty to perform (and to abstain), there corresponds an obligation of the obligee, namely a legal duty to accept performance. And therefore in the sources we find the obligor and obligee designated by exactly the same term; a fact that cannot be disregarded, else many a statement of the medieval legal sources will remain unintelligible.

However, this seems a minor fault in view of all their sterling virtues (of thought, one should add, not of style).

Then one pauses and asks: who in the Middle Ages entertained these clear and distinct ideas? Gierke and company are not analyzing the doctrines of the Four Doctors of the school of Roman law in Bologna or the writings of Gratian in canon law. They are analyzing customaries of Scandinavia and Germany. The nobles and peasants did not entertain these notions. To businessmen, then as now, laws were simply rules they had to live by or try to circumvent. They neither knew nor cared about abstract conceptions of property. These laws were also not being taught and analyzed in any 12th- or 13th-century schools in France, Germany, or Scandinavia, for such schools as existed did not teach Germanic law. Germanic and north Germanic (i.e. Scandinavian) law books are simply transcriptions of what were, to those who first put them in writing, the immemorial practices of their community. One realizes, then, that Heusler, Gierke, and Huebner formulated the meaning of data from the Middle Ages according to the finest standards of legal analysis available at the turn of the 20th century. They also tended, quite naturally, to contrast the notions that they found implicit in Germanic law with those that are explicit in Roman law, the dominant legal system in western Europe for centuries. The result is superb law, but questionable history. This becomes even clearer if one notes the differing perspective of their contemporary, Frederic Maitland and then reads his treatment of the medieval pawn. In *Township and Borough* (Cambridge, 1898), 22, he wrote: 'If we speak, we must speak with words; if we think, we must think with thoughts. We are moderns and our thoughts cannot but be modern. Perhaps . . . it is too late for us to be early English. Every thought will be too sharp, every word will imply too many contrasts.' When he addressed pawnbroking (F. Pollock and F. Maitland, *History of English Law* [Cambridge, 1898], ii. 152–7, 176–83), he struggled at great length to recapture the thoughts of a distant past in all its alterity, to retrieve something of the inchoate medieval notions of 'one's own', in which 'possession' and 'ownership' were somehow indistinguishable and owing and owning were intertwined.

Not surprisingly, a reaction has set in against the clear-cut constructs of the German school. However, that does not affect my analysis. As I have pointed out the issue is not what the facts of Germanic law meant to medieval Germans and Frenchmen, but how these facts would be construed by medieval Ashkenazic halakhists—and that admits of no question. The distinction between ownership and possession is implicit in the Mishnah, as Rashi, seeking to prevent any mistaken contemporary notions from taking root in the Jewish community, pointed out (see footnote 98(*a*)) and is *explicitly* formulated by R. Yoḥanan in the 2nd century in a dictum (*zeh le-fi she-eino shelo, ve-zeh le-fi she-eino bi-reshuto*) that is repeated no fewer than eight times in the Talmud (*Kiddushin* 52a; *Bava Kamma* 68b, 69a, 70a, 111a; *Bava Metsi'a* 7b; *Ḥullin* 134a). That conversion (*sheliḥut yad*) is theft is again a talmudic commonplace. The data of Germanic law would yield to a medieval Jewish scholar exactly the same results as they yielded to Heusler and Gierke some 800 years later.

Some of the facts of medieval pawning have been modified by recent research; however, the crucial ones for my argument are corroborated again and again in medieval Jewish sources. It is clear that in the places of major Jewish settlement, the Germanic laws of pawning as described by the late 19th-century scholars obtained in full. Pawns were regularly re-pawned, sold, and given provisionally as gifts, and Talmudists speak of the 'sale' and 'acquisition' of pawns (see text, pp. 80–2, 87). *Hand muß Hand wahren*, with all its implications for 'ownership', both to the modern and halakhic mind, is repeatedly corroborated from the time of Rabbenu Gershom, at the turn of the first millennium, through the mid-14th century (footnote 98(*a*)). That a pawn is a quit-payment, so that if the pawn is worth less than the debt the creditor can make no claim for the difference, is explicit in the famous proclamation of Rabbenu Tam (footnote 58). That surrender of possession meant surrender of ownership was taken for granted by Ravan and later by an anonymous respondent in *She'elot u-Teshuvot Or Zarua' u-Maharam* (footnotes 60(*c*), 206(*c*)); appendix to note 80, item 3, below.

For recent developments in the understanding of Germanic law, see A. Erler and E. Kaufmann, eds., *Handwörterbuch zur Deutschen Rechtsgeschichte* (*HRG*), i–v (Berlin, 1971–1998), s.v. *Gewere*, *Hand wahre Hand*, *Pfändung*, *Schuld und Haftung*, and references and cross-references there given. (The updated edition of the first volume published in Berlin in 2008, under the editorship of A. Cordes and H. Lück, stops at *Geistliche Gerichtsbarkeit* and does not reach the entry *Gewere*.)

NOTE 58

The repeated confusion of *malveh* and *loveh* in Hebrew texts occurs as a result of both simple scribal error and the fact that in all the other languages that the scribes might have known (French, German, Latin) the terms *deteur*, *Schuldner*, *Schuldiger*, and *debitor* often denoted also the creditor. (See Huebner, *Germanic Private Law* [footnote 12], 466–7; O. von Gierke, *Schuld und Haftung im älteren deutschen Recht*. Untersuchungen zur deutschen Staats- und Rechtsgeschichte 100 [Breslau, 1910], 8, n. 6; P. Viollet, ed., *Établissement de St. Louis*, i [Paris, 1881], 122.) This interchange in common parlance affected even the term *nosheh*, which was used to denote also the debtor (*Teshuvot Ḥakhmei Tsarfat ve-Lotir*, #34: ומסר לו הבעל חוב [=הלוה] שני ראשי פספסין כדרך כל הנושים [fasfasin = festuca], see below). In the case of *nosheh* the anomaly was too great and was ultimately rejected, but the term *ba'al ḥov*, with its inherent ambivalence, grew increasingly to mean debtor until Rashi himself employed it thus in his commentary to Isaiah 58: 3 and again dictated it to his grandson, Rashbam, who was drawing up under his direction a commentary-code on *'Avodah Zarah* (*Or Zarua'*, iv [Jerusalem, 1890], *'Avodah Zarah*, #108; see E. E. Urbach, *Ba'alei ha-Tosafot* [footnote 11], 54–5). It even entered legal formularies as the *shetar ḥov* found in *Maḥzor Vitry*, ii, 2nd edn. (Nuremberg, 1923), # 567; see A. Gulak, *Otsar ha-Shetarot* (footnote 14), 207, n. 2. For several centuries *debitor*, *Schuldiger*, and *ba'al ḥov* showed common meanings and one seemed simply a translation of the other. When in the 13th and 14th centuries *Schuldiger* and *debitor* returned to their original meaning, they pulled *ba'al ḥov* with them, and in the lingua franca of Ashkenazic Jewry, Yiddish, *ba'al ḥov* came to mean debtor only. (The inherent ambiguity of the term *ba'al ḥov* allowed it to be employed for the debtor on rare occasions in the Talmud—see S. Abramson, 'Peshatot', *Leshonenu*, 16 [1948–9], 65–6—and occasionally this use infiltrated even the formulations of so pure a Hebraist as Maimonides, as in 'Hilkhot Malveh ve-Loveh', 1: 3.) The same shift in meaning occurred in koine Greek, the language popularly spoken in Palestine (and much of the Mediterranean littoral) in the Era of the Sages (*Ḥazal*). See S. Lieberman, *Greek in Jewish Palestine* (New York, 1952), 156. (See the appendix to note 56 above for the manner in which German legal historians at the turn of the 20th century treated this inherent ambiguity.)

On *fasfasin*, see A. M. Fuss, 'Rashei Fasfasin = Tally', *Leshonenu*, 24 (1960), 70–2. On the use of a rod or straw, *festuca*, in the creation of obligations, see Huebner, *Germanic Private Law* (footnote 12), 495, 497–503; Brissaud, *A History of French Private Law* (footnote 57), 482–4.

NOTE 62

1. Full title was acquired only via the format ceremony of *Auflassung* (*resignatio*) on the part of the debtor. Theoretically this is beyond question; however, one may entertain doubts as to the actual importance of *Auflassung* in day-to-day moneylending. The seeking out of the debtor before witnesses and the three appearances in court are commensurate with transfers as significant as those of land. However, it seems somewhat implausible that the average pawnbroker went through this process weekly for every piece of household crockery, clothes, agricultural implements, and the like that were given to him as security for short-term loans. We know from Jewish sources that no *Auflassung* was required by Germanic law in the 11th and 12th centuries once the sum of the outstanding principle and interest equaled the value of the pledge. Under such circumstances the pawn automatically became the property of the creditor (*Teshuvot Rashi*, #178; *Ravan*, i, #112). From documents and formularies of land-gages we learn that it was often stipulated in the initial contract that upon default the creditor automatically acquired the gage. The few contracts about movable pledges that have come down to us (see the texts referred to by de Roover, *Money, Banking and Credit* [footnote 15], p. 145, n. 111) contain no such proviso, yet we may conjecture that such provisos were often made. So we find in Glanvill, *De legibus et consuetudinibus regni Anglie* (New Haven, 1932), 10: 6 (see H. D. Hazeltine, *Die Geschichte des englischen Pfandrechts*, Untersuchungen zur deutschen Staats- und Rechtsgeschichte 92 [Breslau,

1907], 197, n. 2), and so we equally find in Jewish sources. We encounter it in a Jewish mobiliagage contract in a Franco-German formulary published by Gulak, *Otsar ha-Shetarot* (footnote 14), 233, #245: **למכור שלא על פי ב[ית] ד[ין] ושלא בהכרזה**. Similarly in a responsum found in MS Montefiore 130 fo. 11a: **אדם שהיה לו ספרי' באפותיקי, והקנה לו בקנין מעכשיו שאם לא יפרענו לאותו זמן שיהיו חלוטי'**, and such an oral proviso was claimed by the defendant in *Teshuvot R. Me'ir mi-Rotenburg* (Cremona), #1. One does not sense, in general, in the numerous responsa that treat pawns, the restrictive presence of *Auflassung* or of a regular delay of a year and a day.

2. For waiver of *Auflassung* in land-gages, see Wigmore, 'The Pledge-Idea' (footnote 56), 338, n. 2; Huebner, *Germanic Private Law* (footnote 12), 445. A simple conditional *Auflassung* was impossible because of *asmakhta* (see *Teshuvot R. Me'ir mi-Rotenburg* (Prague and Budapest), #91), hence the *harsha'ah*; cf. Gulak, *Otsar ha-Shetarot* (footnote 14), 206–8.

NOTE 66

Jay Rosen asked (in a private communication) whether the invocation of *ribbit mi-loveh le-malveh* by R. David of Mainz and Rashi in the instance of the 'pawned pawn' was necessary. One of the three parties is Gentile; more precisely, the debtor in that arrangement is a Gentile. Why not simply say that the case of the 'pawned pawn' is permissible because the debtor is a Gentile? Rava's case in *Bava Metsi'a* (69b, see above, p. 72) treats a situation where all three parties are Jews, hence the permissive factor can only be the triangular relationship; in the case of the pawned pawn discussed by Ashkenazic scholars, however, one party is Gentile.

This question does not lead me to doubt my interpretation of these two scholars' words. Rashi and R. David did claim that a triangular relationship existed. The creditor is clearly Jewish. If the debt is that of the first Jew, and he is also the one physically paying the debt, the only way that Rava's ruling could be invoked is by viewing the first Jew, the payor, as the agent of the Gentile. If so, Rashi and R. David would be claiming *yesh sheliḥut le-goy le-kula*! There is no alternative but to see the Gentile as the debtor of the second Jew. That is to say, the second loan was not actually a loan between two Jews; rather, the first Jew sold the Gentile's debt to the second Jew. Thus the inference that Rashi and R. David viewed the transfer of the pawn as sale of the debt remains intact. The question is: why did they both resort to the sale of debt for this allowance (based on Rava's triangular ruling) rather than to the simple fact that *ribbit* was being paid by a Gentile debtor?

Their choice was tactical, and astutely so. As we shall see (pp. 111–12), *ribbit mi-loveh le-malveh* was the term that Early Ashkenaz employed for economically usurious relations and that was, moreover, the crucial criterion for the existence of *ribbit*. It was also a statement of public policy. Were a genuinely usurious situation to arise by some circumvention or even inadvertently, the courts should find some way to forbid it; and if money had been paid, it should demand restitution. Rashi and R. David were equally of the opinion that usury was determined by legal and not economic categories. *Ribbit* depended entirely on the formal definition of the parties to the loan, by the halakhic categories of 'creditor' and 'debtor' (pp. 99–102, 108–9, 116–17).

They were willing to take a stand in *Schadennehmen* against the conception of usury of Early Ashkenaz. However, they saw no reason to get involved in this question in the controversial matter of the pawned pawn. As we shall soon see (pp. 88–93), its allowance entailed three major changes in Jewish civil law. It demanded the concession that there were property rights in a Gentile pawn and that a sale took place in every re-pawning, even though the parties to the transaction may have spoken of it as a 'loan'. Finally, the transference of the pawn automatically constituted transfer of the debt. From the point of view of usury there were no problems—either from their perspective or from that of their predecessors. The pawned pawn relationship was triangular and economically innocent, as the money came out of the Gentile's pocket. The phrase *lo asrah Torah ela ribbit mi-loveh le-malveh* thus killed two birds—their notion of *ribbit* and the popular one—with one stone.

Had they invoked the permissibility of 'Gentile *ribbit*', they would have had to go further and spell out to the broader community that the money was not just formally but also economically that of the non-Jew, as it came out of the Gentile's pocket. That was the last thing they wanted to do. It would have validated the very outlook they were about to challenge in their next ruling on *Schadennehmen*. *Lo asrah Torah ela ribbit haba'ah mi-loveh le-malveh* disposed of the problem of economic usury without ever mentioning it—and this, to my thinking, is the reason they chose to employ that argument.

Rashi's view that usury was defined formally—not economically—and that this principle was expressed by Rava's ruling became, as did so many of Rashi's conclusions, axiomatic to French halakhic culture. Indeed, in the next century the Tosafists' entire tactic of allowance revolved around splitting the legal parties to a loan from the economic ones. When, in the thirteenth century, various French scholars revived (unknowingly) the old Ashkenazic notion of economic usury, whether on the basis of surety (*'arev*) or on the basis of *aḥarayut* mentioned in the Tosefta—much as Provençal scholars had done from the very outset—they were seeking to alter a climate of opinion that had obtained for some 200 years. Not surprisingly, their ideas met with a mixed reception (see *Halakhah, Kalkalah* [footnote 1], 102–11).

NOTE 79

At first glance, it would seem that towards the close of our period R. Me'ir of Rothenburg demurred from this ruling, a dissent which would have put to question most business practices (*Mordekhai, Bava Batra*, #614, and indeed, some MSS of the *Mordekhai* corroborate the printed version, e.g. London, British Library 537, Parma, de Rossi 929). However, the most authentic text (written in the first person and possessing the signature מ'ב"ב שי') is found in *Teshuvot R. Me'ir mi-Rotenburg* (Lemberg), #404, and *Teshuvot R. Me'ir mi-Rotenburg* (Prague and Budapest), ##354, 989, and reads: חובות תמורת ערבונות. The purchaser did not acquire the Gentile pawn so as to thereby acquire the debt; rather, the purchaser sought to purchase the debt by giving as payment a Gentile pawn taken in a previous loan. That the pawn is that of a Gentile is clear from the end of the responsum. (An expanded version of the text of the *Mordekhai* is found in *She'elot u-Teshuvot Or Zarua' u-Maharam b. Barukh*, ed. Y. Z. Cahana [Jerusalem, 1943], #460. The editor sensed the problem in the text and entered in brackets *temurat* as found in the parallel sources. The Parma manuscript that Bloch refers to in his notes to the Budapest edition of the *Teshuvot R. Me'ir mi-Rotenburg* is Parma, de Rossi 651, and its reading corroborates the reading in *Teshuvot R. Me'ir mi-Rotenburg* [Lemberg].) See also *Teshuvot Maharil*, ed. Y. Satz (Jerusalem, 1980), 115, #75; *Teshuvot Maharil he-Ḥadashot*, ed. Y. Satz (Jerusalem, 1973), ##138, 161; and *Shakh*, 'Yoreh De'ah', 168–9: 60. I hasten to add that forfending this objection of non-transferability cannot be adduced as further proof of the validity of the concretized lien interpretation over the rejected *shetar* analogy; see the appendix to note 80 below, item 3. The latter would, most probably, obviate the same difficulty; see *Teshuvot Maharil he-Ḥadashot*, #138 and nn. 4, 5, 7; and R. Me'ir Eisenstadt, *Teshuvot Panim Me'irot*, ii (Lemberg, 1891), #22, s.v. *ve-'atah*.

NOTE 80

1. One has been sorely tempted in the above discussion to obviate all our difficulties by claiming that they fell back upon the rule of *dina de-malkhuta dina*, especially with regard to the

Gentile's own property. But if this be so, why should they have denied acquisition in cases of inheritance? A similar dichotomy appears later in the rulings of Ravyah (footnote 214). And again when, in the end, the issue of Gentile non-acquisition of pledges was openly raised, Ri employed fairly complicated and problematic lines of argument to circumvent this fact (see text, pp. 141–6), yet it never occurred to him to cut the Gordian knot with *dina de-malkhuta dina*. Medieval Talmudists restricted this notion to foreign relations, as it were: to relations between Jews and their secular rulers, as, for example, taxation, coinage, and maintenance of the public order. They strenuously avoided employing it in intra-Jewish affairs. Any such utilization would have entailed a massive infusion of Gentile legislation into Jewish civil law and undermined the rule of halakhah. This is true not only of the Ashkenazic community, but equally of other Jewish communities in the Middle Ages, irrespective of their assessment of the quality of Gentile law and governance. Note, for example, the sharp reaction in Provence and Spain to Rabad's suggestion to allow Gentile law to fill the lacunae in the halakhic system. See my 'A Response to Rabbi Ephraim Buckwold's Critique of "Rabad of Posquières: A Programmatic Essay", Part I', *Torah U-Mada Journal*, 14 (2006–7), 205 (the essay will appear in the third volume of this series). This is doubly true of Ashkenazic Talmudists. Their highly negative view of Gentile governance led them to constrict—far more than did scholars of other medieval Jewish communities—even the scope of *shetarot ha-'olim be-'arka'ot shel goyim*, which had received talmudic validation on the basis of *dina de-malkhuta dina* (*Gittin* 10b). See S. Shilo, *Dina de-Malkhuta Dina* (Jerusalem, 1975), 312–62, 435–7.

2. Cash sale might have been justified upon the principle of *situmta* (*Bava Metsi'a* 74a), see R. Shimshon b. Tsadok, *Sefer Tashbets* (Warsaw, 1876), #398; ed. S. Angel (Jerusalem, 2011), #398; *Sefer ha-Tashbets ha-Katan: Nusaḥ Maharam Mints u-Veit Yosef*, ed. S. M. M. Schne'orson (Jerusalem, 2005), #345, and the notes of R. Perets ad loc. However, it is clear from the *Teshuvot Ḥakhmei Tsarfat ve-Lotir*, #48, that either the argument of *situmta* hadn't occurred to scholars in this period, or, what is less likely, that they instinctively concurred with the negative doctrine of R. Yeḥi'el of Paris cited by R. Perets.

3. One might contend that the basis for the ruling of assignment via pledges is the doctrine of *otiyot niknot bi-mesirah* (*Bava Batra* 77a), according to the old Ashkenazic version in the Talmud (see *Bava Batra* 77a [ed. Romm], Rabbenu Gershom, s.v. *amar*; ed. Leitner, vol. i, p. 171 ad loc.; Rashbam s.v. *hakhi* and see Rashbam, *Bava Batra* 147b, s.v. *ha-mokher*; *Or Zarua'*, iv [Jerusalem, 1890], *Sanhedrin*, #70), and that *mashkon* should be viewed as analogous to *shetar* on the basis of the measure of guaranteed collection that is provided by both (see *Ravan*, i, #111), and thus see in the transfer of one as in the other an assignment of debt. Even if one were to overlook the difficulties in carrying this analogy over from collection to assignment, this line of reasoning could not be read into R. Meshullam's ruling or that of R. David. It is not quite certain, or, more precisely, I am not quite certain, just what the Rhine doctrine is regarding *otiyot niknot bi-mesirah*, as the remarks of the Mainz commentary (known as the commentary of Rabbenu Gershom) are not quite free of obscurity on this point (see Rabbenu Gershom on *Bava Batra* [ed. Romm], 77a, s.v. *amar*; ed. Leitner, vol. i, p. 171 ad loc.; 76a, s.v. *ve-otiyot*; ed. Leitner, vol. i, p. 169 ad loc., in contrast to Rashbam's parallel comments; see, however, 76b, s.v. *rabbi omer*).

Secondly, even assuming that 11th-century scholars ruled that *otiyot niknot bi-mesirah*, had this doctrine underlain R. David's ruling, he could never have spoken of *meshikhat ha-mashkon*. *Meshikhah* in this context is the direct opposite, the very antithesis of *mesirah* (see *Bava Batra* 75b–76a, Rabbenu Gershom ibid., and Rashbam s.v. *ve-otiyot*), and simply grates upon the ear. (Ri's doctrine ibid., s.v. *iy*, evolved a century later, and even if it is a correct analysis of the amoraic position, this requirement never influenced terminology or speech. The case of

R. Amram Ḥasida, *Bava Batra* 151a, may very well have been according to R. Nathan's doctrine of *meshikhah*. At any rate, the case from 3rd-century Babylonia is the last in which we hear such language.) R. David's use of *meshikhah* indicates that he sees the legal acquisition of the concrete pledge as *ipso facto* resulting in debt transfer, which leads, in my opinion, to the doctrine set above. From a responsum of Ravan (vol. i, #112) we know, at least, that this was the commonly held understanding of debt assignment in the 12th century. Ravan was asked: **ראובן תבע לשמעון מישכנתי משכון ביד גוי ואבדו הגוי והגיע לידך החזירהו לי, ושמעון משיב אני זכיתי בו תחילה ואם לא בכולו מ"מ זכיתי בחוב הגוי**. The defendant's words register the conceptions of the surrounding medieval society: the pawn is the debt reified, and acquisition of the pawn is *ipso facto* acquisition of the debt. Ravan naturally rejects this position on numerous grounds. Note, however, that he does not do so on the basis that as the debt is acquired via *mesirah* and as *mesirah* requires conveyance, there can be no acquisition via *mesirah* with abandoned property (*hefker*). See *Bava Metsi'a* 8b, **אמר רב הונא מוסירה מחבירו קנה, במציאה ובנכסי הגר לא קני, מאי לשון מוסירה, אמר רבא אידי אסברה לי—כאדם המוסר דבר לחבירו, בשלמא מחבירו קני דקא מסר ליה חבריה, אלא במציאה ובנכסי הגר מאן קא מסר ליה**. (I do not believe that one may retroject onto 11th-century, Ashkenazic thought Ri's doctrine proffered—as dialectical resolution—in *Kiddushin* 25b, s.v. *behemah*: *mihu hakh pirkha*. However, if one insists on so doing, one should equally retroject his doctrine articulated in *Bava Batra* 76a, s.v. *iy* end: *ve-af 'al gav*.)

4. One cannot emend the *makhar* that R. Meshullam employed to *masar* because of the context in which it occurs—*u-makhar lo shelish ha-mashkon*. It is improbable that the term *mashkon* is being used in the abstract sense of the word, i.e. several pawns were given and R. Meshullam refers to the *mesirah* of a third of these pawns. When pawnbroking was a daily reality, responsa generally noted whether one or several pawns were used. To give some examples of the use of the plural, *mashkonot*, just from the 11th century: *Teshuvot R. Me'ir mi-Rotenburg* (Prague and Budapest), #794 (by Rabbenu Gershom Me'or ha-Golah; for authorship see footnote 129), #875 (R. Yehudah, Ba'al Sefer ha-Dinim; for authorship see footnote 38(*b*)), and the responsum of Rashi cited above, p. 77.

5. One might argue that the phrase of the defendant in Ravan (vol. i, #112), *zakhiti be-ḥov ha-goy*, means that he acquired rights in the pawn proportionate to the debt owed him, but not the debt itself. Unquestionably that is what the claim would amount to if it were rephrased in classic halakhic terms; and Ravan naturally responded to the claim in these terms. I do believe, however, that the formulation of the defendant reflects the common, lay perception of the realities of the situation. He claims that he has acquired the pawn in its entirety (see above, item 3) or, at the very least, he has acquired the debt for which the pawn was given. Historically, one must always distinguish between the nature of the claims as expressed by the parties, which often mirror popular thinking, and the halakhic formulation employed by the respondent who, like any lawyer or judge, must translate and often transform an unsophisticated and intuitive formulation into halakhic categories so as to address the legal issue presented by the enquiry.

6. Ravan did not here treat the acquisition of the pawn as acquisition of the debt because the issue lies outside the area of relentless business pressure, seeing that it is a question of lost property and not of pawnbroking (see text, pp. 146–9; for Rashi's stand, see footnote 93).

7. As to the authorship of *The Commentary of Rabbenu Gershom on Bava Batra*, see Y. M. Ta-Shma, 'Ha-Perush ha-Meyuḥas le-Rabbenu Gershom Me'or ha-Golah la-Talmud', *Kiryat Sefer*, 53 (1978), 356–65; reprinted in: *Keneset Meḥkarim: 'Iyyunim ba-Sifrut ha-Rabbanit bi-Yemei ha-Beinayim*, i (Jerusalem, 2005), 3–20.

NOTE 81

1. These two lines, **איתביה רבא לרב נחמן: 'קדשה במשכון מקודשת', התם במשכון דאחרים וכדרב יצחק, דאמר רבי יצחק מנין לבעל חוב שקונה משכון וכו'**, are crucial to pawnbroking, as two inferences essential to the conduct of this business may be drawn from them. First, once a pawn has been transferred, the debt cannot be waived. Second, transfer of the pawn automatically entails transfer of the debt. The Talmud states that the creditor can use as *kesef kiddushin* a pawn (of a third party) received as security for a loan. The Talmud states elsewhere (*Kiddushin* 48a) that a debt (of a third party) cannot be used as *kesef kiddushin*. Since the original creditor—who utilized the debt as *kesef kiddushin*—can still waive that debt even after its transfer, the woman legitimately fears that he may subsequently do just that, and that she will be left with nothing. The question naturally presents itself: why then is a pawn valid *kesef kiddushin*? If the debt is waived, the pawn must equally be returned. The inference is that, with the transfer of the pawn, the original creditor loses the right to debt waiver. (*Shitah Lo Noda' le-Mi* [Constantinople, 1751]; *Ḥiddushei ha-Ramban*, ed. I. Z. Meltser [Jerusalem, 1928]; ed. D. Hakohen [Jerusalem, 2005]; *Ḥiddushei ha-Rashba*, ed. A. Lichtenstein [Jerusalem, 1983]; *Ḥiddushei ha-Ritva*, ed. A. Dinin [Jerusalem, 1985], on *Kiddushin* ad loc.) The woman, furthermore, cannot retain the pawn of a third party unless she is the creditor of that party. (If subsequently someone purchased the loan, he could rightfully demand the pawn.) Yet no mention is made in the *sugya* of any debt transfer. Clearly, with the acquisition of the pawn, the woman acquired the debt (*Sefer ha-Terumot* 51: 4: 7; ed. Goldschmidt, p. 1199, whence to 'Ḥoshen Mishpat' 66: 8). Neither of these conclusions was perceived until the 13th century, though they had been previously intuited: the first by the scholars of Early Ashkenaz as discussed in the text, the second by Rabad of Posquières.

2. The inference from *Kiddushin* did not underlie the 11th-century ruling about debt transfer by pawn. First, it is never invoked in the literature of 11th-century Ashkenaz. Second, Rashi writes in his responsum that he believes the cases to be permissible but is afraid to so rule for fear of a 'strong negative reaction' (*la'agei safah*). It would be strange if Rashi, feeling deeply about an issue of considerable social consequence (see text, pp. 77, 94–5), kept his most convincing proof hidden in his back pocket. Admittedly, for the third assumption of his permissive ruling (see ibid.) he had no proof, but there is a world of difference in legal weight and public debate between a single assumption and a triple-decked one. Naftali Lewin has drawn my attention to Rashi's comments in that *sugya*, s.v. *be-mashkon* (see footnote 82). The most that can be said is that at a later date Rashi *may* have detected this principle in the passage in *Kiddushin*. It would be wise, though, to tread cautiously as Rashi's remarks there are anything but clear. See e.g. D. Friedman, *Piskei Halakhot: Yad David*, ii, *Hilkhot Ishut* (Warsaw, 1901), 5: 7, #88 (p. 88); 5: 16, #155; 5: 23, #211; E. Kalir, *Or Ḥadash 'al Kiddushin* (Vienna, 1799) ad loc.

3. As to the first inference, the inability to waive a debt once the pawn has been transferred, see *Sefer ha-Terumot* 51: 6: 3; ed. Goldschmidt, p. 1205: *ve-nish'al ha-Ravad*. Rabad did not perceive the inference from *Kiddushin*, but he was well aware of the universal practice of debt transfer by pawn and felt intuitively that this practice was halakhically correct. Seeking to ground his intuition, as any jurist must, in legal sources, he advanced a weak analogy to a ruling of Alfasi in *Ketubbot* about *matnat shekhiv me-r'a*. Moreover, Rabad infers the inability of the creditor to waive the debt after transferring the pawn by closely parsing the language of Alfasi in an allied issue and then analogizing the case of debt waiver to the one discussed by Alfasi (*Sefer ha-Terumot*, 51: 6: 3; ed. Goldschmidt, p. 1205). This is a strange mode of argument for someone who penned critiques of Alfasi. It is clearly an attempt to link an intuition to an authoritative text, more in the nature of an *asmakhta* than a proof. See my 'Rabad of Posquières: A Programmatic Essay', in I. Etkes and Y. Salmon, eds., *Studies in the History of Jewish Society in the Middle Ages* *and Modern Period Presented to Jacob Katz on his 75th Birthday* (Jerusalem, 1980), 34–5, and 'A Response to Rabbi Ephraim Buckwold' (see the appendix to note 80 above, item 1), 234–6. (Both essays will appear in the third volume of this series.)

NOTE 98

M. Z. Ḥasida in the 1930s was the first to publish *Shibbolei ha-Leket II*. His edition appeared *seriatim* in a mimeographed journal of his entitled *Ha-Segullah*. The penniless author would transcribe some three pages from a photograph of a manuscript of the *Shibbolei ha-Leket II* at the Bodleian Library in Oxford (Bodley 658) together with three pages from each manuscript of several other works at the Hebrew University Library on Mount Scopus, annotate his transcriptions and mimeograph them. When stapled together, these twelve pages or so made for an issue of the journal which he would attempt to sell to libraries and individual scholars to put some bread on his table. This went on for several years (1934–7). Ḥasida numbered the lines of his transcription so as to refer to them in his notes. The notes were quite good but had a slight drawback: Ḥasida could not always keep up the pace of his annotation with the pace of his transcriptions, so the notes to earlier issues would appear at times in later ones. With the advent of Xerox in the 1960s, the pages of the *Shibbolei ha-Leket II* were photostatted and bound as a book (which eased somewhat the problem of correlating notes with text, seeing that both were now found within one binding). The copies were swiftly snapped up, and it was to this edition, issued in 1969, with its numbered lines, that I refer both in the original article and in my book. In 1988 most of the work (but not all) was re-issued in Jerusalem by his descendant, S. Ḥasida, in a version based on all the then-available manuscripts. A number of people have continued to prefer the old, compact, typescript edition with its numbered lines and minimal notes to the bulkier new one. (The Reading Room of the National Library of Israel has kept both editions on the shelf side by side.) I have provided references for both editions in the notes and refer to the later one as 'new edn.'. The lines in the new edition are not numbered but admit of counting.

NOTE 117

The reader will notice that I have not treated *Teshuvot Rashi*, #177, taken from *Mordekhai*, #338. This is because I entertain serious doubts as to its authenticity. While it makes no substantive difference, for precision's sake, one should shift the attribution to Rashi of this responsum to R. Mordekhai and away from R. Tuvyah because MS Jewish Theological Seminary, Rabbinica 674, fo. 42b has the signature 'Tuvyah be-R[abbi] Eliyahu' after *ḥasid shoteh* (in Vilna edn., p. 156b, l. 22). The author of the immediately following *ve-'od mats'ati bi-teshuvot Rashi*, the responsum here under discussion, is thus R. Mordekhai. There is no question but that he believed this to be a responsum of Rashi—the printed text of the *Mordekhai* is corroborated by most manuscripts—but whether he was correct in crediting the attribution is another matter.

1. Any responsum of Rashi's which has only one source is suspect, though not necessarily disqualified. Most responsa had wider diffusion and were picked up in the *Sifrut de-Vei Rashi*, 12th-century Provençal sources, or 13th-century responsa collections. This decision is reported by none of Rashi's pupils. For a man who felt uneasy with a fiction involving a Gentile straw man to have propounded the one of *ein shaliaḥ li-devar 'averah* (there is no agency in crime, i.e. the agent and not the principal is held culpable for any crime perpetrated) is rather strange. A single, rabbinic injunction of *le-ḥumra* is all that one could transgress with the Gentile intermediary. No less than six pentateuchal injunctions could be breached by the *shaliaḥ li-devar 'averah* (see *Bava Metsi'a* 75b, Rashi, s.v. *malveh*). Yet, not only did Rashi suggest employing a Jewish agent, but proposed him unqualifiedly. No conditions were set forth either for ignorance on the part of the creditor or for the need to speak of repurchase at the time of redemption.

2. The use of *ein shaliaḥ li-devar 'averah* was, furthermore, unscrupulous. This principle, which expressed the belief of the halakhah in the absolute moral responsibility of a man for his actions, was here being employed to relieve him (and all others) of that very responsibility. To employ this principle not to fix guilt but to banish it is not clever but foul, not fiction but mockery. Such a device is doomed to failure. Law, in attempting to regulate reality, tends to create a reality of its own, a world of formal status brought into being by symbolic acts. To many a judge the world of his chambers is as real as, if not more real than, the one outside it. When confronted by a situation that it cannot change yet at the same time cannot acknowledge, the legal mind turns from the intractable reality and retreats momentarily to its own universe. There, by the appropriate symbolic acts, the situation is altered and brought into swift alignment with the norm. Any legal fiction must thus be true to the world from which it draws its sustenance. Whatever efficacy or suasion a legal fiction has, it possesses that by virtue of its impeccability. For this reason, few contracts are more iron-clad than the *shetar mekhirah* of *ḥamets*. Reality is tolerated, and the conscience persuaded to ignore it, precisely because of the certainty that legally it doesn't exist. The sale of the State of Israel during the sabbatical year to a penniless Arab by means of a contract duly executed is good legal fiction. It is unfaithful to reality, but true to law. The use of *ein shaliaḥ li-devar 'averah* to acquit of responsibility is false to law itself. A fiction undoubtedly, but one more foul than legal. It was the indignity done to halakhah by this ruling rather than the scope of the allowance—there are fictions of equal or greater compass in *ribbit*, the Gentile straw man, or the *heter 'iska*, for example—which bestirred the opposition. See the glossator to the above-cited *Mordekhai* and the tone of the commentators cited below.

3. Finally, Rashi's rulings are often innovative for their time, but rarely intrinsically radical. Most, once forgotten, were arrived at by others in the course of time. See e.g. Ri's arriving on his own at Rashi's doctrine of creditor ignorance for the allowance of the Gentile straw man (*Or Zarua'*, #212; see text, p. 137). No one in the Middle Ages, whether of French, German, Provençal, Spanish, or Moroccan provenance, ever propounded such an allowance for obvious reasons, and I find it difficult to imagine that the hesitant Rashi, so ill at ease with his Gentile straw man, did. Everything about the ruling seems out of character for Rashi.

4. Doubts as to the responsum's authenticity are not new. Long ago, R. Yosef Caro, R. Mordekhai Yaffe, and R. Eliyahu of Vilna, among others, denied on purely halakhic grounds the attribution to Rashi. (See 'Yoreh De'ah' 160: 16 and the references given by the commentators ad loc.) Other halakhists defended the ruling, but as the argument revolves about the ultimate legal validity of the ruling rather than its appropriateness for Rashi, we need not enter the matter.

NOTE 118

The passage in the *Mordekhai, Bava Metsi'a*—whether the Vilna or Riva di Trento version—from which the responsum is sometimes cited, e.g. *Teshuvot Rabbenu Gershom Me'or ha-Golah* (New York, 1956), #25, is an emended version of Ravyah's abridgment of Riva's handbook in which the decision first appears. Following the *Haggahot Asheri, Bava Metsi'a* 5: 5, the editor attributed the entire, lengthy text to Rabbenu Gershom. However, most of it was authored by Riva, as any perusal of the text in the *Shibbolei ha-Leket* will evince (see text, pp. 118–19). (This mistaken attribution led Ta-Shma to ascribe formulations of the early 12th century to Rabbenu Gershom. See 'Minhag Ashkenaz ha-Kadmon', to be published in the second volume of this series.) The text employed by Shlomo Eidelberg in his edition of *Teshuvot Rabbenu Gershom Me'or ha-Golah* is from the *Mordekhai*. Thus most of the citation was not authored by Rabbenu

Gershom. In addition, ll. 3–4 correspond neither to the Vilna version nor to that of Riva di Trento. One doesn't know, moreover, why the Riva de Trento edition, with its mediocre text, is singled out throughout this edition, as it is equally in Elfenbein's edition of *Teshuvot Rashi* (footnote 42). The first edition of the *Mordekhai* is that of Constantinople, 1509. Admittedly some bibliographical guides, as C. D. B. Friedburg's *Bet 'Eked Sefarim: Leksikon Bibliyografi li-Yedi'at ha-Sifrut ha-'Ivrit* (Antwerp, 1928–31), 414, #2078, gave Riva di Trento as the first printing of that work. However, Friedberg did so because the Constantinople printing of the *Mordekhai* is appended to *Alfasi*, as is still common today. If one is registering separate, bound books, the Riva di Trento edition of 1558 (printed apart from *Alfasi*, after the burning of the Talmud in 1553–4) will appear as the first printing of the *Mordekhai*; this, however, does not make it an *editio princeps*.

NOTE 126

Grossman, in his *Ḥakhmei Ashkenaz ha-Rishonim* (footnote 38(*b*)), 119–20, upholds the dominant view of Rabbenu Gershom's preeminence on the basis of the account in the *Or Zarua'*, ii (Zhitomir, 1862), #275; ed. Or 'Etsyon (Jerusalem, 2006), #275, pp. 205–6. I fail to see how one can base any claim to fame and authority on the basis of such a story. Questions of halakhic stature and authority are tested by how often a thinker's doctrines and rulings are invoked in the subsequent literature and the weight attached to those views. Consider for a moment the plethora of citations of Rabbenu Tam, Ri, Ravyah, and R. Me'ir of Rothenburg in the literature of their successors, and the nigh total absence of Rabbenu Gershom from the literature of his successors in the 11th century becomes even more striking. Indeed, I may be mistaken, but other than one alleged ordinance on his part (*Teshuvot Rashi*, #70), I cannot recall a single instance in that literature where Rabbenu Gershom's ruling or authority is invoked by another Talmudist. If argument be made from the fact that the responsa of Rabbenu Gershom that have come down to us are far more numerous than those of any of his contemporaries, the same argument for preeminence can be made for R. Yehudah Ba'al Sefer ha-Dinim in the next generation. All will agree that Rabbenu Gershom had the same preeminence among his colleagues as had R. Yehudah among his own contemporaries. That preeminence, however, was transient, and neither of the two were cited by their successors. Admittedly, Rabbenu Gershom was the preeminent scholar of the first generation of Ashkenazic halakhists, and thus he may well have put a stamp on Ashkenazic culture. This historic role, however, was unknown to succeeding generations of 11th-century Ashkenaz. In their eyes, he loomed no larger that did R. Yehudah Ba'al Sefer ha-Dinim, and neither was cited by them.

Agus's contention that the heightened reputation of Rabbenu Gershom began with the unbelievably humble Rabbi Ya'akov b. Yakar, who imparted it to his devoted pupil, Rashi, who gave it wide dissemination, makes a great deal of sense. It was due to this new, augmented reputation, that Rabbenu Gershom's responsa were preserved, while those of R. Yehudah, whose fame received no posthumous enhancement, survived by the merest accident in a collection that was incorporated into the Prague edition of the *Teshuvot R. Me'ir mi-Rotenburg* (see footnote 38(*b*)). For R. Ya'akov's humility, see Rashi's characterization: *she-hinhig et 'atsmo ke-askupa nidreset ve-sam 'atsmo sheyarei shirayim* (*Siddur Rashi*, ed. A. Freimann [Berlin, 1910], 80), and the story of his sweeping the ground in front of the Torah ark (*aron ha-kodesh*) with his beard reported in *Sefer Ḥasidim*, ed. Y. Wistinetzki, 2nd edn. (Frankfurt am Main, 1924), #991.

NOTE 176

1. I find it difficult to accept the suggestion of some that Rashbam's posture to usury was influenced by his 'deep involvement' in Christian polemics. First, the depth of that involvement is

dubious. His *Commentary on the Pentateuch* is animated by a desire to lay low the dragon of *derash*, but hardly that of Christianity. Defense of the faith is not only not the *raison d'être* of his book; it is scarcely a shaping factor. The work (on some ten occasions) takes critical cognizance of Christian interpretation; it is not molded by a drive for rebuttal. There are few, if any, cases where one feels that, were it not for Christian commentary, Rashbam would have read the biblical verses differently. Indeed, as David Berger, who has made an intensive study of the matter, has pointed out to me, the measure of preoccupation with Christian polemics in Ashkenazic Jewry was in inverse proportion to the individual's intellectual stature and his attainments in halakhah. Of all those who took up the cudgels against Christianity, Rashbam was clearly the greatest halakhist and his involvement was the least, both in extent and in intensity. Second, even granting deep involvement, *ribbit* does not appear to have been under attack at the time. Unlike Yosef ha-Mekkane or the author of the *Nitsaḥon Yashan*, both of whom wrote a century or two later, Rashbam attempts no vindication of the Jewish–Gentile usury allowance, nor does he seek to emphasize the severity of the law in intra-Jewish loans. In fact, he makes no reference to usury at all in his writings. Rashbam felt that a word was in place for defense of dietary laws but felt no similar need with regard to *ribbit*. This is not surprising as the Church offensive against usury was to begin only a generation or so after his death (see footnote 174). Unable to find any traces of sensitivity to usury in so porous and malleable a field as biblical exegesis and polemics, I am loathe to attribute to it a controlling role in the more rigorous and technical discipline of halakhah.

2. Rashbam's re-emergence in the *Teshuvot R. Me'ir mi-Rotenburg* (Lemberg) is pure literary accident and cannot be correlated with the decline of the *ma'arufya* in the 13th and 14th centuries. If Jewish managerial activity had decreased, Jewish fronting had risen sharply. From the 13th century on, it becomes a permanent feature of the financial landscape of western Europe. (See Hoffmann, *Der Geldhandel* [footnote 15 above], 121; L. Poliakov, *Les Banchieri juifs et le Saint-Siège du XIIIe au XVIIe siècle* [Paris, 1965], 51, n. 2; Nahon, 'Le Crédit' [footnote 15 above], 1127–8.) Rashbam's doctrine was as ill suited to the 14th century as it had been to the early 12th.

NOTE 182

The radical remedy of R. Ya'akov of Orleans (*Haggahot Mordekhai*, #455) was uniformly rejected. People might embrace a radical allowance of Rabbenu Tam, but not one of a minor Tosafist. They desired an allowance for intra-Jewish usury, to be sure, but, desirous at the same time to live by the rule of halakhah, they would accept nothing less than an authoritative go-ahead. See my remarks in '"Religious Law and Change" Revisited' (Chapter 10 below). Stein had already noted that not a single agreement with this remedy is registered in the English *shetarot*, and I would add that over a score of Ashkenazic formularies in manuscript were checked and R. Ya'akov's contract was not to be found. It is found in MS Parma, de Rossi 1237, fo. 153a. This formulary, however, was compiled in 15th-century Italy (see fo. 150b). One can't tell whether the compiler found this document in a formulary or in the *Mordekhai* and added it to round out his collection. To the best of my knowledge the *shetar* is found only in some copies of the notes entitled *Haggahot Mordekhai*. Note that in the printed edition, it is found in the second and not in the first group of *haggahot*. Similarly, it is absent from MS Jewish Theological Seminary, Rabbinica 674, which in *Eizehu Neshekh* fuses the text of our printed *Mordekhai* with that of the printed *Haggahot Mordekhai*. The *haggahot* containing R. Ya'akov's *shetar* made their way into the margins of several manuscripts of the *Kitsur Mordekhai* such as MSS Cambridge, Or. 71, fo. 16b; Hamburg, Staats- und Universitätsbibliothek 194, fo. 14a; Oxford, Bodley 672, fo. 14b. Most copies of the *Kitsur Mordekhai*, however rich they may be in varied glosses, do not contain it, as e.g. MSS Oxford, Bodley 673, fos. 14c–16b; Oxford, Bodley 2444, fos. 8–9; Parma, de Rossi 397 (unfoliated); Parma, de Rossi 1334 (unfoliated); Vatican 324, fos. 121b–124a; Cambridge, Add. 540, fos. 18–20; Moscow, RSL, Günzburg 189, fos. 57–8. One can't speak of two traditions of marginal glosses to the *Kitsur Mordekhai*, as this *shetar* appears in versions of that work considerably different from one another; at the same time, it is absent from manuscripts such as Oxford, Bodley 672, which in many ways is similar to those copies that register this document. The only source, outside the family of *Mordekhai* texts, that has this *shetar* is the 15th-century MS London, Montefiore 108, fo. 100 a–b. However, this work draws heavily upon the *Mordekhai* and hence can scarcely serve as an independent witness to the *shetar*'s diffusion.

NOTE 189

The passages which might indicate such compliance (MS Hamburg, Staats- und Universitäts-bibliothek 45, fo. 183c–d: *u-gedolah mi-zot amar li rabbi* and *u-ma'aseh hayah be-Paris*) are equally explicable by Ri's doctrine of presumed legality (*le-hetera ka-mikhaven*, see text below) or an unconscious infiltration of *Hand muß Hand wahren*. At first blush the latter interpretation seems ineluctable for we read in the Hamburg manuscript; recently published in Emanuel, *Teshuvot Maharam u-Venei Doro*, ii, #411: **ומעש[ה] היה בפריש במעות הר' יוסף ששלח משכון ביד גוי ולוה מישר[אל] בריבית, וכשנודע הדבר למלוה לא רצה להחזיר המשכון, ולא היה כח ביד ב"ד להוציא מידו. ואמרתי לו וכי לא עשה תקנת השוק כמו שגנב גוי או גזל מישר[אל] ונתן או מכר לישר[אל] אחר יש כח ביד ישראל להוציא מידו וכו'**. From its second occurrence, it is clear that the term *koaḥ be-yad bet-din* means not physical power but authorization (*Ketubbot* 96a). If the courts were operating on either Rabbenu Tam's doctrine of *silluk* or Ri's presumption of legality, that is to say if they had assumed a prior waiver or transfer on the part of the owner, the writer's argument would have been wholly beside the point, and he would immediately have been told so. *Hand muß Hand wahren* seems, then, to be operating here. The problem is that while popular thought had often absorbed unawares the notion of *Hand muß Hand wahren*, the Jewish courts were always on guard against it (see footnote 98(*b*)), and the court under discussion is none other than the distinguished one of Paris, perhaps even in the time of R. Yeḥi'el of Paris. Let us note, however, that the narrator did not speak to the judges but to the plaintiff whose claim had been denied (*ve-amarti lo*), who may not have known the reason for the court's rejection of his claim (it was an open question at the time whether the courts had to spell out the reasons for their decisions), or, who may have known it but omitted or forgot it in his complaint. A rejected plaintiff is not always the most accurate reporter. Note should also be taken that the text of Rabbenu Tam's proclamation of *silluk* has come down to us through the good offices of R. Yehudah Sir Leon, head of the Paris court, who took the trouble to sit down and copy it out by hand (*Or Zarua'*, #202, end). To find the Paris court operating with this doctrine is something we might well expect. The author of the passage cited above in the Hamburg manuscript is apparently a pupil of R. Yeḥi'el of Paris (see fo. 183c–d) and may very well be R. Me'ir of Rothenburg himself. These passages are found in what is generally a collection of his writings and responsa.

NOTE 215

1. *Recurrent pattern*. Not only did the men who came after the Tosafists adopt this attitude of legal federalism in their harmonization of the literature of the past, but they continued that tradition in their own works. To give just one example: the two major areas in talmudic commercial law which the communities in Europe had to effectively alter were, first, the non-recognition of many phases of Jewish–Gentile transactions (e.g. property rights in Gentile gages), and second, the refusal to admit the validity of contracts dealing in futures (*davar shelo ba la-'olam*). R. Shelomoh Luria, when discussing the legal status of *arrendas*, the farming-out monopolies, which played a large role in Jewish business life in 16th- and 17th-century Poland, validates such transactions in future profits, among other reasons, on the basis of *situmta* (*Teshuvot Maharshal*, #36 [Jerusalem, 1969], 120b–121a), yet when discussing *situmta* from a general standpoint in his monumental survey of Jewish law, the *Yam shel Shelomoh* (*Bava Kamma* [Prague, 1616–18], 8: 60), he himself denies its effectiveness in the matter of futures. And let note be taken that the responsum and the work on *Bava Kamma* were written less than a year apart; see S. Assaf, 'Mashehu le-Toledot Maharshal', *Sefer ha-Yovel li-Khvod Levi Ginzberg* (New York, 1946), p. 46, n. 11; p. 48, n. 25. (Years later, when treating *arrendas* again, he simply copied out his old responsum. See *Yam shel Shelomoh*, *Kiddushin* [Berlin, 1766], 3: 2. I doubt whether he ever intended to give his passing remark about *situmta* in that lengthy decision normative status over and against his remarks in *Bava Kamma*. Legally—the formal unit of law is often neither time nor intent but opus—there may be a contradiction between the several volumes of the *Yam shel Shelomoh*, but not historically.)

In a soon-to-be-published book on *situmta*, R. Kleinman, while agreeing with the recurrent pattern of 'halakhic federalism', questions whether the example that I gave from Rashal is a valid one. He contends that a close reading of Rashal's responsum indicates that there is no contradiction between it and his position in the *Yam shel Shelomoh*. On the basis of a quick perusal of the page proofs that he was kind enough to send me, I would say that he is correct. The critique will be found in his forthcoming *Darkhei Kinyan u-Minhagei Misḥar ba-Mishpat ha-'Ivri: Mishpat, Re'alyah ve-Historiyah*, 302–4.

2. The term '*halakhic federalism*' struck a responsive chord, and different meanings have since been ascribed to it. As I have been given credit for all of them, I would like to issue here a friendly disclaimer. Jacob Katz has pointed out that the Tosafists, when confronted with the problem of squaring communal conduct with the talmudic texts, as in the matter of Jewish–Gentile relations, proceeded to provide a series of ad hoc allowances in specific areas rather than advocate, as did Me'iri, one new and sweeping allowance. David Berger has written that I have termed this approach 'halakhic federalism'. I have no problem with thus labeling Katz's characterization of the Tosafists, but would simply note that this is not what I had in mind by the term. Katz contended that when confronted with a problem of fairly radical adjustment of talmudic law to changed realities, the Tosafists tended, quite *intentionally*, to rule as narrowly as possible on any issue, as courts usually do when confronted with the choice between an ad hoc ruling and a general one with sweeping implications. In most of this essay, I dealt with the principle of silent incorporation of contemporary realities, such as property rights in Gentile pawns or the right of the creditor to alienate pawns, into the decision-making process of the halakhah. The scholars of Ashkenaz *consciously* integrated these facts of life only in areas of high pressure, such as moneylending, but never in neutral spheres, such as inheritance, for example. This intentional differentiation in civil law runs parallel to that of Katz in ritual law; however, I never termed this phenomenon 'halakhic federalism'. I used the term in the last paragraph of the essay to describe an *intuitive* process that took place in the *exercise of dialectic*—a method intended to unify disparate elements of a system—and highlighted the conduct of the post-medieval writers and commentators on the *Shulḥan 'Arukh*. I noted that these men, reared in cultures far removed from the Germanic world of the Middle Ages and striving to discover and eliminate any inconsistencies in what was rapidly becoming *the* code of Jewish law, never pointed out the contradictions that existed between the assumptions of pawnbroking in the context of usury ('Yoreh De'ah' 169) and those that underlay pawnbroking in the Civil Code ('Ḥoshen Mishpat' 72). Despite a complete unawareness of the practices of medieval pawnbroking, they intuitively sensed that usury was a world apart and should be left to revolve on its own axis, and that many

of its underlying assumptions should not be integrated into the sweeping legal synthesis in which they were so deeply involved. Berger's remarks are found in his 'Jacob Katz on Jews and Christians in the Middle Ages', in J. M. Harris, ed., *The Pride of Jacob* (Cambridge, 2002), 60; 'On the Uses of History in Medieval Jewish Polemic against Christianity: The Quest for the Historical Jesus', in *Jewish History and Jewish Memory: Essays in Honor of Yosef Hayyim Yerushalmi* (Hanover and London, 1998), 38, n. 17. Both essays have been reprinted in his *Persecution, Polemic and Dialogue: Essays in Jewish–Christian Relations* (Boston, 2010). The cited passages are found at pp. 71, 145, n. 17.

Gidon Lebson credits me with characterizing as 'halakhic federalism' the coexistence of conflicting local customs of the widespread Jewish communities in the Diaspora ('Halakhah and Reality in the Gaonic Period', in D. Frank, ed., *The Jews of Medieval Islam: Community, Society and Identity* [Leiden and New York, 1995], 68–9). Again, I have no quarrel with this use of the phrase; however, it's not what I had in mind when I coined it.

3. *Provence's different path.* The Ashkenazic literature on pawnbroking revolves around two basic talmudic rules: *le-ḥumra*—which was the source of many of its problems—and *lo asrah Torah ela ribbit ha-ba'ah mi-loveh le-malveh*—which served as the major avenue of allowance. It is for this reason that I explained and highlighted them at the very outset of the essay. If one turns to the halakhic literature of Provence on pawnbroking, one is struck by the differing importance of these two rules. *Le-ḥumra* is cited by several Provençal scholars, but it is noticeably absent from the responsa of Rabad. *Lo asrah Torah* is cited once by a certain R. Mosheh ha-Nasi b. Todros ha-Nasi (and in a problematic manner at that) and never appears again in the writings of Provençal halakhists.

Much of the reason for these different emphases is that while the Ashkenazic writers of the eleventh, twelfth, and early thirteenth centuries, whom I have discussed at length, ignored the issue of debt collection, Provençal thought, on the whole, saw collection as *the* controlling criterion of *ribbit*. This reduced the role of *le-ḥumra* and that of triangular relationships. If the lender was unaware of the middleman's agency and thought the agent was the principal, the agent would, indeed, be viewed as the principal, seeing that the creditor could bring suit against him. More important, if the debtor's pawn was used, the existence or non-existence of agency was irrelevant, as the payment would always be executed on the pawned property. If the debtor subsequently redeemed the pawn either on his own or by means of an agent, the money would again be coming out of his pocket and he would be viewed as the legal debtor. Why Provence focused from the outset on debt collection is not clear. Perhaps it was simply by intuition; perhaps because of the early importance attached to the Tosefta (independently or via the Yerushalmi), which spoke of *aḥarayut*; perhaps because of the issue of surety (*'arev*) in loans at interest—a common practice in the Midi and a much-discussed issue in its intellectual centers. Be that as it may, Provence generally adopted the principle of economic usury, as did Early Ashkenaz; however, Provençal scholars successfully rooted the principle in talmudic sources. It is scarcely surprising, then, that the course of halakhic thought in Provence on the issue of pawnbroking differed widely from its portrayal in my essay.

For documentation and further details about Provence, see *Halakhah, Kalkalah* (footnote 1), 102–10. For the French focus on debt collection in the 13th century, see ibid. 82–101. For the discussion of surety in Provence, see my "Arev be-Ribbit', *Zion*, 37 (1972), 1–21.

PART III

THE BAN ON GENTILE WINE AND ITS LINK TO MONEYLENDING

CHAPTER SEVEN

Can Halakhic Texts Talk History?

This essay, though published in 1978, was an expansion of a chapter in my Master's thesis, submitted over a decade earlier. Being my earliest venture in writing the history of halakhah, it set forth my approach to the subject, not abstractly but concretely—in the form of *explication de texte*. The step-by-step interrogation of the sources yielded what to my mind were the building blocks of the narrative. The data and the modes of inference were thus opened to scrutiny, and the reader could judge for himself the validity of the conclusions. The same techniques of the textual edition, locating doctrines in their contemporary context and searching for personal posture and external influences by the criterion of 'measurable deflection', have been employed in all my subsequent studies; however, they are never so clearly placed on view as in this essay.

This essay and the preceding one on pawnbroking are studies in detailed reconstruction, and certain patterns emerge. Here too, Rabbenu Tam, alongside Rashi, plays the major role. Indeed, Rabbenu Tam's doctrines dominate the entire field of *yein nesekh*.[1] The leading part he played in shifting halakhah from exegesis to dialectic is common knowledge. Less well known is the fact that this profound involve-

This essay appeared in an amplified form as the fifth chapter in *Ha-Yayin bi-Yemei ha-Beinayim* (below, n. 1). The text is fairly similar but the footnotes in that work—published in 2008, some thirty years after the study originally appeared—are understandably more ample. Though in the notes I have added some cross-references to the book, anyone seeking fuller documentation of the arguments presented here should look to that chapter.

All manuscripts except those of Cambridge University, Hechal Shelomoh, Jerusalem, and the Jewish Theological Seminary of America were viewed at the Institute of Microfilmed Hebrew Manuscripts of the Jewish National and University Library in Jerusalem. I have added two notes at the outset of the essay to document my introductory remarks. All references in the prior literature to these notes should therefore be raised by two, i.e. a statement referring to n. 65 in the original article will be found here in n. 67.

As noted in the preceding chapter, some of the quoted material in the notes below is in Hebrew only. I have only provided English translations for those citations which would be of interest to the general reader. The rest are technical proofs of halakhic arguments. Anyone who cannot follow the Hebrew will not be able to follow the legal argument.

[1] See H. Soloveitchik, *Ha-Yayin bi-Yemei ha-Beinayim—Yein Nesekh: Perek be-Toledot ha-Halakhah be-Ashkenaz* (Jerusalem, 2008), 353–4.

ment in dialectic was coupled with a keen instinct as to when this newly revived method would be of no avail. He intuitively rejected, as we shall see, all distinctions between *gat* and *gigit* as being unpersuasive—as, indeed, the belabored efforts of his successors proved them to be. On another occasion, he swiftly and emphatically stated that dialectics would prove incapable of justifying the widespread practice of accepting Gentile wine (*setam yeinam*) in payment of debts, something that took his disciples anywhere from two to five generations to realize.[2]

The space devoted to Rashi and his predecessors takes up some 60 percent of both studies and for the same good reasons. The views of Early Ashkenaz on *yein nesekh* must be teased out of the sources, and the quiet but transformational role of Rashi comes repeatedly into view—once his words are closely interrogated. In this essay, as in the preceding one on *ribbit*, Rashi is in constant dialogue with his predecessors and contemporaries and, equally, with his religious traditions, with all their stringencies, leniencies, and taboos. We witness in both studies Rashi's growing confidence and his gradual willingness to take issue with established practice. His intuitions were unerring from the outset, but only with time and accomplishment could he break with *minhag avotenu* (the traditions of our fathers). Break he did, but not quickly and not without ambivalence. In the matter of *hamshakhah* (the subject of this essay), he saw to it that his new position was reported by his pupils, but systematically refrained from clearly articulating it in his own oeuvre. In usury, he ended up issuing a bold allowance but shied away from any mention of the word *ribbit* during the transaction, though he knew as well as we do that words neither make nor unmake usury. His genius transfigured what it touched, but he never sought to be revolutionary. If history insists that he nevertheless was one, it should in fairness add that he was a revolutionary *malgré lui*.

IT IS NOT HOW HALAKHIC TEXTS tell stories about other things but how they tell stories about themselves that is our concern here. Confronting us is not the problem of extracting evidence regarding trade or communal organization from law, but the question of how one cracks the colorless and highly impersonal mold into which the thought of the medieval period was cast to reveal a world of individuality, development, and ambivalence. Can the fragmentary and recalcitrant halakhic texts be made to talk history?

Attempting to argue for the affirmative, I would like to trace the origin and fate of one doctrine over the course of some two centuries. Instead of a running account, it seems wisest for our purposes to interrogate each piece of evi-

[2] See H. Soloveitchik, *Yeinam: Saḥar be-Yeinam shel Goyim—'al Gilgulah shel ha-Halakhah be-'Olam ha-Ma'aseh* (Tel Aviv, 2003), 124–5.

dence separately, hoping to see if a continuous narrative emerges from a cross-examination of them, and whether parts of the story are of wider significance. (The importance of the story as a whole would emerge only in the framework of a much larger study.) In brief, I should like to try to reconstruct step by step a small chapter in the history of the halakhah.

To highlight this process of recreation, I have enumerated its steps. Each of the twenty-two texts that join in providing us with a story line is numbered as it is introduced and analyzed.

As the technique employed is that of piecemeal analysis, I hope that the reader will forgive the temporary lapse from brevity. |153|

The topic chosen is an aspect of *yein nesekh*; the time and place—Ashkenaz, in the high Middle Ages.

The Talmud had imposed a severe ban on drinking and trading in Gentile wine or wine that a non-Jew had so much as touched. The social difficulties that this injunction entailed are common knowledge; the economic burdens, though less well known, were no less great.

Wine played a far greater role in the Middle Ages than it does now. Water was not generally drunk, and tea and coffee had not yet come to Europe. Fresh fruit was unavailable for a good part of the year, and whiskey was still undiscovered. Thus thirst could be quenched only by beer and wine. And the thirst was great; partly because meat was heavily spiced (no other method of food preservation was available), partly because drink was the only escape for the poor and the major entertainment of the wealthy. So drink people did, and on a heroic scale. Indeed the quantities consumed stagger the imagination.

The importance of wine in people's daily fare gave to it a role in the economic life of the period that we would scarcely dream of. How were the men of the north, of England and Scandinavia—great drinkers all—to quench their thirst? Mead and beer were available—indeed, in England a full third of the grain crop at the time of the Conquest was used for beer production—but these were looked upon as lower-class drinks. The well-to-do drank wine, and wine was to be had primarily by import. So, as Pirenne first perceived and Dion then magisterially chronicled, wine was a major, and in some places in the eleventh and twelfth centuries the major, commodity of international trade.[3] Many a city grew to prominence and many a merchant attained wealth

[3] H. Pirenne, 'Un grand commerce d'exportation au Moyen Age: Les Vins de France', *Annales d'histoire économique et sociale*, 5 (1933), 225–43; R. Dion, *Histoire de la vigne et du vin en France des*

because of wine. Domestically wine was our water, coffee, and liquor wrapped into one. Economically it was analogous to the modern plastics or electronics industry. The laws of *yein nesekh* did not then regulate some |154| peripheral delicacy or minor foodstuff; they governed a major area of household activity and of daily livelihood.

Basic to any discussion of *yein nesekh*, whether from the point of view of the development of Jewish law or this law's impact on the lives of those who chose to abide by halakhic restrictions, is the question: at what stage of the wine-making process do the manifold restrictions come into play? Halakhically the problem is: at what stage does the must (crushed grapes) cease to be simply grape juice—and, as such, indistinguishable from any other fruit extract (*mei perot, mashkin ha-yotse'in*)—and take on the unique status of wine?[4] Economically, what is at stake is the point up to which it was possible for Jewish and Gentile operations to be meshed and the forms of Jewish enterprise were indistinguishable from the general ones, and the point from which Jewish wine production had to be conducted in isolation and at greater cost.

Tannaitic opinion on this point underwent change. Originally the cut-off stage given was either the liquid's entrance into the wine-pit (*yeridah la-bor, kippuy*) or a later phase, the introduction of the wine into the wine barrel (*shilluy be-ḥaviyot*). Subsequently it was advanced to a stage known as *hamshakhah* and this advancement was ratified by the Talmud.

origines au XIXe siècle (Paris, 1959) (with exhaustive bibliography). The purpose of this essay being methodological, I will keep the technical aspects of wine production to a minimum. Its proper place is in a full-length study of *yein nesekh*. {See now my *Ha-Yayin bi-Yemei ha-Beinayim* (above, n. 1), 59–86.}

[4] The halakhah (like common law) prefers local definitions, and what may be defined as 'wine' in regard to *yein nesekh* may very well be grape juice in other areas of Jewish law, and vice versa. The formulation here presented is medieval, not talmudic. The Talmud did not discuss the problem in terms of 'wine' status; it viewed the juice as wine immediately upon extraction from the grape. It spoke rather of *darkan le-nassekh*—the stage of the wine-making process at which Gentiles began to use it for libation (Tosefta, ed. M. S. Zuckermandel [repr. Jerusalem, 1963], *'Avodah Zarah* 7: 3). Medieval authors saw the matter differently. Rashi (below) spoke of **קרוי יין, שם יין עליו, תחילת ביאתו לתורת יין**, while the commentator *par excellence* of Provence, R. Avraham b. David of Posquières, explained thus: **הוא חשוב להיות עליו תורת יין ולגזור עליו גזי' יינם** (*Perush ha-Rabad 'al 'Avodah Zarah*, ed. A. Sofer [New York, 1961], 148). One may see in this perspective a shift from genuine fear of libation to formal definition, indicative of the transition from libating societies to non-libating ones. One should note, however, that the move to formal definition was begun by the Babylonian Talmud when it defined the stages of the receptivity to libation by the categories of *gemar melakhah* operative in the laws of tithes (see below, pp. 173–4).

1. As the entire discussion in the Middle Ages revolves around seven or eight lines in the Talmud, and as Rashi's position on this problem will occupy a good part of my study, it seems best to cite the relevant passages together with his comments.[5] |155|

RASHI	TALMUD
גת בעוטה. שבעטה ודרכה עובד כוכבים: **שהוא נוטל.** ענבים מתוך יין בעדשים של גת שקורין מיי"ש: **ונותן לתפוח.** אסיפת גל הענבים שתחת הקורה קרי תפוח, ובלע"ז ש"ק, וקסבר תנא דידן לא הוי יין נסך עד שירד לבור: **מה שבבור אסור.** אם נגע בו העובד כוכבים אחרי כן. **בור** היו עושין לפני הגת והכלי נתון שם לקבל היין ויש שטחין הבור בסיד והיין משתמר בתוכו ואינו מאבד טפה, והוא בור סיד.	מתני'. לוקחין גת בעוטה מן העובד כוכבים אף על פי שהוא נוטל בידו ונותן לתפוח, ואינו עושה יין נסך עד שירד לבור. ירד לבור מה שבבור אסור והשאר מותר.
גמ' שהתחיל לימשך. שהגת עשויה במדרון ומשעה שהוא נמשך מצד העליון לצד התחתון קרוי יין: **פקוקה.** שפקקו הצינור ע"פ הבור שלא יכול לירד והיא היתה כולה מלאה ענבים ולא נמשך בה יין ולא זז ממקומו אלא במקום שנסחט שם עומד. **ומקשין.** והא קתני עד שירד לבור אבל לנמשך לא חיישינן: **ה"נ בגת פקוקה ומלאה.** ואשמעינן בגת מלאה אין בה משיכה עד שיטול פקק שלפניה וירד היין והיא משיכתו מיד: **והשאר מותר.** והא הכא דהתחיל לירד והרי נמשך וקתני מה שבגת מותר . . . ולא חיישינן לדרב הונא. . . . דאינו יין עד שירד לבור.	גמ'. אמר רב הונא יין כיון שהתחיל להמשך עושה יין נסך. תנן לוקחין גת בעוטה מן העובד כוכבים ואע"פ שהוא נוטל ונותן לתפוח. אמר רב הונא בגת פקוקה ומליאה. ת"ש 'ואינו עושה יין נסך עד שירד לבור' ה"נ בגת פקוקה ומלאה. ת"ש 'ירד לבור מה שבבור אסור והשאר מותר'. אמר רב הונא לא קשיא כאן במשנה ראשונה כאן במשנה אחרונה. דתניא 'בראשונה היו אומרים . . . דורכים עם העובד כוכבים בגת' ולא חיישינן לדרב הונא 'וחזרו לומר . . . אין דורכין עם העובד כוכבים בגת' משום דרב הונא.
יין משיקפה. הוי גמר מלאכה לענין מעשר ליאסר בו שתיית עראי. משיקפה לשון צף כמו קפא תהומא דמסכת סוכה [דף נג.], שצפין החרצנים על היין כשהוא נח בבור: **ואע"פ שקפה.** מה שבבור קולט מן הגת העליונה ושותה, שאותו שלא ירד לבור לא נגמר מלאכתו: **מן הצנור.** מקום דרך מרזב המקלח היין לבור. **ש"מ קיפוי דבור קאמר.** מדקתני	ואינו עושה יין נסך עד שירד לבור: והתניא 'יין משיקפה'? אמר רבא לא קשיא הא ר"ע הא רבנן דתניא 'יין משירד לבור ר"ע אומר משיקפה'. איבעיא להו—קיפוי דבור או קיפוי דחבית? ת"ש 'יין משיקפה ואע"פ שקפה קולט מן הגת העליונה ומן הצנור ושותה'. ש"מ קיפוי דבור קאמרינן ש"מ. והתני רב זביד בדבי רב אושעיא 'יין משירד לבור ויקפה ר"ע אומר

[5] *'Avodah Zarah* 55a–56a, with two emendations from *Dikdukei soferim* ad loc. All texts cited in this study were checked against manuscripts. For the reader's convenience, however, I have generally cited the printed text, adducing only significant variants. The English translation of the Talmud is based on that of the Soncino Press. As that translation incorporated many of Rashi's explanations into the talmudic text, these elements had to be removed. The translations of Rashi and of all other texts are entirely mine. The *le'azim* in Rashi are taken from A. Darmesteter and D. S. Blondheim, *Les Gloses françaises dans les commentaires talmudiques de Raschi* (Paris, 1929), 92, 126, s.v. *mait*, and s.v. *sac*.

RASHI

ואע״פ שקפה קולט מן הגת דאי בחביות מה עניינו אצל גת. בדבי ר׳ אושעיא. במתני׳ דבי ר׳ אושעיא: משישלה בחביות. לשון השולה דג מן הים [חולין דף סג.], משישלה היין מן הבור להנתן בחביות, וכן מפרש בב״מ בהשוכר את הפועלים [דף צב:], ולעיל קתני לרבנן משירד לבור ולר״ע משיקפה.

TALMUD

משישלה בחביות׳? תרצה נמי להך קמייתא הכי ׳יין משירד לבור ויקפה, ר״ע אומר משישלה בחביות׳ וכו׳.

RASHI

MISHNAH. **A wine-press trodden**: that was trodden by a Gentile. **Even though it was he that lifted up**: the grapes from the wine in the bin of the wine-press which is called *mais* [*mait*] in Old French. **And puts them among the heap (*tapuaḥ*)**: the accumulated pile of grapes under the pressing beam which is called *tapuaḥ* [in Hebrew] and *sac* in Old French. And our *tanna* [i.e. the *tanna* whose views are expressed in the Mishnah] is of the opinion that it [the liquid] does not become subject to *yein nesekh* until it descends into the wine-pit. **What is in the wine-pit is forbidden**: If a Gentile subsequently touched it. A wine-pit used to be built close to the wine-press ... to receive the wine. And there were those who would plaster the wine-pit so that there would be no loss of wine [through seepage], and this is [the origin of the phrase for a retentive memory] 'a plastered wine-pit [which does not lose a drop]' (*Avot* 2: 8).

TALMUD

MISHNAH. A wine-press [containing] trodden [grapes] may be purchased from a Gentile even though it was he that lifted [the trodden grapes] with his hand and put them among the heap; and [the juice] does not become *yein nesekh* until it descends into the wine-pit. When it has descended into the wine-pit, what is in the wine-pit is prohibited but the remainder is permitted.

RASHI

GEMARA. **Begins to flow [*le-himashekh*]**: For the wine-press is sloped, and from the moment that it [the liquid] flows [*nimshakh*] from the upper part to the lower one, it acquires the status of wine. **Stoppered**: They stoppered the pipe above the wine-pit so that [the wine] should not descend, and it [the wine-press] was full of grapes and the wine did

TALMUD

GEMARA. R. Huna said: as soon as the wine begins to flow [*le-himashekh*], it becomes [subject to] *yein nesekh*. But we learn in our Mishnah: 'A wine-press [containing] trodden [grapes] may be purchased from a Gentile even though it was he that lifted [the trodden grapes] with his hand and put them among the heap!'—R. Huna said: this refers to a

not flow in it and did not move from its place but remained in the place where it had been extracted. **And [the Talmud] asks:** did the Mishnah not say 'until it descends into the wine-pit'? However, we are not concerned with what has only 'flowed' [*nimshakh*]. **Similarly here [says R. Huna, the Mishnah deals with] a vat which is stoppered and full**: It teaches us that in a full wine-press there is no flow [*meshikhah*] until the stopper is removed and the wine descends, and this flow [now] occurs immediately. **But the remainder is permitted**: but in this case, since it has begun to descend into the wine-pit, flow has begun; nevertheless, the Mishnah states that 'what is in the wine-press is permitted'. [. . .] **No attention is paid here to the view of Rav Huna:** for it is not [legally] wine until it descends into the wine-pit.

[But we have learnt:] Wine *mi-she-yikpeh*: that is the final stage of food preparation and the wine then becomes subject to tithe and [at this stage] untithed wine becomes forbidden to be drunk. ***Mi-she-yikpeh***: A term denoting 'floating', as in *kafa tehoma* in tractate *Sukkah* [53a]; the grape kernels float on top of the wine, when it [the wine] rests in the pit. **And although he [or it] has *kafah***: what is in the wine-pit, he may draw some off from the above wine-press and drink, for that which has not descended into the wine-pit is not a 'finished product' [and subject to tithe]. **From the pipe**: a tube through which the wine pours into the wine-pit. **Deduce from this that we mean *kippuy* while it is in the vat**: since it says 'although he [or it] has *kafah*, he may draw some off from the wine-press', if *kippuy* [were done] in the barrels, what would 'the wine-press' be wine-press that is stoppered and full. Come and hear: 'and [the juice] does not become *yein nesekh* until it descends into the wine-pit'!—Similarly here [says R. Huna, the Mishnah deals with] a vat that is stoppered and full. Come and hear: 'When it has descended into the wine-pit, what is in the wine-pit is prohibited but the remainder is permitted'!—R. Huna said: here is no contradiction. One teaching is from the older Mishnah and the other from the later Mishnah; for it has been taught: 'At first [the Rabbis] said . . . they may tread grapes together with a heathen in a wine-press.' Consequently no attention is here paid to the view of R. Huna. 'Later [the Rabbis] said . . . [Israelites] may not tread grapes together with a Gentile in a wine-press', for the reason given by R. Huna.

'And [the juice] does not become *yein nesekh* until it descends into the wine-pit.' But we have learnt: wine [with regard to the tithe] *mi-she-yikpeh*!—Raba said: there is no contradiction, because [this latter teaching] is R. 'Akiva's and [that of the Mishnah] is the Rabbis'. For it has been taught: [The liquid is considered to be] wine when it descends into the wine-pit, whereas R. 'Akiva says, *mi-she-yikpeh*.

The question was asked: Does this mean *kippuy* [of the wine] while it is in the vat or when it is in the barrels?—Come and hear! We have learnt: [it is to be considered] wine *mi-she-yikpeh*; and although he has *kafah*, he may draw some off from the upper trough and from the pipe and drink it. Deduce from this that we mean *kippuy* while it is in the vat. Draw this conclusion. But R. Zebid taught in the School of R. Osha'ya: [It is to be considered] wine when it descends

RASHI	TALMUD
doing here. **In the School of R. Osha'ya:** in the collection of tannaitic teachings of the School of R. Osha'ya. ***Mi-she-yishleh be-ḥaviyot***: when it [the wine] is drawn up from the pit to be placed in the barrels, so it is explained in *Bava Metsi'a* in [the chapter with the *incipit*:] 'One who hires the laborer' [i.e. 92b]; whereas the *beraita* says that according to the Rabbis [it becomes wine] when it descends to the pit and according to R. 'Akiva *mi-she-yikpeh*.	into the vat *ve-yikpeh*; whereas R. 'Akiva says: When it is drawn into barrels!—That former [*beraita*] must also be explained in the sense just given, viz.: [It is considered to be] wine when it descends into the vat *ve-yikpeh*; whereas R. 'Akiva says: *mi-she-yishleh be-ḥaviyot*.

|**156**| Rashi's remarks are straightforward enough and passed the intensive scrutiny of the Tosafists without critique or comment.

2. If we leave the printed page of the Talmud to explore the literature of the eleventh century, seeking to enter the milieu that produced Rashi's lucid exposition, the first discussion that we encounter is a private one—between Rashi and his son-in-law, R. Me'ir of Ramerupt.[6] It goes thus:

וששאל לפרש גת וגרגותני ובור. גת הוא שעוצרין בה החרצנים ובדורות הראשונים היו דורכין בו ולא בגיגית. וגרגותני הוא סל שהוא תלוי לפני קלוח הצנור מן הגת והיין נופל לתוכו מן הגת ומסתנן ויורד לבור שהוא עשוי תחתיו שהיין זב בתוכו.
ובמקומותינו אין בור, אך כלי נתון תחת הצנור והוא הבור.
והלכה כרב הונא דאמר משהתחיל לימשך נעשה יין נסך. ואין הדבר אמור אלא במקום שדורכין בגת הוא תחילת ביאתו לתורת יין. אבל במקומנו משנדרך בגיגית שם יין עליו לפי המנהג[!] אבותינו . . . ואין חילוק בין יין נסך לסתם יינם לכל דבר, אלא שהתחילו להקל בו לענין היתר הנאה לפי שאין הגוים שבמקומינו מנסכים יין לעבודה זרה.
יחי חתני ר' מאיר לעד עם בתי והילדים ינובון בשיבה. ושלום.

And he asked [me] to explain *gat*, *gargutni*, and *bor* [*'Avodah Zarah*, 55a–b]. *Gat* is the place where the grape kernels are crushed [i.e. the wine-press], and in previous generations [i.e. in talmudic times] they used to [also] tread there and not in the *cuve* [tub].

[6] *Teshuvot Rashi*, ed. I. S. Elfenbein (New York, 1943), #58, to which add the following manuscripts of the *Issur ve-Heter*: National Library of Israel 8vo 2623 (fo. 42), 4to 749 (#156); Frankfurt Stadt- und Universitätsbibliothek 8vo 69 (fo. 39a–b) (correct *Teshuvot Rashi*, introd. p. XLIX, accordingly). This passage is taken from a larger responsum as MS Bodley 566, fo. 34b demonstrates. {The two National Library manuscripts are copies of the one in Frankfurt and thus of no significance.}

And *gargutni* is the [perforated] basket that hangs in front of the outflow from the pipe of the wine-press; and the wine from the wine-press passes through it and is strained and descends into the pit [*bor*] that lies underneath, so that the wine flows [i.e. should flow] into it.

And in our locale there is no pit; however, the vessel underneath the pipe [from the *cuve*] serves as a pit.

And the law is in accordance with R. Huna, who ruled that when the 'wine begins to flow [*le-himashekh*], it becomes [subject to] *yein nesekh*'. But this applies only to places where they tread in a *gat* [i.e. the wine-press served both as treading floor and press]; there the liquid first acquires the legal status of wine. However in our locales, once it is trodden in the *cuve*, it becomes legally wine according to the custom of our fathers . . .

And there is no difference whatsoever between *setam yeinam* [Gentile wine] and *yein nesekh* [libated wine]. However, people have come to be lax with regard to deriving benefit [from *setam yeinam*], because the Gentiles in our locales no longer libate.

May my son-in-law R. Me'ir live forever together with my daughter, and may the children still bear fruit in old age [Ps. 92: 15]. [May] peace [be with you].

The content is halakhically banal, and it was not by accident that the responsum fell into oblivion.[7] Historically this banality is both informative and explicable. Informative in that R. Me'ir did not at the time possess his father-in-law's commentary; otherwise he would never have had to inquire as to the meaning of *gat*, *bor*, and *gargutni*, since those terms are spelled out at length in that work. As we shall see, Rashi wrote, edited, or dictated no fewer than four commentaries on the tractate *'Avodah Zarah*;[8] this query clearly antedates them all. And as there is every reason to assume that this repeated endeavor was a protracted one—each effort reflecting a rethinking on the part of the author—it would appear that this responsum issues from an early period in Rashi's career and mirrors his initial views before they found formal articulation in his writings.

The 'banality' is explicable by the fact that the tractate *'Avodah* |157| *Zarah* was neither studied nor taught in certain circles, and the Rhine academies generally had but an imperfect knowledge of it. This is a surprising, indeed almost unbelievable, fact in light of the centrality of a tractate that treats *yein nesekh* and all other aspects of Jewish–Gentile relations, but it is a fact nevertheless. No less a figure than R. Eli'ezer b. Yitsḥak, known by his contemporaries as R. Eli'ezer ha-Gadol (the Great), did not know that milk forbade meat products only *be-noten ta'am*, because he had never studied (or had but

[7] Note that outside the *Issur ve-Heter* it was not reproduced in any other work that emanated from Rashi's school, nor is it preserved in later collections.

[8] See below, pp. 187–8.

imperfectly studied) *'Avodah Zarah*.[9] If a scholar of such stature could err on so basic a matter, it was small wonder if men of lesser mold sometimes found themselves at sea in the tractate. Rashi's fourfold efforts in this tractate stem

[9] Rashi reports (*Teshuvot*, #382):

מעידני עלי שמים וארץ שקבלתי מרבינו יצחק הלוי בשחיטת חולין בכל מקום ששנינו בה איסור בשר בחלב בנותן טעם היה רגיל לומר לי לא גמרינן מהא מסכתא ולא עבדינן כוותיה דהא סתמא מתניתין היא בע״ז דבשר בחלב במשהו . . . ואני לא נתתי לבי אז לחקור בדברים, והלא רבינו לא היה שונה מסכת ע״ז, וכשבאתי לכאן ועסקתי במסכת ע״ז.

R. Me'ir b. Shemu'el testified that R. Yitsḥak ha-Levi told him that **רבו ר׳ אלעזר לא למד מסכת ע״ז, ומשום דלא איפשיט ליה החמיר** (*Siddur Rashi* [Berlin, 1912], #594, and parallel passages there cited). These texts prove something only about two leading scholars of Worms. An in-depth study, however, of the literature of the Worms and Mainz academies, found in the *Ma'asei Ge'onim*, *Sefer ha-Pardes*, and *Sefer ha-Oreh*, shows the imperfect grasp that the Rhine scholars had of this tractate, one not even vaguely on a par with their command of *Ḥullin*, for example. A simple example of the heavy-handed belaboring of the halakhically obvious in this period (and inconceivable in any later one) is found in *Ma'asei Ge'onim* (Berlin, 1910), 81: **על שדה איש עצל עברתי**. Contrast this with the one-line disposal of the problem by Rashi towards the close of the responsum cited above. The fact that the Makhirites thought these proofs worthy of being included in their work says a great deal indeed. I am not contending that no commentarial tools on *'Avodah Zarah* were available. Rashi's talents alone could never have divined the meaning of Persian or Greek words; only a commentarial tradition could provide him with this information. The *'Arukh* cites a Mainz commentary on this tractate twice, or possibly four times (s.v. **דגל**, first definition; **מל, סלקנרית**, eighth definition; **לולב**, second definition), but all these are explanations of difficult words or gnomic remarks in the Talmud. Not one is topical or thematic. There is all the difference in the world between a lexical handbook like that of R. Naḥshon Gaon (*Teshuvot Ge'onim Kadmonim* [Berlin, 1848], 39b ff.) or other skeletal aids and an in-depth, running commentary. (A)The statement of R. Me'ir b. Shemu'el is reported thus in MS Bodley 566, fo. 12b: **אבל ר׳ אליעזר החמיר עליו במשהו משום דלא מיפשט פשיט במסכ׳ ע״ז ומשום כבוד רבו החמיר**. I would prefer the common reading of the *Siddur Rashi*, *Pardes*, and *Shibbolei ha-Leket* for the simple reason that no scribe would dream of adding on his own **אבל רבו ר׳ אלעזר לא למד מסכת ע״ז**. Actually the two texts say the same thing. I doubt that R. Eli'ezer ha-Gadol literally never studied the tractate; rather, he did not have a firm grasp of it. Functionally, however, not to be clear about a basic matter and not to have studied it are one and the same thing. {See the extensive discussion of the inadequate knowledge of the tractate in the academies of Mainz and Worms in this period, and the revolution that Rashi wrought in its understanding, in *Ha-Yayin bi-Yemei ha-Beinayim* (above, n. 1), 133–55.} (B) The text of *Teshuvot Rashi*, #81 {taken from MS Bodley 692, fo. 158a} published in the *Monatsschrift* (cited by Elfenbein) also contains the report **והלא רבי׳ לא היה שונה מסכ׳ ע״ז**. However, I have doubts whether this reading is authentic. {See *Ha-Yayin bi-Yemei ha-Beinayim*, p. 134, n. 4 for an explication of these doubts.} (C) R. Ḥanan'el's commentary or fragments thereof *may* have penetrated France during Rashi's lifetime; see J. N. Epstein, 'Perushei ha-Rivan u-Ferushei Worms', *Tarbiz*, 4 (1933), 27 {reproduced in his collected essays, *Meḥkarim be-Sifrut ha-Talmud u-vi-Leshonot Shemiyot*, iii (Jerusalem, 1991). 27}; *Sefer Rashi*, ed. Y. L. Maimon (Jerusalem, 1956), 311, n. 18; E. Kupfer, *Perush Rashi 'al Massekhet Mo'ed Katan* (Jerusalem, 1961), introduction, p. 15, but there is no evidence for such an inroad in the Rhineland. {R. Naḥshon Gaon's authorship of the lexical handbook was determined by J. N. Epstein in 'Die Rechtsgutachten der Geonim, ed. Cassel nach Cod. Berlin und MS Michael', *Jahrbuch der Jüdisch-Literarischen Gesellschaft*, 9 (1911), 220, available in the Hebrew translation in the first volume of his *Meḥkarim* (Jerusalem, 1984), 144.}

from this fact: in *'Avodah Zarah* he was starting from |158| commentarial scratch. Bereft of any guides, R. Me'ir approached the talmudic *sugyot* (passages) treating *yein nesekh* and soon dispatched a request for help.

But if R. Me'ir's first question is comprehensible, his second is not. He inquired of his father-in-law whether the decision lay with the *mishnah aḥaronah* (later *mishnah*) or not. Could the decision possibly lie with the *mishnah rishonah* (older *mishnah*)? If a court reversed its ruling, would any tyro imagine that one had to follow its earlier decision? The *amora* R. Huna, moreover, endorsed the *mishnah aḥaronah* and no dissenting voice is to be found in the Talmud. In light of this what other ruling is conceivable?[10]

Rashi's reply is no less problematic—on closer scrutiny. He explains the structure of the talmudic wine-press and translates it into contemporary terms. The *cuve* (*gigit*, wooden tub),[11] now used for treading, corresponds to the *gat*, the receptacle under the pipe to the *bor*. Rashi then proceeds to inform the inquirer that the decision lies with R. Huna. If the juice becomes *yein nesekh* even in the *gat* (as R. Huna contended) and the contemporary *cuve* is equivalent to the *gat*, the wine in the *cuve* then becomes *yein nesekh* in the strict halakhic sense. Yet Rashi carefully refuses to draw that conclusion and writes instead: שם יין עליו לפי המנהג[!] אבותינו ('it becomes legally wine according to the custom of our fathers'). Note that it becomes *yein nesekh* not by force of law but only as a result of common custom. In sum, we have here an astonishing query from Ramerupt and a reply with a non sequitur.

3. We have no other writings by R. Me'ir to probe for a possible solution, but we do have some by Rashi. As the problem hinges around the application of R. Huna's ruling, let us concentrate our attention there. It will be recalled that Rashi commented on the rule יין כיון שהתחיל להמשך עושה יין נסך ('As soon as the wine begins to flow [*le-himashekh*] it becomes [subject to] *yein nesekh*') thus: שהגת עשויה במדרון ומשעה שהוא נמשך מצד העליון לצד התחתון קרוי יין ('For the wine-press is sloped, and from the moment that it [the liquid] flows from the upper part to the lower one, it is then called [i.e. acquires the legal status of] wine'). However, R. Yitsḥak of Dampierre, the great Ri (d. 1189), in a responsum discovered by R. Ḥayyim Or Zarua' (d. late thirteenth century), reports a different version:[12]

[10] One could object that there is no clear indication that R. Me'ir actually asked a pointed question whether the decision lay with the *mishnah aḥaronah* or not. He may simply have asked for a general clarification of the *sugya*. Personally I do not believe this to be the case; see text, sect. 8. If, however, the reader disagrees, he should feel free to strike this paragraph from the text.

[11] Darmesteter and Blondheim, *Les Gloses françaises* (above, n. 5), 39, s.v. *cuve*.

[12] *Teshuvot Maharaḥ Or Zarua'* (Leipzig, 1860), #174 (fo. 58d). The text was published from what is

וזה כמה שנים שהוקשה מקרה [מסוים] בעיני [מ]מה שמשמע מפי' רש"י וה"ר יהודה בר' נתן תלמידו שהיה חושבה רש"י |159| [לאותו מקרה] המשכה[13] כי פי' התחיל לימשך שהגת עשויה מדרון משעה שהוא נמשך מצד העליון לצד התחתון שנתפנה מן הענבים קרוי יין.

For a number of years [a certain instance] seemed problematic to me in light of what seems implied in the commentary [or commentaries, as the Hebrew has an abbreviated form] of Rashi |**159**| and Rivan [R. Yehudah ben Natan, Rashi's son-in-law]: that Rashi would have considered that instance one of *hamshakhah*, for he [or they—again, the Hebrew has an abbreviated form] explained *hamshakhah* thus: 'For the wine-press is sloped, and from the time that it [the liquid] flows from the upper part to the lower one **and it [the liquid] is cleared of grapes**, it is then called [i.e. acquires the legal status of] wine.' [emphasis added]

The additional three words **שנתפנה מן הענבים** ('and it [the liquid] is cleared of grapes') are no minor matter. *Hamshakhah* means 'flow' and, simply read, R. Huna's doctrine gives the moment of flow, the moment the liquid begins to move, begins to descend downward, as the time when the grape juice assumes the status of wine and becomes subject to *yein nesekh*. And Rashi's comments in the Talmud only locate the first occurrence of such a flow in the normal process of wine production. Not so the doctrine reported by Ri. The principle there enunciated is one of separation of the liquid from the pulp. Grape juice ceases to be just 'grape juice' and becomes 'wine' when the sifting of the juice from the pulp begins. In other words, *hamshakhah* is not a criterion in and of itself, but simply a means to an end. As water seeks its own level, liquids will descend more rapidly than pulp, and the process of separation thus sets in with the onset of this downward flow.

If the halakhah must draw a line between grape juice and wine, it is reasonable to contend that so long as the grape lies interspersed with the juice, the liquid is viewed as grape juice. Only when it is separated does it become an independent entity—wine. Why, however, should liquidity or flow be determinative? True, wine is a liquid, but so is grape juice. Why is flow more a characteristic of one than of the other?

now Frankfurt Stadt-und Universitätsbibliothek 4to 4. Corrections in the citation are from that manuscript (fo. 135). Cf. *Revue des études juives*, 53 (1907), 267–9. The responsum was written between the years 1171 and 1184. Rabbenu Tam had passed away (fo. 59a: **כל הימים בחיי רבינו וגם עכשיו**). Ri's son, R. Elḥanan, however, was still alive (fo. 59d). Rabbenu Tam's death cannot be inferred from the **מ"כ** found after his name; this may easily be a scribal addition. {A new and far better edition of these responsa was published from the same manuscript by M. Avitan in Jerusalem in 2002. Our passage is found at p. 164a. The differences between the two texts are quite minor, but when they occur, Avitan's readings are invariably better. The citations are from this edition.}

13 i.e. Rashi would have viewed this as an instance of *hamshakhah*. {This note was necessary in the original essay which provided no English translations, and Hebrew has no subjunctive mood.}

4. As the doctrine of separation is sharper and more comprehensible than that of liquidity, one might be inclined to suspect that later generations put point and clarity into Rashi's doctrine, and that, as so often happens in legal history, a great jurist (Ri) unconsciously transformed the older doctrine of flow into the more acute one of straining and distillation. An anonymous little handbook on *yein nesekh* found in MS Paris Alliance 482 reports, however, the same version of Rashi, and we read there (fo. 33v):

פירש רש"י וכן הריב"ן משפינה הענבי' אילך ואילך ויין צלול באמצע דהגת עשויה במדרון ונמשך מצד עליון לתחתון כשנתפנו הענבי' אז קרוי יין.

And Rashi explained, as did Rivan: 'when he cleared the grapes to the sides [of the *cuve* or wine-press] and the clear wine is in the middle, for the wine-press is sloped and it [the wine] flows from the upper part to the lower one and the grapes have been cleared away [*nitpanu*], it is then called [i.e. acquires the legal status of] wine.'

The relationship between the two texts merits a few remarks here. Had we only the Alliance manuscript, we could simply disregard it, for the first half of the sentence, **משפינה הענבים אילך ואילך** ('when he cleared the grapes to the sides [of the *cuve* or wine-press]'), is—as we shall see later[14]—the edited version of another work, and we would be justified in assuming |**160**| that the author similarly edited the latter half of that sentence. But his citation corresponds almost precisely with that of Ri. Had we Ri's words alone, we could have suspected him of unconsciously sharpening and sophisticating Rashi's doctrine. Together the two reports seem to corroborate and validate each other. But are they independent witnesses? Ri clearly could not have copied from MS Alliance, for the author of this little guide to *yein nesekh* lived a century later. But could the author of MS Alliance have taken his information from Ri? R. Yitsḥak's responsum was discovered by R. Ḥayyim Or Zarua', that is to say, at the close of the tosafist period. It is not found, to the best of my knowledge, in any other source in print or manuscript.[15] Nor is this late appearance accidental. An investigation of the writings of the Tosafists (Ri's own pupils) on matters of *hamshakhah* shows that they were unfamiliar with this responsum.[16]

14 See below, p. 187.

15 Not even in the encyclopedic work of R. Ḥayyim's father, the *Or Zarua'*.

16 They do not discuss, for example, the problem posed by **נוטל בידו ונותן לתפוח** or that of submerged pulp. Note also that R. Yehudah of Paris attributes to Rabbenu Tam the reasoning of **קודם המשכה אטו אחר המשכה** (*Tosfot R. Yehudah mi-Paris*, in *Shitat ha-Kadmonim 'al 'Avodah Zarah*, ed. M. Y. H. Blau [New York, 1969], i, 266), and is followed in this by our *Tosafot* ad loc. and the *Semag*, ed. E. Schlesinger (Jerusalem, 1989), 295, Injunction #148. From Ri's responsum it is abundantly clear that Rabbenu Tam forbade what he did on emotional grounds, and that the argument of *atu* is Ri's own rationale. See below, n. 96.

To all appearances, it was a private note to an individual party,[17] of which no copy was kept in Dampierre and which surfaced fortuitously a century later. There is nothing to make us suspect that the author of the Alliance manuscript, an epigone of the French school,[18] was aware of it. Certainly the rest of his handbook bears no mark of such an acquaintance. To all appearances, the witnesses are independent.

Unable to shake Ri's report, we turn to the printed text of Rashi and ask whether it might not be in error or whether perhaps the several readings reflect the different editions (*mahadurot*) of Rashi's commentary. *Mahadurot* are a thorny problem in Rashi's studies, but there is little doubt that Rashi did rework his commentary on the tractate *'Avodah Zarah*—although, as Jacob N. Epstein and, more recently, Jonah Fraenkel have insisted, the editing took the form of specific (small-scale) emendations rather than that of actual rewriting.[19] The text in front of the Tosafists was generally uniform |161| and the same uniformity confronts us in the manuscripts. Only one manuscript of Rashi on *'Avodah Zarah* has come down to us, MS Parma, de Rossi 1292,[20] but luckily it would seem to be in some sense a different *mahadurah* or, more accurately, to have retained some readings of another *mahadurah*.[21] In the defini-

[17] Not too much can be garnered from the opening remarks of R. Yitsḥak, *ketav she'elat aḥi*, as the term *aḥi* is used loosely in the tosafist period, at times not even signifying a relative.

[18] The work is wholly derivative of the *Sefer ha-Terumah* and the *Semag*. It is entitled **הלכות יין נסך מה"ר ירוחם** (fo. 33r). This unknown writer should not be confused with the Provençal author of the *Toledot Adam ve-Ḥavvah*, as the most cursory study of the two works will indicate.

[19] J. N. Epstein, 'Perushei ha-Rivan u-Ferushei Worms', above, n. 9(*c*), pp. 189–92 {reproduced in id., *Meḥkarim*, above, n. 9(*c*), iii. 71–3}; J. Fraenkel, *Darko shel Rashi be-Ferusho la-Talmud ha-Bavli* (Ph.D. diss., Hebrew University, Jerusalem, 1968), 1–13 and *passim*. For bibliography on the problem, see A. N. Z. Roth, 'Mi-Perushei R. Yehudah b. Natan', *Sefer ha-Yovel li-Khevod S. K. Mirsky* (New York, 1958), 285–6. See also the remarks of S. Friedman, *Perush R. Yehonatan ha-Kohen mi-Lunel 'al Bava Kamma* (Jerusalem, 1969), 28–9, and J. Fraenkel's rejoinder in the published version of his thesis of the same name (Jerusalem, 1976), 14–19. {See now Friedman's extensive reply, 'Perush Rashi la-Talmud—Haggahot u-Mahadurot', in T. A. Steinfeld, ed., *Rashi: Iyyunim bi-Yetsirato* (Jerusalem, 1993), 147–75.}

[20] MS 172, described by M. Steinschneider in his *Catalog der hebräischen Handschriften in der Stadtbibliothek zu Hamburg* (Hamburg, 1878) as a commentary of Rashi on *'Avodah Zarah*, contains the text of the Talmud only.

[21] Rashi long wavered, for example, over whether *koḥo* of a Gentile forbade wine *be-hana'ah*, and our printed text, being a mixture of two *mahadurot*, shows inconsistencies. See 58b, s.v. *asur* (and *Tosafot* ad loc., s.v. *ela*); 60a s.v. *ḥamra* (and *Tosafot* ad loc., s.v. *'oved*), and the little summary found at the end of the chapter, 61b, s.v. *koḥo*, which, if not actually written by Rashi, was dictated by him to his pupils (see *Piskei ha-Rosh* 4: 13 and *Tosfot R. Yehudah mi-Paris*, pp. 281, 294). The Parma manuscript (fo. 104v) reads for the passage 58b, s.v. *asur*: **אע"ג דלא נגע גזרו רבנן בכחו לאסרו אף בהנאה משום הרחקת עבירה**, and in 60b, s.v. *ḥamra*, lacks the *lishna aḥarina* of the printed text. From the language of all the Tosafists cited above it is clear that they viewed the concluding appendix on 61b as the work of Rashi. However, in MS Mantua Comunità Israelitica 30 (see below, n. 36), the signature *leshon*

tion of *hamshakhah*, however, its reading is identical with the printed text. The Rashi on the Alfasi is of problematic origin, but on *'Avodah Zarah* it too contains readings of different *mahadurot*,[22] and David Blondheim long ago drew attention to the rich manuscript collections of such Rashis. But on our problem, again, they only corroborate the printed version.[23] *Testimonia*, equally, work against us. The printed *Tosafot* ad loc. |162| report Rashi as printed, as do the recently published *Tosafot* of R. Yehudah of Paris.[24] The latter are doubly problematic. These *Tosafot* were written in the *beit midrash* of Ri under his own instruction, as was common in the Middle Ages.[25] This fact, joined with Ri's letter, leads us to the impossible conclusion that Ri cited one text when teaching and another when writing.

Rashbam is found. For the solution to this problem, see text, below, pp. 187–8. {A reproduction of this passage in the Mantua manuscript is found in *Ha-Yayin bi-Yemei ha-Beinayim* (above, n. 1), 145.}

22 For example, Rashi was long perplexed by the problem of whether *roteḥin* and *kins'a* are effective in purging tarred vessels (see *'Avodah Zarah* 33a–b), and in the course of his lifetime held different opinions. In the printed text (33b, s.v. *ve-hilkheta*, and similarly MS Parma and a citation in the *Temim De'im*, in *Tummat Yesharim* [Venice, 1622], #96) he denies the efficacy of both, even *ex post facto*. Rashbam, however, reports that Rashi was willing to admit *kins'a ex post facto* and to go along with the use of *roteḥin* (*Or Zarua'*, iv [Jerusalem, 1890], *'Avodah Zarah*, #170). In addition, in the Rashi on Alfasi the entire section of the printed text from *me-hakha shame'inan* onward is missing; and a similar text was before the Rashba (*Torat ha-Bayit* [Jerusalem, 1963], 5: 6). It is also doubtful whether the passage against *roteḥin* was in the texts that the Tosafists used. See carefully the printed *Tosafot* and *Tosfot R. Elḥanan*, ed. D. Fränkel (Husiatyn, 1901), ad loc., s.v. *kins'a*. {A superior edition of this *Tosafot*, based on a more accurate transcription of MS Montefiore 65 that Fränkel used, was put out by A. Y. Kreuzer (Benei Berak, 2003). Our passage is found at p. 219. The editor of the Rashi on Alfasi has now been identified as a 14th-century German scholar named R. Yisra'el b. Yo'el Süsslein. See A. Ḥavatselet, 'Perush Rashi she-Nidpas Saviv ha-Rif', *Moriyah*, 19 (1993), 106–16. However, the issue of which versions of Rashi's commentary the editor used remains as problematic as before.}

This observation, together with the one in the previous note, points out a lacuna in the current discussion of the problem of *mahadurot*. No doubt the first step is to scour medieval literature to find citations of *perushim aḥerim* or *mahadurot aḥerot* of Rashi and to compare them with the printed text or manuscripts. This alone, however, is inadequate. Only by a close study of the literature of Rashi's school, where his shifts in position are reported, can we ascertain whether other variants in manuscripts or differing citations of Rashi by other medieval scholars are actually instances of other *mahadurot*, though not called so explicitly.

23 Of the seven manuscripts cited by Blondheim (above, n. 5), p. liv, six were available to me. The Livorno manuscript is presently at the National Library of Israel and entered as MS 4to 621. The Turin manuscript was severely damaged in a fire {and the remains do not contain our passage}.

The phrase *she-nitpanah min ha-'anavim* is similarly missing in the commentary of R. Yehonatan of Lunel ad loc. (below, n. 92). For conjectures to which this commentary could give rise, see below, n. 37.

24 See *Tosfot R. Yehudah mi-Paris* (above, n. 16), pp. 264–5.

25 E. E. Urbach, *Ba'alei ha-Tosafot*, revised edn. (Jerusalem, 1980), 22 ff.; cf. B. Smalley, *The Study of the Bible in the Middle Ages*, 2nd edn. (repr. Notre Dame, 1964), 200 ff. {P. Glorieux, 'L'Enseignement au Moyen Âge: Techniques et méthodes en usage à la Faculté de Paris au XIIIe siècle', *Archives d'histoire doctrinale et littéraire du Moyen Âge*, 43 (1968), 175–7, 185–6.}

The solution is a simple one. The commentary of Rivan, Rashi's pupil and son-in-law, was not an independent work, but one written 'before Rashi', under his dictation or tutelage, as is clear from a subsequent quotation ('and Rivan too interpreted it in this manner before Rashi').[26] From a literary point of view, the commentary is Rivan's; halakhically, it is Rashi's. It contains Rashi's views, and it is his authority that gives the work weight. Making halakhic pronouncements, both Ri and MS Paris Alliance could justly quote Rivan's commentary and attribute the views in it to Rashi, for it was the latter who spoke in the work. Any doubts regarding this matter are laid to rest by the opening remarks of the Alliance manuscript—**משפינה הענבים אילך ואילך ויין צלול באמצע** ('when he cleared the grapes to the sides [of the *cuve* or wine-press] and the clear wine is in the middle')—which, as we shall soon see, is a practical halakhic ruling taken directly from Rivan's work, which none can suspect of having appeared in Rashi's commentary.

The task of an editor is completed. He may publish the standard text of Rashi confident that it is the correct one—though with a chastened awareness of the dangers of making literary attributions on the basis of halakhic statements. But the historian's problems have just begun. Why should Rashi have written one interpretation and yet dictated another?

5. Further on in his responsum, Ri cites another passage from Rivan which provides us with a clue.

> **וגם הריב"ן פ' בענין זה לפני רבינו שיחיה [צ"ל רש"י][27] והילך לשונו [ו]פסק שלו: הלכה כמשנה אחרונה, כרב הונא, דיין כיון שהתחיל לימשך עושה יין נסך. ואם גת פקוקה ומלאה היא כגון אנו שדורכין בגיגית, ואין כאן המשכה נראה לומר שאין נעשה יין נסך. אבל [ר'] תולה להחמיר ממנהג שבידינו, ואין רוצה לומר לא איסור ולא היתר.**
> **ואם מפנין החרצנים שבגיגית אילך ואילך כדי שיכנס היין באמצעית כדי לשלותו נראה לר' דאין המשכה גדולה מזו ועושה יין נסך עכ"ל.**

|**163**| And Rivan, too, interpreted it in this manner before Rashi and this is his language and his ruling: 'And the law is in accordance with the later *mishnah* as R. Huna [ruled] "that as soon as the wine begins to flow [*le-himashekh*] it becomes [subject to] *yein nesekh*". And if the wine-press is stoppered [i.e., a stopper has been placed in the drain pipe that leads to the wine-pit] and full [of wine] as is with us since we tread in *cuves*, there is no *hamshakhah*, and one could plausibly rule that [the wine] does not become subject to *yein nesekh*. However, the master [i.e. Rashi] rules stringently in this questionable matter [i.e. forbids it] because of our common practice, and he wishes neither to rule that the wine is permissible nor that it is forbidden.

[26] See the text below, n. 27.

[27] **ר' שי'** became **רש"י** and was then written out in full. The emendation [**ר'**] is made on the basis of the Rashbam. See below, p. 189.

And if one clears the grape kernels to either side, so that the [strained] wine gathers in the middle, so as to scoop it up [more easily from there], it would seem to the master that there could not be a greater instance of *hamshakhah*, and it [that wine] is subject to *yein nesekh*.

Rashi is of the opinion that the principle of *hamshakhah* is that of separation. If so, the contemporary tub (*cuve*) in which the grapes are trodden, and which possesses no spigot to let the juice out, is legally a גת פקוקה ומליאה (a stoppered and full wine-press). Motion and flow do take place (if only as a result of the pressure from the treading), but there is no flow *away* from the pulp, no separation of liquid from solid. Wine in the *cuve* is therefore not subject to *yein nesekh*. Universal custom, however, treats it as such. And Rashi chose to hold his peace out of deference to the *minhag avot*.

This decision for silence was in character with Rashi's retiring nature. While he could, if necessary, battle for his beliefs,[28] there was in him nothing of that imperious urge which so dominated his grandson, R. Ya'akov Tam, to bend his surroundings to his convictions. But here the silence reflected deeper forces. It arose, as we shall see, from an uncertainty on Rashi's part as to the claims of theoretical analysis vis-à-vis those of custom, the accumulated wisdom of the generations. And this hesitancy and ambivalence left their mark on his work. He was willing to have others report in his name the principle of separation—indeed, he saw to it that they did—provided that they also added that he did not intend by this doctrine to alter the current injunctive practice. But in his own writings he refused to challenge overtly or even criticize implicitly the ancient tradition. He explained *hamshakhah* as משעה שהוא נמשך מצד העליון לצד התחתון ('from the time that it [the liquid] flows from the upper part to the lower one') without the key words of שנתפנה מן הענבים ('and it [the liquid] is cleared of grapes'), an interpretation that would imply separation to one already familiar with the idea, but which would be taken by the uninitiated as simply clarifying how the flow ordinarily occurred. Indeed, Rashi's words were read in Germany for close to a century without anyone dreaming of the revolutionary doctrine that they harbored.[29] Logically the posture he assumed was, of course, inconsistent, but psychologically the ambivalence was comprehensible, especially in view of the remarkable emotional force that the traditional injunction had, as we shall see, for Ashkenazic Jewry. Rashi's position could be interpreted as the result of extreme caution, but later evidence will, I hope, show just how long and how deeply he wrestled with himself as to the truth claims of *minhag avot*.

[28] e.g. *Teshuvot Rashi*, ##59–62, 81, 382. [29] See below, p. 212.

The general injunctive custom referred to by Rivan explains R. Me'ir's original inquiry. He too sensed that the principle of *hamshakhah* was one of separation, but if this was so then the contemporary practice of viewing the juice in the *cuve* as subject to *yein nesekh* made no sense. Lacking any commentarial |164| aids he began to question whether he had not misunderstood the Talmud. (The presumption was always in favor of custom.[30]) And so he dispatched an inquiry to Rashi requesting an explanation of the wine instruments mentioned in the Talmud (*gat*, *bor*, *gargutni*) and asking whether the decision indeed lay, as one would naturally assume, with R. Huna. Sensing the thrust of the question, Rashi replied diplomatically. He declined to formulate any critique of regnant practice. Rather, he explained as requested the utensils mentioned in the Mishnah, assured his son-in-law that R. Huna's dictum was binding, and then added that, as for the juice in the *cuves*, **שם יין עליו לפי המנהג[!] אבותינו** ('it becomes legally wine according to the custom of our fathers'), confident that R. Me'ir would catch the critique encoded in the formulation. Rashi's position in the responsum is one with that enunciated by Rivan—with one significant difference. At the time of R. Me'ir's inquiry, he had not yet done any commentarial work on *'Avodah Zarah* (see above, p. 177), and so he declined to confide his criticism even to his inner circle. When dictating to Rivan at a later stage in his career, Rashi was clearly more confident as to his opinions and was willing to have his views brought to public attention, though his feelings were divided as to his own role in their promulgation.

The stages of Rashi's commentarial activity now demand our attention. Before committing ourselves to an interpretation positing an ambivalence that led Rashi to a logically inconsistent public posture, we should explore the simpler alternative: that the responsum and Rivan's work record an early phase in Rashi's thought, and that his commentary without **שנתפנה מן הענבים** ('and it [the liquid] is cleared of grapes') sets forth a later one. The two reports simply reflect a shift in position.

6. Fragments of R. Shemu'el b. Me'ir's commentary on *'Avodah Zarah* have come down to us. On the topic of *hamshakhah* it runs thus:[31]

וכך הלכה (ד) [כ]משנה אחרונה וכרב הונא דיין כיון שהתחיל לימשך עושה יין נסך. ואם גת פקוקה [ו]מליאה הוא (או) כגון שאנו דורכין בגומות (ו)אין כאן המשכה, נראה לומר דאין נעשה יין נסך, אבל רבי תולה להחמיר ממנהג שבידינו ואינו רוצה לומר לא איסור

30 Note too the concluding inquiry whether *setam yeinam* was forbidden *be-hana'ah*, which seems equally to have been generated by the conflict between the simplest meaning of the Talmud and what R. Me'ir witnessed every day. {See now my *Yeinam* (above, n. 2), 42–3, 51–2.}

31 *Or Zarua'*, #213.

ולא היתר לפי שאין לנו גומות אחרים אלא הגומות עצמן שאנו דורכין בהן, ויש שמניחין בהן את היין זמן מרובה כמו בחבית, הלכך אין להתירן.[32]
ואם מפנין חרצנים שבגיגית אילך ואילך שיתכנס היין באמצעיתה או בצדה לשלותו ולסננו, נראה לרבי דאין לך המשכה גדולה מזו ונעשה יין נסך עכ״ל.

|**165**| And the law is in accordance with the later *mishnah* as R. Huna ruled: 'As soon as the wine begins to flow [*le-himashekh*] it becomes [subject to] *yein nesekh*.' And if the wine-press is stoppered [a stopper has been placed in the drain pipe that leads to the wine-pit] and full [of wine] as is our case, since we tread in *cuves* [*gumot*], there is no *hamshakhah*, and one could plausibly rule that [the wine] does not become subject to *yein nesekh*. However, the master [i.e. Rashi] rules stringently in this questionable instance [i.e. forbids it] because this is our custom, and he wishes neither to rule that the wine is permissible nor that it is forbidden. And some leave the wine in the *cuves* for a considerable period of time, as in a barrel, hence one should not permit it.

And if one clears the grape kernels to either side, so that the [strained] wine should gather in the middle or at the side so as to scoop it up or strain it [more easily from there], it would seem to the master that there could not be a greater instance of *hamshakhah* and it [that wine] is subject to *yein nesekh*.

Rashbam's work, no less than Rivan's, was written under Rashi's direction. Indeed a comparison with the passage of Rivan cited above (p. 181) shows that R. Shemu'el's work is simply an emended version of his uncle's (Rivan's) commentary.[33] Taking the unquestioned existence of two *mahadurot* of Rashi's work on *'Avodah Zarah* together with Rivan's and Rashbam's composition, we may conjecture the following pattern of Rashi's literary activity.

Returning home from the Rhineland and its academies, Rashi begins his great commentarial synthesis. *'Avodah Zarah*, a crucial tractate, is without any serious commentary whatsoever, and from his first scanning of the material he finds himself at variance with common practice and popular interpretation. New, however, to his labors, and without accomplishment in the particular

32 This last sentence of Rashbam is explained below, p. 189.

33 This is a pattern which repeats itself in Rashbam's lesser writings. See my remarks in 'Pawnbroking' (Chapter 6 above), n. 174. The material from *'Eruvin* cited by Epstein in 'Perushei ha-Rivan' (above, n. 9(*c*)), pp. 67–8 should be read in this light. See also E. E. Urbach, 'Mi-Toratam shel Ḥakhmei Angliyah mi-Lifnei ha-Gerush', in H. J. Zimmels et al., eds., *Tif'eret le-Yisra'el, Sefer ha-Yovel li-Khevod Y. Brodie* (London, 1967), 28.

In our case, so mechanical was the copying that Rashbam did not realize that he had switched the terms for *cuve* in mid-paragraph (from *gigit* to *guma*) and, more seriously, had been led into stylistic obscurity. His addendum should not have come at the end, for then the section beginning **לפי שאין לנו גומות** seems to be explaining **לא לאיסור ולא להיתר** when actually it refers to why Rashi is **תולה להחמיר** (see below, pp. 189–90). Had Rashbam been writing freely, the passage would have run thus: **ועל המנהג שבידינו אין רבי רוצה לומר לא איסור ולא היתר אלא תולה להחמיר ממנהג שבידינו ולפי שאין לנו גומות אחרים וכו׳.**

topics of the tractate, he absolutely refuses to voice any criticism of reigning ideas *even* to his own pupils and family. Time passes and Rashi's activity begins to encompass *'Avodah Zarah*. He may have begun with a rough basic draft analogous to his work on *'Arvei Pesaḥim*,[34] or he may have bided his time until the full commentary crystallized in his mind and then set it down with his usual brevity and clarity.[35] Rashi continues with his protean labors and, aware that in *'Avodah Zarah* he had begun from scratch, he restudies his commentary and finds to his satisfaction that there is little to correct. He decides that the time has come to provide his people with a vade mecum for this central tractate, so that they may possess for the first time |**166**| not only an extensive commentary but also a briefer, practical guide based on talmudic sources instead of having to rely on the traditional rules of thumb in use up to then. The Spartan literary discipline which he has imposed on himself prevents him from doing this in his own work. So he calls his son-in-law and pupil, R. Yehudah b. Natan (Rivan), and dictates to him a three-tiered commentary of exegesis of the controlling talmudic passages, halakhic decision (*pesak*), and practical application.[36] Time passes. More and more tractates yield up their secrets to Rashi, and he returns once more to *'Avodah Zarah* and revises it here and there. The changes are important but few. Finally, towards the close of his life, he decides to give that tractate a final review and updates the expanded version that he had dictated to Rivan. He calls his grandson, Shemu'el, tells him to take up his uncle's commentary, and together they revise it.

[34] I personally have found inconclusive the objections to the authenticity of the commentary on *'Arvei Pesaḥim*. If the reader differs, he should feel free to strike this sentence from the text.

[35] It is indicative of Rashi's genius that there is no unevenness in his commentary on this tractate, nor does he give any indication of this being a pioneer effort, just as no difference can be detected in Maimonides' writings between the sections on *Sefer Zera'im*, which he hammered out by Herculean labors, and those in *Sefer Mishpatim*, where he built on the work of others.

[36] (A) In the light of my remarks in n. 33, I have taken the liberty of transferring the structure of Rashbam's commentary to the work of Rivan. Too little of Rivan's commentary has survived to establish its structure independently, though our specific citation corresponds to the three-storied structure of Rashbam. Since Rashbam's work was a revised edition of Rivan, it is no wonder that it displaced the latter. (B) A few more citations of Rivan are to be found in *Tosfot Ḥakhmei Angliyah 'al Niddah, 'Avodah Zarah*, ed. S. Sofer (Jerusalem, 1971). Rashbam's commentary on *'Avodah Zarah* is cited *in extenso* in the *Or Zarua'*, and a sizable fragment was discovered by A. Epstein and published in *Otsar Tov. Hebräische Beilage zum Magazin für die Wissenschaft des Judenthums*, 14 (1887), 1–10. {It was republished by M. Y. H. Blau in his *Shitat ha-Kadmonim 'al 'Avodah Zarah*, i (New York, 1969), 273–6.} Large fragments of this work are also to be found in MS Mantua Comunità Israelitica 30, ranged around the text of Alfasi. This voluminous manuscript is unfortunately unpaginated. Our tractate, *'Avodah Zarah*, is found some fifty-five pages before the end. {The manuscript is paginated; however, the numbers are not visible on the microfilm at the Institute of Microfilmed Hebrew Manuscripts of the National Library of Israel.}

The picture I have drawn is speculative and the specific sequence certainly conjectural, but this much seems certain: Rashi dictating to his grandson a revision of his son-in-law's work, itself but an extrapolation of his own, is a scene which occurred quite late in his life. This fact, taken together with the responsum he had written to R. Me'ir before he had undertaken any literary activity, allows us to say that from the earliest period in his career until its close Rashi was of the opinion that the principle of *hamshakhah* was one of separation. Yet he consistently declined to enunciate it in his own oeuvre![37]

7. It was not caution but reverence for the traditions of his fathers that dictated Rashi's position, for throughout his life he sought to understand or, at the very least, find some rationale for the ancient injunctive practice. Success |167| finally crowned his efforts, and he instructed his grandson, R. Shemu'el, to make note of it. And Rashbam wrote:[38]

אבל רבי תולה להחמיר ממנהג שבידינו ואינו רוצה לומר לא איסור ולא היתר לפי שאין לנו גומות אחרים אלא הגומות עצמן שאנו דורכין בהן, ויש מניחין בהן את היין זמן מרובה כמו בחבית הלכך אין להתירן.

However, the master [i.e. Rashi] rules stringently in this questionable instance [i.e. forbids it] because this is our custom, and he wishes neither to rule that the wine is permissible nor that it is forbidden. And some leave the wine in the *cuves* for a considerable period of time, as in a barrel [*be-ḥavit*], hence one should not permit it.

The operative word here is *be-ḥavit*. Since wine was left in the vats (as if it were in a barrel) for some length of time to acquire color and body,[39] it was viewed by his predecessors as falling within the pale of *yein nesekh*, even without separation from the pulp. In other words, if one viewed the tubs as treading floors (as Rashi had hitherto done), then indeed no 'wine' had come into existence. If, however, one looked upon them as barrels, as vessels of storage, the juice contained therein came within the injunctive orbit of *yein nesekh*.

[37] If one should insist contra Epstein and Fraenkel that the *mahadurah kamma* of Rashi was considerably different from the final commentary (see above, n. 19), and further argue (as I never would) that since R. Yehonatan of Lunel in other tractates incorporated Rashi's earlier *mahadurah* into his work, his remarks in *'Avodah Zarah*, ad loc. (see below, n. 90) should be taken as being those of Rashi, then the word 'ever' should be struck from my formulation in the text above. Rashi initially articulated the doctrine of separation, then thought better of it, excised it, and maintained this silence to the end.

[38] *Or Zarua'*, #213, and see above, n. 33.

[39] In MS Modena Comunità Israelitica 30 we find the Rashbam cited thus: **אבל ר' תולה להחמיר . . . ויש שמניחין בהן יין זמן מרובה שבוע(ה) או יותר להחזיק או להאדים**. The same time span is echoed in the *Sefer ha-Terumah* (Venice, 1523), #169. This was about par for the Parisian region as we learn from Olivier de Serres, *Le Théâtre d'agriculture et mesnage des champs*, i (Paris, 1804–5), 275–6. {See *Ha-Yayin bi-Yemei ha-Beinayim* (above, n. 1), 73–4.}

If barrels are the controlling consideration, the halakhic front is shifting from the talmudic requirement of *hamshakhah* to that of *mi-she-yishleh be-ḥaviyot*.

Rashi's interpretation could exist on two premises only. The doctrine of the early *tanna'im*, it will be recalled,[40] had been that grape juice took on the name of wine only when already in the wine-pit or in the barrels. In the wine-pit a process known as *kippuy* was required; in the barrel one described as *shilluy*. The first premise of Rashi's conjecture must be that the doctrines of *kippuy* and *shilluy* were not actually rejected by the later *tanna'im* when they cited *hamshakhah* in the wine-press as the moment of entrance into the class of wine; rather, they had simply advanced that moment. The old definition was still binding, though it would rarely be invoked, since the wine would ordinarily have become subject to *yein nesekh* long before, by virtue of the *hamshakhah* on the treading floor. If, however, the first stage were to be skipped, the old ruling would proceed to subject the wine to *yein nesekh*. The second assumption was that the doctrine of *shilluy be-ḥaviyot* did not embody any principle of separation.

Shilluy means drawing off, drawing up, or removing one thing from the midst of another. It could refer either to the drawing up of the wine in barrels from the pit, or to the removal of impurities from the body of wine. In his commentary on a passage in the tractate *Bava Metsi'a*, identical with the one found in *'Avodah Zarah*, Rashi specifically interpreted *shilluy* as |**168**| separation using these words:[41]

משנתן בחביות והוא תוסס ורתיחתו עולה ומקצת שמרין קופאין למעלה וקודם שיגופו אותן חביות שולין אותן רתיחות ומשליכן.

When it [the wine] is placed in the barrels, and it begins to ferment and the bubbling rises to the surface and some of the lees float on top, and before one stops those barrels, **one draws off those [lees raised] by the fermentation and throws them away**. [emphasis added]

And again in tractate *Betsah*, in his lexical note on *sholeh*, he wrote:[42]

ושולה. מפרש בגמרא שולה הפסולת שצף למעלה כמו משישלה בחביות דהיינו נמי שנוטל חרצנים הצפים ע״פ החביות.

[40] See above, pp. 174–5.

[41] 92b, s.v. *mi-she-yishleh*. The printed text is corroborated by MSS British Library 412, fo. 170b; 413, fos. 98b–99a; Jewish Theological Seminary, Rabbinica 833, fo. 150b; Bodley 429, fo. 111a; Vatican 131 (not paginated); Cambridge Add. 478, fo. 87b. {MS Jewish Theological Seminary 877 is a copy executed in 1727 of a printed Talmud.}

[42] 14b, s.v. *sholeh* (corroborated by MSS Sassoon 517, fo. 31a; Munich 216, fo. 194a; Frankfurt am Main 8vo 158, fo. 30a; Bodley 420, fo. 181; Jewish Theological Seminary, Rabbinica 840. fo. 16a; 841, fo. 13a; Parma, de Rossi 808, fo. 26a; 1299, fo. 164a). In the last manuscript the word *tsafin* is missing; the meaning, however, is the same.

Ve-sholeh [drawing up or off]: in the Talmud this is explained as the drawing off of the impurities that float on top, as in the phrase [*'Avodah Zarah* 56a, *Bava Metsi'a* 92b] 'when it is drawn off in the barrels', which equally means that he **removes** the grape kernels that float on top of the barrel. [emphasis added]

Yet in his commentary on our passage in *'Avodah Zarah*, he defined *shilluy* simply as the introduction of the wine into the barrels:

שישלה היין מן הבור להנתן בחביות וכן מפרש בב"מ בהשוכר את הפועלים.

When it [the wine] is drawn up from the pit to be placed in the barrels, so it is explained in *Bava Metsi'a* in [the chapter with the *incipit*] 'One who hires the laborers' (92b).

Significantly, most commentators, predecessors and successors alike, whether of Spanish, Italian, or Franco-German provenance,[43] concurred with Rashi's other interpretation of *shilluy* as separation.

Rashi's interpretation of the process that takes place in the wine-pit, *kippuy ba-bor*, was similarly colored. **קפה** in the *kal* is an intransitive verb meaning the hardening[44] or the formation of a floating upper crust;[45] in the intensive (*pi'el*) it is a transitive verb, used privatively to denote the removal of that flotage.[46] In the passage in *Bava Metsi'a*, identical with that in *'Avodah Zarah*, Rashi interpreted the term in the latter fashion:[47]

משיקפה. משיקפאו החרצנים על פי הבור כשמתחיל להיות תוסס ונוטלין הזגין ומשליכן.

Mi-she-yikappeh: when the grape kernels float on the face of the [wine in the] pit when it begins to ferment and **he takes [i.e. removes] these grape kernels and throws them away**. [emphasis added]

Indeed, the remark there of the Talmud when discussing *kippuy*, 'he that draws it [up] is the one who does the *kippuy*', clearly indicates that *kippah* is a transitive verb that denotes an action performed by a person, rather than an intransitive verb denoting a process that occurs with the wine. Rashi moreover states that the surfacing referred to takes place during the process of fermentation,

43 (A) Maimonides, *Mishneh Torah*, 'Hilkhot Ma'asrot' 3: 14; id., *Perush ha-Mishnayot*, ed. J. Kafiḥ (Jerusalem, 1963), *Ma'asrot* 1: 7; and see Alfasi, *'Avodah Zarah*, #1240 (Vilna edn., fo. 13a). (B) *Perush Ri Malki Tsedek* (of Simponte), *Ma'asrot* 1: 7; see the first explanation in *Sefer 'Arukh ha-Shalem*, ed. A. Kohut (repr. New York, 1955) s.v. *k-f-h*, fourth definition. (C) *Perush Rash mi-Shants*, *Ma'asrot* 1: 7.

44 Maimonides, *Perush ha-Mishnayot*, *Terumot* 4: 11. See W. Bacher, 'Beiträge zur semitischen Sprachvergleichung bei Moses Maimuni', in *Recueil des travaux rédigés en mémoire du Jubilé Scientifique de M. Daniel Chwolson* (Berlin, 1899), 135 (referred to in *Tosafot he-'Arukh ha-Shalem*, ed. S. Krauss [Vienna, 1937], 369).

45 Rashi on *'Avodah Zarah*, ad loc., and numerous parallel remarks cited in Y. Avineri, *Millon Perushei Rashi* (Tel Aviv, 1949), s.v. *k-f-h*, to which add *Zevaḥim* 6a, s.v. *kufya*.

46 Above, nn. 43–4.

47 92b, s.v. *mi-she-yikpeh* (readings corroborated by all manuscripts cited above, n. 41).

some time after the entrance of the liquid into the wine-pit. In *'Avodah Zarah*, however, he writes on the *identical* passage, and again he stands almost alone among |**169**| commentators:[48]

משיקפה: לשון צף, כמו קפא תהומא דמסכת סוכה, שצפין החרצנים על היין כשהוא נח בבור.

Mi-she-yikpeh: A term denoting 'floating', as in *kafa tehoma*, in the tractate *Sukkah* [53a]; the grape kernels **float** on top of the wine, when it [the wine] rests in the pit. [emphasis added]

Thus the mixed juice is brought within the injunctive domain of *yein nesekh* briefly after its introduction into any vessel, precisely as custom had it.

Rashi's general interpretation would have yielded a unified interpretation of the *sugya*: *hamshakhah*, *kippuy*, and *shilluy* are all stages in the process of purification. The controversy among the *tanna'im* is, as it were, intramural: which stage of separation marks the advent of wine? In our *sugya* in *'Avodah Zarah* Rashi realizes the implications of his insights and systematically eliminates the notion of separation in each and every term.

Caution might have led Rashi to muffle his doctrine of *hamshakhah*, but it could never have induced him to misinterpret the Talmud, to distort his life's work, or to compromise his artistic integrity. Only a profound conviction that *minhag avot*, the tradition of our forefathers (or this tradition at least), was one manifestation of truth and that a proper reading of the Talmud must allow for[49] the accommodation of this truth could have led Rashi to redefine *kippuy* and *shilluy* and to code into his oeuvre a potential vindication of ancient custom.

The fact that Rashi is not alone in his comments, that Maimonides in his work on the Mishnah understood *kippuy* after the manner of Rashi and that the *'Arukh* adduces a similar explanation of *shilluy*,[50] shows that Rashi's remarks were lexically sound and contextually valid. Any lingering doubts are

[48] Only Me'iri (*Bet ha-Beḥirah* [Jerusalem, 1965], 202) explains *kippuy* as Rashi. Maimonides in the first *mahadurah* of his *Perush ha-Mishnayot*, printed in the standard edition of the Talmud, interprets *kippuy* as floating, as does R. Naḥshon Ga'on in *Teshuvot Ge'onim Kadmonim*, fo. 40a. However, the surfacing they refer to takes place after the fermentation has begun. {For the authorship of R. Naḥshon Gaon, see above, n. 9(*c*).} Rabad (*Perush ha-Rabad 'al 'Avodah Zarah*, p. 152) explains it as the settling of the lees, which even in the warmest climate takes place some time after Rashi's *kippuy*.

[49] Though not necessarily oblige.

[50] Lexically, that is. For *kippuy*, see n. 44; for *shilluy*, see *'Arukh*, s.v. *k-f-h*, fourth definition. *Shilluy* is explained not as separation but as transfer from barrel to barrel. This occurs after *kippuy*, which, according to the *'Arukh*, is separation. Doctrinally, then, there is no relation between this explanation and that of Rashi; lexically they are one. Me'iri adopts Rashi's explanation of *kippuy in toto*.

laid to rest by Rashi's comments passing 800 years of intensive scrutiny without question or comment.[51] Yet a careful reconstruction of the literature of his school shows his writings to be equally a vindication |170| of contemporary mores. Rashi's commentary, like all great works of art, is multileveled in meaning. It here moves simultaneously on the plane of timeless commentary and on that of contemporary reference. It has the dimension of objective clarification and that of a defense of the traditions of the world from which he came. Rashi in the matter of *hamshakhah* is both an immortal commentator and a faithful son of the pre-Crusade Ashkenazic community.

To all appearances, no work seems less tinctured with the character and attitudes of the author than that of Rashi. More than any other figure of the Middle Ages, he resembles Keats's poet, in that he seems 'to have no self, to have no identity but to be constantly informing and filling another body'. The historian contemplating his oeuvre, which baffles all searches for personality and posture, knows the despair that Schiller spoke of in his encounter with the classics.

> Wholly unconfiding [the classical poet] flees the heart that seeks him . . . The object possesses him utterly . . . Like a Deity behind this universe, he stands behind his work . . . Misled as I was through acquaintance with modern poets to seek at once the poet in the work . . . I could not bear that in this instance the poet could nowhere be seized and would nowhere abide my question.[52]

Yet, unless we succeed in 'seizing the poet', in perceiving the personal in the objective, unless we uncover the polysemy of the work that forms a watershed in Jewish history, seeing its contemporary import alongside its permanent meaning, we shall never truly understand Rashi, or fathom his greatness, or begin to write the history of halakhah.

The practical implications of Rashi's interpretation were considerable. Grapes, upon harvest, were placed in cylindrical baskets (*hôtes*) that were strapped to the back, carried to the *cuve*, and emptied into it. When the vat was filled and closely packed, the treading began and the liquid was emitted via a spigot near

51 In the course of close to a millennium, several scholars did note in passing some of these contradictions, e.g. R. Shelomoh Algazi, *Leḥem Setarim* (Venice, 1664), *'Avodah Zarah*, ad loc.; R. Shelomoh Luria, *Ḥokhmat Shelomoh*, *Bava Metsi'a*, ad loc.; R. Mosheh Sofer, *Ḥiddushei Ḥatam Sofer* (New York, 1957), *Bava Metsi'a*, ad loc.; R. Shemu'el Strashun (in the Vilna edition of the Talmud), *'Avodah Zarah*, ad loc. They made, however, no ado about them.

52 Cited in M. H. Abrams, *The Mirror and the Lamp: Romantic Theory and the Critical Tradition* (New York, 1958), 238.

the base of the vat. Only then was the pulp taken to a press for the last drop of wine to be extracted.

If the spigot remained closed, no separation of wine from pulp would occur, and the entire first phase of wine production would be released from the injunctive domain of *yein nesekh*. In other words, so long as the crushed grapes |171| remained interspersed with the wine—and since the reddish color and the 'body' of wine are obtained from the skin, the pulp was in fact left in for a week or so[53]—one need not guard against Gentile contact. Non-Jewish labor could be employed without a qualm, and wine transported and stored without the onerous requirements of special and double seals. Vineyards that might previously have been left untended because of the impossibility of ensuring Jewish supervision could now be cultivated and harvested.[54] Jews could contract wine from Gentiles, requesting only that it be delivered in a mixed state.

Jewish communities were generally tiny, averaging from a handful to a score of families, and tended (in the Champagne region) to make their own wine. As the crude state of barrel-making made the aging of wine and its long-term storage impossible,[55] wine was usually produced anew every fall. An entire year's consumption had to be provided for in the treading of September and early October, but since the High Holidays and Sukkot fell in these months, the time available for grape pressing was limited indeed. In contrast, the quantities of wine consumed in this age were (as I have already noted) enormous, and it was taxing in the extreme to tread so large a quantity in so short a time with so little manpower. It is difficult to see how this could have been accomplished without the concerted effort of the entire community.[56]

53 See above, n. 39.

54 Suggested by *Ma'aseh Ge'onim*, p. 81. This would have allowed them to make full use not only of their own distant vineyards but also those offered in mortgage to them. {For the wide scope and importance of such mortgages, see *Yeinam* (above, n. 2), 68–90.}

55 M. W. Labarge, *A Baronial Household of the Thirteenth Century* (New York, 1965), 106. Rashi himself makes reference to the short lifespan of wine in a query on another matter to R. Yitsḥak b. Yehudah: **ובעשר שנים ובט"ו שנים שהחמרנו על עצמ[נ]ו והדבר[!] מאד קשה, כי הדרכים המשובשים[!] ואין יהודי יוצא ובא, ויין שלנו אין מתקיים לקדוש ולהבדלה וצריך להביאו ממרחק**. MS Bodley 566, fo. 35b. {The passage is cited in full in *Ha-Yayin bi-Yemei ha-Beinayim* (above n. 1), 255. For details and full documentation of the brief shelf life of wine, see ibid. 82–4.}

56 It is this (rather than any professional occupation as a vintner) that explains Rashi's oft-cited remarks (*Teshuvot*, #382), **הלב יודע טרד המצוי באגור ביקבים, על כן לצדק יכריעני אדוני ר' עזרא את קוצר מילי**. The average Champagne household in the month of September very much resembled our own before Passover. The second passage usually cited in support of Rashi's supposed occupation (*Sefer ha-Oreh*, p. 214, *Teshuvot*, #159) refers most probably to R. Yitsḥak b. Yehudah. In the literature of his school Rashi is never called *rabbenu ha-gadol*, but the former scholar is regularly referred to this way by the Makhirites in the *Ma'asei Ge'onim*. Indeed, the presumption is against anyone being a vinegrower in Troyes. Its deeply fissured soil is to this day inhospitable to viticulture, and, not surpris-

The use of non-Jewish help in the treading and the possibility of |172| contracting wine deliveries constituted an enormous lightening of the load. The ruling would have been a boon to any age, but it was particularly advantageous in the waning years of the eleventh and early years of the twelfth century as the Jewish community began its retreat from landowning[57] and its control over wine production became progressively more difficult.

An allowance such as this cannot long be suppressed. If Rashi rendered tacit obedience to those customs in which he had been raised and whose validity had been unquestioned in the academies where he had studied, these held no sway over the minds of the young scholars who had gathered around him, whose thinking he had shaped, and whose halakhic world was his teachings. Rashi's reservations were primarily emotional and these stand little chance of survival when opposed by both logic and convenience. Law by its nature tends to adopt articulated positions and discount personal hesitations. His pupils dutifully noted his reservations but themselves joined, apparently, in promulgating the doctrine that freed wide tracts of wine production from all restraints.[58]

8. The next development is the appearance of the doctrine of R. Ya'akov of Ramerupt (more commonly called Rabbenu Tam). Ri reports:[59]

ואין נראה . . . אלא כפירוש ר"ת, יין משהתחיל לימשך פירוש שהתחיל לקלח מגת קודם שירד לבור תנן לוקחין גת בעוטה אע"ג שהוא נוטל בידו וכו' משמע אפילו התחיל לימשך בגת פקוקה ומלאה שאינו מקלח כלל.

ingly, E. Chapin has found no reference to vines in local documents (*Les Villes des foires de Champagne des origines au debut du XVIe siècle* [Paris, 1937], 5, 97–8). Contrast this with their frequent mention in the Bar-sur-Aube region (ibid. 77–92.). A generation or so before Rashi there seems to have been only one solitary owner or, perhaps, more accurately, only one major owner of vineyards among the Jews of Troyes (*Teshuvot R. Me'ir mi-Rotenburg* [Prague and Budapest, 1895], #941 and note ad loc.). Undoubtedly, there were some local vines, probably for private use (Rashi's words almost imply as much), but that they should have regularly produced a surplus sufficient to afford a living is asking a great deal of them. Despite all this, Rashi may nevertheless have been a vintner; but by the same measure he may have been an egg salesman. {See now *Ha-Yayin bi-Yemei ha-Beinayim* (above, n. 1), 46–50. In the original article, I mistakenly wrote that the 'chalky soil' of Champagne was inhospitable to viticulture. This is an error and a bad one; I have substituted here 'deeply fissured' for 'chalky'.}

57 B. Blumenkranz, *Juifs et Chrétiens dans le monde occidental 430–1096* (Paris, 1960), 20; id., 'Cultivateurs et vignerons juifs en Bourgogne du IXe au XIe siècle', in *Bulletin philologique et historique du Comité de travaux historiques et scientifiques* (1959), 131–6.

58 *Or Zarua'*, #215, cited in main text, below, p. 207. I say 'apparently' because the respondent's remarks about Rashi are not quite accurate; see text below, p. 209. However, I do not believe we would be justified in questioning the statements about R. Me'ir and R. Shemu'el. In light of my analysis of R. Me'ir's query (above, p. 186), his joining in on the promulgation of the allowance would be expected.

59 *Tosfot R. Yehudah mi-Paris*, p. 264.

> And this [i.e. Rashi's interpretation] is not plausible . . . but rather, as Rabbenu Tam explained, [the phrase] 'As soon as the wine begins to flow [*le-himashekh*], it becomes [subject to] *yein nesekh*' means when it begins to pour out of the treading floor before it descends into the wine-pit. And the Mishnah's ruling that 'A wine-press [containing] trodden grapes may be purchased from a Gentile even though it was he that lifted [the trodden] grapes with his hand' includes the case when it [the wine] flows within a stoppered and full wine-press, provided that it does not pour out of the wine-press.

Hamshakhah, according to Rabbenu Tam, is not the downward flow of the juice *on to* the pressing floor, but the flow of the juice *out* of that place. The unique category of wine came into existence only when the liquid left the press. While on the treading floor, it remained ever grape juice (*mashkin ha-yotse'in*). Only when removed from its place of origin could it assume the independent category of wine.

This was no academic doctrine. Care would have to be taken, according to Rashi's interpretation, that no pulp was ever pushed to the side or scooped out to make for easier treading, for then *hamshakhah* would take |173| place and the wine would be subject to *yein nesekh*.[60] Ideally, a Jew would have to be constantly present to ensure that no such minor scoopage took place. Doubts naturally arose as to just how feasible such control was. It is easier at times to observe a blanket injunction than to confine an allowance within a framework of onerous precautionary measures. Rabbenu Tam's doctrine swept away the need for any such measures. So long as the wine remained in the *cuve* where it was initially trodden, it was totally immune to any injunction.

The question that immediately presents itself is: what was the relationship of this doctrine to the felt needs of the time? The bearing of halakhah towards reality—the patterns of resistance and response, of attentiveness and indifference—is a complex one and forms too large a topic to be treated here. For the moment let me say that nothing could be farther from the mind of any religious person, let alone of a man of the Middle Ages, than an attempt of set purpose to align a Divine norm with temporal needs.[61] Response, when it came, flowed from the conjunction of a distinctive communal self-image with certain premises of the dialectical method, and as often as not halakhah turned a deaf ear to common need. But under certain specific conditions, circumstances did play a role (if only mediately) in the birth of ideas, and the question that arises is whether Rabbenu Tam's doctrine of *hamshakhah* was an instance of this.

60 *Tosfot R. Yehudah mi-Paris*, p. 265; ומאד יש לתת לב לצידי המשכה and the printed *Tosafot* 55b, s.v. *amar*, end.

61 See the important remarks of H. H. Ben-Sasson in *Beḥinot*, 9 (1957), 46–9.

Every case is of course unique, but two criteria can be mentioned. The first is temperament: is such awareness in character with the propounder of the doctrine? Some scholars are oblivious to reality, others are well aware of it. The second is an uncharacteristic flaw, and I emphasize the word 'uncharacteristic'. Is there some defect in the doctrine that leads one to infer that unless something had impinged, wittingly or not, upon the mind of the author, he would not have arrived at what he did?

The criterion of character is in most cases circular. We know next to nothing about the temperament of most halakhists. Fortunately this is not the case with Rabbenu Tam. His intense awareness of his people's needs and his boldness in thought and action are well documented.[62] Ravyah (R. Eli'ezer ben Yo'el of Mainz, d. *c.*1225) leveled against Rabbenu Tam's doctrine of *hamshakhah* a critique from the Tosefta.[63] But this proves nothing. Even the |174| great Rabbenu Tam could overlook a Tosefta. More damning is the well-nigh universal stricture that *hamshakhah* simply does not mean 'pouring' in mishnaic Hebrew; the word for 'pouring' is *kiluaḥ* or, in our case, *yeridah la-bor* (descent into the wine-pit).[64] Had R. Huna wished to express what Rabbenu Tam claimed he did, he should simply have said *mi-she-hitḥil la-redet la-bor* ('when it [the wine] begins to descend into the wine-pit'). *Hamshakhah* refers invariably to a flow *across* a surface as Rashi had explained it. Few men in the Middle Ages had a finer lexical sense than Rabbenu Tam, and it is difficult to see his explanation other than as an attempt, conscious or unconscious (and subject to the restrictions I have outlined elsewhere), to ratify general practice and to insulate much of Jewish wine production from any religious proscription.[65]

[62] S. Albeck, 'Yaḥaso shel Rabbenu Tam li-Ve'ayot Zemano', *Zion*, 19 (1954), 103–41. The article should be qualified by Ben-Sasson's observations referred to in the preceding note.

[63] MSS Bodley 637, #1069 {*Sefer Ravyah le-Massekhet 'Avodah Zarah*, ed. D. Deblitski (Benei Berak, 1976), #1069; *Sefer Ravyah*, ed. D. Deblitski (Benei Berak, 2005), iv, #1069} cited in *Or Zarua'*, #214; 'Sefer Amarkal', in S. Eppenstein et al., eds., *Le-David Tsevi. Festschrift zum siebzigsten Geburtstage David Hoffmanns: gewidmet von Freunden und Schülern* (Berlin, 1914), Hebrew section, p. 13.

[64] See the critique of the Spanish and Provence school and that of R. Asher: *Ḥiddushei ha-Ramban 'al 'Avodah Zarah* (ed. C. D. Chavel, Jerusalem, 1970) ad loc.; *Ḥiddushei ha-Rashba 'al 'Avodah Zarah* (Jerusalem, 1966) ad loc.; *Ḥiddushei ha-Ritva* and R. Nissim of Gerona's commentary to Alfasi, ad loc.; *Bet ha-Beḥirah 'al 'Avodah Zarah* (Jerusalem, 1965), 205–6; *Piskei ha-Rosh*, 4: 3. (As to the identity of the author of the *Ḥiddushei ha-Rashba 'al 'Avodah Zarah*, see A. Rosenthal's remarks in *Kiryat Sefer*, 42 [1967], 132–9.) The only medieval scholar known to me to endorse Rabbenu Tam's position is Ri (*Tosfot R. Yehudah mi-Paris*, loc. cit.), but his position was influenced by the difficulties he encountered in explaining *notel be-yado ve-noten le-tapuaḥ* of the Mishnah (see his responsum cited above, n. 12). There is no evidence that Rabbenu Tam was motivated by this consideration.

[65] H. Soloveitchik, 'The Tosafist Conception of Law'. Paper presented at the annual meeting of the Association of American Law Schools, Houston, Texas, December 28, 1976. {An expanded ver-

Such may be our conclusion—if Rabbenu Tam's pupils understood him properly. R. Ya'akov's own words have not come down to us. Our knowledge of his position comes from reports of the Tosafists, and they, inspired primarily by the formulation of R. Yehudah of Paris, who wrote his *Tosafot* at the feet of R. Yitsḥak of Dampierre (no mean source!), speak uniformly of *kiluaḥ*, and by so doing expose the doctrine to withering lexical criticism. It is an even chance, however, that Rabbenu Tam was imperfectly understood. Wine in talmudic times did not pour out of a press into a pit. The press was built on one level, the pit on a lower one, and a pipe connected the two. In a letter which I shall presently discuss[66]—though unfortunately not one in |175| which he presses his own position—Rabbenu Tam evinces an awareness of this fact, writing נמשך ויורד דרך הסילון לבור ('it flows and descends through a pipe to the wine-pit'). The exit of the liquid from the press did not then entail pouring, but a downward motion across the inner surface of the pipe, precisely as implied by the term *hamshakhah*. R. Ya'akov Tam's pupils inadvertently formulated his doctrine in terms of medieval realia and thus came to speak of pouring (*kiluaḥ*).[67] The flaw may be in the tosafist transmission rather than in Rabbenu Tam's initial position, in which case one of our two criteria (for detection of influence) has not been met. One could contend that despite the appropriateness of the term *hamshakhah*, Rabbenu Tam's interpretation was still too apposite to contemporary need to be wholly fortuitous. This may well be, but there is no way of proving it, for one lacks the crucial 'measurable deflection' that is necessary for any demonstration that extraneous factors were impinging upon the course of immanent developments.

In brief, if no breakdown occurred in tosafist communication, if no misunderstanding arose in the central *yeshivah* of Dampierre, Rabbenu Tam's interpretation bears the imprint of contemporary challenges. If such a mis-

sion of this lecture was published as 'Religious Law and Change: The Medieval Ashkenazic Example', Chapter 9 below.} See below, p. 219, for the measure of inner conviction that this interpretation carried for Rabbenu Tam. In passing, I should add that there is no evidence, to the best of my knowledge, that Rabbenu Tam earned a living from the sale or production of wine. Cf. Urbach, *Ba'alei ha-Tosafot* (above, n. 25), 62. The presence of a large cask (*pitam*) in a house proves nothing, especially in view of the quantities then consumed. Moreover the R. Ya'akov there mentioned is not Rabbenu Tam but a prominent member of his community. See *Temim De'im*, #86: מעשה אירע בבית הנדיב ר' יעקב . . . ושאלו לרבי' יעקב ד"ל והתיר, and this reading is corroborated by MS London Beth Din 14, fo. 146b: הנדיב ר' יעקב . . . ושאלו לר"ת וכו'. {On Rabbenu Tam's superb lexical sense, see now *Ha-Yayin bi-Yemei ha-Beinayim* (above, n. 1), 357–8.}

66 Below, pp. 207–8.

67 It will not do to argue that *k-l-ḥ* can also mean motion across a surface as in *Zevaḥim* 25b. It almost invariably does not, and the Tosafists did not use Hebrew after an archaic or idiosyncratic fashion, certainly not when writing expository prose.

understanding did indeed arise and Rabbenu Tam's doctrine is actually lexically sound, there is no way of evaluating its genesis, other than by personal intuition. It would be wisest, perhaps, to eschew such divination in the initial phase of halakhic historiography and to adhere as closely as possible to the criterion of 'measurable deflection' if we wish to avoid the pitfalls of a simplistic sociology of law. Let us lay the foundations of Jewish legal history with insights possessing some measure of certainty and only then fill in the interstices with impressions. Only after the halakhic terrain has been charted with some certainty, and skills acquired and intuitions tested in the course of that arduous mapping, should we venture into the territory of conjecture and surmise.

Be that as it may, Rabbenu Tam's allowances were after all but the capping stone of Rashi's. What of that initial revolutionary doctrine? Was it a product of the felt needs of the time? Recall Rashi's guarded language in his early responsum to R. Me'ir, his protracted silence, his excision of the words '[the liquid] is cleared of grapes' (*she-nitpanah min ha-'anavim*), and his novel explanations of *kippuy* and *shilluy*. If ever a man sought to hide his discovery it was Rashi. What emerges is the picture of a great commentator arriving, on this occasion as on hundreds of others, at the precise nuance of a term. Perceiving the consequence of the downward |**176**| flow in terms of the unequal rate of descent of liquids and solids, he transformed sharpened fact into principle (that of separation), and invested the law with coherence. And then he stopped dead in his tracks! It was his pupils—whose halakhic world was his teachings and who felt no deference to a Rhineland where they had never studied—who promulgated the new creed, one which the people rapidly and profitably embraced. While the acceptance of this major innovation, almost revolution, in *yein nesekh* and, possibly, its refinement by later hands is attributable to circumstance, its inception is not. The initial breakthrough was here an immanent development. And lest anyone attempt to generalize, let me add that in the next case the situation could be the reverse and in the one after that altogether different.

In any event, the joint doctrine of Rashi and Rabbenu Tam liberated much of the production, transportation, and storage of wine from the injunctive domain of *yein nesekh*. Small wonder that the old injunctive custom was swept away! The new doctrine won such wide acceptance in Champagne that by the last quarter of the twelfth century the great R. Yitsḥak of Dampierre (Ri) neither knew nor had even heard of the original custom, and added that in Rabbenu Tam's day the allowance was equally universal.[68]

[68] *Teshuvot Maharaḥ Or Zarua'*, #174, fo. 59a; p. 165a in Avitan's edition (above, n. 12): ועל אותו

9. But we are anticipating. Our printed *Tosafot* reports, in the name of R. Yehudah of Paris:

> ויש שהיו רוצין למצוא חן בעיני העובדי כוכבים והיו העובדי כוכבים דורכים עמהם בגיגיות קודם המשכה, ושמע ר' יעקב והקפיד ורצה לנדותם אם לא ישמעו וישובו ולא יעשו עוד.

And there were those who sought to find favor in the eyes of the Gentiles, and Gentiles would tread in the tubs with them . . . And R. Ya'akov [i.e. Rabbenu Tam] heard of this and wished to excommunicate them if they would not obey and desist [from what they were doing] and not repeat it.

R. Mosheh of Coucy, R. Yehudah's pupil, gives a similar report in his code, *Semag*.[69] In the actual *Tosafot* of R. Yehudah the evaluation 'who sought to find favor in the eyes of the Gentiles' is not found, and Ri, too, in a report that we shall soon consider, omits this assessment.[70] The problem is both textual (what is the correct reading in the *Tosafot* of R. Yehudah?) and historical (is the report a later evaluation or an actual description of the motivation of the participants?).

Yein nesekh had long been considered a classic example of *insolentia Judaeorum*. One of the earliest anti-Jewish (possibly antisemitic) tracts written in the Middle Ages, that of Agobard of Lyons, mentions with bitterness that Gentile touch defiled liquids and made them unfit for Jewish consumption. From *privilegia* granting to the Jews the right to sell their wine, one can see |177| how deeply resented was the implied Jewish superiority contained in the *yein nesekh* ban. No less a person than Innocent III lashed out at this presumptuousness.[71] Whether the specific merchants mentioned by R. Yehudah

מנהג [ש]אמר שנהגו להחמיר ולכך לא רצה לומר רבי(נו) בדבר לא איסור ולא היתר, גם על זה נפלאתי, כי לא ראיתי ולא שמעתי שום אדם שהיה מחמיר חומרא זו . . . וכדברי רבינו יעקב . . . ראיתי נוהגים במדינה הזאת כל הימים בחיי רבינו וגם עכשיו.

[69] *Tosafot*, ad loc., s.v. *amar*, end; *Semag*, ed. E. Schlesinger (Jerusalem, 1989), 295, Injunction #148. A similar report is found in *Tosfot R. Perets* cited in *Teshuvot Ri Kolon*, #2. Another pupil of Ri, the editor of MS Bodley 1408, gives a similar report (in #154). Parts of this work were published by S. Assaf in *Sefer ha-Yovel li-Khevod A. Marx* (New York, 1950), 9–22, from MS Schocken 19520. {The full text was published from the Bodley MS by M. Y. H. Blau in his *Shitat ha-Kadmonim 'al 'Avodah Zarah*, iii (New York, 1991), 165–279. Our passage is at p. 260. MS Bodley 1408 was itself copied from MS Bodley 884. Our passage is found in the latter work at fo. 167b.} On the relationship of the manuscripts, see Urbach, *Ba'alei ha-Tosafot* (above, n. 25), 228, n. 7. R. Yehudah of Paris may be the editor of this collection; see ibid. 229, n.10.

[70] *Tosfot R. Yehudah mi-Paris*, pp. 265–6; *Teshuvot Maharaḥ Or Zarua'*, #174.

[71] *Patrologia Latina*, ed. J. P. Migne, vol. civ, p. 826. {Agobard of Lyons, *Opera Omnia*. L. van Acker, ed., Corpus Christianorum, Continuatio Medievalis 52 (Turnhout, 1981), 193}; *Patrologia Latina*, vol. cxvii, p. 170; J. Aronius, *Regesten zur Geschichte der Juden im Fränkischen und Deutschen*

were motivated by the desire 'to find favor in Gentile eyes' or not is not really important; that *yein nesekh* engendered disfavor is. And this is the point of significance. Gentile goodwill was needed by all; *yein nesekh* was an omnipresent irritant and everyone had much to gain by its allowance. Any evaluation of developments in *yein nesekh* must take into account the high price in Christian bitterness that Jews were willing to pay for this injunction. Too often our attention focuses on the allowances made, forgetting that these were ad hoc alleviations within an injunctive framework, and that that framework was maintained despite its contributing to and exacerbating antisemitism—which in this period translated itself rapidly into persecution. Occasion presented itself to the Tosafists to wipe *yein nesekh* from the books, and it was rejected with shock.[72] Spanish Jews, for example, were lax in their observance of this injunction, and attempts were made to rid themselves of this annoying restraint.[73] I have found, however, no evidence for any of this in France or Germany. The Ashkenazic community was animated by a fierce sense of the heroic in the face of persecution and intensely felt its dissimilarity to the heathen world around it. *Yein nesekh* seemed to these Jews an appropriate symbol of this distinctiveness, and they did not begrudge the price they had to pay for it. The people's identification with the injunction and their pain-filled and costly efforts to maintain it go a long way to explaining, psychologically, the inclination of the halakhists to alleviate points of particular stress.

10. In his responsum, Ri provides us with further details of the story:[74] |**178**|

> **וכבר היו בני אדם מסביבות עיר מיץ שהלכו לארץ אשכנז והיו דורכים גתותיהם על ידי גוים, וקבלו בני המלכות שביניהם לרבינו יעקב, וכעס ביותר על המקילין המקלקלין מנהג קדושים וכשרים, ואמר לנדותם אם לא ישמעו שלא לעשות עוד.**

And there were once people from the environs of Metz who went to Germany and used to employ Gentiles to tread their wine-presses [*cuves*]. And the men of the

Reiche bis zum Jahre 1273 (Berlin, 1902), 90; R. Hoeniger, 'Zur Geschichte der Juden Deutschlands im Mittelalter', *Zeitschrift für die Geschichte der Juden in Deutschland*, 1 (1887), 141; S. Grayzel, *The Church and the Jews in the XIIIth Century*, revised edn. (New York, 1966), 73, 127–8. See also R. S. Lopez's remarks in *Speculum*, 42 (1967), 343. {For the later Middle Ages, see G. Mentgen, *Studien zur Geschichte der Juden im mittelalterlichen Elsaß*, Forschungen zur Geschichte der Juden 2 (Hanover, 1995), 560, 612.}

72 See J. Katz's discussion in *Bein Yehudim le-Goyim* (Jerusalem, 1960), 55–6. {The passage is found in the English version of that work, entitled *Exclusiveness and Tolerance* (Oxford, 1961), at pp. 46–7.}

73 e.g. Maimonides, 'Hilkhot Ma'akhalot Asurot', 11: 10; *Teshuvot ha-Rambam*, ed. J. Blau (Jerusalem, 1960), ii, #269; Avraham b. Natan ha-Yarḥi, *Sefer ha-Manhig*, ed. Y. Rafael (Jerusalem, 1961), 660.

74 *Teshuvot Maharaḥ Or Zarua'*, #174, fo. 59b; p. 165b in Avitan's edition (above, n. 12). It is worth noting that though Metz was part of the Empire, culturally we see it was under French sway. The

empire complained to Rabbi Ya'akov, and he was extremely angry with those who treated lightly [*mekilin*] [the injunction against Gentile treading] and who were destroying [*mekalkelin*] the custom of the holy and proper ones [i.e. ancient custom]. And he declared that he would excommunicate them if they would not obey [him] never to do this again.

He reports that 'the men of the empire complained'. The complaint and outcry were general, but from Ravyah we know that the actual letter was written by R. Shemaryah of Speyer.[75] The letter was sharp enough to put Rabbenu Tam on the defensive. And writing thus to Rabbenu Tam was no simple matter. The spirit of talmudic dialectics which had been dormant (in any significant fashion) since the fifth century had sprung to life again in Rabbenu Tam, and in him and through him the halakhah embarked upon a new period of massive creativity. He was working a revolution and he knew it; and through him flowed the imperious sense of bringing a freshly wrested vision of truth to the world. His contemporaries (even his critics) sensed this, and their relationship to him was not one simply of respect or reverence, but of awe—awe before the unforeseeable and the unique. Fear of his intellectual thunderbolts and the force of his leonine personality often made timid men of those who had dealings with him.

11. The report of another encounter of Rabbenu Tam with R. Shemaryah has come down to us, and from it we may hazard a guess that when the time had come for Germany to register a protest in Ramerupt, the choice of R. Shemaryah was not wholly accidental. R. Yitsḥak Or Zarua' relates:[76]

> **אני יצחק המחבר בר' משה שמעתי שבא מעשה לפני רבי' תם זצ"ל בראובן שהיה חייב לשמעון מנה ומת ראובן. ונסתפק רבינו תם זצ"ל אם מן הדין יכול לעכב שלא לקוברו עד שיפרעו לו המנה שחייב לו, שהיה ידוע שהיה חייב לו, או שמא אינו רשאי (לנולוו) [לנוולו]. ונמלך ברבינו שמריה בר מרדכי זצ"ל. והשיב לו שהדין עם שמעון ויכול מן הדין לעכב את קבורתו עד שיפרעו לו הואיל וידוע שהוא חייב לו כמסקנ' דשמעתין דיכלי למימר זוזי יהבינן לינוול ולינוול. וקיבל רבינו תם את דבריו.**

And I the author, Yitsḥak ben Mosheh, heard that a case came before Rabbenu Tam,

exact boundaries of *Tsarfat* and *Ashkenaz* have yet to be delineated, just as the halakhah still awaits its Klimrath line setting off northern France (*Tsarfat*) from Provence. Until we have such maps we will not be able to use properly the growing number of place names that manuscripts are beginning to provide us with. A question coming from a city under French influence might be insignificant, but if it arose in a German area it could indicate a major change.

[75] *Sefer Ravyah*, #1050, published by I. A. Agus in *Teshuvot Ba'alei ha-Tosafot* (New York, 1954), 75–6 {and in *Sefer Ravyah 'al 'Avodah Zarah*, 16; *Sefer Ravyah*, iv. 10}.

[76] *Or Zarua'*, iii (Jerusalem, 1887), #199, correction from MS British Library 530, fos. 278–9, from which the text was published.

may his memory be blessed, concerning Re'uven, who owed Shim'on money, and Re'uven died. And Rabbenu Tam, may his memory be blessed, was in doubt whether one [i.e. Shim'on] could properly delay his burial until the money owed him was paid, for it was known that he [Re'uven] owed him [the money]. Or perhaps one was not allowed to disgrace [the corpse in this way]. And he consulted with Rabbenu Shemaryah ben Mordekhai, may his memory be blessed, who replied that Shim'on was right, he could hold up the burial until he was paid, since it was known that he [i.e. Re'uven] owed him [the money]; [the case is] similar to the [instance in the Talmud, *Bava Batra* 154b] where 'they can say "we have given *zuzim* [i.e. money], let the [body of the debtor] be disgraced"'. And Rabbenu Tam accepted his ruling.

R. Shemaryah was certainly not the greatest German scholar of his time. R. Eli'ezer ben Natan and R. Yo'el far surpassed him. It has been suggested that R. Shemaryah happened to be then passing through Troyes or Ramerupt, and this is what occasioned the inquiry.[77] And indeed, had Rabbenu Tam dispatched a letter to Speyer, there would have been an automatic delay of burial for at least a week or so. But even granting R. Shemaryah's presence at the time in the Champagne, the story is still remarkable. First, Rabbenu Tam was the last man to ask for advice regarding a decision. Indeed, this is the only case known to |179| me where he did so. Not that he did not find himself in quandaries at times, but he invariably found his own way out of them. Second, the passive role described in 'and Rabbenu Tam accepted his ruling' is also out of character, especially in view of R. Shemaryah's astounding line of reasoning, which constitutes the third surprising aspect of this encounter. The case at hand involved the suspension of two pentateuchal *mitsvot*: the imperative of 'Be sure to bury him that same day' and the injunction of 'You must not leave his body on the tree overnight' (Deut. 21: 23). Argument was made from permission granted by the Talmud to open a grave for a moment to ascertain whether the deceased was a minor or not. The nature of the ban on grave-opening remains obscure to this day,[78] but it is probably not pentateuchal and certainly not even vaguely on a par with the injunction against leaving a body unburied. Opening a grave briefly and leaving the dead unburied are two totally different things, and no one needed to be told this less than

[77] Urbach, *Ba'alei ha-Tosafot* (above, n. 25), 191.

[78] See Y. Y. Greenwald, *Kol-Bo 'al Avelut* (repr. New York, 1973), 217 ff., 223 ff. and *Pitḥei Teshuvah*, 'Yoreh De'ah', 363: 7–8. M. Elon, in his *Ḥerut ha-Perat be-Darkhei Geviyyat Ḥov ba-Mishpat ha-'Ivri* (Jerusalem, 1964), 238–40, has already raised this point. {The expanded and more readily available version of Elon's book, now entitled *Kevod ha-Adam ve-Ḥeruto be-Darkhei ha-Hotsa'ah la-Po'al* (Jerusalem, 2000), retains the same pagination as the original edition. The enlargement is in the lengthy introduction.}

Rabbenu Tam. How he could have accepted such an argument is little less than astonishing.

The solution to these problems may lie in an observation of E. E. Urbach, who noted that all that we possess of R. Shemaryah are reports of practical rulings—*pesakim*.[79] Indeed, his judicial talents—his ability to chart the appropriate path to the desired decision—displayed themselves even in his student days,[80] and his practical orientation earned for him the sobriquet (unique among the Tosafists) of *ba'al ma'asim*. R. Shemaryah, in other words, was a *posek* (decisor, judge), not a dialectician; a man who operates with ideas rather than creating them. The mind of the *posek* does not so much focus on the ultimate implications of an idea (and its coherence with others) as on its optimal implementation. More than it examines ideas, it assesses their place in a world of men and things. Such an intellect weighs the contending claims of tradition, opinion, and practical effect against the monolithic demands of logic. Balance rather than acuity is its hallmark. Few contrasts could be greater than that between R. Shemaryah, the practically oriented *moreh hora'ah* (decisor, judge), and Rabbenu Tam, the boldest halakhic iconoclast of the Middle Ages and possibly the period's greatest revolutionary.[81] The two types represent |**180**| two principles that are found in any legal system—stability and dynamics, tradition (precedent, if you will) and theoretical (shifting) truth, practicality and logic. When personalities clash, the *posek* looks upon the dialectician, especially the revolutionary one, as an unsettling element in the system and perhaps even too clever by half, while the theoretician looks down on the *moreh hora'ah* as a technician and a dullard to boot. When sympathetic relations reign, however, each may see in the other a necessary complement to his own work and call upon him for aid when he feels his own tools unequal to the task at hand.

People in the Middle Ages felt no strong obligation to pay off debts, and even respectable members of the community defaulted without qualms of conscience. It has already been noted in this connection that delaying burial

[79] Urbach, *Ba'alei ha-Tosafot* (above, n. 25), 191.

[80] **מעשה היה שישב רבינו שמריה לפני ריב"א הלוי, וחבל אדם בחבירו, ותפס הנחבל כוס של כסף מן החובל ובאו לדין לפני ריב"א והיה ריב"א מצטער על הדין, ואמר לו רבינו שמריה, רצונך שאפטר אותך מן הדין. אמר לו אין, אמר לו לנחבל, יודע אתה כמה עשה לך הפסד, אמר אין. ובזמן הזה אין שום אדם יודע לשער על כן הוא פטור, שאין דנין דיני קנסות בבבל. אמר ליה תנוח דעתך [שהנחת] דעתי.** (cited ibid.).

[81] Objection will immediately be made that Rabbenu Tam himself was a great *posek* (decisor). Indeed he was (see above, n. 62), but he was a creative *posek*, not a manipulative one. He did not balance multiple factors or seek technical shortcuts to a goal, but forged bold new doctrines and ruled on their basis. His greatness in this area stemmed from the fact that his daring and creativity were not confined to theory but overflowed into practice.

was at the time an accepted form of coercion for the liquidation of debts.[82] Among Jews, of course, the obligation was clear-cut and a dictum held that paying one's debt was not simply a monetary obligation but also a religious one (*peri'at ba'al ḥov mitsvah*),[83] but waywardness in these matters is often infectious. Rabbenu Tam was apparently confronted with a recalcitrant debtor. (Note the twice redundant phrase 'for it was known that he [Re'uven] owed the money', which occurs in the question and again in R. Shemaryah's reply.[84]) The question arose whether some new means of constraint could be applied, and the common delay of burial seemed the most effective one at hand. No one knew better than Rabbenu Tam the seriousness of the injunction involved; yet no one in the Middle Ages was more aware of contemporary forces and needs. Caught between the contradictory pulls of logic and the need for pressing action, he turned to a well-known *posek* and *ba'al ma'asim*, R. Shemaryah, who happened to be passing through. If this distinguished representative of the Rhineland would recommend holding up burial, he, Rabbenu Tam, would go along with that. Working from analogy rather than deduction as jurists (though not dialecticians) do, R. Shemaryah suggested just that, on the basis of the talmudic dictum 'let the [body of the debtor] be disgraced'. And, in the words of R. Yitsḥak Or Zarua', וקיבל ר"ת את דבריו ('and Rabbenu Tam accepted his ruling'). Quite intentionally this ruling was not a product of Rabbenu Tam's halakhic initiative, but one in which he purposely chose to play a subsidiary role. |**181**|

Be that as it may (our reconstruction is after all only a conjecture), Rabbenu Tam relied on R. Shemaryah in no less a matter than suspending a biblical injunction. If the burial story antedated our case of tub-treading, the choice of R. Shemaryah to pen a letter of protest to Rabbenu Tam was a shrewd one. The imperious genius of Ramerupt could hardly claw his critic and try to prove him a fool (as he had done to others who dared question his ways), for that would mean that he had relied upon a fool previously. If the case of the debtor occurred after the one of *yein nesekh*, it speaks doubly of the respect that R. Shemaryah commanded and, incidentally, of Rabbenu Tam's character. This encounter ended, as we shall see,[85] with Rabbenu Tam's discomfiture; yet that proud scholar still esteemed his critic enough to turn to him later for guidance. At all events, a professional *posek* of conventional thought was

82 M. Elon, *Ḥerut ha-Perat* (above, n. 78), 238–40.

83 *Ketubbot* 86a.

84 Strike both phrases from the text and the responsum reads naturally. The opening has already stated מעשה . . . בראובן שהיה חייב מנה לשמעון ומת. If the debt were in doubt, one could not have collected it from Re'uven even if he had been alive, not to speak of the disgrace that it would have heaped on his body after his death.

85 Below, p. 219.

chosen, one who would have to be replied to on his own terms, and upon whom the dialectical thunderbolts of Rabbenu Tam would be wasted.

12. The text of R. Shemaryah's letter has not come down to us, but we do possess a letter of his to R. Yo'el describing the correspondence:[86]

גם אודיעך חביבי מה שהעידו לפני עדים כשרים שהתיר ר"ת זצ"ל לדרוך ענבים לגויים ולמלאות בגיגית גדולה עד שהיתה מליאה, והניחו ביד גוי עד שיהא (כח) [נח] מרתיחתו, והיו ישראל לוקחין הכל ומפנין הענבים למעלה בגיגית, ולוקחין אותן, (ומאז) [ולא] החמיר הרבה על שמירתו עד (שלא) שפינו. [ש]היה אומר שהיתה הגיגית כמו גת מליאה ופקוקה דלוקחין מהן. ושלחתי כתב לר"ת על מה עושין כן, והקשיתי על מה דאמרינן לוקחין גת בעוטה מן הנכרי היאך לא חיישינן ליין נסך, ליחוש שמא עירב הגוי יין נסך עד שלא ידע או החליפו? ותו היכי ידעינן דגת טהור הוה דגוי טיהרו? עד שמצאתי בירושלמי [א]הך מתני' לוקחין גת וכו' תני ר' חנין הדא דאת אמרת בשלא העלים ישראל ממנו, אבל העלים ישראל ממנו לא בדא . . . ומתחילה היה מודה לי ר"ת שודאי היה מתיר, אבל כשהקשיתי לו מן הירושלמי לא באתה לידי תשובתו. ואעפ"כ לא תקל במגע גוי.

שמריהו ב"ר מרדכי

I will further inform you, dear friend, what reliable witnesses have attested to, namely, that Rabbenu Tam, may his memory be blessed, allowed Gentiles to tread grapes and to fill a large *cuve* [with more harvested grapes to be trodden] until the *cuve* was full, and [subsequently] to leave it in Gentile hands until the fermentation was completed. And Jews would then purchase everything [i.e. the entire contents of the *cuve*], separate out the grapes [i.e. grape kernels floating] on top of the [contents of] the *cuve* and cart it away. And he was not very stringent about [Jewish] supervision [of the *cuve*] until the removal [of the grape kernels]. For he was of the opinion that the *cuve* has the legal status of a stoppered and full wine-press that one is permitted to purchase from them [i.e. Gentiles].

And I sent a letter to him [questioning] the basis of such a practice. And I raised the question, 'How can the Mishnah state that 'a wine-press [containing] trodden grapes may be purchased from a Gentile'? Why should one not fear the possibility of *yein nesekh*—perhaps the Gentile mixed some *yein nesekh* [with the wine juice in the *cuve*]? Furthermore, how do we know that the *cuve* is kosher, that the Gentile [took care to] kosher it [by scraping it thoroughly so as to remove any wine residue of previous treadings]?' Until I found a [passage in the] Yerushalmi on the *mishnah* 'A wine-press [containing] trodden grapes' [which stated:] 'R. Ḥanin taught that this

[86] See above, n. 75. The first emendation is from the manuscript; the second is my own. I would not attach too much importance to the זצ"ל after Rabbenu Tam's name found in the text. This could easily be a scribal addition. Rabbenu Tam is referred to as מ"ע in R. Yo'el's reply that follows immediately in the manuscript (fo. 287v). I have learned, however, to be very wary of such notations. (See below, n. 88, and note the surprising absence of any mention of Rabbenu Tam's doctrine of *bittul be-shishim* for *ḥamets*.) See above, n. 12 and below, n. 117.

allowance [of the Mishnah] applies only if the Jew has kept the *cuve* under his constant supervision; if he hasn't, [the allowance] is not applicable.' . . . At first, Rabbenu Tam admitted to me that he had, indeed, allowed [the aforesaid case]. However, though I objected [to his allowance] on the basis of the Yerushalmi, I have yet to receive a reply from him. Nevertheless do not be lenient [*takel*] in [instances of] Gentile touch.

Shemaryah ben R. Mordekhai

From the opening remark ('what reliable witnesses have attested to'), we can gauge the depth of the shock that the German community experienced when it encountered the French practice. R. Shemaryah, the esteemed scholar of the Rhineland, fears to be disbelieved by his friends, and so, like anyone else about to tell a scandalous story, he prefaces it with the remark that he has it on good |182| authority. Gentile tub-treading is simply *inconceivable* to them, as is any Gentile contact with the *cuve*.

From his report it would appear that R. Shemaryah dispatched two letters to Rabbenu Tam. In the first he challenged the latter's decision on the basis of the possibility of an admixture of *yein nesekh*. Later he found a passage in the Yerushalmi that supported his position, and dispatched this proof to Rabbenu Tam. This second note went unanswered, at least at the time of his communication to his colleague.

13. Rabbenu Tam's reply has been preserved by the *Or Zarua'*, and as we shall have to make a detailed analysis of it, it is best to cite it at length.[87]

ועל היין שכתבת שאנו מקילין כך הנהיג רבינו שלמה זצ"ל ורבי' שמואל זצ"ל. ואבא מרי זלה"ה [לא] היה מקפיד על שממלאים הגוים הגיגיות, שאמרו רבותינו שאין תורת גת שייך בגיגיות וכל זמן שאין מסננין כלל אין מקפידין על מגע גוי דגת פקוקה ומלאה הויא הגיגית דאין לה המשכה עד שיסננו. ופשיטא דהילכת' כרב הונא דמשהתחיל לימשך עושה יין נסך, וזהו בגת שיש לה פה כעין סילון ומיד נמשך הימנה אם אינה פקוקה, אבל גיגיות שלנו אין להם המשכה כי אם ע"י הסל שמסננין על גביו. דהא מתרץ רבי (יהודה) [הונא] . . . בגת פקוק' ומלאה פ' שהיתה פקוקה ומלאה שלא הוציא מן היין כלום על ידי גרגותני ועומדת הגת במלואה, שכל הענבים שנתנו בגת עדיין בתוך הגת, וכן הוא נראה היתר גמור . . . וכן היא משנה אחרונה אין דורכין עם הנכרי בגת משום שמיד כשדורך נמשך ויורד דרך הסילון לבור כיון שאין הגת פקוקה, ואפי' היה גוי שואב בכלי ושותה היינו אוסרין אותו, דההיא פורתא קרינן התחיל לימשך.

ותימה לי מה דעתך שאתה כתבת דלית לן דרב הונא? אית לן ואית לן! והרבה אנו מחמירים ביין, אבל בגיגית אין אנו מקפידין אם הגוי . . . משבר הענבים במקל . . . אבל ליכנס הגוי ולדרוך אפי' בגיגית או בגת פקוקה חלילה לנו. ושלום עליך.

יעקב בר מאיר

As to the [Gentile] wine, which you contended in a letter that we treat lightly [or leniently—*mekilin*]. Thus [i.e. our practice] was instituted by R. Shelomoh [i.e.

[87] Sect. 215; the correction **לא** is made on the basis of the *Mordekhai*, #845, and see above, n. 58.

Rashi] and R. Shemu'el [i.e. Rashbam] and my father, R. Me'ir, may their memory be blessed. They were indifferent to Gentiles filling the *cuve* [with grapes]. For our teachers held that the status of [our] *cuve* was not the same as that of the [talmudic] wine-press, and as long as no straining [of the liquid from the grape kernels and husks] takes place, one may be indifferent to Gentile touch, for it [the *cuve*] has the status of 'a stoppered and full wine-press', as there is no *hamshakhah* until it [the wine] is strained.

Of course the law is according to Rav Huna's view that 'as soon as the wine begins to flow [*le-himashekh*], it becomes [subject to] *yein nesekh*'! [However] this [only] occurs in a wine-press with an opening and a drain pipe [to the pit], for then *hamshakhah* takes place immediately, if it [the drain pipe] is open. However, no *hamshakhah* takes place in our *cuves* [which have no drain pipe at all], unless one strains the content with a [porous] basket. For Rav Huna replies [in the Talmud] . . . that the [allowance of] the Mishnah refers to a wine-press floor that is full and stoppered, where no wine escapes from the wine-press into the basket-strainer [*gargutni*] and the wine-press is full to the gills, and all the grapes that have been deposited in the wine-press remain there. And this [i.e. Gentile touch in such a wine-press] would seem to be perfectly permissible . . . And this is the ruling of the later *mishnah*, 'One may not tread with a Gentile in a treading floor', for the wine flows immediately through the drain pipe to the pit since the wine-press has not been stoppered.

If, however, the Gentile were to scoop up a small quantity of wine [from the *cuve*], we would forbid the entire *cuve*, for that small quantity of wine that he has drawn off [with his cup and separated from the grape kernels] would meet the requirements of 'the onset of separation' [*hitḥil le-himashekh*].

I am astonished. What did you have in mind when you wrote to us that we 'do not rule like Rav Huna'? We certainly do rule like Rav Huna! And we are quite stringent in matters of wine. However, in the case of a *cuve*, we are indifferent if a Gentile . . . [packs in the grapes in the *cuve*] with a rod [and in doing so] breaks the grapes [and thus some wine is created in the tub] . . . God forbid, however, that a Gentile should go in and tread—even if it be in a *cuve* or stoppered wine-press. Peace be upon you.

Ya'akov b. Me'ir

There is no reference whatsoever to either of R. Shemaryah's objections. This clearly is a reply to another letter that R. Shemaryah did not mention to R. Yo'el. Rabbenu Tam here answers two charges: first, a general one that he was lax in matters of *yein nesekh* ('As to the [Gentile] wine, which you contended in a letter, that we treat lightly [or leniently—*mekilin*]'); second, that French practice controverted R. Huna's ruling of *hamshakhah* ('I am astonished. What did you have in mind when you wrote to us that we "do not rule like Rav Huna"?'). Clearly this was R. Shemaryah's opening salvo. Only when shown that these practices did not violate an explicit talmudic dictum did R. Shemaryah advance the second contention—that they ran the danger (*ḥashash*) of an admixture.

To return to the rebuttal. Rabbenu Tam feels compelled to emphasize that he, too, is stringent (*maḥmir*) in matters of *yein nesekh*. This is the only case known to me where the great Rabbenu Tam had, as it were, to explicitly assert his religiosity. One |183| can see how deeply the Ashkenazic community felt about *yein nesekh* when a suspicion of laxity could put even leonine Rabbenu Tam on the defensive. Aware, perhaps, of his reputation as a revolutionary,[88] Rabbenu Tam opened by pointing out that the current practice was not his innovation. Behind him, no less than behind R. Shemaryah, stood a tradition ('thus [i.e. our practice] was instituted by R. Shelomoh [i.e. Rashi] and R. Shemu'el [i.e. Rashbam] and my father, R. Me'ir, may their memory be blessed'). While the merchants of Metz may have given Rabbenu Tam's name as authority and cover, the allowance was not of his making. It would seem, however, that he shaded the story a bit by stating that Rashi 'instituted' (*hinhig*) the practice. As far as we know (barring a radical change of heart in his last days), Rashi provided the theoretical basis for the allowance but hardly advocated or instituted it. Personal hesitations, however, have no place in law. (The Tosafists, for example, cited Rashbam's report without mentioning the tale of Rashi's self-imposed silence.[89]) Legally Rashi did make the allowance, and so pressure of circumstance together with legal outlook allowed Rabbenu Tam to write as he did and in a sense quite accurately. This is not historical but legal narration. Historical narration, as we conceive it, hardly existed at the time, certainly not among halakhists. R. Shemaryah, as we shall soon see, acted after a similar fashion. To our mind this might seem a cloak for personal discomfiture. Perhaps it was, but it was a cloak worn naturally and with a sense of honor.

Rabbenu Tam then turned to the basis of French practice and presented the *sugya* of *hamshakhah* as interpreted in France. Note, however, that he did not set forth his own doctrine of *hamshakhah* but that of Rashi.[90] It may be that at this time his own interpretation had not yet crystallized, or his writing

88 Note incidentally the concluding remarks of R. Shemaryah (Agus, *Teshuvot Ba'alei ha-Tosafot*, p. 76 {*Sefer Ravyah 'al 'Avodah Zarah*, 16; *Sefer Ravyah*, iv. 10}). No halakhic discussion follows. This is simply the report of one German rabbi to another of Rabbenu Tam's activities as a *posek*. In each of these decisions, Rabbenu Tam was breaking with either German tradition or that of his fathers (*min be-mino*). See the vociferous German reaction to his ruling that *ḥamets* was *batel be-shishim* in *Ravan*, ed. S. Z. Ehrenreich (Simleu Silvaniei, 1926), i, #10; ed. S. Albeck (Warsaw, 1905), #10.

89 *Tosafot* 55b, s.v. *amar*.

90 There is no mention of flow out of the press; rather, straining (*sinun*) is made the criterion.

here may be an instance of a skillful fusion of tact and legal accuracy. The Germans were mounting a frontal attack on the French practice, and an effective defense demanded a presentation of Rashi's doctrine. Rabbenu Tam's own position was, for practical purposes, but a fine point, a further insulation of the wine in the *cuve* from *yein nesekh*. Why then complicate the defense, especially since he strove to present a French tradition over and against the injunctive one of the Germans?

Having shown how his countrymen's practices were rooted in R. Huna's |184| dictum, Rabbenu Tam wrote perplexedly to R. Shemaryah: **ותימה לי מה דעתך שכתבת דלית לן דרב הונא** ('I am astonished. What did you have in mind when you wrote us that we "do not rule like Rav Huna"?'). We may infer from this, as already noted, that R. Shemaryah first challenged Rabbenu Tam by claiming that French conduct ran counter to R. Huna's ruling. And this is of triple significance. First, the objection makes sense only on the assumption that *hamshakhah* means flow or liquidity—both of which occur in a closed *cuve*. Indeed, my remarks at the outset of the essay that the Rhineland communities interpreted *hamshakhah* thus (i.e. that the reigning injunctive custom had a theoretical basis) were largely based on R. Shemaryah's query. They were founded also on the citation of R. Huna's dictum without comment in the *Sefer ha-Pardes* (which on the subject of *yein nesekh* contains Rhineland rather than French traditions).[91] If *hamshakhah* is merely 'flow', then R. Huna's remarks are indeed self-evident, for that is simply what the word means; if, however, *hamshakhah* is but a means to an end and that end is separation, this obviously requires articulation. Eleventh-century thought, in other words, is not self-contained, and anything but articulate. While an intensive study of the *Pardes*, *Ma'asei Ge'onim*, and the like is certainly a desideratum, it will rapidly prove inadequate. In our case the existence of an injunctive custom is mentioned nowhere in the literature of the period. Our knowledge comes from the fragment of an eleventh-century work (Rivan) cited by a twelfth-century scholar (Ri) whose writings surfaced in the late thirteenth century (R. Ḥayyim Or Zarua'). More significantly, the theoretical basis for the practice, which served as a starting point for all halakhic developments, can be educed only from an assumption contained in a reconstructed query sent by a scholar of the twelfth century taken together with an earlier commentarial silence. Yet reconstruct the eleventh century we must. For without a knowledge of pre-Crusade thought we shall never fully grasp the activity of Rashi and his school,

[91] *Pardes* (Constantinople, 1802), fo. 16a, s.v. *lokḥin*; (Warsaw, 1890), #259. See also *Teshuvot Ḥakhmei Tsarfat ve-Lotir*, ed. J. Müller (Vienna, 1881), #9; *Teshuvot Rabbenu Gershom Me'or ha-Golah*, ed. S. Eidelberg (New York, 1957), #22.

and significant developments in Germany in its more famous centuries will go undetected.

Second, it is noteworthy that R. Shemaryah omitted telling R. Yo'el of this first letter. The innate superiority of the principle of separation as the dividing line between wine and grape juice over that of flow or liquidity was apparent to all halakhists. Once promulgated, Rashi's doctrine swept the field entirely and was adopted by all schools, whether of French, German, |185| Provençal, or Spanish provenance.[92] And R. Shemaryah was no exception. His objection, he realized, was groundless, and the old Rhine doctrine was now of unproven worth. But why publicize tradition's problematic nature? A responsum is a halakhic communiqué, not a diary or a historical narrative. The substantive parts of the correspondence were the later ones, and these he conveyed to R. Yo'el.

The third point that may be inferred from R. Shemaryah's use of R. Huna is that the commentaries of the Rashbam (or Rivan) had not yet penetrated Germany to any sizeable extent.[93] If they had, German scholars would have known full well the basis for the French practice. A generation later, in Ravyah's time, these works were common knowledge. Determination of the date (or period) of a doctrine's diffusion is prejudicial to all questions in the history of halakhah. We tend to assume the influence of an idea to begin with its publication, but little could be farther from the truth. Some fifty to seventy years after their composition neither Rivan's work nor that of the Rashbam had penetrated some 150 miles eastward. Rashi's work did reach Germany; Ravan used it constantly. Since it is highly doubtful whether the

[92] (A) *Sefer Ravyah*, #1069; *Sefer ha-Rokeaḥ*, #492; *Piskei ha-Rosh* 4: 3; *Or Zarua'*, ##213–15; R. Yehonatan of Lunel on *Alfasi*, ad loc. (found in the edition of the Talmud published by El ha-Mekorot and Pardes-Israel [Jerusalem, 1963]); *Bet ha-Beḥirah*, ad loc. Both Naḥmanides (*Ḥiddushim*, ed. Chavel, ad loc.) and R. Yonah Gerondi (*Ḥiddushei Talmidei Rabbenu Yonah*, ed. Z. H. Zherkovsky [New York, 1957], ad loc.) realized Rashi's accomplishment and added this accolade: **זו היא שיטת רש"י ויפה למד ויפה פירש דרך השמועה**. Anyone familiar with the writings of medieval halakhists knows how rare compliments are. (B) Rabad, too, perceived the principle of separation, but could not explain as smoothly as Rashi did how this process inevitably occurred on the treading floor (*Perush ha-Rabad 'al 'Avodah Zarah*, p. 149, s.v. **ל"ק**, cited in *Temim De'im*, #107). His successor, R. Yehonatan, abandoned the Provençal explanation for that of Rashi.

[93] R. Yo'el apparently had sections of either Rivan's or Rashbam's commentary, which had penetrated Germany anonymously. See his closing remarks (MS Bodley 637, #1050; {*Sefer Ravyah 'al 'Avodah Zarah*, 20; *Sefer Ravyah*, iv. 12}): **ומצאתי בשם גאון בענין זה ונראה לו לאיסור יותר מלהתיר[!] ומסיים דבריו ואם מפנין חרצנים שבגיגית אילך ואילך שיתכנס היין באמצע היינו המשכה גמורה**. The term *ga'on*, as is well known, was used in 13th- and 14th-century Germany for distinguishing predecessors, especially of the period before the rise of the Tosafists. But apart from this fragmentary reference there is no evidence of penetration. From Ravan's remarks on *'Avodah Zarah* 55b–56a, it is equally clear that he does not know of any doctrine of separation.

German scholars would have fired off a sharp letter to Rabbenu Tam without first checking Rashi's comments, one can further see how well Rashi had succeeded (by the elision of the three words *she-nitpaneh min ha-'anavim*—'cleared of grapes') in camouflaging his revolutionary doctrine.[94]

14. Rabbenu Tam concluded his letter with these words: אבל ליכנס הגוי ולדרוך אפי' בגיגית או בגת פקוקה חלילה לנו ('God forbid, however, that a Gentile should go in and tread—even if it be in a *cuve* or stoppered wine-press'). The French allowance had extended to Gentile |186| touch only; it had never countenanced tub-treading. And Ri tells us that Rabbenu Tam proceeded to act upon his words:[95]

> וכעס [ר' יעקב] ביותר על המקילין המקלקלין מנהג קדושים וכשרים, ואמר לנדותם אם לא ישמעו שלא לעשות עוד. ואולם מתוך ההלכה לא שמעתי שמיחה בידם כיון שלא היו מקילין בנתינת גרגותני לתוך הדריכה,[96] כי גם במדינה מעשים בכל יום שאין נזהרים ממגע גוי קוד' המשכה של נתינת גרגותני. אך דבר מגונה ומכוער ביותר אם ידרוך גוי יין של ישראל.

And he [Rabbenu Tam] was extremely angry with those who treated lightly [*mekilin*] [the injunction against Gentile treading] and were destroying [*mekalkelin*] the custom of the holy and proper ones [i.e. ancient custom that was still in force]. And he declared that he would excommunicate them if they would not obey [him] not to do this any more.

However, I did not hear that he objected to their conduct on halakhic grounds, as they did not permit [Gentile treading] once the basket strainer had been inserted into the *cuve* [and strained its contents]. And it is a daily occurrence in our parts that one pays no heed to Gentile touch prior to the *hamshakhah* of the basket-strainer. However it is a most disgraceful and ugly thing that a Gentile should tread the wine of a Jew.

Legally, as Ri himself noted, the merchants of Metz were correct. If wine in the *cuve* was not subject to *yein nesekh*, why not have Gentile treading? Indeed, when the doctrines of Rashi and Rabbenu Tam were studied in Spain, scholars

94 Similarly, Ravan never elicited this doctrine from Rashi's words (see previous note).

95 *Teshuvot Maharaḥ Or Zarua'*, #174, fo. 59b; p. 164b in Avitan's edition (above, n. 12).

96 In the light of Ri's explicit statement here and elsewhere (ibid., fo. 59c bottom), one should discount the report of R. Yehudah of Paris in his *Tosafot* (ad loc.) that Rabbenu Tam forbade treading because of the *mishnah aḥaronah*. This was Ri's conjecture as to a possible legal basis for Rabbenu Tam's ban. Law, however, dislikes visceral reactions and soon Ri's thoughts were viewed as the reason motivating Rabbenu Tam's stand. In some schools, though, memory of the non-halakhic nature of Rabbenu Tam's stand lingered on even after its transformation, and we read in the *Semak Zurich*, ed. Y. Y. Har-Shoshanim (Jerusalem, 1978), ii. 357: ושמע רבינו תם והקפיד ורצה לנדותם אם לא ישובו כי אולי יש לאסור לפי [משנה] אחרונה, גזירה לפני המשכה אטו אחר המשכה. אך משמע מתוך פ' ר"ת שלא הקפיד אלא דווקא על הבני אדם אבל היין לא נאסר.

there considered this obvious inference.[97] Nevertheless the French community declined this allowance, despite the enormous conveniences that it offered! Within less than one month wine had to be made for twelve, and we must remember the quantities consumed in the Middle Ages. The use of Gentile labor, not to speak of the possibility of ordering outright trodden *cuves*, would have lightened the load considerably. Yet throughout the twelfth century, while Jews were being forced out of landholding and wine production was becoming ever more difficult for them, they stubbornly declined to avail themselves of the permissible. This refusal on the part of the people to maximize their allowances, |187| their desire to uphold at heavy cost even that which could be discarded, must be taken into account when evaluating the posture of the Tosafists towards communal needs.

The idea of Gentiles treading Jewish wine awakened revulsion in the Ashkenazic psyche, and the anger of Rabbenu Tam and the language of Ri—**דבר מגונה ומכוער ביותר** ('a most disgraceful and ugly thing')[98]—only reflected a general repugnance. The roots of this sentiment are difficult to uncover[99]

[97] R. Nissim of Barcelona wrote: **ורבותינו הצרפתים ז״ל מקילין לומר דרב הונא כי קאמר מכיון שהתחיל לימשך דוקא משהתחיל לימשך לבור, אבל מתחתונה לעליונה של גת אינה המשכה לעשות יין נסך, ולפיכך הם מתירים לדרוך עם העכו״ם בגת פקוקה כל שלא ירד ממנה כלום לבור** (Alfasi,adloc.). Naḥmanides (*Ḥiddushim*, ad loc.), followed by R. Aharon ha-Levi (*Perush ha-Rah* in *Shitat ha-Kadmonim 'al 'Avodah Zarah*, ed. M. Y. H. Blau [New York, 1969], ii. 135), does indeed forbid treading on the basis of the *mishnah aḥaronah*. However, their views were not accepted by their own disciples. See *Torat ha-Bayit*, 5: 2; *Ḥiddushei ha-Rashba 'al 'Avodah Zarah* and *Ḥiddushei ha-Ritva* ad loc. It must also be remembered that even Naḥmanides' doctrine (and that of Rah) is premised on the assumption that *hamshakhah* can take place on the treading floor. This being so, a precautionary ordinance against Gentile treading makes sense. Rabbenu Tam's doctrine, however, ruled out such a possibility and R. Yitsḥak subscribed to it (see above, n. 64).

[98] This phrase should be taken quite literally. There may be an allusion to *harḥek min ha-ki'ur*, for the full sentence reads: **אך דבר מגונה ומכוער ביותר אם ידרוך גוי יין של ישראל, כי פעמים שימשך ולאו אדעתיה . . . וגם כל הרואים אותו דורך לא ידעו כי קודם המשכה דווקא דורכים**. These are but rationalizations, and poor ones at that, for if there is a fear of *hamshakhah* or of *mar'it 'ayin*, Gentile touch should then be forbidden equally, and Ri explicitly permits it. Indeed, treading possibly creates a less serious danger of *yein nesekh* than touch does, for **נסיך דרגל לא שמיה נסוך** (*'Avodah Zarah* 56b).

[99] It is possible that the repugnance was heightened by the fact that Gentiles trod barefoot (F. von Bassermann-Jordan, *Geschichte des Weinbaus unter besonderer Berücksichtigung der Bayerischen Rheinpfalz*, i [Frankfurt, 1907], 255–6; id., *Geschichte des Weinbaus* [Frankfurt am Main, 1923], 351), while the Jews, as Innocent III had already noted, wrapped sheets around their feet (Grayzel; above, n. 71). It would further appear, as Bassermann-Jordan notes in both his works, that in the Rhineland even Gentiles did not tread barefoot, but rather beat the grapes with sticks; this might explain the utter shock of German scholars at the French practice (note Rabbenu Tam's concluding remarks to R. Shemaryah, above, p. 207).

I would add that the Ashkenazic reaction to tub-treading has little in common with that which Rabad of Posquières registered in *Temim De'im*, #83. In the case under discussion there, the upshot of

(it clearly antedates all literary remains of the community), but one suspects that this aversion played its part in Rashi's stubborn efforts to sustain, or at least understand, the custom of [our] fathers (*minhag avot*). It was not simply a question of ancient custom. Rashi, like any other halakhist, took issue at times with established practice. But here he realized that his interpretation of *hamshakhah* allowed Gentile tub-treading, and he asked himself in amazement whether it was possible that the religious sensibilities of the entire Ashkenazic community had gone astray. Could so deeply felt an injunction be a figment of the imagination, and had the toll in drudgery and antisemitism all been paid in vain? It was, one suspects, questions like these and the conflicting pull of intellectual certainty that led Rashi into ambiguity.

15. Rabbenu Tam's letter presenting the French position had its impact. The |188| parting words of R. Shemaryah to his colleague were **ואעפ"כ לא תקל במגע גוי** ('nevertheless, do not be lenient in [instances of] Gentile touch').[100] Note that he did not write **ומ"מ מגע גוי אסור** ('nevertheless, Gentile touch renders [the wine] forbidden'); rather, he advised maintaining the old injunctive practice. Rashi's doctrine of separation had an innate persuasiveness that R. Shemaryah fully realized, and in fact tacitly conceded by his silence regarding his first critical letter to Rabbenu Tam. But the difficulty in accepting an allowance running counter to habit and upbringing, and the instincts of a *posek*, which insist that time must elapse before even the most plausible new idea proves itself, led R. Shemaryah to counsel holding fast to the traditional ruling.

16. Time passes, and a generation arises that comes into early contact with the theory of separation. It comes as no surprise if, in the works of Ravyah and even in that of R. Ele'azar of Worms (who represents a far more conservative school), we find Rashi's doctrine accepted without demur.[101]

17. And then we read in the *Takkanot Shum* (signed by both the above writers), **ולא יניח הגוי לדרוך היין** ('one should not allow a Gentile to tread the wine').[102] The acceptance of the principle of separation left the ancient pro-

a certain doctrine would be to destroy a good deal of the *raison d'être* of *yein nesekh*. That is to say, the logical conclusions of a theory are so startling that they cast overwhelming doubts as to the validity of its premise—a common enough mode of reasoning. In Gentile treading, however, no accepted principle of *yein nesekh* is endangered, and no premise is in turn challenged. The repugnance is self-contained and logically indefensible. I can see no other basis for it other than a religious (and possibly an aesthetic) one. {See my discussion in *Yeinam* (above, n. 2), 113–21.}

[100] See above, p. 206.

[101] *Sefer Ravyah*, #1069; *Sefer ha-Rokeaḥ* (Fano, 1505), #492.

[102] L. Finkelstein, *Jewish Self-Government in the Middle Ages* (repr. New York, 1964), 225.

hibition without a leg to stand on, and German merchants in and around 1220 began to draw the same conclusions as had those of Metz some half-century earlier. Lacking any figure of the awesome proportions of Rabbenu Tam, the scholars of the Rhineland fell back on communal ban to shore up faltering custom. Were they successful? We do not know. Rabbenu Tam's threat was effective for some time, though by the latter half of the thirteenth century it had spent its force.[103] It would be an ironic ending to our story if Gentile treading had succeeded in establishing itself in Germany before it made headway in France.

18. But tub-treading, it will be remembered, was not the only thing R. Shemaryah |**189**| had objected to. The French also left *cuves* unsupervised in Gentile houses, and that exposed them, R. Shemaryah contended, to the danger of Gentiles mixing genuine *yein nesekh* in the vat. Rabbenu Tam, as far as we know, brushed this aside.[104] Then R. Shemaryah came across the passage in the Yerushalmi prohibiting wine (even if still mixed with the pulp) that had been left unsupervised with non-Jews, and dispatched this objection to Rabbenu Tam. At the time of his communiqué to R. Yo'el, R. Shemaryah had had no reply from Rabbenu Tam. But it would *seem* that an answer was finally forthcoming, and that in it Rabbenu Tam admitted that his critic was in the right.

103 (A) R. Yitsḥak of Corbeil makes no mention of Rabbenu Tam's ban or any injunction against treading in his influential *Semak* (Constantinople, 1509, #225; in many later editions #223). His contemporary, R. Perets, reports: **ומ"מ בדיעבד אין לאסור, ובצרפת ובפרובינציא נהגו לדרוך ע"י גויים** (*Teshuvot Ri Kolon* [Venice, 1519], #32). As R. Perets, to the best of my knowledge, never referred to Provence in his *Tosafot*, we might suspect that the closing remark is a later gloss. This report of French practices, however, is corroborated by R. Aharon of Lunel, who wrote disapprovingly in his *Orḥot Ḥayyim, Ḥelek Sheni* (Berlin, 1902), 248: **ובצרפת נהגו לדרוך גיגיות על ידי גויים, ומנהג שטות הוא**. {The passage in the *Orḥot Ḥayyim* is taken from the *Sefer ha-Dinim* of R. Perets, MS Vienna Österreichische Nationalbibliothek 66, fo. 135b.} (B) The printed text of the *Semak*, with the absence of any mention of Rabbenu Tam, is corroborated by all manuscripts of the work that I checked. (C) On the Provençal practice, see *Bet ha-Beḥirah*, p. 206, top; *She'elot u-Teshuvot min ha-Shamayim*, ed. R. Margulies (Jerusalem, 1957), 30. It is possible, however, that Me'iri's statement refers to northern France.

104 In the century-long discussion by the French Tosafists of the Yerushalmi (see below, n. 119) no mention is made of the fear of admixture (with the exception of *Tosfot R. Yehudah mi-Paris*, under the special circumstances that *yein nesekh* is adjacent and would ordinarily be added). Their entire discussion revolves around the fear of *hamshakhah*. Rabbenu Tam's rejection was probably based on the fact that the Mishnah ruled that *lokḥin gat be'utah*. If R. Yehudah ha-Nasi did not fear an admixture, it would be gratuitous for others to do so. See also *'Avodah Zarah* 12a and the discussion in the *Or Zarua'* ad loc.

The German school, i.e. Rokeaḥ (in #492) and Ravyah (in #1069) interpreted the fear of the Yerushalmi as being one of admixture. In other words, the instinctive apprehensions to which R. Shemaryah gave voice in the first letter became the interpretational basis of the second. {As to #492 in Rokeaḥ, see below, n. 123, end.}

And this is the evidence for my last statement: after reproducing the critique leveled by Ravyah against Rabbenu Tam's understanding of *hamshakhah*, the author of the *Sefer Amarkal* (a pupil of R. Asher) concludes with the following:[105]

נמצא בתשובות ר"ת שהי' נוהג להתיר ורבי' שמריה החזירו מכל אילו הראיות.

It was found in the responsa of Rabbenu Tam that his custom was to allow such a practice; however, R. Shemaryah got him to change his mind by force of these proofs.

If this report is taken at face value, we must postulate three more letters. First, after he had taken care not to present his own doctrine of *hamshakhah*, Rabbenu Tam changed his mind for some reason and informed R. Shemaryah of his position.[106] R. Shemaryah then anticipated Ravyah's proofs from the Tosefta and wrote of them to Rabbenu Tam, and finally received another letter from Rabbenu Tam admitting the cogency of the objections. The old warning against multiplying entities beyond necessity comes immediately to mind. The entire discussion, moreover, was irrelevant to the issue at hand. The French practice could do quite well on the basis of Rashi's doctrine alone. Aptowitzer has already noted that *Amarkal* is not to be relied on,[107] so we need never infer such heavy communication between Speyer and Ramerupt. Inaccurate the author of *Amarkal* may be, but he is not a liar. He |**190**| had heard some report of a retraction by Rabbenu Tam in matters of *hamshakhah* and naturally assumed it to be a retreat by that scholar from his own doctrine. On this basis alone I would hesitate to state that Rabbenu Tam actually conceded, but there is a difficult passage in the *Mordekhai* that now claims our attention.

After citing Rabbenu Tam's letter to R. Shemaryah defending the French position (above, p. 207), R. Mordekhai wrote:[108] ואני מצאתי בשם ר"ת להחמיר בגיגיות כמו גבי גת ('and I found in the name of Rabbenu Tam that one should be as stringent with a *cuve* as with a wine-press'). If the juxtaposition is taken seriously the note could mean one of two things, both equally difficult. The new equation of *gigit* and *gat* may be referring to the opening remarks of Rabbenu Tam שאין תורת גת שייך בגיגית ('that the status of [our] *cuves* was not the same as that of the [talmudic] wine-press'), which would mean that Rabbenu Tam subsequently abandoned not only his own but also Rashi's analysis of

[105] 'Sefer Amarkal' (above, n. 63), p. 13.

[106] Or if Rabbenu Tam only arrived later at his doctrine of *hamshakhah* (see text, above, pp. 195–6), then we must assume that he hastened to inform R. Shemaryah that France was moving yet one more step towards leniency.

[107] V. Aptowitzer, *Mavo le-Sefer Ravyah* (Jerusalem, 1938), 152.

[108] Sect. 845, thus in MSS British Library 537, Vienna, Österreichische Nationalbibliothek 73. The printed text reads 'ומורי ה"ר מרדכי מצא בתוס. See below.

hamshakhah, even though no cogent criticism had been leveled against the latter. Or it may be referring to his closing remarks (as found in the printed text) about basket-carrying and the beating of grapes with sticks:

והרבה אנו מחמירין בגת אבל בגיגית אין אנו מקפידין אם העובד כוכבים שואב ומביא והיין מזלף או אפילו משבר ענבים במקל.

And we are quite stringent in matters **of the wine-press**. However, in the case of a tub, we are indifferent if the Gentile brings [baskets of grapes] and the wine in the baskets [coming from the crushed bottom grapes] drips [into the *cuve*] or even if he [the Gentile] [packs in the grapes in the *cuve*] with a rod [and in doing so] breaks the grapes [and thus some wine is created in the *cuve*]. [emphasis added]

The trouble with this reading is that in Rabbenu Tam's time grapes were never brought to a wine-press but to the *cuve*,[109] and so there was nothing to be stringent about. In the *Or Zarua'* the passage runs thus: **הרבה אנו מחמירין ביין** ('And we are quite stringent in matters of **wine**'). Its correctness is evident: this is a reply to the charge mentioned by Rabbenu Tam in his opening: **על היין שכתבת שאנו מקילין** ('As to the [Gentile] **wine**, which you contended in a letter, that we **treat lightly** [or **leniently**]'). And indeed, most manuscripts of the *Mordekhai* itself contain the *Or Zarua*'s reading.[110] |191| Even granting

[109] All Hebrew and Gentile sources attest to this. See text, sect. 2; Bassermann-Jordan, *Geschichte des Weinbaus unter besonderer Berücksichtigung* (above, n. 99), i. 254 ff.; id., *Geschichte des Weinbaus* (above n. 99), 349–51; R. Billiard, *La Vigne dans l'Antiquité* (Lyons, 1913), 439–42. The average person could hardly afford to build a wine press, even if he lived in an area where the right of press was not one of the lord's *banalités*. I have been unable to find one manuscript illumination or frieze from the Middle Ages showing *contemporary* treading in any place other than a *cuve*. {See now M. Lachiver, *Vins, vignes et vignerons: Histoire du vignoble francais* (Paris, 1988), 214–20; P. Mane, *Le Travail à la campagne au Moyen Age: Étude iconographique* (Paris, 2006), 222–40.} I say contemporary treading, for an illustration of a biblical verse where a wine press is mentioned would, not surprisingly, portray a wine press. See J. C. Webster, *The Labors of the Months in Antique and Medieval Art till the End of the Twelfth Century* (Evanston and Chicago, 1938) and the literature there cited; J. Senecal, 'Les Occupations des mois dans l'iconographie du Moyen Age', *Bulletin de la Société des Antiquaires de Normandie*, 25 (1924), 33–90 (the illustrations given on pp. 38–40 are symbolic and not descriptive). All the manuscript illuminations referred to by O. Hassel in his unpublished *Subject Index of Illuminations in the Bodleian Library* under the headings 'pressing' and 'treading' were personally checked and no press was found. I would like to thank Mr. Hassel and his staff for the unfailing courtesy that they extended to me.

[110] MSS Budapest, Hungarian National Museum 2° 1, fo. 234a; Sassoon 534, fo. 244c; British Library 537, fo. 160d; Vienna, Österreichische Nationalbibliothek 72, fo. 185c; 73, fo. 139a; Hechal Shelomoh, Jerusalem, 4; 5 {both are currently lodged at the National Library of Israel and entered as MSS 4to 6695 (fo. 146a); 4to 6696, (fo. 9b)}. The only manuscripts known to me to contain the reading *gat* are that of Hechal Shelomoh 3 {= National Library of Israel, 8vo 6697}, fo. 8d, and apparently some copies of the *Or Zarua'* used by the printers of the 1598 Cracow edition of the *Mordekhai*. (Our printed *Or Zarua'* is an accurate transcription of MS British Library 531, fo. 62b.) {Cambridge Add. 490.1, fo. 159a, has *gat* in the text and emended by gloss to *yayin*.}

the printed text of the *Mordekhai*, no objection was ever raised against stick-beating or against a Gentile's carrying grapes. Why Rabbenu Tam should have had a change of heart on the matter is incomprehensible.

There is, furthermore, a puzzling lack of uniformity in R. Mordekhai's note. The printed text reads 'and my teacher, Rabbi Mordekhai'. Some manuscripts have it in the first person, 'and I found'; others phrase it simply as 'there are those that say', and some omit it altogether.[111]

The section immediately following in the *Mordekhai* reads thus:

> גרסינן בירושלמי על מתני' לוקחין גת בעוטה. תני רבי חנן והוא שלא העלים ישראל עיניו ממנו. ובסמ"ג מסתפק אולי הירושלמי מיירי שאין הגיגית מליאה אבל אם הניחה מליאה אז נ[י]כר חסרונה

We read in the Yerushalmi on the *mishnah* 'A wine-press [containing] trodden grapes may be purchased': 'R. Ḥanan taught: provided that a Jew has kept the wine-press under his supervision all the time.' And R. Mosheh of Coucy in his *Semag* has his doubts whether or not the Yerushalmi refers to a less than full *cuve*, but were a full *cuve* left [unsupervised in Gentile hands], any loss of the wine [in the *cuve* as a result of Gentile depletion] would be noticed.

R. Mordekhai, we know, did not live to complete his work. His students, upon his martyrdom, rounded it out from his notes.[112] R. Mordekhai, I suggest, came across a report of Rabbenu Tam's letter of retraction to R. Shemaryah and made a note of it[113] alongside his *following* discussion of the Yerushalmi's requirement of super-vision of the wine for future reference and expansions which, tragically, never came. And copyists acted as copyists do with glosses. Some omitted it altogether, others quoted it cautiously as 'some say' (*yesh omrim*), and some simply incorporated it into the text. It was the students and copyists, unaware of the meaning of the cryptic note, who appended it, quite naturally, to the *preceding* letter of Rabbenu Tam (in which *gat* and *gigit* are manifestly contrasted and Rabbenu Tam explicitly mentioned) rather than to the *subsequent*, fragmentary discussion of the Yerushalmi's ruling on unsupervised wine, for which it was originally intended. What the words שיש להחמיר בגיגית כמו בגת ('one should be as stringent with a *cuve* as with a

[111] MSS Budapest, Hungarian National Museum 2° 1, fo. 234a; Vienna, Österreichische Nationalbibliothek 72, 185c; Vienna, Österreichische Nationalbibliothek 73, fo. 138b; British Library 537, fo. 160d have it in the first person. The citations from the *Mordekhai* in the commentary ranged around the Blondheim *Alfasi* (above, n. 23) have *ve-yesh omrim*, while the passage is missing entirely in MSS Sassoon 534, Cambridge Add. 490, Hechal Shelomoh 5 {=National Library of Israel 4to 6696}.

[112] S. Cohen, 'R. Mordekhai b. Hillel ha-Ashkenazi', *Sinai*, 12 (1943), 103–4.

[113] In MS Hechal Shelomoh 5 {=National Library of Israel 4to 6696} it actually appears as a gloss in the margin, though this could have arisen simply from a scribe who, having skipped it in his initial transcription, then proceeded to add it to the margin.

wine-press') meant was that Rabbenu Tam anticipated (and not for the first time)[114] later attempts by the Tosafists to distinguish between *gat* and *gigit* and thus neutralize the Yerushalmi.[115] He rejected them and said that the Yerushalmi's ruling applied equally to the contemporary *cuve*. It was this that he communicated to R. Shemaryah, and it was |192| echoes of this concession that were picked up by the author of the *Amarkal* some hundred and fifty years later.

Rabbenu Tam's conduct here may perhaps serve as a useful reminder of the measure of inner conviction that a thinker requires before he sets forth a doctrine which, to our eyes, appears to be (and may in a sense ultimately be) a justification of the status quo. If the reports of the Tosafists are accurate,[116] Rabbenu Tam *would* interpret *hamshakhah* as pouring, but he would *not* distinguish between a wine-press and a *cuve*. To our minds the reverse might seem more reasonable. *Hamshakhah* as pouring ran contrary to the basic use of mishnaic Hebrew; a distinction between *gat* and *gigit* ran contrary to nothing. It was always a legal possibility. But to Rabbenu Tam things appeared differently, and the fact that the equation of *cuve* with the press condemned French practices could not move him to assent to a doctrine of which he was not convinced.

19. But if subscribe he could not to the vindication of contemporary practice, neither would he proclaim its guilt. It will be noted that French sources knew nothing of Rabbenu Tam's retraction, and even Germany had but the barest notion of it. I suspect he delayed his reply until the tumult subsided and then, out of intellectual honesty, sent a quiet note to R. Shemaryah[117] conceding the point, but made no mention of the matter to his pupils. Ever the realist, he knew that the authority of a Yerushalmi could not roll back long-entrenched forms of Jewish wine production, and he saw no need to proclaim to his people, struggling at high cost to uphold *yein nesekh*, the problematic nature of their conduct.

114 A close study of the *Sefer ha-Yashar* will show just how much of subsequent tosafist thinking Rabbenu Tam anticipated. The printed *Tosafot* do not reflect the protean nature of Rabbenu Tam's thought. (See now *Ha-Yayin bi-Yemei ha-Beinayim* [above, n. 1], 216–22, 261–7, 354.)

115 Below, n. 119.

116 See text, above, p. 198.

117 If someone insists that Rabbenu Tam was no longer alive at the time of the correspondence (see above, n. 86), he may either discount my reconstruction or assume that Rabbenu Tam quietly notified someone, but not R. Shemaryah, of his retraction, and that reports of this note were picked up by late 13th-century editors. I suspect that the abbreviation **בתוס'** (above, n. 108) should be read **בתוספת**, i.e. in a gloss, and should not be understood as a reference to any of the famed novellae of the French academies. No one in France, to the best of my knowledge, was aware of Rabbenu Tam's retraction.

20. But the Yerushalmi passage was discovered independently in France. The aged R. Yosef Porat came across it and showed it to Ri.[118] The simultaneous emergence of the text in both countries indicates that its surfacing was more than coincidental. It was a hallmark of the broadening of the halakhic horizons of the twelfth century, which confronted the previously insulated Ashkenazic community with a wealth of new material, the content of which did not always concur with common practice. And upon the |**193**| successors of Rabbenu Tam fell the task of explanation. While uniformly recommending precautionary measures, all the Tosafists nevertheless did their utmost to defend established practice.[119] This phenomenon of vindication repeats itself again and again in their discussion of *yein nesekh* and of other contemporary problems. A proper understanding of it is essential to any evaluation of the mentality of the Tosafists and of the relationship of their thought to the world around them. But it is too large a topic to be treated here.

21. The Yerushalmi posed problems in France, but it only bolstered tradition in Germany. Thanks to it and to the strong stand taken by the rabbinic authorities, Germany continued to abstain from leaving vats unsupervised with Gentiles well into the early years of the thirteenth century. Or so it would seem from Ravyah. He wrote:[120]

> **ובירושלמי דמסכת ע"ז גרסינן לוקחין גת בעוטה וכו' תני ר' חנין והוא שלא העלים ישראל את עיניו ממנו אבל אם העלים ישראל את עיניו ממנו [לא בדא], ודכוותה צריך לומר בגיגית פקוקה ומליאה, ולהוציא מיושבי ארץ צרפת שלוקחין גיגיות בעוטות מן הנכרי---כי יש לחוש לתערובת יין נסך אפילו כפי משנה ראשונה, וגם יש לחוש אולי יין מסונן מן הבור היה בגיגית בתחילה ולא הודחה, ואיכא עכבת יין נסך. ובארץ אשכנז החמירו מימים קדמונים אפילו בגיגיות. וכשר הניהוג[!] ולא מהלכה רופפת אלא מאמיתה של הלכה.**

And the Yerushalmi in *'Avodah Zarah* reads thus: '[Mishnah] "A wine-press [containing] trodden grapes": R. Ḥanin taught: provided that a Jew has kept the wine-press under his supervision all the time. However, if the Jew has not kept up such supervision, [the allowance is not applicable].'

[118] *Teshuvot Maharaḥ Or Zarua'*, #174, fo. 59c; p. 165b in Avitan's edition (above, n. 12).

[119] Ibid. #174, fo. 59c–d; *Tosfot R. Yehudah mi-Paris*, pp. 264–6, 294–6; *Sefer ha-Terumah*, #169; *Semag*, ed. E. Schlesinger (Jerusalem, 1989), 295, Injunction #148; *Semak*, #225 (or #223; see above, n. 103); *Tosafot*, ad loc.; 'Sefer Amarkal' (above, n. 63), 13–14; *Piskei ha-Rosh* 4: 3.

[120] Sect. 1069. Deblitski, in both of his editions of the *Sefer Ravyah* (above, n. 63), mistakenly chose the reading of the British Library MS: **ודכוותיה צריך לומר בגת**, rather than that of the Bodley MS: **ודכוותיה צריך לומר בגיגית**. He also completed the missing words of Ravyah's quotation of the Yerushalmi with his own rather than that of the Yerushalmi—**לא בדא**.

One must similarly rule with regard to the stoppered, full *cuve*, **contrary to the practice of the Jews of France**, who purchase *cuves* trodden by Gentiles—for one should fear of an admixture of *yein nesekh* even according to the older *mishnah*. And one should also fear that initially there may have been in the *cuve* some strained wine from the pit; for [the *cuve*] may not have been [thoroughly] scrubbed [after its prior use by Gentiles], and it thus contains traces of this *yein nesekh*. And in the land of Ashkenaz, from the earliest times, they were stringent [in this matter] even with *cuves*, and correctly so, not [simply] on the grounds of custom **but on those of halakhic truth**. [emphases added]

The implication is that this is a French and not a German practice. Note too the shift in argument that has occurred. The ancient ban knew nothing of the Yerushalmi (remember R. Shemaryah's words *'ad she-matsati ba-Yerushalmi*—'until I found [a passage] in the Yerushalmi'), but was rooted in R. Huna's dictum and included not only unsupervised storage but Gentile touch and tub-treading as well. Yet within one generation (from R. Shemaryah's note to R. Yo'el to the work of the latter's son, Ravyah) the old injunction was transformed, and the Rhineland interpretation of *hamshakhah* simply evaporated. Only somewhat less remarkable than the retentive capacity of a traditional society is its ability to forget at times what it must. It then innocently pours new content into old forms and renews their mandate.

22. Ravyah's pupil, R. Yitsḥak Or Zarua', treats at length the problem of *hamshakhah*, and that discussion, like Gaul, may be divided into three parts.[121] He opens with a full citation of Rashbam's commentary on |**194**| *'Avodah Zarah* (cited above, pp. 186–7), then quotes *in extenso* the critique that Ravyah directed against Rabbenu Tam's doctrine of *hamshakhah*, and concludes with the latter's reply to R. Shemaryah defending French practices. There is nothing new in what he says, but what is of great significance is his silence. No mention is made of the Yerushalmi. Indeed, he copies the text of Ravyah up to the passage cited above—and then stops. There is no reference to the injunctive tradition of Germany or to the problematic French custom. This pattern repeats itself many times over in the *Or Zarua'*. Ravyah and R. Ele'azar of Worms (Rokeaḥ) represent a German tradition. R. Yitsḥak Or Zarua' belongs as much to France as to Germany. There is a great deal of Germanic material in that work, but it is not a work of Germanic tradition. From the days of Rabbenu Tam and Ri, French influences press hard on the Rhineland culture and in the second quarter of the thirteenth century succeed in overwhelming it. R. Me'ir of Rothenburg is intellectually no more German than

[121] ##213–15.

French, and the same holds true for R. Mordekhai. As for R. Asher (Rosh), who would know of the achievements of Ravan and Ravyah if he took his instruction from the *Piskei ha-Rosh*? There is far more of Spain and Provence in that work than there is of his homeland. Germany as a distinct halakhic culture ceased to exist somewhere after the year 1230,[122] and the disappearance of the old injunctive tradition from the pages of the *Or Zarua'* is just an example of this general dissolution.

If R. Yitsḥak Or Zarua', R. Me'ir of Rothenburg, and their successors one and all did not think the ancient ban worthy of mention,[123] it is difficult to see how the ordinary businessman could feel himself much bound by it. We have every reason to assume that now, like his French compatriots, he too left his *cuves* unsupervised.

France and Germany melded into one halakhic community, and as the awesome figure of Rabbenu Tam receded into memory and the emotional bias against |195| treading waned,[124] the people began to reap the rich fruits of R. Ya'akov Tam's labors and those of his grandfather. The curtain falls on Ashkenaz around the year 1300 with Gentiles treading and Gentiles touching and Gentiles handling the entire first phase of Jewish wine production.

In the still of the fourteenth century, after all the titans had departed, a last protesting murmur was heard—almost as an epilogue—in the now empty halls of the Tosafists. The editor of a much-copied compendium ranged around the Alfasi[125] could not refrain from interrupting his transcription of Rashi on our *sugya* with this resigned note: והאידנא נוהגין שלוקחין גיגיות מלאות ענבים דרוכין מן הגויים וסומכין על המשנה וטועין ('Nowadays people are accustomed

[122] Intellectually, that is. Distinctive German practices and customs continue for centuries.

[123] R. Me'ir of Rothenburg, the *Tashbets* and the *Haggahot Maimuniyot* make no mention at all of the matter, while R. Asher (ad loc.) adopts the French position. R. Mordekhai cites Ravyah's fears of admixture alongside the French allowance and makes no mention of the ancient injunctive custom. The first sign of the weakening may be found in *Sefer ha-Rokeaḥ*, #492, if our printed text is correct. It is corroborated by the one extant manuscript of the *Sefer ha-Rokeaḥ*, MS Paris Bibliothèque Nationale 363, fo. 188a. One would much prefer better support, since this is a late 15th-century copy and closely related to the manuscript from which the *Sefer ha-Rokeaḥ* was published. Personally, I suspect that a gloss has crept into the text. I should add that if the text is authentic, our case is not typical. The *Sefer ha-Rokeaḥ* is generally a very conservative work and free of substantive French influences. See H. Soloveitchik, 'Three Themes in the *Sefer Ḥasidim*', *AJS Review*, 1 (1976), 348–9. {See *Ha-Yayin bi-Yemei ha-Beinayim* (above, n. 1), 126, n. 21, for my strong reservations as to whether the lengthy treatment of the laws of *yein nesekh* found in the concluding section of the *Rokeaḥ*, #492, was indeed authored by R. Eli'ezer of Worms.}

[124] See above, n. 103(*a*).

[125] The Alfasi MSS referred to above, n. 23.

to purchasing from Gentiles *cuves* filled with trodden grapes, relying upon the Mishnah erroneously.)[126]

In the Bodley manuscript[127] of this work the scribe has omitted the last word. Intentionally?

[126] Popular practice relied, apparently, upon the language of flat allowance found in the Mishnah. See above, n. 104.

[127] MS Bodley 548, fo. 64a.

AFTERWORD

PAGE 189

To avoid misunderstanding, I changed the phrase 'itself but an expanded version of his own [work]' to 'itself but an extrapolation of his own [work]', in light of Y. Fuchs's strictures in 'Ketav Yad Mantova, ha-Kehillah ha-Yehudit 30 u-Terumato', *Tarbiz*, 79 (2011), 398–401. From the numerous citations of Rashbam's commentary in the *Or Zarua'* on *'Avodah Zarah*, it is clear that it was not a full-fledged commentary on the tractate. It consisted rather of an explication of the gist of the *sugya* together with the final ruling (much like Alfasi), which was followed by the practical applications of the stated ruling to contemporary circumstances (*halakhah le-ma'aseh*). As the section heading makes clear, I addressed here the sequence of Rashi's writings and contended that a revised version dictated by Rashi to his grandson of a work that he, Rashi, had previously dictated to his son-in-law—both of which were based on prior revisions of his own commentary—constituted Rashi's fourth or fifth commentary, as it were, on the tractate. It had to have been composed late in life. I was treating the time of composition of the Rashi/Rashbam commentary, not its structure. However, the sentence that I wrote—'Rashi dictating to his grandson a revision of his son-in-law's work, itself but an expanded version of his own, is a scene which occurred quite late in his life'—gives the impression that that work was a full-fledged commentary on the tractate (that also contained practical contemporary applications). Fuchs quite justly argued that this is not so. Whence the change in formulation. I also expanded a sentence or two in the preceding paragraph to make clear that Rashi's own commentary was lengthy and comprehensive whereas Rashbam's was brief and selective

PAGE 204

When the article first appeared, Chimen Abramsky of University College London wrote to me that my analysis of the encounter between Rabbenu Tam and Rabbenu Shemaryah in the case of the recalcitrant debtor was an application of the story told by S. Zevin in *Ishim ve-Shitot: Shurat Ma'amarim 'al Ishei Halakhah ve-Shitotehem ba-Torah* (Tel Aviv, 1952), 58–9, about my great-grandfather, R. Ḥayyim Soloveitchik, and R. Yitsḥak Elḥanan. I replied that if my construction was a retrojection it had been an unconscious one, and, more importantly, whether or not it was, was irrelevant. The test of a historical reconstruction is not from where the historian got the idea, but whether there is a persuasive correspondence between the data being interpreted and the interpretation proffered.

PAGE 220

The significance of the repeated vindications of popular practice is the subject of the essays 'Religious Law and Change: The Medieval Ashkenazic Example' (Chapter 9 below), and '"Religious Law and Change" Revisited' (Chapter 10 below).

CHAPTER EIGHT

Halakhah, Taboo, and the Origin of Jewish Moneylending in Germany

I SPENT many of my student years researching both usury and the laws forbidding wine touched by a Gentile (*setam yeinam*). The first was the subject of my doctorate, the second that of my Master's thesis. I never dreamt, however, that the two might be related. In the late 1990s I began to prepare for publication a much-expanded version of my Master's thesis, and naturally had to read up on the literature that had accumulated on subjects related to viticulture in the thirty years that had elapsed since I had last engaged with the topic. Works from the Arye Maimon Institut für Geschichte der Juden were also beginning to appear, and they changed my perspective on a number of issues. One of them was the possible relationship between the ban on benefiting in any manner from *yein nesekh* and the fateful Jewish involvement in moneylending. I developed the argument in a book in Hebrew, but presented the gist of it in the following lecture.

SO LARGE A TOPIC AND SO SHORT A LECTURE! Yet it is only appropriate that the thesis be first presented here in Speyer, even though the constraints of the conference allow only twenty-five minutes for its presentation. I am about to offer a bold thesis drawing lines between points stretching over hundreds of years. Most of these points are known to many here, and to some better than to me. More importantly, the lines between these points traverse territories known to many here far better than they are to me. I am an intellectual historian, not an economic one, and by no possible stretch of the imagination a historian of medieval German agriculture. The value of my remarks depends entirely on the degree of persuasive correspondence

This essay in its original form did not have footnotes, only a bibliography at the end entitled 'Further Reading', which listed titles alone without page references. This format has been preserved here. However, I have added page references to the works listed, and they effectively serve as documentation of the major points of my argument. I have further added several footnotes to document some statements that I felt required proof.

between the thesis advanced and the data with which many of you here are so intimately familiar.

It is also fitting that the presentation be made here as it draws on the researches of the past two decades of the Trier school generally, and, more specifically, on that of the Arye Maimon Institut für Geschichte der Juden of the University of Trier, which have transformed our understanding of German Jewry in the late Middle Ages and ineluctably challenged some of our received notions of German Jewish history in the high Middle Ages. The case at hand is an excellent example. In one sense, my entire argument is an attempt to solve jointly the difficulties posed by my own researches in the history of halakhah and the ones posed by the results of the researchers of the Trier school.

I should emphasize at the outset that the subject of this lecture is the developments in Germany; those in France are an entirely different story and lie beyond the scope of my presentation. |295|

The Taboo on Gentile Wine

Let me begin with the results of my own researches. Jewish law strictly enjoins trade in Gentile wine (*setam yeinam*)—indeed, deriving any benefit whatsoever from such wine. Jews in medieval Germany lived in wine-growing areas and both payment in kind and trade in wine were ubiquitous. A report from the mid-tenth century states that a compromise was reached. Wine would be accepted as payment of a debt, but not as an object of trade. Surprisingly enough, the injunction against trade was, to all appearances, upheld until at least the beginning of the fourteenth century. All sources report with regret that Gentile wine is accepted in payment of debts; not one source reports that there is trade in this commodity. The communal ordinances of Shum (Speyer, Worms, and Mainz) of 1221–3 attempt to repair several breaches in the observance of *setam yeinam*, but no mention is made of trade in it. Even the German Pietists, who castigated their communities unceasingly for every imaginable sin, make no mention of trade in Gentile wine.

Indeed, the aversion to Gentile wine assumed the dimension of a taboo, that is to say, an abhorrence that cannot be explained by the rational postulates of the culture itself. Generation after generation of halakhic thinkers in medieval Ashkenaz arrived at the conclusion that all forms of benefit are permitted from Gentile wine—including trade. However, this conclusion was rejected with shock, even though no convincing rationale could be adduced for its repudiation.

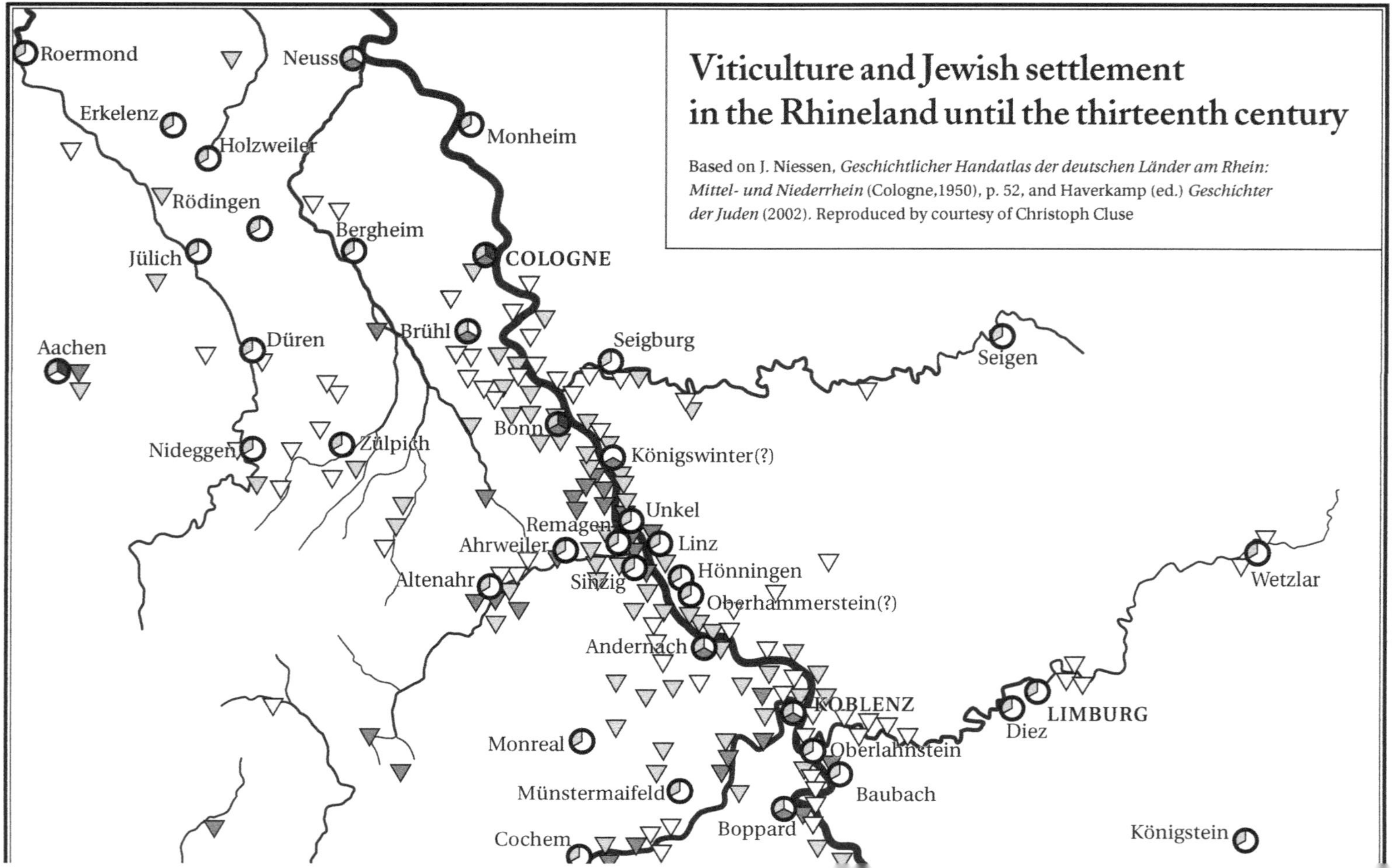
Viticulture and Jewish settlement
in the Rhineland until the thirteenth century
Based on J. Niessen, *Geschichtlicher Handatlas der deutschen Länder am Rhein: Mittel- und Niederrhein* (Cologne,1950), p. 52, and Haverkamp (ed.) *Geschichter der Juden* (2002). Reproduced by courtesy of Christoph Cluse
Roermond
Neuss
Monheim
Erkelenz
Holzweiler
Rödingen
Bergheim
Jülich
COLOGNE
Brühl
Seigburg
Seigen
Aachen
Düren
Bonn
Königswinter(?)
Nideggen
Zülpich
Unkel
Remagen
Linz
Ahrweiler
Hönningen
Sinzig
Altenahr
Oberhammerstein(?)
Wetzlar
Andernach
KOBLENZ
LIMBURG
Diez
Monreal
Oberlahnstein
Baubach
Münstermaifeld
Boppard
Cochem
Königstein

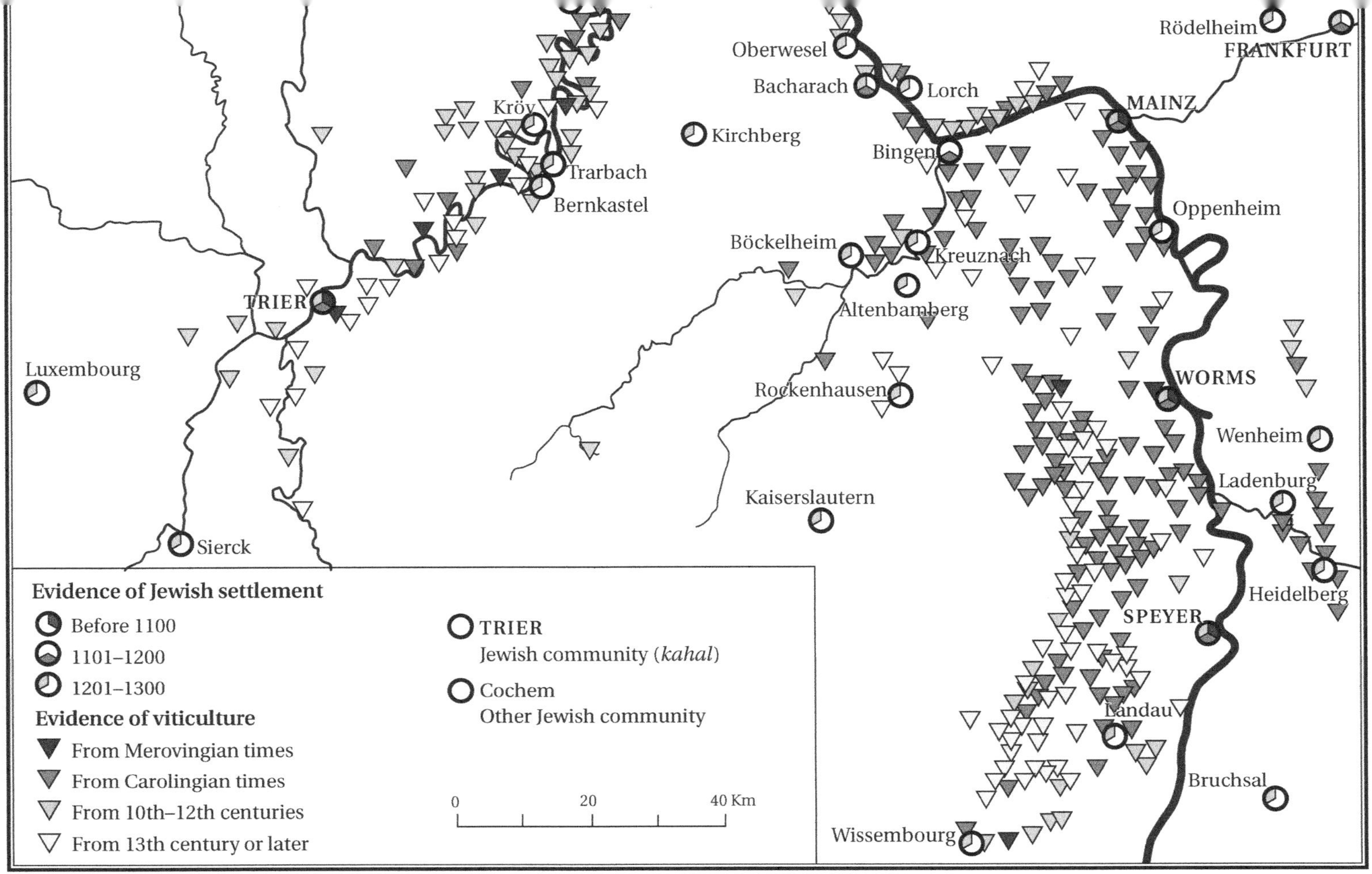

Rödelheim
FRANKFURT
Oberwesel
Bacharach
Lorch
MAINZ
Kröv
Kirchberg
Bingen
Trarbach
Bernkastel
Oppenheim
Böckelheim
Kreuznach
TRIER
Altenbamberg
Luxembourg
WORMS
Rockenhausen
Wenheim
Ladenburg
Kaiserslautern
Sierck
Heidelberg
SPEYER
Landau
Bruchsal
Wissembourg
Evidence of Jewish settlement
Before 1100
1101–1200
1201–1300
Evidence of viticulture
From Merovingian times
From Carolingian times
From 10th–12th centuries
From 13th century or later
TRIER
Jewish community (kahal)
Cochem
Other Jewish community
0
20
40 Km

Jews in the German Empire lived in wine-growing areas and were in the tenth and eleventh centuries, and possibly even in the twelfth, a trading class. One need only look at the maps of Jewish settlement in the German Empire and that of German medieval viticulture to see to what extent Jewish habitation was congruous with that of the classic wine-growing areas of Germany (see map above). How could such a group abstain from trade in the most important and profitable commodity of its area? One can be a peddler, selling rings and things and buttons and bows, or a trader, a man of substance dealing in a recognized, profitable commodity. The overall impression given by sources is that the Jews were, until their large-scale entry into moneylending, a trading class. How, then, could they not trade in wine?

The Omnipresence of Wine

The trade in wine was massive and widespread. In the eleventh and early twelfth centuries it was one of the most important articles of trade in northern Europe. It was then surpassed by wool, but remained throughout the period a staple of national and international trade. Nor is the reason difficult to seek. Water was viewed as the drink of animals, or of peasants, who differed little from beasts, but not of self-respecting men. Such imports as tea and coffee were still unknown, whiskey had yet to be discovered, and fresh fruit was unobtainable for much of the year. Only wine could slake the thirst, and the thirst was great as drink was both a physical need and an escape. Meat had to be heavily spiced or salted in order to preserve it, and |**296**| alcohol was the major consolation of the lower classes and the primary entertainment of their betters. So drink they did, and on a scale that is difficult for us to grasp.[1]

The canons of St. Paul's, honorable men all and unsullied by any charge of gluttony, were allotted 17(!) liters of beer a day. The regulations of the monastery of Battle, whose monks were no less well thought of than the men of St. Paul's, specifically stipulated a corrody (daily food allotment) of 'no less'—thus in the *regula*—than 16 liters of wine a day.[2] Admittedly, not everyone in the Middle Ages drank, or could afford to drink, 16 liters of wine a day, and the average consumption of wine per person is estimated at the very minimum of 0.7 liters a day. But note what these modest figures mean in the aggregate. A city with 25,000 to 30,000 inhabitants above the poverty line (for

[1] I have altered the formulations in this paragraph so as not to repeat a few sentences in 'Can Halakhic Texts Talk History?' (Chapter 7 above).

[2] D. Knowles, *The Monastic Order in England: A History of its Development from the Times of St Dunstan to the Fourth Lateran Council, 940–1216* (Cambridge, 1940), 717 (Appendix XX).

the poor could ill afford wine) consumed at least some 6,387,500 to 7,650,000 liters of wine a year. And wine, north of the Alps, could be obtained only by trade.

The vine is a sub-tropical plant; indeed, 'wild vines', growing on their own, are common in countries bordering the Mediterranean. For proper ripening, grapes require a steady supply of sunshine in the final months of maturation. This is easily found on the Mediterranean littoral, where clouds are scarcely to be seen in the months of July and August. One of the characteristics of a temperate climate, however, is the instability of the weather. Days, occasionally weeks, can pass without steady sunshine. The winters, furthermore, are too harsh and the summers too humid for the natural growth of the vine. Only in a few select regions can the vine flourish, and there only if cultivated by professional vintners who possess the expertise acquired slowly over centuries of raising a precious crop in a notably hostile environment, of exploiting every incremental advantage of the *terroir*. Those few regions in northern Europe favored by the gods for the careful cultivation of wine became centers of trade, of wealth, and of power. And few localities were more favored in vine-growing than was the Rhineland—especially the Middle and Upper Rhine, the very center of the major Jewish communities in the Middle Ages (see map).

The wine trade was the economic lifeblood of the region, yet the uniform impression given by all Jewish sources—legal, hortatory, and institutional—is that the ban on Jewish trade in Gentile wine was upheld. The conclusion from the Hebrew sources was ineluctable, but it made no sense. How could a trading class abstain from trading in the most common and profitable item of commerce in the regions where they lived? Such was the problem posed by my researches into the history of Jewish law.

The researches of the Arye Maimon Institut für Geschichte der Juden have shown the deep Jewish involvement in viticultural credit in the fourteenth and fifteenth centuries. Some of the worst massacres in Germany occurred in the vine-growing areas, yet no sooner did they stop slaughtering Jews than they turned to them for credit. Why were Jews allowed to be major players in this one area long after they had been driven out of |**298**| other forms of commercial credit? If Jews were not expelled from viticultural credit, it was not for lack of will, not because the Gentiles did not wish to expel them, but because they could not. But why couldn't they?

Second, if Jews played such a major economic role in the late Middle Ages when what has been called 'pathological or chimerical antisemitism'—with its charges of blood libel and poisoning of wells—was rampant, what was their role in earlier centuries, when only 'rational antisemitism' reigned, that is to say, when Jews were only accused of 'sins' to which they would have proudly admitted—infidelity, blasphemy, and being children of those who killed, or approved of the killing of, one deemed by them to be a false messiah?[3] Is this large-scale involvement some strange efflorescence of the late Middle Ages or simply the first documentation that we possess of a long-standing activity? This is a question that cannot be avoided.

To this witches' brew of new problems, let us add three old ones: in the tenth and eleventh centuries, German Jews were a trading class; by the thirteenth, they were a moneylending one. What were the stages of this metamorphosis? Second, how is it that this transition left no traces? Third, where did they get the money to lend? Whence the initial capital formation that enabled them to enter finance? |**299**|

From Wine Trade to Viticultural Investment

Keeping these six large questions in mind—How did Jewish traders in the Rhineland avoid participating in the ubiquitous wine trade? Why did Jews still command a prominent place in viticultural credit in the late Middle Ages? Was this involvement recent or of long standing? What was the transition from trader to lender and why has it left no traces in the historical record? and, finally, Whence the capital formation that enabled them to be lenders?—let us now step back into the Carolingian period, when the curtain first rises on the Jews in north-western Europe.

In what is arguably the first anti-Jewish (as opposed to anti-Judaic) tract of the Middle Ages, Agobard's *De Insolentia Judaeorum*, the author complains that Jews sell to Christians wine that they consider defiled or contaminated (*immundus*) and will not themselves drink. He further informs us that Jews provide wine to high royal officials and boast of their access to the corridors of power. His successor Amulo writes that Jewish wine is drunk everywhere and some clerics go so far as using it for the Mass. The first sizeable record of Jewish landholding comes from the Mâconnais in the first two decades of the tenth century, and there 65 percent of Jewish landholding was of vineyards, while the general ratio in Burgundy of vineyard to arable land was some 25 percent.

The Carolingian reports are credible. Jewish law forbids drinking wine touched by Gentiles. Consequently, Jews had to produce their own wine—no small task considering the enormous quantities that were consumed during

[3] G. I. Langmuir, *Toward a Definition of Antisemitism* (Berkeley, 1990), 63–99, 195–310.

the Middle Ages. In the Mediterranean lands, this was purely a question of manpower—as the grape is a sub-tropical fruit and grows there naturally. In northern Europe, however, viticulture is a constant struggle against the natural environment. Vineyards seem so natural a part of the German landscape that we forget that vines are as natural to the Rhineland as palm trees. When Jews first crossed the Alps or when any of them first moved into any new location in the temperate zone, they had to ensure for themselves a steady supply not only of kosher meat but also of kosher wine. The first was no problem; the second could be achieved only by either acquiring the skills of the vintners or forming a close tie with this relatively elite group of workers with whose accumulated skills, handed down from father to son over the centuries, no lord could dispense.

Jews in the Carolingian era, or at least the Jews we know of, were traders, often of luxury items. They swiftly realized that their necessary skill in viticulture or their long-standing contacts with vintners could be put to very lucrative use and, as one way to a ruler's heart is through his stomach, purveying quality wine could also give them access to power—so crucial for their physical safety. If Jews were associated with quality wine, Amulo's charge makes sense: should God's table be inferior to that of man? Some clergy thought not and intentionally used Jewish wine for the Mass, for the greater glory of God.

At the end of the tenth century trade began to revive. In northern Europe wine was one of the major commodities of international trade in the eleventh century, and |**300**| throughout the Middle Ages it remained a staple of north European commerce. Few places in northern Europe were better suited to or had longer traditions of viticulture than the Rhineland, and none had a better waterway to the wine-starved countries bordering the North Sea. Once wine became a major, if not the major, item of trade, Jewish merchants in the Rhineland were in danger of being marginalized and of being reduced to peddlers. How were they to maintain their position in trade if the ban on trade in Gentile wine remained in place? Just about this time, the mid-tenth century, we hear of the compromise position being reluctantly adopted in the Jewish community of Lotir, i.e. Lotharingia. Gentile wine as payment would be tolerated; initiating trade—never and under no circumstances. And this flimsy distinction, to all appearances, held for centuries, with all the potent power of a taboo. Given this taboo and its force, the only way Jews could maintain their position in the trade of the most profitable commodity in the Rhineland was to extend credit to the vineyard owners and stipulate that payment be made in wine. If the current financial needs of the owners were already spoken for, as was often the case, Jews *had* to finance viticultural expansion. Only thus could they be assured of a steady supply, a *sine qua non* of trade. Hence, Jewish trade in the Rhineland is inextricably bound up with Jewish credit. There was no period of transition. From the outset, Jews were equally involved both in trade and in credit. Jews did not see themselves as creditors but rather as traders, as they were not interested in the interest from the loans but in the produce that they obtained through them and the profits that would be made by its sale. Interest, let us remember, is calculated in percentages, while trade mark-ups are calculated in multiples. Moreover, in an era before Jews came to be identified with credit, their Christian neighbors did not see them as creditors either, any more than the customers of today view Bloomingdale's or Marks & Spencer as creditors rather than as merchants. When Jews began to be pushed out of trade they naturally concentrated on its flip side—credit—in which they had long experience, and moneylending, once wholly ancillary to their commercial activities, became *the* dominant mode of Jewish enterprise.

What was the scope of their viticultural credit? If, as Professor Matheus has written, Jews were already playing an important role in the wine trade by the year 1000, then they were also playing a significant role in viticultural investment by that date. There was scarcely a riskier or more long-term investment in the Middle Ages, or a more labor- and capital-intensive one. Unlike grain crops, which one ploughs and sows (little skill is demanded for either operation), and then waits several months to harvest, vines in the temperate zone require year-round, skilled toil as one is attempting to raise a crop in an environment hostile to its growth. The most one can hope for is one good crop every three years or so. Thus one waits not six months for a return on one's investment but often twenty-four or thirty-six costly, labor-filled months. If viticultural credit was expensive, risky, and long-term, financing viticultural expansion was infinitely more so. It takes anywhere from three to seven years to develop a new vineyard, and some three years of maturation are needed simply to expand an existing one by layering (*marcottage*). Once mature, the new |**301**| vineyard has the same chance of success as the old—one in every two, possibly three, years. One is talking of three to five, realistically even five to seven, expense-laden years of waiting. Indeed, five to seven years of free rent was the standard period extended by landowners to tenant cultivators of new vineyards. Throughout this protracted span of time there are constant crises and a need for continuous supervision. The vineyards in the Mâconnais in the tenth century studied by Blumenkranz are all within some 12 to 15 kilometers of the place of Jewish settlement, and the vineyards held by the investment group of Vesoul of the fourteenth century studied by Annegret Holtmann are no further away from Vesoul. For whether one is an owner or an investor, one can never be more than a day's journey from the crisis-prone vineyards. The investor was constantly confronted with the question of whether to sink in further money to save or improve the harvest or to cut his losses. Someone without viticultural expertise and intuition born of a deep familiarity with vine-growing would swiftly lose his shirt. But constant supervision did not in itself guarantee success. Equally necessary for the investor was the merchant's ability of intuiting what the crop—if successful—would be worth at harvest time. This in turn demanded some network of information on conditions in neighboring areas, as they determined the overall supply at the time of sale. Added to all the above is a final prerequisite: the money manager's sense of whether a further outlay—even if the harvest is successful—is the optimal use of his capital at a given moment. This combination of viticultural expert, merchant, and money manager, coupled with a network of information provided by co-religionists, was, I suggest, more frequently found among Jews than among Christians.

The Law of Unintended Consequences

If all this is so, we can understand why Jews continued to play an important role in viticultural credit in the late Middle Ages, even after they had long been demonized and exiled from society and from all its untainted professions. They were not *admitted* into viticultural credit in the late Middle Ages; rather, they could not be *expelled* from it, because they had been in it for so long. The sums at risk in viticultural credit were simply too large, the prospective profits too great, and Jewish expertise too long and well established for their persecutors to forgo. We can equally understand that there was never an initial phase in which the Jews amassed capital. This question, like the one regarding the missing transitional phase from trading to lending, has received no good answer because it assumes what never was, namely, that Jews were lending their own capital. Jewish investors received their money, as do all good investors, from other people—who are only too happy to have someone else increase their wealth.

If my analysis is correct, we have uncovered a Jewish expertise and profession some half a millennium old—the viticultural expert and investor—that has hitherto gone unnoted. In addition, if Jewish involvement in the wine trade was as extensive as has recently been portrayed, we have also brought to light a significant Jewish contribution |302| to German medieval agriculture, which had also slipped into the abyss, the oblivion of time.

It should be emphasized, however, that these are two separate and distinct conclusions: the first hinges on both the geographical extent of Jewish involvement in viticultural credit and the period for which it lasted, the second on the significance of this involvement in the overall picture. One may readily assent to both an early and an extensive Jewish participation in viticultural credit, and yet deny that this activity had any significance in the expansion of German viticulture during the Middle Ages

Finally, we witness anew the one law that does obtain in history—the law of unintended consequences. For the origins of both the centuries-old profession and the possible agricultural contribution lay in a religious injunction enacted in the pagan Mediterranean at the beginning of the Common Era that worked its unanticipated effects some thousand years later in central Europe of the high Middle Ages. And the impact of the injunction may not have stopped there. For if the credit extended to viticulture paved the way in Germany for the eventual concentration of Jews in moneylending—a profession that shaped in no small measure the fate of the Jews in the coming centuries and their image for close to another millennium—then the talmudic ban on Gentile wine and the potent taboo that attended it played, in a wholly unforeseen though not mysterious way, a truly remarkable role in the history of the Jews in Christian Europe.

FURTHER READING

Blumenkranz, B., 'Cultivateurs et vignerons juifs en Bourgogne IXe au XIe siècles', *Bulletin philologique et historique du Comité des travaux historiques et scientifiques* (1960), 129–36. Reprinted in id., *Juifs en France: Écrits dispersés* (Paris, 1989), 111–16.

Holtmann, A., *Juden in der Grafschaft Burgund im Mittelalter*, Forschungen zur Geschichte der Juden, vol. xii (Hanover, 2003), 153–82, 242–61.

Matheus, M., 'Wein', in *Lexikon des Mittelalters*, vol. viii (Munich, 1997), col. 2119.

Mentgen, G., *Studien zur Geschichte der Juden im mittelalterlichen Elsaß*, Forschungen zur Geschichte der Juden, vol. ii (Hanover, 1995), 557–74.

Pirenne, H., 'Un grand commerce d'exportation au Moyen Age: Les Vins de France', *Annales d'histoire économique et sociale*, 5 (1933), 225–43.

Postan, M., 'Trade in Northern Europe', in *The Cambridge Economic History of Europe*, ii: *Trade and Industry in the Middle Ages*, 2nd edn. (Cambridge, 1983), 119–256.

Rohrbacher, S., and M. Schmidt, *Judenbilder: Kulturgeschichte antijüdischer Mythen und antisemitischer Vorurteile* (Reinsbeck, 1991), 41–147.

Soloveitchik, H., *Yeinam: Saḥar be-Yeinam shel Goyim—'al Gilgulah shel Halakhah be-'Olam ha-Ma'aseh* (Tel Aviv, 2003), 31–90.

Toch, M., 'Wirtschaft und Verfolgung: Die Bedeutung der Ökonomie für die Kreuzzugspogrome des 11. und 12. Jahrhunderts. Mit einem Anhang zum Sklavenhandel der Juden', in A. Haverkamp, ed., *Juden und Christen zur Zeit der Kreuzzüge* (Sigmaringen, 1999), 253–85.

Ziwes, F.-J., *Studien zur Geschichte der Juden im mittleren Rheingebiet während des hohen und späten Mittelalters*, Forschungen zur Geschichte der Juden, vol. i (Hanover, 1995), 232–7.

AFTERWORD

1. This essay is not an argument but a suggestion which would solve a number of large questions in the history of medieval German Jewry. It would be an argument had we actual documents of Jewish viticultural credit; private loan documents, however, are usually destroyed upon payment. Rabbinic sources document the abstention from initiating trade in Gentile wine until the early years of the fourteenth century. The taboo thus lasted some 350 years, with Jewish involvement in viticultural credit continuing for well over another century. Whether the taboo was equally maintained over this period of time is an open question. Rabbinic sources dwindle dramatically in the fourteenth and fifteenth centuries, and those that we have are silent on the subject. It is clear from Gentile sources that the taboo was on the wane in the latter half of the fifteenth century, and by the sixteenth century Jews were actively initiating trade in Gentile wine.[1] Where the taboo stood in the fourteenth century is unclear.

I further doubt that such records as those of the wine fair of Cologne will be of much help. Given the prestige surrounding wine and the intense, indeed 'pathological' antisemitism of the late Middle Ages, it seems improbable that Jewish creditors in Germany would have been allowed to bring the wine to market, lest any prestige or good repute attend these less than human, sadistic torturers of God. I very much suspect that the Jewish involvement was terminated immediately after the harvest, and a long distance placed between the Jews and the pride of the Rhineland. After the wine was sold, the Jew received his payment for the credit he had extended. It was, however, the Gentile landowner or his estate manager who, wishing to be seen as the master of wine and vine, brought the precious cargo to the fair.

2. It is interesting to note, though I do not know how to go about proving anything with the information, how many European Jewish family names are linked to three commodities—gold, silver, and wine: Gold, Goldstein, Goldberg, Goldman, Goldfarb, etc.; Silver, Silber, Silverman, Silverstein, Silberg, etc.; Wein, Weiner, Weinberg, Weinstein, Weinreich, etc.

3. In a symposium on my book-length study of this problem, *Yeinam: Saḥar be-Yeinam shel Goyim—'al Gilgulah shel ha-Halakhah be-'Olam ha-Ma'aseh* (Tel Aviv, 2003), Berachyahu Lifshitz questioned whether this essay does not conflict with one of the basic facts presented in my essay on pawnbroking (above, pp. 84–5). If in Germanic law a pawn (be it mobilia or real estate) became the property of the creditor, then every possessory mortgage (even if immediately rented back to the original owner) became the property of the Jewish creditor, and thus it should have been forbidden to Jews to trade in the wine produced by the current Gentile occupant (the original owner) and his laborers. Let us recall, however, one of the central points of the essay on

[1] M. Toch, 'Wirtschaft und Geldwesen der Juden Frankfurts im Spätmittelalter und in der Frühen Neuzeit', in K. E. Grözinger, ed., *Jüdische Kultur in Frankfurt am Main von den Anfängen bis zur Gegenwart* (Frankfurt am Main, 1997), 25–46.

pawnbroking. When necessary, the halakhah will silently incorporate the dominant law of the surrounding areas under heavy economic pressure, as were pawnbroking and credit transfer (sale of debt) in medieval times and as the stock market would be today. Outside the area of pressure, as in matters of family inheritance or *kesef kiddushin* (objects of value employed in the marriage ceremony, such as the wedding ring), the classic rules of the halakhah reasserted themselves, and no title whatsoever was granted to pawns taken from Gentiles. The taking of wine as debt repayment was unquestionably an issue under intense pressure in medieval Germany. However, to enable such payments, the halakhah needed only to treat the possessory mortgage taken from the Gentile debtor as it is classically viewed by the halakhah; namely, it was simply a security taken to ensure repayment of a loan. It was purely accessorial, without a scintilla of ownership being attached to it. The halakhah was here only too glad to oblige. The silent incorporation of external realities is what halakhah does as a consequence of *force majeure*; it naturally prefers to rule on purely internal premises, as here.

PART IV

SOME GENERAL CONCLUSIONS

CHAPTER NINE

Religious Law and Change

The Medieval Ashkenazic Example

THIS PAPER, written in 1982, summed up my views consequent on my researches in usury, martyrdom, *yein nesekh*, and the laws regulating Jewish–Gentile relationships. I emphasized, I believe rightly so, the lengths to which the Tosafists went to justify communal practice. I equally pointed out that this relentless defense of common practice went hand in hand with, indeed, was sustained by, the ongoing acceptance of the new halakhic demands created by the tosafist dialectic. I did not then perceive the contradiction between these two phenomena. Every new demand was an implicit criticism of past practice. How could the Tosafists have defended to the death, as it were, the religious practices of the Ashkenazic community in the realm of usury, martyrdom, *yein nesekh*, and the like, yet massively reform the religious practice of the same community in other areas of Jewish law? I address this problem in the next essay, '"Religious Law and Change" Revisited'.

My overall understanding of the relationship between the Ashkenazic self-image and the communal reality has been the subject of an extensive critique by David Malkiel in his *Refashioning Ashkenaz: The Human Face of Franco-German Jewry, 1000–1250* (Stanford, 2009), 148–99. My reply is found in Chapter 12, 'On Deviance', below.

IF LAW IS CONCEIVED, as religious law must be, as a revelation of the Divine will, then any attempt to align that will with human wants, any attempt to have reality control, rather than be itself controlled by, the Divine norm, is an act of blasphemy and is inconceivable to a God-fearing man.

The first half of this article is a condensed version of a paper given at the annual convention of the Association of American Law Schools, Houston, Texas, 28 Dec. 1976, entitled 'The Tosafist Conception of Law'. The essay here presented was a lecture delivered at the Center for Israeli and Jewish Studies of Columbia University, 7 Dec. 1982. The lecture is printed as delivered, and no attempt has been made to alter the oral—if you wish, the rhetorical—nature of the presentation. I would like to thank Professors Jacob Katz, Ya'akov Sussman, and I. M. Ta-Shma for commenting on the paper.

As the Middle Ages was a time of faith among Jews no less than among Christians and Muslims, the unalignability, the non-adaptability if you wish, of religious law is a premise that must underlie all our investigations |205| and our understanding of the history of halakhah in the Middle Ages. Yet the contention of this paper is that at times the very intensity of religious conviction and observance can be conducive to a radical transformation of religious law, and that the very depth of religious attachment can play a supportive role in deflecting the Divine norm from the path of its immanent development, bringing it into line with the needs and practices of the time.

A few prefatory remarks may, however, be in order before beginning the argument. First, the subject of the lecture is conscious change—reinterpretation of a set purpose to achieve a given goal. Second, our subject is not the responsa literature. We will not deal with actual judicial rulings—a sphere where there has always been a strong interplay between circumstances and legal principles—but rather with the theoretical writings of the halakhah, a literature one might expect to be most immune to pressure. My remarks will center about the classic super-commentary on the Talmud: the work of the Tosafists, the great series of Franco-German glosses composed in the twelfth and thirteenth centuries, printed alongside the Talmud in every edition of that work, and indissolubly associated with every attempt to understand that complex corpus, from the Middle Ages to the present day. So central are the works of the Tosafists that one may well paraphrase Whitehead and say that all subsequent halakhic thinking has been a series of footnotes to the *Tosafot*. Which brings me to the third and final point by way of introduction: medieval halakhic thought, in fact medieval Jewish culture generally, can be divided roughly into four units. There is the culture of Muslim Spain, which began to flourish in the mid-tenth century, and was then annihilated in one fell swoop by the Almohads in the 1140s; its greatest product, Maimonides, fled as a boy from Cordoba to settle eventually in Egypt. The second culture is the north European one, centered in France and Germany and usually called Ashkenaz. The third is that of Provence, located roughly in what is now called the French Riviera; a culture apart, both in Jewish and in general history, from the one of northern France, at least until the thirteenth century. And finally there is the halakhic thought of Christian Spain, which began with the Reconquista in the late twelfth century and achieved great heights, possibly the greatest intellectual heights of the Jewish Middle Ages, in the thirteenth and fourteenth centuries. It is these four separate cultures (the two Spains—Muslim and Christian—as well as Provence and Ashkenaz) that form the foci of the lecture. My remarks will be directed towards drawing out the uniqueness of the approach to certain problems of law and reality of the Franco-German |206| (Ashkenazic) culture, in contrast to the responses of the other three cultures—cultures no less creative, no less daring than that of Franco-Germany, but ones which chose, in the inevitable clash between need and theory, a path wholly different from that of the Ashkenazic community.

Anyone who has studied the writings of the Tosafists will have noticed that often when they introduce a radical and occasionally unconvincing interpretation of a talmudic passage they conclude with 'and therefore we may allow this or that practice'. If one takes the *Tosafot* on the printed page of the Talmud, this is most noticeable in the tractate *'Avodah Zarah*, but if one studies other works of the school, such as the *Sefer Ravyah* or the *Or Zarua'*, or uses earlier *Tosafot*, such as those of R. Shimshon of Sens or R. Yehudah of Paris, one will perceive that in other areas the seemingly neutral words of the printed *Tosafot* have on many occasions a similar purpose in mind.

Many have inferred, and reasonably so, that as the Tosafists were not only scholars but also communal leaders (in this community religious and lay leadership were intertwined), like all true leaders they shaped the law to meet the needs of their people.[1] It was noted, however, that often the practices referred to were actually ones of long standing, and that the remarks of the Tosafists did not constitute any innovation but were rather a ratification of the status quo.[2] Furthermore, detailed study will show that often the practices referred to were ones that were not under heavy economic or social pressure. A good many of the practices allowed by the Tosafists certainly were products of such pressures (especially those in the areas of trade or business), but others were not at all. A few that were legitimized were even contrary to the material interests of the community. And so the question presents itself (and I emphasize that we are dealing here with commentaries and theoretical writings): what legitimized, in the eyes of the Tosafists, this radical reinterpretation?[3] 'Reinterpretation' is actually a misleading term. More accurately, one should ask what led them to read the Talmud, to *perceive* the Talmud, in a fashion that can be construed only as a justification |207| of the status quo. And we are not dealing with a few isolated instances. There are numerous occasions—indeed, in the fields of *yein*

[1] E. E. Urbach, *Ba'alei ha-Tosafot*, revised edn. (Jerusalem, 1980), 90–1, 740–1 and *passim*; S. Albeck, 'Yaḥaso shel Rabbenu Tam li-Ve'ayot Zemano', *Zion*, 19 (1954), 103–41.

[2] J. Katz, review of E. E. Urbach, *Ba'alei ha-Tosafot*, *Kiryat Sefer*, 31 (1956), 12–13.

[3] See the important remarks of H. H. Ben-Sasson, 'Hanhagatah shel Torah', *Beḥinot*, 9 (1957), 46–9.

nesekh (the injunction against drinking wine touched by Gentiles) or *hilkhot 'avodah zarah* (the laws regulating social and commercial relations between Jews and Gentiles found in tractate *'Avodah Zarah*), entire *areas* of talmudics —in which one may say, without fear of exaggeration, that the Tosafists overtly fashioned the law so as to align it better with regnant practice and need.[4]

Perhaps we can best understand this phenomenon if we follow a course of reasoning that may well have occurred to the Ashkenazic community. Jewish law has very stringent regulations regarding rules of martyrdom. In a few extreme instances martyrdom is absolutely mandatory. In those cases where it is not mandatory it is forbidden, and most probably one who suffers voluntary martyrdom should be viewed as having committed suicide.[5] Life is not optional in Judaism, and one knows of no allowance for committing suicide to avoid forced conversion. Yet from numerous Crusade chronicles, both Jewish and Christian, it is perfectly clear that the Ashkenazic community—men, women, and children—did not all abide by these regulations. Scholars and simple folk alike committed suicide rather than have baptism forced upon them, rather than be dipped in what they called 'contaminated waters'. And let it be noted that we are not dealing with instances of mass hysteria, but with a pattern of conduct persisting over the course of centuries. They went yet further. Parents slaughtered their own |**208**| children to prevent them from falling into Christian hands and from being raised as Christians, and even recited a

[4] J. Katz, *Bein Yehudim le-Goyim* (Jerusalem, 1960), 35–56. {English version: *Exclusiveness and Tolerance: Studies in Jewish–Gentile Relations in Medieval and Modern Times* (Oxford, 1961), 24–47.} H. Soloveitchik, *Minhag, Metsi'ut ve-Halakhah be-Maḥshavtam shel Ba'alei ha-Tosafot: Yein Nesekh, Nituaḥ le-Dugma* (MA thesis, Hebrew University of Jerusalem, 1967). {A much-expanded version of this study appeared as *Ha-Yayin bi-Yemei ha-Beinayim: Yein Nesekh: Perek be-Toledot ha-Halakhah be-Ashkenaz* (Jerusalem, 2008).}

[5] See *Mishneh Torah*, 'Hilkhot Yesodei ha-Torah', 5: 1–5. I have adopted, both from conviction and for presentational purposes, the Maimonidean position on voluntary martyrdom as being the straight and simple interpretation of the halakhah (just as *yehareg ve-'al ya'avor* expresses an imperative, so similarly does its companion statement, *ya'avor ve-al yehareg*). And indeed a reading of the *Semak* (Constantinople, 1509) would indicate just how aware R. Yitsḥak of Corbeil was of the cogency of this argument. Opinions, however, can legitimately differ on this matter. The question here addressed is not the legal validity of the positions adopted, but the mind-frame that shaped those positions. Murder of one's children to avoid baptism is legally inadmissible, yet it is evident that this centuries-old practice possessed the full tacit approval of the Tosafists (see below, n. 8). A culture that assents to child murder as preferable to baptism is one that, I believe, will inevitably view voluntary martyrdom as permissible, indeed commendable. Be that as it may, my argument is made on the basis of child murder rather than voluntary martyrdom. (Josephus' account of Masada has recently generated considerable literature on suicide; see L. H. Feldman, *Josephus and Modern Scholarship* [Berlin, 1984], 779–80. For our purposes, see below, n. 8.)

blessing on the murder of themselves and of their own children, as they would on the performance of other Divine commandments, such as the eating of matzah on Passover night.[6] One of the most tragic documents to come down to us from the Jewish Middle Ages is an inquiry sent to the great Rabbi Me'ir of Rothenburg (d. 1293) concerning the appropriate penance for a man who slaughtered his children as a pogrom was in progress, in order to prevent them from falling into Christian hands, and then failed in his own attempt at suicide. Rabbi Me'ir was hard put to find a reply.[7]

The magnitude of this halakhic breach is enormous. Whether one is permitted to suffer voluntary martyrdom is highly questionable; suicide is forbidden beyond question, and the permissibility of murder needs no discussion. Thus if the law were to be followed, the scholars of these communities would have had to rule that all the martyrs—*kedoshim*, or 'holy ones', as they were called—were not only not holy, but were 'self-killers' and murderers; that not only should they not be buried with honor, but perhaps they should even be

[6] {*Hebräische Berichte über die Judenverfolgungen während des Ersten Kreuzzugs*, ed. E. Haverkamp, Monumenta Germaniae Historica, Hebräische Texte aus dem mittelalterlichen Deutschland 1 (Hanover, 2005)}; *Gezerot Ashkenaz ve-Tsarfat*, ed. A. Haberman (Jerusalem, 1945). The English translation is that of S. Eidelberg, *The Jews and the Crusades: The Hebrew Chroniclers of the First and Second Crusades* (Madison, 1977). See now R. Chazan's translation in his *European Jewry and the First Crusade* (Los Angeles, Berkeley, and London, 1987), 223–97. Suicide and slaughter of children are attested to by Albert of Aix, *Recueil des historiens des croisades, historiens occidentaux*, iv (Paris, 1879), 293. {See now J. Riley-Smith, 'The First Crusade and the Persecution of the Jews', in W. J. Shields, ed., *Persecution and Toleration*, Studies in Church History 21 (Oxford, 1984), 51–72; E. Haverkamp, '"What Did Christians Know?": Latin Reports on the Persecutions of Jews in 1096', *Crusades*, 7 (2008), 59–86.} Recitation of the blessing: *Gezerot*, 41, 45, 46, 78, 96 (see also pp. 62, 113); *Hebräische Berichte*, 285, 395, 417, 419, 441. See S. Abramson, 'Nusakh Berakhah 'al Kiddush ha-Shem', *Torah she-Be'al Peh*, 14 (1972), 159–63. I have found no evidence for viewing this as a later exaggeration (cf. Y. Baer, introduction to *Gezerot*, 4). On the radically different responses to martyrdom and conversion on the part of the Spanish community, see G. D. Cohen, 'Messianic Postures of Ashkenazim and Sepharadim', in M. Kreutzberger, ed., *Studies of the Leo Baeck Institute* (New York, 1967), 115–58. See also B. Lewis, *Jews in Islam* (Princeton, 1984), 82–4. {See now E. Carlebach, *Between History and Hope: Jewish Messianism in Ashkenaz and Sepharad*, Victor J. Selmanowitz Memorial Lecture 3, Touro College Graduate School of Jewish Studies (New York, 1998); and David Berger's cautionary remarks in 'Ha-Meshiḥiyut ha-Sefaradit ve-ha-Meshiḥiyut ha-'Ashkenazit bi-Yemei ha-Beinayim: Beḥinat ha-Maḥloket ha-Historiografit', in J. Hacker et al., eds., *Rishonim ve-'Aḥaronim: Meḥkarim be-Toledot Yisra'el Mugashim le-'Avraham Grossman* (Jerusalem, 2010), 11–28; English translation in id., 'Sephardic and Ashkenazic Messianism in the Middle Ages: An Assessment of the Historiographical Debate', in id., *Cultures in Collision and Conversation: Essays in the Intellectual History of the Jews* (Boston, 2011), 289–311.}

[7] *Teshuvot, Pesakim u-Minhagim shel R. Me'ir mi-Rotenburg*, ed. Y. Z. Cahana, ii (Jerusalem, 1960), *Teshuvot*, #59 {I gave the example of Koblenz from memory and it failed me. The actual case was even more tragic. The father slaughtered his children to prevent their being seized and baptized by the rioters; the riot, however, was put down before it reached his home.}

denied burial, or at best be buried at the far end of the cemetery where the most vile criminals are interred. Such a conclusion, needless to say, was an emotional impossibility, and we need not be surprised if the Franco-German community evolved, in the course of time, a doctrine of the permissibility of voluntary martyrdom, and even one allowing suicide. They did this by scouring all the canonized and semi-canonized literature for supportive tales and hortatory aggadah, all of **|209|** dubious legal worth. But by massing them together, Ashkenazic scholars produced, with a few deft twists, a tenable, if not quite persuasive, case for the permissibility of suicide in times of religious persecution. For murder of one's children few could find a defense, and almost all passed that over in audible silence.[8] **|210|**

[8] See reference in Katz, *Bein Yehudim* (above, n. 4), 91, n. 8; *Exclusiveness and Tolerance* (above, n. 4), 84, n. 3 to which may now be added: *Tosfot Sens*, *'Avodah Zarah* 18a, s.v. *mutav*, in *Shitat ha-Kadmonim 'al 'Avodah Zarah*, ed. M. Y. H. Blau, i (New York, 1969); *Gilyonei Tosafot*, cited in *Ḥiddushei ha-Ritva 'al 'Avodah Zarah*, ed. M Goldstein (Jerusalem, 1978), 18a, s.v. *ha*; *Semak Zurich*, ed. Y. Y. Har-Shoshanim, i (Jerusalem, 1973), Imperatives 3 and 6; *'Arugat ha-Bosem*, ed. E. E. Urbach (Jerusalem, 1939), i. 222; *Tosafot ha-Shalem 'al ha-Torah*, ed. E. Y. Gliss, i (Jerusalem, 1982), on Gen 9: 5 (*Orḥot Ḥayyim, Ḥelek Sheni*, ed. M. Schlesinger [Berlin, 1902], i. 26–7) {and, of course, the responsum of R. Me'ir discussed above and cited in the preceding note}.

Significantly, this defense is made by no less a figure than Rabbenu Tam; and the striking formulation of the *Tosafot* (*'Avodah Zarah* 18a), מצוה לחבל בעצמו ('it is a meritorious deed to hurt [i.e. kill] oneself'), which might be suspect as being a later heightening of a more measured formulation by possibly the greatest Talmudist of the time, is confirmed by the *Tosafot* of Ri's son, R. Elḥanan, the earliest and most direct *reportatio* of the Dampierre: ואומר רבי יעקב . . . סברא היא דשרי ומצוה היא ('R. Ya'akov [i.e. Rabbenu Tam] says it is both logical that it is permitted and it is a meritorious deed'). *Sevara* can be either deductive, inductive, or axiomatic. Clearly, no principle has been stated from which this conclusion has been deduced, nor can this conclusion be inferred from the facts. (Indeed to the extent that there are talmudic data, they point to the opposite conclusion, as the very existence—or the very necessity, one should say—of the *Tosafot* ad loc. indicates.) Rather, suicide is simply axiomatic to Rabbenu Tam. Similarly, when argument is made from *ben sorer u-moreh*, which, as is well known, *lo hayah ve-lo nivra*, no legal argument is being advanced but a religious truism asserted. The same holds true for citing tales of R. Yehudah he-Ḥasid and midrashim on legal issues of life and death.

Subsequent formulations de-emphasized the imperative nature of suicide, but almost all asserted that it was permissible and that those who did so act were *kedoshim*. The defense for murdering children is far more muted. It is absent from the classic works of Ashkenaz but found in scholia. Ritva assumes Rabbenu Tam to be of this opinion, though the text of the *Gilyonei Tosafot* is far from clear on the matter. Indeed, as all other reports of Rabbenu Tam's doctrine confine it to suicide, the concluding remarks ומכאן לומדים לשחוט הנערים ('from here they learn [that it is permissible] to kill the youths') would appear to be those of the *Gilyonei Tosafot*. R. Mosheh of Zurich attributes such a defense to Ravyah. Be that as it may, the practice clearly had popular rabbinic sanction. Needless to say, differing voices on so traumatic an issue were heard, as the passage in the *Tosafot ha-Shalem* indicates, but the protests are anonymous or from men of no consequence (מהר"ש בר' אברהם המכונה אוכמן—Maharash b. Avraham, also called Uchman). {See Afterword.}

R. Shelomoh Luria saw Ri of Dampierre as opposing suicide (*Yam shel Shelomoh, Bava Kamma*

What had taken place was that law and logic had led men to an emotionally intolerable conclusion, one that denied their deepest feelings and, more significantly, their deepest religious intuition, and so the law was reinterpreted. Let us carry this process a step further. Suppose that in the study of talmudic texts the new dialectical method that had emerged in the twelfth century discovered, with its freshly found acuteness, that a number of the practices in the realm of *kashrut*, for example, or in the realm of Sabbath observance, had been in egregious error. Suppose that some practices of centuries, rooted in a monotextual understanding of the Talmud, were now subjected to the harsh glare of dialectic, with its sweeping collation and sharp distinctions, and that these practices were now weighed and found wanting—as wanting they would be found to be. Yet the people who had lived by these practices, who had shaped their lives in the law's accord, were the very same ones who had gone willingly, indeed avidly, to their death, who had lived lives of intense religious observance, climaxed by their giving the ultimate measure of devotion. These same people were now to be shown to have lived out their lives in sin, to have desecrated the Sabbath, to have eaten non-kosher food, to have drunk non-kosher wine, to have poured out their hearts in improper and meaningless prayers. Could such a conclusion be accepted by these communities?

8: 59), but this is highly questionable. Logically, if suicide is not permitted as an escape from fear, then whether that fear is of murder or of baptism should make no difference. The very essence of the Ashkenazic position, however, was that baptism did make a difference. Significantly, Ri is never mentioned in contemporary sources as differing with the regnant opinion. We possess, moreover, two direct reports of Ri's teachings on this subject (*Tosfot R. Elḥanan 'al 'Avodah Zarah*, ed. A. Y. Kreuzer [Jerusalem, 2003] and *Tosfot Sens* in *Shitat ha-Kadmonim 'al 'Avodah Zarah* 18a), and no demurrer is there registered against his uncle's doctrine. Just how deep feelings ran may be seen from the *Yam shel Shelomoh* itself. R. Shelomoh combats at length, and with all his characteristic power, the acceptance of suicide as a legitimate alternative to baptism and then concludes by stating that it is permissible to set one's house on fire, engulfing both oneself and one's family in the flames, in order to avoid baptism. By remaining in the house until the flames reach him, this person would be legally passively *allowing* himself and his family to be killed rather than actively taking life. (Note 27 in the printed *Semak Zurich* is not part of the text itself and is not found in other MSS of the work. It was written in a different hand, as are all the other sundry notes. It claims that a lengthy discussion of the slaughter of children is to be found in the *Mordekhai* on *'Avodah Zarah*. I have not found any such discussion either in the printed *Mordekhai* or in fifteen of the sixteen MSS of that work on file at the Institute of Microfilmed Hebrew Manuscripts of the National Library of Israel. MS Vatican 141 was not available.) {That microfilm is now available, and the passage is not to be found there. Such a passage is, in fact, cited in the name of the *Mordekhai* by Avraham Zakut in *Sefer ha-Yuḥasin* (Frankfurt am Main, 1925) fo. 51a–b. I was referred to this citation by A. Gross, "Al ha-Tismonet ha-Ashkenazit shel Kiddush ha-Shem be-Portugal bi-Shenat 1497', *Tarbiz*, 64 (1995), 96–7. As Gross remarks (n. 34), one does not know whether Zakut saw an actual manuscript of the *Mordekhai* or read a report similar to that of the note in the *Semak Zurich*.}

The answer again is no. And so a similar process of reinterpretation began—of justifying the past in light of, and by means of, the intellectual tools of the present.

The process I have described is, of course, a schematic one and has been used primarily as an expositional device. Self-images are seldom the product of simple linear thinking. But what we unquestionably have before us is the way in which a community's self-image can change the course of its legal thought. The Franco-German community was permeated by a profound sense of its own religiosity, of the rightness of its traditions, and could not imagine any sharp difference between its practices and the law that its |211| members studied and observed with such devotion.[9] The Provençal Jewish community and the Spanish communities, on the other hand, wrestling as they were with, or with what they perceived to be, widespread religious laxity,[10] had no such self-image, and it never occurred to the scholars of these communities, many of whom were in every sense the intellectual heirs of the French Tosafists, to seek to align their people's practices with the written word. Or, more accurately, they never imagined that contemporary conduct was informative of talmudic law, that the deeds of the common folk were revelatory of the Divine intent. The Franco-German community, in its state of intense religiosity, saw the word of God as being, as it were, incarnated in two forms: first, in the canonized literature (i.e. the Talmud); second, in the life of its people. If the new dialectical method, with its sweeping collation of the most varied sources, with its constant juxtaposition of contradictory passages, discovered that among the contradictions uncovered was one not simply

[9] See above, n. 4, and J. Katz, 'Ma'ariv bi-Zemano ve-Shelo bi-Zemano: Dugma le-Zikah bein Minhag, Halakhah ve-Ḥevrah', *Zion*, 35 (1971), 35–60; and now A. Mintz, *Hurban: Responses to Catastrophe in Hebrew Literature* (New York, 1984), 84–108. {Katz's study was reprinted in his collection of essays entitled *Halakhah ve-Kabbalah: Meḥkarim be-Toledot Dat Yisra'el 'al Medoreiha ve-Zikatah ha-Ḥevratit* (Jerusalem, 1984), 175–200. English translation in J. Katz, *Divine Law in Human Hands: Case Studies in Halakhic Flexibility* (Jerusalem, 1998), 88–110.}

I do not perceive a similar attitude reflected in the responsum of R. Hai Ga'on, *Otsar ha-Ge'onim, Rosh ha-Shanah*, ed. B. M. Levin (Jerusalem, 1938), 60–8. First, the thrust there is polemical, a defense of rabbinic traditions about shofar-blowing against Karaite criticism. More significantly, I have not discovered any systematic reworking of *areas* in the halakhah of *issur ve-heter* in the writings of the Ge'onim so as to align them with communal practice. Intellectual history is the study of the actual intellectual work of a period, not of occasional proclamations. This point cannot be overemphasized. The Ge'onim did revise commercial law extensively. This area, however, creates no legal or religious problems, for *hefker bet din hefker*. No such rule obtains in the area of ritual law, and *minhag* can never cancel out an unquestionable *issur*. It is in this area that the communal self-image must arise, systematically raising common practice to the level of a quasi-text, and thus allowing its integration into the halakhic process.

[10] Y. Baer, *A History of the Jews in Christian Spain*, i (Philadelphia, 1966), 236–61 and *passim*.

between a passage in the first volume of the Talmud and another passage in the last, but between a passage in the Talmud and the practice of a God-fearing community, to the Tosafists the problem was one and the same. The resolutional tool of dialectic was and is distinction, and whether the conflict was between two passages in the law or between life and law, to the Tosafists the solution to both was a radical interpretation of the halakhah.

This self-image was unique to the Ashkenazic community and was not shared by other European Jewish communities in the medieval world. But |212| its origins elude us. The Crusade experience, while strongly reinforcing this image, did not in itself create it. It is already reflected in the earliest writings issuing from the Rhineland, those of Rabbenu Gershom Me'or ha-Golah.[11] Coeval with its literary remains, the source of this self-image perforce lies beyond the realm of documentation and decipherment. But that which sustained this image falls within this realm, and now demands our attention.

Clearly, so large a topic exceeds the format of a lecture, and it would be a bold man indeed who would claim to know in full what nurtures and sustains a collective psyche. I would simply like to draw attention to four factors that were possibly conducive to this Ashkenazic mentality.

First, the simplicity of religious beliefs. The Ashkenazic community never developed, possibly never wrote, a line of religious philosophy. This is bad for philosophy, but good for religiosity, if we define religiosity, as Geertz once did, as 'being held by religious ideas rather than holding them'. For religious philosophy is an act of justification. It seeks to make the beliefs and practices of a religion comprehensible in the terms of another system. Implicit in the act of translation is the assumption that the categories of the other system are the dominant ones. They are the notions that yield comprehension and bestow value. Otherwise why translate? The surrounding civilization had made few cultural inroads. And even at the point of direct encounter, that of Christian–Jewish polemics, the issues were exegetical, not philosophical.[12] One problem

[11] H. Soloveitchik, 'Pawnbroking: A Study in *Ribbit* and of the Halakhah in Exile', *Proceedings of the American Academy for Jewish Research*, 38–9 (1972), 235–9, esp. 239. {The passages are found in the expanded version of the article in this volume, Chapter 6 above, esp. pp. 112, 138. I offer a suggestion as to the origin of this self-image in '"The Third Yeshivah of Bavel" and the Cultural Origins of Ashkenaz: A Proposal', which will appear in the second volume of this series.}

[12] Note the absence of Ashkenazic writers in D. Lasker, *Jewish Philosophical Polemics Against Christianity in the Middle Ages* (New York, 1977). Contrast this with D. Berger, *The Jewish–Christian Debate in the High Middle Ages* (Philadelphia, 1979). Whether philosophy played the major corrosive role in Spain that Yitsḥak Baer attributed to it is an open question. Certainly it did not help. For bibliography on this issue, see B. Septimus, 'Narboni and Shem Tov on Martyrdom', in I. Twersky, ed.,

did arise, that of anthropomorphism, |213| but significantly this is of internal rather than external origin. We have, however, no way of knowing on which side of the matter the bulk of the community—scholars and simple people alike—stood. Indeed, the total silence in all other sources on what, to our way of thinking, is a fundamental theological issue, the absence of any attempt to marshal support, political or rabbinic, against positions that to each side were the rankest heresy, makes one suspect that the celebrated controversy between R. Mosheh Taku and the Pietists[13] was, if not quite a tempest in a teacup, then an in-house affair, and that most people knew little and cared less one way or the other. When they prayed, they prayed to the God of their fathers—as most men do.

Second, correlative with this simplicity was the absence of religious alternatives. Conversion as a cultural phenomenon was not perceived as being an actuality. People did convert—a good number of them,[14] some from conviction, some from desire for advancement, and some, possibly most, from sheer weariness. But at no time did the Tosafists see the ground being eroded from

Studies in Medieval Jewish History and Literature (Cambridge, Mass., 1984), 447, n. 1. (My remarks are confined to the 12th and 13th centuries, the period of the *ba'alei ha-Tosafot*, which in Germany comes effectively to an end in 1303 with the emigration of R. Asher and decisively to an end in France with the expulsion of 1306. I must, however, register here my misgivings about the exaggerated inferences that have been drawn from E. Kupfer, 'Li-Demutah ha-Tarbutit shel Yahadut Ashkenaz ve-Ḥakhameiha ba-Me'ot ha-Yod Dalet ve-ha-Tet-Vav', *Tarbiz*, 42 (1973), 113–47. My own study has confirmed what I initially heard from Professor Mordekhai Breuer: an examination of the origins of the individuals involved, and of their concentration in one culturally unique city, Prague, would mitigate considerably the far-reaching conclusions that have been drawn from the material published by Kupfer. H. H. Ben-Sasson's position on the extent of the currents of philosophical speculation in Germany at the end of the 14th and through the 15th century {in *Perakim be-Toledot ha-Yehudim bi-Yemei ha-Beinayim* (Tel Aviv, 1962), 205–6, and in id., *Trial and Achievement—Currents in Jewish History* (Jerusalem, 1974), 155} may be in need of some modification but has not, to my mind, been effectively shaken.

13 *Ketav Tamim* in *Otsar Neḥmad*, 3 (1860), 54–90. For literature and discussion, see Y. Dan, *Ketav Tamim MS Paris H 711* (Jerusalem, 1984), introduction.

14 e.g. references given by Katz, *Bein Yehudim* (above, n. 4), ch. 6; S. W. Baron, *A Social and Religious History of the Jews*, v (Philadelphia, 1957), 112–14, 340–1; R. Chazan, *Medieval Jewry in Northern France* (Maryland, 1973), 146–7, 189–90, 195–6. {A. Haverkamp, 'Baptized Jews in German Lands during the Twelfth Century', in M. A. Signer and J. Van Engen, eds., *Jews and Christians in Twelfth Century Europe* (Notre Dame, 2001), 234–54; C. Levin, 'Jewish Conversion to Christianity in Medieval Northern Europe: Encountered and Imagined, 1100–1300' (Ph.D diss., New York University, 2006).} I personally would treat with some reservations the reports of 16th-century chroniclers, such as Ibn Yaḥya and Usque, who, fresh from the Spanish trauma, wrote of the 1182 expulsion by Philip II, *ve-rubam hemiru*. No contemporary source records this, and the Latin sources cited by Chazan specifically state that few converted. See also A. David, 'Mif'alo ha-Historiografi shel Gedalyah Ibn Yaḥya, Ba'al Shalshelet ha-Kabbalah' (Ph.D. diss., Hebrew University of Jerusalem, 1976), 335, n. 11.

under the feet of Judaism.[15] The basic allegiance of the populace was unquestioned, and this finds expression in the historiography of the period. |214|

For all their vividness, the crusade chronicles are hortatory: they describe martyrdom so as to induce emulation. Yet despite their desire to emphasize and extol, and by so doing to educate and inspire, there are repeated accounts of apostasy—in Kerpen and Geldern, in Mors and Treves, a large number in Metz; and in the venerable city of Regensburg, the entire community went, albeit unwillingly, to the baptismal font.[16] To all the various narrators—writing, it should be emphasized, at different times and in different places—such events were forced, momentary lapses, moments to be pitied rather than to be feared.[17] It never occurred to any of them that what had transpired was a result of anything other than overwhelming duress.

[15] The report of R. Yonah of Gerona expressed vividly the Ashkenazic viewpoint about the inherent improbability of voluntary conversion to Christianity (*Teshuvot She'alot le-ha-Rashba* [*sic*], Rome *c.*1470, #179; ed. A. Zalaznik, Jerusalem 2001, vii. 179):

> עוד מפ׳ ה״ר יונה ז״ל פסק בענין יין נסך. ששמע (לפסוק) [לפסק] לחכמי צרפת: כי משומד לע״ז והוא הולך ממקום למקום, ובעיר אחת הוא מאמין בע״ז בפני גוים, ובעיר אחרת נכנס בבית ישראל ואומר שהוא יהודי, ואין אנו יודעים אם הוא יהודי אם לאו . . . הפסק כן הוא: יען שהוא אומר לנו שהוא יהודי אינו עושה יין נסך, והטעם כי הע״ז מלתא דמסתבר הוא שיהיה שקר. וכשהוא אומר שמאמין בה, הוא עושה להנאת יצרו הרע ואינו מאמינו בלבו. וכשהוא אומר לנו שהוא ישראל, הוא אומר בלב טוב מפני שאמונתו היא אמונה ישרה וטובה ונכונה ואמתית ומילתא דמסתבר היא.

> Another ruling of R. Yonah, may he rest in peace, in the matter of *yein nesekh*, one that he heard from the French scholars. An apostate goes from place to place; in one city he [states] that he believes in idolatry [i.e. Christianity] and in another city he enters Jewish homes and says that he is a Jew, and we don't know whether he is or is not a Jew . . . This is the ruling: since he tells us that he is a Jew, [his touch] does not make *yein nesekh*. The reason being that it is [only] reasonable that idolatry [i.e. Christianity] is false, and [when] he says that he believes in it, [he does so] for his own wicked, personal advantage but doesn't really believe in it. When [however] he says that he is Jewish, he says it with a good [i.e. honest] heart for his belief [i.e. that what he believes in] is straight, good, correct and true, and it is a reasonable thing.

Not everyone would go this distance and turn this perspective into an absolute legal presumption. There are all types of people, and specific cases should be treated individually, especially in such weighty matters as *'agunah* (*Mordekhai*, *Ketubbot*, #306). My attention was drawn to both these sources by E. E. Urbach, *Ba'alei ha-Tosafot* (above, n. 1), 245.

[16] *Gezerot* (above, n. 6), 25, 43, 51, 56, 73, 80, 94–6. {*Hebräische Berichte* (above, n. 6), 445, 461 ('Mere' and not 'Mors'—see ibid. 39, n. 13), 467, 479, 481.} See now R. Chazan, *European Jewry* (above, n. 6), 99–136.

[17] The considerable effort that has been expended over the past century in determining the priority of the several chronicles, their common or different sources, and the roles of the different editors is a consequence of their sharing a common view, and a common religious and historical outlook. All chronicles being of the same hue, differentiation has had to be made on the basis of minor cracks in the narrative and variations in historical detail and emphasis. (For the literature, see Y. Hacker, 'Li-Gezerot Tatnu', *Zion*, 31 [1966], 233, n. 1, to which one should add the recent research of R. Chazan, 'The First-Crusade Chronicles', *Revue des études juives*, 133 [1974], 235–54; 'The Hebrew First-

When a person harbors within him conflicting sentiments, and an overwhelming force emerges from without, the question will inevitably arise (and unsolvable it will remain) to what extent the individual was simply a victim of circumstances and to what extent his conduct was a consequence of his inner ambiguities. Such a question, which arose constantly in Spain, haunted its history, and still hovers over its historiography,[18] never raised its head in Ashkenaz. *All*, to the chroniclers, was the result of outside circumstances,[19] and, as the fidelity of the converts was unquestioned, no ill word |215| was to be uttered against them (והמדבר עליהם רעה, כאילו מדבר [!] פני השכינה).[20] It furthermore never occurred to any of these chroniclers that in recording these lapses, in praising the religious observance of the apostates during the period of enforced Christianity,[21] and in emphasizing that those who failed the test were beyond rebuke they might awaken in the minds of their readers the notion that there existed in times of persecution, if not a viable, at least a tolerable alternative to excruciating martyrdom. Rightly or wrongly, the Ashkenazic community was convinced of the basic loyalty of its people and that, irrespective of what individuals might do, the community as a whole would stick fast to the course, even if it meant its physical doom.

Third, there was an ongoing and ever-broadening acceptance of the law by the people. It is in the tosafist period that the Jewish kitchen was fettered. As a

Crusade Chronicles: Further Reflections', *AJS Review*, 3 [1978], 79–99.) {See now *Hebräische Berichte* (above, n. 6), 34–244.}

18 See Y. H. Yerushalmi, *From Spanish Court to Italian Ghetto* (New York, 1971), 21–42, for a full discussion.

19 See now Mintz, *Hurban* (above, n. 9), ch. 2, esp. pp. 90–2. The chroniclers' view of *anusim* differs little from that of Rashi (*Teshuvot Rashi*, ed. Y. S. Elfenbein [New York, 1943], #168). (Note the tone of the query and that of the reply.) See also R. Asher in *Zikhron Yehudah* (Berlin, 1846), fos. 50v–51v; ed. A. Y. Ḥavatselet (Jerusalem, 2005), #92: 65, 69 (pp. 124–5). (It should be noted that R. Asher's opponents did not question the unfaltering allegiance of the *anusim* but rather his assumption that *every* infraction committed during their enforced Christianity was a consequence of direct duress and that they were, therefore, legally spotless. His opponents contended that the *anusim* occasionally breached the law—to which they aspired to return and subsequently did—either out of fatigue or convenience. And this had legal repercussions.)

20 {*Hebräische Berichte* (above, n. 6), 481, 483}; *Gezerot* (above, n. 6), 56–7 and *passim*.

21 Ibid. ועתה נאה לנו לספר בשבח הנאנסים ('and now it is only appropriate for us to speak in praise of the coerced ones [i.e. the forced converts]'). Christian chroniclers confirm the fact that most converts returned to the fold. Sources are excerpted in J. Aronius, *Regesten zur Geschichte der Juden im Fränkischen und Deutschen Reiche bis zum Jahre 1273* (Berlin, 1903), ##189, 202, 203, 206, 218. B.-Z. Dinur, *Yisra'el ba-Golah*, i (Jerusalem and Tel Aviv, 1965), 1, 31, 43–5. Baron, *Social and Religious History* (above, n. 14), iv. 284 n. 12, and 293 n. 21. (Let me be clear. I am not stating that all three chronicles describe specific conversions in different cities to the same degree, but this is a function of the respective degrees of historical detail and geographic emphasis of the several narratives. All, however, speak openly and unabashedly about conversion.)

result of the dialectical approach, conclusion after conclusion was being drawn from the Talmud and the religious norm expanded to undreamt-of frontiers. It was during the era of the Tosafists that the few lines in the Talmud about salting meat were transformed into much (though not all) of that comprehensive set of regulations that confronts us in the *Sha'arei Dura*, and that the few pages and half-pages in *Kol ha-Basar* yielded up the complex halakhic universe of *basar be-ḥalav* (the laws of milk and meat).

But in saying this are we not assuming that this theoretical efflorescence was swiftly translated into practice? That Jewish life in the time of R. Mosheh Isserles in sixteenth-century Poland was effectively regulated by tosafist thought is unquestioned. But what evidence do we have of contemporary conduct?

Unquestionably, the great men of Dampierre thought their words of practical significance, and R. Barukh of Worms, possibly at R. Yitsḥak's request, wrote the *Sefer ha-Terumah*.[22] When the itinerant preacher |216| R. Mosheh of Coucy decided to put into writing what he had preached, what he inscribed was pure tosafist doctrine (laced with considerable Maimonideanisms),[23] as was R. Yitsḥak of Corbeil's *Semak*, the most copied and annotated Ashkenazic code of the Middle Ages.

We come closer to the popular when we turn to the host of tiny handbooks found primarily in manuscript (and most probably destined to remain there). In the absence of any authoritative code before the middle of the thirteenth century, scholars or would-be scholars would compile for their own use a little compendium of some three or four pages on *yein nesekh* or some aspect of *kashrut* or Sabbath observance. These works are bereft of any value, but they amply demonstrate that the conception of Talmud, even in the mind of the most mediocre writer, was wholly a tosafist one. If people thought like a Tosafist, they were likely to act like one.

Any doubts on the matter are laid to rest by the responsa literature. I do not refer to simple statements of 'and we follow Rabbenu Tam's opinion'. Such a simplistic approach towards the history of halakhic praxis would not get us far. I refer instead to the fact that numerous queries would make no sense unless one assumed that this doctrine of Rabbenu Tam or that one of Ri was common practice, and many replies would be incomprehensible without the assumption that Ravan's doctrine or that of R. Simḥah held sway in a certain region. It is still difficult to chart the pattern of penetration—which doctrines penetrated when and how quickly—but that contemporary tosafist thought

22 Urbach, *Ba'alei ha-Tosafot* (above, n. 1), 349.

23 *Sefer Mitsvot Gadol*, 2 vols., ed. S. Schlesinger (Jerusalem, 1989, 1995).

was percolating downward is the ineluctable conclusion of any study of the unarticulated assumptions of the literature of the period. The academies were not speaking to themselves. The contours of religious conduct were being effectively shaped by tosafist thought, and the people were slowly but surely accepting an ongoing thickening of the heavenly yoke.

Fourth, there was a refusal on the part of the people to maximize their allowances. Given the centrality and omnipresence of wine in medieval society, the injunction against *yein nesekh* imposed an enormous economic burden. Moreover, *yein nesekh* had long been considered a classic example of *insolentia Judaeorum*. One of the earliest anti-Jewish (possibly antisemitic) tracts written in the Middle Ages, that of Agobard of Lyons, mentions with bitterness the rule that Gentile touch defiled liquids and made them unfit for |217| Jewish consumption. From *privilegia* granting to the Jews the right to sell their wine one can see how deeply resented was the implied Jewish superiority assumed to be contained in this injunction. No less a person than Innocent III lashed out at this presumptuousness. Gentile goodwill was needed by all; *yein nesekh* was an omnipresent irritant, and Jews had much to gain by its allowance.[24] Occasion presented itself to the Tosafists to wipe *yein nesekh* from the books, but the idea was rejected with shock.[25] Spanish Jews, for example, were lax in

[24] *Patrologia Latina*, ed. J. P. Migne, vol. civ, p. 826 {Agobard of Lyon, *Opera Omnia*. L. van Acker, ed., *Corpus Christianorum*, Continuatio Medievalis 52 (Turnhout, 1981), 193}; *Patrologia Latina*, vol. cxvii, p. 170; Aronius, *Regesten* (above, n. 21), 90; R. Hoeniger, 'Zur Geschichte der Juden Deutschlands im Mittelalter', *Zeitschrift für die Geschichte der Juden in Deutschland*, 1 (1887), 141; S. Grayzel, *The Church and the Jews in the XIIIth Century*, revised edn. (New York, 1966), 73, 127–8. {For the later Middle Ages, see G. Mentgen, *Studien zur Geschichte der Juden im mittelalterlichen Elsaß*, Forschungen zur Geschichte der Juden 2 (Hanover, 1995), 560, 612.} See also the remark of R. S. Lopez in his review of I. A. Agus, *Urban Civilization in Pre-Crusade Europe* (New York, 1965), in *Speculum*, 42 (1967), 343. {In this paragraph I have borrowed the formulations found in 'Can Halakhic Texts Talk History?' (Chapter 7 above).}

[25] *Tosafot*, *'Avodah Zarah* 57b, s.v. *le-apukei*. See H. Soloveitchik, *Minhag, Metsi'ut* (above, n. 4), ch. 3 {*Ha-Yayin bi-Yemei ha-Beinayim* (above, n. 4), 363–4}. The German Pietists were unabashed in their criticism of the shortcomings of their people, yet no mention is to be found in *Sefer Ḥasidim* of drinking *yein nesekh*. There were, of course, people who drank, as there were those who transgressed other injunctions, but *yein nesekh* is mentioned in only three of some seventy penitentials (MSS Vatican Heb. 183, fo. 177b; Munich Heb. 232, fo. 22b; Parma, De Rossi, 1048, fo. 17a). A more accurate gauge would be to say that it is wholly absent from the HTR genre, found in one contaminated text of the HTRB group, and in two of the three MSS of the IT genre. On this classification and for the list of MSS, see I. G. Marcus, 'Ḥasidei Ashkenaz Private Penitentials: An Introduction and Descriptive Catalogue of Their Manuscripts and Early Editions', in Y. Dan and F. Talmage, eds., *Studies in Jewish Mysticism: Proceedings of Regional Conferences held at the University of California, Los Angeles, and McGill University in April, 1978* (Cambridge, Mass., 1982), 57–83. The text of MS Vatican Heb. 183 was published in typescript in a sourcebook for a course at the Hebrew University by Y. Hacker, entitled

their observance of this injunction,[26] and made attempts to rid themselves of this annoying restraint. I have found, however, no evidence for anything similar in France or Germany.

I have chosen *yein nesekh* as illustration because it constitutes an entire injunctive area, and its costs were dramatic. But there are numerous issues in other areas where practice was *far more conservative* than theory. This is significant both psychologically and religiously. Every restriction is an added burden, and a host of voluntarily assumed burdens can create the image of a people struggling to live its religious life amid a recalcitrant reality. To entertain the idea that this endeavor might end in failure is a |218| psychological impossibility for many, and some halakhists will see in the people's need a Divine mandate for action, and in the course of time the intractable will be rendered permissible.

I have used the phrase 'Divine mandate' advisedly. The oft-cited words of Rabbenu Tam, the greatest Tosafist (d. 1171), are without parallel in medieval literature for their explicitness. He proclaimed that he was openly embarking upon a radical judicial construction in order to alleviate the Jewish economic plight: **נראה בעיני היתר גמור ומצוה מן המובחר לתת מחיה לבני ברית** ('I deem it perfectly permissible, indeed a Divine mandate, so as to provide sustenance for my co-religionists'). These famous words were addressed not simply to the public at large—they had reasonably sufficient allowances at their disposal—but to those deeply observant Jews who—in the mid-twelfth century, when moneylending was fast becoming the staff of Jewish life—still refused to avail themselves of previous legal fictions that had unfettered intra-Jewish credit, and were eking out their living faithful to the old injunctive teachings of the Rhineland. It was *their* plight, the plight of the pious and devout, that inspired this unprecedented boldness, and it was to overcome *their* hesitancy in availing

Be'ayot Nivḥarot be-Ḥeker Yahadut Ashkenaz, i, produced by the student organization's Akademon Press (Jerusalem, 1974), 41.

[26] e.g. Maimonides, 'Hilkhot Ma'akhalot Asurot', 11: 10; *Teshuvot ha-Rambam*, ed. J. Blau (Jerusalem, 1960), ii, #269; Abraham b. Nathan ha-Yarḥi, *Sefer ha-Manhig*, ed. Y. Rafael (Jerusalem, 1978), ii. 660. More qualifiedly, *Teshuvot Rivash*, ed. D. Metsger (Jerusalem 1993), i, #180; *Teshuvot Tashbets*, ed. Y. Katan (Jerusalem, 1998), i, #29; *Teshuvot Rashba*, ed. A. Zalaznik (Jerusalem 1998), iv, #149. *Teshuvot Rashba*, ed. A. Zalaznik (Jerusalem, 1997), i, ##717, 813, and *Teshuvot Tashbets*, i, #85, cannot be cited as evidence of actual practice. *Teshuvot ha-Rashba*, ed. A. Zalaznik [Jerusalem, 2001], vii, #528) is not by Rashba but is one of a series of excerpts from the *Orḥot Ḥayyim, Ḥelek Sheni* (above, n. 8). {On the composite nature of what is commonly called 'volume seven' of the *Teshuvot ha-Rashba*, see the editor's introduction to the Jerusalem edition, p. 9, and the introduction of S. Z. Havlin to the reproduction of the *Teshuvot She'elot le-ha-Rashba, Defus Rishon, Roma c.1470*, published by the National Library of Israel (Jerusalem, 1977), 25.}

themselves of existing allowances that that impatient genius wrote at uncharacteristic length, emphasizing that this was no abstract allowance on his part, but that he himself had personally so ruled in cases involving members of his own family, and concluded: **הארכתי בדבר למען דעת כל אדם שהוא היתר גמור** ('I have dwelt on this arrangement at length so that **everyone** should know that it is **fully** permissible'; emphasis added).[27] |219|

On another level the refusal of the people to maximize their allowances may be taken as the workings of a religious intuition alongside which the written word pales.[28]

This final point is an important one; it can perhaps best be brought home by making it more contemporary. I remember my own shock when, after studying 'Yoreh De'ah', I realized that there is no need for separate milk and meat dishtowels, dishracks, or cabinets, and that if food is served cold, there is no need for separate dishware altogether. Again, there is all the difference in the world between not having *ḥamets* (bread) in the house (*bal yera'eh u-val yimatse*) and the house being what we call *pesaḥdik* (fit for Passover use).[29]

[27] *Or Zarua'*, iii (Jerusalem, 1887), *Bava Metsi'a*, #202. I must here modify the assessment I made in 'Pawnbroking: A Study in *Ribbit*' (above, n. 11), 251 (the modification has now been incorporated in the expanded version of the article in this volume at p. 133). I did not then notice the insistently suasive element in Rabbenu Tam's declaration: his emphasis that he *himself* ruled thus, in cases involving members of *his own* family. And finally, I missed the significance of the two words **כל** (all) and **גמור** (fully) in his concluding remarks cited in the text. People in search of an allowance needn't be assured that it is **היתר גמור** (fully permissible); the word 'permissible' from the lips of Rabbenu Tam would have more than sufficed. Nor would they be interested in knowing whether the respondent himself practiced these allowances. The entire thrust of the declaration now seems to me to be aimed at the group that still abided by the century-long tradition of the Rhineland, which had now received new and emphatic validation from Rabbenu Tam's elder brother, Rashbam ('Pawnbroking: A Study in *Ribbit*' [above, n. 11], 241–2; expanded version, above, p. 129). To be sure, Rabbenu Tam's sweeping allowance answered a general need by removing the highly inconvenient restrictions still present in Rashi's legal fiction (and I have no doubt that Rabbenu Tam was fully aware of this). This, however, does not now seem to me to be the motivating force behind Tam's declaration, and certainly it is not the general audience that he is here primarily addressing, but rather one that he strongly feels needs persuading. To sum up, I would say that his doctrine abolishing the law of *le-ḥumra* (ibid. 252; expanded version, above, pp. 130–2) was indeed motivated by the desire to unfetter completely intra-Jewish credit by use of the Gentile straw man. For most people an allowance by Rabbenu Tam sufficed. Others felt his doctrine to be too radical and without sufficient basis, and if rejecting it entailed major financial losses, that had to be accepted. It is to this group that Rabbenu Tam addressed his famous declaration, though of course it had implications for all. And in time the doctrine of *silluk* became the standard form of intra-Jewish credit.

[28] This lecture was written in 1982. Since then Jacob Katz has traced the presence and complexities of what he terms 'ritual instinct' in his superb *Goy Shel Shabbat* (Jerusalem, 1984); English translation: *"The Shabbes Goy": A Study in Halakhic Flexibility* (Philadelphia, 1989).

[29] I am using the traditional east European kitchen as an expositional device and am not here claiming that eastern Europe reproduced the cultural milieu of Ashkenaz that I have attempted to

The simple truth is that the traditional Jewish kitchen and pre-Passover preparations have little to do with halakhic dictates. They have been immeasurably and unrecognizably amplified by popular religious intuition. We all know this, but our religious sense, our religious experience, belie this knowledge, and our instincts reject this fact out of hand. To serve cold cuts on a 'dairy' dish is *treif*—everything in 'Yoreh De'ah' to the contrary notwithstanding.

The prevalent has not here expanded the normative, it *is* the normative, and anything less is inconceivable. Once the existing becomes identified with the appropriate (as it does in any vibrant traditional society), this identity can easily spill over and legitimize practices that fall beyond the halakhic perimeter. But legitimacy there beckons only because at the halakhic center the prevalent, the accepted, the traditional is far richer and 'righter' than the skeletal written word. The greater the increment of religion-as-practiced over religion-as-known, the broader and richer the domain of religion-as-experienced |**220**| over religion-as-prescribed, the greater the confidence in the religious intuition of the people.

But in talking about religious simplicity, undivided allegiance, thickening of the heavenly yoke, and refusal to maximize allowances, have we not forgotten that there were murderers, lechers, apostates, informers, thieves, and Sabbath violators in Ashkenaz, no less than in Sefarad? There was hardly a charge leveled in Spain, except perhaps that of religious skepticism, that did not find its counterpart in Germany. Have I not painted an idealized portrait of Ashkenaz? Or, if my analysis is correct, did not Ashkenaz have an idealized image of itself?

Frankly, one is hard pressed to answer that question. For, like most large questions, it is actually composed of a number of smaller, subtler ones. When is an unreflecting faith 'religiosity', and when is it philistinism? When is cowering before a hideous death simply a failure of nerve, and when does it betoken a weakness of the spirit? When is a series of breaches just that, and when does it signify erosion? When does a mute cry for help arise from an inability to cope, and when from a lack of will to cope? When is a refusal to live life as freely and fully as sanctioned by the law a mark of religious intuition,

outline in this paper. (There are certain similarities and filiations, and these have been set forth in a paper delivered at the Kotlar Institute for the Study of Contemporary Judaism of Bar-Ilan University. This, however, is a wholly separate issue and is neither related to nor in any way implied by my argument here. {The paper was subsequently expanded and published as 'Rupture and Reconstruction: The Transformation of Contemporary Orthodoxy', *Tradition*, 28 (1994), 64–131; the essay will be included in my forthcoming volume of the same title.}

and when is it a misplaced, foolish piety? In each case the line between the alternatives is too fine, for me at least, to perceive from a distance of over half a millennium. Perhaps these questions *are* best left to the judgment of contemporaries.

Whether Ashkenaz was right in her pride or Sefarad wrong in her sense of guilt, I cannot say. I believe that we can say that their different self-images shaped, in many areas, the respective courses of their halakhic thought. |221|

AFTERWORD

NOTE 8

I took as self-evident the weakness of the tosafist arguments justifying suicide when fearing that one might apostatize and gave only the basic documentation and relegated that to a footnote. I swiftly discovered that many of my contemporaries felt differently about the matter, and felt rather strongly. For example, A. Grossman, 'Shorashav shel Kiddush ha-Shem be-Ashkenaz ha-Kedumah', in I. F. Gafni and A. Ravitzky, eds., *Kedushat ha-Ḥayyim ve-Ḥeruf ha-Nefesh: Kovets Ma'amarim le-Zikhro shel 'Amir Yekuti'el* (Jerusalem, 1991), 99–130; I. M. Ta-Shma, 'Hit'abdut ve-Retsaḥ ha-Zulat 'al Kiddush ha-Shem: li-She'elat Mekomah shel ha-Aggadah be-Masoret ha-Pesikah ha-'Ashkenazit', in Y. T. Assis et al., eds., *Yehudim mul ha-Tselav: Gezerot Tatnu ba-Historiyah u-va-Historiografiyah* (Jerusalem, 2000) 150–6; reprinted in id., *Keneset Meḥkarim*, i (Jerusalem, 2005), 388–94; E. Kanarfogel, 'Halakha and *Metziut* (realia) in Medieval Ashkenaz: Surveying the Parameters and Defining the Limits', *Jewish Law Annual*, 14 (2003), 193–224; I. Marcus, 'The Dynamics of Jewish Renaissance and Renewal', in M. Signer and J. Van Engen, eds., *Jews and Christians in Twelfth-Century Europe* (Notre Dame, 2001), 36.

As a consequence of this sustained critique, I felt the need to set forth my reasoning in much greater detail. It appeared as 'Halakhah, Hermeneutics and Martyrdom in *Ashkenaz*', *Jewish Quarterly Review*, 94 (2004), 77–108, 278–99. In the Afterword of that essay, I also present the basis of my claim that the Tosafists were of the opinion that *ben sorer u-moreh lo hayah ve-lo nivra*. The essay will appear in the second volume of this series.

PAGE 242

The statement 'Life is not optional in Judaism' should be qualified by the remarks in 'Halakhah, Hermeneutics and Martyrdom in *Ashkenaz*', p. 90, n. 27 (see continuation of note 8 above).

NOTE 12

See now D. J. Lasker, 'Jewish Philosophical Polemics in Ashkenaz', in O. Limor and G. Stroumsa, eds., *Contra Judaeos: Ancient and Medieval Polemics between Christian and Jews* (Tübingen, 1995), 195–213. The most that can be said is that there *may* be some *hints* of philosophical polemic in two texts of the mid-13th century, but no philosophical argument is to be found in the Ashkenazic literature of the period under discussion, 1000–1300, the era of pre-Crusade Ashkenaz and that of the Tosafists.

D. Lasker has expanded somewhat his claims in 'Popular Polemics and Philosophical Truth in the Medieval Critique of Christianity', *The Journal of Jewish Thought and Philosophy*, 8 (1999), 243–59, and argues (p. 254 ff.) that polemicists themselves had a knowledge of philosophy but did not bring it to the fore in view of the limitations of their audiences. I find myself in full agreement with David Berger's evaluation of this argument and more generally with his overall assessment of the attainment in philosophy of all classes in Ashkenaz. See D. Berger, 'Polemic, Exegesis, Philosophy and Science: On the Tenacity of Ashkenazic Modes of Thought', *Jahrbuch des Simon-Dubnow-Instituts*, 8 (2009), 27–40; reprinted in id., *Cultures in Collision and Conversation: Essays in the Intellectual History of the Jews* (Boston, 2011), 152–66. One sentence of his (*Jahrbuch*, p. 28; *Cultures*, p. 153) bears quoting and remembering in light of the recurrent tendency in scholarship to revisionism: 'Exceptions remain exceptions; allusions remain allusions; rejection of anthropomorphism is in itself not rationalism; and reading a few books does not necessarily alter deeply entrenched modes of thought.'

PAGES 248–9

In the past decade or two some historians have claimed that baptism constituted a serious temptation for the Ashkenazic community. I feel that its attraction was, perhaps, somewhat greater than the Tosafists perceived, but still far less than contemporary historiography portrays it as being. I hope to address this issue in a separate essay.

NOTE 25

In this note I documented the refusal of the Ashkenazic community to abolish de facto the injunction against *yein nesekh*. This would have been a radical step, though one taken by many in the Jewish communities of Spain and Italy and later in Moravia. More significant, perhaps, is the refusal of Ashkenazic Jewry to utilize numerous allowances within the injunctive framework of *yein nesekh* as, for example, employing Gentile labor in the backbreaking work of treading the tubs of grapes (see above, p. 213). In the next essay, '"Religious Law and Change" Revisited', I have detailed their refusal to adopt other allowances offered to them by their halakhists, Rashi and the Ba'alei ha-Tosafot.

CHAPTER TEN
'Religious Law and Change' Revisited

FROM QUERIES RECEIVED over the years about 'Religious Law and Change', it is clear that I should have prefaced that article with a distinction that Jacob Katz used to make between two terms: *minhag* and *nohag*. These may be roughly translated as 'custom' and 'customary practice'; better yet, 'custom' and 'habitual practice'. The exact terminology isn't significant; the different concepts conveyed by these two words are. Custom (*minhag*) has a recognized threefold place in halakhah. It may adjudicate between two halakhic views, as in 'The custom of Ashkenaz is to follow *Tosafot*; that of Sefarad to follow Maimonides'. It may tilt the balance of an issue in which the law is unclear (*be-makom she-ha-halakhah rofefet*).[1] Finally, it may determine conduct in the interstices of the halakhah, there being no directives in the normative literature on the subject. Much of our daily prayer is custom, and such phrases as 'in Poland it is customary not to recite *av ha-raḥamim* on this Sabbath' or 'at this point in prayer the Sefardim add . . .' abound in the literature. What characterizes *minhag*, custom, in all these three instances is that the practices described are both legitimate and recognized by their practitioners as part of the religious inheritance of the community. When it comes to local *minhag*, all Jewish communities are remarkably tenacious in defending their customs and vindicating their religious traditions, and little distinction can be drawn among different Jewish cultures of the Middle Ages, or of the modern period for that matter. *Nohag*, 'habitual practice', on the other hand, refers to conduct that is not viewed as custom, not perceived as part of a conscious religious tradition, but simply the way people of a community have traditionally acted on the *assumption* that these practices are legitimate, are in accord with the halakhah.

The subject of both this essay and 'Religious Law and Change' is *nohag*.

[1] JT *Pe'ah* 7: 6; fo. 20c, in the Venice edition; col. 108 in the edition of the Academy of Hebrew Language (Jerusalem, 2001).

What happens when a received practice is discovered to contravene the halakhah? This question is made even more acute when the matter touches upon something enjoined by the halakhah (*issur ve-heter*), as consumption of non-kosher foods, in view of the unquestioned rule that neither custom nor habitual practice can allow that which the halakhah clearly forbids.[2] It is in its attitude towards habitual practice that Ashkenaz parts company with other Jewish cultures.

In my essay 'Can Halakhic Texts Talk History?' I dealt at length with the issue of *hitḥil le-himashekh*, which Rashi, and all commentators in his wake, interpreted as expressing a principle of separation,[3] namely that grape juice ceases to be simply 'grape juice' and becomes 'wine' and subject to *yein nesekh* when the process of separation of the liquid from the crushed grapes begins.

This ruling caused R. Yitsḥak of Dampierre, the famed Ri, considerable soul-searching. He was bothered by the fact that all too often in the course of the exhausting treading—easily the most arduous process in wine production, in which women and children were never to be employed, only able-bodied men—the treader took a drink by dipping a cup into the vat (*cuve*) and filling it with juice. Should this cupful be reckoned as the 'onset of separation'? On the one hand, some of the wine in the tub has been strained off. On the other hand, this is not the onset of the *process* that will separate the rest of the juice from the crushed grape. That will occur when a strainer is put over large bowls placed under the spigot, the spigot is opened, and strained wine flows into these receptacles.[4]

This was not a theoretical question. The French community, it will be remembered, had allowed Gentiles to be involved in the transportation and handling of the open *cuve*—which inevitably involved some contact with the wine it contained—until the moment the spigot was opened.[5] If cup-dipping constituted *hamshakhah*, Gentiles regularly touched Jewish wine well after the onset of that process, and most 'kosher wine' was not at all kosher. Nevertheless, Ri wrote:

[2] As to the oft-cited remarks of R. Eizik Tirna (Yitsḥak mi-Tirnau) in his *Sefer ha-Minhagim*, ed. S. Y. Spitzer (Jerusalem, 1979), 2, about the permissibility of eating the fat of the rumen (*ḥelev ha-keres*), they refer to custom, to its right to adjudicate between two different views in all areas of the halakhah, including that of *issur ve-heter*. On the controversy over the permissibility of eating the fat of the rumen, see Y. E. Zimmer, *'Olam ke-Minhago Noheg* (Jerusalem, 1996), 250–61.

[3] Above, pp. 180, 185, 211.

[4] *Teshuvot Maharaḥ Or Zarua'*, ed. M. Avitan (Jerusalem, 2002), #174, p. 165, s.v. *u-khe-divrei*.

[5] 'Can Halakhic Texts Talk History?' (Chapter 7 above).

היה נראה בעיני לאסור והלואי שהיו נוהגין להחמיר בדבר . . . אבל אין בידי לאסור אחר שנוהגים כולם היתר מימי רבותינו נוחי נפש. וכמו שנוהגים בשלהם נוהגים גם בשלי כשקונין לי יין. וצורינו יצילנו מכל מכשול חטא ועונש וידריכנו בנתיב מצותיו לקיימם כמאמרם.

And it would appear to me that the [instance of the inserted cup] is forbidden, and I wish that the custom in such cases were to forbid [the wine in the tub] . . . However, I do not feel sufficiently empowered to forbid [this wine] since the custom has been to allow [it] since the days of our teachers, may they rest in peace. And as they act with their *cuves* so they act with mine, when they purchase wine for me. May our Rock save us from all stumbling, sinful error and punishment and may He lead us in the way of His commandments to fulfill them properly.[6]

Ri's conduct highlights the striking identification of the Tosafists with the religious standards of their community, a solidarity displayed most noticeably when they have serious reservations about those standards. In almost every phase of wine production—in supervision of the *cuves* after the treading, in transportation of the wine by Gentile wagoners, in the purging (*hakhsharah*, *hag'alah*) of the vessel that contained *yein nesekh*, and in the sale of Gentile wine that had been given as payment in kind for outstanding debts, the Tosafists advised taking extra precautions and not relying on common practice, writing: 'it is best to act more stringently in this matter', 'it is proper to act more stringently', and 'may he who acts more stringently be blessed'.[7] The same phrases or their equivalent are strewn throughout the first two chapters of *'Avodah Zarah*, which deal with Jewish–Gentile relations.[8] What is never found in their writings are such phrases as: 'The scholar [*talmid ḥakham*, *tsurva de-rabbanan*] should here act more stringently', or 'he who has an ounce of Torah [*re'aḥ torah*] in him should abstain from this'.[9] The intellectual elite of Ashkenaz never saw itself as constituting the religious elite.[10] Its level of

[6] *Teshuvot Maharaḥ Or Zarua'*, #174, p. 165, s.v. *u-khe-divrei.*

[7] e.g. *'Avodah Zarah* 31b, s.v. *ha-sholeaḥ*; 55b, s.v. *amar*; 74b, s.v. *de-havah*.

[8] e.g. *Tosfot R. Elḥanan 'al 'Avodah Zarah*, ed. A. Y. Kreuzer (Jerusalem, 2003), 2a, s.v. *laset ve-latet* (p. 5); ibid. 15b, s.v. *ein* (p. 85).

[9] As in *Yam shel Shelomoh, Bava Kamma* (Prague, 1616–18), 8: 9.

[10] This has already been noted by J. Katz in 'Ma'ariv bi-Zemano ve-she-lo bi-Zemano—Dugma le-Zikah bein Minhag, Halakhah ve-Ḥevrah', *Zion*, 35 (1970), 47–9; reprinted in id., *Halakhah ve-Kabbalah: Meḥkarim be-Toledot Dat Yisra'el 'al Medoreiha ve-Zikatah ha-Ḥevratit* (Jerusalem, 1986), 187–8. English version in id., *Divine Law in Human Hands: Case Studies in Halakhic Flexibility* (Jerusalem, 1998), 107–9. Ri's remarks in *Ḥagigah* 22a, s.v. *ke-m'an*, are revelatory. The *beraita* had ruled that one could not include an *'am ha-arets* in the *birkat ha-zimmun* (*Berakhot* 47b). The sharp religious and social split that existed in talmudic times between *ḥaverim* and *'amei ha-arets* did not exist in the Middle Ages, certainly not in the small Ashkenazic communities. When called upon to reconcile this dictum with the popular practice of scholars and ignorant folk joining in one *zimmun*, R. Elḥanan invoked another talmudic passage (*Ḥagigah* 22a), which stated that one could treat *ḥaverim* and *'amei ha-arets* in an equal manner to reduce resentment and social tensions (*mi-shum*

observance was one and the same as that of the community from which it sprang and in which it dwelt, and it never occurred to the Tosafists that they should act 'better' than their co-religionists. Individuals might practice a heightened ritual observance and would undoubtedly reap their reward in the world-to-come. But no group, however scholarly, need stand higher than did the community in its level of observance. The Ashkenazic community appeared to the Tosafists as a *kehillah kedoshah*, a holy congregation, whose religious practices were a living embodiment of the dictates of the Torah. Any contradiction between its practices and the demands of the halakhah was illusory. This cultural axiom outweighed the community's cognitive conclusions. Again and again in the field of *yein nesekh*, its members raised serious questions about the common practice, but each and every time they concluded by endorsing it.[11] And so, despite all his deep reservations, Ri still wrote: 'And as they act with their *cuves*, so they act with mine, when they purchase wine for me.'

I drew attention to this phenomenon in 1967 in my work on *yein nesekh*.[12]

eivah). Ri, however, did not like the tone of superiority implicit in the invocation of the *Ḥagigah* passage. He preferred to invoke the passage in *Berakhot* 16b that forbade religious presumptuousness—*lo kol ha-rotseh litol et ha-shem yitol*. No one nowadays should have the presumption to call himself a 'scholar' vis-à-vis his co-religionist, regardless of the latter's level of knowledge. (דלא כל הרוצה ליטול את השם, להחזיק לעצמו כתלמיד חכם שלא לזמן על ע"ה, בידו ליטול, ואין אנו מחזיקין עצמינו כתלמיד חכם לענין זה. He adds *le-'inyan zeh* because with respect to some other matters, such as exemption from taxes, the category of *talmid ḥakham* was still applicable.) Technically speaking R. Elḥanan's answer is superior. The Talmud in *Ḥagigah* provides a specific allowance for erasing the line between learned and ignorant. The passage in *Berakhot* about religious presumptuousness is stated with regard to a totally different matter, *keri'at shema'*. One can use it by analogy only and by a broad analogy at that. R. Elḥanan's colleague, R. Yehudah Sir Leon of Paris, sought the better of two worlds, by citing the tannaitic formulation in *Ḥagigah* (שלא יהא כל אחד בונה במה לעצמו) rather than the amoraic one of *eivah*, a formulation that turned the meaning of the passage in *Ḥagigah* into something very much akin to Ri's explanation. *Tosfot Rabbenu Yehudah Sir Leon 'al Berakhot*, ed. N. Sachs, ii (Jerusalem, 1972), 47b, s.v. *amar rav huna*. (To forfend misunderstanding, I should add a methodological note. R. Elḥanan's position does not evidence elitism or contemporary tension. Noting a discrepancy between a talmudic dictum and popular practice, he cites another talmudic passage to solve the problem. That passage employs the phrase *mi-shum eivah*, which he simply reproduces. In Ri's distant and superfluous analogy of *keri'at shema'*, we have a 'measurable deflection', which is entirely lacking in R. Elḥanan's argument. R. Yehudah Sir Leon's position is more difficult to assess. After all, he too but invokes a talmudic passage. To my eye, however, R. Yehudah's citation is too elegantly apropos to be entirely unconscious. Opinions, however, could differ on the matter. Cf. D. Malkiel, *Reconstructing Ashkenaz: The Human Face of Franco-German Jewry, 1000–1250* [Stanford, 2009], 177.)

[11] See my *Ha-Yayin bi-Yemei ha-Beinayim—Yein Nesekh be-Ashkenaz: Perek be-Toledot ha-Halakhah be-Ashkenaz* (Jerusalem, 2008), 169–320.

[12] 'Minhag, Metsi'ut ve-Halakhah: Yein Nesekh, Nituaḥ le-Dugma' (MA, Hebrew University, 1967).

This assessment was confirmed by my subsequent studies of pawnbroking and of martyrdom, together with Lau's study of the *ḥadash* injunction (*ḥadash be-ḥuts la-arets*).[13]

One question, however, poses itself immediately. The vast halakhic synthesis of the Tosafists drew hundreds, if not thousands, of new conclusions from the Talmud, conclusions that in the course of time the Ashkenazic community accepted and that changed the face of religious life in Ashkenaz. Anyone who compares the skeletal rules of Passover or of Sukkot in the *Siddur Rashi* with the complex set of regulations found in *Sefer Mitsvot Gadol*, or the elementary dictates of *basar be-ḥalav* (milk and meat) in the *Sefer ha-Pardes* with the immense and intricate regulative universe found in the *Sefer ha-Terumah* or the *Sha'arei Dura*, sees immediately the vast transformation. Nor was this acceptance simply theoretical, as one sees from questions asked in medieval Ashkenaz that have meaning only if one assumes that doctrine 'X' or 'Y' of the Tosafists was the common practice. A similar picture emerges from minor handbooks found in manuscript, trivial works of no intrinsic worth but that mention in passing what the local practice was. The doctrines of the Tosafists had, indeed, seeped downward and become part of the habitual religious life of the Jewish community. Every one of these innumerable changes was an implicit criticism of past practices, yet the Tosafists never hesitated to propagate their new conclusions nor had they any qualms about writing codes whose peremptory tone proclaimed that these new observances were obligatory. Why did not the notion of *kehillah kedoshah* operate here? Why in all these areas did the Tosafists not view the received, habitual conduct of their communities 'as informative of talmudic law' as they did in *yein nesekh*? Why did they not see here 'the deeds of the common folk as revelatory of the Divine intent' as they did in *kiddush ha-shem*?

Take Rabbenu Tam, for example. No one tried harder than he did to justify popular practice in *yein nesekh* or *kiddush ha-shem*.[14] Yet he did not hesitate to disqualify all the Torah scrolls (*sifrei Torah*) of Germany as they were written in

[13] 'Pawnbroking: A Study in *Ribbit* and of the Halakhah in Exile', *Proceedings of the American Academy for Jewish Research*, 38–9 (1971–2), 203–68. A much-amplified version of the study appears as Chapter 6 above. *Halakhah, Kalkalah ve-Dimmuy 'Atsmi: Ha-Mashkona'ut bi-Yemei ha-Beinayim* (Jerusalem, 1985) is a Hebrew version of the pawnbroking article but carries the analysis of Ashkenazic thought through the 13th century and, more to our purposes, treats in detail the contrasting developments in Provençal and Spanish thought. 'Halakhah, Hermeneutics and Martyrdom in *Ashkenaz*', *Jewish Quarterly Review*, 94 (2004), 77–108, 278–99. (This essay will appear in the second volume of this series.) B. Lau, 'Ḥadash be-Ḥuts la-Arets: Le-Darkhei Hitmodedut ha-Poskim be-Mikrei Pa'ar bein Halakhah le-Metsi'ut' (Ph.D. diss., Bar-Ilan University, 1997).

[14] See *Ha-Yayin bi-Yemei ha-Beinayim* (above, n. 11), 185–9, 215–22, 261–6, 298–303, 353–4; 'Halakhah, Hermeneutics and Martyrdom', 85–96.

ink that he deemed unfit for sacred scrolls.[15] The same boldness and indifference to long-standing, entrenched practice exhibited itself in the realm of *issur ve-heter*. His remarks about the kosher status (*kashrut*) of a certain lesion of the lobes of the lung, *unah ha-serukhah be-'umah* are well known. Rashi and his revered teacher R. Ya'akov ben Yakar had declared that such a lesion did not render an animal un-kosher (*terefah*). The *Tosafot* reports that not only did Rabbenu Tam disagree but that he went so far as to proclaim that 'anyone who permits such a lesion feeds Jewry un-kosher foods [*terefot*]'.[16] Rashi's allowance, however, was neither his innovation nor that of his teacher. R. Yitsḥak Or Zarua' informs us that 'Rabbenu Gershom, R. Shelomoh b. Shimshon of Worms, Rashbam, R. Yitsḥak ben Yehudah all allow the lesion of *unah be-umah* and the custom in Mainz is also to allow it'.[17] Rabbenu Tam was ready to proclaim publicly that both the French and German communities had been eating *terefot* for some two hundred years, yet refused to admit the possibility that they had at the same time drunk *yein nesekh*.

The difference lay in the cost of the observance. *Yein nesekh* exacted from Jews a far higher price than did kosher meat or the keeping of the Sabbath. It had long been seen as an instance of *insolentia Judaeorum*. In the halcyon days of the ninth century, Agobard, bishop of Lyons, wrote in anger that Gentile touch defiled wine in Jewish eyes and made it unfit for their consumption. From the many *privilegia* that specifically granted to the Jews the right to sell their wine—and Jews paid handsomely for each and every right granted—one may gauge just how widely resented was the implied Jewish superiority contained in the *yein nesekh* ban. Innocent III himself inveighed against this presumptuousness, and one did not take lightly the anger of Innocent III.[18] In a period of rapid devolution of Jewish status, in the atmosphere of growing

[15] *Tosafot*, *Megillah* 19b, s.v. *'al*; *Niddah* 20a, s.v. *pali*; *Or Zarua'*, i (Zhitomir, 1862), #542: **דלא מיקרי דיו אלא דיו הקרוש של קוצים שעושים בצרפת**. See M. Z. Bat-Yehoudah, *Les Encres noires au Moyen Age* (Paris, 1983), 103, n. 16, 117–21.

[16] *Sefer Ha-Yashar*, *Ḥelek ha-Ḥiddushim*, ed. S. S. Schlesinger (Jerusalem, 1955), #449 (pp. 267–8); *Ḥullin* 47a, Rashi, s.v. *afilu*; *Tosafot*, 46b, s.v. *heinu* (end).

[17] *Or Zarua'*, i, *Ḥullin*, #411, fo. 112b (end). See *Sefer Ravyah 'al Ḥullin*, ed. D. Deblitski (Jerusalem, 1976), #1089; *Sefer Ravyah*, ed. D. Deblitski (Benei Berak, 2005), iv, #1069. (Rabbenu Gershom's allowance was his final position on this question. Initially he forbade such a lesion, then he began to have doubts, and finally he allowed it. See *Ma'aseh ha-Ge'onim*, ed. A. Epstein [Berlin, 1910], 82, and MS Oxford, Bodley 566, fo. 18a. See also the language of Rabbenu Gershom cited in *Teshuvot u-Fesakin me'et Ḥakhmei Ashkenaz ve-Tsarfat*, ed. E. Kupfer [Jerusalem, 1973], 1–2.)

[18] *Patrologia Latina*, ed. J. P. Migne, vol. civ, p. 826; Agobard of Lyons, *Opera Omnia*; L. van Acker, ed., Corpus Christianorum, Continuatio Medievalis 52 (Brepols, 1981), 193; J. Aronius, *Regesten zur Geschichte der Juden im Fränkischen und Deutschen Reiche bis zum Jahre 1273* (Berlin, 1902), 90; R. Hoeniger, 'Zur Geschichte der Juden Deutschlands im Mittelalter', *Zeitschrift für die Geschichte der Juden in Deutschland*, 1 (1887), 141; S. Grayzel, *The Church and the Jews in the XIIIth Century*, revised

belief in ritual murder and in the blood libel, Gentile goodwill became ever scarcer. *Yein nesekh* was a constant provocation and there was everything to gain by its allowance.

And allowances presented themselves repeatedly to the Ashkenazic community. Rashi's time witnessed the first appearance in Ashkenaz of the very plausible geonic ruling that since neither Christians nor Muslims libated, benefit (*hana'ah*) from *yein nesekh* was permissible. This allowed unrestricted trade in Gentiles wines, with all its enviable profits. Nonetheless, it was restricted by Rashi and the Tosafists, both French and German, to acceptance of Gentile wine only as payment in kind for a pre-existing debt. Entrepreneurial initiative in the growing wine trade, the major source of wealth in the cities along the Rhine and the Mosel, was ruled out, and with popular approval, for the Ashkenazic community strictly avoided any such commerce for over three centuries.[19] In the days of Rabbenu Tam and Ri, a second and yet greater opportunity presented itself—to eliminate not simply the ban of benefit but the ban of *yein nesekh* altogether, to lift from the shoulders of Ashkenaz once and for all the heavy burden of this injunction. The argument, as posed in a pointed question from Ri to Rabbenu Tam, was simple and convincing and the permissive conclusion begged to be drawn; indeed, other communities did draw it. Ashkenaz, however, rejected it with shock.[20] A generation later, a third allowance appeared. Ashkenazic scholars learnt of the Maimonidean view that wine that had an admixture of honey was not subject to *yein nesekh*. One could allow all cases of Gentile touch by the simple expedient of adding beforehand a touch of honey to the wine, as Jews in Spain and North Africa actually did. Maimonides further added that this was not a personal holding of his; all the 'great scholars of the Maghreb' had ruled thus. The *Mishneh Torah* was readily available in Ashkenaz in the latter half of the thirteenth century, as the Ashkenazic glosses to it, the *Haggahot Maimuniyot*, attest.

Those unfamiliar with the contents of Maimonides' code would have learnt of the 'honey allowance' through the agency of the *Mordekhai*, one of the most influential works in the later Middle Ages.[21] Yet Maimonides' allow-

edn. (New York, 1966), 73, 127–8. For the later Middle Ages, see G. Mentgen, *Studien zur Geschichte der Juden im mittelalterlichen Elsaß*, Forschungen zur Geschichte der Juden 2 (Hanover, 1995), 560, n. 612.

[19] See my *Yeinam: Sahar be-Yeinam shel Goyim* (Tel Aviv, 2003), 31–90.

[20] See the extensive discussion in *Yeinam*, 104–21, and J. Katz's discussion in *Bein Yehudim le-Goyim* (Jerusalem, 1960), 55–6. (The passage is found in the English version of that work entitled *Exclusiveness and Tolerance* [Oxford, 1961], 46–7.)

[21] Maimonides, 'Hilkhot Ma'akhalot Asurot', 11: 10. *Mordekhai*, *'Avodah Zarah*, #841, Vilna edn., fo. 43b (top). The printed text is confirmed by numerous manuscripts of the *Mordekhai*, including what is far and away the best one, MS Budapest, National Museum 2° 1, fo. 234 (bottom).

ance was ignored completely. In the first quarter of the thirteenth century, R. Yehudah of Paris (d. 1224) received a report that adding a touch of honey to the wine to forestall *yein nesekh* was standard practice of Jews in Islamic countries. R. Yitsḥak Or Zarua' arrived independently at this position on the basis of a passage in the Yerushalmi and mentioned in conclusion the report from Islamic countries. His position, however, had no more influence, won no more acceptance than did that of Maimonides. Indeed, R. Yitsḥak's permissive argument was never cited in the subsequent literature. What was cited from the *Or Zarua'* was the exotic appendix, not the proof. 'I **think** that **some people heard** from my teacher R. Yehudah of Paris that in the lands of Yishma'el and Egypt they are accustomed to add honey to the wine and *yein nesekh* no longer applies' (emphasis added). His own son, in his abridgment of his father's massive compendium, cited the reported practice of Islamic lands, not the allowance based on the Yerushalmi, as did similarly R. Yisra'el Krems (latter half of the fourteenth century) in his widely disseminated *Haggahot Asheri*.[22] Even this report of the doings in distant lands was heard no more. Not for lack of relevance. Wine laced with spices and honey (*hypocras*) was a favorite medieval drink and was also thought to have medicinal properties. Sweeteners, moreover, were often used in northern climes either to counter the acrid taste of the tannins or to cover the onset of spoilage, which occurred quite early, as the wine was exposed on all sides to air because of the poor construction of the barrels.[23] Yet Maimonides' allowance was never invoked, nor that of the *Or Zarua'*, not even as a last resort position, as in cases of severe financial loss, *hefsed merubbeh*.[24] It was stillborn; its permissive conclusions apparently interested few in Ashkenaz, either in the high or the late Middle

[22] *Or Zarua'*, iv (Jerusalem, 1890), *'Avodah Zarah*, #189. R. Ḥayyim Or Zarua', *Piskei Or Zarua'*, in *Shitat ha-Kadmonim 'al 'Avodah Zarah*, ed. M. Y. H. Blau (New York, 1991), iii. 289, #74. *Haggahot Asheri*, *'Avodah Zarah*, 2: 12. (I have corrected the name of his teacher found in our text of the *Or Zarua'* on the basis of the citation in the *Haggahot Asheri*.) I should add that if something is composed in equal measure of wine, honey, and spices, or has sizeable quantities of these ingredients, it constitutes a new product known as *inomlin* (*'Avodah Zarah* 30a) and is not subject to *yein nesekh*. At bar here is either wine with a trivial amount of honey or a wine *laced* with spices and honey. The product is clearly wine and is viewed as such—wine with an added sweetness and tang.

[23] Hypocras: *Le Mesnagier de Paris*, ed. G. E. Brereton and J. M. Ferrier (Paris, 1994), 776–8; H. E. Sigerist, ed., *The Earliest Printed Book on Wine, by Arnold of Villanova* (New York, 1943), 34–44; S. Pegge, ed., *The Forme of Cury: A Roll of Ancient English Cookery, compiled about A.D. 1390, by the Master-Cooks of King Richard II* (London, 1780), 86–7; Olivier de Serres, *Le Théâtre d'agriculture et mesnage des champs*, ii (Paris, 1804–5), 613–14; reprinted (Paris, 1996), 1168–9. On hiding the taste of spoilage: J. Strayer, ed., *Dictionary of the Middle Ages*, vi (New York, 1985), s.v. 'Honey', p. 28. B. Pferschy, 'Weinfälschung im Mittelalter', in *Fälschungen im Mittelalter*, Proceedings of the International Congress of Monumenta Germaniae Historica, Munich, 16–17 Sept. 1986, v (Hanover, 1988), 670–6.

[24] See below, n. 40.

Ages. A report that there was some correspondence between a late fifteenth-century German glossator of the *Mordekhai* and his friend or relative in Crete only corroborates the silence of the sources:[25]

> כתב לי אחי ה"ר שלמה מקנדיא שהם מתירים שם יין בתערוב' מעט שמן או דבש כפי המיימוני, ולא מצאו הגה עליו [ז"א הגהות מיימוניות]. וזה דלעיל כתבתי לו לפי דעתי. וכן נ"ל שאנו נוהגי' אסו' מכח הראיו' שהבאתי ולא יכולתי להאריך כאן.

My brother, R. Shelomoh of Candia, wrote to me that they permit (in Candia) wine laced with some honey or oil following the Maimonidean view, as they found no *haggah* [gloss] upon it [i.e. German Jews in Candia had adopted the Maimonidean position, as they found no dissent in the authoritative German gloss on *Mishneh Torah*, the *Haggahot Maimuniyot*]. And I wrote to him what I have said previously. It seems to me that we are accustomed [*nohagim*] to forbid such cases on the basis of the arguments that I have presented. I can't go into further detail here.

Not only was Ashkenazic Jewry uninterested in allowing *yein nesekh*, it did not even seek to allow the customary injunction on wine condiments and substitutes—verjuice (*boser*) and vinegar (*ḥomets*). Popular convention in Ashkenaz had expanded the scope of the *yein nesekh* injunction to include *boser* and *ḥomets* touched by a Gentile. To our mind this appears as a trivial extension; it was anything but that in the Middle Ages and constituted a major inconvenience.

Both the French and German palates in medieval times sought a balance of two primary tastes—the heavily spiced and the sour.[26] More than 50 percent of the *Vivandier*, a late medieval French cookbook that included many older recipes, was based on the combination of spicy and sour; another 25 percent of its recipes were based on one or the other taste exclusively. The acidic or sour taste was obtained in northern climes by liberal use of vinegar in cooking and, even more so, by the fermented juice of unripened grapes, which was called 'verjuice', the juice of green (*vert*) grapes. Not surprisingly, a vibrant market for such grapes developed. North-east of Rheims, for example, between the Vesle river and the Retourne, where the sun was insufficient to bring grapes to full ripening, farming concentrated on grains and green grapes, and for a month or

[25] Jerusalem, National Library of Israel, Goldschmidt 4[to] 6697 (*Min ha-Genazim*, #3) fo. 10a. *Aḥi* in medieval correspondence may mean either friend or relative.

[26] B. Laurioux, *Manger au Moyen Age* (Paris, 2002), 31. See also B. S. Rose, 'A Medieval Staple: Verjuice in France and England', *Oxford Symposium on Food and Cookery 1989* (Oxford, 1990), 205–12. German recipes differ in no way from the French, see M. W. Adamson, 'Medieval Germany', in M. W. Adamson, ed., *Regional Cuisines of Medieval Europe: A Book of Essays* (New York and London, 2002), 163, 185. On the older origins of many of the recipes found in the *Taillevant*, see B. Laurioux and O. Redon, 'Emergence d'une cuisine médiévale: Le Témoignage des livres', in H. Bresc, ed., *Matériaux pour l'histoire des cadres de vie dans l'Europe occidentale (1050–1250)* (Nice, 1984) 97–9.

so, from early August to early September, wagonloads of verjuice wended their way to the markets in Rheims.[27]

Verjuice was occasionally drunk, as, more frequently, were sour, old wine and simple vinegar, either straight or with some admixture, usually wine. This sounds quite strange to our ears and, indeed, in the Middle Ages it would have sounded equally strange to people living in Mediterranean countries. However, wine is a subtropical fruit and requires several months of uninterrupted sunshine for full ripening. In the temperate zone, the sky is often cloudy, and successful viticulture is possible only in selected areas. Those who lived outside these areas or who were too poor to purchase the produce of the labor-intensive vines had to make do with whatever alcoholic beverages they could if they wished to escape momentarily from the troubles of this world. Few wines lasted more than a year, most only six months or so,[28] and many regions were short of wine by the late spring. In England the shortage was chronic.[29] Medieval viticulture had made great strides in growing grapes in an adverse climate; medieval cooperage (barrel-making), however, was still primitive. There were gaps between the staves and the base and between the individual staves—all of which were stopped up by rags, grass, or whatever came to hand.[30] The air seeped into the barrels from all sides, and the acetous fermentation ('vinegarization') began early on. If one wanted wine in the late

27 J.-P. Devroey, *L'Éclair d'un bonheur* (Paris, 1989), 83, 146–7.

28 This was first argued by Y. Renouard in 'Le Vin vieux au Moyen Age', *Annales du Midi*, 76 (1964), 447–55; reprinted in id., *Études d'histoire médiévale*, 2 vols. (Paris, 1960), 249–56. It ran against the considerable authority of F. von Bassermann-Jordan (*Geschichte des Weinbaus*, 3 vols., 2nd edn. [Frankfurt am Main, 1923], 471–2), whose views were to be seconded in G. Schreiber, *Deutsche Weingeschichte. Der Wein in Volksleben, Kult und Wirtschaft*, Werken und Wohnen. Volkskundliche Untersuchungen im Rheinland 13 (Cologne, 1980), 295–6. However, Renouard's views have won general acceptance. See e.g. H.-J. Schmitz, *Faktoren der Preisbildung für Getreide und Wein in der Zeit von 800 bis 1500*, Quellen und Forschungen zur Agrargeschichte 20 (Stuttgart, 1968), 62, 67, 70; M. Lachiver, *Vin, vigne et vignerons en région parisienne du XVIIe au XIXe siècle* (Pontoise, 1982), 114–15; R. Matheus and M. Matheus, '"Je älter der Rheinwein, je mehr Firne bekömmt er, welches dem Kenner am meisten gefällt": Beobachtungen zum Geschmackswandel im Mittelalter und in der Frühen Neuzeit', *Mainzer Zeitschrift*, 96–7 (2002) (Festschrift Schütz), 73–4; R. van Uytven, 'Der Geschmack am Wein im Mittelalter', in M. Matheus, ed., *Weinproduktion und Weinkonsum im Mittelalter*, Geschichtliche Landeskunde 51 (Stuttgart, 2005), 124–5; see though D. Kerber, 'Der Weinbau im mittelalterlichen Koblenz', in M. Matheus, ed., *Weinbau zwischen Maas und Rhein in der Antike und im Mittelalter* (Mainz, 1997), 279. For the few wines that constituted the exceptions to this rule, see M. Lachiver, *Vins, vignes et vignerons: Histoire du vignoble français* (Paris, 1988), 77; J. Verdon, *Boire au Moyen Age* (Paris, 2002), 152–5.

29 See the remarks of R. Yitsḥak b. Perets of Northampton cited by R. Ya'akov Ḥazan in his *'Ets Ḥayyim: Halakhot, Pesakim u-Minhagim*, ed. Y. Braude (Jerusalem, 1962), i. 196.

30 *Ha-Yayin bi-Yemei ha-Beinayim* (above, n. 11), 82–3.

summer, one had to drink wine that was well on its way to becoming vinegar, and the line dividing two- or three-year-old wine from vinegar was thin and fleeting indeed. Not surprisingly, sour old wine fetched a good price. In 1389, Richard Piques, bishop of Rheims, died; the audit of the episcopal estate listed 'fifty *queues* [1 *queue* = 400 liters] at 30 *sous* a *queue*, twenty *queues* of old wine, not worth anything'.[31] The 'auditors', as it were (*commissaires-prisaires*), assessed the old wine from the viewpoint of episcopal consumption; a less elevated perspective would have been more realistic (and profitable). Tax records from the Rémois registered wine prices from a year or two earlier (1387–8): new wine sold at 48 *sous* a *queue*; two-year-old wine at 20 *sous* a *queue*; three-year-old wine from 14 to 24 *sous* a *queue*. Some ten years later (1394–5), new wine sold at 36 to 56 *sous* a *queue*; two-year-old wine at 40 *sous* a *queue*.[32]

The Talmud had expressly exempted vinegar from the *yein nesekh* ban,[33] and logic would suggest that verjuice was equally excluded. Early Ashkenaz banned both—understandably, as only the thinnest of lines now separated slightly acid old wine from verjuice and souring wine from vinegar. Besides being drunk, both were regularly employed in the preparation of foods. Care then had to be taken that the Gentile help—Jewish communities were far too small to supply all the numerous hands needed in running a household in an age before plumbing and electricity—never touched, even inadvertently, these ubiquitous liquids. Rashi, in the commentary-code that he dictated to Rashbam, pointed out that vinegar was specifically permitted.[34] This commentary-code achieved wide dissemination, but people never seized upon this allowance and maintained their old prohibitive posture. Somewhere in the years between 1149 and 1153, R. Meshullam of Melun, a Provençal scholar who had settled in northern France, attempted to allow, among other things, both vinegar and verjuice. Rabbenu Tam was outraged, and a correspondence in high and angry tones ensued.[35] Their loud voices guaranteed that the purely

[31] 'Old wine' meant wine over a year old; see Renouard's article cited above, n. 28. In medieval Hebrew sources the terminology is flexible. 'New wine' generally meant wine that had not yet fermented or had just fermented, what was called 'must' in Middle High German (*yayin ḥadash she-korin most*); 'old wine' denoted wine less than a year old. Last year's wine was often called just that—*yayin de-eshtakad*. See ibid. 85, n. 264.

[32] Devroey, *L'Éclair* (above, n. 27), 117–18.

[33] *'Avodah Zarah* 29b–30a.

[34] *Or Zarua'*, #152. On this commentary-code, see 'Can Halakhic Texts Talk History?' (Chapter 7 above).

[35] *Sefer ha-Yashar, Teshuvot* (Berlin, 1892), ##45: 1, 46: 3, 47: 4, 48: 4. On the date see A. Reiner, 'Rabbenu Tam u-Venei Doro: Kesharim, Hashpa'ot ve-Darkhei Limmud' (Ph.D. diss., Hebrew University, 2002), 284–6.

consuetudinary nature of the ban became widely known, yet there is not a whisper in the sources that this resulted in any relaxation of the widespread ban.[36]

Not only did the Ashkenazic community not seek to free itself of the injunction against *yein nesekh*, it did not even seek any policy of judicial leniency in this area, never endeavoring to ensure that questions of *yein nesekh* would be decided according to the more lenient view. R. Mosheh of Coucy, the author of the *Sefer Mitsvot Gadol*, discovered a dictum in the Yerushalmi stating *ein medakdekim be-yein nesekh*—one should not be too punctilious, i.e. one should not be too strict, in matters of *yein nesekh*.[37] He applied it, however, to one—classically problematic—case only, the leaking barrel that a Gentile had instinctively plugged,[38] and made no further use of it, even though the dictum was a policy statement and invited, possibly demanded, broader application. His code had very wide circulation, yet no further mention is made of this dictum in the entire printed literature of Ashkenaz. One person and one person alone invoked this passage, an unknown R. Elyakim ha-Kohen of Friedburg, as reported in MS Oxford, Bodley 566. He, however, construed it economically—that one should rule leniently in *yein nesekh* in instances where the inquirer was a poor man.[39] This reduced the dictum of the Yerushalmi to a subset of the well-known principle of *hefsed merubbeh*, namely, that in ritual law there is leeway for the decisor to render a lenient judgment when a strict one would entail serious loss.[40] The only difference was that in most areas the principle of *hefsed merubbeh* was an option, whereas, according to this unknown scholar, in matters of *yein nesekh* it would be an obligation. Someone somewhere on the periphery advocated leniency for the poor, but no one advocated it for anyone else.

Of all the laws of *yein nesekh*, the most annoying and constraining was that

36 *Ha-Yayin bi-Yemei ha-Beinayim* (above, n. 11), 376–80.

37 *Sanhedrin* 4: 7; fo. 22b in the Venice edition; col. 1287 in the edition of the Academy of Hebrew Language (Jerusalem, 2001); *Sefer Mitsvot Gadol*, ed. E. Schlesinger (Jerusalem, 1989), 298, Injunction 148 cited in *Haggahot Maimuniyot* (with regard to this specific problem), 'Hilkhot Ma'akhalot Asurot', 12: 4, n. 3.

38 The problem was discussed and differing opinions offered by the widest range of scholars; see *Ha-Yayin bi-Yemei ha-Beinayim* (above, n. 11), 83, n. 253.

39 Fo. 34b. The construction was based on what he took to be its context in the Yerushalmi. See *Ha-Yayin bi-Yemei ha-Beinayim* (above, n. 11), 365. No one by the name of Elyakim ha-Kohen of Friedburg is mentioned either in E. E. Urbach's *Ba'alei ha-Tosafot*, revised edn. (Jerusalem, 1980), or in I. Elbogen, A. Freimann, and H. Tyckocinski, eds., *Germania Judaica*, i (Breslau, 1917–34; 2nd edn. Tübingen, 1963). Simcha Emanuel informs me that to the best of his knowledge this name appears nowhere else in the literature of the period.

40 See *Entsiklopediyah Talmudit*, x (Jerusalem, 1961), s.v. *hefsed merubbeh*, pp. 32–41.

of *nitsok*.[41] If the Gentile helper opened the spigot of the barrel to fill a pitcher, not only was the wine in the pitcher forbidden, but also the wine in the barrel. If the maid poured herself a glass of wine from the pitcher, not only the wine in the glass was forbidden, but equally that in the pitcher. Worse yet, if the glass of the Gentile was not washed after she had drunk from it, and someone poured some wine into it, the traces of wine in the glass proceeded to render the contents of the pitcher forbidden, and if someone used the glass to pour himself a drink from the barrel, a common enough occurrence, the contents of the entire barrel were forbidden.

Jewish communities in the Middle Ages were, as I have said, far too small to supply all the hands necessary to run a household in the days before plumbing and electricity. Gentile help was indispensable. As neither coffee nor tea had yet arrived in Europe, and water was viewed as fit only for beasts (or for the poor, who differed little from beasts),[42] wine was the daily drink, at least of all those who could afford it. Germs were an unknown hazard at that time, and people regularly ate the leftovers of others.[43] There is no reason to assume that if someone drank wine from a glass and a little was left over, people would bother to wash it out before filling it again with wine for their own consumption. Yet now Jews had to insist that their helpers wash out all glasses from which they had drunk wine. The resentment this must have generated is obvious. Moreover, if anyone picked up a glass that someone had drunk from and poured himself a drink, and later it was discovered that the glass had been used by the helper, the contents of the entire pitcher or the entire barrel were forbidden. Such occurrences were inevitable and intolerable.

The law of *nitsok* is unique to *yein nesekh* and exists in no other area of ritual law. Not surprisingly, there developed in Provence a school that held that as *nitsok* was singular, every attempt should here be made to be as lenient about it as possible. It was further claimed that this was the stance of the great R. Zeraḥyah ha-Levi, Ba'al ha-Ma'or, though his actual statement on the matter is ambiguous.[44] No hint of such a doctrine is to be found in Ashkenaz. Indeed,

41 See *Ha-Yayin bi-Yemei ha-Beinayim* (above, n. 11), 277–8.

42 Ibid. 99–100.

43 N. Elias, *The Civilizing Process* (Oxford and Cambridge, Mass., 1993), 51, 55.

44 *Orḥot Ḥayyim*, *Ḥelek Sheni*, p. 255. R. Ya'akov b. Mosheh of Bagnols in his *Issur ve-Heter* (in *Shitat Kadmonim 'al Ḥullin*, ed. M. Y. H. Blau [New York, 1989], 129) contends that R. Zeraḥyah allowed *nitsok* only in cases of *hefsed merubbeh*. The latter's words are cited in *Ba'alei Asufot*, MS Moscow, RSL, Günzburg 73, fo. 61a (**ודין (רחוק) ניצוק רחוק ועמוק ומצוה וחוק שלא לטעון ולא לפרוק, וכן שמענו כל שיש להקל לעירוב ולניצוק, ויגיד המקל אם בעקלקלה או בעקל**). As to *Sefer Ravyah 'al 'Avodah Zarah*, ed. D. Deblitski (Benei Berak, 1976), #1069 (p. 62); *Sefer Ravyah*, ed. D. Deblitski (Benei Berak, 2005), iv, #1069 (p. 41); and *Teshuvot ha-Rosh*, ed. Y. S. Yudlov (Jerusalem, 1994), 19: 1, see my remarks in *Ha-Yayin bi-Yemei ha-Beinayim* (above, n. 11), 366, n. 86.

if anything, the developments there are somewhat the reverse. The existence of the law of *nitsok* was a matter of debate in the Talmud. Jewish communities the world over—Babylonia, Egypt, the Maghreb, Spain, Provence, Italy, and Ashkenaz—ruled, one and all, that the holding was that *nitsok* obtained in *yein nesekh*. Rabbenu Tam came along and, unimpressed by universal consensus, argued with his customary power that all this was a mistake.[45] It was clear from the Talmud that *nitsok* did *not* obtain in *yein nesekh*. So convincing were his arguments that Naḥmanides wrote that, were it not for the rulings of the Ge'onim and R. Alfasi, he would follow Rabbenu Tam. Not surprisingly, the major halakhic decisors in thirteenth-century France, such as R. Mosheh of Coucy, R. Yitsḥak of Corbeil, and Rabbenu Perets, either ruled in accordance with or were strongly inclined to Rabbenu Tam's view. However, other Ashkenazic scholars adhered to the old injunctive perspective. Some advocated a compromise position: *nitsok* was operative in *yein nesekh*, but allowance would be made for instances of *hefsed merubbeh*, major loss. An unknown French author of the latter half of the thirteenth century by the name of Yeruḥam wrote simply, 'The custom is to forbid *nitsok*.' Despite the enormous lightening of the load that Rabbenu Tam's view would have allowed, there is no evidence that the Ashkenazic community hastened to the gate to adopt it.[46]

This was scarcely the case with other Jewish cultures. Jews under Islam, at least those of Muslim Spain, the Maghreb, and Palestine (and one should probably add Egypt), freely invoked the allowance of a honey admixture. This view had not only been unopposed by the rabbinic authorities, it had even received their full approval.[47] The 'honey allowance' survived the Reconquista, and Jews of Christian Spain conducted themselves as had their predecessors.[48]

45 *Sefer ha-Yashar, Teshuvot*, #76: 4; *Sefer ha-Yashar, Ḥelek ha-Ḥiddushim*, #719; *Teshuvot Ḥakhmei Tsarfat ve-lotir*, ed. J. Müller (Vienna, 1881), #1; *Tosfot R. Yehudah mi-Paris* in *Shitat Kadmonim 'al 'Avodah Zarah*, ed. M. Y. H. Blau (New York, 1969), ii, 72b, s.v. *amar* (p. 346); *Ravyah*, p. 90; *Or Zarua'*, #215.

46 *Ha-Yayin bi-Yemei ha-Beinayim* (above, n. 11), 303–4.

47 *Teshuvot ha-Rambam*, ed. J. Blau (Jerusalem, 1960), ii, #269. Menaḥem Ben-Sasson has drawn my attention to J. Blau, 'Etslenu be-al-Andalus, Etslenu ba-Magreb', *Mesorot*, 7 (1953), 43–50.

48 See the passage in MS Paris, Bibliothèque Nationale 1391 published by I. Levi in 'Un recueil de[s] consultations de[s] rabbins de la France méridionale', *Revue des études juives*, 39 (1899), 237:

וזכורני כי בילדותי היו מוכרים יין בבתינו ובאים סוחרים עברים ספרדים וקנו ממנו יין ומלאו כלים גדולים, ואחר כך לקחו דבש ונתנו כזית בכל כלי וכלי. ושאלתי להם למה עשו כן. ואמרו לי שלא יאסור עוד במגע גוי.

And I recall, in my childhood they used to sell wine in our houses and Spanish Jewish merchants would come and buy wine from us and fill large vessels [with it]. Subsequently, they would take honey and put [a quantity] the size of an olive in each vessel. I asked them why they did this. They replied so that the wine would not become forbidden by Gentile touch. Simcha Emanuel drew my attention to this passage.

When Ri's shocked inquiry to Rabbenu Tam[49]—'Do you realize that if you combine two plausible rulings, Rashi's and your own, the injunction of *yein nesekh* disappears?'—became common knowledge, it provided the rationale for the abolition of *yein nesekh* first in Spain, and later on in Italy and Moravia.[50] There isn't a hint of such conduct in France or Germany. As I have written: 'The Ashkenazic community was animated by a fierce sense of the heroic in the face of persecution and intensely felt their dissimilarity to the heathen world around them. *Yein nesekh* seemed to them an appropriate symbol of this distinctiveness, and they did not begrudge the price they had to pay for it.'[51]

The cost of *yein nesekh* was high; how much more so was the cost of *kiddush ha-shem*, with its murders, suicides, and parental killing of children lest they fall into Christian hands and be raised as idolaters?[52] Not surprisingly, in no area did the Tosafists defend communal practice more. The greatest Tosafists—Rabbenu Tam, Ri, R. Shimshon of Sens, possibly Ravyah, certainly R. Me'ir of Rothenburg—all justified their people's conduct, even if this entailed sanctioning suicide; some even found a justification for the slaughter of children.

The attitude towards Christianity evinced by the Ashkenazic community and the extreme price it was willing to pay for it shaped the attitude of the Tosafists towards communal practice in allied areas, and I emphasize the word 'allied'. Fifty years ago, Jacob Katz pointed out the Tosafists' policy of justification of many of the popular allowances in Jewish–Gentile relations.[53] They justified such things as trade with Gentiles on Sunday, trade in animals and selling of weapons throughout the year, serving as Gentile nursemaids and having Gentiles serve as Jewish nursemaids—all practices that had been forbidden in the Talmud.

The bifurcation that takes place here between the Tosafists and the

49 *Tosafot*, *'Avodah Zarah*, 57b, s.v. *le-apukei*; *Tosfot R. Yehudah mi-Paris 'al 'Avodah Zarah*, 57b, s.v. *le-apukei*. For a full discussion of the issue, see *Yeinam* (above, n. 19), 105–15.

50 Spain: Avraham b. Natan ha-Yarḥi, *Sefer ha-Manhig*, ed. Y. Rafael (Jerusalem, 1961), 660. Italy: K. Schlesinger, 'Maḥloket be-'Inyanei "Setam Yeinam" be-Italyah bi-Shenat Shasah (365)', in B. Kurzweil, ed., *Yuval Shai: Ma'marim li-Khevod Shemu'el Yosef 'Agnon be-Hagi'o le-Sevah be-Yom Tet be-Av Tashyaḥ (718)* (Ramat Gan, 1958), 281–348; G. Kohen, 'Le-Toledot ha-Pulmus 'al Setam Yeinam be-Italyah u-Mekorotav', *Sinai*, 39 (1975), 62–90. Moravia: *She'elot u-Teshuvot Ramah*, ed. A. Ziv (New York, 1970), #126; see also the *Haggah* of R. Shelomoh Luria (Rashal) to the *Tur* cited in R. Yo'el Sirkes, *Bayit Ḥadash*, 'Yoreh De'ah', #114, s.v. *kol*.

51 'Religious Law and Change' (Chapter 9 above).

52 Ibid. A full discussion of the sources and their analysis can be found in 'Halakhah, Hermeneutics and Martyrdom' (above, n. 13).

53 *Bein Yehudim le-Goyim* (above, n. 20), 35–45. In the English version of that work, entitled *Exclusiveness and Tolerance* (above, n. 20), the passage is found on pp. 24-36.

scholars of Provence, Catalonia, and Spain is noteworthy. In the matter of trade on Christian holidays, scholars from all cultures participated equally. The Talmud had forbidden trade three days before a religious holiday and three days after, not to speak of on the holiday itself. In the Roman world such holidays were few. Christianity, however, had adopted the seven-day week of the Jews, and every Sunday was a religious holiday. This meant that no trade was ever possible with Christians. This was patently absurd: could God have sent His people into exile and denied them the basic means of sustenance? So scholars from every culture sought the means of allowing Jewish–Gentile commerce. The Tosafists, however, proceeded to find halakhic justification for a wide range of business practices, trade in problematic items, and Jewish–Gentile interactions, as the ones previously mentioned. The Tosafists sought to justify in detail the varied initiatives taken by the members of their community to earn their keep from the surrounding Gentile society and to legitimate the web of Christian–Jewish relations that existed in their time. The sages of the other cultures would have little of this. That the halakhah permitted Jewish economic survival was unquestioned; however, this scarcely meant that the specific steps that Jews of Provence or Spain had taken to earn their livelihood were in full accord with the halakhah. It certainly did not mean that one should justify closer and warmer relations with the surrounding society, not to speak of adopting some of its latitudinarian attitudes. The problems of religious observance and of freethinking were too widespread in their communities for the scholars of southern Europe to entertain the notion that the prevalent was the true, that popular practice was the living embodiment of halakhic norms, and that any proper interpretation of the law's dictates must take these practices into account.

The same parting of the ways took place in the matter of usury. To the framework question—Is the lending of money at interest to Gentiles permitted?—there was a common response. True, some opinions in the Talmud forbade it; however, it was inconceivable that Jews should be condemned to live in the Diaspora, pressed into the role of lenders, and forbidden to earn their living from this profession.[54] The Tosafists moved from there to justify a wide range of specific financial arrangements practiced by members of the Ashkenazic community. The Talmudists of other cultures studiously refrained from following suit. R. Shemu'el ha-Sardi (of Cerdaigne) asked Naḥmanides in Gerona: On what basis do Jews rely on Rava's opinion in the Talmud and employ one type of mortgage to avoid the usury injunction, when it seems clear that the talmudic holding is against this position? Naḥmanides replied in

[54] See 'The Jewish Attitude to Usury' (Chapter 5 above).

astonishment: Jews are openly taking interest from their co-religionists, and you are bothered that they conduct themselves in some business dealings in line with opinion 'A' in the Talmud when it seems that the ruling is in favor of opinion 'B'![55]

Not only did the Catalonian and Spanish scholars not justify the practices of their communities, they declined even to cite the justifications advanced by the Tosafists. The school of Naḥmanides and his disciples, Rashba, Ritva, Rah, and Ran, constituted the second stage of the dialectical revolution in halakhah. The first stage was Rabbenu Tam and Ri, the second, the Spanish-Catalonian school. The works of Naḥmanides and his disciples invariably open with the problems raised by the Tosafists, present the tosafist solutions, and proceed either to amplify them or suggest new ones. However, when it comes to questions of communal practice, these works systematically refrain from reproducing the solutions of the Tosafists. Their authors embraced the method of the Tosafists, refined their thought, and gave it its most sophisticated expression. They fully acknowledged their debt and proclaimed that 'They [the Tosafists] are the teachers, they are the instructors, and they are the revealers of all hidden things.'[56] However, no hidden halakhic insights were to be found, to their thinking, in the habitual religious practice of the people.

To be sure, there is a tendency among the Tosafists to justify communal practice in other areas too, as in the time of the evening prayers or clapping (*hashma'at kol*) on the holidays—certainly more than is found among Provençal scholars or those of the Spanish-Catalonian school.[57] Ashkenaz *did* have a more positive communal self-image than did other cultures. However, one must be careful not to exaggerate its extent or the scope of these occasional justifications. One must equally never forget that implicit in the new and ever-expanding norms of the Tosafists was a vast criticism of the practice of their contemporaries and even their revered forefathers. The inclination that we find among the Tosafists in these other fields does not differ substantively from that of Rashi. He, too, occasionally defended a widespread practice, and his pupils even report:[58]

[55] *Teshuvot Ramban*, ed. C. B. Chavel (Jerusalem, 1975), #42.

[56] *Ḥiddushei Ramban le-Massekhet Makkot ve-Dinei Garmi*, ed. M. Hershler (Jerusalem, 1975), 106: *hem ha-morim, hem ha-melammedim, hem ha-megalim kol nitman*.

[57] Katz, 'Ma'ariv bi-Zemano' (above, n. 10); *Tosafot, Betsah* 30a, s.v. *tenan*.

[58] *Ma'aseh ha-Ge'onim*, p. 83, and in the parallel passages cited by I. S. Elfenbein in his edition of *Teshuvot Rashi* (New York, 1943), #163. The editors of the *Ma'aseh ha-Ge'onim* drew here upon a lost work entitled *Likkutei Rashbam* as evidenced by MS Cambridge, Add. 2580, fo. 106b, gloss. If our passage is typical, Rashbam, no less than R. Shemayah and several anonymous pupils, engaged in disseminating Rashi's rulings.

וכשישראל המקבל(ו) מן הגוי משגרו לר[בי] בימים טובים, אין ר[בי] חושש בדבר לבדוק אחרי יהודי בשום איסור והיתר ולשאול הימנו אם קיבל מן הגוי בראיית עין, שלא נחשדו ישראל על כך, כי כל העדה כולם קדושים.

If a Jew received from a Gentile a present [of mulberry wine, to which grape wine was often added before drinking] and sent it on to another Jew, our teacher [i.e. Rashi] does not require [the second Jew] to check [whether or not the wine added was kosher] for Jews are not suspected [of being lax in this matter, and one may assume that the original recipient checked this out] for 'all the community are holy, all of them' [Num. 16:3].

Yet at the same time Rashi's sweeping interpretive enterprise dictated a major revision of established practice. We are familiar with the *sifrut devei Rashi*, a series of works of Rashi's pupils, such as the *Siddur Rashi*, *Maḥzor Vitry*, and *Sefer ha-Oreh*—parts written at Rashi's dictation, most based on the students' own observations and inferences—that cover all of what would be now called 'Oraḥ Ḥayyim' and significant sections of 'Yoreh De'ah'. What are these if not an attempt at the reconstruction of Jewish ritual? To us these works appear banal, but in their time they were anything but that. They appear wholly redundant to us because we take Rashi's interpretation as a given. After all, this is the way we understood the *sugya* from the outset. (That is why most were not published until the late nineteenth and early twentieth century.) However, at the time, these works were transformative. Rashi's disciples were only too well aware that his great commentary had far-reaching implications for proper religious practice and felt duty-bound to publicize them. It is difficult to imagine that they would have done so without his consent.

The major change in the attitude to religious praxis comes, as in so many other areas, with Rabbenu Tam and Ri. One suspects that the events—or their perception of the events—of 1096 played no small role in this transformation of perspective. They, however, systematically justified communal practices only in those areas that demanded major sacrifices and had elicited conduct that could only be characterized as supererogatory. I confess to being incautious in my formulations in 'Religious Law and Change'. To be sure, I took care not to attribute this attitude to scholars of the eleventh century, including Rashi—though this was widely attributed to me—and carefully confined it to the Tosafists and to the Tosafists alone. However, I spoke of a general attitude on the part of these thinkers. I based my remarks on my researches in *yein nesekh*, usury, and martyrdom. What eluded me was that I had studied these topics precisely because the Jews were here subject to relentless pressure, and I had been interested in observing how law and praxis responded to powerful constraints. In *yein nesekh* and martyrdom, the Ashkenazic community acted above and beyond the call of duty. In matters of *ribbit* its conduct was not supererogatory, but it maintained full compliance with that onerous injunction under progressively more trying circumstances and equally refused allowances which were not deemed authoritative.[59] It was for this reason that the Tosafists defended the apparent 'breaches' in religious conduct. They systematically vindicated communal conduct so that it should never be thought that the centuries of sacrifice paid for the observance of *yein nesekh* and the abstention from taking interest from their fellow Jews had all been in vain, for all the while people had been drinking that despised and forbidden drink and had for centuries transgressed all the numerous injunctions against *ribbit*. The Tosafists thought and wrote as they did about martyrdom because they could never entertain the notion that the 'holy ones' (*kedoshim*) who had committed suicide rather than be touched by the 'slush waters' of the baptismal font were self-murderers. They also knew beyond all doubt that the parents who, before committing suicide, had slaughtered their children so that they might die as Jews and go to an eternal life, rather than be raised as Christians, live as idolaters, and suffer an eternal death, were not vile murderers who should be buried at the far end of the Jewish cemetery. They were the true children of the Patriarch. Like Abraham, they had been called to immolate their primordial instincts on the altar of God; unlike him, they had received no last-minute reprieve. They deserved, the Tosafists believed, burial with full honors, and their final resting place was deservedly in the 'bosom of Abraham'.

[59] See Chapter 6 above, pp. 126–8, 133–4, that chapter's Appendix, note 182, and Chapter 9 above, pp. 253–4 and n. 27 ad loc.

AFTERWORD

PAGES 262–3

Adiel Schremer in 'Shikul Da'at Hilkhati: "Pelugat ha-Re'ah" u-Meḥkar ha-Halakhah ha-Bikorti', *Diné Israel: Studies in Halacha and Jewish Law*, 28 (2011), 138, n. 153, argues that from much the same numerous *privilegia* permitting Jews to sell meat to Gentiles, no less than to sell them wine, one sees that Gentiles were equally resentful of the laws of *terefot* (un-kosher meat). *Terefot* meant, in effect, that meat unfit for Jewish consumption was still good enough for Gentiles. Not surprisingly, then, Jews had to pay handsomely for the right to sell such meat to Christians.

Schremer's point is well taken and one that I should have anticipated and neutralized in advance.

Both *terefot* and *yein nesekh* were resented by Gentiles, but not to the same extent and scarcely with the same intensity. *Terefot* was known to Gentiles; it was not regularly experienced by them. Few Gentiles witnessed or would have wanted to witness the rites of the Jewish abbatoir, as the inspection of the lungs (*bedikat ha-re'ah*) and occasionally that of the intestines (*benei me'ayim*)—an odoriferous procedure. Gentiles could touch Jewish meat, handle it, and do with it whatever they wished, without any untoward halakhic effect. This was scarcely true of the ubiquitous wine. Jews refused every proffered cup, the symbol of hospitality and good fellowship. (The refusal of alcoholic drink is usually seen as a calculated insult.) If a Gentile so much as touched or poured any wine, that wine became unfit for Jews to drink. So long as the wine was in existence, a safe distance had to be kept between it and the Gentile. Nor can we tabulate the enormous bitterness that this engendered among those employed in Jewish homes, most of whom were Gentile (the Jewish community was too small to supply the number of hands necessary to run a home that had neither electricity nor plumbing). If a servant poured himself a drink from a pitcher, the entire pitcher was forbidden. If he failed to wash out the cup from which he drank—and before the existence of germs was known, this was usually the case—and someone then used the cup to draw wine from the cask, all the wine in the cask became forbidden. Human forgetfulness being what it is, such cases were frequent. In an age when corporal punishment was routinely practiced by masters upon servants and apprentices—and such rights continued well into the eighteenth century—many a servant was beaten for such lapses. Christian servants must have hated the *yein nesekh* injunction and shared their feelings with their co-religionists.

Moreover, the second central consideration is the willing, indeed, voluntary maintenance of the injunction. In *terefot*, there were no ready allowances waiting to be employed; in *yein nesekh* there were several. Jews could not have banished *terefot* from the law books; their religion demanded its observance. They could very well have abolished *yein nesekh* altogether or greatly restricted its scope. They did neither.

CHAPTER ELEVEN

A Note on Deviance in Eleventh-Century Ashkenaz

Avraham Grossman has argued that the traditional picture of a deeply observant Ashkenazic community in the eleventh century is an exaggeration, for the responsa literature of that era shows that the community was constantly contending with criminals (*'avaryanim*) and violent men (*alamim*).[1] The evidence he adduces may be entered under four headings: (1) Repeated instances throughout the eleventh century of resistance to communal ordinances. (2) The need of communities to impose fines and excommunication to control their members. (3) Recourse by individuals to Gentile courts. (4) References in responsa to thieves, perjurers, and occasional strong-arm tactics.

If the purpose of the essay was to counteract the pathos-laden description of pre-Crusade Ashkenaz by Yitsḥak Baer,[2] I have no quarrel with the antidote that Dr. Grossman has prescribed. If it is presented as a rounded portrait of Ashkenaz in the eleventh century, I would like to register a qualified demurral.

Let us analyze each phenomenon separately.

1. In an important article Grossman demonstrated that Yitsḥak Baer's portrayal of communal organization was in error.[3] It was not the case, as Baer had contended, that Jewish self-government in Ashkenaz initially required that decisions be made unanimously, with the principle of majority rule evolving only in the course of the thirteenth century. Rather, from the very outset, the

[1] A. Grossman, ''Avaryanim ve-Alamim ba-Ḥevrah ha-Yehudit be-Ashkenaz ha-Kedumah ve-Hashpa'atam 'al Sidrei ha-Din', *Shenaton ha-Mishpat ha-'Ivri*, 8 (1981), 135–52.

[2] 'Ha-Yesodot ve-ha-Hatḥalot shel Irgun ha-Kehillah bi-Yemei ha-Beinayim', *Zion*, 15 (1950), 28–35; reprinted in his *Meḥkarim u-Masot be-Toledot 'Am Yisra'el*, ii (Jerusalem, 1986), 87–95.

[3] A. Grossman, 'Yaḥasam shel Ḥakhmei Ashkenaz ha-Rishonim el Shilton ha-Kahal', *Shenaton ha-Mishpat ha-'Ivri*, 2 (1975), 175–99; Y. Baer, 'Ha-Yesodot ve-ha-Hatḥalot (above, n. 2), 1–41; 'Meḥkarim u-Masot' (above, n. 2), 60–100.

governing principle was majority rule, as I. A. Agus had contended long ago.[4] However, contrary to Agus, Grossman convincingly argued that the Jewish community was not democratic but oligarchic. The 'little people' (*ha-ketanim*) were to listen to the 'great ones' (*ha-gedolim*) and to their 'elders' (*zikneihem*). Majority rule was simply a practical way of resolving differences among the *maiores*. In his presentation Grossman was so interested in making the important point, contra Baer, that majority rule obtained throughout the course of the eleventh century that he presented that period statically, as if communal power and its reach had been one and the same at the outset and at the close of that century.

If communal authority was fully in place and widely recognized at the outset of this period, in the days of Rabbenu Meshullam (fl. latter half of the tenth century) and Rabbenu Gershom (d. 1028), the numerous instances of non-compliance with communal ordinances that Grossman cites portray, indeed, a deviant and recalcitrant community. If, however, the eleventh century witnessed the slow growth and emergence of communal self-government, each new stage reflecting an expansion of the scope of its authority, we are then confronted not with a breach of mores and of the traditional code of conduct but resistance to new and growing claims of power. Deviance is the violation of a prevailing social norm, a failure to live up to what is rightfully expected. The norm needs to have attained broad acceptance before its breach can be termed deviant. A novel claim to authority over people is invariably perceived by some as an infringement of personal liberty, and resistance is only natural.

I believe that communal self-government was scarcely in place at the outset of our period. It evolved slowly and, over the course of the eleventh century, expanded its reach dramatically. I have described this transformation in detail in my *Shut ke-Makor Histori*[5] and will simply summarize its major stages in a paragraph.

The earliest Ashkenazic text dealing with communal organization that we possess comes from Lucca at the end of the tenth century—if one thinks that northern Italy in this period should be viewed as part of Ashkenaz. It speaks of the community (*kahal*) establishing a tariff of fines for acts of personal violence. This is simply elementary group discipline without which no collectivity, human or wolf pack, can survive. Another text speaks of what later came

[4] 'Democracy in the Communities of the Early Middle Ages', *Jewish Quarterly Review*, 43 (1952), 153–76.

[5] H. Soloveitchik, *Shut ke-Makor Histori* (Jerusalem, 1990). See 'The Authority of the Babylonian Talmud and the Use of Biblical Verses and Aggadah in Early Ashkenaz', which will appear in the second volume of this series.

to be called *ma'arufya*, namely, the right of an established dealer to have exclusive contact with his customers and not to be subject to competition. This right appears equally in the responsa of Rabbenu Gershom Me'or ha-Golah of Mainz. Also found in those responsa is the right of a community to declare that all lost goods found by Gentiles and purchased by other Jews must be returned to their original owner. Land seized from a Jew by a Gentile and sold to another Jew also had to be returned.[6] All these are but forms of restoration of property to its original owner. (Analogously, the Gentile customer of the *ma'arufya* was perceived as being 'owned', as it were, by the *ma'arufya*, and one had no right to dispossess him of 'his' customer.) These norms express group solidarity. The shift from group help to group governance and coercion came with the advent of taxation. With the growth of population, Gentile authorities began to impose taxes not on families or clans as before, but upon collectivities of Jews residing in one place. This compelled the group to apportion the burden among its members, i.e. to impose upon them individual taxes. Monetary exactions and military service are the hallmarks of 'state' power. This shift from solidarity to coercive authority was a watershed; it inevitably raised a series of allied problems that can be observed vividly in the responsa of R. Yosef Tov 'Elem.[7] Not surprisingly, the opposition to this transformation of communal authority was strong. By the second quarter of the eleventh century the *kahal* claimed the right not only to demand the surrender of fungible money, but also to order a member to rid himself of a specific quarrelsome servant (or serf). By the end of the century, the community was seeking (under certain circumstances) to interfere in the private lives of its members. Rashi and his teacher, R. Yitsḥak b. Yehudah, both upheld, independently of one another, the right of the *kahal* to force a young man to go through with a marriage, because breaking off the betrothal would have brought shame to the family of the bride.

Is it surprising that at each stage of this evolution of authority there was resistance to the new claims of empowerment by the *kahal*? Each phase entailed an unprecedented loss of liberty on the part of the individual. What people were struggling against was not a recognized prerogative but a novel arrogation. Resistance is here instinctive and has little to do with *'avaryanut*, crime, or transgressive behavior.

[6] See the text from MS Montefiore 130 published by Grossman in 'Yaḥasam shel Ḥakhmei Ashkenaz ha-Rishonim' (above, n. 3), 194.

[7] *Teshuvot R. Me'ir mi-Rotenburg*, ed. R. N. N. Rabbinowicz (Lemberg, 1860), #423; *Teshuvot R. Me'ir mi-Rotenburg* (Prague and Budapest), #941; *Teshuvot Ba'alei ha-Tosafot*, ed. I. A. Agus (New York, 1954), #1.

Once this is clarified, the remaining examples of deviancy adduced by Grossman lose much of their evidentiary value. To continue with the enumeration of his arguments:

2. A state is defined by its coercive power, by its monopoly of legitimate force. The Ashkenazic 'state' in the Middle Ages had no power of life-threatening corporal punishment. The only legitimate force it possessed was monetary fines and social sanction, i.e. excommunication. When taxation was first introduced, individuals resisted and the community placed them under ban. R. Yosef Tov 'Elem upheld this ban for the simple reason that 'in these times [i.e. in contrast to talmudic times] there is no way to coerce the wicked other than by fines and excommunication'. This is not a testament to widespread deviancy but a statement of the facts of life in the Ashkenazic Diaspora.

3. Recourse to Gentile courts. Nowadays, there is a common misapprehension about civil suits. Accustomed to submitting to religious authority, religious Jews (and secular Jews in their wake) view resistance to rabbinic rulings as seriously recalcitrant. They forget that currently they submit only in ritual law. Asking a question of the rabbi means that the individual has, from the outset, yielded of his own free will to rabbinic authority. In civil cases defendants are hauled into court against their will. Even more important, one's ego and social standing are not at stake in a question of ritual law. Civil law, however, is a zero-sum game: one loses to another party. The opponent has triumphed, and that is always an embarrassment, especially in a small, face-to-face community. Considerable sums of money can be at stake in civil suits, far more often than in ritual matters. People dislike losing; doubly so when money is at stake. When losing a case, or when seeing the prospects of such loss in one system of law, one naturally seeks redress in another. For this reason, no problem is more pervasive in Jewish history than the appeal to *'arka'ot*, Gentile courts. To point out that some members of the eleventh-century Ashkenazic community turned to *'arka'ot* is only to say that this generation, like the tens of generations that followed, was all too human.

4. Which brings us to Grossman's final argument: there are references to perjurers, strong-armed individuals, and occasionally even thieves in eleventh-century sources. When we speak of 'England's finest hour' in the Second World War, we speak of how ordinary British people acted in a moment of historic testing, how they defied all odds in a heroic stand for their nation's values and way of life. There was looting and fraudulent claims after the bombings, the black market flourished because of rationing, and the crime rate

increased by 57 percent between 1939 and 1945.[8] However, this has not altered the historic image. In the thing that counted most, Britain in 1940 was weighed and not found wanting.

The same holds true for the generation of 1096, and for the three preceding generations that had created the religious culture that was tested in the First Crusade. Heroes are human, and we should not be at all surprised if the responsa literature—with its snapshots of daily life—vividly details their frailties.

I believe that Dr. Grossman would agree with these last two points and that the difference between us is simply one of emphasis and presentation.

APPENDIX

The manuscripts of the Jewish Theological Seminary had not yet arrived at the Institute of Hebrew Microfilms in Jerusalem in the mid-1970s. Grossman, in his study of eleventh-century communal self-government,[9] employed my transcription of R. Shemayah's important report of the rulings of Rashi and R. Yitsḥak b. Yehudah concerning communal organization in MS JTS, Rabbinica 1077, fo. 75a, which I had made during my stay in New York in 1971. I subsequently printed that transcription in my *Shut ke-Makor Histori*.[10] The transcription had a number of minor errors and has now appeared in print twice. I take this opportunity to correct an entrenched error for which I was responsible.

מפי הרב ר׳ שמעיה. שאלו את ר׳ על בני אדם שקופצין ונודרים ונשבעין שלא ישמרו ולא יעמדו על גזירת הצבור וכפייתם, או אפי׳ הם עשרה בני אדם. ואחר כך גזרו צבור עליו, אם חלה הגזירה עליו או לא. והשיב ר׳ ואמ׳ ברי חלה וחלה עְלֵיה[11] ואינו אלא נשבע לבטל המצוה דכת[י׳] הט אזנך ושמע דברי חכמים. ולא עוד אלא שאין נמנעין הצבור מלגזור עליו לכתחילה אלא גוזרין ומחרימין ומטעינין על צוארו דאין איסור בכך כל עיקר. ומעשה באחד באַבֲלון שקִדש ריבה אחת ורצה לחזור וקפץ ונשבע שאם גוזרין עליו לא יקבל. וגזרו עליו בנו קהלו והסכימו עמהם בני מיאויינינא וכנסה לחופה. ואף רבנו ר׳ יצחק ב״ר יהודה הסכים על ידם, והוא הזקיקן לכך. וגם אני ראיתי שני פעמים באנשים שקפצו ונשבעו להיפרש מן הצבור שלא ליתן כלום באותה מתנה. ואחר כך הטעינן ר׳ שבועה חמורה ולא חש לשבועת הבלים.

8 See Juliet Gardiner, *Wartime Britain* (London, 2004), 504–22.

9 See Grossman (above, n. 3), 187–90.

10 *Shut ke-Makor Histori* (above, n. 5), 121.

11 The diacritics or what seem to be diacritics here and in אבלון are found in the manuscript.

CHAPTER TWELVE

On Deviance

A Reply to David Malkiel

IN AN AVOWEDLY REVISIONIST HISTORY entitled *Refashioning Ashkenaz: The Human Face of Franco-German Jewry, 1000–1250*, David Malkiel, a well-known historian of early modern Jewry, devotes an entire chapter to demonstrating how widespread deviance was in the Ashkenazic community of the Middle Ages.[1] I would like to first examine some of his underlying assumptions and then turn to the specific criticisms leveled against my article 'Religious Law and Change: The Medieval Ashkenazic Example'.[2]

Dr. Malkiel posits the existence of a vast grid of religious requirements and argues that anything that is in the slightest way incongruous with this grid is deviance—whether it be more than the letter of the law demanded (*le-ḥumra*), less than the law demanded, or even simple custom, if the popular practice did not originate in the canonical literature. Thus, the deviance of Ashkenazic Jewry comes to the fore (*a*) in its *supererogatory conduct*, for example its voluntary martyrdom and slaughter of its children lest they be baptized, its refusal to abrogate the irksome ban on Gentile wine (*yein nesekh*), and its more limited use of Gentile services on the Sabbath (*goy shel Shabbat*) than was allowed by law; (*b*) in *breaches*, for example the widespread trade with Gentiles in the Friday markets; trade with Gentiles at any time in objects that the Talmud has forbidden, such as horses and oxen; women braiding their hair on the Sabbath; women wearing jewelry outside the home on that day, something the Talmud bans for fear that they might take off a brooch or bracelet to show to friends and take a few steps with it (to get better light for viewing, for example) and thus carry an object in the public domain (*reshut ha-rabbim*) on the Sabbath—an act forbidden by halakhah; (*c*) finally, in such *customs* as women immersing themselves, after their menses, three times in the ritual bath (*mikveh*), rather than just once as is required by the law; their not doing work on the day of the New Moon (Rosh Hodesh); and their similar refraining from labor while the Hanukah candles burn.

[1] (Stanford, 2009), 148–99. [2] Above, p. 239.

If custom is deviance, then Jewish life throughout the ages has been grossly deviant, as law provides religious life with only a skeletal framework. There is the widest variety of ritual behavior which is textually rootless, or rooted textually much after the fact. As large tracts of our prayer book (*siddur*) are pure custom, 'Yekum Purkan' is then deviant, *Pirkei Avot* is deviant, as is the singing of *zemirot* on the Sabbath. Much of the traditional Jewish kitchen is without foundation in the normative literature, as I noted in my essay.[3] There is no need for separate milk and meat tablecloths or napkins, no need for separate dishracks, and if one is washing up by hand, one can wash milk and meat dishes together. Halakhically speaking, the traditional Passover preparations are mostly superfluous. The emptying of cupboards holding the year-round plates and dishes and the scouring of their shelves, as well as the obsessive cleaning of every nook and cranny of the house, are entirely the product of Jewish housekeeping traditions handed down through generations from mother to daughter. All these are both customary and supererogatory and should be labeled 'deviant'.

Dr. Malkiel dwells at length on the fact that early modern women did not have access to the written literature, and hence all their transmissions were mimetic rather than learned and did not necessarily derive from the canonized texts. I would advise my distinguished colleague that in a traditional society, unlike the religious society of today, everything is transmitted mimetically: male conduct was imparted in a way that differed little from that of women. One no more learns how to pray or put on *tefillin* from law books than one learns how to speak or dress by following written instructions. Putting on shoes and putting on a *tallit katan* are part of the unreflective repertoire of daily conduct that is absorbed by the child from his earliest days. They are not 'learned' but acquired by living among people who habitually conduct themselves in this way. They are simply part of the socialization of the child (here the Jewish child) that begins with infancy, as patterns of conduct become ingrained and norms of behavior are instilled. This initiation into the group's way of life (*oraḥ ḥayyim*) is inevitable and unremitting, and the continuous instruction imbibed from home and street is coterminous with conscious life itself. I will dwell no further on the subject as I have written an entire essay on the difference between a mimetically acquired religiosity and one that is text-based, and simply refer the reader to it.[4]

[3] Above, p. 254.

[4] H. Soloveitchik, 'Rupture and Reconstruction: The Transformation of Contemporary Orthodoxy', *Tradition*, 28 (1994), 64–131; the essay will be included in a forthcoming volume of the same title.

Even in a text-based society much of the religious education is mimetic and largely unrelated to the normative literature. To give but one example: one of the first religious notions instilled in a child is that of *muktseh*. Not only is work on the Sabbath forbidden, but so too is any contact with utensils and the appurtenances of work or business such as money, pens, or light fixtures. Such objects are called *muktseh*. As soon as the child begins to crawl, he is warned off handling or even touching on the Sabbath any number of things that he may freely handle during the week. By the age of 3, certainly by 4, the child has internalized this sharp divide of everyday objects and already recoils from touching them on the Sabbath. What he has learned by then is all he needs to know for the rest of his life. Anything learned subsequently about the subject will serve only to confuse, for the exact definition or, more accurately, the exact definitions, of *muktseh* and *issurei tiltul* are extremely complex. Indeed, R. Avraham Yesha'aya Karelitz, also known as the Ḥazon Ish, first made his reputation among scholars with a study of *muktseh*, a pioneering attempt to bring some order into that complex halakhic universe.[5] It would be no exaggeration to say that in previous generations only the greatest of Talmudists could make claim to familiarity with this abstruse field or, indeed, showed any interest in it. Nor was such abstruse knowledge necessary. The mimetic tradition on the matter is clear and simple, the normative texts anything but that, and legal discussion would only compound the confusion.

Let us dispense then with the categories of 'custom' and 'stringency' as indicators of deviance, and focus on what is generally termed 'deviance', namely malfeasance and nonfeasance—breaking the law and failing to live up to its demands.[6]

If we seek 100 percent observance of the law by the entire community, we will seek and never find. There were wayward Ashkenazic Jews as there were wayward Puritans. No one ever claimed that there was no serpent in the garden of Ashkenaz. Everything is a question of proportion, and that is precisely what is lacking in Dr. Malkiel's presentation. He cites, for example, women braiding their hair and wearing jewelry on the Sabbath.[7] What is their significance however? What was the general level of Sabbath observance in

[5] *Sefer Ḥazon Ish 'al Oraḥ Ḥayyim* (Benei Berak, 1991), *Hilkhot Shabbat*, ##40–9. The study first appeared in 1923.

[6] I will forbear treating here the serious breach of the Seventh Commandment committed by parents when confronted with the prospect of the baptism of their children subsequent to their own martyrdom, as I have treated it extensively in 'Halakhah, Hermeneutics and Martyrdom in *Ashkenaz*', *Jewish Quarterly Review*, 94 (2004), 77–108, 278–99. (The essay will appear in the second volume of this series.)

[7] *Refashioning Ashkenaz* (above, n. 1), 155–60, 162–3.

Ashkenaz? *Sefer Ḥasidim* spells out some breaches[8]—are these serious or trivial? More importantly, what were the practical consequences of the dialectical revolution of the Tosafists in the area of Sabbath observance? What allowances were possible in the new doctrines and which were declined? Which were embraced, and at what cost? Who bore the brunt of these changes—men or women? How did the novel doctrines of the Tosafists with regard to *shehiyah* and *hatmanah*, for example, impact on the Jewish kitchen, on women's provisioning of their families on the Sabbath? Did they swiftly adopt these new regulations; did they even go further and act here, as in the matter of the *goy shel Shabbat*, in a supererogatory fashion? Without answers to such questions, one can't assess the significance of the breaches. If the general level of observance was high, if the new demands were being absorbed slowly but steadily into popular practice, and if women bore willingly these fresh burdens, indeed, incorporated them on their own initiative into their housekeeping traditions, one can well understand why halakhists were loath to deny their desire for a bit of primping and preening on their well-earned day of rest.

Moreover, in a traditional society, where the present receives its empowerment from the past, the conduct of one's parents and teachers is never 'wrong'. No Jewish housewife (*yidishe bale-boste*[9]) could have entertained the idea that her mother and grandmother fed their families non-kosher food (*treyfes*) all their lives. The most one might persuade her to admit was that another way of doing it was somewhat preferable. That too would be a considerable accomplishment, and few rabbis would even attempt it. There was a saying among rabbis: 'A *yidishe bale-boste* takes instruction from her mother only.' If this seems strange to the contemporary ear, consider a college course in ethics. A commonly used tool in teaching the subject is to present, at the outset of the course, a series of cases and ask students for their reaction as to who in these stories acted rightly and who wrongly. The instructor then shows them how self-contradictory the students' answers are. Living the 'unexamined life', their values are shown to be a welter of contradictions. Yet no one has become a criminal as a result of a course in ethics. Our sense of right and wrong has been so deeply instilled in us that it is immune to intellectual criticism, for abstract reasoning generally affects only what is 'learnt'. We have acquired our values, however, not by instruction but by osmosis, imbibed them unawares from home, street, and early schooling. What's right is right and what's wrong is wrong; sophisticated arguments change nothing. The sense of religious 'right'

[8] See e.g. *Sefer Ḥasidim*, ed. Y. Wistinetzki, 2nd edn. (Frankfurt am Main, 1924), ##272, 356, 591.

[9] As stated in the Introduction, Yiddish words are transliterated according to YIVO's guidelines.

and 'wrong' is scarcely different in an enclosed and deeply entrenched mimetic society.

The *bale-boste* is, then, emblematic rather than unique. To give a simple example: no one had greater authority and prestige in nineteenth-century Lithuania than the Gaon of Vilna. Yet his writ did not run in his own home town, let alone in Lithuania. It ran only in his own small synagogue, the Gaon's *kloyz*. For example, in the late nineteenth century, seeking to demonstrate to an elite Lithuanian audience the singularity of his father and uncle, the writer A. Y. Fromkin pointed out that they were among the very few who systematically followed the rulings of the Gaon.[10] Very few apparently did. People tend to think that Ashkenazim in Israel generally follow the Gaon's rulings. However, this is only true for a dozen or so practices in the public arena, predominantly in synagogue ritual, although the Gaon's writings demand hundreds of alterations of practice in every aspect of Jewish life—Sabbath, Passover, Sukkot, and the like. Similarly, he effected little change in the deeply settled communities of Lithuania, whose traditions stretched back many centuries, some close to half a millennium, and whose members did not lightly entertain the idea that their past practices had been deviant and their revered ancestors unwitting sinners. Not squaring with contemporary halakhic thought, even the best of contemporary halakhic thought, is one thing; error and wrongdoing another. My distinguished colleague uses the term 'deviant' somewhat too freely in discussing a traditional society.

Furthermore, even conduct which is, indeed, recognized by a society as deviant is not always the object of rectification. No society enforces all of its rules, or even tries to. Wrongdoing is failing to reach a level of attainment that is seen as achievable, and 100 percent compliance by the community is generally viewed as unachievable. There is a strong inclination in any establishment to overlook certain long-standing infractions or ones that are hard to correct. There is an equal awareness that the 'crooked timber of humanity' will never be made entirely straight. Human nature being what it is, some laxity in the broader society is inevitable, and the attempt to enforce religious purity, to attain perfect congruence between deed and norm, is simply counterproductive.

In enforcement one must pick and choose, and perspective is essential. This holds true even in the historically novel situation of today, where religiosity is not mimetic but text-based, where the canonical literature is, as Justice

[10] See my 'Rupture and Reconstruction' (above, n. 4), 111, n. 20(*c*). For the range of the Gaon's sweeping reassessment of proper ritual practice, see Zvi Hirsch ben Shelomoh [Lempert], *Piskei ha-Gra 'al Shulḥan 'Arukh*, 'Oraḥ Ḥayyim' (Vilna, 1875).

Holmes once characterized the United States Constitution, 'a brooding omnipresence in the sky', and where traditional performance is generally under a critical referent.[11] To give an example: eating meat on the holidays is a religious imperative. According to Maimonides, it is even a pentateuchal one (*mi-de-oraita*).[12] Yet Ashkenazic Jews eat milk products on Shavuot. By Dr. Malkiel's standards, eating *blintzes* is deviance. Admittedly, some rationales have been found for this anomaly, but my learned colleague would correctly argue that these are but *ex post facto* justifications. Furthermore, the absence of any anti-*blintzes* campaign would highlight, to Dr. Malkiel's way of thinking, the recalcitrance of popular practice and the weakness of contemporary Torah leadership. Perhaps, indeed, it does. I suspect, however, that most rabbis and *rashei yeshivah* would reply:

> Look, this generation has witnessed an enormous appreciation both in the level of Torah study and that of religious observance. Forty years ago, the daily *minyan* (the ten-man quorum required for public prayer) was a dying institution. Torah study groups (*ḥavrutot*) of laymen were rare, as was any form of post-yeshiva 'learning'; as for the page-a-day study of the Talmud (*daf yomi*)—most had never even heard of it. The morning *minyanim* are now packed, learning in *ḥavrutot* is widespread, daily Talmud classes are found everywhere, and thousands are engaged in the *daf yomi* study. Numerous organizations presently guarantee the *kashrut* of thousands of items, whereas previously one had to rely on reading the list of ingredients. A generation or two ago one had to plead with parents to give their children a Jewish education. Nowadays, day schools and yeshivas are flourishing, and many parents go heavily into debt to provide a yeshiva education for their children. So, everything considered, if they want to do as their parents did and eat *blintzes* on Shavuot, let them eat *blintzes*.

Context and perspective are everything, and that is precisely what Dr. Malkiel cannot provide, as he is a historian of early modern Jewish history and has done little or no research into the primary sources of medieval Ashkenaz, at least as far as I can discern. He has collected, mostly from secondary sources, a number of infractions, or what he believes to be infractions, that frequently occurred there. Useful as such a list is, without some placement in a larger setting it says very little.

Towards the end of the chapter on deviance, Dr. Malkiel specifically addresses my argument in 'Religious Law and Change':[13]

[11] See my 'Rupture and Reconstruction' (above, n. 4), 70–4.

[12] 'Hilkhot Yom Tov', 6: 17–18.

[13] D. Malkiel, *Refashioning Ashkenaz* (above, n. 1), 195–6.

Soloveitchik suggests four factors contributed to this self image of excellence. The first is 'the simplicity of religious beliefs.' This may be an oblique reference to the absence of philosophy in contrast to its alleged pernicious impact on the Jews of Spain, in Yitzhak Baer's classic dichotomy. Whether or not this model ought to be accepted as true, the nexus between this simplicity and righteous self-image is not mandated by logic and it remains unclear.

It is one thing to contend, as did Baer, that philosophy was the font of all the religious ills of Spanish Jewry. It is wholly another to assert, as I did, that the perception of the mechanistic universe set in motion by an Unmoved Mover is less conducive to religious beliefs and observance than that of a religious cosmology governed by a personal God. A God, moreover, who has revealed and covenanted himself to man, and whose daily intervention in human affairs, both his reward and punishment, is taken as a given. Philosophy may not spell the end of religious conviction, as Baer posited; however, the notion that the performance of religious obligations (*mitsvot*) is simply a means to attain certain moral and spiritual ends (as the followers of Maimonides contended) is less conducive to religious observance than the perception of *mitsvot* as divinely ordained ends in and of themselves (as most other Jews believed). The simple reason for this is that there is invariably more than one way to achieve any given goal; why not then substitute the eating of matzah with some spiritual exercise? If such fears are unrealistic, then what was the Maimonidean controversy about?

There is, indeed, no logical nexus, as my distinguished colleague says, between '[religious] simplicity and righteous self-image'. There is, however, a logical nexus between religious simplicity and piety, certainly an empirical one between simple, unquestioning faith and scrupulous observance of the dictates of that faith. The greater the piety of the community, the better its religious self-image will be.

Dr. Malkiel continues:

The second factor is undivided allegiance—the universal assumption that the Ashkenazic community was and would always remain faithful, notwithstanding the existence of some apostates. The First Crusade comes into play here, because this aspect of the Ashkenazic self-image rests on the record of mass martyrdom in 1096. The closest connection between the 1096 experience and faithful observance is the passage from *Sefer Hasidim* that makes the argument that a Jew ought to meet his quotidian religious obligations because were he to live through a period of religious persecution, obviously he would suffer death rather than transgression [*sic*], that is, baptism. How widespread this image of the First Crusade experience was in the twelfth century is uncertain; recent scholarship has highlighted the significance of apostasy and has downplayed the scope of mass martyrdom. Moreover, the extent of the impact of German Pietists on the Ashkenazic society is another murky problem. A third problem with this argument is that it is tautological. The Jews of Ashkenaz, argues Soloveitchik, saw themselves as absolutely faithful to Judaism because they believed they are and would always be faithful to Judaism.

I don't know what German Pietism has to do with the matter. I certainly never invoked it. Can anyone read the *piyyutim* written in the wake of the First Crusade, recited in Ashkenaz for centuries (and still recited to this day) on Tishah be-Av and again on the most solemn day of the year, Yom Kippur, and not believe that this conduct was held up as the pinnacle of religious devotion, surpassing a hundredfold the *'akedat Yitsḥak* (Abraham's sacrifice of Isaac), and proudly presented as the singular achievement of the Ashkenazic community and of that community alone? Can one imagine that this does not shape a community's self-image?[14] Of course there were communities, such as Kerpen and Geldern, even the ancient one of Regensburg, that went to the baptismal font, and the chronicles of the First Crusade do not hide this fact. However, as I have pointed out elsewhere, 'To all the various narrators—writing, it should be emphasized, at different times and in different places—such events were forced, momentary lapses, moments to be pitied rather than to be feared. It never occurred to any of them that what had transpired was a result of anything other than overwhelming duress.'[15] The issue is not, as my learned colleague would have it, how recent scholarship has reconstructed the events of 1096, but how the collective memory of Ashkenaz portrayed them.

Dr. Malkiel further questions whether the events of 1096 resonated in the twelfth century. What were the mass suicides and murder of children in York in 1179 if not a replay of 1096? The events of 1096 set the pattern for communal response to forced baptism for the next 250 years.[16] Obviously not every community engaged in suicide and the murder of its children; more fortunately, not every situation demanded such a line of conduct. (Such situations could usually arise only when there was either a breakdown of governmental

[14] See D. Wachtel, 'The Ritual and Liturgical Commemoration of Two Medieval Persecutions' (MA thesis, Columbia University, 1995); S. Goldin, *The Ways of Jewish Martyrdom* (Turnhout, 2009), 123–62. Indeed, some are of the opinion that the Crusade chronicles themselves had initially a liturgical function. See Y. Baer's introduction to *Gezerot Ashkenaz ve-Tsarfat*, ed. A. M. Haberman (Jerusalem, 1950), 3–4; G. D. Cohen, 'The Hebrew Chronicles and the Ashkenazic Tradition', in M. Brettler and M. Fishbane, eds., *Minḥah le-Naḥum: Biblical and Other Studies Presented to Nahum Sarna in Honour of his 70th Birthday* (Sheffield, 1993), 51.

[15] Chapter 9 above.

[16] See A. Gross, *Struggling with Tradition: Reservations about Active Martyrdom in the Middle Ages* (Leiden, 2004), 20–7, 103–6.

authority or a tacit allowance of mob rule by the powers that be.) The martyrs of Mainz and Worms were portrayed as the apotheosis of religious devotion, this image was then inculcated by the incorporation of the tale of their sacrifices into the yearly ritual, and the conduct of 1096 was emulated often enough for the Ashkenazic community to believe that this response was typical. The narrative that the Ashkenazic community wove of itself was one of religious heroism. Whether this self-told tale was any more true than other national narratives is an open question. It unquestionably contributed to an elevated self-image. Linking valor with pride and stalwartness with self-esteem may be obvious, but it is not tautological.

Dr. Malkiel then writes: 'Soloveitchik's third factor is what he terms "the thickening of the heavenly yoke". We are told that the commoners increasingly heeled to talmudic law and that "tosafist thought was percolating downward". Our sources for this are limited to rabbinic literature, which can hardly be taken at face value.' I must confess that I am baffled. My learned colleague has written a chapter of over fifty pages documenting what he believes is religious deviance. All the sources he cites are from rabbinic literature. Why does he find rabbinic sources credible when they speak of deviance but not so when they speak of compliance? Moreover, these sources do not *speak of* compliance, they do not state overtly how observant the community is—a complimentary, even self-congratulatory observation that might be suspect. Source after source *presumes* a compliance with a relatively new demand of the Tosafists. Why would an inquirer pose a question to a religious authority that makes sense only if one assumes that the practice was to forbid, for example, *noten ta'am bar noten ta'am* (*nat-bar-nat*) if both stages are *ḥamin* (an innovative doctrine reported in the name of Rashi[17]), if this wasn't the case? Was the query a practical joke or an attempt to harass a busy *posek*?

'More significant,' writes Dr. Malkiel,

> is the fourth factor, the 'refusal to maximize allowances.' . . . Soloveitchik pursues this line of inquiry and sees in this pattern 'the workings of a religious intuition alongside of which the written word pales.' This argument leads to a conclusion very much in conjunction with the argument of this chapter, for both religious intuition and ritual instinct are explanations that justify deviant behavior. We have seen that the Jews of medieval Franco-Germany adhered to a code of behavior that was, to a surprising extent, autonomous and recalcitrant rather than submissive to talmudic and rabbinic authority.

[17] *Tosafot*, *Ḥullin* 111b, s.v. *hilkhata*; *Tosfot ha-Rosh 'al Ḥullin*, ed. A. Lichtenstein (Jerusalem, 2002), 111b, s.v. *u-shemu'el*; *Or Zarua'*, i (Zhitomir, 1862), *Hilkhot Basar be-Ḥalav*, #467.

I have already registered my dissent from Dr. Malkiel's definition of deviance in view of the strong presumption of rectitude in a traditional society of any long-standing norm of conduct, and further remarked on the relative autonomy of most religious practices in a mimetic society. What my learned colleague calls 'recalcitrance' I would term 'resilience'. The deep embeddedness of religious life in habit and tradition does indeed make it resilient, and rabbinic authority over the ages has been the first to give that tenacity its due.

'Soloveitchik concedes', concludes Dr. Malkiel, 'that "there were murderers, lechers, apostates, informers, thieves and Sabbath violators in Ashkenaz no less than in Sefarad" and he [i.e. Soloveitchik] asks, "Have we not painted an idealized portrait of Ashkenaz?" The foregoing discussion suggests that this question must be answered in the affirmative.' Perhaps it is egotism on my part, perhaps I am simply too old to change my spots, but I still prefer my original answer:[18]

> Frankly, one is hard pressed to answer that question. For, like most large questions, it is actually composed of a number of smaller, subtler ones. When is an unreflecting faith 'religiosity', and when is it philistinism? When is cowering before a hideous death simply a failure of nerve, and when does it betoken a weakness of the spirit? . . . When does a mute cry for help arise from an inability to cope, and when from a lack of will to cope? . . . In each case the line between the alternatives is too fine for me, at least, to perceive it from a distance of over half a millennium. Perhaps these questions *are* best left to the judgment of contemporaries.

Assessments of credibility or sincerity—indeed, any evaluation of another person's attitude and beliefs—are best determined by actual observers. In law, such indications of inner states are called 'demeanor evidence'. Only the trial judge or jury who saw and heard the conflicting witnesses can determine who should be believed and who distrusted; who spoke honestly and whose words inspired no confidence. Courts of appeal, having before them only the written record, can rule on issues of law, not on ones of fact. They can never rule that A's testimony should be preferred over that of B if the trial court thought otherwise. In these matters, as in those that I raised in the above-cited passage, the contemporary observer has a decisive superiority over the historian.

The advantage that the historian possesses is perspective. He writes long after the event, knowing how things turned out decades or centuries later. He is able, then, to discern trends, to sift attention-grabbing epiphenomena from events which proved to be pregnant with consequence. A historian who notes, for example, instances of deviance in the German Jewish community of the

[18] Above, pp. 255–6.

seventeenth century and knows of the large defections of the next century can raise the question: are the earlier instances of deviance the first signs of what were later to become massive erosions, or are they still the random deviance found in any society, and does religious observance begin to wane only with the Enlightenment? In our instance, however, perspective yields nothing. The deviance in the Ashkenazic community in 1400 is not noticeably different from that of 1200. To be sure, societies change over time, and every age has its own problems. As a result of the frequent expulsions within the German Empire, family stability, for example, was shaken and the number of marital breakups rose dramatically in the late Middle Ages.[19] However, in most areas (including martyrdom) the level of religious observance remained remarkably stable. If anything, there was a turn to greater stringency—in the running of the Jewish kitchen and in the realm of *kashrut* generally. Garnering no insight from the perspective of centuries, I suggested then and still suggest now that modesty may be wisdom, and that the historian would do well to defer here to the judgment of contemporaries.

[19] Y. Y. Yuval, 'Takkanot Neged Ribbui Gerushin be-Germanyah ba-Me'ah ha-Tet Vav', *Zion*, 48 (1983), 177–215.

REVIEW ESSAY

Yishaq (Eric) Zimmer, *'Olam ke-Minhago Noheg*

Jerusalem: Merkaz Zalman Shazar, 1996. 328 pp.

THIS TWO-PRONGED STUDY is a work of sound and sober scholarship and of sterling honesty. The first section comprises an analysis of the course and fate of ten religious requirements or customs. Among those addressed are the history of the male head covering (*yarmulke* or *kippah*), a topic previously subjected to all types of tendentious studies, which receives here its first objective and comprehensive presentation, and the wearing of *pe'ot* (earlocks) and its fate over the course of two thousand years of Jewish history. Next comes a fascinating history of prayer gestures—bowing or prostration, closed or open eyes, clasped, folded, or outstretched hands, immobile or swaying body (*shokln* in Yiddish). All these stances were adopted by one community or another over the course of the past two millennia and, in a path-breaking examination, Zimmer provides us with a comprehensive survey of the Jewish postures of prayer. Certain strange practices in some communities on the afternoon of the Ninth of Av are then investigated, as is the fate of a number of variant texts in the prayer book. Eating indoors, rather than in the *sukkah*, on Shemini Atseret, a practice we associate with hasidic groups, is traced, in all its vicissitudes, back to a family in eleventh-century Rhineland. The section concludes with an enlightening discussion of the disappearance in European Jewry of one of the standard requirements of mourning, *'atifat ha-rosh* (covering one's face up to the eyes).

The second section of the book addresses the issue of cultural cleavage—the rift in many areas of religious practice that occurred in the late Middle Ages between western and eastern Germany—known as Minhag Rheinus and Minhag Ostreich. This split continued until the Holocaust, as Poland adopted the 'Rite of Ostreich' early on, while Germany west of the Magdeburg–Regensburg line, which included such famed communities as Mainz, Worms, and Frankfurt am Main, remained true to the old Rhineland traditions. The differences between the rites are many and seem to form no pattern. Zimmer presents the first systematic study of nine of these different practices, from menstrual and postnatal sexual abstinence to the order of lighting Hanukkah lights (left to right or right to left) and seeks to come up with some common denominator.

Zimmer cautiously suggests an idea or two, but candidly admits that they remain unproved and that no clear explanation has been found for this cultural rift; nor has any pattern been discovered in the strange and manifold ways that this fissure expressed itself. This is not surprising, as cultural cleavages and boundary formations are among the most baffling problems in history, and in their final forms they often combine the most central with the seemingly trivial. That the geographical line that linguistically divided northern and southern France into the lands of *langue d'oc* and *langue d'oïl* should roughly coincide with the line of demarcation between Romanesque and Gothic architecture seems to us, if not explicable, at least credible. That both should approximate the geographical line separating sharply sloped roofs made of flat tiles from gently sloped ones made of curved tiles seems somewhat ridiculous. Or take a more apt example, drawn from law. France in the Middle Ages was divided not only linguistically but also legally; it housed two different legal systems. The famed Klimrath line dividing *pays de droit écrit* (country of Roman law) from *pays de droit coutumier* (country of Germanic law) is almost identical with the one separating the zones using different terms for a mare (*cavale* or *jument*). (No disagreement, mind you, about what one called male horses—or dogs or cats, or any other animal for that matter—just the word for female horses.) And when one adds to the problem of cultural cleavage that of the diffusion of legal customaries—such disseminations often hinge on the origins of the early settlers, marriage alliances among elites who made or interpreted the laws and enforced practices, and on zones of shared culture as reflected by common dialect and pronunciation—it seems naïve to expect that an initial survey, seeking to trace for the first time the origins and course of nine such differences, should yield the whys and wherefores of the complex cultural cleavage that occurred during one of the least (internally) documented periods in central European Jewish history: the harrowing 150 years that followed the Black Death.

Zimmer draws attention to six factors that had a significant impact on religious praxis: Palestinian traditions, which were especially active in Ashkenazic culture in the high Middle Ages; German Pietism, which strongly influenced the Austrian and Polish rite (Minhag Ostreich) in the late Middle Ages; Safed mysticism, which often generated new rituals or swung the balance in favor of one competing practice over another in the course of the late sixteenth and the seventeenth centuries; cultural milieu, such as that which led to the abandonment of *'atifat ha-rosh* in mourning; physical environment, as in the instance of the colder climate in Poland leading to the abandonment in many circles of eating in the *sukkah* on Shemini Atseret; and finally, the pervasive presence of the 'ritual instinct'—popular intuition as to what was or was not religiously appropriate—that has been so carefully detailed by Jacob Katz in *The Shabbes Goy*.

The scholarship manifested throughout the study is meticulous, the integrity in acknowledging the help of others and the circumspection in drawing conclusions simply admirable. There is little that this reviewer can do except make a correction or register a demurral here and there, and then share some thoughts about some of Zimmer's larger conclusions. If I have reservations about a number of Zimmer's inferences, it is not because he has expressed them incautiously—far from it, he is the very soul of caution—but because of the strange alchemy of grammatical mood that occurs in scholarly citation. Conclusions stated by an author in the subjunctive mood often emerge in the writings of others in the indicative.

First, some addenda, corrigenda, and demurrals:

Pages 72–113. The chapter on prayer gestures would be enhanced if it were placed alongside Rudolph Suntrup's *Die Bedeutung der liturgischen Gebärden und Bewegungen in lateinischen und deutschen Auslegungen des 9 bis 13 Jahrhunderts* (Munich, 1978). Jews may well have consciously avoided commonality with Christian religious gestures; they would, however, have shared the common gestures of the surrounding society, much as Jews today, for example, show approval by clapping. For this reason, Suntrup's study should be complemented by François Garnier's *Le Langage de l'image au Moyen Âge*, ii: *Grammaire des gestes* (Paris, 1982), a veritable encyclopedia of what each gesture and body position then meant.

Pages 83–4. One should add the outspread hands described by R. Mosheh of Coucy, the author of the *Semag*, in the prayer published by Yitsḥak Gilat in *Tarbiz*, 27 (1958/9), 56. This source, in turn, would be illumined by Heinz Demisch's *Erhobene Hände: Geschichte einer Gebärde in der bildenden Kunst* (Stuttgart, 1984).

Page 129. Spanish influence on the rites of fourteenth-century Bohemia seems to me implausible.

Page 136. The author of the *Commentary on Tamid* is not R. Barukh of Worms, who wrote the *Sefer ha-Terumah*. E. E. Urbach's arguments (*Ba'alei ha-Tosafot*, revised edn. [Jerusalem, 1980], 354–60) on the matter are convincing. The author is, however, a pupil of R. Shemu'el he-Ḥasid, which is yet more to Zimmer's point. Nevertheless, I fail to see what evidence there is that Ḥasidei Ashkenaz were instrumental in the desuetude of the daily priestly blessings (*nesi'at kappayim*). If they demanded *tevilat ba'alei keriyin* (ritual immersion after seminal emission) for prayer and, a fortiori, by Zimmer's conjecture, for *nesi'at kappayim*, they obviously met that requirement regularly, for they certainly prayed daily. Why then should they not have had priestly blessings daily? If Zimmer wishes to attribute to Ḥasidei Ashkenaz the strange doctrine of the *Sefer Miktsa'ot*, why then did they bless on holidays? Do menstrual cycles cease on *yamim tovim*?

Pages 163–74. In his treatment of *sukkah* on Shemini Atseret, our author has omitted the characteristically original position of R. Yehudah ben Kalonymus in his *Yiḥusei Tanna'im ve-Amora'im*, ed. Y. L. Maimon (Jerusalem, 1963), 329–30. It deserves wider currency, as it is the most cogent argument ever made for eating indoors on Shemini Atseret.

Pages 194–5. Zimmer's bibliographical references to medieval dress are adequate but somewhat dated; for example, H. Weiss, *Kostümkunde* (Stuttgart, 1872). He might consider updating them in a subsequent edition, using the bibliography found in J. Bumke, *Höfische Kultur*, ii (Munich, 1986), 821–3. {English translation: *Courtly Culture: Literature and Society in the High Middle Ages* (Woodstock and New York, 2000), 720–2.}

Page 216. The geographical divide between Minhag Rheinus and Minhag Ostreich presented by Zimmer, based, I assume, on the information contained in the discussion of suet (pp. 250–61), is practically identical with the line between Ashkenaz and Kena'an drawn by Max Weinreich in his *History of the Yiddish Language* (Chicago, 1980), 46. Weinreich's discussion of the origins of the 'Knaanite' settlement (pp. 79–91 and *passim*), while certainly open to question, is directly relevant to the problem that Zimmer addresses (e.g. pp. 234–5), and use of Weinreich's work on this issue, not to speak of his discussion of Lotir (p. 330 ff.) and the relationship between eastern Yiddish and east-central German (p. 448 ff.), would have enriched Zimmer's argument. One cannot overemphasize the fact that while the differences between Ostreich and Rheinus express themselves in halakhah and liturgy, the divide itself is cultural, and such cultural determinants as language and demographic origins need to play a large role in any analysis of these fissures.

Pages 233–5. The attribution to Ḥasidei Ashkenaz of the growing tendency in eastern Germany to abstain from sexual relations during the entire postnatal period (*yemei tohar*, forty days after the birth of a son, eighty days after that of a daughter) seems to me forced. An ambiguous line in a manuscript of the *Pa'aneaḥ Raza* (a late thirteenth-century collection of Ashkenazic Bible commentaries) seems somewhat thin evidence in the absence of any corroboration in either *Sefer Ḥasidim* or the writings of Rokeaḥ. Indeed, R. Ele'azar Rokeaḥ explicitly permits sexual congress during this period (p. 234). Ḥasidei Ashkenaz were very stringent with regard to contact between a menstruant woman and any *sancta*—sacred objects (*sifrei Torah*), places (synagogues), and acts (prayer). Full distance (*harḥakah*) between spouses during the menstrual period was also advocated to best avoid sexual temptation, a human failing of which Ḥasidei Ashkenaz were only too well aware. However, to the best of my knowledge, there is no evidence that the German Pietists advocated sexual abstinence over and above what the law demanded. For all its asceticism in other matters, *Sefer Ḥasidim* manifests an ample, almost lusty, endorsement of marital sex. If the widespread practice of postnatal abstinence obtained, Ḥasidei Ashkenaz might well have gone along with it, but I have difficulty envisioning them initiating such protracted continence.

I would also caution Zimmer on citing T. B. Auerbach's edition of the *Sefer ha-Eshkol* (Halberstadt, 1869) (pp. 31, 221, 226, 244, 253). The early years of the twentieth century witnessed a bitter conflict over its authenticity. Shalom Albeck, the editor of a second, and much smaller, text of the *Eshkol*, launched a vituperative attack on Auerbach after his death, questioning not only Auerbach's judgment, but also his integrity and that of his widow. Not surprisingly, some leading scholars sprang to the defense of Auerbach's good name and published a pamphlet entitled *Tsidkat ha-Tsaddik*. Upon its appearance, Auerbach appeared to have been vindicated. But, with all respect to the goodwill of these truly distinguished scholars, the pamphlet is long on encomia and short on argument. Seen now, from the perspective of some three-quarters of a century, Auerbach's *Eshkol* appears to be a clear forgery, incorporating arguments found in sixteenth-, seventeenth-, and even eighteenth-century writings. This is not to say that Auerbach himself forged the manuscript. He may well have been duped. When he began working on it, in the mid-nineteenth century, manuscript publication of medieval halakhic works was in its infancy, and little was then known of the state of halakhic thinking in mid-twelfth-century Provence. Be that as it may, the work remains a forgery and should not be used for historical purposes. I should, perhaps, add that Zimmer's citations of

Auerbach's *Eshkol* are never crucial to his argument. Their elimination in no way alters the portrait he has drawn.

And now to the larger conclusions:

I would take exception to Zimmer's occasional penchant for explaining an inexplicable development by attributing it to 'Palestinian influence'. For example, I do not see the evidence for the Palestinian origins of swaying, shaking bodily gestures in prayer (pp. 211–12). A reference or two (pp. 100–1) to the literature of the *yordei merkavah*, the Palestinian visionaries of ecstatic ascent, seem inadequate support. Ecstatic visionaries may well have trembled in prayer, but have we any evidence whatsoever, from the midrashim or the Talmud Yerushalmi, that ordinary Palestinian Jews swayed and '*shokl*ed' in their prayers? (Truth to tell, we cannot even find the putative reference in the *heikhalot* literature; see p. 100 n. 164.) There is, indeed, a Palestinian substratum to many Ashkenazic practices. This was pointed out in the earliest days of Wissenschaft des Judentums, and has been emphasized, perhaps overemphasized, in recent years. However, unless a Palestinian origin can be shown, adducing it without proof is, to my mind, to proffer a panacea rather than a solution. In fairness, one should add that on the several occasions that Zimmer does tender this solution, he cautiously tags it with a 'perhaps'.

Zimmer attributes to the colder climes of Poland the disappearance, in many hasidic circles, of the practice of sitting in the *sukkah* on Shemini Atseret. If climate were a sufficient explanation, the custom of sitting in the *sukkah* should have disappeared on Sukkot itself. Climate, then, is a necessary but scarcely sufficient condition for this deviation from the norm. I would suggest that *sukkah*-sitting on Shemini Atseret was established on an original fault line, and its observance ultimately cracked under the joint pressure of a colder climate and the change in religious calendar that occurred in eastern Europe as the Safed kabbalah made ever greater inroads, especially among hasidim.

Allow me to explain.

The Talmud (*Shabbat* 23a), when discussing the second day of *yom tov* (*yom tov sheni shel galuyot*), states that, strictly speaking, one should not recite a blessing on the commandments performed that day, as, for example, on the second *seder* night. However, were the rabbis to have instituted the second *seder*, for example, without the appropriate blessings over matzah and *maror*, people would not take the second-day ceremonies seriously (*de-lo le-zilzulei bah*). They made one exception to this policy, *sukkah* on Shemini Atseret—where they instituted sitting without the blessing—and, in the fullness of time, the exception proved the wisdom of the rule. It did not have to happen, and, indeed, in most lands it did not happen. In Poland, however, the frequently bitter autumn cold made *sukkah*-sitting a genuine burden. Jews had sacrificed much for their faith, and no one dreamed that severe chills suspended the demands of religion, so Jews dutifully sat in *sukkot* throughout the Sukkot holiday. Shemini Atseret, however, was a different matter. *Sukkah*-sitting on that day was clearly a second-class commandment. Evidence: it did not even merit a blessing, unlike all other second-day *mitsvot*. And by the 1640s the laxity in *sukkah*-sitting on Shemini Atseret was widespread in Poland, as the remarks of the super-commentators on the *Tur* and *Shulḥan 'Arukh* clearly indicate (pp. 168–9).

Common though it was, this laxity was not yet characteristic of any one group. In the course of the next century, the growing influence of Safed kabbalah transformed Hoshana Rabbah into a day equal to—indeed, greater in its momentous irreversibility than—Yom Kippur. On this day, the final and irrevocable judgment on every individual was rendered. The tension of Judgment Day stretched now not from the first of Ellul (when *seliḥot* began) to Yom Kippur, but some fifty-two days—all the way to Hoshana Rabbah. Just as *motsa'ei* Yom Kippur in Temple times became an occasion for celebration, as the accumulated tensions of that awesome day found release, so *motsa'ei* Hoshana Rabbah, the night of Shemini Atseret, became an eve of hasidic celebration. *Hakkafot* were shifted from Simhat Torah, and the festivities of Shemini Atseret far exceeded those of its sister holiday. Such celebrations could scarcely be held outside in the cold October nights, and the festive eating and drinking could take place in the *sukkah* only with difficulty. And so, *sukkah*-sitting on Shemini Atseret fell into desuetude among large bodies of hasidim. The northern climate, indeed, played a role in this disuse, but without the original fault line of 'no *berakhah*' and the shift in date of the religious climax of the year, the sharp autumn cold, by itself, I would suggest, would have been insufficient to effect any large-scale change.

Zimmer draws upon Ta-Shma's important article on the presence of numerous pupils of R. Yehudah he-Ḥasid in Slavic countries. Ta-Shma conjectured that R. Yehudah he-Ḥasid moved from Speyer to Regensburg because of the opposition that he encountered in the old Rhineland city to his radical program and sought out the 'frontier' zone as being more receptive to his innovative ideas. Similarly, pupils of his settled in the east precisely because in the new settlements there was a greater chance of instituting hasidic doctrines. Adopting this line of thought, Zimmer sees in German Pietism a major force in shaping the rite of Ostreich and Poland. It is an interesting thesis and certainly worth pursuing. It should be noted, however, that Regensburg in the twelfth century was a burgeoning commercial center. Situated on the Danube, it was a gateway city to trade with south-eastern Europe and the lands of Islam, and quite possibly was also already playing a central role in financing the *Ostsiedlung* (eastward migration and settlement of Germans). And Jewish settlement in medieval times often followed commercial opportunity. To ask why R. Yehudah he-Ḥasid settled there is equally to ask why other prominent Tosafists, such as R. Yitsḥak ben Mordekhai (Rivam), R. Yitsḥak ben Ya'akov (Ri ha-Lavan), R. Efrayim, R. Barukh, and R. Shemaryah, had all made their new homes in Regensburg. Moreover, Regensburg, while considerably east of the Rhineland, was no *tabula rasa*, waiting for the imprint of some eminent émigré. It housed a distinguished line of German Tosafists, who antedated R. Yehudah in residence by a half-century. More significantly, it was the seat of one of the most venerable Jewish communities in Germany, whose recorded history stretched back as far as that of the Rhineland cities. It is customary to picture the expansion of the German Jewish community as radiating eastward from the settlements on the Rhine. The written record, however, documents the simultaneous emergence in the tenth century of Jewish communities both along the Rhineland and in the trading centers near and along the eastern borders of the Empire—Regensburg, Magdeburg, Merseburg, and Prague. True, the oldest academies were in Mainz and Worms, but the other ancient communities were scarcely deferential about their local customs and practices. R. Yitsḥak Or Zarua'—who numbered R. Yehudah he-Ḥasid among his teachers—juxtaposes, with no sense of inferiority, the traditions of his native Bohemia with those of the Rhineland.

As to the alleged influence of German Pietism on the Eastern Rite, we would do well to remember two things. First, rich and important as Ta-Shma's article is in the new information that it provides about little-known medieval Polish scholars, the connections between these erudite men and Ḥasidei Ashkenaz remain, nevertheless, conjectural. For example, the idea that the scholar R. Ya'akov ha-Kohen belonged to the circle of German Pietists is based on the assumption that the Ya'akov ha-Kohen (not a very rare or distinctive name) mentioned in the halakhic sources is one and the same person as the Ya'akov ha-Kohen mentioned in a now lost kabbalistic manuscript. All that we know for certain is that R. Yehudah he-Ḥasid had Slavic pupils in his Bible classes. There is no evidence that these eastern students were scholars of any standing or that they exercised any authority in their homeland. Second, and more generally, we should be open to the presence of French influence on the eastern border of the Empire, a notion not as surprising as it may at first sound. In the latter half of the twelfth century some German scholars traveled to France to study under Rabbenu Tam, and in the thirteenth century this westward student migration became widespread. Indeed, there is scarcely a single thirteenth-century German scholar of note who did not spend considerable time in French academies.[1] This means that German and French scholars not only formed one intellectual circle, but also experienced school-bonding, and friendships formed from living and studying together in adolescence and early adulthood have proven to be among the firmest bases of future contacts.

French halakhic culture, moreover, was continuously rising in prestige, as German students flocked to France, while few French students, if any, studied in Germany. In the mid-thirteenth century Magdeburg, on the eastern periphery, referred a question to Normandy, to R. Shemu'el of Falaise, who, sick at the time, asked his pupil, the future R. Me'ir of Rothenburg, to copy out his response;[2] and in 1291, a plaintiff in Goslar wanted his case judged by 'French rabbis'.[3] The fortunes of French Jewry declined steadily under Louis IX and Philip the Fair, and many people looked about for other lands of opportunity. We know of a steady stream southward; is it unreasonable to think of a migration, at least of the elite, eastward? The new German settlements needed men of learning, and the 'old-school network' was in place—a skein of friendships thickening here and there into nodes of influence that could ease the placement of past comrades and colleagues, the would-be French émigrés.

It is not surprising, then, that R. Ḥayyim Palti'el became the rabbi of Magdeburg.[4] His *Sefer ha-Minhagim* may well underlie that of R. Avraham Klausner, which played so decisive a role in the formation of the Minhag Ostreich. If this is correct, we would be faced with a major French component in the Eastern Rite.[5] And let us not forget the settlement in Regensburg in the

[1] See my article, 'Three Themes in *Sefer Hasidim*', *AJS Review*, 1 (1976), 349. (The article will be reprinted in the third volume of this series. See also 'The Halakhic Isolation of the Ashkenazic Community', Chapter 3 above.)

[2] *Teshuvot R. Me'ir mi-Rotenburg*, ed. R. N. N. Rabbinowicz (Lemberg, 1860), #386.

[3] Ibid., #476.

[4] Cf. Henri Gross, *Gallia Judaica: Dictionnaire géographique de la France d'après les sources rabbiniques* (Paris, 1897), with supplement by S. Schwartzfuchs (Amsterdam, 1969), 482.

[5] A half-century ago, Daniel Goldschmidt established that the *Sefer ha-Minhagim* of R. Avraham Klausner was based heavily on that of R. Ḥayyim Palti'el, which he discovered and published with an introduction in *Kiryat Sefer*, 23 (1947/8), 73–83. Recently, Simcha Emanuel has contended that the *Sefer ha-Minhagim* of Ḥayyim Palti'el is itself based on a prior one by R. Ḥezkiyah of Magdeburg found in a Bodley manuscript (Neubauer, 1150). If this is so, the influential rite of R. Klausner would be entirely German. As Emanuel analyzed the provenance of the Bodley manuscript rather than its contents—whether the practices there reflected French or German usage—only

course of the twelfth century of the prominent German Tosafists, noted before, most of whom were pupils, in one form or another, of Rabbenu Tam and kept up an active correspondence with him.[6] A beachhead may have been established, an opening wedge created, even at that early date, for French influence. It is too early to speak with any confidence of these matters, but it illustrates how complex a process was at work. The spread of swaying in prayer (*shokln*) in the fourteenth and fifteenth centuries is attributed by Zimmer to Ḥasidei Ashkenaz (p. 101), though it seems more a French practice than a German one. In a similar vein, the famed, perplexing abstention from eating legumes (*kitniyot*) on Passover, universally accepted in eastern Europe, is a French practice and not a German one.[7] This Gallic custom found

the publication of the manuscript will settle the issue. (Simcha Emanuel, 'Sefarim Avudim shel Ba'alei ha-Tosafot', Ph.D. diss., Hebrew University of Jerusalem, 1993 263–4.) {The thesis has since been published as *Shivrei Luḥot: Sefarim Avudim shel Ba'alei ha-Tosafot* (Jerusalem, 2007). The above discussion is at pp. 219–28.}

[6] See now the fine MA thesis by Rami Reiner (written under the direction of I. M. Ta-Shma), 'Rabbenu Tam: Rabbotav (ha-Tsarfatiyim) ve-Talmidav Benei Ashkenaz', Hebrew University, 1997, 82–98. {If the stormy and polemical R. Efrayim of Regensburg, also known as R. Efrayim ha-Gibbor (the Warrior), was still alive at the time of R. Yehudah he-Ḥasid's move, one shudders to think of his reaction to some of R. Yehudah's novel rulings. On R. Efrayim, see E. E. Urbach, *Ba'alei ha-Tosafot* (Jerusalem, 1980), 199–206.}

[7] R. Shemu'el of Falaise (fl. latter half of 13th century) in *Or Zarua'*, ii (Zhitomir 1862), #256, fo. 58c, and R. Perets of Corbeil (d. 1297/9) in *Sefer Mitsvot Katan* (Constantinople, 1509), #221 end {#222 in many later editions} are the first writers to mention the practice, though it clearly antedates their compositions. Both R. Mordekhai ben Hillel (Vilna edn., *Pesaḥim*, #588; Jerusalem edn. [2008], 73–4) and R. Me'ir ha-Kohen (*Haggahot Maimuniyot* in the first edition of *Mishneh Torah* [Constantinople, 1509], 'Hilkhot Ḥamets u-Matsah' 5: 1) know of it through the work of R. Perets, which they cite. The writings of R. Me'ir of Rothenburg and R. Asher (Rosh) make no mention of it; it is equally absent from the code of R. Alexander Susslein, the *Sefer ha-Aggudah*, the last German work written before the Black Death. {My formulation here was far too elliptical. Both R. Mordekhai and R. Me'ir ha-Kohen cite the work of R. Yitsḥak of Corbeil, *Sefer Mitsvot Katan*, as forbidding *kitniyot*. No such passage is found in most printed editions of that work. It is equally absent from what is possibly the oldest text of the *Semak*, still lacking the notes of Rabbenu Perets (MS British Library 1056, ca. 1280). The passage is found, however, in the printed *Haggahot* of R. Perets to that work, and is corroborated by an early manuscript of the *Haggahot*, written during R. Perets' lifetime (Nîmes, Bibliothèque Municipale 26, fo. 82b). (No argument can be made either way from the 1509 Constantinople edition of the *Semak* as it fuses here the original text of the *Semak* with that of the *Haggahot* of R. Perets and presents both as one unit.) On this basis I attributed the injunctive reports of R. Mordekhai and R. Me'ir to R. Perets. I would add, however, that MSS Parma, de Rossi 189, dated 1297, fo. 178a, and Hamburg, Levi 70, dated 1298 (unfoliated), contain the injunctive passage in the text of the *Semak*. Though it is of no matter to my argument which of the two late 13th-century rabbis in Corbeil recorded the *kitniyot* injunction, I am still inclined to attribute the report to Rabbenu Perets as the tendency of glosses by Rabbenu Perets to be absorbed into the text of the *Semak* is well known to anyone who uses the manuscripts of this work, especially as many manuscripts have the glosses not in a side-box (as in the printed *hassagot* of Rabad) but in the body of the text, preceded by the word

endorsement at the eastern perimeter of the Empire by one of the architects of the reconstruction of Jewish life after the Black Death, R. Shalom of Neustadt. By dint of his influence and that of his pupil, the famed R. Ya'akov Moellin, the injunction spread both eastward into Poland and westward back to the cities of the Rhineland. Again the pattern is: France to eastern Germany and then on to the plains of Poland. It is good to point out the possible influence of R. Yehudah he-Ḥasid on the Eastern Rite, but one has equally to note other forces that may have been no less formative.

Much of the purported influence of the German Pietists, in Zimmer's analysis, rests upon their bent for stringency, for *ḥumrah*. However, not every tendency to *ḥumrah* needs to be attributed to Ḥasidei Ashkenaz. The impulse for a thickening of the heavenly yoke, a discontent with the religious standards of the common herd, and the sense of the inadequacy of the received norms to summon the full measure of the believer's devotion are recurring features of all religions and spring from quite varied sources, most of which are unrelated to any pietistic movement in the Rhineland. One may have little use for notions of the *retson ha-bore* or for the Pietists' radical social program, yet, for one's own reasons, one may share their aspirations of maximizing religious compliance. Even explicit statements made at much later dates, such as that of R. Yo'el Sirkes,[8] should be carefully assessed. For time had passed and the more radical bent of the medieval Pietists had long been forgotten. Little now remained of the Pietists' legacy in the collective memory of pre-Chmielnicki Poland other than sensitivity in human relations, personal humility, rites of penance, and an inclination toward *ḥumrah*. A new culture finding its voice (as Poland did then) is often in search of distinguished antecedents, and in this case a claim was easily made for descent from the venerated Ḥasidei Ashkenaz. Such assertions, however, may be more in the nature of acquired heraldry than actual lineage, or, if that be too harsh a metaphor, more a pious self-image than a fact.

In specific instances, moreover, the impulse towards stringency may well come from wholly different sources. Zimmer himself has pointed out that the atmosphere of sexual abstinence that obtained in Germany in the century following the Black Death had its influence upon Jewish practice, especially

haggah. See, for example, in the case under discussion, MS National Library of Israel 4to 6702, fo. 123a, where the passage on *kitniyot* appears in the text of the *Semak* after a two-letter abbreviation: *heh gimel*. The omission of those two letters (or three—*heh, gimel, heh*—if the word is written out) moves the gloss into the body of the text. (On the date of MS British Library 1056 see Emanuel, *Shivrei Luḥot* [above, n. 5], 199 n. 55.) See Afterword for further remarks on the ban on *kitniyot*.}

[8] *Teshuvot ha-Baḥ ha-Yeshanot* (Frankfurt am Main, 1697), #79.

with regard to postnatal sexual relations (p. 235). In sexual matters, furthermore, what appears to us as a *ḥumrah*, and undoubtedly is one from a legal point of view, may well have been a birth control measure instituted by women, who, via *issur niddah* and *yemei toharah*, ultimately controlled their sexual availability. Halakhically, the woman has full credibility as to the *issur niddah* and may announce at any time that she has experienced a minute flow, and women's mode of counting *shiv'ah nekiyim*, regardless of how protracted it may be, is legally binding, as evidenced by *takkanat* Rav Ze'ira in talmudic times and the four- to seven-day medieval extensions. Sexual subordination of the woman in principle, but her frequent control of sexual congress in practice, is a central, if unnoticed, feature of Jewish domestic relations. And, one may add, the future historian who would essay to write its history (as Zimmer does not) would do well to pay heed to this fact.

Finally, I would suggest that any treatment of the menstruation injunction, especially of practices for which one is hard-pressed to find any normative justification, involves some use of anthropology. The taboo is nigh universal, and certain recurring patterns in human conduct may hold out as much enlightenment as possible filiations with Karaism or with some long-lost Jewish sects. Not all solutions in halakhic history are textual. Admittedly, anthropology has no magic wand, and its current fashionability among historians is, indeed, a bit much; nevertheless, it may have much to offer the student of Jewish family life of the fourteenth and fifteenth centuries, a period in general history that is sometimes known as the 'waning of the Middle Ages', but which in Jewish history is no less than the crucible of eastern European culture.

These are some of the thoughts elicited by this rich, sober, and scrupulous work. Zimmer's clearly written study is not always easy going, but it more than amply repays a close reading.

AFTERWORD

Simcha Emanuel, in his introduction to *Derashah le-Pesaḥ le-R. Ele'azar mi-Vormaiza* (Jerusalem, 2006), 51–2, has questioned my claim that the ban on *kitniyot* is of French origin and that it traveled first to the eastern border of the German Empire and then moved backward to the Rhineland. He both advanced the date of this ban and challenged its place of origin by pointing out that R. Ele'azar of Worms (d. *c.*1227) stated in his Passover sermon that the current custom was to refrain from eating legumes. Clearly, he argues, the ban originated in the Rhineland and was not a late thirteenth-century invention, as I had suggested, but was already being observed, at the very latest, in the early decades of that century. Emanuel further relates the emergence of the *kitniyot* injunction to the switch from a two-field system of crop rotation (with no regular sowing of legumes) to a three-field system (with legumes forming part of the yearly harvest) on the basis of Lynn White's observation on the shift to a three-field system in north-western and central Europe over the course of 'several centuries after 800'. I would like to make two technical points and then enter three reservations.

First, the passage Emanuel cites in the name of R. Yitsḥak of Corbeil should, to my mind, be attributed to Rabbenu Perets (see above, n. 7). Second, the reason given for that injunction in a newly discovered manuscript of Rokeaḥ—the fear of admixture to the beans of some kernels of grain—is found already in the *Haggahot Maimuniyot* of the 1509 Constantinople edition of *Mishneh Torah*. Subsequent editors could not understand the reason given, and deleted it or replaced it with ones found in other versions of that work.

Reservations: first, I would hesitate to advance the advent of a serious ban on *kitniyot* to that early a date on the basis of R. Ele'azar's remarks. Let us first note that R. Ele'azar failed to mention this ban in his own work, *Sefer Rokeaḥ*. Moreover—and this fact is even more telling—no one else in Germany knew of such a ban: R. Me'ir of Rothenburg and R. Asher (Rosh) were unaware of it, and R. Mordekhai and R. Me'ir ha-Kohen, author of the *Haggahot Maimuniyot*, cited French sources. This means that the *bet midrash* of Maharam, for all its vast eclecticism, knew nothing of the abstention of Worms, and neither did Rokeaḥ's pupil, the encyclopedic R. Yitsḥak Or Zarua', who cited the ban in the name of R. Shemu'el of Falaise.[9] To all appearances, it seems to have been some local—possibly even group—*ḥumrah*, unique to Rokeaḥ's personal (hasidic?) community whom he addressed in his Passover sermon. What spread to the eastern part of the Empire and then on to Poland was the widely acknowledged French ban, not the unknown local one mentioned by R. Ele'azar of Worms in a sermon.

Second, I would warn against tying the ban on *kitniyot* too tightly to the spread of the three-field system. Lynn White speaks very cautiously of the spread of the three-field system, and emphasizes that only the broadest generalizations are possible. To state that by the late thirteenth century the three-field system was widespread in north-western and central Europe is one thing; to explain the *kitniyot* ban on this basis is another, as generalities cannot be drawn upon to explain specific events. Any correlation must relate the ban in a

[9] *Or Zarua'*, ii (Zhitomir, 1862), *Pesaḥim*, #256, fo.58c. See also Urbach, *Ba'alei ha-Tosafot* (above, n. 6), 464 n. 18.

particular time and place to the advent at the same date of a three-field system and in the same locale. This is a heavy burden of proof. In the mid-1980s I began exploring this correlation between the three-field system and *kitniyot* and found it impossible to map a clear linkage because of the intermingling of the two systems of crop rotation. For example, the Rhineland is generally considered to have reverted to a two-field system in the later Middle Ages.[10] Yet three-field systems can be found in the Upper Rhine[11] and, I can now add, also in the Upper Middle Rhine.[12]

Finally, the issue is complicated by 'broadcast sowing' (*semer à la volée*) mentioned by Robert Fossier.[13] Legumes, because of their nitrogen-fixing ability, make the earth more fertile. Seeds of leguminous vegetables (peas and beans, for example) would be scattered over the cereal crops, especially barley, and the crops would be harvested together. Kernels of grain were thus interspersed with those of peas and beans. They were subsequently separated; however, no one could be certain that the division had been absolute. Thus, legumes always carried with them the danger of a cereal admixture, and one cannot fix any particular date when broadcast sowing first began or became widespread.[14]

In brief, the spread of the three-field system unquestionably played a role in the *kitniyot* ban; but how large a role is difficult to say.

[10] See G. Schröder-Lembke, 'Wesen und Verbreitung der Zweifelderwirtschaft im Rheingebiet', *Zeitschrift für Agrargeschichte und Agrarsoziologie*, 7 (1959), 14–31; H. Hildebrandt, 'Zum Problem der Rheinischen Zweifeldwirtschaft: Bemerkungen zur Genese des Zweifelderbrachsystems im deutschen Raum', *Mainzer Naturwissenschaftliches Archiv*, 16 (1977), 7–34.

[11] H. Ott, *Studien zur spätmittelalterlichen Agrarverfassung im Oberrheingebiet*, Quellen und Forschungen zur Agrargeschichte 23 (Stuttgart, 1970), 104–7.

[12] O. Volk, *Wirtschaft und Gesellschaft am Mittelrhein vom 12. bis zum 16. Jahrhundert*, Veröffentlichungen der Historischen Kommission für Nassau 63 (Wiesbaden, 1998), 278–80.

[13] *Peasant Life in the Middle Ages* (Oxford and New York, 1988), 103–4.

[14] Private communications of Robert Fossier to the author, October 16 and November 11, 1998. For a botanical analysis of the reasons set forth for the *kitniyot* ban by R. Manoaḥ of Narbonne, and a suggestion that it may apply equally to northern France and Germany, see A. O. Shemesh, 'Shorasheiha ha-Botniyim shel Gezerat Kitniyot be-Pesaḥ 'al pi Rabbenu Manoaḥ mi- Provens', *Sidra*, 21 (2006), 99–111.

Bibliography of Manuscripts

Most manuscripts have been cited by the catalogue number of the Institute of Microfilmed Hebrew Manuscripts at the National Library of Israel, not by the shelf mark of the library of origin, the reason being that, given the Institute's vast collection of microfilms from all over the world, for decades most scholars worked there rather than moving around to different libraries in a host of countries. They naturally cited the manuscripts as they were registered in the Institute's catalogue, and these numbers have entered the scholarly literature.

Generally there are three numbers in the lists below: the catalogue number registered at the Institute in the left-hand column taken from the catalogues of the respective libraries of origin; the library of origin's shelf mark in the middle column; and the reel number of the microfilm at the Institute in the right-hand column (where the catalogue number is not that of the Institute this is noted in the relevant left-hand column heading).

Where the library of origin did not have a catalogue, the Institute registered the manuscripts by the library's shelf mark, and the only references given below are that library's shelf mark and the Institute's reel number. Where the library of origin arranged its manuscripts by the order of its catalogue, the catalogue number together with the Institute's reel number are the only references.

The collections of London Beth Din and Beth Hamidrash, Jews' College (Montefiore), London, and the Sassoon Library, Letchworth, have been sold and the manuscripts dispersed, many to private parties. Such manuscripts are nevertheless entered below as they are registered in the card catalogue of the Institute. Thus, the manuscript of *Sefer Asufot*, currently in the hands of David H. Feinberg, New York, was originally Montefiore 134 and is so registered in the Institute's card catalogue and in this volume.

Budapest, Hungarian National Museum
(Magyar Tudományos Akadémia—Hungarian Academy of Sciences)

Catalogue no.	Shelf mark	Reel no.
2° 1	—	31445

Cambridge, University Library

Stephan C. Reiff's catalogue of Cambridge University Library's manuscripts came out long after the microfilms of Cambridge had been accessed by the Institute. These manuscripts were therefore registered at the Institute by Cambridge's shelf mark. For these manuscripts, the shelf mark appears in the left-hand column, Cambridge's catalogue number in the middle, and the Institute's reel number on the right.

Catalogue no.	Shelf mark	Reel no.
SCR 203	Add. 478	15946
SCR 297	Add. 489	16783
SCR 283	Add. 490	16784
SCR 335	Add. 498	16791
SCR 286	Add. 540	16829
SCR 359	Add. 667.1	16997
SCR 274	Add. 2580	17534
SCR 285	Or. 71	18701
SCR 473	Or. 786	18717
SCR 262	Or. 791	18722
SCR 314	Oo 6.70.1	16285

Frankfurt am Main, Stadts- und Universitätsbibliothek

Catalogue no.	Shelf mark	Reel no.
72	8vo 69	25909
166	8vo 158	22024

Hamburg, Staats- und Universitätsbibliothek

Catalogue no.	Shelf mark	Reel no.
45	hebr. 235	1041
194	hebr. 247	1051

Hamburg, Staats- und Universitätsbibliothek, Levy Collection

Catalogue no.	Shelf mark	Reel no.
70	—	1533

Jerusalem, Hechal Shelomoh: transferred to Jerusalem, National Library of Israel

Catalogue no.	Shelf mark	Reel no.
3	8vo 6697	38502
4	4to 6695	38531
5	4to 6696	38514

Jerusalem, National Library of Israel

Catalogue no.	Shelf mark	Reel no.
—	8vo 90	B310 (90 = 8)
—	8vo 6697	38502
—	4to 621	B636 (4to 621)
—	4to 6695	38531
—	4to 6696	38514
—	4to 6702	38478

Jerusalem, Schocken Institute for Jewish Research

Catalogue no.	Shelf mark	Reel no.
—	19520	45431

Letchworth, Sassoon Library

Catalogue no.	Shelf mark	Reel no.
517	—	9300
534	—	9334

London, Beth Din and Beth Hamidrash

Catalogue no.	Shelf mark	Reel no.
14	—	4685

The manuscript was acquired by the Jüdisches Museum, Berlin, shelf mark VII.5.262

London, British Library

Catalogue no.	Shelfmark	Reel no.
412	Or. 73	5914
413	Add. 27196	5863
530	Or. 2859	6408
531	Or. 2860	6409
532	Add. 27297	6085
537	Add. 19972	5018
1056	Add. 11639	4948G

London, Jews' College, Montefiore Collection

Catalogue no.	Shelfmark	Reel no.
65	—	4583
67	—	4585
98	—	4613
108	—	4622
130	—	4642
131	—	5134
134	—	7304

Mantua, Comunità Israelitica

Catalogue no.	Shelfmark	Reel no.
30	D65	810

Moscow, Russian State Library, Günzburg Collection

Catalogue no.	Shelfmark	Reel no.
—	73	6753
—	189	6867

Munich, Bayerische Staatsbibliothek

Catalogue no.	Shelfmark	Reel no.
95	hebr. 95	41375

216	hebr. 216	23132
232	hebr. 232	1656

New York, Jewish Theological Seminary

Catalogue no.	Shelfmark	Reel no.
Rabbinica 673	—	41418
Rabbinica 674	—	41419
Rabbinica 833	—	42271
Rabbinica 840	—	42275
Rabbinica 877	—	34145

Nîmes, Bibliothèque Seguier Municipale

Catalogue no.	Shelfmark	Reel no.
26	—	4424

Oxford, Bodleian Library

Catalogue no.	Shelfmark	Reel no.
420	Opp. Add. Qu. 23	18408
429	Opp. 387	18573
446	Opp. 99	18490
548	Mich. 613	19419
566	Opp. 276	19437
637	Opp. 66	20218
641	Opp. Add. fo. 34	20557
658	Opp. 315	20574
668	Opp. 60	20584
672	Opp. 300	20588
678	Opp. 42	20593
683	Opp. 313	20598
692	Opp. 317	17285
781	Mich. 46	20318
800	Opp. 94	20337
884	Opp. 337	21843
1150	Opp. 672	16610

Catalogue no.	Shelf mark	Reel no.
1408	Opp. 49	22432
1566	Opp. 111	16934
1606	Opp. 563	17184
2444	Christ Church 196	15588

Paris, Alliance Israélite Universelle

Catalogue no.	Shelf mark	Reel no.
482	—	12872

Paris, Bibliothèque Nationale

Catalogue no.	Shelf mark	Reel no.
380	Héb. 380	4359
1391	Héb. 1391	34252
1408	Héb. 1408	15770

Parma, Biblioteca Palatina

Giovanni B. De Rossi published a catalogue of his personal Hebraica collection in 1803. That collection was acquired by the Biblioteca Palatina. In 2001 a more precise and detailed catalogue was published by Benjamin Richler, long after the collection had been accessed by the Institute. Its card catalogue registers the De Rossi number.

De Rossi catalogue no.	Shelf mark	New catalogue no.	Reel no.
86	Parm. 2758	Richler 859	13607
189	Parm. 1940	Richler 804	13095
397	Parm. 2241	Richler 850	13406
651	Parm. 2606	Richler 858	13307
808	Parm. 2224	Richler 743	13409
929	Parm. 2902	Richler 829	13795
1033	Parm. 3057	Richler 1554	13823
1048	Parm. 2410	Richler 1552	13275
1133	Parm. 3280	Richler 1367	13957
1237	Parm. 2092	Richler 881	14236
1292	Parm. 3155	Richler 727	13896
1334	Parm. 1809	Richler 851	13031

Rome, Biblioteca Nazionale Centrale Vittorio Emanuele

Catalogue no.	Shelf mark	Reel no.
53	Or. 53	403

Vatican, Biblioteca Apostolica

Catalogue no.	Shelf mark	Reel no.
141	Ebr. 141	11627
183	Ebr. 183	8698

Vienna, Österreichische Nationalbibliothek

Catalogue no.	Shelf mark	Reel no.
66	hebr. 180	1447
72	hebr. 2	1294
73	hebr. 208	1470

Source Acknowledgments

The following essays were originally published as detailed below.

CHAPTER 1: 'The Printed Page of the Talmud', in Sharon Mintz, ed., *Printing the Talmud: From Bomberg to Schottenstein* (New York, 2005), 37–42.

CHAPTER 2: 'Catastrophe and Creativity: 1096, 1240, 1306', *Jewish History*, 12 (1998), 71–85.

CHAPTER 3: 'The Halakhic Isolation of the Ashkenazic Community', *Jahrbuch des Simon-Dubnow-Instituts/Simon Dubnow Institute Yearbook,* VIII (special issue 'Science and Philosophy in Ashkenazi Culture: Rejection, Toleration, and Accommodation', ed. Gad Freudenthal) (2009), 41–7.

CHAPTER 4: Originally published as an entry in J. R. Strayer, ed., *Dictionary of the Middle Ages* (New York, 1982–9).

CHAPTER 5: 'The Medieval Jewish Attitude to Usury', in Diego Quaglioni, Giacomo Todeschini, and Gian Maria Varanini, eds., *Credito e usura fra teologia, diritto e amministrazione: Linguaggi a confronto (Sec. XII–XVI)*, proceedings of an international conference held at the Istituto Trentino di Cultura, Trento, 4–5 Sept. 2001 (collection of the École Française de Rome 346) (Rome, 2005), 115–27.

CHAPTER 6: 'Pawnbroking: A Study in Ribbit and of the Halakhah in Exile', *Proceedings of the American Academy of Jewish Research*, 38–9 (1972), 203–68. (The version in the present volume is greatly expanded and almost twice as long as the original.)

CHAPTER 7: 'Can Halakhic Texts Talk History?', *AJS Review*, 3 (1978), 153–96.

CHAPTER 8: 'Halakhah, Taboo, and the Origin of Jewish Money Lending in Germany', in Christoph Cluse, ed., *The Jews of Europe in the Middle Ages (Tenth to Fifteenth Centuries)*, proceedings of an international symposium held at Speyer, 20–25 Oct. 2002 (Cultural Encounters in Late Antiquity and the Middle Ages 4) (Turnhout: Brepols, 2005), 295–304.

CHAPTER 9: 'Religious Law and Change: The Medieval Ashkenazi Example', *AJS Review*, 12 (1987), 205–23.

CHAPTER 10: A free translation of chapter 9 of *Ha-Yayin bi-Yemei ha-Beinayim—Yein Nesekh: Perek be-Toledot ha-Halakhah be-Ashkenaz* (Jerusalem, 2008), 321–9.

Index of Names

A
Aaron of Lincoln 61
Abelard, on Jewish usury 47
Abravanel, R. Yitsḥak, on usury 55
Agobard of Lyons, *De Insolentia Judaeorum* 200, 230, 252, 263
Agus, I. A. 113 n. 126, 162 n. 126, 279
R. Aharon ha-Levi of Barcelona (Rah):
forbids Gentile grape treading 213 n. 97
novellae of 32
on property rights in distraint pawns 147–8 n. 209
Alconstantini 61
Alfasi 60, 91 n. 77(*c*)
Amulo, on widespread use of Jewish wine 230
R. Asher ben Yeḥi'el (Rosh) 22, 128, 141, 143–4 n. 204, 303 n. 7
defense of forced converts 250 n. 19
flight to Spain 12, 22, 32
Sefer Pesakim 32
Tosafot on *'Avodah Zarah* 16 n. 9
Auerbach, T. B., controversy over his edition of *Sefer ha-Eshkol* 298
R. Avraham ben David of Posquières (Rabad):
commentary on the Talmud 4, 24, 25, 37
creativity of 14–15
did not invoke *ribbit mi-loveh le-malveh* 164–6 n. 215 #3
on filling lacunae in halakhah 156–7 n. 80
lack of influence in Ashkenaz 37
lost commentary on *Mo'ed Katan* 28, 37
on mourning 28
on sale of debt and subsequent waiver thereof 89 n. 71, 91 n. 77(*a*), 159–60 n. 81 #3
R. Avraham ben Efrayim 18, 34
R. Avraham ben Yitsḥak, Av Bet-Din 142–3 n. 204(*b*)
R. Avraham Farissol 50
R. 'Azri'el ben Avraham of Bohemia 21, 34, 36

B
Ba'al ha-Ma'or, *see* R. Zeraḥyah ha-Levi of Lunel
Ba'al Sefer ha-Dinim, *see* R. Yehudah ha-Kohen of Mainz
Ba'al ha-Turim, *see* R. Ya'akov ben Asher
Baer, Yitsḥak 48 n. 15, 247 n. 12, 278, 289
R. Barukh of Worms:
Sefer ha-Terumah 8–9, 16–17, 18, 251
Tosafot of 8, 16
Berger, David, 163, 165–6, 257
Bernard de Feltre 54

C
Cavalleria 61
Chanter, Peter, condemnation of usury 54
Charlemagne 53, 85 n. 58
Chazan, Robert 23 n. 22, 130 n. 175
on conversion of Jews in Spain 248 n. 14
Christiani, Pablo 55
Cooperman, B. 56 n. 41
Creslin of Provence 61

D
R. David ben Kalonymus, commentary by a pupil of 20 n. 17
R. David ha-Levi of Mainz:
on *ma'arufya* 108, 112–13
on pawned pawn 77–82, 87, 90, 97, 102, 139, 149, 155 n. 66, 157–8 n. 80 #3
on *Schadennehmen* 77–82, 87, 88 n. 66, 90, 97, 102, 117–19, 124, 155 n. 66

E
R. Efrayim of Bonn 14 n. 6
R. Efrayim of Regensburg 14 n. 6, 303 n. 6
Eidelberg, S. 161–2 n. 118
R. Ele'azar of Worms (Rokeaḥ) 298, 305

R. Elḥanan 8, 15, 16, 98
R. Eli'ezer ben Natan of Mainz (Ravan) 22, 83 n. 54(*b*), 124–5
  commentary on prayers 21, 36
R. Eli'ezer of Touques, *Tosafot* of 10
R. Eli'ezer ben Yo'el ha-Levi (Ravyah) 13 n. 2, 14 n. 6, 21, 22, 71 n. 38(*b*), 162 n. 126
  abridged work of Riva 118, 125
  de facto acceptance of contemporary reality 59, 149–50
  exegetical method 36
  pawns 83 nn. 53, 54(*b*), 149 n. 214
  silent incorporation of contemporary reality 148–9
R. Eliyahu of Vilna (Gaon of Vilna) 160 n. 117 #4
  changes to ritual practice 287
R. Elyakim ha-Kohen of Friedburg 269
Emanuel, Simcha 130 n. 176, 269 n. 39, 302 n. 5, 305–6

F

Fossier, Robert 307

G

Gaon of Vilna, *see* R. Eliyahu of Vilna
R. Gershom (Me'or ha-Golah) 4, 59, 76, 81 n. 49
  Ashkenazic self-image, shares 112
  Hand muß Hand wahren 98 n. 98(*a*)
  influence in 11th cent. less than supposed 113, 162 n. 126
  ma'arufya 109
  ratification of contemporary practice 110, 112
  responsa of 280
  reverse agency 110–14, 139; *see also* Index of Subjects: agency: reverse construction
  Schadennehmen 110 n. 118(*b*)
  surety ruling 114–15, 137–8
  usury, attitude to 97, 115–16
Gratian, on usury 54
Grossman, A. 162 n. 26, 282
  on deviance in Early Ashkenaz 278–9, 281
  on intellectual impact of First Crusade 23 n. 22
  on Rashi's liturgical commentaries 21 n. 18

H

R. Ḥanan'el 100 n. 99(*c*)
  commentary may have penetrated in Rashi's lifetime 178 n. 9(*c*)
R. Ḥanan'el ben Shemu'el 24
R. Ḥayyim Palti'el, *Sefer ha-Minhagim* 302
Ḥazon Ish, *see* Karelitz, R. Avraham Yeshaya
R. Ḥezkiyah of Magdeburg 86 n. 60(*c*), 302 n. 5
Holtmann, Annegret, study of Vesoul vineyard investment 232
Huebner, R. 152–3

I

Ibn Yaḥya, on expulsion from France 248 n. 14
Innocent III condemns law of *yein nesekh* 200, 252, 263
Isserles, R. Mosheh (Rema) 37, 134–5 n. 186(*b*), 251

J

Juan de Peronnes 17

K

R. Kalonymus: creditor cannot compel redemption of the pawn 92 n. 78
Karelitz, R. Avraham Yeshaya (Ḥazon Ish) on *muktseh* 285
Karo, R. Yosef 161 n. 117 #4
Katz, Jacob 51 n. 25, 56 n. 41
  concept of ritual instinct 254 n. 28, 296
  distinction between *minhag* and *nohag* 258
  on Gentile–Jewish relations 272
  on Tosafists' allowances 164–5 n. 215 #2
Kimḥi, R. David (Radak), on charging interest to Gentiles 50–1
Klausner, R. Avraham, *Sefer ha-Minhagim* 302
Kleinman, R. 163–4 n. 215
Kleinman, Y., edition of *Mordekhai, Bava Metsi'a'* 151 n. 42 #4
Krems, R. Yisra'el 265

L

Langmuir, Gavin, rational and irrational antisemitism 54

Lasker, D., on philosophical knowledge of polemicists 256–7
Lebson, G. 164–6 #2
Lifshitz, Berachyahu 93 n. 83, 235
Lopez, R. 46 n. 6
Louis IX 302

M
Maharam Schiff 58
Maimonides (Rambam) 60
commentary on the Talmud 4, 5, 24–5, 25 n. 26, 26
count of biblical commandments 9
ignored in Ashkenaz 33–4, 38
influence in Spain 33, 289
Mishneh Torah 21–2 n. 20, 33, 37–8
Sefer Mada' 21 n. 20
theology of 289
wine mixed with honey is not subject to *yein nesekh* 264
Maitland, F. 152–3 n. 56
Malkiel, David 239, 283, 288
R. Me'ir ben Kalonymus, pupil's commentary on *midreshei halakhah* 20 n. 17
R. Me'ir ha-Kohen 21
attempt to facilitate the reception of *Mishneh Torah* 21
Haggahot Maimuniyot 37
on *kitniyot* 303 n. 7, 306
R. Me'ir of Rothenburg 22, 98, 162 n. 126, 303 n. 7
attempt to broaden Ashkenazi thought 37–8
authority of 37
collections of his responsa contain many responsa of other decisors 71 n. 38(*b*) #2
Hilkhot Semaḥot 28
imprisonment of 12, 22, 32
responsa of 21
school of 21
students of 22
R. Me'ir ben Shim'on of Narbonne 55
Me'iri, *see* R. Menaḥem ha-Me'iri
R. Menaḥem ha-Me'iri 24, 62, 119 n. 140, 123 n. 155(*b*)
R. Meshullam ben Kalonymus, on pawned pawn 46 n. 6, 76, 81–2, 87, 88 n. 66, 96 n. 93(*a*), 156–8 n. 80 #4
R. Meshullam of Melun 268
R. Meshullam ben Ya'akov of Lunel:
commentary on the Yerushalmi 20 n. 17
work on pawnbroking 65
Moellin, R. Ya'akov 304
R. Mordekhai ben Hillel:
florilegium of, *see* Index of Subjects: *Sefer Mordekhai*
on *kitniyot* 306
martyrdom of 12, 22, 32
student of R. Me'ir of Rothenburg 22
Morel de Falaise, *see* R. Shemu'el of Falaise
R. Mosheh of Coucy:
on prayer gestures 296
preaches in Spain 18, 33
Sefer Mitsvot Gadol 9, 17, 18, 34
selective use of *Mishneh Torah* 17, 33–4
trial of the Talmud 9, 18
R. Mosheh ha-Nasi b. Todros ha-Nasi 164–6 n. 215 #3
R. Mosheh of Paris 50

N
Naḥmanides (Ramban) 7, 65
Catalonian school of 32, 37, 274
on charging interest to Gentiles 50–1
critique of tosafist position on pawns 147 n. 208
lack of influence in Ashkenaz 37
novellae on the Talmud 12 n. 1, 32

P
R. Peraḥyah 24
R. Perets of Corbeil 10, 32
notes to *Sefer Mitsvot Katan* 303–4 n. 7
Tosafot of 10, 17
Philip II, expulsion of Jews from France 248 n. 14
Philip the Fair 302

R
Rabad, *see* R. Avraham ben David of Posquières
Rabbenu Gershom, *see* R. Gershom (Me'or ha-Golah)
Rabbenu Tam (Ya'akov ben Me'ir of Ramerupt) 71 n. 38(*b*), 149, 163
anticipated later doctrines of the Tosafists 219

Rabbenu Tam (*cont.*):
authority of 10, 13, 17, 25, 36
awareness of contemporary problems 94 n. 83, 129, 133, 197, 204–5, 219, 253
business transaction with Ri 140
correspondence with R. Shemaryah of Speyer 202–19; concession to R. Shemaryah 216–19; differing talents of the two 203–4
debt not assignable by pentateuchal law 95 n. 87
dialectical exegesis of Talmud 6–7, 13, 35, 169–70
emotional qualifications to bold allowances 107, 136
fronting 140–1
Gentile straw man 42, 130–6, 141, 253–4
Gentiles, permissibility of engaging in usury with 42, 45, 46 n. 4
German students of 301, 303
hamshakhah, doctrine of 195–6; immanent development or response to felt need 196–9, 219; practical implications 196, 199; widespread acceptance 192
justification of contemporary practice 131–6, 139–41, 244 n. 8, 275
le-ḥumra: abolition of 131–2, 253–4; neutralization of 135
lexical sense 197
little familiarity with Riva's writing 13 n. 2
ma'arufya allowance 140–1
nitsok rejected by 271
pawned pawn 139–40, 141; see also *silluk* below
personal nature of debt 91 n. 77(*b*), (*c*)
personality 7, 13, 14–15, 202, 204–5
posek (decisor), nature of his role as 204 n. 81
responsa of 7 n. 3, 13–14
revulsion at idea of Gentiles treading grapes for Jewish wine 212–13
Sefer ha-Yashar, reasons for difficulty of 7, 14
shi'abud ha-guf ve-shi'abud nekhasim 91 n. 77(*a*), (*c*)
silluk (renunciation) 94 n. 83, 99 n. 98(*b*), 107, 133–7, 140, 164 n. 189
wine dealer, no evidence thereof 197–8 n. 65
Radak, *see* R. David Kimḥi
Rah, *see* R. Aharon ha-Levi of Barcelona
Rambam, *see* Maimonides
Ramban, *see* Naḥmanides
Rash mi-Shants, *see* R. Shimshon of Sens
Rashba, *see* R. Shelomoh ibn Aderet
Rashbam, *see* R. Shemu'el ben Me'ir
Rashi (R. Shelomoh Yitsḥaki) 71 n. 38(*b*), 149, 155 n. 66, 160 n. 117 #4
Andalusian thought never in dialogue with 60
authority of 24–5; in early responsa 77–8, 94; in later responsa 103
commentary on the *Alfasi* 183
commentary on the liturgy 21 n. 18
commentary on the Talmud 3–5, 7, 12 n. 1, 17, 19, 23, 35; artistic dimension to 192–3; on *'Arvei Pesaḥim*, authorship in doubt 188; on *'Avodah Zarah*, manuscript of 182; *Commentary of Rashbam*, written under Rashi's direction 187–8; *Commentary of Rivan*, written under Rashi's direction 184; consummates Rhineland commentaries 23; different editions (*mahadurot*) of 182; sets French pattern of *explication de texte* 35, 36
communal authority, bolsters 280
R. David of Mainz, inquiries of and support by 77–8, 94 n. 84, 102, 108
debt assignment: *otiyot niknot bi-mesirah* 96 n. 93(*b*); by transfer of pawn 90–3, 96 n. 93(*b*), 139
defense of communal practice 274; *see also* relationship to ancient traditions *below*
doctrine of *hamshakhah* 170, 176–93; muffles 189–92; plays major role 169, 173–95; practical implications of 193–5; prefers students to state it explicitly 170, 185; principle of separation 180–1; problematic text of 179–84
Early Ashkenaz, in constant dialogue with 60
economic significance of his rulings on *ribbit* 102–3
education 4, 19, 21 n. 18, 23

Gentile straw man 42, 103–7; emotional qualification to bold allowance 107
growing confidence 103–5, 170, 187–8
le-ḥumra 99–101, 105–6, 129; as a penalty (*kenas*) 100 n. 99(*a*), 105–6; as reinstituting agency 100 n. 99(*b*)
ma'arufya (Jewish factotum) 94 n. 84, 107–8, 129
oscillation of position: on *koḥo shel goy* (Gentile force) in *yein nesekh* 182 n. 21; on *roteḥin*, use in purging tarred vessels 183 n. 22
pawned pawn 77–9, 82 n. 51, 88 n. 66, 94, 102, 155 n. 66
personal character of debt 91 n. 77(*a*), (*c*)
personality 59, 107, 160–1 n. 117 #3, 170, 185, 189, 192–3
property rights in contract and distraint pawns 83–8
reaction to *Hand muß Hand wahren* 98 n. 98(*a*)
relationship to ancient traditions (*minhag avot*) 170, 176–7, 185, 189, 192–3, 195
resolution of contradictions 26
responsa: neither collected by nor known to Tosafists 20, 35; probable misattribution of 160–1
revolutionary role in halakhah 59, 170, 199
revulsion at idea of Gentiles treading grapes for Jewish wine 214
rulings disseminated by students 195, 274 n. 58, 275
Schadennehmen 77–8, 94 n. 84, 97–9, 104–5, 114, 116, 155–6 n. 66
sifrut devei Rashi 275
silent incorporation of contemporary reality 94–6
terminology: precision of 58, 121; purism of 82 n. 51, 100 n. 99
usury, view of 96–7, 99–102, 104 n. 107(*b*), 105–6, 108–9, 155–6 n. 66
vintner, no evidence thereof 194 n. 56
Ravan, *see* R. Eli'ezer ben Natan of Mainz
Ravyah, *see* R. Eli'ezer ben Yo'el ha-Levi
Rema, *see* Isserles, R. Mosheh
Ri (R. Yitsḥak ben Shemu'el of Dampierre) 6, 19, 23, 25, 27, 162 n. 126
authority of 10, 13 n. 2, 15, 17, 35
Ba'al ha-Tosafot 7, 23
debt not assignable by pentateuchal law 95 n. 87
dialectical exegesis of Talmud 35
firstborn, inheritance of pawns 86 n. 60(*c*)
Gentile straw man, allowance requires creditor's ignorance of subterfuge 137
halakhic federalism 59, 140–50
le-ḥumra 137
little familiarity with Riva's writing 13 n. 2
pawned pawn 141–5
permits charging interest to Gentiles 46 n. 4
personality 7, 15
presumption of legality, doctrine of 136–9, 164 n. 189
property rights in distraint and contract pledges 147
report of the merchants of Metz 201–2
*reportatio*s 8, 9, 15
responsum on *hamshakhah* 179–82
restriction of rights in pledges 147 n. 209
revulsion at idea of Gentiles treading grapes for Jewish wine 212–13
silent incorporation of contemporary reality 142, 145–7
thinking in contemporary terms 86 n. 60(*c*)
Tosafot of 7–8, 10, 15–16
unaware of Rashi's responsum 137 n. 190
Ritva, *see* R. Yom Tov Al-Sevilli
Riva, *see* R. Yitsḥak ben Asher
Rivam (R. Yitsḥak ben Mordekhai) 13 n. 2
Rivan, *see* R. Yehudah ben Natan
Rosen, J. 93 n. 83, 143–4 n. 204, 155
Rosh, *see* R. Asher ben Yeḥi'el

S

St Louis, anti-usury ordinances 55
Schremer, Adiel 276
Schwarzfuchs, Simon 23 n. 22
R. Shalom of Neustadt 304
R. Shelomoh ibn Aderet (Rashba) 32
R. Shelomoh of Château Landon 83 n. 53, 148
R. Shelomoh Luria 164 n. 215

R. Shelomoh ben Shimshon (Rabbenu Sasson) 26
R. Shelomoh Yitsḥaki, *see* Rashi
R. Shemaryah of Speyer:
correspondence with Rabbenu Tam, 202–19, 221
intellectual characterization 204, 214
R. Shema'yah, disseminates Rashi's rulings 274 n. 58, 282
R. Shemu'el of Falaise 62, 302, 303 n. 7, 306
R. Shemu'el he-Ḥasid 20 n. 17
R. Shemu'el ben Me'ir (Rashbam) 76
commentaries reached Provence in 12th cent. 36
commentary on *Avodah Zarah*: circulation in Germany delayed 211–12; reasons for Rashi's directing this commentary 188; revision of Rivan's commentary 187; sources of 188 n. 36(*b*); structure 188, 189, 223; written under Rashi's direction or dictation 187
disseminates Rashi's rulings 274 n. 58
firstborn inheritance of pawns 86 n. 60(*c*)
Gentile straw man, ban on 129–30
incorporeality of debts 91 n. 77(*b*)
insistence on halakhic purity in the face of facts 129–30
jus mercatorum, parallel to 95
le-ḥumra, rejects Rashi's interpretation of 129
Likkutei Rashbam 274 n. 58
ma'arufya (Jewish factotum), ban on 129, 162–3 n. 176 #2
polemic, Christian–Jewish 130 n. 176(*b*), 162–3 n. 176 #1
transfer of debts: *ma'amad sheloshtan* 95 n. 89; *otiyot niknot bi-mesirah* 96 n. 93(*b*)
R. Shemu'el ha-Sardi (of Cerdagne) 141, 150 n. 215, 273
pawn transfer as sale of debt 93 n. 82
reliability of citations 103 n. 105(*d*)
R. Shimshon of Sens (Rash mi-Shants):
commentary on *mishnayot* 9
indifference to non-Ashkenazi authors 33
intellectual stature of 33
responsa collection not preserved 19–20
settles in the Land of Israel 17
Tosafot of 8, 10, 16, 17
R. Simḥah of Speyer 20 n. 17, 83 n. 53
Sirkes, R. Yo'el 304
Sombart, W. 44 n. 1
Soncino, Gershom 10
Susslein, R. Alexander, *Sefer ha-Aggudah* 303 n. 7
Sussman, Y. 19 n. 15

T

Tachau, R. Mosheh:
commentary on Yerushalmi 20 n. 17
controversy with Pietists over anthropomorphism 248
Taku, R. Mosheh, *see* Tachau, R. Mosheh
Ta-Shma, I. M.:
on Maimonides' commentary 25 n. 26
on the students of R. Yehudah he-Ḥasid 300, 301
on R. Yehonatan of Lunel 24 n. 24
R. Tsidkiyahu ha-Rofe 100 n. 99(*c*)
R. Tuvyah b. Eliyahu of Vienne (Burgundy) 77 n. 42, 160 n. 117

U

Urbach, E. E. 16 n. 10, 20 n. 17, 297

V

Vilna Gaon, *see* R. Eliyahu of Vilna
Vitalis, Salamon Mayr of Perpignan, *see* R. Menaḥem ha-Me'iri
Vivelin of Strassburg 61

W

Weinreich, Max 297
White, Lynn 306

Y

R. Ya'akov ben Asher (Ba'al ha-Turim) 22, 32, 93 n. 82
R. Ya'akov of Courçon 20 n. 16
R. Ya'akov ben Elyah 55
R. Ya'akov ha-Kohen 301
R. Ya'akov ben Me'ir of Ramerupt, *see* Rabbenu Tam
R. Ya'akov of Orleans, circumvention of usury 132 n. 182(*b*), 163 n. 182

R. Ya'akov ben Yakar 263
excessive humility of 162 n. 126
R. Ya'akov ben Yitsḥak ha-Levi 80 n. 48(*a*), 82 n. 51
Yaffe, R. Mordekhai 160 n. 117 #4
R. Yeḥi'el of Paris 28, 32, 164 n. 189
R. Yehonatan of Lunel 24
R. Yehudah of Barcelona, commentary on the Talmud 24
R. Yehudah he-Ḥasid 300
influence on Minhag Ostreich 304
move from Speyer to Regensburg 300–1
Slavic students of 300–1
R. Yehudah ben Kalonymus, *Yiḥusei Tanna'im ve-Amora'im* 14, 21, 36, 297
R. Yehudah ha-Kohen of Mainz (Ba'al Sefer ha-Dinim) 89 n. 72, 90 n. 74, 116 n. 136
authority of 162 n. 126
halakhic federalism in rulings of 59
Sefer ha-Dinim 71 n. 38(*b*), 83 n. 53, 88 n. 65, 89 n. 72, 90 n. 74
silent incorporation of contemporary reality 90 n. 73(*a*)
R. Yehudah ben Natan (Rivan), commentary on *Avodah Zarah* 184, 186–8
written under Rashi's direction or dictation 184, 188
R. Yehudah of Paris (Sir Leon) 181 n. 16, 198, 260–1 n. 10
*reportatio*s 8
Tosafot of 8, 9, 16, 17, 27
on *yein nesekh* 200, 212 n. 96, 265
R. Yitsḥak ben Asher (Riva) 13 n. 2, 26, 149
author of *Tosfot ha-Rav* on *Mo'ed Katan* 28
criticized by Rabbenu Tam 29
dialectical method, he or Rabbenu Tam as originator of 13 n. 2, 26–9
Gentile straw man, forbidden by 120, 123, 124
Hand muß Hand wahren 98 n. 98(*a*), 120
handbook on pawnbroking 65, 118–29
le-ḥumra, use of 100 n. 99(*c*), 123
misrepresentation and false fronting 119, 126
Schadennehmen 119, 122, 124
Tosafot of 26–8
Tosefta, use of 123–4
usury as economic moralism/realism 121–2
R. Yitsḥak Campanton 12 n. 1
R. Yitsḥak of Corbeil:
on martyrdom 242 n. 5
sale of Jewish–Christian promissory notes 63 n. 13
Sefer Mitsvot Katan (*Semak*) 9, 18; most copied halakhic work of Ashkenaz 251; need for conveyance of pawned pawn 137
R. Yitsḥak of Dampierre, *see* Ri
R. Yitsḥak ha-Levi of Worms 58, 111
R. Yitsḥak ben Mordekhai (Rivam) 13 n. 2
R. Yitsḥak of Oppenheim 99 n. 98(*a*)
R. Yitsḥak Or Zarua' of Vienna 13 n. 2, 21, 36, 301
French scholars unaware of writings of 31 n. 2
on *kitniyot* 306
use of *Mishneh Torah* 34
R. Yitsḥak of Simponte 17, 33
Yitsḥak ben Yeda'yah 56 n. 43
R. Yitsḥak ben Yehudah 280
R. Yo'el ha-Levi 14 n. 6, 83 n. 53
R. Yom Tov Al-Sevilli (Ritva) 32
R. Yonah of Gerona, ruling concerning apostate 249 n. 15
R. Yosef Bonfils (Tov 'Elem):
communal organization, 102 n. 104, 280, 281
responsum to Troyes, date of 102 n. 104
usury, alleged attitude towards 47
R. Yosef ibn Megas 26, 60
R. Yosef ha-Mekkane 162–3 n. 176 #1
Yosef ben Mosheh (author of *Leket Yosher*) 56 n. 43
R. Yosef Tov 'Elem, *see* R. Yosef Bonfils

Z

R. Zeraḥyah ha-Levi of Lunel (Ba'al ha-Ma'or) 36–7, 270
Zimmer, Yishaq (Eric) 294–305 *passim*

Index of Places

A

Ashkenaz 62
- attitude to martyrdom 242–4, 249, 275–6, 289–91
- communal self-image 112, 246, 247, 255–6, 274, 289–90
- emigration to southern Europe 37
- involvement in commerce 69
- isolation, cultural and halakhic 31, 32, 35–7, 247
- philosophy, absence of 247, 256 n. 12, 289
- religious beliefs, simplicity of 247
- *see also* Early Ashkenaz; Germany

B

Bar-sur-Aube region 194–5 n. 56
Bonn 19

C

Catalonia, scholars of 32, 37, 273, 274
Champagne 6, 7, 12, 69
- moneylending in 100 n. 99, 102, 103–4 n. 107(*b*), 113
- winemaking in 194, 199

Cologne 19
- wine fair, records of 235

Corbeil 17

D

Dampierre 7, 10, 12, 36, 147, 198, 251
Danzig 61

E

Early Ashkenaz (*c*.950–1096):
- *'Avodah Zarah* not part of curriculum 177–9
- difficulty in eliciting its halakhic positions 58–9, 170, 210–11
- economic problems confronted as result of usury injunction 69–71
- exegesis, talmudic: deficiencies in 59; of entire Talmud, including *Seder Kodashim* 59
- halakhic intuitions 59
- halakhic terminology: danger of retrojection of later concepts, 58–9; lack of certainty as to meaning of 58; looseness of 111 n. 121(*a*), 121; *yotse mi-kiso shel*: *see* Index of Subjects: usury, definition
- *hamshakhah*, doctrine of 185–6, 210
- importance for understanding of Rashi and *Tosafot* 60, 210–11
- Jewish self-government in 278–80
- judicial boldness and flexibility 59
- Rashi's thought rooted in 60
- re-evaluation of 26
- religiosity of the community, contested by Grossman 278
- *see also* Ashkenaz; Germany

eastern Europe 13 n. 2, 37, 199
Egypt, influence of Rashi 25
England, expulsion from 31
Evreux academy 17

F

Falaise academy 17
France 6, 10
- academies 17, 36, 301
- cultural exclusivity 34, 35–6
- emigration from in 13th cent. 302
- *explication de texte* central feature 19, 21, 35
- expulsion from 12, 18, 31
- indifference to responsa literature 19–20
- prestige of German yeshivas overshadowed by those of 24, 25, 302
- reception of *Mishneh Torah* 33–4
- shift of centers of learning from Germany to 24, 25

G

Germany:
- academies, *see* Index of Subjects: academies
- characterization of tosafist works of 13 n. 2, 21, 36

Germany (*cont.*):
cultural exclusivity 36–8
emergence of dialectic 13 n. 2, 19, 26–9
Jews live in vine-growing areas 225, 228
loss of distinct halakhic culture in 13th cent. 22, 221–2
migration between cities 300–1
origin of moneylending in 224–36
pogroms 12, 22, 32
prestige of French yeshivas overshadows those of 24, 25, 302
Rashi displaces Rhineland commentaries 25
reception of *Mishneh Torah* 21, 33–4, 37–8
responsa literature 21, 36
split in communal practice between east and west 294–5
wine trade in 228–9
see also Ashkenaz; Early Ashkenaz

I
Île-de-France 12
Israel, Land of 16–17
Italy 10, 25

L
Lotharingia 19, 231, 297
Lotir, *see* Lotharingia
Lucca, responsa on moneylending 46

M
Mâconnais 230, 232
Mainz 4, 19, 25, 30, 46
Mannheim, school of (music) 30
Metz 201–2, 209, 212

N
Normandy 12, 17, 18

P
Paris 17, 18, 98 n.98(*b*), 164 n.189
Poland 61, 164–5 n. 215, 251
adopts Minhag Ostreich 294
communal self-image 304
eating indoors on Shemini Atseret 296, 299–300
influence of German Pietists 304
Provence:
commentators 24
communal self-image 246, 273
cultural impact in Germany, absence of 36
halakhic culture of 13 n. 2, 37
influence of Ashkenazic thought 25, 36–7
laxity of observance 273
responsa on moneylending 46

R
Ramerupt 12
Regensburg 19
forced baptism of community 25
German Tosafists settle in 300, 303
R. Yehudah he-Ḥasid settles in 300–1
Rhineland:
academies 4, 21 n. 18, 23
map of viticulture and Jewish settlement in 226–7
vine-growing and wine trade in 229, 231

S
Sefarad, *see* Spain
Sens 17
Simponte, influence in Ashkenaz 33
Spain:
Almohads' annihilation of Jewish culture in 240
Catalonian school (of Naḥmanides) 32, 37, 273, 274
communal practices not justified by scholars 274
communal self-image 246, 256, 273
edition of Talmud 12 n. 1
flight of Rosh and son to 12, 22, 32
French influence 25, 36–7
halakhic culture of 13 n. 2, 37
laxity of observance 273
R. Mosheh of Coucy in 18
Naḥmanides' influence 32
no cultural impact in Germany 36
philosophy, adverse religious effects of 289
responsa literature 21, 36
Speyer 19, 26, 300

T
Toledo 32
Toulouse 53–4
Touques 17

Troyes:
academy of 12, 36
opposition to Rashi's views on pawnbroking in 101–2, 114, 116
viticulture in 194–5 n. 56

V

Vesoul, vineyards in 232–3

W

Worms 4, 19, 26, 30, 111, 117

Y

Yemen, dominance of Rashi 24–5

Index of Subjects

A

academies (*bet midrasho shel*; schools of thought):
- of R. Me'ir of Rothenburg 21, 142–3 n. 203(*b*)
- of Naḥmanides 32, 37, 274
- of Provence 197 n. 64
- of Rashi 123 n. 22, 193, 194 n. 56, 210
- of Spain 12 n. 1, 197 n. 64

academies (yeshivas, institutions):
- Corbeil 17
- Dampierre (Ri) 7, 10, 12, 36, 147, 198
- destruction in First Crusade 22–3, 24, 29–30
- Evreux 17
- Falaise 17
- French academies, German study in 36, 301–2
- Mainz 19, 23, 24, 35, 178 n. 9, 301
- of Rabbenu Sasson 26
- Rhineland 4, 21 n. 18, 23, 177
- of Riva 26
- Sens 147
- Touques 17
- Troyes 12, 36
- Worms 24, 26, 35, 178 n. 9, 301

agency: Gentile non-agency (*ein sheliḥut le-goy*) 71–2, 79, 99, 105, 109–11
- *le-ḥumra*, see *le-ḥumra*
- *ma'arufya* (Jewish factotum) 70, 94 n. 84, 107–9, 112–14, 129, 140–1, 162–3 n. 176 #2
- straw man, *see* straw man

agency: reverse construction (Rabbenu Gershom) 110
- contrasted to Ri's automatic nullifier 139
- R. David's expansion of 113–14
- dissenting views in Worms 111–12
- French tosafist literature, absence from 113 n. 126
- Riva's expansion of 122–4
- Tosefta seen as confirmation of 123

Alfasi, commentaries on:
- by R. Ḥanan'el ben Shemu'el 24
- by Rashi 184
- by R. Yehonatan of Lunel 24

'Amudei ha-Golah, see *Sefer Mitsvot Katan*

Anonymous Commentaries of Mainz, see *Commentary of Rabbenu Gershom*

antisemitism:
- contribution of moneylending to 56
- contribution of *yein nesekh* to 200–1, 252
- in *De Insolentia Judaeorum* 200, 252
- in medieval Germany 229–30, 235
- in Wilhelminian Germany 46

anusim 250 nn. 19, 21
- *see also* conversion

apostasy, *see* conversion

Arba'ah Turim:
- author of 22, 32
- limited acceptance in Ashkenaz 32
- supercommentary on 300

'arev, *see* surety

'arka'ot (Gentile courts) 83–4, 278, 281

'Arugat ha-Bosem 21, 34, 36

'Arukh, see *Sefer he-'Arukh*

Arye Maimon Institut für Geschichte der Juden 224, 225, 229

Auflassung, *see* Germanic law

'Avodah Zarah 8, 16 n. 9
- not part of curriculum of Early Ashkenaz 177–9
- Tosafists justify radical rulings in 241

B

ba'alei ha-Tosafot, *see* Tosafists; *Tosafot*

Babylonian law 42, 53

Babylonian Talmud, *see* Talmud

baptism, see *anusim*; conversion

Bavli, *see* Talmud

bet midrash, *see* academies (*bet midrasho shel*; schools of thought)

broadcast sowing, see *kitniyot* ban

C
child murder in order to avoid baptism 242–3, 276, 290
as a form of deviance according to Malkiel 283
rabbinic views on 244 n. 8
see also martyrdom
Christianity:
conversion to, *see* conversion
as idolatry 249 n. 15
Christian(s):
charging interest to 45–51
Jewish attitude towards 50–1, 272
not considered idolaters 264
polemics with 50, 130 n. 176(*b*), 162–3 n. 176, 247
selling non-kosher meat to 276
trade with 273
usury condemned by 42, 50, 52, 54, 55, 121, 129 n. 174
viewed as foreigner (*nokhri*) in matters of usury 41, 45
yein nesekh an insult to 200–1, 230, 252, 263, 276–7
chronicles, *see* Crusade, First
commenda 41, 126, 134 n. 186(*a*)
commentaries, *see* liturgy; *midreshei halakhah*; *and individual authors*
Commentary of Rabbenu Gershom Me'or ha-Golah 4, 23, 25
Commentary on Tamid, authorship of 296–7
commerce, *see* trade
communal practice, see *nohag*
communal self-image 289, 290
in Ashkenaz 112, 138 n. 103, 246, 247, 255–6, 274, 291
in Poland 304
in Spain 246, 256, 273
conversion:
anusim 250 nn. 19, 21
child murder in order to avoid 242–3, 244 n. 8
forced 25, 242, 249, 250 n. 19, 289–90
instances of 249, 250 nn. 19, 21, 290
not seen as an actual danger 248
temporary only 250 n. 21
tempting to Ashkenazi community 257
courts:
civil suits 281
Gentile: Jewish recourse to 83–4, 278, 281
Jewish in Paris 98–9 n. 98(*b*), 164 n. 189
credit:
pressures to equalize sources of 103
sources of 70
viticultural, Jewish involvement in 229, 231–2, 233–4, 235
crime 278
as distinct from resistance to new communal ordinances 280
as resistance to established norms 280
theft 278, 281
violence 279
Crusade, First 11, 12, 19, 25
chronicles of: Christian 242, 250 n. 21; Jewish 242, 249, 250 nn. 19, 21, 290
cultural impact, actual or challenged, of 12, 22, 23 n. 22, 24, 28 n. 31, 29, 247, 275
general significance in Jewish history 23 n. 22
image in Ashkenazi memory 22, 289, 290
martyrdom during 242, 289–91
custom, see *minhag*
cuve (tub), *see* wine

D
De Insolentia Judaeorum 230, 252
debt assignment:
direct transfer of note from hand to hand 96 n. 93(*b*)
Germanic law, status of assignment in 62
incorporeal entity not subject to sale 91
mi-de'oraita invalid 95
personal obligation between parties 91
resistance to payment 204–5
shi'abud ha-guf, *shi'abud nekhasim* (*in personam*, *in rem*) 91 n. 77(*a*), (*c*)
talmudic period, difficulties in assignment 95
via acquisition of note of indebtedness 96 n. 93(*b*)
via *agav* 88 n. 68, 90 n. 73(*b*)
via cash sale 90
via *situmta* 156 n. 80
via transfer of Gentile's note of indebtedness 62–3

via transfer of Jew's note of indebtedness (*mesirah* or *ketivah u-mesirah*) 88, 89 n. 71, 90, 92 n. 80, 95, 96 n. 93(*b*), 156–8 n. 80 #3
via transfer of pledge 80, 88, 89, 90 n. 74; challenge to 142–5; *dina demalkhuta dina*, not invoked 92 n. 80, 156 n. 80 #1; mistaken instance of 156 n. 79; pledge transfer as *otiyot niknot bi-mesirah* 96 n. 93(*b*), 156 n. 80 #3; rationale 91–2; Ri's use of Rabbenu Tam's doctrine of *silluk* 142–5; validation 92–3, 159 n. 81 ##1, 2
via triple presence (*ma'amad sheloshtan*) 88, 89, 92 n. 79, 95
debtor, recalcitrant, left unburied 202–5
decisor, see *posek*
deviance 278–9, 283, 285, 287, 292–3
see also crime
dialectics:
differences between France and Germany 19–20, 35
eliminated in *Sefer Mitsvot Katan* 18
emergence of 12–13, 13 n. 2, 24, 25, 26–7
French preoccupation with 19–20, 29, 35
revival of, central role of Rabbenu Tam in 6–7, 13, 29, 45, 202
in Riva's writing 28–9
shift from exegesis to 19, 23
of the *Tosafot* 5, 6–7, 8, 15, 246

E
Eastern Rite, see *minhag*: Minhag Ostreich
excommunication 200, 278, 281
expulsion:
from cities within German Empire 293
from England 31
from France 12, 18, 31; reports of Ibn Yaḥya and Usque about 248 n. 14

F
false fronting, *see* misrepresentation
fasfasin (tally) 154
First Crusade, *see* Crusade, First

G
Gentile(s):
authorities, Jews informing on each other to 61
charging interest to 41–2, 45, 47, 49, 50–1
courts, Jewish recourse to 83–4, 278, 281
non-agency of Gentile (*ein sheliḥut le-goy*), *see* agency
resentment of *terefot* 276
resentment of *yein nesekh* 200–1, 230, 252, 263, 276–7
straw man, *see* straw man
wine, see *yein nesekh*
Ge'onim:
method of resolving talmudic contradictions 26
responsa of 19, 35
German Pietists (Ḥasidei Ashkenaz) 65 n. 17, 290
connection to Polish scholars 301
on Gentile wine 225
influence on Ashkenazi practices 295, 297, 298, 300, 303
Sefer Ḥasidim, see *Sefer Ḥasidim*
stringency of 304
unaware of allowance of Gentile straw man 126
views on usury 48–50, 126
Germanic law 62, 84–5, 87–8, 152–3 n. 56
Auflassung 87 n. 62, 154 n. 62
bailee may return either the object or its equivalent 145
Haftung 84 n. 56(*b*)
Hand muß Hand wahren 89, 98, 120, 145 n. 206(*a*), 164 n. 189
pawn, redemption of 98, 145–6; status of 84–7, 145–6
possession of mobilia in 98 n. 98(*a*), 145–6
restrictions on debt transfer 91 n. 77(*b*)
Sachhaftung 84
Schuld 84 n. 56(*b*)
translated into halakhic categories 84 n. 56(*a*), 85, 145–7, 152–3 n. 56(*a*)
Greek Orthodox Church, on usury 53

H
Haggahot Asheri 20, 265
Haggahot Maimuniyot 13 n. 2, 20, 37–8, 306
halakhah:
abdication of regulatory role 138–9
dialectical revolution in 6–7, 13, 21 n. 18, 202, 274, 286

halakhah (*cont.*):
in exile 96, 147–50
influence of common practice on 92–3, 110
justification of common practice, see *nohag*: Ashkenazic defense of
legal fictions in 105–7, 135–6, 160–1 n. 117 #2
personal outlook yielding halakhic interpretation 106
recognition of the customs of merchants (*jus mercatorum*) 95–6; medieval, *de facto* 96; talmudic, *de jure* 96
resistance to economic pressures 125–8, 129–30
responses to economic pressure in 70–1, 87–8, 103, 148; *de facto* only 147–9
silent incorporation of contemporary reality into: assignment of debt 90 n. 73, 94–5, 145–50; ownership of Gentile pawns 87–8, 93 n. 83, 94–5, 96 n. 93(*b*), 142, 145–50
translating facts of Germanic law into categories of 84 n. 56, 85, 145–7, 152–3 n. 56(*a*)
halakhic federalism:
definition 150
implicit in ruling of R. Yehudah Ba'al Sefer ha-Dinim 59
of the Tosafists 59, 140–50, 164 n. 215 ##1–2
halakhic flexibility as function of level of religious observance 134
Ḥasidei Ashkenaz, *see* German Pietists
hasidim, not eating in *sukkah* on Shemini Atseret 299–300
Ḥiddushei ha-Ritva 'al Bava Metsi'a, actual and alleged versions of 99 n. 98(*d*)
historiography, methodology of:
'measurable deflection' 60, 151 n. 6, 199
problems in understanding 11th-cent. rabbinic texts 58
problems in understanding *Sefer Ḥasidim* 58
retrojection: criterion for use 223; danger of 60–1
holy ones, see *kedoshim*
ḥumrah (stringency), tendency to 304–5, 306

I
inheritance:
firstborn's, of pledges 86 n. 60(*c*)
property rights in Gentile pawns 88
Issur ve-Heter shel Rashi, editions of 151 n. 42

J
Jewish community:
deviance in 278–9, 283, 285, 287, 292–3
excommunication from 278, 281
fines imposed by 278, 281
interferes in private lives of members 280
oligarchy in 279
ordinances, resistance to 279, 280
principle of majority rule in 278–9
self-government in Early Ashkenaz 278–9
taxation in 280, 281
see also *nohag*

K
kahal, *see* Jewish community
kedoshim (martyrs) 243, 244 n. 8, 276
kitniyot ban:
broadcast sowing 307
as *ḥumrah* 306
R. Me'ir of Rothenburg and Rosh unaware of 306
origins of 303, 304 n. 7, 305–7
three-field system 306–7

L
landowning, 11th-cent. retreat from 195
law, *see* Babylonian law; Germanic law; Muslim(s); Roman law
le-ḥumra 72, 166 n. 215 #3
fence against usurious relations 115–16, 129
R. Ḥanan'el on 120 n. 149
Maimonides on 106 n. 110
Rabbenu Tam on 131–2, 135
Rashbam on 129
Rashi on 99–101, 105–6; as reinstating agency 100 n. 99(*b*), 104 n. 107(*a*); as penalty (*kenas*) 100–1 n. 99(*a*), 105–6, 116
Ri on 137
Riva avoids invoking 100 n. 99(*b*), 123; understanding *le-ḥumra* in light of Tosefta, 121–2
Likkutei Rashbam 274 n. 58
liturgy, commentaries on 20, 21, 36

M

ma'arufya (Jewish factotum) 70
  R. David's allowance of 108
  Gentile non-agency 107
  mar'it 'ayin 122 n. 153
  Rabbenu Gershom's reverse agency as allowance of 109–10; opposition to reverse agency 111
  Rabbenu Tam on 140–1
  Rashbam's prohibition of 129, 162–3 n. 176 #2
  Rashi's misgivings about 108
  Riva's allowance of 119, 122–4; expansion to varying interest rates 124
  role in Jewish economic life 108
  Tosefta, application to 122–3
Ma'aseh ha-Ge'onim, difficulty of 58
maḥatsit sekhar maḥatsit hefsed (similar to *commenda*) 126
martyrdom:
  Crusade chronicles on 249
  en masse 289–90
  of the Jews of Mainz 25, 291
  of the Jews of Worms 291
  laws regulating 242
  Maimonides' position on 242 n. 5
  seen as ideal in Ashkenaz 242 n. 5, 249, 276, 290–1
  Sefardic view on 243 n. 6
  the *Semak* on 242 n. 5
  Tosafists' response to 244, 276
  voluntary 242–3 283, 290; permitted in Ashkenaz 244; Rabbenu Tam's justification of 244 n. 8
  see also child murder; *kedoshim*; suicide
martyrs, see *kedoshim*
massacres, *see* pogroms
Mekhilta, see *midreshei halakhah*
mesirah (informing), fear of 61
midreshei halakhah, commentaries on 20, 36
mimetic transmission:
  society and 292
  of tradition 284–5, 286–7
minhag (custom):
  as deviance (Malkiel) 283–4
  distinction between *minhag* and *nohag* 258
  factors affecting diffusion of 295–6
  Minhag Ostreich vs. Minhag Rheinus 294–5, 297, 302
  'Olam ke-Minhago Noheg 294
  prayer book heavily based on 284
  role in halakhah 258
  see also *nohag* (communal practice)
Mishneh Torah 21–2 n. 20
  cited in *'Arugat ha-Bosem* 34
  cited in *Or Zarua'* 34
  clear Hebrew in 33
  purpose of the glosses by R. Me'ir ha-Kohen 37–8
  reception in northern Europe 21, 33–4, 38
  Zera'im and *Toharot* ignored by R. Shimshon of Sens 33
misrepresentation (false fronting) 119, 126–8, 129 n. 174
Mo'ed Katan, lost commentaries on 28, 29 n. 36, 37
monasteries:
  alcohol consumption in 228
  as moneylenders 53, 70
moneylending:
  Christian attacks on 42, 54, 55
  connection to *setam yeinam* 224, 230
  to Gentiles 41, 45–7, 49, 50, 232–3
  Jewish involvement in 42, 47 n. 11, 54, 232; Champagne in 11th cent. 69, 102; France 130 n. 175, 225; Rhineland in 11th cent. 102
  monasteries involved in 53, 70
  as moral question: change in Christian view 53–4; not seen thus by Jews 45–9, 51, 52
Muslim(s):
  charging interest to 45
  countries, Jewish moneylending in 42
  law, does not stigmatize usury 42
  not considered idolaters 264
  Spain, Jewish culture in 240
  viewed as foreigner (*nokhri*) in matters of usury 41
mysticism, influence on Ashkenazic practices 295, 299, 300

N

Nimukei R. Kovil 83 n. 54(*c*)
nohag (communal practice):
  Ashkenazic defense of 239, 241, 260, 274–6; in commerce 272–3;

nohag, Ashkenazic defense of (*cont.*):
in the face of new knowledge 220; in martyrdom and suicide 244, 272; out of respect for ancient traditions (*minhag avot*) 192; significance of 223, 239–77; in usury 110
distinction between *nohag* and *minhag* 258
factors impacting on 295–6
in Spain not justified by scholars 274
see also *minhag* (custom)
nokhri, *see* Gentile(s)

O

'Olam ke-Minhago Noheg 294
Or Zarua' 21, 46 n. 4
lost for many centuries 38
Machon Yerushalayim edition 83 n. 53
Maimonidean citations 21 n. 20

P

Palestinian Talmud, *see* Yerushalmi
Palestinian traditions, impact on Ashkenazic practice 295, 299
pawnbroking:
difference between banking and 63–4
Germanic law applied in instances of Jewish–Gentile 153
importance of 65–6
interest rates 64, 66–8
legal issues involved 57
pawn-taking not indication of 69
pawn ticket (*reconnaissance*) 65 n. 17
similarity of medieval and modern 66
pawned pawn 73–4
as assignment of debt, challenged 141–5
R. David ha-Levi of Mainz on 77–82, 87, 88 n. 66, 90, 96 n. 93(*a*), 97, 102, 139, 149, 155 n. 66, 157–8 n. 80 #3
economic significance of the allowance of 102
Rabbenu Meshullam ben Kalonymus on 76, 81–2, 87, 88 n. 66, 96 n. 93(*a*), 156–8 n. 80 #4
Rabbenu Tam on 142–5; renunciation (*silluk*) 94 n. 83, 99 n. 98(*b*), 107, 133–7, 140, 164 n. 189
Rashi on 77–9, 82 n. 51, 88 n. 66, 94, 102, 155 n. 66
Ri on 141–5
R. Yitsḥak of Corbeil, on need for conveyance of 137
pawns (pledges):
analogy to *shetar* 156–7 n. 80 #3
assignment of pawn as assignment of debt, *see* debt assignment
circulation of 87
compulsion on borrower to redeem 92 n. 78
force majeure (*onsin*), responsibility for 86 n. 60(*a*), 247 n. 209
Gentile pawn, no acquisition of 81–4, 87–8, 141, 142 n. 203(*b*), 143, 146, 148–9
in Germanic law, *see* Germanic law: pawn
in Provence, borrower defined by ownership of 142–3 n. 203(*c*), 164–6 n. 215 #3
right of possession of 143 n. 204
sale of 89–90, 109; impossibility of debt waiver after 159 n. 81 ##1, 3; traffic in 148
value, greater than debt 85 n. 58, 97–8 n. 96, 120
pawns, acquisition of:
compulsory redemption 92 n. 78
concretion of the lien perceived as 92, 156–8 n. 80 #3
contract pawn (*be-sha'at halva'ah*) 82–3, 88, 147
distraint pawn (*shelo be-sha'at halva'ah*) 83, 88, 147
Pentateuch:
debt sale invalid by law of 95
injunction against usury 42, 45, 81
Perush Rabbenu Gershom 59
multiple authorship of 156–8 n. 80 #7
philosophy:
absence of, in Ashkenaz 247, 256 n. 12, 289
influence of, in Spain 247 n. 12, 289
Pietism, German, *see* German Pietists
pledges, *see* pawns
pogroms:
Armleder 22
Good Werner 22, 32
Rintfleisch 12, 22, 32
in vine-growing areas 229
polemics, Jewish–Christian 130 n. 176(*b*), 162–3 n. 176, 247

posek (decisor), methodology of 204
presumption of legality (Ri's doctrine) 136–9
promissory notes 62–3

R
reconnaissance, *see* pawnbroking
Refashioning Ashkenaz: The Human Face of Franco-German Jewry, 1000–1250 283
Reformation, stigma on usury 42, 54
religious beliefs in Ashkenaz, simplicity of 247, 289
reportatio 8, 15
responsa (*teshuvot*):
of Early Ashkenaz 19, 35
of Ge'onim 19, 35
German Jews send questions to French rabbis in 13th cent. 302
importance in Germany 21, 36
importance in Spain 21
of Rabbenu Tam 7 n. 3, 14, 19
of Rashi not preserved by Tosafists 20, 35
reflect middle echelon of society 62
reflect tosafist influence 251–2
of Shimshon of Sens, collected but not preserved 19, 20 n. 16
viewed as *livres de circonstance* and not preserved by French Tosafists 19–20, 35
ribbit, *see* usury
ribbit mi-loveh le-malveh, *see* usury, definition: bilateral arrangement
Roman law 42, 53, 62 n. 12, 91 n. 27(*b*), 145 n. 206(*b*)

S
Sages (*ḥazal*) on debt assignment 95–6
Schadennehmen 71, 73, 75
R. David ha-Levi of Mainz on 77–82, 87, 88 n. 66, 90, 97, 102, 117–19, 124, 155 n. 66
economic significance and limitations of 102–3
Rabbenu Gershom on 110 n. 118(*b*), 118 n. 138
Rashi on 77–8, 94 n. 84, 97–9, 104–5, 114, 116, 155–6 n. 66
Riva on 119, 122, 124
science, awakens little interest in Ashkenaz 31
Sefer 'Amudei ha-Golah, unused title of *Semak* 8 n. 14
Sefer he-'Arukh 192
pawned copy of 134 n. 186(*a*)
Sefer ha-Dinim, identification of 71 n. 38(*b*)
Sefer ha-Dinim shel Rabbenu Perets 215 n. 103(*a*)
Sefer ha-Eshkol, controversy over editions of 298
Sefer Ḥasidim:
ban on sexual relations during *yemei tohar* not mentioned 298
on breaches of law 286
endorses marital sex 298
on martyrdom 289–90
reasons for difficulty of 58
on usury 48–9
yein nesekh not mentioned as a problem 252 n. 25
Sefer ha-Minhagim (R. Ḥayyim Palti'el), may underlie work of R. Avraham Klausner 302
Sefer Mitsvot Gadol (*Semag*) 9, 17, 18, 34
focus on dialectic 35
lack of availability 38
tosafist doctrine in 251
Sefer Mitsvot Katan (*Semak*) 9, 18, 303 n. 7
first real Ashkenazic code 35
on martyrdom 242 n. 5
popularity of 34
tosafist doctrine in 251
Sefer Mordekhai 13 n. 2, 20, 21–2
alleged discussion of child murder 245 n. 8
completed by his students 218
Sefer ha-Oreh 22, 275
Ḥelek Sheni, identification of 150 n. 42
Sefer ha-Pardes 22
on topic of *yein nesekh* mostly German material 210
Sefer Ravyah 14, 21, 38
Sefer Rokeaḥ:
conservative work 222 n. 123
on the *kitniyot* ban 306
Sefer ha-Terumah (R. Barukh of Worms) 8–9, 16–17, 18, 251
Sefer ha-Terumot (R. Shemu'el ha-Sardi, of Cerdagne):
edition of A. Goldschmidt 151 n. 42 #1
reliability of citations 103 n. 105(*d*)

Sefer ha-Yashar, reasons for difficulty of 7, 14
Semag, see *Sefer Mitsvot Gadol*
Semak, see *Sefer Mitsvot Katan*
setam yeinam, see *yein nesekh*
sexual relations:
abstinence from 295, 298, 304–5
endorsed by *Sefer Ḥasidim* 298
women's control over 305
Shabbes Goy, The, concept of ritual instinct in 296
Shibbolei ha-Leket II, edition of M. Z. Ḥasida 160 n. 98
Shitah on *Mo'ed Katan* (of R. Yeḥi'el of Paris), employed Rabad's lost commentary 28
Shum, ordinances of 225
see also Index of Places: Mainz; Speyer; Worms
Siddur R. Shelomoh mi-Germaiza by R. Eli'ezer of Mainz (Ravan) 21 n. 18
Sifra, see *midreshei halakhah*
Sifrei, see *midreshei halakhah*
sifrut devei Rashi as attempt to revise established practice 275
silluk (renunciation) 93–4 n. 83, 98–9 n. 98(*b*), 164 n. 189
becomes standard form of intra-Jewish credit 140, 254 n. 27
definition of 133–7
employed by R. Yitsḥak of Corbeil in promissory notes 62–3 n. 13
introduced by Rabbenu Tam 107, 133
straw man (Gentile) 42, 46
German Jewry's apparent compliance with ban on 125–8
Rabbenu Tam's radical allowance of 130–6, 254 n. 27; French and English Jewry's reliance on 132
Rashbam's prohibition of 129–30; adherents to 133–4
Rashi's allowance 103–5; demand for creditor's ignorance of the subterfuge 105–6, 130–1; his emotional qualifications 106–7; French acceptance of 133
Ri's demand for creditor's ignorance of subterfuge 137
Ri's 'presumption of legality' doctrine 137
Riva's prohibition of 119–22, 125
suicide:
during Crusades 242
permitted in Ashkenaz during persecution 244, 276
voluntary martyrdom seen as 242, 243
in York 290
see also martyrdom
sukkah, use on Shemini Atseret 299–300
surety, circumvention of usury injunction by means of:
employed in Germany 115 n. 132, 137–8
Rabbenu Gershom seeks to prevent 114–15, 137–8

T

Talmud:
Bomberg edition 12 n. 1
burning of 12, 17
commentary of R. Yehudah of Barcelona 24
contradictions in 5, 26–7
Fez edition 12 n. 1
French exegesis of 19, 21, 35
German exegesis of 20, 21, 36
Maimonides' commentary 4, 5, 24, 25 n. 26
old Rhineland commentaries 25
printed page of 3, 12, 25
Rabad's commentary 4, 24
Rabbenu Gershom's commentary 4, 23
Rashi's commentary 3, 4–5, 7, 12 n. 1, 17, 19, 23
Soncino edition 3, 10, 12 n. 1
Spanish edition 12 n. 1
telegrammatic style 3, 5
Yerushalmi, *see* Yerushalmi
taxation, by Gentile authorities 280
teshuvah/*teshuvot*, *see* responsa
Teshuvot Rabbi Me'ir mi-Rotenburg, misnomer 71 n. 38(*b*)
Teshuvot ha-Rashba, vol. 7, composite nature of 81 n. 48(*b*)
theft 278, 281
three-field system, see *kitniyot* ban
Tosafist(s) 3, 5, 12
anonymity of 6
areas not treated by 9
attitude to martyrdom 244, 276

as communal leaders 241
criticism of contemporary practice, implicit 274, 275
defense of communal practice 223 n. 220, 239, 241, 260, 275–6; in commerce 273; in the face of new halakhic knowledge 220; in martyrdom and suicide 244, 272
elite religious practice not entertained by 260–1
impact on halakhic practice 286
intellectual revolution 17
lack of interest in responsa 19–20
Naḥmanides' school, true heirs of 32
period, end of 248 n. 12
question practice of lending money to Gentiles 45
radical interpretation of halakhah 246–7
shape our conception of *sugya* 60
see also *Tosafot*

Tosafot:
dialectic in 5, 6–7, 8, 15, 19, 26–7, 35
editing of 9, 10
see also Tosafists *and individual Tosafot*

Tosafot of R. Elḥanan 8, 15, 16
on *'Avodah Zarah*, editions of 183 n. 22

Tosafot of R. Eli'ezer of Touques 10

Tosafot of R. Perets 10, 17, 27
on *'Avodah Zarah*, citation from 200 n. 69

Tosafot of Ri 7–8, 10

Tosafot of Ri Sir Leon, see *Tosafot* of R. Yehudah of Paris

Tosafot of Riva 26–9

Tosafot of Rosh on *'Avodah Zarah* 16 n. 9

Tosafot of R. Shimshon of Sens 8, 10, 16, 17, 27

Tosafot of R. Yehudah of Paris 8, 9, 16, 17, 27

Tosfot R. Perets, see *Tosafot* of R. Perets

Tosfot ha-Rav on *Mo'ed Katan* 28, 29 n. 36

Tosfot Ri ha-Zaken ve-Talmido 29 n. 36

Tosfot Shants, see *Tosafot* of R. Shimshon of Sens

Tosfot R. Yehudah mi-Paris, see *Tosafot* of R. Yehudah of Paris

trade:
between Jews and Gentiles 59, 273, 283
on Christian holidays 272, 273
Jews' exclusion from 42, 47
significance for Jews in 11th cent. 69, 89 n. 72, 231
in wine, *see* wine trade

tradition, mimetic transmission of 284–5, 286–7

Tur, see *Arba'ah Turim*

U

ukimta (mode of distinction) 26, 29

University of Trier, research on German Jewry 225

usury:
biblical ban on 45, 50, 51 n. 24
Christian ban on 51, 52, 53, 54, 70, 121–2
Christians viewed as foreigners (*nokhri*) in matters of 41, 45
compliance with laws of 276
condemned by Christians 42, 50, 52, 54–5, 121, 129 n. 174
economic pressure on halakhists 70–1, 103, 133, 141–2, 273
from Gentiles 41, 45–7, 49, 50
monasteries involved in 53, 70
split interest allowances 120 n. 147, 124–5
technical nature of, in Talmud 52–3
terminology, 11th cent., *see* usury, definition of: *yotse mi-kiso shel*
see also usury, attitudes towards; usury, definition

usury, attitudes towards 96, 121–2 n. 152, 273
R. David 96–7, 99
German Pietists 126 n. 167
German Tosafists 124–5, 276
judicial constructions reflect the predisposition of the jurists: pawned pawn 96–7; reverse agency 110–13, 115
Rabbenu Gershom 115–16
Rashi 96–7, 99–102, 108–9
Riva (and German Tosafists) 119–22, 124

usury, definition 41
bilateral arrangement (*ribbit mi-loveh le-malveh*), as defined by the fiscal relationship 111–12, 116; see also *yotse mi-kiso shel* below
bilateral arrangement (*ribbit mi-loveh le-malveh*), as defined by the legal parties 116–17, 121
general definition in talmudic law 41

usury, definition (*cont.*):
trilateral arrangement (*eino ribbit mi-loveh le-malveh*) 72–3, 77, 80–1, 113; central means of allowance in Ashkenaz 163–6 n. 215 #3; rarely employed in Provence 163–6 n. 215 #3
yotse mi-kiso shel (out of the pocket of): out of the Gentile's pocket/*ma'arufya* 108, 111, 113, 115; out of the Gentile's pocket/pawned pawn 72–3, 77–8, 97; out of the Jew's pocket/*Schadennehmen* 99; out of the Jew's pocket/surety 114–15; Rabbenu Gershom on 115–16 n. 137

V
verjuice:
Ashkenazic ban on Gentile 268–9
popularity in medieval cuisine 266–7
vinegar, Ashkenazic ban on Gentile 268–9
vine-growing, *see* viticulture
viticulture:
difficulties of, in northern Europe 231, 232, 267
and Jewish settlement in Rhineland, map 226–7
in Troyes 194–5 n. 56
viticultural credit, Jews' involvement in 229, 231–2, 233–4, 235
Vivandier (French cookbook) 266

W
wine:
cuves (tubs) for treading grapes 176–7, 179, 184–9; Gentiles allowed to handle open *cuves* 259; pressed grapes soaked in 189
drunk in large quantities 171, 194, 228
economic importance of 171–2, 228, 229, 231
Gentile, see *yein nesekh*
halakhic definition 172–6
honey and spices added to 264–6, 271
Jewish family names linked to 235
nitsok 269–71
shortage of 267
time pressure on production of kosher wine 194
treading grapes 176, 177, 178; barefoot 213 n. 99; *cuves* (tubs) used for 176–7, 179, 184–9; revulsion at Gentile treading 207, 208, 212–15, 257
see also viticulture; wine trade
wine fair, Cologne, records of 235
wine trade:
Jews abstain from 228, 230
Jews' involvement in 231–3, 235, 264
see also *yein nesekh*

Y
Yad ha-Ḥazakah, see *Mishneh Torah*
yein nesekh:
accepted as payment of debt 231, 264
ban abolished in Spain, Italy, Moravia 257, 272
connection to moneylending 224, 229–34
laxity of Spanish Jews in observance of 252–3
nitsok, *see under* wine
resented by Gentiles 200–1, 230, 252, 263, 276–7
Sefer Ḥasidim, not mentioned as a problem in 252 n. 25
as taboo 225, 231, 234, 235, 252, 264
Tosafists refuse to abolish 252, 264, 269
trade in 225, 229, 235
upheld willingly by Jews 213, 225, 235, 272
Yerushalmi's lenient position on 269
see also *yein nesekh*
Yerushalmi 299
appearance in Ashkenaz in 12th cent. 220
on *ha'alamat 'ayin* 206–7, 215, 218–20
lenient position on *yein nesekh* 269
tractate *Shekalim*, commentary on 20, 36
yeshivas, *see* academies
Yiḥusei Tanna'im ve-Amora'im 14, 21, 36
eating indoors on Shemini Atseret 297

Printed and bound by CPI Group (UK) Ltd, Croydon, CR0 4YY
09/06/2025
14685814-0004